With cordial regards

Graham H. Stuart

AMERICAN DIPLOMATIC
AND
CONSULAR PRACTICE

American Diplomatic

AND

Consular Practice

GRAHAM H. STUART

Stanford University

SECOND  EDITION

New York

APPLETON-CENTURY-CROFTS, INC.

To the
Department of State
and the
Foreign Service of the United States
Agencies Extraordinary and Plenipotentiary
for the
Promotion of Peace and Prosperity among States

Preface

THE AIM OF THIS STUDY, now presented in completely revised form, is to afford an adequate survey of the organization and workings of the machinery employed in conducting the foreign relations of the United States. Former Secretary of State Hughes aptly designated skillful diplomacy as preventative medicine. The best of medicine is of little avail, however, if its use is limited and its application suspected. Unfortunately, the man in the street in our democracy not only looks askance at diplomatic medicine, but he is still more suspicious of the physicians who prescribe it. This attitude restricts the effective work of the State Department at home and that of the diplomatic and consular service abroad.

Perhaps the most important reason for this feeling is the aura of secrecy which is thrown about the practice of diplomacy. The citizen is not permitted to appreciate sufficiently the fact that diplomacy is merely the conduct of a nation's business abroad. Nor does he have it brought home to him that diplomacy has an additional function of even greater importance in that it must maintain the friendly atmosphere between states without which commercial, intellectual, and social relations are impossible. A little more publicity would do much to dispel the atmosphere of suspicion with which the conduct of diplomacy is unfairly beclouded.

The present study is an effort to present the machinery of diplomacy as an effective scientific agency of government. It attempts to show the practical utility and fundamental necessity of the work of the Department of State and the Foreign Service by giving a firsthand account of what they are doing and how they are doing it. The personnel, past and present, has furnished the material. Although the author concedes that he has approached his task with a sympathetic attitude, he has constantly endeavored to remain objective and critical.

This edition is based largely upon material obtained in Washington and abroad since World War II, although the author has drawn extensively upon the previous volume written sixteen years ago.

The volume could not have been written without the wholehearted support and assistance of the officers both in the Department of State and in the diplomatic and consular services abroad. Their sympathetic and cordial coöperation has been continuous and unfailing. If a small part of the valuable information furnished has been fairly presented, the study will not fail in its purpose. To express his gratitude individually would require the author to name personally many of the personnel in the Department of State and a goodly number of the staffs of our embassies, legations, and consulates abroad.

A special expression of gratitude is due to his colleague and friend, Professor James T. Watkins IV, who read the manuscript carefully and made many valuable suggestions. His thanks are also due to Miss Grace McClimans for her careful proofreading, and to Mrs. Lorraine Stumm and Mrs. Marguerite Colte for arranging and typing the manuscript.

G. H. S.

Contents

AMERICAN DIPLOMATIC
AND
CONSULAR PRACTICE

1

The Control of Foreign Relations
in the United States

THE CONDUCT AND CONTROL of its foreign relations has become a problem of paramount importance to the United States. The Second World War sounded the knell of American isolationism. Henceforth the formulation of a sound foreign policy would be just as important as the formulation of a successful domestic policy. The Marquis Curzon, an authority on the subject, has declared that "foreign affairs are really the most domestic of all our affairs, for it is in relation to foreign affairs that every man and woman in this country secures immunity from war, relief from the heavy burden of taxation, prosperity of trade and industry."

But to achieve a successful foreign policy it is not sufficient merely to formulate it. It is absolutely essential to have a well regulated system of control for the proper conduct of such a policy. In autocratic systems the control is simple since it is automatically vested in the head of the state. But in democracies where fear of absolutism always exists, numerous checks are imposed upon autocratic control of foreign relations by the head of the state. The result unfortunately is to make the conduct of foreign relations in a democracy both difficult and cumbersome. Perhaps in no country is this situation more evident than in the United States.

When first set up under the Articles of Confederation the government of the United States vested the control of foreign relations in a committee of the Congress. This was found to be so unsatisfactory that when the Constitution was formulated it was decided to give the control of foreign relations to the President but with very careful checks against possible abuse. He was made Commander in Chief of the Army and Navy but only Congress could declare war or appropriate money to wage it. The President could make treaties but two-thirds of the Senate had to approve them. He could appoint ambassadors and ministers but the Senate must approve his choice. Nevertheless the President was vested with the executive power and history has shown that a strong president can to a considerable extent determine the foreign policy of the United States.

1

Presidential Formulation of Foreign Policy. The reason for the great power over foreign relations which is now vested in the hands of the President is due partly to the failure of the Constitution to assign the formulation of foreign policy to any one instrumentality of government. Some of the most important foreign policies which the United States has enunciated, such as the Monroe Doctrine and the so-called Doctrine of Isolation are essentially presidential policies. Since such policies are primarily political matters they are not subject to review by the courts. Furthermore, since the President has full executive power and command of the Army and Navy to enforce his decisions, the Congress has only indirect methods of control. It may express its opinion by resolution but the President can use his own discretion as to whether he will accept such advice. In his annual messages to the Congress the President regularly expresses his opinion upon the foreign policy to be pursued by the United States and unless such policy violates national or international law the President can usually make his policy effective.

The fundamental doctrine of American foreign policy, the doctrine that kept us out of the League of Nations, was the doctrine of isolation enunciated in his farewell address by President Washington and supported just as fervently by Presidents Adams and Jefferson who succeeded him. The fact that subsequent presidents have refused to follow this long established policy when they regarded it inexpedient as, for example, President Theodore Roosevelt's action preceding and during the Conference of Algeciras is further evidence of the presidential power. When President Wilson logically and in accordance with the new position of the United States attempted to throw the doctrine overboard he only failed because of an unfortunate combination of political circumstances at home and the fact that his bitter personal enemy, Henry Cabot Lodge, was chairman of the Foreign Relations Committee of the Senate. Subsequently a much less forceful President was able to make the United States a full fledged member of the United Nations with overwhelming senatorial approval.

The Monroe Doctrine, another cardinal foreign policy of the United States is essentially a presidential policy. It has been extended, amended, revised, reinterpreted, disregarded, and renewed by subsequent presidents. It was not mentioned by President Lincoln during its contemptuous violation by the Maximilian expedition in Mexico. It could serve President Grant as a claim for an American isthmian canal. President Cleveland made it sound like a clarion call for American hegemony in the western world. The first President Roosevelt used it as a big stick policy to keep order in the Caribbean. President Wilson tried to make it a truly Pan-American policy. President Hoover reduced it to its original meaning. President Franklin D. Roosevelt made it practically obsolete by his new commitments to the Latin American states in accordance with the Good Neighbor Policy.

Although the so-called Truman Doctrine granting aid to Greece and Turkey was originally drafted in the Department of State it was revised by President Truman and presented forcefully to the Congress as a vital requirement for the protection of the United States.

Legislative Interference. The President it must be conceded does not possess this initiative in the formulation of foreign policy wholly free from the suggestions and advice of the legislative body. In fact the President upon numerous occasions must appeal to the Appropriations Committee, to the Foreign Relations Committee of the Senate, and to the Foreign Affairs Committee of the House to win their support in behalf of important matters of foreign policy. Individual senators often possess overwhelming influence, as evidenced by the rôles played by Senators Vandenberg and Connally in the formulation of policies pertaining to international organization during and after World War II.

Both the Senate and the House of Representatives feel free at any time to offer gratuitous advice in the form of resolutions, and many examples might be cited. A Senate resolution of 1835 requested the President to negotiate treaties with other governments for the protection of companies attempting to construct an isthmian canal. A Senate resolution of 1888 asked President Cleveland to open negotiations with China regarding immigration. Perhaps the most famous Senate resolution was introduced in 1912 by Senator Lodge as a sort of corollary to the Monroe Doctrine. It attempted to prevent the sale of any territory in the western hemisphere so situated as to threaten the safety of the United States if occupied by a foreign state for naval or military purposes.[1]

The House has been equally prolific with resolutions regarding foreign policy. It, too, attempted to support the Monroe Doctrine by declaring in reference to the Maximilian expedition into Mexico "that it does not accord with the policy of the United States to acknowledge a monarchical government erected on the ruins of any Republican government in America under the auspices of any European power."[2] In this case the Secretary of State in a note to the French Minister repudiated this statement of policy as being wholly without the constitutional prerogatives of the House.

In the field of legislation the Congress may seriously impair the President's powers to conduct an effective foreign policy. The Johnson Act of 1934, which provided that no persons under American jurisdiction could make a loan to any government defaulting in its debt to the United States,

[1] For text see *American Journal of International Law*, VI, 937 (1912).
[2] *Congressional Globe*, XXXIV, 1408 (April 4, 1864).

is an example of legislative initiative in the control of foreign relations without executive wish or support and it remained a serious handicap until the Lend-Lease legislation sidestepped its provisions, and the later Bretton Woods bill nullified them.

The various so-called neutrality acts passed between 1935 and 1940, which were aimed at keeping the United States out of war, practically nullified President Franklin D. Roosevelt's efforts to curb the aggressor states. In somewhat similar fashion the Congress materially restricted President Truman's administration of the European Recovery Program by delaying appropriations and sending a House Committee to Europe in 1947 to determine at firsthand the needs of the respective countries. A more recent type of legislative interference has been the statutory establishment of all powerful interdepartmental committees such as the National Security Council and the National Security Resources Board which tend to decentralize responsibility.

Presidential Responsibility. In this connection it should be noted that according to American constitutional law the President is legally responsible for the acts of the heads of the executive departments. Therefore any policy initiated by a Secretary of State is in reality a presidential policy. Consequently Secretary Hay's policy of the Open Door, Secretary Hughes's policy of limitation of armament, Secretary Hull's policy of tariff reciprocity and Secretary Marshall's policy of aid to Europe to check communism owed their existence to presidential sanction. In conclusion it may be stated that the President possesses the initiative in the formulation of foreign policy and his success in achievement is limited only by his intelligence and his will.

It should be noted that upon certain occasions the presidential initiative has brought about unfortunate incidents. The famous indiscretion of President Harding during the Washington Arms Conference of 1922, when he gave a statement to the Japanese with regard to the island status of their country in direct violation of the stand taken by Secretary Hughes, is a well remembered incident. The very unfortunate result of the Hoover-Laval conversations regarding the debts would never have arisen if the affair had been handled by trained diplomats who would have had accurate notes as to exactly what was said and an initialed memorandum as regards the decision reached.

The failure of the allies to specify in writing the right of ingress and egress to Berlin through the Soviet Zone by land and water transportation was a mistake which the trained State Department officials would not have made, but President Roosevelt thought it inadvisable to insist that Stalin commit himself further than a tacit acceptance.

The President as the chief executive of the United States is the only legitimate functionary to carry on negotiations with foreign states. Thomas

Jefferson referred to the President as "the only channel of communication between the United States and foreign nations." [3] John Marshall called him "the sole organ of the nation in its external relations, and its sole representative with foreign nations," and a report from the Foreign Relations Committee of the Senate asserted that "the executive is the sole mouthpiece of the nation in communication with foreign sovereignties." [4] Of course, in this connection the President ordinarily acts through the Department of State. Except in cases of personal communications to foreign heads of state, usually of a ceremonial nature, all written communications to foreign governments are signed by the Secretary of State or American foreign diplomatic representatives. Here again the President's position in the direction of foreign policy is paramount, for the action of the President in such matters of policy is binding on the Congress, the courts and all public officials both Federal and state. It should be noted that the Logan Act passed January 30, 1799, forbidding unauthorized private citizens to negotiate upon matters of state with foreign governments is still the law of the land, and its application was suggested with reference to Henry Wallace when he spoke against the Truman Doctrine while touring Europe in the spring of 1947.

The Appointment of Foreign Representatives. Among the specific powers conferred by the Constitution upon the President is the appointment of ambassadors and other public ministers and consuls.[5] Such appointments, however, are subject to the approval of a majority of the Senate. Due to the fact that senatorial approval is required a certain amount of political pressure is sometimes put upon the President with reference to choice diplomatic posts. The posts of London and Paris are the two most important in the American Foreign Service and there is always keen competition for these positions. Therefore, these posts are almost always filled by political appointees. The position of the President in making these appointments is a most unenviable one. There are so many outstanding supporters of the party and so few adequate awards available. It is a well known fact that George Harvey, who perhaps did more than any other Democrat to bring about the election of Woodrow Wilson, became his bitterest enemy when refused the position of Ambassador to the Court of St. James's. He later threw his influence to the election of President Harding, a Republican, and achieved his desire of becoming our Ambassador to London. Incidentally, his reputation was not enhanced by his service.

The United States has never adopted the policy of limiting appointments in the diplomatic service to career men and until the Foreign

---

[3] J. B. Moore, *Digest of International Law* (Washington, 1906), IV, 680.
[4] See Q. Wright, *The Control of American Foreign Relations* (New York, 1922), 21.
[5] Article II, Sect. I.

Service Act of 1946 it was almost an unwritten law that upon the inauguration of a new President all American ambassadors and ministers should submit their resignations to the new President. The tendency in recent years, however, has been to refuse to accept the resignations of the career men in the service and to fill a good share of the posts of minister and a few ambassadorial posts with experienced men.

On the whole the Senate is inclined to grant approval of diplomatic appointments in a purely routine fashion. There is no doubt that influential senators are often able to obtain certain diplomatic posts for their protégés. It is also true that a senator who fails of reëlection is often taken care of by being given a diplomatic appointment. But such procedure is to be expected so long as the diplomatic service is not placed wholly upon a career basis. Upon rare occasions a political appointee is so manifestly unsuited to represent the United States abroad that public opinion compels withdrawal of the nomination. Such an outcry of protest arose when President Roosevelt in 1943 nominated Democratic National Chairman Edward J. Flynn as Minister to Australia that Flynn himself requested the President to withdraw his name.[6]

Congressional Limitations on the Appointive Power.   The Congress has from time to time placed certain limitations upon the appointment power of the President but it is a moot question as to how far the President is bound by such legislation. For example, the law of March 1, 1855, attempted to limit the President's power to the appointment of American citizens only as envoys extraordinary and ministers plenipotentiary. It also stated to which countries they were to be sent and the specific annual compensation for each. Attorney General Cushing construed the act to be merely recommendatory and not mandatory. He declared that in his judgment the President might employ a person if the public interest required it whether he were a citizen or not. Nor could "Congress by law constitutionally require the President to make removals or appointments of public ministers on a given day, or to make such appointments of a prescribed rank or to make or not make them at this or that place." [7]

The Congress, however, continued to make legislation controlling diplomatic appointments. It was made impossible to appoint aliens as either diplomatic or consular officers by refusing compensation to such officers not citizens of the United States. Inasmuch as the President had never utilized his specifically granted powers to appoint ambassadors, the Congress by an Act of March 3, 1893, making appropriations for the Diplomatic and Consular Service, authorized him in his discretion to appoint the same class of diplomatic agent as any foreign government appointed to the United States. The Act provided for the Congress of Vienna classi-

[6] Graham H. Stuart, *The Department of State* (New York, 1949), 386-7.
[7] *Opinions U.S. Attorney General*, 214.

fication: ambassador, envoy extraordinary, minister plenipotentiary, minister resident and chargé d'affaires. It also added the position of special envoy. The long delay on the part of American presidents in making ambassadorial appointments was due primarily to the popular opposition in a democracy to the ceremonial inherent in such positions.

An even more restrictive act was passed by the Congress in 1909 which stated that "hereafter no new ambassadorship shall be created unless the same shall be provided for by an act of Congress." In accordance with this mandate ambassadorships have been established by special authorization as follows: Spain in 1913, Argentina and Chile in 1914, Belgium in 1919, and Cuba in 1923. Here again, however, this act of Congress has been construed as merely recommendatory, for President Wilson raised the post at Lima, Peru, to an ambassadorship without the authorization of Congress.

The greatest limitations upon the President's appointive power have been taken by presidential initiative and consent. In order to establish a career service based entirely upon the merit system a series of congressional statutes have been passed placing all positions below the rank of minister in the diplomatic and consular services upon a permanent civil service basis. At the present time all consular officers and all diplomatic officers under the rank of minister are appointed as a result of competitive examination to a position of Foreign Service officer and they are promoted strictly upon a merit basis. The Act of February 23, 1931 provided that the Secretary of State might recommend promotions from Foreign Service officers to the position of minister, and both Presidents Hoover and Franklin Roosevelt availed themselves of this provision. As examples, Norman Armour, formerly Counselor of the Embassy in Paris, was appointed Minister to Canada and later Ambassador to Argentina, and George Messersmith, formerly Consul General at Berlin, was named Minister to Austria, and subsequently Ambassador to Cuba and then to Mexico. In accordance with the Foreign Service Act of 1946, Foreign Service officers who had served as chiefs of missions or in comparable positions were eligible to be appointed to the class of Career Minister; that is, they could serve as ministers or ambassadors and retain their status of Foreign Service officers regardless of changes of administration. In January, 1947, about 60 per cent of United States ambassadors and ministers were career officers.

Presidential Agents. Another interesting example of the President's appointive power is the practice of sending special presidential agents abroad without consulting the Senate in any way. These diplomatic or secret agents are not strictly officers of the United States nor public ministers, but they are usually given the same privileges and immunities by foreign governments as are accorded to public ministers. Such agents are usually sent for secret negotiations and are paid out of a secret contingent fund of the President, for the expenditure of which he is not required to give an accounting.

President Washington began this practice almost immediately after the ratification of the Constitution when he sent Gouverneur Morris, then in Paris, as his special agent to London to "converse with His Britannic Majesty's Ministers as to certain matters affecting the relations between the two countries." [8] A report of the Senate Foreign Relations Committee in 1888 stated that some 438 persons had been appointed or recognized by the President without the advice or consent of the Senate or the express authority of Congress to conduct negotiations and conclude treaties. [9]

As outstanding examples of such procedure we might note the mission of Commodore Perry in 1853 to conclude a treaty with Japan, the missions to the Hague Conferences of 1899 and 1907, the mission of Colonel House to Germany in 1916 and France in 1917, and the entire peace commission headed by President Wilson to conclude a treaty of peace with Germany in 1919. President Hoover after his election but before his inauguration constituted himself a sort of special agent on a good will trip to Latin America. President Franklin D. Roosevelt sent William C. Bullitt as his special agent to the Soviet Union in advance of its recognition and Norman Davis served as presidential agent with the rank of Ambassador as America's chief representative to the disarmament conference.

President Franklin D. Roosevelt utilized Patrick J. Hurley, William J. Donovan, W. Averell Harriman, Harry Hopkins, and numerous others on *ad hoc* missions. The appointment of Myron C. Taylor as Envoy to the Vatican aroused considerable Protestant objection but President Truman retained him although conceding that the position was not a permanent one.

The Senate has protested many times and vigorously against this practice. In 1882 in consenting to the ratification of a treaty with Korea the Senate resolved that "it does not admit or acquiesce in any right or constitutional power in the President to authorize or empower any person to negotiate treaties or carry on diplomatic negotiations with any foreign power unless such person shall have been appointed for such purpose or clothed with such power by and with the consent of the Senate...." [10]

The Congress also has attempted to restrict the President's power. In a clause in the deficiency bill of March 4, 1913, the Congress declared that "Hereafter the executive shall not extend or accept any invitation to participate in any international congress, conference or like event without first having specific authority of law to do so." [11] Such limitation is an

---

[8] Wright, *op. cit.*, 328.
[9] *Senate Document* No. 231, 56th Cong., 2nd sess., Part 8, 337-62.
[10] Malloy, *Treaties*, I, 340.
[11] 37 *U.S. Statutes at Large*, 913.

unconstitutional infringement upon the President's control of foreign relations and as such has been violated with impunity by subsequent presidents.

Power to Receive Foreign Representatives. Correlative with the President's power to appoint and send diplomatic representatives is the power to receive ambassadors and other public ministers. The vital difference is that in the case of reception of foreign envoys the President would seem to have absolute power untrammeled by any legislative control. This unrestricted power of receiving foreign public officers imposes a great responsibility upon the President because through it the President has the power of recognizing new foreign states and governments. A premature recognization of a belligerent or revolutionary government by the President might well be regarded as a just cause of war by the parent state. In this way the President could plunge the country into war without any check on the part of Congress.

This power of recognition was first used by President Washington in 1793 when by receiving Citizen Genêt he recognized the new revolutionary government of France. In our relations with Latin America the President has used the power of recognition very often as a means of exerting pressure upon various Latin American states. In the case of Central American republics an effort has been made to prevent revolutions by refusal to recognize governments which have come into power through unconstitutional means. In the case of Mexico the United States was able to cause the downfall of the Huerta government and to impose important reservations regarding the Mexican constitution upon the government of President Obrégon. The government of Dr. Grau San Martin in Cuba, which was overthrown in January, 1934, claimed that its downfall was due to the refusal of President Roosevelt to accord recognition. The recognition of the Soviet Government by President Roosevelt in 1933 was made upon his own initiative and was in direct opposition to the policy followed by his two predecessors, Presidents Coolidge and Hoover.[12]

A flagrant abuse of the power of recognition occurred when President Truman in 1948, allegedly to obtain political support in the forthcoming presidential election, recognized Israel before a formal request for recognition had been received and before the American representatives at Lake Success who were debating the Palestine problem had been informed of his precipitate action.

The power of recognition goes further than the recognition of new states and new governments. Ever since President Washington issued the first proclamation of neutrality in 1793 Presidents have on their own initiative recognized a state of war as existing by proclamations of neutrality. The

---

[12] The settlement of claims in connection with presidential recognition is now accepted as an executive prerogative. See U.S. *v.* Belmont, 301 U.S. 324, 330-1 (1937).

United States through a proclamation by President Franklin D. Roosevelt recognized a state of war existing between Italy and Ethiopia in 1935 even before the League of Nations had so decreed. The President has also assumed the power to determine by the character of his proclamation whether a status of belligerency or insurgency exists. It naturally follows that the President can determine when such warlike conditions end by proclaiming the termination of American neutrality. Finally, through diplomatic correspondence carried on by the Department of State the President has recognized the establishment of protectorates and the acquisition of territory.

Here, again, the question has arisen as to the exclusiveness of the President's power. Since premature recognition of a revolutionary government as a belligerent or the recognition of a state as independent before acceptance of such a change in the *status quo* by the parent country is a just cause for war, should not the Congress which alone can declare war participate in the attendant negotiations? In fact, upon certain occasions as, for example, in the case of the recognition of Texas, which ultimately brought about war with Mexico, the President did consult with and ask the coöperation of Congress. Nevertheless, the consensus as expressed by Secretaries of State, by the courts, and by the Senate itself concedes that the power of recognition is vested solely in the hands of the executive.[13]

War Powers of the President. The powers of the President as Commander in Chief of the Army and Navy of the United States are another important element in his control of foreign relations. He can move the forces of the United States as he sees fit even though such disposition may provoke an outbreak of hostilities. It is generally conceded that President Polk's order sending American forces to the east bank of the Rio Grande into territory claimed by Mexico was the spark which touched off the war with Mexico. President Cleveland unquestionably prevented hostilities with Spain when he warned that if the Congress should declare war he would refuse to mobilize the Army. It has also been argued that if President McKinley had not sent the battleship *Maine* to Havana harbor the war with Spain might have been averted.

But since the President is expected to use the military and naval forces of the United States to defend American territory and to protect the rights of Americans abroad and on the high seas he must use his own discretion as to how these objects may best be accomplished. Professor Borchard in his scholarly study on the *Diplomatic Protection of Citizens Abroad* gives it as his opinion that "the Executive has unlimited authority to use the armed forces of the United States for protective purposes abroad in any

[13] Moore, *op. cit.*, I, 244-7.

manner and on any occasion he considers expedient." [14] President Taft has declared "the President is made Commander-in-Chief of the Army and Navy by the Constitution, evidently for the purpose of enabling him to defend the country against invasion, to suppress insurrection and to take care that the laws be faithfully executed. If Congress were to attempt to prevent his use of the Army for any of these purposes, the action would be void." [15]

An outstanding use of the President's military power which has been much criticized was the despatch by President Theodore Roosevelt of an American cruiser into Colombian waters with orders to keep the Panamanian railway open even though it necessitated prohibiting Colombian troops from disembarking into their own territory. The result was the success of the Panama revolution and the construction of the Panama canal by the United States. A less successful example of the use of the President's military power was the sending of American forces into Mexico to capture the bandit Villa who had crossed into American territory and murdered a number of American citizens.

Perhaps the most radical use of this power occurred when President Truman despatched Army, Navy, and Air Forces into Southern Korea in July, 1950, as a United Nations police force to repel the attack of the Communist armies of North Korea against the South Korean Republic, which was still under the protection of the United States. Although not very popular with the Congress at this time, President Truman received almost unanimous support from both Republicans and Democrats in this unprecedented action.

In times of war, the Executive has such a vital responsibility for the security of the state that he must seek advice from every source available —not only public officials but from private sources where warranted. Harry Hopkins, Samuel Rosenman, and Bernard Baruch often influenced President Franklin D. Roosevelt in historic decisions, and the occupation problems in postwar Germany were made infinitely more difficult by the inexcusably inept advice of Secretary of the Treasury Henry Morgenthau, Jr.

The Treaty-making Power. Finally, the last and perhaps most important power possessed by the President in the control of foreign affairs is based upon the constitutional provision which states: "He shall have power by and with the advice and consent of the Senate to make treaties provided two-thirds of the Senators present concur." [16] Inasmuch as

[14] E. M. Borchard, *The Diplomatic Protection of Citizens Abroad* (New York, 1915), 452.
[15] W. H. Taft, *Our Chief Magistrate* (New York, 1925), 128-9.
[16] Article II, Sect. 2, clause 2.

treaties have become the fundamental basis of international law, jurisdiction over the treaty-making power is essential to the control of foreign relations. It is in this field that the President and the Senate have had some of their greatest struggles and unfortunately for the foreign policy of the nation the Senate is too often victorious.

James Bryce in his remarkable interpretation of the American Government has cogently expressed this situation: "The Senate has been mainly guided by its Foreign Relations Committee, a fluctuating body, usually containing a few able men among others who know little or anything outside their own country and may regard the interests of their own state rather than those of the Union. Jealous of its powers and often impelled by party motives the Senate has frequently checked the President's action, sometimes with unfortunate results." [17]

When the constitutional fathers provided for a joint control of the treaty-making power they had in mind a small body of some twenty-six eminent and intelligent men in the Senate (indirectly elected and therefore not subject to popular prejudice) who would confer in a judicial fashion with the President as to the best interests of the country in entering into engagements with the rest of the world. Hamilton pointed out in *The Federalist* the reasons why the lower house could not share this power because "Accurate and comprehensive knowledge of foreign politics; a steady and systematic adherence to the same views; . . . decision, secrecy and dispatch are incompatible with the genius of a body so various and so numerous." [18] Never was it visualized at that time that the Senate would grow into a body of ninety-six members directly elected from the forty-eight states, an unwieldy advisory group which would often permit politics to take precedence over the general interests of the country as a whole.

Even at the beginning, however, the procedure of consulting the Senate in the actual formulation of a treaty was found to be a failure. The story is told of President Washington at an early period of his administration having gone to the Senate with a project of a treaty to be negotiated and having been present at their deliberations upon it. "They debated it and proposed alterations so that when Washington left the Senate Chamber he said he would be damned if he ever went there again. And ever since that time treaties have been negotiated by the Executive before submitting them to the consideration of the Senate." [19]

John Hay when Secretary of State had a number of unfortunate experiences with the Senate's attitude towards the approval of treaties and became very pessimistic about it. "A treaty entering the Senate," he wrote, "is like a bull going into the arena; no one can say just how or when the

[17] James Bryce, *Modern Democracies,* 2 vols. (New York, 1927), II, 373.
[18] *The Federalist,* P. L. Ford, ed. (New York, 1898), 502.
[19] J. Q. Adams, *Memoirs,* 12 vols. (Philadelphia, 1874-77), VI, 427.

final blow will fall—but one thing is certain, it will never leave the arena alive." [20] President Wilson had one of the bitterest struggles with the Senate in his effort to obtain the ratification of the Treaty of Versailles. There is little doubt but that a small group of senators led by Henry Cabot Lodge fought the treaty and prevented its adoption partly through personal antagonism to President Wilson and partly through a narrow partisanship spirit. In a study made by the Department of State it was estimated that in the period between 1789 and 1931 the Senate caused the failure of some 160 treaties, either by outright rejection, or by amending them so as to cause their rejection, or by not taking final action. [21]

In the negotiation of a treaty the President has a free hand, although it is still argued by some authorities that the Senate should be consulted even from the beginning. Nevertheless the practice has become established for the President to carry on all the negotiations and sign the treaty before submitting it to the Senate for its approval. On one occasion when President Jackson sought the advice of the Senate on an Indian treaty prior to signature he apologized for departing from a long and unbroken usage in similar cases. [22]

On a number of occasions, however, the Secretary of State has consulted with senators individually and informally, particularly members of the Foreign Relations Committee, as to their attitude towards a possible treaty. On other occasions senators have been chosen on the commission to conclude the treaty under consideration, thus making them to a certain extent responsible in advance for its acceptance by their fellow members. President Wilson might have had greater success if he had given the Senate some representation at the Versailles Conference. President Harding was careful to name senators from both parties to conclude the Washington Arms Agreements. Secretary Kellogg depended upon Senator Borah to steer his Pact at Paris through the Senate—in fact Washington wiseacres declared that the Secretary of State could be seen daily ringing the doorbell of the Senator from Idaho. President Truman depended as much upon Republican Senator Vandenberg as he did upon Democratic Senator Connally to secure senatorial approval of the North Atlantic Pact—the first treaty of armed alliance ever signed by the United States in times of peace.

An interesting question arises when the treaty requires the appropriation of money to carry out its provisions. Since Congress has the sole right to appropriate money, is it bound by a treaty made without its knowledge or consent? This is a much disputed point but in actual practice Congress has never yet failed to appropriate the necessary funds to make a treaty

[20] W. R. Thayer, *Life of John Hay* (New York, 1915), II, 293.
[21] *Miscellaneous Publications of the Department of State,* No. 382 (Washington, 1932).
[22] Wright, *op. cit.*, 250.

effective. However, when President Johnson made a treaty in 1868 with Denmark for the purchase of the Danish West Indies for $7,500,000, the Senate refused to approve it because of personal and political hostility towards the President. The result was that when the United States finally obtained the islands in 1917 they had to pay more than three times as much, namely, $25,000,000. Petty partisan politics sometimes comes very dear.

On certain occasions the Senate has refused to act upon treaties which successive presidents have earnestly desired to make a part of the law of the land. A notorious example of such flouting of executive purpose occurred with regard to the Hay-Quesada Treaty, signed with Cuba in 1904, relinquishing all American claim to the Isle of Pines. Although every subsequent American president favored its acceptance the Senate, hearkening to the outcry of the American landowners on the island, was not prevailed upon to pass it until 1925.

The delay in the ratification of treaties due to dilatory action by the Senate is such that in its instructions to its diplomatic officers the government of the United States declares as regards ratification of treaties it is preferable that the exchange of ratifications shall be effected "as soon as possible" rather than within a specified time.

On the other hand, presidential initiative has brought about the abrogation or revision of some treaties of vital importance to the United States. For example, the 1934 treaty with Cuba practically abrogating the Platt Amendment was passed unanimously by the Senate after only two days discussions in order to carry out President Roosevelt's Good Neighbor Policy.

Although the Senate may reject a treaty outright the more common procedure is for it to qualify the treaty with amendments, reservations or interpretations. In some cases the amendments or reservations are of such character as to nullify completely the proposed aim of the treaty. In such a case the President is at liberty to withdraw the treaty from any further action. President Taft was forced to withdraw a number of arbitration treaties which he had made when he found that the Senate was not disposed to accept them without restrictive amendments. President Taft resented bitterly the Senate's attitude and later explained his action by declaring that the Senate had "truncated them and amended them and qualified them in such a way that their own father could not recognize them. ... So I put them on the shelf and let the dust accumulate on them in the hope that the Senators might change their minds, or that the people might change the Senate; instead of which they changed me." [23]

Sometimes the Senate's amendments are not acceptable to the other party which refuses to accept the treaty in its amended form. Great

[23] J. M. Mathews, *American Foreign Relations* (New York, 1928), 197.

Britain refused to accept a convention signed in 1803 for settling the northern boundaries of the United States because the Senate had expunged one article. A convention for the suppression of the slave trade signed in 1824 was also refused by Great Britain due to the conditions imposed by the Senate.[24]

At the present time the custom of the Senate seems rather to make reservations instead of amendments. Reservations are distinguished from amendments in that they involve no formal or textual changes in the treaty. The United States was kept out of the World Court because of five reservations appended by the Senate of the United States to the protocol of adhesion. Four of them were accepted unconditionally by the other signatory powers, and a modified form of the fifth proposed by Elihu Root was subsequently approved. However, although on January 9, 1935, the Senate Committee on Foreign Relations by a vote of 14 to 7 recommended that the Senate advise and consent to the adherence of the United States, and President Roosevelt threw his influence strongly behind the proposal, the Senate refused by a vote of 52 to 36. Jingoistic nationalism aroused by the Hearst press and misleading radio appeals were sufficient to stampede a small group of spineless senators. On the other hand after World War II cordial coöperation took place between the executive and legislative branches on a nonpartisan basis as regards the United Nations Charter and the United States entered both the U.N. and the World Court by almost unanimous senatorial approval.

There has never been complete agreement as to the extent of the treaty-making power in the United States. According to the dicta of the courts, "the treaty-making power in the United States extends to all proper subjects of negotiation between our Government and the governments of other nations."[25] It is generally conceded that the President may make a treaty which violates any law passed by Congress but he may not make a treaty in violation of the Constitution.

Executive Agreements. There is one possible procedure eliminating senatorial interference which is sometimes available to the President in dealing with a foreign state. Since the Constitution prescribes that treaties shall receive the consent of the Senate, but does not define the term, and later refers to agreements or compacts which the states may enter into with the consent of Congress, the President has assumed the power of making executive agreements which are not submitted to the Senate for its approval. Sometimes such agreements are under authority expressly delegated to the President by Congress but sometimes he may make such agreements in direct violation of the expressed will of the Senate.

Perhaps the most famous of such agreements was the one made by

[24] Moore, *op. cit.*, V, 199, 200.
[25] Geofroy *v.* Riggs, 133 U.S. 258, 267 (1890).

President Theodore Roosevelt in 1905 for administering the customs collection in the Dominican Republic. Although the President sent two messages to the Senate urging immediate approval of the protocol, the Senate adjourned without action. President Roosevelt thereupon decided to carry out the arrangement as an executive agreement. Santo Domingo accepted the *modus vivendi* and President Roosevelt in his next message to Congress declared the arrangement would last until the Senate acted upon the treaty. The Senate did not take kindly to this alleged executive usurpation and Senator Tillman violently arraigned the President for his unconstitutional abuse of authority. But the agreement worked and the Senate finally but grudgingly gave its consent.

Another famous agreement was the so-called "Gentleman's Agreement" of 1908 with Japan regarding Japanese immigration. This was merely a declaration of policy between the two Governments but it was faithfully adhered to until abrogated in a most arbitrary and ungentlemanly fashion by the Immigration Act of 1924. The Root-Takahira and the Lansing-Ishii agreements with Japan regarding American policy in the Far East are also well known examples of executive agreements.

The arrangement between the United States and Great Britain which provides for the nonfortification of the 3,000 miles of frontier between the United States and Canada has never been put into the form of a formal treaty. The peace protocol with Spain which ended the war of 1898 and provided for the evacuation of Puerto Rico and its subsequent cession to the United States was an executive agreement entered into by the President as the Commander-in-Chief of the Army.

The so-called Hull reciprocal trade agreements, although not subject to the Senate's approval, are not strictly executive agreements inasmuch as an act of Congress specifically placed in the hands of the President the power to negotiate such agreements and at the same time limited his powers and the duration of the grant of power.

President Franklin D. Roosevelt made numerous executive agreements, some of which were of most vital importance to the nation. The exchange of fifty outmoded destroyers with Great Britain for naval and air bases of great strategic importance in the Caribbean and off the northeast coast of the United States was the act of a far-seeing, courageous statesman. On the other hand, the commitments made at Yalta to Stalin, when the President acceded to the Soviet's taking over territory conquered from Japan or belonging to her ally China, was an example of reckless chance-taking which had the most grievous consequences for the United States. According to Dr. Wallace McClure, treaty specialist in the Department of State for many years, by 1941 more than 1,200 executive agreements had been entered into by the United States.[26]

[26] See Wallace McClure, *International Executive Agreements*, (New York, 1941).

Such examples of presidential powers could be multiplied but illustration enough has been given to show that in the American system of government the control of foreign relations is largely within the President's hands. With his appointive power, his treaty-making power, his war powers, and his power to dictate policy he can direct the foreign policy of the United States into the channel wherein he wishes it to flow. Since the President is the only man in the American system who represents the United States as a whole, the power is well placed. Even President Harding who had served longer as a Senator than as President dared to tell the Senate that from his own experience he at last realized that "to the executive comes the closer view of world relationship." There have been many occasions when a majority of the American people have wished that the President were the sole director of the foreign policy of their country.

2

The Department of State—I

HISTORICAL DEVELOPMENT OF THE DEPARTMENT

IN TAKING UP the organization of the machinery of international intercourse it is necessary first to consider the agency which directs the foreign relations of a state. This administrative and policy-determining agency is usually called the Foreign Office or the Ministry of Foreign Affairs. In the United States, for reasons which will be given later, it is called the Department of State.

Preconstitutional Development of the Department of State. The State Department of the United States may claim an interesting, if limited ancestry. Its origin can be traced to the Committee of Secret Correspondence chosen by the Continental Congress in 1775 with the illustrious Benjamin Franklin as its chairman. This committee distinguished itself by undertaking the negotiations which subsequently led to the very advantageous alliance with France of 1778. The Committee's name was changed in 1777 to the Committee for Foreign Affairs and under this title it functioned intermittently and rather ineffectually until 1781. At that time it was thought that "the extent and rising power of these United States entitles them to a place among the great potentates of Europe," and a plan of organization was submitted to the Congress on January 10, 1781.[1]

The plan began with establishing an office "for the department of foreign affairs to be kept always in the place where Congress shall reside," and it provided for "a secretary for the despatch of business of the said office, to be styled secretary for foreign affairs." After considerable debate the office was established, but the first secretary, Robert R. Livingston of New York, was not selected until August 10 of the same year. The department as originally organized consisted of the secretary with a salary of $4,000 a year, a first undersecretary at $800, and a second undersecretary at $700, a clerk and translator at $500, and another clerk at $500.[2]

---

[1] *Journals of the Continental Congress,* Library of Congress ed., XIX, 43.
[2] For the historical development of the Department see Gaillard Hunt, *The Department of State of the United States* (New Haven, Conn., 1914) and Graham H. Stuart, *The Department of State* (New York, 1949).

An act enlarging the secretary's powers was passed in 1782, but by the end of the year, Livingston, finding that his expenses exceeded his salary by several thousand dollars and preferring to be Chancellor of the state of New York, resigned. He retained his position for over six months until Congress could choose a successor, but when they failed to do so the office was vacant for over a year until John Jay was elected and took over the duties in December, 1784. Jay carried on the work so ably begun by Livingston until the government under the Articles of Confederation came to an end.

Establishment of the Department of State. The new Constitution did not specifically provide for executive departments but it clearly took them for granted. The Congress elected according to its terms, therefore, did not hesitate to set up executive departments by its statutory authority. The first executive department to be established was named the Department of Foreign Affairs and the Congressional Act creating it became law by the signature of President Washington July 27, 1789.[3] A little later in the same year when it was found that no provision had been made in the departments of Foreign Affairs, Finance, or War to keep the records and seals of the United States or to publish the acts of Congress, it was decided to entrust those duties to the Department of Foreign Affairs. To make the name of the department include its new domestic functions, the law extending its jurisdiction (the act of September 15, 1789)[4] changed its name to that of the Department of State, and the principal officer was to be known as the Secretary of State. John Jay, appointed Chief Justice of the Supreme Court, had carried over the functions of the foreign office merely until his successor could be appointed and inducted into office. Thomas Jefferson, then on a mission to France, was named by the President as the first Secretary of State and he accepted and entered upon his new duties late in March, 1790.

Early Functions and Prerogatives. Although the Department of State was primarily the department to advise with the President in the conduct of foreign affairs, it was also made the repository of all domestic functions which could not properly be assigned to the Departments of Finance or War. In fact, Jefferson described the Department as embracing the whole domestic administration (war and finance excepted). For example, the Secretary of State was made custodian of the laws, the records and the Seal of the United States. It was his duty to promulgate the laws and resolutions of Congress; subsequently he was authorized to promulgate and publish the treaties to which the United States is a party and amendments to the Constitution. President Washington not only referred to the

[3] 1 *U.S. Statutes at Large,* 28.
[4] 1 *U.S. Statutes at Large,* 68.

new department all correspondence within its jurisdiction but also copies of most of his own letters. The Department regularly served as the medium of correspondence between the President and the governors of the states.

An Act of Congress of March 1, 1792, provided that in case the offices of President and Vice President should both be vacant, the Secretary of State should notify the governors to choose electors within a specified time, but the Act of January 19, 1886, vested the succession in case of death, removal, resignation, or inability of both President and Vice President, in the members of the Cabinet successively beginning with the Secretary of State. This law although now superseded clearly established the primacy of the Department of State over the other departments.

A number of duties of a domestic character which were assigned to the Department of State shortly after its organization have passed out of its jurisdiction with the establishment of other departments.[5] By acts of Congress dated April 10, 1790, and February 21, 1793, the State Department was charged with the issuance of patents and this work remained under its jurisdiction until the Department of Interior was established in 1849 and the patent business assigned to it. Copyrights were also placed under the jurisdiction of the State Department insofar as it served as a repository for all maps, charts, books, engraved prints, and musical compositions whose titles had been deposited in the clerks' offices of the various United States District Courts. These publications were transferred in 1859 to the Department of Interior and in 1870 to the Library of Congress.

The first taking of the census was undertaken by the Federal marshals but the publication of the returns was placed under the supervision of the Secretary of State. The Department continued to exercise this function until the work was transferred by Congress in 1850 to the Department of Interior. It was in the same year that all petitions for executive pardons which up until this time had been received by the Secretary of State were transferred to the office of the Attorney General. The State Department continued, however, to act in an administrative capacity for the Department of Justice until 1893.

The direction of territorial affairs was also given to the Department of State until the Act of March 1, 1873, transferred all such duties to the Secretary of the Interior. From 1796 to 1812, the Secretary of State was required to sign land patents and record them but this function was taken over by the General Land Office in the Treasury Department.

Other duties of the Secretary of State which lasted for brief periods were: management of the mint, from 1792 to 1799; serving as the transmitting agency for sending of quarterly returns of ships' manifolds from

[5] See Hunt, op. cit., Chap. VI, for a detailed account.

the collectors of the districts to the Congress regarding impressments of American seamen from 1799 to 1812; control of the immigration service from 1846 to 1868; publication of the annual volume known as *Commercial Relations of the United States* from 1856 to 1903, and the issuance of letters of marque and reprisal from 1798 to 1863. It should be noted, however, that no such letters have been issued since 1815.

Reorganizations of the Department. As Jefferson organized the Department in the first year of his incumbency, it consisted of one chief clerk, three ordinary clerks, and a French translator. After ten years of service the Department in 1800 consisted of a total force of ten men including the Secretary.[6] In 1820 the personnel of the Department had increased to fifteen as follows: the Secretary, the Chief Clerk, ten clerks, two messengers, and an assistant.[7]

A reorganization took place under Secretary McLane in 1833 and a more substantial one under Secretary Fish in 1870, when the first geographical agencies were set up. The most complete reorganization preceding World War I was initiated and carried out by Secretary Knox and Assistant Secretary Huntington Wilson in 1909, when the Department was definitely organized upon a regional basis. However, the Department still remained very small, with only 35 ranking officers and 135 clerks, which with all other employees made a total of 210 persons. It was well said that at the outbreak of World War I, Assistant Secretary of State Alvey A. Adee carried the "whole machinery of foreign policy under his hat."

The coming of the war produced an overwhelming increase in the Department's work. Citizens abroad must be protected, vast numbers of passports had to be issued, foreign interests were put in charge of the United States, but no opportunity was given for an orderly reorganization till after the war was over. Then, due to a penny-pinching policy on the part of the Congress, the State Department was not given sufficient funds to perform even its most essential duties efficiently. It was not until 1932 that President Hoover and Secretary of State Stimson were able to obtain sufficient personnel and adequate salaries to meet the minimum requirements of the Department. The total number of employees at this time was about 800 and the depression reduced it to 753 by January 1, 1936.

A slight reorganization of the Department was inaugurated in 1937-38 by Assistant Secretary of State George Messersmith, when, for the first time, ranking officials as advisers in various fields were given the opportunity to consider problems of long-term policy, and the Department at last recognized the importance of cultural relations.

When World War II broke in the fall of 1939, the Department, which still numbered less than one thousand in personnel, was only able to carry

[6] Hunt, *op. cit.*, 191.
[7] *Ibid.*, 203.

out its duties by putting in over 20,000 hours of overtime work. When, in the year 1940, the officials of the Department worked 156,000 hours of unpaid overtime, the need for expansion was finally recognized. A rapid increase in personnel followed, particularly in agencies of an economic character. Economic operations mushroomed to a point where, at the end of the war, some five hundred State Department officials were engaged in some phase of this work. New passport regulations, new visa-control procedure, a vast increase of every sort of communication compelled a continuous expansion. For example, the number of incoming airgrams and telegrams received and acted upon per month increased from 246 in January, 1942, to 4,397 in January, 1944.

The need for a complete reorganization of departmental machinery could not await the end of the war, and on January 15, 1944, a serious attempt was made to remedy outstanding defects. However, so many faults were found, due to undue haste and inadequate preparation, that another complete reorganization was made by Secretary Stettinius on December 20 of the same year. This, although still unsatisfactory, was an improvement and remained, with a few fundamental changes introduced by Secretary Marshall in 1947, until the recommendations of the Hoover Commission were made effective early in 1950.[8]

Streamlining the Department.   The Department of State was the first Federal agency to be reorganized in accordance with the recommendations of the Hoover Commission on the Organization of the Executive Branch of the Government. A Task Force report pointed out that the work of forty-six executive agencies involved some aspect of the conduct of foreign affairs, and that for the budgeted expenditure of 7 billion dollars for the fiscal year 1949, approximately 95 per cent represented amounts allocated to agencies other than the Department of State.

The report noted that an appalling burden of work had fallen upon the Secretary and Under Secretary, and to remedy this situation it was proposed to delegate greater responsibility for policy-making to Assistant Secretaries and to increase the number of these officers to ten. A law to carry out the recommendations of the Commission was passed May 6, 1949, and Secretary of State Acheson moved immediately to put the reorganization plan into effect. Except for the controversial proposal to amalgamate the personnel above a certain level in the State Department with the personnel of the Foreign Service, the implementation of the reorganization program was practically completed by the end of the year.

The Department of State has expanded in functions in approximately

8 Commission on Organization of the Executive Branch of the Government, *Foreign Affairs, a Report to the Congress* (Washington, 1949); also *Task Force Report on Foreign Affairs* (Washington, 1949).

the same ratio as it has in size. No longer is it merely responsible for assisting in the formulation of policy and for the guidance of our diplomatic and consular representatives abroad. It is equally responsible for furnishing to the American public and to the peoples abroad the nature and objectives of the foreign policy of the United States. From time to time it has also been given the responsibility for operational activities such as the liquidation of United States Foreign War surplus property, and Greek-Turkish Aid Program, and the civil administration of the United States occupation of Germany.

Housing the Department of State. The Department's first home was a two-story residence building in Philadelphia. From there it was moved to New York then back to Philadelphia, then to Trenton and finally to Washington. Here it remained but not in one place. In fact it moved eight different times before it was finally established in the vast granite pile on Pennsylvania Avenue next to the White House as a cotenant with the Departments of the Army and Navy. This location was expected to be permanent and remained so from 1865 until the end of the Second World War. But this building large as it was could not possibly house the ever-expanding Department of State even after the Navy and Army had moved to new quarters of their own. In fact by the end of 1945, the eight thousand employees of the Department of State were scattered through forty-seven different buildings.

On January 22, 1947, the Department began to move its principal agencies into a new modernistic building built originally for the War Department at the corner of Twenty-first Street and Virginia Avenue. By May, 1948, the Department's buildings were reduced to seventeen, all within approximately a mile radius of the so-called New State Building in Foggy Bottom. As of January 1, 1950, the Department of State proper had about 6,800 employees, of whom some 3,000 were administrative officials, 2,000 were policy-determining officers, and the rest engaged in research, public relations, or informational affairs. The cost of operating this first department of the government—the "Department of Peace," as Secretary Hughes called it—amounted to only $24,510,000 for domestic service for the year 1950. If we include the Foreign Service the total was $78,152,100.

OFFICE OF THE SECRETARY

In attempting to describe the great organization which carries on the relations between the United States and the rest of the world it seems desirable for the sake of convenience to separate the Department of State into two parts on a functional basis. It is not necessary that the division be hard and fast but it will simplify the task before us if we may describe first the officials and divisions whose duties are largely concerned with the determination of policy and then take up the part of the organization which is more purely administrative in character.

It goes without saying that such a classification is necessarily arbitrary and that many officials in the Department perform both types of services. Nevertheless the work of the Department permits a fairly logical separation into the two divisions and the added convenience in simplifying the description may justify the attempt.

It should also be noted that we are concerned at this time with the Department of State proper and not with its agencies in the field nor with the various international commissions or other agencies engaged in related activities.

Although as we have already noted the President is largely responsible for the foreign policy of the United States, he must depend upon others to assist him in the formulation of this policy, and it is to the Secretary of State that he first turns for counsel and advice. But no one person can possibly be in a position to advise intelligently upon the innumerable and complex problems which arise constantly in the relations of modern states. Therefore the Secretary must have assistants, and as the United States grew from a small isolated state to a vast world power, the number of assistants increased in number and in the variety of their work.

Thus there has grown up an efficient organization to aid the President in the conduct of our foreign affairs which is equipped to cope with the most difficult political or technical problems in international relations. As a result, although the Secretary and perhaps Under Secretary of State must be political appointments in the sense that they must fit in with the President's political views, all other officials who may be called upon to aid the President in the formulation of foreign policy must be specialists trained by long experience. The Department of State, therefore, has remained perhaps the least influenced of any of the executive departments by partisan politics.

Although the various duties of the Department of State are treated in subsequent pages, it might be advisable at this point to summarize briefly, with particular reference to the formulation and conduct of foreign policy, the duties as they exist today.

Among the more specific functions of the Department under this category we may list the following:

1. To assist the President with advice in the formulation of the foreign policy of the United States;
2. To carry on the diplomatic correspondence of the United States with other sovereign states;
3. To direct and administer the Foreign Service of the United States;
4. To advise regarding the acceptance, recall or dismissal of foreign diplomatic agents and to assist in their reception;
5. To aid in the negotiation, interpretation, enforcement and termination of all international agreements;

6. To assist in the protection of American citizens and their rights and interests in foreign countries;
7. To be ready to give information regarding the political, economic and social conditions as they exist in the world.

Unless the Department of State is competent to perform these varied and difficult duties both tactfully and efficiently, the well-being of the United States may be seriously jeopardized. The Department of State is essentially the department of the government concerned with the maintenance of peace and the United States must depend upon the wisdom of its personnel to maintain a position of respect and honor abroad.

The Office of the Secretary of State in the United States is noticeably different from the position of foreign minister as it exists in the majority of states in two particulars. In the first place, the jurisdiction of the office still covers certain important domestic duties such as the publication of the laws and resolutions of Congress and the conduct of relations between the President and the governors of the states, and it is the Secretary of State who serves as the medium of communication in these instances. In the second place, the head of the office is, theoretically at least, merely the spokesman of the President and therefore cannot legally be held responsible for the foreign policy which he may sponsor. Nevertheless, in practice the respective personalities and interests of President and Secretary of State largely determine the rôle of each in the formulation and conduct of the foreign policy of the United States. For example, President Wilson paid very little attention to Secretary Lansing in working out his foreign policies while President Harding permitted Secretary Hughes to have almost a free hand.

President Franklin D. Roosevelt in his first two administrations did not interfere with Secretary Hull but from 1941 on he was to a considerable degree his own Secretary of State. President Truman was seemingly ignored at times by Secretary Byrnes, whereas Secretary Acheson made no important policy decision without first consulting President Truman.

The Secretary of State enjoys the position of being *primus inter pares* in relation to the other members of the President's cabinet. He is usually the President's closest adviser and right hand man and in cabinet meetings he occupies a seat immediately at the right of the President. The Secretary of State also takes first place among cabinet members in all matters pertaining to ceremonial. The Department of State was the first executive department to be established by Congress and it is still customary to find the Secretary of State named first among cabinet officers in congressional acts. We have already noted that the Act of January 19, 1886, placed the succession if a vacancy should occur in the offices of both President and Vice President in the members of the cabinet successively, beginning with the Secretary of State.

The Presidential Succession Act of 1947 however placed the Speaker of the House next in line to the Vice President, after him, the President pro tempore of the Senate, and last, heads of departments beginning with the Secretary of State.

The organic act governing the duties of the Secretary of State in the conduct of foreign affairs may still be said to be the Act of July 27, 1789, which set up the Department of Foreign Affairs. In accordance with the provisions of this act the Secretary was to "perform and execute such duties as shall from time to time be enjoined on or entrusted to him by the President of the United States, agreeable to the Constitution, relative to correspondences, commissions or instructions to or with public ministers or consuls, from the United States, or to negotiations with public ministers from foreign states or princes, or to memorials or other applications from foreign public ministers or other foreigners, or to such other matters respecting foreign affairs, as the President of the United States shall assign to the said department...." [9]

Although the Secretary of State is not legally responsible for the conduct of foreign affairs, he is publicly responsible, and if necessary, he should try to prevent the President from making mistakes in the conduct of foreign affairs. Secretary Hamilton Fish went so far as not to promulgate a proclamation signed by President Grant recognizing Cuban belligerency lest it involve the United States in war with Spain. Grant was appreciative of the wise judgment of his Secretary of State and praised him for the "steadiness and wisdom which have kept me from mistakes into which I should have fallen."

As the problem of conducting our foreign affairs has become increasingly complex, the Secretary himself has been compelled to depend more and more upon his subordinates so that at the present time only the most important state papers come before him, and he signs only such correspondence and documents as he cannot properly delegate others to sign in his name. The unfortunate phase of this situation is that the American representative in the field is never sure that his communication will reach the Secretary's eye even though it may be a matter of most vital import. Miles Poindexter, a former United States Ambassador to Peru, once told the writer that Secretary Hughes had never read the despatch which he sent advising strongly against the holding of a plebiscite in Tacna-Arica. The United States might have been spared much trouble if his advice had been followed. Henry P. Fletcher always telegraphed from Santiago, Chile, when he wanted to be sure that Secretary Bryan would read his despatch, as Bryan usually read telegrams. Frederic J. Stimson, former United States Ambassador to Argentina, declared that neither Bryan, Lansing, nor Hughes had ever read one of his despatches, but that he found that if he gave the Associated Press correspondent the pressing

[9] 1 *U.S. Statutes at Large,* 28.

matter of a despatch, the Secretary was likely to get the information the next morning in the *Washington Post*.[10]

In defense of the Secretary of State it must be said that no Secretary of State even though a superman would be physically able to read daily even a small percentage of the despatches coming into the Department from some seventy ambassadors and ministers. In fact the demands upon his time from the President, the Congress, the press, the members of the Cabinet, senators and representatives who must be received scarcely leave him time to read all the telegrams received from the diplomatic missions and consulates. Therefore he must delegate the responsibility of reading all but the most important communications to competent Assistant Secretaries and Chiefs of Divisions.

The Secretary of State, however, does occupy himself with the negotiation of important treaties, with urgent questions of American policy in all parts of the world, with the protection of American interests abroad, and with such problems as recognition of governments, relations with the United Nations, and the establishment of better commercial relations with foreign states. It is a custom rigorously followed that all official communications from the President to other governments shall be signed by the Secretary of State. The sole exceptions are the so-called ceremonial notes of congratulation or condolence which may be signed by the President in person and sent directly to the head of a foreign state. In the same way all communications from American representatives abroad or foreign representatives in the United States which pertain to foreign affairs are addressed to the Secretary of State.

In these days when public opinion is of such importance in relation to foreign affairs, a good press is of the greatest value. Of course, the relations between the Secretary of State and the press depend considerably upon the personality and attitude of the Secretary of State, but no Secretary can afford to ignore the value of maintaining the best possible relations with the press. Secretary Hay inaugurated the practice of meeting representatives of the press personally, Secretary Hull met them almost daily and Secretary Acheson saved a half hour or more for them every Wednesday.

The Secretary must also be available for visits of foreign representatives, and Thursday between eleven and one o'clock was formerly set aside for this purpose. However, the Secretary must be ready to receive a foreign representative on an urgent mission at the earliest possible moment, and at the present time he receives diplomats on request.

The Secretary of State is the President's representative in dealing with the Congress in questions relating to foreign policy. He must testify at committee hearings, and it is his responsibility to maintain cordial relations with members of the legislative body. This is not always easy of

[10] F. J. Stimson, "An Intimate Discussion on Our State Department," *Scribner's Magazine*, LXXXV, 163 (February, 1929).

accomplishment, and as great a Secretary of State as John Hay was never popular with the members of the Senate Foreign Relations Committee. Secretary Acheson, although courteous and diplomatic to the highest degree, found it difficult at times to endure the barrage of trivial and inconsequential questions which partisan congressman were prone to lay down. On the other hand, Secretary Root was a past-master in dealing with Congress, and in spite of serving under an obstreperous President, he was able to gain senatorial approval for all but three of the one hundred and three treaties which he presented to that august body.

The Secretary of State is by departmental regulations required to sign important correspondence relating to the formulation and interpretation of foreign policy, reports to the President for transmission to Congress, letters and memoranda addressed to the President, letters to members of Congress and all important letters, instructions, notes, and telegrams of such importance as to require his signature. However with the vital need in recent years of time to formulate policies and secure their acceptance these routine requirements are almost entirely delegated to the Secretary's assistants.

The Secretary of State must still perform a few functions of a domestic nature. He is the medium for correspondence between the President and the chief executives of the several states of the United States. He publishes the laws and resolutions of Congress, amendments to the Constitution, and proclamations of the admission of new states into the Union. In presidential elections the Secretary of State is officially informed by the governors of the states of the votes cast for presidential electors; he certifies these votes to the President of the Senate and the Speaker of the House of Representatives, and publishes the governors' certificates. He is custodian of the laws of the United States. It was due to the assumption of these duties as provided by Act of September 15, 1789, that the title, Secretary of Foreign Affairs, was changed to that of Secretary of State. John W. Foster, who for a short period ably filled this position, has declared that "it was an unwise and misleading change, as the name indicates that the main business of the department was of a domestic character, whereas it is almost wholly international in its functions, and should be termed the Department of Foreign Affairs, as provided in the original law . . . it is unfortunate that the name should have been changed, as the new duties might have been added without altering the character of the department, and the misnomer which has adhered to it for more than a century might have thus been avoided." [11]

Inasmuch as the President is responsible for all acts performed by the Secretary of State the relationship between the two is usually very close, but the rôle of the Secretary of State depends largely upon the interest

[11] John W. Foster, A Century of American Diplomacy (New York, 1900), 124.

of the President in foreign relations and his confidence in his Secretary of State. Often upon receiving an important document from Secretary of State Seward, President Lincoln merely asked where he should sign his name.[12] According to Mr. Thayer, "Mr. Hay used to tell his friends that often President McKinley did not send for him once a month on business, but that he saw President Roosevelt every day."[13] Although Secretary Hay had a much freer hand in the formulation of policy under McKinley than under Roosevelt, there is no doubt but that both presidents depended to a considerable extent upon his counsel. On the contrary, President Wilson depended very little upon Secretary Lansing for counsel or advice, but rather used him as a trained expert in international law to see to it that the president's communications and instructions were couched in the proper legal phraseology.

During periods when Secretary of State Hull was ill President Franklin D. Roosevelt got into the habit of utilizing Under Secretary of State Summer Welles, and when the President continued this procedure after Secretary Hull returned to the Department it brought about a serious split between the Secretary and Under Secretary which ultimately resulted in the resignation of the latter.

President Franklin D. Roosevelt liked to act as his own Secretary of State at times and resented any criticism from the Department. On one occasion when the President sent one of his fireside chats to the Department for comment and the Department recommended various changes he became quite irate. Where for example the Department suggested the omission of a sentence accusing American citizens—many in high places— for aiding the agents of the fifth column in the United States President Roosevelt not only kept the original sentence but added the phrase "especially in the State Department."[14]

Although Lord Bryce once wrote that "the President has a Secretary of State to advise him who is . . . frequently only a politician selected because of his party standing and possessing little knowledge of world affairs,"[15] the appointment of men like Hay, Root, Hughes and Marshall belies the contention. Writing concerning Secretary Olney, Montgomery Schuyler, himself a former diplomat, declared that "the Secretary of State should be a man so big and so able to accept responsibility and make decisions that only in rare cases should matters of foreign policy be referred to the President and then only with a statement of the policy advocated by the Secretary."[16]

[12] Frederick W. Seward, *Reminiscences of a War-Time Statesman and Diplomat* (New York and London, 1916), 148.

[13] W. R. Thayer, *The Life of John Hay* (New York, 1915), II, 297.

[14] Robert Sherwood, *Roosevelt and Hopkins* (New York, 1949), 227-8.

[15] James Bryce, *Modern Democracies* (New York, 1927), II, 373.

[16] Samuel Flagg Bemis, ed., *The American Secretaries of State and Their Diplomacy* (New York, 1928), VIII, 321.

The Secretary of State is *ex officio* a member of the Export Import Bank, the Foreign Service Buildings Commission, the Smithsonian Institution, the National Gallery of Art, and the National Munitions Control Board, but he rarely attends meetings of these agencies. However, he does attend regularly cabinet sessions and meetings of the National Security Council and the National Security Resources Board. Unquestionably the Secretary's most important engagement is his daily meeting with the members of his staff to plan the day's program. With Mr. Acheson as Secretary, the Under Secretary, the two Deputy Under Secretaries, the Directors of the Policy Planning Staff and the Executive Secretariat, the Ambassador-at-Large and a Special Assistant to the Secretary regularly attend these sessions.

A critical evaluation of the achievements of approximately sixty incumbents who have filled the important position of Secretary of State in the United States would show their vital influence upon the development of American foreign policy. John Quincy Adams as Secretary of State gave us the Monroe Doctrine, James Buchanan formulated the doctrine of expatriation, William Seward by the purchase of Alaska, our first non-contiguous territory, launched the United States upon a policy of imperialism, James G. Blaine was the father of Pan-Americanism, John Hay made the Open Door a fundamental basis of American foreign policy, Elihu Root laid the foundations for the Foreign Service as a career and Charles Evans Hughes initiated the policy of limitation of armament. Although it may be presumptuous to evaluate the work of the more recent Secretaries of State, history will not be able to overlook Secretary Kellogg's stubborn advocacy of the reunuciation of war as an instrument of national policy, Secretary Stimson's policy of nonrecognition of states organized in violation of treaty commitments, Secretary Hull's efforts to break down commercial barriers by reciprocal trade agreements, Secretary Marshall's success in aiding Europe to help herself and Secretary Acheson's efforts to contain the aggressive advances of Soviet Communism.

In the words of a former American consul general, the Secretary of State is "the pivot of the entire system, with enormous powers sufficiently within his control to give the stamp of his personality to the whole range of transactions to which the nation is a party during his incumbency." [17]

Special Assistants to the Secretary. Each recent Secretary of State has determined how many special assistants he needs in addition to the regular members of the Department. Secretary Stettinius had at least a dozen advisors and special assistants whereas Secretary Marshall had six. Secretary Acheson has one Consultant and three Special Assistants.

The Consultant until 1951, when he was appointed special representative with rank of ambassador to negotiate the Japanese Peace Treaty, was

[17] Tracy Lay, *The Foreign Service of the United States* (New York, 1928), 74.

John Foster Dulles, eminent authority on international affairs, who as a well known Republican was partly instrumental in maintaining a certain bipartisan approach in foreign policy matters.

One Special Assistant, Lucius D. Battle, attends all meetings and does such follow-up work as is necessary, checks commitments and approves all appointments to see the Secretary. A second, Bromley K. Smith, takes care of such *ad hoc* projects as the Secretary deems advisable. The third Special Assistant for Press Relations is in reality a top flight agency serving as the logical successor of the one-time Division of Current Information. The present head, Michael J. McDermott, has been the chief press officer in the Department since 1927. His agency is the domestic outlet for all information regarding the foreign policy of the United States. It deals with up to three hundred correspondents, radio announcers, photographers, and others interested in foreign policy information. Mr. McDermott or his Executive Assistant, Lincoln White, has a daily noon meeting with the press when information on the activities and policies of the Department is released to the various news media. The Special Assistant is also responsible for briefing the Secretary of State for his weekly conference with the press.

This agency maintains liaison with the press-relations sections of the White House and other Federal agencies and acts as the clearing agency of the Department for speeches, news releases, and material issued by other Federal agencies but which bears on foreign policy.

It prepared and distributed over 1,000 press releases annually during 1949 and 1950. It also prepares and distributes to the Department a daily summary of news stories on international relations that have a bearing upon the Department's activities. It also publishes summaries of the Secretary's weekly press and radio news conferences. As at present organized the Special Assistant for Press Relations has eight officers including the Executive Assistant and an Assistant on Economic Affairs.

International Security Affairs. Although the administration of the Marshall Plan was not placed under the direction of the Department of State the foreign-aid program known as the Mutual Defense Assistance Program came under its jurisdiction. As the rearmament program for Western Europe was stepped up, the Department, on January 8, 1951, set up the Director of International Security Affairs and made his office responsible for the functions performed by MDAP. In other words this unit directed and coördinated all State Department activities relating to collective and mutual defense, military assistance, the export and sale abroad of military material, and the commitment of United States military resources for United Nations purposes.

This agency works with an interagency Committee on International Security Affairs which includes representatives of the Department of

State, the Department of Defense and Economic Cooperation Administration merged subsequently into Mutual Security Administration. Since most of the military aid given under the program has gone to the North Atlantic Treaty countries a regional office paralleling the organization in the Department has been set up in Europe.

Although this unit is small in numbers and may only possess a temporary existence its Director, Thomas D. Cabot, ranks as a consultant to the Secretary of State and the agency is given a position in the Office of the Secretary above even that of the Policy Planning Staff.

Policy Planning Staff. It had long been appreciated that the procedure of "making policy on the cables" was no longer possible, and that long range planning was vital to successful policy-making. An attempt to meet this need was made in 1937 when Advisers on Political Affairs and International Economic Affairs were appointed, but the results were not satisfactory and the positions were subsequently abolished. Another attempt made in 1945 when the Secretary's Staff Committee was set up was equally unsuccessful. When General Marshall became Secretary of State in January, 1947, he decided to establish a Policy Planning Staff modeled somewhat upon a section of the General Staff of the Army. Its purpose was not only to formulate long-term plans for the achievement of American foreign policy objectives, but also to anticipate problems which might face the Department and to evaluate the adequacy of current policy in relation to the existing international situation. To ensure its freedom from administrative duties, the staff was not permitted to issue directives or instructions either to departmental agencies or to missions in the field.

As Director of the Policy Planning Staff a brilliant Foreign Service Officer, George F. Kennan, of Career Minister rank, who had had over twenty years experience in European posts, was chosen. The staff consisted of a small number of Foreign Service officers and members of the State Department staff, and it was to be assisted by special advisers from other branches of the government and by experts outside of the government. When Kennan was granted a leave of absence early in 1950 for research purposes Deputy-director Paul H. Nitze was made Director. Several former ambassadors have served on this body including Cavendish Cannon and George H. Butler. Miss Dorothy Fosdick, a specialist in United Nations Affairs, is the only woman who has been a regular member of the Staff. The Staff meets at least once daily to discuss questions of high policy. Its work is varied and of a highly confidential nature. It is too early to evaluate its achievements, but its establishment was unquestionably an attempt to meet a very vital need in the Department.

Under Secretary of State Webb has described the Staff as "a capsule of concentrated brain power and experience in diplomacy . . . sometimes known as crystal gazers," but at the same time he declared that "this little group has done such valuable work and has become so indispensable it is hard to imagine how the Department ever got along without it."

The Executive Secretariat. The Executive Secretariat is a sort of control mechanism for the entire office of the Secretary of State. It was introduced by Secretary Marshall March 1, 1947, who collected under its jurisdiction such agencies as the Division of Coördination and Review and the Division of Protocol as well as certain servicing units such as the Committee Secretariat Staff and the Policy Reports Staff. Its primary responsibility is to ensure that all matters coming to the Secretary are in proper form and that the decisions of the Secretary are properly implemented and carried out. Policy decisions and reports necessary to the formulation of policy are disseminated by this agency. If joint consultation is necessary the committee structure is utilized.

In order that all outgoing communications may adhere to established policy and standards, those of the Secretary and Under Secretary are reviewed by Director W. S. McWilliams and his assistants while all others are reviewed by the Chief of the Correspondence Review Staff, Blanche Halla, and her assistants, Sarah D. Moore and Helen L. Daniel. Chief Halla and Assistant Chief Moore of the Correspondence Review Staff have each served in the State Department for more than thirty years and by training and ability are peculiarly well equipped to prevent the issuance of contradictory or ill considered statements which might return later to plague the writer.

Committee and Planning Staffs. The Committee Secretariat Staff was set up to control the cumbersome and unwieldy committee system which had mushroomed in the Department. With authority to advise regarding the establishment, operation and termination of all committees of the Department or those in which the Department participated, the Committee Secretariat was enabled to eliminate duplication and to coördinate the activities of such committees as were deemed essential.

The Policy Reports Staff fills the need of a policy liaison agency in a Department which has expanded from less than a thousand to over six thousand in less than a decade. The principal activity of the Policy Reports Staff is to circulate within the Department and between the Department and the missions abroad such policy informational material as may be necessary to the proper functioning of the Department and the missions. It directs and supervises the preparation of policy statements, maintains a comprehensive indexed policy record file of official policy decisions and is prepared both with materials and visual aids to brief such persons as the Secretary may direct.

Protocol Staff. Although diplomatic ceremonial has always been a necessary adjunct of diplomatic missions and foreign offices abroad, in the United States it has generally been regarded as being in some way a monarchical or court practice,—a puerile deference to mere form—and therefore unworthy of our democratic institutions. This attitude has been so pronounced with us that it was not until 1893 that the Congress permitted any foreign representative of the United States to be given the rank of ambassador, and even today our diplomatic representatives are not permitted to wear the resplendent costumes and regalia which is customary with foreign nations. This same sentiment prevented for more than a century the appointment of an official in the Department of State whose duty it should be to act as master of ceremonies at diplomatic receptions and on other state occasions.

Writing as late as 1906, John W. Foster, who had served both as Secretary of State and on numerous diplomatic missions abroad, declared that "the new diplomats coming to Washington have often felt the need of such an official, and even the resident people of society would be grateful to the government if it would provide them some authorized person who could solve for them the many vexed questions of precedence which are continually arising." [18]

It was not until the end of World War I that a ceremonial section was created in the Department of State. On August 18, 1919, Mr. Charles Lee Cooke was named "Ceremonial Officer" and placed at the head of the ceremonial section in the office of the Third Assistant Secretary of State. This protocol service was found to be so valuable to the Department and Mr. Cooke's flair for that type of work so pronounced that for seventeen years he remained Ceremonial Officer and final arbiter on matters of precedence and protocol.

In 1928 a full-fledged Division of Protocol was established and the following year it added international conferences. In 1937 it was relieved of its conference work, and under George T. Summerlin, a Foreign Service Officer, the Division of Protocol remained almost unchanged until 1945. When Secretary Marshall established the Executive Secretariat in March 1947, the Division of Protocol was included as a Protocol Staff. Stanley Woodward, who had entered the Division of Protocol as Assistant Chief in 1937 and had been named Chief in 1946, remained in charge as Chief of Protocol until he was relieved by Foreign Service Officer John Farr Simmons in 1950.

The duties of the Protocol Staff are exceedingly varied as the following brief summary indicates: The Staff is charged with all matters pertaining to the presentation to the President of ambassadors and ministers accredited to this Government. This service includes correspondence pertaining to the *agréation* or acceptability of these officials to the American Govern-

[18] John W. Foster, *The Practice of Diplomacy* (New York, 1906), 57.

ment. All the details of the presentation, such as the time, the appointment of the necessary aides, the acceptance of the credentials, the preparation of the President's speech of welcome and the final arrangements in the White House are under the jurisdiction of this Staff. All questions regarding the rights and immunities of foreign representatives accredited to the United States are decided here; also arrangements for such courtesies as the freedom of the port and other similar privileges granted to distinguished foreigners are taken care of by the Staff. The task of entertaining and protecting visiting foreign officials, foreign naval vessels and their officers, and foreign military organizations is included. It operates the sumptuously furnished Blair House and the Blair-Lee House for the housing and entertainment of distinguished foreign guests.

In one week Richard Southgate, Chief of Protocol from 1935 to 1937, had to go to New York to meet Ambassador Le Breton of Argentina and to return to Washington with him. Later in the same week he went to New York to meet Hjalmar Schacht, and came back with him. On Saturday of the same week he left for the Pacific Coast to meet the Japanese delegation, which in those days meant four days on the train each way. Southgate is said to have remarked, "When I die, I want placed on my grave a stuffed shirt and a battered top hat, with the inscription: 'He rode with Ambassadors.'"

When a foreign head of state, or minister of foreign affairs, or some other outstanding dignitary makes a formal visit, the arrangements for his reception must not only insure his safety but also preclude the appearance of any hostile manifestation which might reflect upon this Government's courtesy and hospitality.

The Protocol Staff also assists the American diplomatic official who goes abroad. It finds out whether he is *persona grata* to the foreign government; it prescribes the method of presenting his credentials, subject, of course, to foreign customs; it makes arrangements for his participation in international conferences or ceremonial functions. It answers questions concerning the acceptance of medals and decorations conferred by foreign governments upon military, naval, or civil officers of the United States.

All ceremonial letters from the President of the United States to the heads of foreign governments are prepared in this agency. It is responsible for the preparation of the *Diplomatic List* and must be exceedingly careful that no foreign representative's name is omitted. It is equally important that the name of no individual who has not a bona fide official connection with a foreign government appear on the *List*.

The Protocol Staff has charge of the seals of the United States and the Department of State and sees to it that the seal of the United States is affixed to all treaties, executive proclamations and other documents required by law. The seal of the State Department is used to authenticate numerous documents such as powers of attorney, trademarks and patents, certificates of fraudulent naturalization, courier letters, extradition papers and many others. The Protocol Staff also maintains custody of decorations and awards conferred by foreign governments upon officers of the United States and determines when such individuals are legally entitled to receive such decorations or awards.

The present Chief of Protocol is John Farr Simmons, a Foreign Service Officer of Career Minister rank, who has had some thirty-five years experience in the State Department and Foreign Service of the United States. The total staff as of September 15, 1950, was twenty-six persons. Raymond D. Muir, Chief Ceremonial Officer and Assistant Chief, was former chief usher at the White House.

Correspondence Review Staff.   A small but vitally necessary cog in the machinery of the Department of State is the Correspondence Review Staff. For many years preceding World War I all outgoing correspondence from the Department came under the careful scrutiny of Alvey A. Adee. But when the daily output of letters increased from about a hundred to over a thousand, a more elaborate organization was required. Designated as the Office of Coördination and Reviews, its first director was Miss Margaret Hanna, who had served under Assistant Secretary of State Adee for some twenty-eight years. After heading this agency for another thirteen years she was succeeded by Mrs. Blanche Rule Halla who, after nine years as Assistant Chief, has been in charge of it for the past fourteen years. The Correspondence Review Staff sees to it that every important outgoing piece of mail is reviewed, edited and carefully coördinated as to accuracy and style and in correct form for signature. In order that consistent decisions and uniform policy be insured and diplomatic errors avoided, the Correspondence Review Staff makes certain that every interested party has initialed the draft before it is signed and dispatched.

This agency has prepared and is the custodian of the *Official Style Book* of the Department of State which prescribes the forms of address and correspondence carried on by the Department, "the departmental lingo" as Secretary of State Day called it. A ready reference file of diplomatic precedents is maintained so as to avoid action contrary to well established precedents without the necessity for prolonged research. An up-to-the-minute file of names of all ambassadors, ministers, and heads of missions in Washington and abroad is kept so that the Department may know at all times the names, titles and rank of responsible persons to whom communications may be addressed.

A few examples will show the advantages of the review procedure. When the American Minister in Lisbon in 1941 requested the Department to instruct him as to whether he could permit American officials who had been interned in Germany or Italy to be interviewed by British Legation officials as they passed through Lisbon, one division drafted a reply declaring it to be undesirable and another declared the Department found no reason to object. Without the reviewing by this agency, the two contradictory instructions might have been dispatched to Minister Fish. On another occasion when an American citizen inquired of the Department regarding Canton and Enderbury Islands, an inexperienced official curtly replied that the Department of Interior had jurisdiction. As a simple courtesy, the Review Staff added a sentence stating that the letter had therefore been referred to the Interior Department for attention. The young drafting officer resented the action, but he was overruled.

On one occasion when a young vice consul who was being transferred sent in a batch of clippings from the local press quite laudatory in tone and expressing keen regret at his departure, he was sarcastically informed by a Department official that his excellent standing was recognized without need of further evidence. Mrs. Halla saw no reason for such a communication to be sent since the vice consul was already in the States and could be reprimanded orally if it was thought necessary. Her position in the matter was approved.

During the drastic reorganization of the Department made by Secretary Stettinius in 1944, this agency was temporarily eliminated. The bad results were so quickly evident that within a month a complete restoration was effected. The excellent work performed by this agency is due largely to the long experience and great ability of the Chief and two Assistant Chiefs. Mrs. Halla, the Chief, has served in the Department continuously for thirty-four years, Assistant Chief Sarah D. Moore for thirty-three years, and Assistant Chief Helen L. Daniel for twenty-nine years.

3

The Department of State—II

THE SECRETARY OF STATE, as we have already indicated by virtue of his close relationship with the President, must be a political appointee of the President. In fact, the President has almost a free hand in this appointment and rarely does the Senate refuse an immediate confirmation. On the contrary, although there is no legal requirement to this effect, it was generally hoped when the office of Under Secretary was first created that since the Secretary of State must be a political nominee, the Under Secretary should be a permanent appointee from the career service or from the experienced personnel in the Department whose tenure might give a greater degree of continuity to the work of the Department. It may be said that although this hope has not been realized in respect to permanency, it has not been disappointed in the qualifications and ability of the incumbents.

The office of Under Secretary of State was first provided for by law in 1919.[1] For the preceding ten years a position known as Counselor to the State Department existed, but with the advent of the new office the position of Counselor was dropped. In 1923 the situation was regularized by the following provision in the annual appropriation act: "Undersecretary of State and the counselor for the department shall hereafter be designated 'Undersecretary of State' to be appointed by the President by and with the advice and consent of the Senate. . . ." [2]

The first Under Secretary of State was Frank Lyon Polk, an able lawyer who had already served as Counselor in the Department of State for four years, and for six months had been Acting Secretary of State while Secretary Lansing was in France. He was succeeded by Norman H. Davis, who had represented the United States abroad as financial commissioner, and had served both on the Armistice Commission and upon the Supreme Economic Council. Of the fifteen subsequent appointments up to date (1951) Under Secretaries Fletcher, Phillips, Grew, Castle, and

[1] 40 U.S. *Statutes at Large*, 1224.
[2] 42 U.S. *Statutes at Large*, 1068.

Welles were from the career service. Of the others, one, J. Reuben Clark, had served previously as solicitor for the Department of State and was an outstanding authority on international law, and the other, Joseph P. Cotton, was appointed by President Hoover at the request of Secretary Stimson to help reorganize the Department. Under Secretaries Stettinius, Clayton, and Acheson had all served as Assistant Secretaries before being named as Under Secretaries. Robert A. Lovett, former Assistant Secretary of War, had proved his administrative ability, and as international banker, was thoroughly informed regarding European economic and financial affairs. James E. Webb, who was appointed Under Secretary of State January 27, 1949, was a lawyer and businessman who had served from 1946 to 1949 as Director of the Budget. He was particularly well equipped to reorganize the Department in accordance with the Hoover Committee's recommendations. Up to the present time, career officer Sumner Welles has served the longest period as Under Secretary of State—having held the position from 1937 until 1943. Joseph Grew and William Phillips, both career officers, have had the honor of having each held the office upon two separate occasions.

The Under Secretary of State is the principal assistant and adviser to the Secretary of State. He aids the Secretary in the discharge of his various functions, such as formulating and executing the foreign policies of the Government and in the reception of the representatives of foreign governments. He has general direction over the work of the Department, and the heads of the geographical divisions quite commonly confer with him in the formulation of policies. In fact, where the Under Secretary is particularly familiar by experience and training with certain fields, the heads of those geographical divisions report directly to him. For example, since Under Secretary Phillips was particularly familiar with the European situation and to some considerable extent with the Far East, the heads of these two geographical divisions conferred regularly with him. In the same way Under Secretary Welles generally assumed responsibility for the relations with Latin America. In passing it should be noted that for a short period a second Under Secretary for Economic Affairs was appointed, and William L. Clayton held this position from August 17, 1946, until October 14, 1947.

The Under Secretary customarily acts for the Secretary in matters which do not require the Secretary's personal attention and in the absence of the Secretary he becomes Acting Secretary of State. In fact even with the Secretary present the Under Secretary acts as a sort of deputy of the Secretary, signing some correspondence and performing any other function possible to relieve the strain on the Secretary. With a department as highly centralized as State the Under Secretary is the Secretary's *alter ego* and must be ready to substitute for him upon any occasion.

During the administration of Under Secretary Webb certain new problems of an international character were put under the jurisdiction of the Under Secretary's office. Problems of foreign relations pertaining to atomic energy were assigned to Special Assistant to the Under Secretary R. Gordon Arneson, who had served as advisor to the United Nations Atomic Energy Committee from 1946 to 1948. Another Special Assistant to the Under Secretary was Wilbert M. Chapman, who had as his field fisheries and wild life. The threat to United States interests in the seals of the Pribiloff Islands, to the salmon fisheries of the Columbia River by the Japanese, the migratory bird laws and treaties required the formulation of policy and action to safeguard the rights of American citizens in these fields.

The so-called Point Four program of President Truman, which required planning, implementation and managing, brought another Special Assistant into the Under Secretary's Office. The Act for Technical Coöperation and Development in undeveloped areas upon a coöperative basis was placed under the Department of State for administration and Ambassador Capus M. Waynick as Administrator was at first made Special Assistant to the Under Secretary.

A third Special Assistant Floyd A. Lehrbas, a former foreign correspondent and one-time Director of the Department Office of International Information, was named by Under Secretary Webb to improve public relations with the press. It was felt that the correspondents did not have enough personal contacts with the Secretary, Under Secretary, and Assistant Secretaries. Lehrbas determined to remedy this situation and within four months he had arranged five hundred conferences where the representatives of the press were able to get better acquainted with the top side departmental officials. He also arranged that the Foreign Service Institute should give a course on public relations to Foreign Service officers in the Department. It was determined that every effort should be made to counteract the widely spread critical attitude of the public towards both the Department and its representatives abroad.

During the period towards the end of the Second World War when Secretary of State Stettinius was attending the many international conferences which required his presence in person, Under Secretary Grew served as Acting Secretary of State for five and one-half months. Under Secretary Acheson had an even more difficult assignment, since his chief, Secretary Byrnes, was compelled to spend more time in the capitals of Europe than in Washington. It was fortunate for the United States that in the first case the Acting Secretary outclassed his superior in both experience and ability, and in the second case, the Department was in equally able and experienced hands. Under Secretary of State James E. Webb, who had made an exceptional record of administrative ability as Director of the Bureau of the Budget, was appointed to aid in the reorganization program. Inasmuch as Secretary Acheson was familiar with every phase of departmental policy-making as well as administration, Under Secretary Webb's lack of experience in international affairs was not the handicap that it might otherwise have been. However, since the Secretary of State often does not have previous diplomatic experience, it would seem the part of wisdom that under normal conditions the Under Secretary's appointment be based upon experience in the field of international affairs as well as upon tested ability.

The Counselor. The position of Counselor in the Department of State has been an intermittent one. It was first established by Secretary Knox in 1909, and its incumbent was expected "to investigate and report on such important questions as required legal and technical skill and uninterrupted consideration." [3] When the office of Under Secretary of State was established in 1919, Frank Lyon Polk, who had been serving as Counselor since 1915, added this new title which the Department preferred, and the situation was regularized by the elimination of the title of counselor in 1923.

The position was reëstablished in 1936 in order to satisfy Secretary Hull, who wanted R. Walton Moore as his Under Secretary of State. President Franklin D. Roosevelt wanted Sumner Welles as Under Secretary and when he appointed Welles Under Secretary he named Moore as Counselor with equal rank and salary as special adviser to the Secretary. However, in the absence of the Secretary, the Under Secretary became Acting Secretary of State. When Moore died in 1941 at the age of eighty-one, no one was named to succeed him and the position again lapsed. It reappeared in 1945 when Secretary Byrnes named his Special Assistant, Benjamin Cohen, Counselor of the Department. When Cohen resigned in 1947, Secretary Marshall appointed Charles E. Bohlen, a Foreign Service Officer of nineteen years service, to the post.

The duties of the position had gradually changed and under Bohlen its principal activity was in conducting general liaison work with the Bureau of the Budget and the Congress, following up pending legislation and keeping officers of the Department advised of legislative developments relating to their activities. Nevertheless the Counselor still served as a top flight political adviser to the Secretary whenever the situation warranted.

When Bohlen was sent as Career Minister to Paris in 1949, George Kennan, Director of the Policy Planning Staff, was named Counselor as well. After the latter resigned his position as head of the Policy Planning Staff in 1950 in order to take a much needed rest and to engage in private research for a period, he still retained the title of Counselor. However, since liaison with Congress had now become the duty of the Assistant Secretary of State for Congressional Relations, the position of Counselor

[3] Graham H. Stuart, *The Department of State* (New York, 1949), 213.

reverted to a specialist adviser's position and in the spring of 1951 Mr. Bohlen was recalled from Paris to fill this rôle. The importance of the position was shown when Mr. Bohlen was sent in the fall of 1951 as adviser to General Omar Bradley in his trip to Korea to determine what policy should be followed in the stalemated Korean truce negotiations.

The Ambassador-at-Large. One of the problems recognized by the Hoover Commission was the necessity for the Secretary of State or the Under Secretary to attend numerous international conferences requiring long continued absences from the Department. For example, Secretary Byrnes spent 350 out of his 562 days as Secretary of State in international conferences. To remedy this situation there was created on March 2, 1949, the Office of Ambassador-at-Large who could assist the Secretary in important international negotiations as well as attend important conferences abroad when an experienced representative of high rank was required. The Department was fortunate in persuading Dr. Philip C. Jessup, Professor of International Law at Columbia University, to accept this position. He had served upon many occasions as consultant to the Department and other governmental agencies and at the time of his appointment was serving as deputy chief of the United States mission to the United Nations. Ambassador-at-Large Jessup has been able to reduce the burden of international conferences and negotiations formerly resting upon the Secretary of State to a very considerable degree.

Dr. Jessup was one of those accused by Senator McCarthy of Wisconsin of having an "unusual affinity for Communist causes." Dr. Jessup was cleared both by the State Department's Loyalty Security Board and by the President's Loyalty Review Board. The accusations were shown to be wholly unmerited and unworthy of serious consideration. In fact Generals Marshall and Eisenhower both attested to Jessup's devotion to America and his opposition to communism, and President Truman and Secretary of State Acheson gave him their loyal support.

The Deputy Under Secretaries of State. The position of Deputy Under Secretary of State dates from the Hoover Commission's reorganization plan, which recommended the strengthening of the Secretary and Under Secretary level by the addition of two Deputy Under Secretaries, the one to act in matters of substance and the other as "general manager" to administer the Department and the overseas service.

The first person to serve as Deputy Under Secretary in charge of political affairs was Dean Rusk, who at the time of his appointment was serving as Assistant Secretary of State in charge of United Nations affairs. Mr. Rusk was succeeded in 1950 by Career Minister H. Freeman Mathews, a Foreign Service Officer with twenty-seven years experience.

In addition to his responsibilities as assistant to the Under Secretary in the fields of coördination and policy the Deputy Under Secretary for Political Affairs acts as consultant for the Department in the National Security Council and maintains liaison between the Department of State and the Department of Defense. Although in his immediate office the Deputy Under Secretary has a staff of only ten including the various bureaus and offices under his general direction, the personnel as of January 1, 1950, numbered 1,792.

The Deputy Under Secretary for Administration is the official largely responsible for the operations of the Department and of the Foreign Service. All questions of personnel management, budget estimates, operation facilities, and the security program of the Department are under his jurisdiction. The total staff for these various activities numbered 2,922 as of January 1, 1950.

John E. Peurifoy, who had been acting as Assistant Secretary of State in charge of administration, became the first Deputy Under Secretary for Administration. Mr. Peurifoy, whom Congressman Judd of Minnesota held up "as evidence of what a man can do even in the government if he has the ability," had advanced from a $2,000 a year job as an economic analyst to this important position in a little over a decade. When in the summer of 1950, Mr. Peurifoy was sent as Ambassador to Greece he was succeeded by Carlisle H. Humelsine, who had been serving as Deputy Assistant Secretary for Administration. The Deputy Assistant Secretary was Walter K. Scott, who had already served in several important administrative posts in the Department before he was named to this position.

The Deputy Under Secretary for Administration has numerous offices and divisions under his jurisdiction, some of which, like the Office of Budget and Finance and the Division of Central Services, are exceedingly important but whose activities are not immediately germane to the work of the Foreign Service officer; hence we shall limit our consideration to those agencies and activities in which he has a more direct interest. In presenting these agencies the order followed has been largely in accord with the classified directory of the Department.

ADMINISTRATION OF THE FOREIGN SERVICE

Director General of the Foreign Service. The present organization in the Department of State for the administration of the Foreign Service is based upon the Foreign Service Act of 1946 as modified by the reorganization effected in accordance with the Hoover Commission Report of 1949. At the top is the Director General of the Foreign Service, who as adviser to the Deputy Under Secretary of State for Administration represents the interests of the Foreign Service. He evaluates the effectiveness of the departmental policies and activities which concern the overseas operations of the Department and appraises the effectiveness of the

Foreign Service in carrying out departmental policies. He also helps in the formulation of policies governing the administration of the Foreign Service and in coördinating the activities of the Foreign Service with the needs of the Department and other Federal agencies. He supervises the inspectors of the Foreign Service establishments abroad, the foreign reporting services, the secretariat of the interdepartmental board of the Foreign Service and serves as Chairman of the Commission of the Foreign Service Institute.

This "chief of staff" position of the Service must be filled according to the Foreign Service Act of 1946 by appointment by the Secretary of State from among Foreign Service officers of career minister or class I designation, and he may not hold the office for more than four years. Up to the present time there have been four Directors General of the Foreign Service: Selden Chapin, Christian M. Ravndal, Richard P. Butrick, and Gerald Drew. The effectiveness of the position has been somewhat handicapped by the uncertainty regarding the amalgamation of the personnel of the Foreign Service with that of the Department of State.

The Division of Foreign Service Personnel.   In line with the recommendations of the Hoover Commission a new Office of Personnel was established in 1949 so as to consolidate the separate personnel facilities for the Foreign Service and the Department of State. Haywood P. Martin, who had been serving as Director of the Office of the Foreign Service, was made Director of the combined agency. The Division of Foreign Service Personnel numbered approximately 175 persons, whereas the Division of Departmental Personnel numbered only 75. Foreign Service Officer Elbridge Durbrow was named Chief of the former and Arch K. Jean remained Chief of the latter.

The Division of Foreign Service Personnel is the agency in the Department which is closest to the Foreign Service officer and which has the most direct control over his position in the field. This Division is the planning agency of the Foreign Service officer's career. It takes into consideration the aptitude of the officer, his language qualifications, his particular interests, his predilection for diplomatic or consular work, his previous experience, his length of service at the post, any necessary commitments that he may have made, his health, and even on occasion the health of some close member of his family.

For example, on one occasion where a consul's wife was stricken with such a serious illness that it was essential that she be returned to the States, the Foreign Service officer was transferred to the Department without his making a formal request. By this procedure the expense of transportation was eliminated, a matter of considerable importance to the consul since he had already expended some $3,000 in meeting the cost of his wife's illness. The Foreign Service officer was not unappreciative at the Department's action and stated publicly that he probably owed his wife's life to Foreign Personnel's consideration and prompt action.

As might be expected the Division sometimes makes transfers which seem fantastically foolish from the point of view of the officer concerned. The classic example is the case of the consul with seven children who was transferred from Vladivostok to Singapore in the middle of winter after the family wardrobe had already been bought. But cases on the other side might also be cited.

An organization with its personnel distributed as is that of the Foreign Service in all parts of the civilized world, subjected to every sort of climatic condition, from equatorial Nairobi to wintry Winnipeg, and liable to be transferred from Paris to Port-au-Prince at a moment's notice, must pay some attention to morale. It is the function of the Division of Foreign Service Personnel to keep in such close and intimate contact with the officers of the service that transfers and promotions shall be made as far as possible both for the good of the service and to the advantage of the individual. It is hardly advantageous to the service that an officer who has spent a good share of his career in Spanish-speaking countries and has shown particular ability in such posts be transferred to a Far Eastern or Near Eastern assignment. If a change is thought desirable, a post in another Latin country or an English-speaking country would be more advantageous. Neither is it good policy to give certain officers a monopoly of the popular posts while certain others are asked to accept more than their share of undesirable assignments.

Of course, the primary basis for recommendation both for transfers and promotions is the carefully prepared efficiency reports sent in by supervising officers. These reports must be studied and filed to serve as the officer's character *dossier*. But personal interviews are also an important factor in evaluating an officer's services and the Division makes a particular point of interviewing all visiting officers home on leave. Every year hundreds of officers visit the Department for periods varying from several days to a few weeks and are interviewed by one or more officers of the Division.

In addition to the reports from the officers in charge of each post, the Department keeps a number of inspectors in the field who travel from post to post and keep the Division in personal touch with the force in the field. Men chosen for inspectors are men of experience in the service, endowed not only with keen perceptions and administrative ability, but possessed of personalities which command affection and respect. An inspector will often perceive and report upon undesirable conditions which would never have been mentioned in an official report. He is also in a position to listen to grievances and to see that they are corrected if justifiable.

According to Howard K. Travers, Director of the Foreign Service Inspection Corps, "the inspector acts as the eyes and ears of the Director General in order to keep him fully informed concerning field conditions and should pass on to him any suggestions or constructive criticisms from the field which would result in an improvement in the Service."

Perhaps a word should be said concerning the Board of the Foreign Service, which was first set up by an executive order of June 8, 1931. This Board, which at present consists of three Assistant Secretaries of State, the Director General of the Foreign Service, and representatives from the Departments of Agriculture, Commerce, and Labor, receives the efficiency ratings of the Foreign Service officers from the Division of Foreign Service Personnel and recommends all assignments and promotions from the information thus furnished. Not only may recommendations be made for promotion within the Foreign Service, but those officers who have demonstrated special capacity may be recommended for promotion to the grade of minister or ambassador.

Division of Foreign Reporting.   This agency first set up in 1945 has as its primary responsibility the supplying of full and timely information on foreign developments to the various governmental Departments such as Commerce, Labor, and Interior which they might request or find useful. In carrying out this task the Division establishes standards regarding data to be reported and priorities regarding requests for information. One branch develops for each country in which the Foreign Service operates basic reporting plans to meet the informational requirements of the various governmental agencies to be serviced. Another branch handles the communications originating in the governmental agencies requesting information from the Foreign Service officers.

The other vital function of Foreign Reporting Division is one of evaluation of the reporting performance of Foreign Service posts. All political and economic reports prepared abroad for the various governmental agencies are received and checked for promptness and effectiveness. Thus the Division is the focal point through which the Department controls the reporting activities of the Foreign Service officers.

Division of Foreign Buildings Operations.   For more than a century the record of the United States Government in providing adequate living and working quarters for its diplomatic and consular representatives abroad left much to be desired. For some reason until quite recently it has been regarded as undemocratic for the United States to house its ambassadors and ministers adequately and to give them suitable chanceries in which to perform their functions. Up until the First World War period the United States possessed but one suitable embassy building and one adequate legation—the former at Constantinople, the latter at

Peking. The situation as regards consular establishments was even worse. The result of this situation was that only wealthy men could afford to accept the top positions in our diplomatic service. The Congress was not unaware of this situation and Congressman Nicholas Longworth from Ohio pointed out in 1906 that no one but a very rich man could be an ambassador of the United States in any European capital and that even to be a minister the appointee had to be comparatively wealthy. In fact he concluded that the United States in its top diplomatic personnel abroad had "an aristocracy purely and solely of the dollar."

Even as late as 1933, Francis White in resigning as Minister to Czecho-slovakia is said to have given as one of the reasons for his resignation the fact that the American legation was housed in a building whose chimney was falling down, whose roof was tumbling in, and where the chinks in the walls let in the sunshine and the rain. As a consequence Mr. White had been forced to reside in a hotel.

The first important legislation to remedy this situation was the Lowden Act of February 17, 1911, which provided a maximum of $500,000 annually to be used by the Secretary of State for the acquisition of suitable sites and buildings abroad. The first appropriations under this act were made in 1914 for the purchase of embassies in Tokyo and Mexico City. Subsequent progress was so slow that after fourteen years only eight embassy and legation buildings had been acquired, of which one was a gift by John Pierpont Morgan of his magnificent home in London. The United States Government delayed so long in accepting this generous gift that Mr. Morgan's son finally telephoned the Department of State that the offer had been withdrawn. Under Secretary Henry P. Fletcher, knowing how much the Department wanted the building, replied that it was too late as the President had already accepted the offer. He quickly drafted a letter of acceptance on White House stationery thanking Morgan for his generosity, rushed over to the White House and got President Harding's signature and dispatched the letter forthwith to Morgan in New York.

The next legislative step was the Foreign Service Buildings Act of May 7, 1926, which empowered the Secretary of State, subject to the direction of a Foreign Service Buildings Commission established by the Act, to acquire property and buildings and to alter, repair and furnish such buildings for the use of diplomatic and consular establishments. The amount to be appropriated, not to exceed $10,000,000, was to be known as the Foreign Service Building Fund of which not more than $2,000,000 was to be expended in any one year. The Foreign Service Buildings Commission was to consist of the Secretary of State, the Secretary of Treasury, the Secretary of Commerce, the chairman and ranking minority members of the committees on foreign affairs of the Senate and the House.

A month after the passage of the Act, the Foreign Service Buildings Office was set up in the Department and on June 23, 1926, Keith Merrill, a Foreign Service Officer, was appointed Chief.

In 1937 the present Chief, Frederic A. Larkin, was made head of the Office, which since 1944 has been known as the Division of Foreign Buildings Operations. The Chief serves as the executive secretary of the Foreign Service Buildings Commission of the Congress. At present (1951) there are five operating branches in the Department, (1) Property Leasing Branch, (2) Property Acquisitions, (3) Administration, (4) Furniture and Furnishings, and (5) Building Projects. There are also nine regional overseas offices: Rio de Janeiro, Manila, Tokyo, New Delhi, Vienna, Paris, The Hague, London, and Rome.

A tremendous expansion in acquisition of buildings abroad occurred after World War II as a result of foreign currency assets which were available to the United States arising from the disposal of war surplus, lend lease settlements, and the utilization of ECA counterpart funds. From 1947 through 1950 some 540 projects were completed in seventy-two countries at a cost of approximately $93,000,000 of which the American taxpayer contributed only about 3 per cent or about $2,300,000.

A summary of properties owned by the United States at the beginning of 1951 would show 8 office buildings, 3 residential properties and 2 combined office and residential properties in the American Republics; 27 office buildings, 120 residential properties and 9 combined office and residential properties in Europe; 19 office buildings, 100 residential properties and 7 combined office and residential properties in the Near East and Africa; and 9 office buildings, 53 residences and 4 combined office and residential properties in the Far East.[4]

Strangely enough, in spite of this great improvement in housing facilities for American Foreign Service officers abroad, probably no agency of the Department is criticized more bitterly and constantly than the Division of Foreign Service Buildings Operations. One of the causes of disagreement is the tendency of the Division to disregard the ideas of the officials at the various posts in order to follow a consistent policy of construction along American lines, which, it must be conceded, does not always harmonize with the existing architectural styles. It is also alleged that the Division fails to take advantage of opportunities presented by the resident officers and is forced later to pay more for less satisfactory sites. Finally, even if this Division is somewhat highhanded in its methods, on the whole American personnel abroad today is housed as well or better than other foreign representatives and it is improving steadily.

The Division of Communications and Records. The Division of Com-

---

[4] Department of State Appropriations for 1952, Hearings H. R. 82nd Cong., 1st sess., 485.

munications and Records was until 1931 known as the Bureau of Indexes and Archives. Its new title is better in that it indicates that this division is a living organism rather than the mortuary of archaic or obsolete documentary materials. Actually this division is the distributing and filing agency of the Department. It receives, records, classifies, distributes, and preserves the correspondence, written and telegraphic, of the Department. It is the vital link between the Foreign Service in the field and the officers of the Department.

· For the fiscal year 1950-1951 the Division of Communications and Records processed 522,626 telegrams, handled about 3,000,000 written official communications, and sent or received 83,548,813 words or groups of words. The statisticians have figured that DC receives or sends 95 words every minute of every day.

The incoming and outgoing messages are read by analysts familiar with the various agencies of the Department who decide to which a message shall be assigned for action and which for information only. The Division also provides a service for fast intergroup communication by radio-teletype between Washington and certain major Foreign Service posts. For example officers in Washington and London may get together in their respective conference rooms and see their incoming and outgoing messages transmitted by radio-teletype projected upon a screen an instant after receipt or transmission. This permits an exchange of ideas almost as speedily as if the two groups were in the same room.

Every form of communication is utilized by this Division. Although telephone service is now available to almost every corner of the earth, the Department relies primarily upon the mail and telegraph services. Secrecy is a vital factor, and the scrambler telephone is not as safe as a message sent in code by telegraph or wireless. If absolute secrecy is essential, a diplomatic pouch and special courier system is used. Couriers now fly regular routes spanning every continent and the airgram is utilized almost as much as the telegram. The courier service is under the general direction of this Division.

Although the outsider might think that the courier has the most glamorous job in the Division the life of a courier is not one to envy. For example, a courier on the North American routes flies monthly about twice as many hours as the flight personnel of the airlines. In fifteen days the courier on the A route makes a round trip from Washington to Rio de Janeiro stopping to leave or pick up pouches at more than a dozen Caribbean, Central American or South American posts. One of the most famous courier trips was made by Courier Horton R. Telford from Bern to Istanbul in 1940 after Italy had declared war on Greece. It included twenty kilometers on foot over mountains with porters carrying five sixty-pound pouches, being strafed by planes, bogged down in the mud in an automobile, hiring an oxcart to get to a railway and then flagging a train to Istanbul. But the pouches arrived intact.[5] It has been estimated that the present group of almost a hundred couriers flies 10,200,000 miles a year which equals over four hundred times around the earth at the equator.

When a communication is received by this Division, if a letter or dispatch, it is opened, analyzed and sent to the office, division, or person interested in the subject matter. If a telegram, it is decoded and then sent on. Before it leaves the Division, however, it is turned over to a record clerk who makes a brief description of it for filing as well as an index card. If previous correspondence is referred to or seems relevant to take proper action, such papers are withdrawn from the files and attached to the piece of correspondence. If the communication goes to several agencies, all are noted, and each time the piece returns to DC and is again routed on its way. Once the communication has completed its routing, it is returned and filed in its proper place in the permanent archives.

If the communication is vitally important it may be sent directly to the Secretary of State, to the Under Secretary or to one of the Assistant Secretaries; but more often the desk officer of the area or subject-matter particularly concerned is the first to receive it, and he may indicate its subsequent routing.

The Division of Communications and Records is one of the largest agencies in the Department. At present the Division has three branches: Telegraph, Records, and Liaison. The pressure of work imposed by World War II forced a reorganization of this Division both in procedures and in equipment. When for example the Telegraph Branch got as far as two days behind in the coding and decoding of messages, the War Department stepped in with trained code clerks to help out. With the aid of new high speed equipment—decoding machines that could function more than six times as fast as by the manual method—the average time for a message in the code room was reduced from forty-eight hours to six. The backlog of as many as 15,000 documents in the Records Branch was eliminated, and a more efficient functional organization was put into operation with a tally system which kept the Division informed at all times of the location of papers. The Liaison Branch both processes and distributes all telegrams, airgrams, dispatches and reports from the Foreign Service and maintains liaison with some fifty governmental agencies.

With the vast volume of incoming communications it can well be understood that messages do not always reach the proper person as quickly as the representative in the field would like. Ambassador Miles Poindexter claims that a vital message which he sent from Lima in regard to the Tacna-Arica situation not only did not reach the Secretary of State but disappeared completely in the Department's complicated records filing

[5] See the article by Couriers Jack Grover and Ed Pierce in the *Saturday Evening Post* (March 13, 1948) describing the couriers' work.

system. On another occasion the request by the Soviet Government for a loan was mislaid and the reply drafted only six months later.

Various devices are used by United States representatives in the field to get their reports into the hands of the proper officials in the Department as quickly as possible. A common method is to overclassify the document. Utilizing the classification now in operation for State Department documentation: unrestricted, restricted, confidential, secret, top secret and eyes only, the officer in the field by raising the classification one or two places may obtain consideration at a higher level.

As a result of the highly technical character of the work in this Division, changes of personnel have been reduced to a minimum. David A. Salman, who came over from the War Department to instal a new system of filing in 1906, was made Chief ten years later and remained as head until 1943 and then served as consultant on cryptography until the end of 1948, a total service in the Department of forty-two years. Unfortunately, this record has not been maintained during the period of World War II when one chief followed another in yearly or biannual intervals. The present Chief, Robert E. Stufflebeam, was appointed in January, 1949, after three years' experience in the Department in administrative work. His staff currently numbers about 725.

Division of Cryptography. Cryptography in the Department dates back to the days of Benjamin Franklin, but the first code book was not used until 1876. The work was at first an integral part of the Division of Communications and Records, but in 1934 in order to obtain greater security the work was put directly under the jurisdiction of Assistant Secretary of State G. Howland Shaw with David A. Salmon in charge. In 1944 a survey directed by Secretary Hull recommended mechanico-electric equipment instead of the hand-operated equipment then in use and a better system of accounting for secret documents. It was also recommended that the two codes which had been in use for some considerable time be used no longer for confidential communications.

As a result of this survey a Division of Cryptography was established in the fall of 1944 and Commander Lee Wood Parker, who was serving as Assistant Security Officer in the Department, was named Chief. As set up the operations section was responsible for the devising and implementing of the Department's cryptographic systems; the security section reviewed telegraphic communications and was responsible for the detection of security violations.

There is necessarily a close relationship between the Department and the Foreign Service posts abroad in this vitally important field. The code room in the Division of Communications and Records must be informed whenever a new post is established or an old one eliminated so that messages will be sent out in the proper code or cipher. If a post is closed suddenly because of threatened seizure by an enemy certain equipment and material explaining its use must be destroyed and the Department notified.

Every effort has been made to improve and protect the Department's cryptographic systems. The present methods of classifying materials and administering security controls are as rigorous as can be devised, and every effort is being made to keep up to date on technical improvements in cryptographic methods and to work out the best possible security system for protecting vital information.

OFFICE OF CONSULAR AFFAIRS

This office formerly known as the Office of Controls is the result of the desire on the part of certain administration officials to centralize under one head various agencies which have no particular relation one to the other and which usually could function more effectively autonomously. At the present time it has under its jurisdiction the following divisions: Passport, Visa, Protective Services, Security, and Munitions. Certainly no one would question Ruth Shipley's ability to run the Passport Division without any direction from above, and for many years the Visa Division although headed by regularly rotating Foreign Service officers has been ably directed by its two permanent Assistant Chiefs, Eliot B. Coulter and Robert C. Alexander. Inasmuch as the divisions of this office of particular interest to the Foreign Service are discussed below, there is no need at this time to consider the office as an administrative entity. Its present Director is Samuel D. Boykin.

The Passport Division. The Passport Division is one of the largest and one of the most autonomous divisions of the Department. Before World War I when passports were the exception rather than the rule, the duties of the Division were largely carried on by the Bureau of Citizenship. During the war, the Bureau increased in size until it had as many as 250 employees. To remedy this situation, a departmental order of Secretary Lansing, August 13, 1918, divided the work. The Bureau of Citizenship was henceforth to be known as the Division of Passport Control and was to retain jurisdiction over all matters pertaining to passports and citizenship. At the same time a Visa Office was established to take care of all matters relating to aliens coming to the United States. The present organization of the Passport Division is based upon Secretary Kellogg's order of April 17, 1926, which merely changed the name to Passport Division.

At the outbreak of World War II the Passport Division was given the responsibility for controlling the movements of American citizens in accordance with our neutrality laws and with getting governmental personnel to various areas required by their duties. A new green passport more difficult to forge was issued to replace the outstanding red passports thus removing from circulation all fraudulent or altered passports as well as invalidating those in the hands of persons engaged in activities not in the best interest of the United States. Another security provision was the issuance for the first time of passports to American seamen. This requirement alone necessitated the issuance of more than 300,000 seaman passports during the war period. During the war the Division also issued certificates of identity where desirable to defense workers and to American nationals required to go back and forth across the Mexican border.[6]

Since the issuance of passports is the primary function of the Division, it is perhaps worthwhile to show the constantly increasing number of passports granted to American citizens. In 1914 the United States issued and renewed 20,320 passports. In 1920 when steamship and railway routes were once more open to travel 160,488 were issued. Ten years later before the ravages of the depression the peak year was reached and in 1930 some 203,174 passports were issued and renewed. World War II again practically stopped civilian travel and the record of 1930 was not equalled until 1949 when over 260,000 passports were required. All records were broken in 1950 with the issuance and renewal of 306,871 passports.

For convenience to the public passport agencies have been established in New York, San Francisco, Boston, Chicago, and New Orleans, all of which are supervised by the Division in Washington. It should be noted, however, that these agencies only issue emergency passports after authorization has been obtained from the Division in Washington. Ordinarily they merely take the application and the Division issues the passport. As a further convenience, an application for a passport may also be executed before any clerk of a Federal or state court authorized to naturalize aliens.

Although most travelers get their passports before leaving the United States, sometimes their passports expire while they are abroad and there are also many American citizens living abroad who desire passports. In these cases the American consular officers issue the desired passports.

Inasmuch as passports are at present issued only to persons who are citizens or owe allegiance to the United States, various accompanying documents are required. The application must give the pertinent facts regarding his birth, residence, marital status, citizenship, the objects of his journey and his destination. He must supply photographs of himself and those accompanying him. In making his application he must be accompanied by an American witness who can make a supporting affidavit.

[6] For a more detailed account see Graham H. Stuart, "Safeguarding the State through Passport Control," *Department of State Bulletin* (June 10, 1945), 1066-70.

A native citizen must submit a birth certificate or its equivalent, while a naturalized citizen must submit his certificate of naturalization. If there is the slightest possibility of fraud, all of these documents must be checked as to their authenticity.

The work of a clerk examining a passport application is extremely complicated. He must keep in mind the various laws, regulations and treaty provisions which apply and at the same time be on the lookout for fraud and deception. Particular attention must be paid to original applications coming from abroad because fake or altered birth certificates have become a regular stock in trade in certain countries of Europe.

The Passport Division is very active in its efforts to prevent fraud. Not only is every document scanned and checked but when fraud is discovered the Division acts in procuring indictments and assists in the prosecution. It has also worked out in certain fraud centers abroad a special technique for the identification and authentication of documents. It has made the alteration of passports exceedingly difficult by the use of a special paper and of a new type of flexible cover, by the employment of special type in the passport writing machines, and by a varicolored impression stamped on the photograph at the same time sealing it to the page.

The Division works constantly with the Department of Justice in checking citizenship and in submitting evidence looking towards the deportation of aliens guilty of passport frauds. Since the recent immigration laws have restricted so rigidly the entrance of aliens, the responsibilities of the Division in connection with the issue, renewal and amendment of passports has naturally increased along these lines.

The Division is necessarily divided into various sections equipped to carry out the technical character of the work. In addition to the chief and several administrative assistants there is a European Section, a Western Hemisphere Section, a Restricted Area Section, and a Military Personnel Section. There is an Information Section, a Passport Processing Section, a Research and Records Section, and a Fraud Section. The largest section is the Foreign Branch with forty-five in its personnel. The total number of authorized regular positions is 205.

The Chief of the Passport Division is Ruth B. Shipley, who has been in the Department of State since 1914. She has held her present position as Chief of the Division since 1928, and under her direction the Division has been administered efficiently, and without fear or favor.

Few officials of the Department come under more pressure or are subjected to greater criticism without being able to explain than the Chief of the Passport Division. A case in point occurred when a Polish priest with a Communist background, the Reverend Orlemanski, applied for a passport to go to Russia. He was refused even though much pressure was brought to bear from many high places. The passport was issued only upon an order direct from the White House. A storm of protest arose in the press on the ground that since a group of Baptist ministers had been refused passports to go to South America to work with the Indians the Division had shown rank discrimination. Mrs. Shipley made no effort to defend herself. What was her surprise a few days later to read in the press that President Roosevelt commended the "wonderful ogre" in the Passport Division for her rigorous enforcement of the law.

The Visa Division. The Visa Division is essentially the development of an organization due to the vast amount of work entailed by the rigid restriction of immigration to the United States after World War I. The Visa Office was set up August 13, 1918, in the Division of Passport Control and detached December 1, 1919 to be operated as a separate unit. On January 1, 1931, a departmental order changed its name to Visa Division.

Before World War I the only control of immigration was at our ports of entry which was a very harsh and unfair system for the alien who was not permitted to enter. When the restrictive Immigration Act of May 19, 1921, placed the entrance of aliens upon a quota basis, the Visa Office and the Department of Labor worked out a policy whereby consuls should issue visas to eligible immigrants abroad. Profiting by the experience of the Act of 1921, Congress provided by the Immigration Act of 1924 that an immigrant could only be admitted after first procuring a consular visa on his passport and the consul had to pass upon the eligibility of the alien under both the qualification tests and the allotted quotas.

Although the consul abroad is made responsible for the proper administration of our immigration laws, it is the function of the Visa Division to advise the officers in the field as to the interpretations of law in connection with questions which have arisen in the case of individual aliens. This problem was increased considerably by the period of the depression when it was found advisable to restrict immigration drastically under a strict interpretation of the clause in the Act of 1917 classifying as inadmissible all aliens who are likely to become public charges.

As might be expected, this drastic restriction policy, which reduced immigration to about 10 per cent of the allotted quotas, brought about protests on the part of interested parties in the United States. Not only were consuls and the Visa Division bombarded by letters from relations and friends of disappointed aliens, but members of Congress took up cudgels in their behalf, regardless of the fact that both consuls and the Department were merely enforcing a law which Congress itself had passed. The correspondence carried on by the Division along these lines has been a considerable and a somewhat thankless task.

As a matter of fact, while it has been the policy of the Government to protect the interests of the American wage-earner, at the same time the

Visa Division must see to it that the immigration laws are administered as humanely as is consistent with the restrictive provisions of the law. Every effort is made to avoid needless separation of husbands and wives, parents, and children. There are certain provisions of the Act of 1924 which allow American citizens to obtain on behalf of certain immigrant relatives a non quota or preference within the quota status. Such a status is obtained by filing a petition with the Department of Justice which, if approved, goes to the Visa Division for transmission to the consul in the field. The Visa Division has a so-called "Petition Room" where a record is kept of the petitions approved by the Department of Justice and which forwards the authorizations to the proper consular officer abroad.

This Division reviews all visa correspondence from consular officials to interested persons in the United States. Such a review permits the maintenance of a fixed policy and also a check on any incomplete statement of fact or misinterpretation of law. In cases where visas have been refused on questionable grounds or unnecessary delays have occurred, the Division takes up the case with the consular official and the question is carefully reviewed.

Investigations of fraud in connection with immigration documents or other phases of the illegal entry of aliens is another important activity of the Visa Division. It also coöperates with the Department of Justice in regard to the deportation of aliens, with the Treasury Department regarding matters concerning smugglers of narcotics, with the United States Public Health Service concerning the medical examination of aliens by their surgeons, and with the Department of Justice regarding the prosecution of persons engaged in procuring the illegal entry of aliens into the United States. If the Department considers it desirable to recommend changes in existing immigration legislation to the Congress, the Secretary and Assistant Secretary of State utilize the services of the Visa Division in an advisory capacity.

During World War II, in order to prevent the entry of persons who might be prejudicial to the security of the United States, a new procedure was established whereby aliens entering the United States were required to submit to the Visa Division a biographical statement and two affidavits of sponsorship. An interdepartmental committee considered these cases from the standpoint of national security and made appropriate recommendations. A formal review procedure was established with a board of appeal for cases where the committee's action was adverse. The "Alien Registration Act of 1940" required the fingerprinting and registration of all aliens.

The Displaced Persons Act of June 25, 1948, which authorized the issuance of immigration visas to 205,000 displaced persons during the period from July 1, 1948, to June 30, 1950, instead of utilizing the Visa

Division for its administration set up a Displaced Persons Commission in Washington, D.C., whose responsibility it was to certify to the consular officers that an individual was a displaced person and eligible to entry under the act.[7]

Although the principal visa task of the Division pertains to the granting of visas for immigrants' passports, there is also a certain amount of work pertaining to the visaing of the passports of temporary visitors. Many aliens, unable to obtain entrance as immigrants, try to get in as tourists, for alleged business purposes or to visit relatives. Ordinarily the consul can decide these cases directly but occasionally he finds it advisable to consult with the Division.

Finally, the Division issues diplomatic visas to members of foreign missions in Washington who desire to go abroad and return to the United States.

There were in March, 1951, one hundred twenty-three employees in the Visa Division and during the fiscal year 1950, 2,665 passports were visaed in the Division and 6,682 advisory opinions rendered. When it is remembered that over 300,000 visas are issued in the field annually of which over 150,000 may be quota visas the work done by the Division can be appreciated. Hervé J. L'Heureux, the present Chief of the Division, is a Foreign Service Officer of some twenty years service. Because of the pressures and strains of this position it has become the custom to rotate the position of chief so that no one will hold it for more than a period of about three or a maximum of four years. On the other hand the two Assistant Chiefs, Eliot B. Coulter and Robert C. Alexander, have been with the Division for periods of twenty-one years and ten years respectively. Mr. L'Heureux has administered his office so fairly and satisfactorily that the Congress recently made a special dispensation in his case to permit him to remain for five years as Chief of the Visa Division.

Division of Protective Services. The Division of Protective Services might be said to trace its ancestry back to the Welfare and Whereabouts Section set up in the Consular Bureau at the outbreak of World War I to assist Americans stranded in the war areas. In World War II it was known as the Special Division and it did a remarkable job in repatriating Americans and protecting them and their interests in the countries at war. As World War II gradually merged into the "cold war" the necessity continued for the Department to protect the interests and property rights of Americans abroad, so the Special War Problems Division became the Special Projects Division and later the Division of Protective Services. In

---

[7] For an excellent account of the work of the Division see Eliot B. Coulter, "Visa Work of the Department of State and the Foreign Service," *Department of State Bulletin* (October 10, 1949).

all the reorganizations we find the name of Madge M. Blessing, who has been handling welfare and whereabouts cases in the Department for some thirty-five years.

Other specific duties of the Division include matters of representation of foreign governments by the United States and of the United States by other governments in times of war and seeing to it that the provisions of the General Convention for Prisoners of War and the Hague Conventions regarding laws of warfare are observed by belligerents. With the Iron Curtain countries flagrantly violating practically every accepted principle of international law in their treatment of foreigners under their jurisdiction, this Division has been almost continuously engaged in trying to locate missing Americans and in evacuating American citizens from dangerous areas. As an example of the success of the methods perfected in the Department, within sixty hours after the forces of North Korea had crossed the thirty-eighth parallel some 1,800 Americans were evacuated to Japan without injury to anyone. When an allegation was made that top officials came out first an investigation was made and the findings indicated that the Ambassador and his staff remained in Korea. Learning of one subordinate official who had come out on the last flight, the investigation showed that the individual was so afraid of airplanes that he had remained until compelled to get on the last plane.

The present head of the Division of Protective Services is Edward E. Hunt, who has had a long record abroad and at home in Red Cross and civilian relief work and served as Associate Chief both of the Special Projects Division and the Protective Services Division before becoming Chief in 1949. The Division is subdivided into the following branches: representation, public services, property and notarials, and emergency services.

Division of Security. One of the new divisions of the Department resulting from Communist activities and alleged infiltration into key positions in the Government is the Division of Security set up in 1947 in accordance with the President's Loyalty Program established by Executive Order 9835 issued March 21, 1947. Assistant Secretary of State Peurifoy was given authority by Secretary of State Marshall to rid the Department of any disloyal or undesirable persons in the Department or any who might be regarded as security risks.

The established procedure was to check all employees of the Department and the Foreign Service against the files of the Federal Bureau of Investigation. A Loyalty Security Board of nine members, later raised to sixteen, served as a panel from which boards of three acted in all hearings of persons regarded as security risks. The chairman of the Department's Loyalty Board was an eminent New Hampshire jurist, Conrad E. Snow; the members were carefully selected from Foreign Service officers and

State Department officials. The administration of this policy was placed under the direction of the Division of Security.

This Division comes under the general direction of the Office of Consular Affairs in the Department and its chief is a former official of FBI, Donald L. Nicholsen, chosen because of his excellent record. The Division has a competent staff in Washington and a field force covering all the sections of the United States. Every new appointee is carefully investigated by the field force before being put upon the rolls of the Department. In the year 1950 the Division of Security investigated 5,914 American applicants and rejected 52 persons as security risks and 259 for character and suitability reasons.[8] If any question of loyalty is raised regarding any employee of the Department the FBI makes the investigation. From the period of January 1, 1947 to January 1, 1951, there were separated from the Department and Foreign Service, which totaled 28,500 persons in 1951, some 158 persons, of which 14 were for security reasons and 144 for homosexuality.[9]

The question of security risks in the Department was given considerable notoriety early in 1950 by a series of speeches by Senator McCarthy of Wisconsin who declared that there were some fifty-seven card-carrying Communists in the Department at that time. Deputy Under Secretary of State Peurifoy forthwith requested by a telegram to Senator McCarthy that he name the employees to whom he referred. He failed to answer the telegram. When later he gave certain names to the press it was quickly proved that eminent persons like Dr. Harlow Shapley and Professor Owen Lattimore, whose card-carrying activities have never been proved, had never been employed by the Department of State. In fact, Senator McCarthy has never been able to name a single one of his fifty-seven card-carrying Communists. Some of the accusations were so far-fetched, as for example the accusation of guilt by association in the case of Ambassador-at-Large Philip Jessup, that to fair minded people the whole McCarthy performance became ridiculous. Unfortunately, to many of those falsely accused the results were tragic.

It should be noted that in serious cases of loyalty where important officials were concerned, if the Department's Loyalty Board was unable to return a satisfactory finding the accused might appeal to the head of the agency to which he was attached and if still dissatisfied, to the Loyalty Review Board, whose findings were final. Although the Secretary of State was given by law the absolute discretion to terminate the employment of any officer when deemed advisable in the interests of the United States, the Loyalty Board procedure with appeal to the Loyalty Review Board was the normal procedure.

[8] Department of State Appropriations for 1952, Hearings H.R. 82nd Cong., 403.
[9] *Ibid.*, 400-1.

THE FOREIGN SERVICE INSTITUTE

The idea back of the Institute dates from the same period as the establishment of a career consular service. Secretary of State Root in 1906 began the reorganization of the consular service on a merit basis and th following year the newly appointed consular officers were given a thirty day course of instruction in the Department before proceeding to their posts. According to Mr. Carr, at that time Chief Clerk, the purpose was "to give novitiates in the service some practical training in the running of a consular office before sending them to their posts. This is mutually helpful, for it saves the new appointee from making many embarrassing mistakes and saves the Department from conducting a sort of correspondence training school."

Two years later in 1909 newly appointed diplomatic secretaries were also assigned to the Department for instruction although in practice their training largely consisted of visiting the various divisions and bureaus of the Department and reading reports, rather than in having more formal instruction.

The Rogers Act of May 24, 1924, provided for "a suitable period of probation in an unclassified grade" thereby permitting the successful candidates to be assigned to the Department for instruction for as long a period as should be deemed necessary. The executive order of June 7, 1924, authorized the creation of a School in the Department of State to afford a period of instruction and probation for new appointees to the Foreign Service of the United States. The instruction was to be essentially of a practical nature, and the courses were selected primarily for their value as essential background material for the regular work in the field. The lecturers were to be officers of the Department and of the Foreign Service with a few specialists from the outside when this was deemed advisable.

William Dawson, a career officer of many years' standing was appointed chief instructor and took up his duties February 1, 1925. The first class worked in the Department for a period of five months but the term was gradually increased to seven or eight months. The students followed a regular routine of lectures, work in a Division of the Department, French conversation, quizzes and study. Experts from the various geographical divisions outlined American policies as they related to the various parts of the world. Lectures were given on such subjects as economic policies, foreign loans, raw materials, political reporting, electrical communications, and many other political and technical problems. But perhaps the most important part of the students' preparation was the opportunity to spend from one to three weeks in each of the important divisions of the Department. In this way the new appointees not only obtained a valuable insight into the details of departmental organization and operation but established useful contacts with their older colleagues.

When Consul General James B. Stewart took over the School, October 1, 1928, it was decided to curtail the course to six weeks, but when that period was found to be too short it was lengthened to three months. One other change occurred when at the suggestion of Mr. Byington the appointees were given several months' training in the field before being assigned to the Department for work in the School.

With the passage of the Foreign Service Act of 1946 a more comprehensive training program was authorized, and on March 13, 1947, the Department established the Foreign Service Institute. In addition to the traditional basic training for newly appointed officers, the Institute provided more advanced and specialized training for experienced officers both in the Department and in the Foreign Service. Other agencies, such as ECA, Labor, Agriculture, and Defense have made limited use of the agency's facilities. As many as five thousand people annually receive some type of instruction for variable periods from the staff of the Institute.

The Institute's School of Basic Officer Training offers a nine to twelve weeks orientation course aimed to acquaint the newly appointed officer with the requirements and duties of the Foreign Service. Advanced officer training is of various types. Refresher courses may be taken by officers who have been abroad for many years so that they may familiarize themselves with recent developments in the United States in the fields of history, economics, and political science. Some officers with particular interests are given special work in functional specialization in the Institute or are assigned to university graduate schools with specialized programs. The Institute is very well equipped for language training and offers full time intensive instruction in eleven foreign languages and part time semi-intensive instruction in thirty-one. The present Director of the Institute is Harry C. Hawkins, a former high ranking Foreign Service Officer who has also held many important positions in the Department of State.[10]

Technical Coöperation Administration. We have already mentioned the much publicized Point Four Program initiated by President Truman. Although the administration of this program of technical assistance to backward areas by the Department of State was at first uncertain, the Technical Coöperation Administration was organized in October, 1950 and placed under the jurisdiction of the Department. The TCA as it is called is responsible for the planning, launching, and management of technical-assistance programs. It receives the assistance of the regional bureaus, the Bureau of United Nations Affairs, certain specialized agencies, and of the Office of Educational Exchange for its trainee programs.

---

[10] Hawkins was succeeded by Deputy Director Norman Burns on March 3, 1952.

4

The Department of State—III

FOR MORE THAN half a century after the Department of State was established, the Chief Clerk served as Assistant Secretary of State and acted as Secretary in the absence of his chief. In fact, his duties as stated were to be such in all respects as pertained to an Under Secretary of State. By the Act of March 3, 1853, we find provision made for the first time establishing an Assistant Secretary of State. A Second Assistant Secretary of State was created by the Act of July 25, 1866, and a Third Assistant Secretary of State by the Act of June 20, 1874. No further changes occurred until the Rogers Bill of May 24, 1924, eliminated the numerical distinction of rank among the secretaries and authorized the appointment of an additional assistant secretary to take over the duties of the Director of the Consular Service, an office which was thereby abolished.

As a result of the two reorganizations carried through by Secretary Stettinius in 1944, two additional assistant secretaries were authorized and appointed. The addition of four more assistant secretaries came as a result of the Hoover Committee's recommendations, which were authorized by the law of May 6, 1949. Two of the new assistant secretaries were given supervisory status—one to serve as Deputy Under Secretary charged with policy, and the other as Deputy Under Secretary in charge of administration. A third was made responsible for liaison activities with the Congress, and a fourth was to be in general charge of economic and social policy. Of the other six, four supervised the geographical Offices of American Republic, European, Far Eastern, and Near Eastern and African Affairs, one was responsible for United Nations Affairs, and one was in charge of the Office of Public Affairs.

It is in the office of Assistant Secretary of State that we find the best examples of permanency in the Department. William Hunter, who had been in the Department since 1829 and by 1852 had become Chief Clerk, was made Second Assistant Secretary of State in 1866 and held the office for the next twenty years. He was succeeded by Alvey A. Adee, who, entering the Department in 1874, had become Third Assistant Secretary of State in 1882; at the death of Mr. Hunter in 1886, Adee was promoted to the position of Second Assistant Secretary of State. He held this position for the next thirty-eight years until he was made Assistant Secretary of State on July 1, 1924, three days before his death. Adee became such an important cog in the machinery of the Department that he came to be known as the permanent Under Secretary. Fluent in the use of French, German, Italian, and Spanish, an expert in English diplomatic phraseology, he was generally conceded to be America's greatest expert in both the content and technique of diplomacy. The story is told that Gaillard Hunt, then Chief of the Bureau of Manuscripts in the Library of Congress, went to Adee to see about transferring certain documents from the Department to the Library. "Mr. Adee," he said, "the law entitles us to withdraw from the Department to the Library all ancient, historical and no longer useful material." "If that is so," replied Adee, "you will have to take me along too." He served in the Department in one capacity or another during the incumbencies of twenty-two Secretaries of State, and it was John Hay who called him "Semper Paratus" Adee.

Wilbur Carr to a certain extent carried on the Adee tradition. Entering the Department as a clerk in 1892, he served as Chief of the Consular Bureau, as Chief Clerk, as Director of the Consular Service, and was appointed Assistant Secretary of State in 1924. After twelve years in this position and after forty-five years in the Department, Carr was named Ambassador to Czechoslovakia in 1937.

Assistant Secretary—Congressional Relations. The position of Assistant Secretary for Congressional Relations may perhaps be dated from 1941 when Assistant Secretary of State Breckinridge Long relinquished his administrative duties and took over the supervision of liaison activities with the Congress and general representation of the Department at hearings of congressional committees. Upon his resignation in 1944, Assistant Secretary Dean Acheson took over this work and when the latter became Under Secretary in 1945, the functions of congressional liaison were carried on by his staff. In January, 1947, the Office of Legislative Counsel was established under the Legal Adviser to take over liaison duties with Congress. When Foreign Service Officer Charles E. Bohlen became Counselor on August 1, 1947, he was given official responsibility for relations with Congress and the staff of the Legislative Counsel came under his direction. With the Hoover reorganization of 1949, Foreign Service Officer Jack K. McFall was named Assistant Secretary of State for Congressional Relations and authorized to devote his entire attention to this field.

The duties of the office are such as the name indicates. The Assistant Secretary for Congressional Relations supervises the legislative program of the Department and serves as a channel for the receipt of requests from Congress for assistance in departmental matters. He consults with members of Congress and congressional committees concerning international situations and foreign policy developments which are in any way concerned with legislative enactments. He presents the views of the Department with regard to contemplated legislation which bears upon the foreign policy of the United States. A useful function of this office is a legislative reference service concerning congressional activities which includes a digest of the Congressional Record.

Mr. McFall felt that his agency must combat the idea that the State Department operated in a vacuum and that its personnel held aloof from the Congress. Late in 1949 in a series of meetings between the top-level members of the Department, congressmen and senators were arranged at Prospect House, in the Department and in the Capitol. At these meetings congressmen and State Department officials got acquainted, and the Department's organization and work was discussed informally and frankly. The Assistant Secretary urged that every Foreign Service officer upon his return from his post get in touch with his home senators and congressmen, and similarly members of the Department should get in touch with members of the Congress who had returned from trips abroad. As a result of this effort in the direction of closer relations between the Department and the Congress some 1,500 congressional contacts were made monthly by personal meeting, by telephone, or by letter. When it is considered that during a single session of the Congress the Department of State was interested to a greater or lesser extent in about 50 per cent of the 10,000 public and private bills introduced in that session, the importance of close liaison between the Congress and the State Department is appreciated.

The staff of the Assistant Secretary for Congressional Relations is relatively small—twenty-four in all—but all of the officers are experienced specialists in dealing with the "Hill."

Assistant Secretary—Bureau of United Nations Affairs. The Assistant Secretary for United Nations Affairs is a recent post dating from the Hoover recommendations for the reorganization of the Department. The Bureau of United Nations Affairs as it is now designated may be said to stem from the Office of Special Political Affairs set up in 1944 to prepare plans for a postwar international organization. The Dumbarton Oaks Conference and the San Francisco Conference were to some considerable extent results of its work. When the United States entered the United Nations this agency became known as the Office of United Nations Affairs. Perhaps its best-known directors have been Alger Hiss and Assistant Secretary of State Dean Rusk. Its present head is Assistant Secretary of State John D. Hickerson, a Foreign Service Officer of more than thirty years experience—the only career officer among the current Assistant Secretaries of State. His Deputy Assistant Secretary is Durward V. Sandifer, who has served in the Department for seventeen years and in the field of international organization ever since 1944.

As organized in 1951 the Bureau of United Nations Affairs has directly under the Assistant Secretary, an Executive Staff, a United Nations Planning Staff, and a Refugees and Displaced Persons Staff.

Four offices, Dependent Area Affairs, International Administration and Conferences, United Nations Political and Security Affairs, complete the Washington organization. Affiliated with the Bureau is the staff of the United States mission to the United Nations headed by Senator Warren R. Austin. The Bureau in the Department numbers approximately 225, the mission in New York about 180. The relationship between the organizations in the Department and in New York as described by Mr. Sandifer is that the Mission is a front-line operational and representational office which negotiates on the spot while the Bureau develops the policies and instructions and does the backstopping. The work of the Bureau covers not only matters pertaining to the United Nations but also all other international organizations and conferences in which the United States participates. It should be noted that in the Department of State the UNESCO Relations Staff comes under the jurisdiction of the Assistant Secretary of State for Public Affairs.

United States Membership in International Organizations. Perhaps it is pertinent at this point to note the vast expansion of international organizations since World War I and the cost of their maintenance as of the year 1950 to the United States. The United Nations has an annual budget of between $34,000,000 and $40,000,000, of which the contribution of the United States is approximately 40 per cent. UNESCO's budget is about $8,000,000 and the United States contributes about 38 per cent. World Health Organization costs $7,000,000 and the United States paid 36 per cent while Food and Agricultural Organization with a budget of $5,000,000 received 27 per cent from the United States. The International Labor Organization with gross assessments totaling $6,000,000 obtained 22 per cent from the United States. The International Refugee Organization in 1949-1950 required the vast sum of almost $123,000,000, but the following year it was cut to about $43,000,000. The quota of the United States for each year was slightly over 57 per cent. The only other organization budgets of over a million dollars a year are the Pan-American Union and the Pan-American Sanitary Bureau where the United States' contribution amounts approximately to 70 per cent.[1] These amounts seem to

[1] For a complete account of all international organizations of which the United States is a member and the assessments, see Department of State Appropriations for 1952, Hearings Committee on Appropriations, H.R., 81st Cong., 1st sess., 287-327.

be quite considerable but if they are compared with the huge sums required for security in the form of armaments they are infinitesimal.

Assistant Secretaries—Geographical Bureaus. The seed of the geographical divisions was sown by Secretary of State Hamilton Fish in 1870 when he set up a First Diplomatic Bureau to take care of correspondence with Western Europe and the Far East, and a Second Diplomatic Bureau charged with correspondence with the rest of the world. Secretary Philander C. Knox carried the geographical idea further in 1908-1909 by establishing four divisions in the Department of State covering Far Eastern, Near Eastern, Western European, and Latin American Affairs.

In the first Stettinius reorganization of 1944 the four geographical divisions were raised somewhat in importance—they were named offices and placed under directors who were directly responsible to the Under Secretary of State. The Hoover reorganization emphasized the responsibility and importance of the geographical agencies still further and made an assistant secretary of state responsible for each of the geographical areas.

The general responsibilities for the four assistant secretaries for regional bureaus are approximately the same. They are charged with the conduct of foreign relations with the countries of the region specified and with seeing to it that the Secretary, Under Secretary, and the various Assistant Secretaries are advised of the major policies formulated. They supervise the relationships with foreign missions in the United States representing the countries within their regional jurisdiction. In similar fashion they direct the operation of Foreign Service establishments within their geographical areas abroad and prepare and review all communications to them.

It should be noted that each bureau has special advisers on public affairs, economic affairs, United Nations affairs and questions of intelligence. Under the existing arrangement it is hoped to make each bureau the final arbiter of policy in all ordinary conditions subject of course to review by the Under Secretary, the Secretary, and the President if the situation warrants it.

Assistant Secretary—Bureau of European Affairs. The Bureau of European Affairs is the largest of the geographical agencies with a total professional and clerical staff of over three hundred. It is divided into four offices—British Commonwealth and Northern European Affairs, Eastern European Affairs, Western European Affairs, and European Regional Affairs. The latter office has jurisdiction over such subjects as the North Atlantic Treaty, questions concerning the United Nations in

Europe, or activities concerning three or more countries not in the same office. This agency exercises jurisdiction over 116 overseas posts.

The Bureau of European Affairs in its almost half century of existence has with only two exceptions been headed by career Foreign Service officers. One of these exceptions was William R. Castle, Jr., whose qualifications were easily the equivalent, and the other is the present Assistant Secretary of State George W. Perkins, a businessman who had been acting as chief of industries branch for ECA in Paris before his appointment. His immediate predecessors were Foreign Service Officers James C. Dunn, H. Freeman Mathews, and John D. Hickerson.

A brief summary of some of the recent problems which the Bureau of European Affairs has considered in its routine assignments will perhaps give an idea of the work carried on by each one of the geographical agencies. For example, the Office of the British Commonwealth and Northern European Affairs has been conducting negotiations for a Treaty of Friendship, Commerce, and Economic Development with Australia and has concluded a Treaty of Friendship, Commerce, and Navigation with Ireland. It has secured implementation of the Fulbright Program for educational exchanges in Australia and New Zealand. The economic specialists of the Office are responsible for all questions concerning British exchange control regulations and if advisable must direct the American Embassy in London to protest any ruling which is harmful to the interests of the United States.

The Office of Eastern European Affairs has been particularly concerned with the plight of certain American citizens incarcerated behind the Iron Curtain. In the case of Robert Vogeler more than a score of *démarches,* written and oral, were initiated by the Office on Mr. Vogeler's behalf, and retaliatory actions against the Hungarian Government were suggested to the Secretary of State. In the case of Rumania, where a progressive series of harassments and annoyances of the United States' Mission was being carried out, a policy of strict retaliation was adopted towards the Rumanian officials in Washington. Official travel and even pleasure trips were curtailed in exact relation to similar treatment of our Legation officials in Bucharest.

The divers problems handled by the Office of Western European Affairs extends from assisting American Minister Perle Mesta to obtain transportation for a group of American students stranded in Luxembourg to keeping an eye upon the stability of the French cabinet with its traditionally high center of political gravity. The relationship of the United States with Spain under Franco has been a constant and long continuing problem, and the Office of Western European Affairs has been under constant pressure to facilitate economic and financial deals. A number of senators proposed that United States surplus agricultural commodities should be exchanged for Spanish strategic materials. The Office noted that Spain's supply of such materials was comparatively limited and frequently failed to meet Federal Supply Service specifications and were priced out of the United States market because of the artificial exchange rate of the Spanish peseta. American consulates in Spain have been troubled by the Spanish Government applying bounties to the exports of Spanish almonds to the United States. When the United States placed a countervailing duty upon Spanish almonds it practically eliminated Spanish almond exports to the United States. The Office carried on long and arduous negotiations to remedy the situation.

Although the desk officers in geographical agencies are individualistic in their methods of work the procedure for routine reports from diplomatic and consular officers abroad is approximately as follows: the correspondence or despatches go first to the officer in charge of affairs for the country in which the documents originate. He reads them carefully and if he thinks certain passages should receive the attention of the Director, he marks them or prepares a memorandum upon the question as a whole. However, if no action is required and the matter is of a routine character, the officer in charge makes the information a part of his background and has the correspondence filed away for possible future reference. If a situation arises which concerns any particular country the Director may request the responsible officer to prepare a memorandum or he may call him into an oral conference. In either case, the assistant in charge is expected to be prepared with all the relevant information.

It is quite customary for representatives of foreign missions in Washington to call personally upon the Director of a geographical bureau for information when the matter is not of sufficient importance to go directly to the Secretary or Under Secretary of State. As a result, a considerable amount of the Director's time is taken up by such conferences.

The announced basic objective of the Bureau of European Affairs for 1952 has been to preserve world peace and protect American interests through aiding freedom-loving European nations to resist Communist, political, economic, or military aggression. As steps in this direction the Bureau has supported the North Atlantic Treaty Organization as a focus around which common defense programs could be built; it has worked to increase the unity of non-Soviet Europe; it has supported democratic elements behind the Iron Curtain, and it has helped integrate western Germany into the Western orbit.

Assistant Secretary—Bureau of Inter-American Affairs.   Ever since the promulgation of the Monroe Doctrine in 1823, the United States has evinced a profound interest in its Latin American neighbors. In fact, most of the catch phrases descriptive of American foreign policy have been related in some way to the Latin American republics. The Doctrine of

Two Spheres, Paramount Interest, Big Stick Policy, Dollar Diplomacy, and Good Neighbor Policy, all are closely associated with the desire of the United States to distinguish between its political interests in the New World and the Old.

The roster of names of those who have headed this agency will indicate that experience, training, and ability have been the criteria to appointment—Thomas C. Dawson, Leo S. Rowe, J. Butler Wright, Sumner Welles, Dana G. Munro, Laurence Duggan, and Paul C. Daniels are among those who have directed the Bureau.

The present Assistant Secretary for Inter-American Affairs is Edward G. Miller, Jr., who was born in Puerto Rico, speaks Spanish as well as English and who had had considerable experience in the Department as a divisional assistant in the Latin American field in 1938; he has advanced by reason of experience and merit. The Bureau has, in addition to the regular advisers found generally in all geographical agencies, the United States Representative to the Council of the Organization of American States and the United States Representative to the Inter-American Economic and Social Council. There are four offices in the Bureau: Middle American Affairs, East Coast Affairs, North and West Coast Affairs, and Regional American Affairs. The latter office initiates and coördinates policy regarding the Inter-American System and its agencies and conferences.

The Bureau of Inter-American Affairs has played in the past a very important rôle in the policy of reciprocal trade agreements sponsored by Secretary of State Hull and his successors, and at present it is looking forward to aiding in a similar fashion the Point Four Program which has been inaugurated by President Truman.

Assistant Secretary—Bureau of Far Eastern Affairs. The Bureau of Far Eastern Affairs was the earliest of the policy-forming geographical agencies to be established. It was first set up under William Phillips on March 20, 1908, and during its history it has been directed by such outstanding authorities on the Far East as E. T. Williams, J. V. A. MacMurray, Nelson T. Johnson, Stanley K. Hornbeck, and Joseph W. Ballantine. The present head of the Bureau is Assistant Secretary of State Dean Rusk, who has had military service in the Far East and was acting as Deputy Under Secretary of State for Political Affairs when he was transferred to this post. The critical relations with Communist China and the war with Korea added to the bitter criticism of the State Department's Far Eastern policy has made this position one of the most difficult to handle satisfactorily. The Deputy Assistant Secretary is Livingston T. Merchant.

Inasmuch as diplomatic and consular officers assigned to the Far Eastern posts find it difficult to perform their duties without a knowledge of the language, under the direction of the Bureau of Far Eastern Affairs a system of training for personnel to be stationed in China and Japan was worked out. According to regulations issued in 1926 a certain number of Foreign Service officers were chosen to be attached for two years to the Embassies in Tokyo and Peiping to study the Japanese and Chinese languages. From these specially trained language officers most of the consular offices and certain posts in the diplomatic missions in these countries were staffed. The Division itself also draws about half of its officers from the career service in the field.

With the establishment of the Foreign Service Institute excellent courses in all Oriental languages could be obtained here which permitted the so-called language students to do a considerable part of their preliminary specialization in Washington.

Inasmuch as the problems of the Far East are exceedingly complex, and there is less familiarity with them than with political problems of Latin America or Europe, the Bureau acts as a general clearing house in Far Eastern Affairs for the Department in its contacts with other departments, with other governments, and with the public. The protection of businessmen, travelers, and missionaries, the policy of the open door, the critical relations between China and the United States, the formulation and implementation of a peace treaty with Japan, the administration of the newly acquired territories and trusteeships in the Pacific require the attention of the Division.

As currently organized, the Bureau in addition to the Deputy Assistant Secretary and the Executive Director has four Advisers: Intelligence, United Nations, Economic and Labor, and Public Relations officer. It has three Offices: Chinese Affairs, Northeast Asian Affairs, and Philippine and Southwest Asian Affairs. When it is remembered that the latter agency includes Thailand, Indo-China, the Netherlands East Indies, and Indonesia, all potential points of world conflagration, the problems facing this agency can be appreciated.

Assistant Secretary—Bureau of Near Eastern, South Asian, and African Affairs. As originally established and until the reorganization, January 15, 1944, this agency was limited in area to what was generally designated as the Near East—confessedly a somewhat ambiguous term.

As a specialized intensive training is required to understand properly the peculiar problems of the Near East, G. Howland Shaw, Chief of the Division of Near Eastern Affairs, in 1926 inaugurated a policy of specialization for officers interested in and adapted to service in the Near East. Certain experienced men of ability were picked and new students made aware of the possibility of such specialization. If a prospective candidate was interested and seemed suited to the work he was given a probationary assignment in the Near East and then upon his return to the Department examined carefully as to his physical and mental reactions. The need of language training was recognized by an executive order issued May 8, 1928, establishing regulations to govern the selection, training and promotion of Foreign Service officers for language assignments in the Near East, in Eastern Europe and North Africa. Under this order provision was made for the assignment to the consul general in Paris as language officers of a certain number of candidates who for three years as a part of their duties should study Arabic, Turkish, modern Greek, and modern Persian at the École des Langues Vivantes Orientales. At the present time this language training is for the most part given by the Foreign Service Institute of the Department of State. Such officers were expected to remain in the Near Eastern field although they might be given a relief assignment at a port like London after a considerable period of service.

The story is told of a certain young Foreign Service officer from a western state who desired service in the Near East but was not thought adapted to it. However, merely by chance he received a Near Eastern assignment, but was not permitted to qualify for study in Paris. Nevertheless, he kept insisting, and as his work was quite satisfactory, he was finally given the opportunity. His work was so exceptionally brilliant that upon its completion he was invited to become a member of the staff of the school, an almost unbelievable honor for an American student. He remained in the service, however, and received an assignment where his exceptional talents might be properly utilized.

The work of the Division used to be rendered somewhat more complicated by the fact that the so-called capitulatory rights still exist in certain countries of the Near East. In addition to the "capitulations" granted by treaty, other extraterritorial privileges have grown up by custom and usage. These survive today however only in Morocco.

Another factor of special interest in the Near East is the large number of American educational and research institutions which have been established there. Although Robert College, the Constantinople College for Women, and the American University of Beirut are perhaps best known, there are a number of other American institutions of higher learning, as well as archaeological expeditions actively at work in Greece, Egypt, Mesopotamia, and Iran.

The heads of this agency have been largely drawn from the Foreign Service and have included John Van A. MacMurry, Warren D. Robbins, Allen W. Dulles, G. Howland Shaw, Wallace Murray, and Loy W. Henderson. The Office of Near Eastern and African Affairs played a very important part in the invasion of North Africa in World War II when through its well formulated and executed policy the French possessions in North Africa were kept intact and served as the spearhead for the successful invasion of Europe.[2]

[2] Graham H. Stuart, *The Department of State* (New York, 1949), 365-71.

The present Assistant Secretary for Near Eastern, South Asian, and African Affairs is George C. McGhee, a businessman with some experience in the Department of State who served as coördinator for aid to Greece and Turkey. There are three offices: Greek, Turkish, and Iranian Affairs; South Asian Affairs; and African and Near Eastern Affairs. The latter Office includes the entire Arabian Peninsula, Egypt, Palestine, Israel, Libya, Tangier, and the Spanish, British, Belgian dependencies and colonies in Africa.

Director—Bureau of German Affairs.   The Bureau of German Affairs differs from the other geographic bureaus primarily in that it is headed by a Director instead of by an Assistant Secretary of State. Shortly after the end of World War II political matters within the jurisdiction of the State Department with regard to Germany and Austria were under the direction of the Division of Central European Affairs in the Office of European Affairs. However as Germany and Austria were under military jurisdiction it was thought wise to appoint one Assistant Secretary of State for Occupied Areas from the Army and Brigadier General Charles E. Saltzman, who had been Chairman of the United States delegation for Bizonal Arrangements for Germany, was named. However, this was a temporary arrangement and in June, 1949, President Truman directed that the military government under the Army be changed to a civilian government under the Department of State. He named John J. McCloy as the United States High Commissioner to Germany with the rank of Chief of Mission, Class I. Meanwhile Career Minister Robert D. Murphy, who had been serving as the United States political adviser at Frankfort on the Main, was brought back to the United States and made Acting Director of the newly established Office of German and Austrian Affairs in the State Department.

When the new organization plan recommended by the Hoover Commission was put into effect in November, 1949, Austria remained in the Office of Western European Affairs under the jurisdiction of the Assistant Secretary for European Affairs, whereas Germany was given a separate administration set up under a special bureau headed by a Director who was given the status as an Assistant Secretary of State. Colonel Henry A. Byroade, who had been serving as deputy-director under Murphy, was made Director of the new Bureau of German Affairs and Murphy named Ambassador to Belgium.

As explained by Acting Director G. W. Lewis the job of the Bureau of German Affairs is to consolidate all the policy-making functions of the Department for the support of Mr. McCloy's operations, and to handle his requests for information or guidance when they come into the Department of State. The Bureau also supplies the High Commissioner with all necessary administrative and program services including assistance to recruit his staff. When the existing State Department personnel in Germany numbering 638 is drastically reduced as is planned, the Bureau of German Affairs, which currently has about sixty persons, will be reduced to approximately a dozen and probably revert to the Office of Western European Affairs.

As organized today the Bureau of German Affairs has three geographic offices: the Office of Eastern European Affairs, the Office of Western European Affairs, and the Office of British Commonwealth and Northern European Affairs. A fourth office called the Office of German Public Affairs is concerned with matters of international information, educational exchange, and domestic public affairs activities, which includes efforts to reëducate the German people in the direction of peace and democracy.

Assistant Secretary—Economic Affairs. The Department has paid some attention to economic affairs ever since a statistical office was set up in 1854 to report upon changes in foreign commercial systems. After World War I when economic experts were assigned to various geographical divisions to deal with their individual problems the Office of the Economic Adviser was established to advise the Department on all matters of general economic policy. World War II brought about such a vast increase of economic problems that the Office of the Economic Adviser became a bottleneck through which the stream of economic affairs could not possibly pass. Whereas at the beginning of the war less than one hundred persons were concerned with international economic affairs towards its conclusion about five hundred were employed in this field. The reorganization of the Department on January 15, 1944, placed all economic matters under the general direction of an Assistant Secretary of State. Dean Acheson, who held that position at the time, found himself responsible for eleven divisions concerned with some phase of economic matters.

At the end of World War II, with the establishment of such international agencies as the Economic and Social Council of the United Nations, the International Monetary Fund, the International Bank for Reconstruction and Development, and with the complicated problems of lend-lease, surplus war property, and economic security controls, the temporary position of Under Secretary of State for Economic Affairs was established while the position of Assistant Secretary for Economic Affairs was still retained. Assistant Secretary William L. Clayton became Under Secretary and Willard L. Thorp, an economic expert, was named Assistant Secretary. The position of Under Secretary for Economic Affairs was dropped in 1947 with Clayton's resignation; nevertheless the organization, still headed by Assistant Secretary Thorp, remained one of the largest agencies in the Department. Although subsequently a considerable number of the economic experts were transferred to various area divisions it was necessary to retain a substantial number to cover matters of a multilateral character.

Beginning early in the year 1951, the Assistant Secretary, in addition to assistants and advisers, had four offices under his direction. The Office of Financial and Development Policy, under Director Leroy D. Stinebower, as its name indicates is charged with financial and economic policy affairs of the Department at home and abroad, also with dealing with interagency bodies and interdepartmental committees, with the Export-Import Bank, and the National Advisory Council. Matters relating to lend-lease and surplus property were under its jurisdiction. The Office of Transport and Communications Policy covers the fields of aviation, inland transportation, shipping, and telecommunications. Its director is Walter A. Radius. The Office of International Materials is responsible for policy concerning petroleum, agricultural products, metals, and minerals. The Office of Economic Defense and Trade Policy has under its direction the large commercial policy staff which is charged with making reciprocal trade agreements and economic treaties.

One of the thorny problems which faced this agency was to obtain the return of lend-lease ships from Russia. Some ships were finally obtained but only a small number of frigates and merchant ships and one ice breaker were given back. When countries fail to live up to the trade agreements the branch in charge must get compliance or terminate the agreement. Currently a most important problem has been to reduce the flow of raw materials to the Soviet Union particularly from those states receiving Marshall Plan help. With security considerations resulting from the "cold war" requiring the tightening of export controls to prevent shortages in strategic materials, and the necessity for further control of foreign financial transactions, the work of this agency is again expanding.

Assistant Secretary—Public Affairs. The United States did not appreciate the crying need for an agency to explain our policies until World War II. It was then that the effectiveness of Nazi propaganda was brought home to us and the Office of War Information established. With the close of the war and the development of the even greater menace of a Communist campaign of villification, a more vigorous effort was begun to combat it. A Division of Cultural Relations had been set up in the Department of State in 1938, but it was largely concerned with a program of exchange of students and professors. It was not until the reorganization of January 15, 1944, that an Office of Public Information was established utilizing the newer means of communication to furnish the American public and other nations unbiased information regarding the foreign policy of the United States.

As organized in 1951 under Assistant Secretary of State Edward W. Barrett, domestic matters were under the direction of the Office of Public

Affairs headed by Director Francis H. Russell. The work of this Office was carried on by four operating divisions. The Division of Public Studies is responsible for keeping the Department informed regarding the trend of public opinion. It collects and analyzes newspaper editorials, magazine articles, and radio opinion and prepares reports regarding its findings. Its acting chief is H. Schuyler Foster. Closely allied to this agency is the Division of Public Liaison, which establishes contacts with nongovernmental organizations, arranges for speeches to be given by Departmental officers and answers public mail on foreign policy. Its chief in 1951 was Margaret R. T. Carter.

The Division of Historical Policy Research, under the direction of Chief G. Bernard Noble, edits basic documents on foreign policy including the series known as the *Foreign Relations of the United States*. The Division has recently edited captured Nazi and Japanese documents for public distribution. The Division of Publications produces and distributes all the official publications of the Department except press releases. These include the *State Department Register,* the *Foreign Service List,* the *Diplomatic List,* the *Department of State Bulletin* and various pamphlet series on various phases of foreign policy. Its chief is Robert L. Thompson.

The public affairs work abroad is under the general direction of Charles M. Hulten, who serves as general manager of the Office of International Information and the Office of Educational Exchange. The former, headed by Director Orvill C. Anderson, is responsible for the development, coördination, and execution of the United States information policies pertaining to international relations. The most publicized and best financed agency of the Office of International Information is the Division of International Broadcasting, under Chief Foy D. Kohler, which broadcasts the Voice of America to practically all of the countries of the world. This Division to carry on its "Campaign of Truth" utilizes over thirty different languages, employs over one thousand persons and costs over $15,000,000 annually. The nuisance value of the Voice of America to the Soviet Government may be estimated by the fact that some 250 Russian stations are used to jam the Voice at a cost of approximately as much as the United States spends upon its whole radio output. The jamming is so extensive that on one occasion the entire speech of Mr. Malik before the Security Council of the United Nations was blotted out. On the other hand the Voice of America broadcast to Russia the recorded voice of Andre Vishinsky to correct *Pravda*'s report of what the Soviet Foreign Minister told the United Nations about Soviet atomic development.

The Division of International Motion Pictures produces and distributes motion pictures estimated at reaching audiences numbering ten to twelve million monthly. Some of these films pertain to questions of major policy such as "Why the United Nations Aids Korea," which appeared within a month of the outbreak of the Korean War. Several of its productions have won prizes in international exhibitions as for example the "Tanglewood Story" and the "Shipbuilders of Essex."

The Division of International Press and Publications aims to present the American scene through the printed word in such a way as to explain American policies. Its *Wireless Bulletin* sent by Morse Code is received by all the United States embassies and legations abroad, which decode and distribute it and utilize it directly or in translation to fit the situation. Its slick magazine, *Amerika,* printed in the Russian language sells fifty thousand copies monthly in the Soviet state. It has a considerable pamphlet program covering such titles as *Education for Freedom, Toward World Peace and Progress,* and the *Outline of American History* printed in several languages and distributed widely. Over 600,000 copies of the latter title were distributed. It also provides a feature news program and a photographic program.

The other principal agency directing informational activities abroad is the Office of Educational Exchange, headed by William C. Johnstone, Jr. Under the authorization of the Smith-Mundt and Fulbright Acts a very considerable exchange of persons between the United States and foreign countries was put into operation. During the year 1950 the United States brought over some 4,300 teachers, students, research scholars, and leaders from foreign countries and at the same time awarded grants to some 1,250 Americans to go abroad for study, lecturing, or to serve as specialist advisers in foreign countries.

Another vital activity was the establishment of information centers and libraries abroad where American books and magazines on open shelves might be available to the public. By the end of 1950, the United States had established 140 information centers and libraries in sixty-one different countries. On one occasion the Mexican Foreign Minister informed former Assistant Secretary of Public Affairs George Allen that the United States information program was the "finest activity the United States could possibly carry on in his country." The United States Information Center in Prague became so popular that some seven thousand Czechs visited it every month. As a result the Czechoslovak Government forced it to close.

Other agencies under the jurisdiction of the Assistant Secretary for Public Affairs are the UNESCO Relations Staff, the Interdepartmental Information Staff, and the Public Affairs Policy Advisory Staff. As an unbiased report on the success of the informational program and its administration by the State Department the second semiannual report by the United States Advisory Commission on Educational Exchange (January 1—June 30, 1949), after reaffirming its belief in the major importance of the international exchange of ideas between this country and others declared that the program as conducted by the Department of State was making "a substantial contribution" to the foreign relations of this country in those areas where it is in operation.

Legal Adviser. The Legal Adviser is a bulwark of protection to the Foreign Service officer. It instructs him regarding the proper procedure in preparing certifications, treaties, authentication, and letters rogatory. It will advise him in regard to any legal difficulty in which he may become involved. If he loses any property through no fault of his own he has recourse to the claims board, on which a member of the Legal Adviser's staff sits, and if the board approves, the Department, through the Legal Adviser, will ask Congress for an appropriation.

A member of the staff is Assistant Legal Adviser for United Nations Affairs, and the Headquarters Agreement with the United Nations has raised some interesting questions of international and constitutional law. The establishment within the State of New York of an inviolable area which is under the general jurisdiction of the United Nations rather than under Federal, state, or local authorities, yet wherein Federal, state, and local law of the United States applies, has already produced many problems of legal interpretation.

The first Legal Adviser, appointed in 1931, was Green H. Hackworth, who had entered the Department as a law clerk in 1916 and had become Solicitor for the Department in 1925. Hackworth served until 1946, when he was elected a judge in the World Court. His immediate successor was former Solicitor General of the United States Charles Fahy, and he was followed by Ernest A. Gross in 1947. The present Legal Adviser is Adrian S. Fisher, former counsel for the Atomic Energy Commission, who was appointed June 22, 1949. The staff as of 1950 numbers slightly over one hundred, of whom forty are attorneys.

The name "Legal Adviser" for the legal division of the State Department is to a certain extent a misnomer inasmuch as the work is far broader than the name implies. Not only does this Office give legal advice to the members of the State Department, but it regularly represents the Government before international tribunals and courts of claims. It must be prepared to support with cogent arguments one administration on its policy of non-recognition of a foreign government and make an equally strong case for recognition by the next. It must protect the executive in his direction of foreign policy from the constant encroachments on the part of the legislative branch.

It is interesting to note that in the early days of the Department, the Secretary of State handled the legal work personally and Jefferson, who was a well trained lawyer as well as a remarkable statesman, laid down policies with respect to neutrality and recognition of governments which are followed to this day. The first law officers date from 1848, and were called examiners of claims, while from 1891 to 1931 the law officer was called Solicitor for the Department of State while he was at the same time nominally under the Department of Justice. The present status of the Office is based upon the Act of Congress of February 23, 1931, as amended October 15, 1949.

The corps of lawyers who assist the Legal Adviser is regularly confronted with so many types of cases of international law that it may well be denominated an organization of specialists. There is not a law office in the country to which more varieties of legal cases are referred. They run the gamut of every branch of law—international, admiralty, Federal, state, and common law. Not only must the Legal Adviser's staff handle the strictly legal problems presented to it, but it must also give advice to the Secretary of State, his assistants and the heads of political and administrative divisions on mixed questions of law and policy.

For the most part, the work is allocated to the more experienced men according to geographical areas, distributed approximately on the same basis as those in the Department of State. For example, a case involving an alleged breach of contract in a railway concession in Peru would be assigned to one of the assistants specializing in the Latin American field. On the other hand, certain types of cases which come before the Department constantly and in great numbers, such as claims, extradition, and citizenship are assigned to specialists in these fields.

There are various ways of handling the problems presented. Sometimes a memorandum is prepared for the Secretary or the Under Secretary; again the action may take the form of a note addressed to a foreign diplomatic mission in the United States or an instruction to one of our missions abroad. A senator may introduce a resolution inquiring into the religious policy of the Mexican Government as it affects American citizens and the State Department finds it necessary to send a diplomatically worded letter pointing out that the President, rather than the Congress, is given the authority by the Constitution to direct the foreign policy of the United States.

The problem of claims takes a considerable part of the Legal Adviser's time. In the first place, the legal phase of negotiations leading up to the signature of agreements for the submission of claims to arbitration must be handled. Then the preparation and presentation of the cases follows. During the years 1930-1933 inclusive, the Legal Adviser's Office conducted five international arbitrations in which it received on behalf of American nationals upwards of $700,000. In connection with each of the arbitrations there was voluminous correspondence incidental to the collection of evidence in the foreign country where the claim arose, as well as considerable diplomatic correspondence and numerous conferences at the State Department and in the foreign capital as to the terms of the arbitration, the selection of arbitrators, rules of procedure and similar questions. An interesting example of international claims was the settlement with Germany of claims arising from the Black Tom explosion in New Jersey during World War I. The Legal Adviser has compiled a complete register of outstanding international claims which permits the formulation of an intelligent policy with regard to their systematic consideration and settlement.

The services of the office are used in the drafting of all treaties and agreements. It was this agency which drafted the North Atlantic Pact, the foundation of the West against Soviet aggression. The legal implications of treaties, their interpretation, their violation by other countries, the limits to which the treaty-making power may extend consistent with the Constitution and the laws of the United States, are passed upon by the Legal Adviser.

Inasmuch as legal advisers are not maintained by the Department of State in foreign countries,[3] the more complicated legal problems arising in the American embassies, legations, and consulates abroad are referred to the Legal Adviser. These questions may range from the probate procedure in Morocco to the real property laws of Poland, from the question of our right under international law to protect American stockholders in a foreign corporation to the legality of embargoes, from the effect of foreign laws and decrees in existing stipulations to the question whether a court decision against an American national in a foreign country constitutes a "denial of justice" under international law. Questions are constantly arising concerning the rights and privileges of diplomatic and consular officials abroad and of foreign diplomatic and consular officers in the United States.

The Legal Adviser has much to do in cases of extradition. A preliminary finding must be made as to whether a demand shall be made on a foreign government for the extradition of a fugitive from the justice of the United States. The treaty governing the case, the laws of the several countries and the states of the United States must be examined. In these cases the duties of the office are essentially juridical in character.

In fine, the Legal Adviser must attend to the protection of the government's interest in a boundary dispute which may jeopardize the national domain, and at the same time satisfy John Citizen that his claim which may have very little merit in law is receiving the most careful possible attention. All cases of protection of a public nature, whether large or small, important or insignificant, on behalf of the government or in support of a citizen, must be given impartial and careful consideration by this office.

Special Assistant—Intelligence. Although a successful foreign policy requires a complete and accurate knowledge of all pertinent facts, no

[3] The term *counselor of embassy* or *legation* should not be confused with the term *Legal Adviser;* the former designation refers to the highest ranking secretary in the more important posts.

centralized agency existed in the Department of State to perform this function until the Office of Strategic Services was liquidated in September 1945. Thereupon a Special Assistant to the Secretary of State in charge of Research and Intelligence was established and a considerable number of the O.S.S. personnel transferred to the State Department. This agency after numerous changes in direction and various reorganizations as to administration had become stabilized by the end of 1949 as it exists today.

The duty of this agency is to provide the Department of State with a centralized research service able to insure that all available sources are explored and the facts marshaled and analyzed so as to present a complete picture upon which to formulate an intelligent and effective foreign policy. Furthermore, in accordance with the provisions of the National Security Act of 1947 the Department of State is required to furnish the Central Intelligence Agency with political and economic intelligence, which combined with military, naval, air, and other pertinent intelligence will permit the National Security Council to formulate policies aimed at strengthening the security of the United States. The work of this agency has become increasingly difficult due to the censorship imposed in Iron Curtain countries and the distortion prevalent in the information obtained from those areas.

The intelligence agency is divided into two offices, the first, Intelligence Research, the second, Libraries and Intelligence Acquisition. The first which has a number of divisions set up to cover the principal geographical areas of the world receives the raw materials of information and produces intelligence studies for the use of the policy officers of the Department. The second acquires and processes the materials, maintains the library and reference services, and obtains data for biographic reports on foreign personalities. Special Assistant W. Park Armstrong, Jr., who heads the intelligence work, has been in the Department intelligence work since 1946.

5

The Development of the American Foreign Service

IT HAS ALREADY been shown that the President is the controlling factor in determining the foreign policy of the United States. But to carry out this policy it is not sufficient to have at home an able Secretary of State with capable and well trained assistants; there must also be a corps of experienced men abroad, specialists in the various international services, experts trained to achieve results in accordance with long established international procedure. Conceding that a man brilliantly successful in business or politics at home may at times be equally successful abroad, nevertheless he must have the assistance of the career officer to counsel and advise him in the many intricate details of diplomatic practice.

Eminent Diplomats of the Revolutionary Period. In its early history the United States appreciated the advantages of being well represented abroad. Fortunately for the new republic, although the Congress under the Articles of Confederation was notoriously inept and inefficient in its conduct of foreign relations, at no period of our history do we find more eminent names in the list of those representing the United States abroad.

Benjamin Franklin had a remarkable diplomatic career. His first experience of this nature began in 1757, when he was sent by the Pennsylvania Assembly to London, where he remained for five years. Two years later he returned to London as the representative of Pennsylvania, Massachusetts, New Jersey, and Georgia, and for eleven years until 1775 he carried on every sort of negotiation in behalf of these colonies. At the outbreak of the war he was first sent to Canada to gain the support of the northern colonies and in 1776 he was appointed Commissioner to France. The following year he was commissioned to the court of Spain but never completed this mission. In 1778 he was named Plenipotentiary to the court of France and became the reigning sensation of the day. In 1782 Franklin acted with John Jay as Joint Commissioner to negotiate peace, and it was during these delicate negotiations that he wrote his famous reply to Vergennes, who had complained justly that France had not been informed of the preliminary articles of peace. It was a masterpiece of diplomatic finesse and while avoiding a break with France it maintained the advantages of treating directly with England. In 1782 at the age of seventy-six he was appointed Plenipotentiary to negotiate a treaty of amity and commerce with Sweden and he was entirely successful in his mission. Commissioned again two years later to sign similar treaties with European countries and the Barbary States, he was able to sign a treaty with Prussia in 1785. With more than twenty-five years of diplomatic experience, oftentimes serving simultaneously upon several different commissions, Franklin well deserves the title of America's first career diplomat.

John Adams served as Commissioner to France in 1777 and as Plenipotentiary to negotiate peace with Great Britain in 1779. He was commissioned to negotiate a treaty of amity and commerce with the Netherlands in 1780 and the following year was again appointed Joint Commissioner to make peace with Great Britain. In 1785 he was commissioned as the first Minister Plenipotentiary of the United States to Great Britain and served for three years under the most trying circumstances. Although John Adams possessed a temperament hardly suited to diplomacy and was reputed to have said that no man will ever be pleasing at court in general who is not depraved in his morals or warped from his country's interest, he was successful in matters where patience and dogged determination were required. His achievement in obtaining a commercial treaty with the Netherlands was declared by a European foreign minister to have been "the greatest blow struck in the American cause, the most decisive." [1]

John Jay was appointed Plenipotentiary to the court of Spain in 1779 and left Madrid in 1782 as a Joint Commissioner to negotiate peace with Great Britain. His substantial achievements at this period are too often overlooked because of his subsequent unpopularity resulting from his mission to Britain and the Treaty of 1794.

Thomas Jefferson was commissioned Joint Plenipotentiary with Franklin in 1784 to sign treaties of amity and commerce with European and Barbary States and signed treaties with both Prussia and Morocco at Paris, the first on July 28, 1785, and the second on January 1, 1787. His subsequent brilliant career as Secretary of State and as President should not make us forget his earlier success in representing his country abroad.

To Silas Deane, however, goes the honor of having been the first diplomatic agent appointed to represent the new revolutionary government. His letter of instructions was dated March 3, 1776, and was prepared by the Committee on Secret Correspondence. He was to assume the character of a merchant engaged in West Indian trade, put himself in contact with friends of the colonies abroad and to secure audience with

---

[1] John Adams, *Works*, 10 vols. (Boston, 1851-65), III, 309.

the Count de Vergennes, French Minister of Foreign Affairs.[2] He used invisible ink in his correspondence, writing his despatches to Congress between the lines of supposed business letters which the officials at home could easily read after subjecting the letters to an acid bath.[3]

John W. Foster, although conceding that the young republic was not always well represented by its agents and diplomatic representatives, places Franklin, Adams, Jay, and Jefferson on a par with the best trained diplomats of Europe, and in reviewing the history of the Revolutionary period gives it as his opinion that the place in the public esteem and in value of service to our country, next to Washington, must be given, not to that patriot John Adams, not to Patrick Henry, Thomas Jefferson, nor to any military hero, but to Benjamin Franklin, our first and greatest diplomat.[4]

Slow Development of the Diplomatic Service. After the Federal government was set up under the Constitution in 1789, the diplomatic service developed slowly. Under the Constitution (Art. II, Sec. 2) the President was given the power to nominate and by and with the advice and consent of the Senate to appoint ambassadors and other public ministers and consuls. It was over a century, however, before any ambassadors were appointed, and in his first appointments President Washington limited the rank of his foreign representatives to that of chargé d'affaires. The first two appointments were made April 20, 1790, before an Act of Congress made any provision for foreign representation. William Short and William Carmichael were commissioned as Chargés d'Affaires to France and Spain respectively, "the designation of the officer being derived from the law of nations and the authority to appoint from the Constitution." [5]

When in 1790 President Washington proposed to send a chargé d'affaires to Lisbon the Portuguese Government objected on the ground that the grade was "of little privilege or respectability by the rules of their court and held in so low estimation with them that no proper character would accept it to go abroad." [6] The President thereupon decided to nominate David Humphreys as Minister Resident but with no increase in salary.[7]

On July 1, 1790, the Congress passed an act authorizing the President "to draw from the Treasury a sum not exceeding forty thousand dollars annually for the support of such persons as he shall commission to serve the United States in foreign ports, and for the expense incident to the

---

[2] Francis Wharton, *Diplomatic Correspondence of the American Revolution* (Washington, 1889), II, 78.

[3] John Jay, *Correspondence and Public Papers*, 4 vols. (New York, 1890-93), I, 84.

[4] John W. Foster, *A Century of American Diplomacy* (New York, 1910), 102.

[5] 7 *Opinions U.S. Attorney General*, 194.

[6] *American State Papers, Foreign Relations*, I, 127.

[7] It should be noted, however, that chargés d'affaires were sent later between the years 1825-1854 and 1876-1882.

business in which they are employed." [8] It should be noted that in the beginning Congress appreciated the need of an expense account, in fact an outfit was allowed each minister equal to the total of his salary. Unfortunately, the total of salary and outfit for a minister was not to exceed $9,000, a sum hardly adequate even in those days for the necessary equipment and expense. Robert Livingston when Secretary of Foreign Affairs in his annual report as to the needs of his Department had pointed out "Justice suggests that the salaries of officers who are engaged in so delicate and difficult a department . . . should have such appointments as to free them from embarrassment with respect to their private affairs," [9] but Congress was just as unwilling then as it is today to appropriate adequate expense allowances for our foreign representatives. Jefferson dipped into his private fortune and finally went bankrupt as a result of his diplomatic expenses and John C. Calhoun refused both the London and Paris posts because his private fortune would not stand the cost.

During Washington's administrations there were only a half dozen European countries where the United States felt it essential to send diplomatic representatives—France, Great Britain, Spain, Portugal, the Netherlands, and Prussia. The first American minister to Russia was commissioned in 1809, a minister was sent to Sweden and Norway in 1814, while Austria did not receive a diplomatic representative from the United States until 1838.

The Congress in this early period neither created diplomatic offices nor did it determine grades or ranks, although certain grades of diplomatic officers were mentioned in some of the appropriation acts. It was the President's right to appoint public ministers of any rank or denomination which the public interest might require. [10] Thus we find the Minister Resident to Portugal, David Humphreys, also accredited as Commissioner Plenipotentiary to Algiers. A special minister was sent to Denmark in 1811. Until 1814 the United States representive to the Netherlands had the rank of minister resident, but subsequently he ranked as envoy extraordinary and minister plenipotentiary. We have already noted that Washington's first diplomatic appointees were commissioned as chargés d'affaires to France and Spain.

In 1818, however, the Congress specified the names of the diplomatic posts already established or those to be filled and certain sums of money were allotted to each in the appropriation acts. [11] Realizing, however, the necessity of a certain degree of flexibility, an additional sum as a contingent fund was placed at the disposal of the President. The first law

[8] 1 U.S. Statutes at Large, 128.
[9] Samuel Flagg Bemis, American Secretaries of State and Their Diplomacy (New York, 1928), I, 126.
[10] 7 Opinions U.S. Attorney General, 195-196.
[11] 3 U.S. Statutes at Large, 422.

definitely regulating the diplomatic and consular services was not passed until March 1, 1855.

Early Development of the Consular Service. No attempt was made in the early period of the United States to set up a consular service entirely separate from the diplomatic service. The minister was expected to act also as the consul general in the country to which he was accredited and to supervise all other consular officers serving there. Since Congress at first failed to appoint any consular officers, the diplomatic representative had to serve also as a commercial agent. John Adams while Commissioner in France urged the appointment of consuls, and Franklin was very emphatic in his suggestions that the plan of appointing French merchants as commercial agents was bad and expensive.[12]

Our first Consul, William Palfrey, was appointed in 1780 in accordance with the terms of the Treaty of Commerce with France signed in 1778 but he never arrived at his post, as his ship was lost in a storm. Thomas Barclay was thereupon sent to France in 1781 with a commission as Vice Consul which was subsequently changed to Consul when Palfrey's death was definitely ascertained. Although Thomas Barclay is generally considered to have been the first American to serve as Consul under a formal appointment, Richard Harrison, an American merchant at Cadiz, was appointed early in 1781 and called Consul by Chargé d'Affaires William Carmichael.[13]

Unquestionably the most colorful of our early consuls was William Eaton, who served as Consul at Tunis from 1797 until 1803. Later as Navy Agent on the Barbary Coast with a heterogeneous army of Arabs, Greeks, and Italians under his command he marched 500 miles across the desert of Libya and captured the Tripolitan port of Derna.

The first action taken by Congress regarding a consular service was the resolution of March 16, 1784, declaring it to be "inconsistent with the interests of the United States to appoint any person not a citizen thereof to the office of minister, *chargé des affaires,* consul, vice consul, or to any civil department in a foreign country." [14] In spite of requests by our foreign representatives that the two services be separated, however, a resolution of October 28, 1785, authorized the ministers plenipotentiary of the United States in Europe and, where there was no minister, the chargé d'affaires, to exercise the powers of a consul general.[15] But inasmuch as the resolution did not prohibit the appointment of consuls, in January, 1786, Samuel Shaw was chosen Consul and Thomas Randall Vice Consul to serve in Canton, China.

[12] E. R. Johnson, "The Early History of the United States Consular Service, 1776-1792," *Political Science Quarterly,* XIII (March, 1898), 24-25.

[13] Bemis, *op. cit.,* I, 179.

[14] *Journals of the Continental Congress,* IX, 60.

[15] Johnson, *op. cit.,* 32.

During the first three years of his administration Washington appointed seventeen consuls and five vice consuls whose remuneration came solely from fees and profits of their commercial activities.[16] Realizing the need for further legislation, in his address to Congress December 8, 1790, Washington urged the expediency of regulating by law both the jurisdiction and the functions to be permitted to consuls. The Congress thereupon passed the first law regulating consuls and their duties on April 14, 1792, which was to remain the organic law on the subject for more than half a century.

Consular Service Established on Fee System.   The act of 1792, however, did little more than recognize the existence of the consular service, prescribe the duties to be performed and provide a schedule of fees which the consular officers might collect for their official services. Consuls and vice consuls could receive protests and declarations and give copies duly authenticated; they could settle the estates of Americans dying within their district if the laws of the country permitted; they were expected to take jurisdiction over stranded vessels flying their flag and over goods saved from these vessels; to serve as depositories for ships' papers and to offer relief to shipwrecked seamen. There were restrictions neither as to nationality nor as to the right to engage in trade. In fact, except in the Barbary States, consuls received no salaries and had to depend upon fees and their business for their livelihood.

Apparently no one would accept the position of consul in Tunis, Tripoli, or Morocco unless a salary should go with the post. As these were important posts at a time when the Barbary corsairs were constantly seizing American ships, cargoes, and crews, the Congress authorized salaries of $3,000 to be paid to consuls in these countries. Algiers was added to the list of salaried posts in 1797.[17] An act of May 1, 1810, provided that the consuls in the Barbary States should not engage in trade, the first law of its kind on the statute books.

A combination of the spoils system and the fee system was not a sound basis for satisfactory and efficient consular service, and numerous complaints came to the State Department. The personnel was alleged to be incompetent and the fees unequal and exorbitant. Secretary of State Edward Livingston made a careful investigation into the whole situation in 1833, and in a lengthy and critical report emphasized the need for a stricter definition of consular functions and pointed out the viciousness of the fee system.

As a remedy for the situation, Secretary Livingston suggested that the consular officers be compensated by adequate salaries. "They will never then by their countrymen be suspected of acting towards them as their

[16] Eugene Schuyler, *American Diplomacy* (New York, 1895), 45.
[17] Jones, *op. cit.*, 5, 6.

commercial interest, not as their duty requires, and their complaints in behalf of their fellow citizens will be attended to, because they will not be liable to the suspicion of advocating their own interest. . . . [18]

A list of the ministers, consuls, and other diplomatic and commercial agents of the United States in foreign countries as of December 15, 1830, appended to this report indicates the rapid growth of the consular and commercial services as contrasted with the diplomatic. In the diplomatic group we find only five posts—Great Britain, France, Russia, Spain, and Colombia, with envoys extraordinary and ministers plenipotentiary, and only one—the Netherlands—with a minister. In all the other capitals, twelve in number, where the United States had diplomatic representation the post was filled by a chargé d'affaires. As against these eighteen diplomatic posts the United States had 156 consuls, vice consuls, and commercial agents in as many different capitals or ports.

One of the most famous Americans representing the United States abroad at this time was Washington Irving, who while attached to the Legation at Madrid from 1826 to 1829 wrote *The Conquest of Granada* and *The Alhambra*. He later served as Secretary of Legation in London and Minister to Spain.

Defects in the Diplomatic Service. Secretary Livingston also made a fine report to President Jackson on the unfortunate predicament of our diplomatic officers. He indicated to what a serious extent the failure to provide adequate salaries was handicapping our representatives abroad, pointing out that at home heads of bureaus had offices, messengers, clerks, stationery, in fact, every convenience for carrying on the business in hand, while "to represent the dignity of the country, and on a scanty salary to transact its most important concerns abroad we send a man whom we provide with none of these necessaries for the transaction of his business; we force him to do all the drudgery of the office with his own hands, and either to live in some obscure place, where his countrymen blush to find him fixed . . . or at the expense of his own fortune, to provide what is necessary for the interest and dignity of the Government." [19] Livingston's conclusions are as pertinent today as when they were made: "If the mission is useful, it ought to be supported at the public, not at private expense; and the representatives of a great nation ought not to be obliged to employ, in devising parsimonious expedients for their support, that time and those talents which ought to be occupied in the service of their country." [20]

Until the year 1831 since there were no salary appropriations for secre-

[18] *Senate Document* No. 83, 22nd Cong., 2nd sess., 3.
[19] *House of Representatives Ex. Document* 94, 22nd Cong., 2nd sess., 5.
[20] *Ibid.*, 6. See part B of this document for numerous examples of inadequacy of salaries.

taries of legations each minister paid his own secretary and therefore regarded the copies of his despatches and sometimes his instructions as well as his own personal property. When the minister left his post he took the records with him and as a result the early records of many of the important posts are missing. Secretary Livingston in his report of 1833 found that "the archives of most of our legations exhibit only a beggarly account of empty boxes" and in an appendix cited statements from our diplomatic representatives abroad to the effect that the proceedings of the different missions to England from the first mission to August 1, 1826, were not recorded in the legation; that all despatches from our legation in France prior to March, 1810, were missing; and in Russia neither records nor despatches before 1823 were on file.[21]

To make the position of minister attractive as a political reward on occasions the appointee was permitted to be paid for considerable periods of time when he was away from his post. In this way the representative might draw salary for a year or two and spend only a few weeks at his post. The mission of John Randolph of Roanoke to St. Petersburg has been cited as a notorious instance of this abuse. Henry Adams thus describes the incident: "In September, 1829, John Randolph of Virginia was offered and accepted the mission to Russia; he sailed in June, 1830, remained ten days at his post, then passed near a year in England; and returning home in October, 1831, drew $21,807 from the Government, with which he paid off his old British debt. This act of Roman virtue, worthy of the satire of Juvenal, still stands as the most flagrant bit of diplomatic robbery in the annals of the United States Government."[22]

More than twenty years elapsed before the Congress took definite action to improve the conditions in the foreign service. A beginning was made when a Senate resolution of January 31, 1851, requested the Secretary of State to communicate any information which he might possess relative to the adoption of a graduated scale of diplomatic salaries based upon the combined considerations of the importance of the mission and the expenses of residence.[23] Secretary of State Webster thereupon sent a circular letter to the various American diplomatic representatives requesting a statement of their expenses. The replies indicated that with few exceptions the American representative had to draw upon his own private means in order to maintain his position even in the most economical fashion.[24] Whereas the normal salary of a minister was $9,000 and that of a minister resident was $4,500, Abbott Lawrence in London was spending over $20,000, W. C. Rives in Paris $16,500, Neill Brown estimated that $12,000 was the minimum, George Folsom at The Hague

---

[21] *Ibid.*, 5, 12-13.
[22] Henry Adams, *Life of John Randolph* (Boston, New York, 1882), 302.
[23] *Senate Ex. Document* No. 93, 32nd Cong., 1st sess., 1.
[24] *Ibid.*, 2-53.

had an exact budget of $12,479.86. Stanhope Prevost, diplomatic agent at Lima, averaged $11,360 annually, but conceded that by suppressing carriage, coachman, and one wet nurse he could save about one thousand dollars a year.

No action was taken until 1854, however, when the House Committee on Foreign Affairs favorably reported out a bill which was made law on March 1, 1855. This law prescribed grades, posts and salaries in both the diplomatic and consular services and limited all such appointments to citizens of the United States. Attorney General Cushing declared that the Congress only could recommend such limitations; otherwise it was usurping the constitutional powers of the President.[25] This act was thereupon repealed the following year and a new law adopting some of the recommendations of the Attorney General was passed.

The Act of 1856. The act of August 18, 1856,[26] was a landmark in the development of the foreign service of the United States and many of its provisions still hold. Salaries for ambassadors, envoys extraordinary, and ministers plenipotentiary appointed to Great Britain and France were fixed at $17,500; those to Russia, Spain, Austria, Prussia, Brazil, Mexico, and China at $12,000; all others at $10,000. Ministers resident and commissioners were to receive 75 per cent of these amounts, and chargés d'affaires 50 per cent. The President was authorized to appoint secretaries of legation at various posts with compensation ranging from $1,500 in Europe to $5,000 in China.

Consuls and commercial agents were also to be granted fixed compensation ranging from $500 in such posts as Cobiga and Tabasco to $7,500 in Liverpool and London. The bill further provided that no consul or commercial agent receiving $1,500 or more should be engaged in mercantile business. An interesting innovation of the law was the provision authorizing the President to appoint a maximum of twenty-five consular pupils at $1,000 a year to be assigned to consulates, these appointments to be made only after an examination by the Secretary of State of the qualifications and fitness of the candidate for the office. This provision looked towards the building up of a career service. But Congress failed to make the appropriation necessary to carry out this provision and shortly afterwards repealed it. In 1864, however, another act provided for the appointment of thirteen consular clerks who were to be subject to removal only for cause stated in writing and submitted to Congress.[27] The underlying purpose to secure trained men to be advanced in the service failed be-

[25] 7 *Opinions U.S. Attorney General,* 215, 267.
[26] 11 *U.S. Statutes at Large,* 52.
[27] 13 *U.S. Statutes at Large,* 139. For the full story of this effort to provide more efficient consular officers see Henry Brooks Adams, *Civil Service Reform* (Boston, 1869), 21-32.

cause the clerks preferred small salaries and permanency to large returns and uncertainty.

The duties of both diplomatic and consular officers were prescribed in some detail and a tariff of fees for consular services established. A careful accounting of all fees was required. Perhaps one of the most important provisions of the law was that it granted the President authority to prescribe from time to time any regulations or instructions not contrary to the law in relation to the duties of diplomatic and consular officers which he might think conducive to public interest. Much of the subsequent development of the diplomatic and consular services has been based upon such regulations.[28]

Further Efforts at Reform.   The outstanding defect in the law was that appointment still rested upon political influence rather than on merit, and tenure of office depended largely upon the political situation at home. De B. Randolph, United States Consular Inspector, brought a scathing indictment against the service in his report published in 1882. He asserted that "almost every consulate has some defects in its history owing to the incompetency, low habits and vulgarity of some of its officers during the endless round of evils incident to rotation." Among the particular abuses he cited were the collection of illegal fees in settling estates of Americans abroad, the issuance of illegal passports and the selling of the American flag. In conclusion, he declared that "if all could be told of the consular service of the United States as illustrated in the conduct of its officials, the excess of bad over good would be so great that the most cold and indifferent citizen would blush for the name of his country." [29] Reports of committees on bills in Congress to remedy this situation were prepared in 1868, 1872, 1884, and 1886 but no action was taken. It was not until the second administration of President Cleveland that further definite progress was made and then solely by executive order.

It is only in recent years that the sterling statesmanlike ability of President Cleveland has been properly appreciated. During his first administration his diplomatic appointments were for the most part above the average, nor was there the clean sweep in the consular service that had been generally expected.[30] He was an ardent advocate of government ownership of diplomatic residences abroad and in one of his messages he declared that he was "thoroughly convinced that in addition to their salaries our ambassadors and ministers at foreign courts should be provided by the government with official residences.... The usefulness of a

[28] A detailed account of the developments under the law in the consular field may be found in C. L. Jones, *The Consular Service of the United States* (Philadelphia, 1906), 13-26.

[29] William Slade, "Attractions and Flaws in Our Consular Service," *Forum*, XV, 163 (April, 1893).

[30] Bemis, *op. cit.*, VIII, 49.

nation's diplomatic representative undeniably depends to a great extent upon the appropriateness of his surroundings, and a country like ours, while avoiding unnecessary glitter and show, should be certain that it does not suffer in its relations with foreign nations through parsimony and shabbiness in its diplomatic outfit." [31]

It should be noted that on March 1, 1893, just three days before President Cleveland was inaugurated, the Congress had inserted a clause in one of the regular appropriation bills to the following effect:

> Whenever the President shall be advised that any foreign government is represented in the United States by an ambassador, envoy extraordinary, minister plenipotentiary, minister resident, special envoy, or chargé d'affaires, he is authorized in his discretion, to direct that the representative of the United States to such government shall bear the same designation. This provision shall in no wise affect the duties, powers or salary of such representative.[32]

President Cleveland took immediate advantage of this provision and as a result for the first time in its history the United States appointed ambassadors to London, Paris, Berlin, and Rome and received from these capitals representatives of similar rank.

President Cleveland was also keenly interested in the consular service and, according to report, when the copy for the 1888 edition of the *Consular Regulations* was sent to him he read the *Regulations* before approving them and said that he found them interesting.[33] In his presidential messages of 1888 and 1893, he had urged the reorganization of the consular service in order that it might become a more proficient agency. Apparently business interests at this time had become insistent upon some action being taken to improve the consular service. On January 23, 1894, the National Board of Trade passed a resolution agitating for the reform of the consular service in disregard of political affiliations. The *Century Magazine*, taking this resolution as a basis, sent a circular letter to a considerable number of ex-ministers of the United States asking their opinion. It published this symposium of opinions from such men as Robert T. Lincoln, former Minister to Great Britain, James B. Angell, former Minister to China, J. L. M. Curry, former Minister to Spain, and Oscar Straus, former Minister to Turkey. Only one of about a dozen interrogated found the service satisfactory and all the rest agreed unanimously upon the need to divorce the system from politics. J. R. Young, former Minister to China, who was personally familiar with most of the posts in Europe and the Far East declared that from his observations "in no branch of public service does the present system do more harm than in the management of our relations with foreign nations." [34]

[31] *Senate Document* No. 128, 54th Cong., 2nd sess.

[32] 27 *U.S. Statutes at Large*, 497.

[33] Gaillard Hunt, *op. cit.*, 333.

[34] "Consular Service and the Spoils System," *Century Magazine*, XLVI, 306 (June, 1894).

Consular Reform by Executive Order.   When the Senate failed to act on the bill for the reorganization of the consular service on a merit basis favorably reported by Senator Morgan on February 6, 1895, President Cleveland decided to make a start by executive order. As a basis of justification for his action the order was prefaced by the declaration that it was "of great importance that the consuls and commercial agents of the United States shall possess the proper qualifications for their respective positions to be ascertained either through a satisfactory record of previous actual service under the Department of State or through an appropriate examination." [35]

The order provided in substance that any vacancy in a consulate or commercial agency where the salary ranged from $1,000 to $2,500 should hereafter be filled either by transfer or promotion from another State Department position or after a suitable examination.

This order was a step in the right direction but a very short one. Examinations were held but only after the candidate had been selected and few failed to pass. Only one candidate failed out of 112 who took the examinations between March 3, 1897, and March 3, 1898. Furthermore, the political pressure upon the executive for consular posts was very great and since it was claimed that the rules were proclaimed only after a considerable change in the consular personnel, the new administration of President McKinley changed 238 out of 272 salaried consuls.[36] Harry A. Garfield, writing in 1900, told of the experiences of a friend who in following the trail of a defaulter had required the assistance of the American consular personnel. This representative of a business concern declared that of the twenty consuls and commercial agents that he sought out, fully one half were unfit for the position and some of them were disreputable. Another businessman with important interests abroad had found the American consul absent from his post the last two months of his term, and his successor, "a large, thick set man with the face of a retired bartender who spoke no foreign language and affected to despise all but his own—and that was peculiarly his own" wholly incompetent to help him. He had to appeal to the British consul who gave him the necessary assistance.[37]

Theodore Roosevelt had gone on record as favoring a career foreign service as far back as 1894 when addressing the National Board of Trade [38] so that when he became President it was expected that he would take

---

[35] *Senate Report* No. 1073, 54th Cong., 1st sess.

[36] George McAneny, "How Other Countries Do It," *Century Magazine*, XXXV, 611 (February, 1899).

[37] Harry A. Garfield, "The Business Man and the Consular Service," *Century Magazine*, LX, 268 (June, 1900).

[38] A. H. Washburn, "Some Ends of Our Consular Service," *Atlantic Monthly*, LXXIV, 241 (August, 1894).

action. In his first message to Congress on December 3, 1901, President Roosevelt recommended a reorganization of the consular service based upon "the just principle that appointments to the service should be made only after a practical test of the applicant's fitness, that promotion should be guided by trustworthiness, adaptability and zeal in the performance of duty, and that the tenure of office should be unaffected by partisan considerations." [39] He again reverted to the subject in his annual message of December 6, 1904, when he declared that our consular service needed improvement and that salaries should be substituted for fees, and proper classification, grading and transfer of consular officers should be provided.[40]

President Roosevelt cast aside completely the spoils system in making his appointments to diplomatic and consular posts. Francis B. Loomis, Assistant Secretary of State under President Roosevelt, declared that "every vacancy that has occurred since Mr. Roosevelt became President has been filled, so far as was practicable by promoting deserving men already in the service, and such promotions have been made, generally speaking, without reference to politics or political influence." Loomis also spoke highly of the assistance rendered towards the accomplishment of this end by the two Secretaries of State who served under President Roosevelt: "No man fought more persistently and valiantly to lift the Consular Service from the plane of partisan politics than Mr. Hay.... His successor, Mr. Root ... has taken up the work at the advanced point where Mr. Hay laid it down, and already his influence has made itself felt to the great advantage of the whole American foreign service." [41]

The first tangible evidence of a change in appointment procedure came with the issuance of two executive orders dated November 10, 1905. The first extended the scope of the executive order of September 20, 1895, as regards examinations for the consular service to include all officers whose compensation was not less than $1,000 annually. The second required that vacancies in the office of secretary of embassy or legation should be filled thereafter by transfer or promotion or by appointment after an examination.[42] A departmental order issued the same day by Secretary Root set up an examining board to determine the qualifications of applicants designated by the President. The order further provided for oral and written examinations in international law, diplomatic usage, and modern languages. President Taft and succeeding Presidents followed and extended this excellent precedent.

[39] J. D. Richardson, *Messages and Papers of the Presidents,* IX 6672 (December 6, 1904).
[40] *Ibid.,* 7024.
[41] Francis B. Loomis, "The Proposed Reorganization of the American Consular Service," *North American Review,* CLXXXII, 359 (March, 1906).
[42] *Senate Document* No. 359, 59th Cong., 2nd sess., 9.

The Statute of April 5, 1906.   Congress also was finally convinced of the need for reform in the consular service and on April 5, 1906, it passed an act completely reorganizing this branch of the foreign service.[43] Consuls general and consuls were classified and graded in nine classes ranging in salary from $2,000 in such small posts as Niagara Falls, Rouen, and Gibraltar to $12,000 for the ports of London and Paris. To achieve efficiency five inspectors of consulates were to be appointed by the President and every consular establishment was to be inspected at least once in every two years.[44] Positions in the service paying $1,000 or more a year were to be held by Americans only, nor were any officers of this class to carry on any private business. Fees for notarial services were prescribed and all fees had to be accounted for and paid into the Treasury.

President Roosevelt followed this act by an executive order dated June 27, 1906, prescribing regulations governing appointments and promotions in the consular service in accordance with the provisions of the Civil Service Act of January 16, 1883. All appointments to classes 8 and 9 were to be filled either (1) by the promotion of vice consuls, consular clerks, deputy consuls or consular agents, or (2) by new appointments of candidates who had passed a satisfactory examination for appointment as consul. Vacancies in all classes above 8 and 9 were to be filled by promotion based upon efficiency "as shown by the work that the officer has accomplished, the ability, promptness and diligence displayed by him in the performance of all his official duties, his conduct." [45]

Inasmuch as the appointments under the civil service were dependent entirely upon presidential prerogative, there was some fear lest the next administration would revert to the spoils system. President Taft, however, not only continued the merit system but by an executive order dated November 26, 1909, conferred a similar civil service status upon all diplomatic officers below the rank of minister.

The foreign service of the United States had at last been established on a merit basis for the entire consular branch and for all diplomatic officers beneath the rank of minister. As a result the quality of the service rapidly improved and businessmen and travelers no longer had to look up the British consul rather than the American for help in solving serious or technical problems. At the outbreak of World War I our foreign service compared favorably with that of great Britain and France even though we spent much less upon its development and its equipment.

The Spoils System Returns.   When Woodrow Wilson became President in 1913 the Democrats had been out of office for sixteen years and

[43] 34 *U.S. Statutes at Large,* 99.

[44] Secretary Root instituted this improvement basing it upon his experience with the Army while Secretary of War. Philip C. Jessup, *Elihu Root* (New York, 1938), II, 101.

[45] *Senate Document,* No. 359, *op. cit.,* Sect. 10.

it was but natural that considerable pressure should be put upon him to return the consular service to the spoils system. He refused categorically and the executive order of Elihu Root was maintained in force. In the diplomatic service, however, the record was not so satisfactory. William Jennings Bryan, the new Secretary of State, was a politician and as such appreciated party services. As a result many career diplomats who held positions as ambassadors or ministers, particularly in Latin American countries, were forced to surrender their posts to new appointees who were little more than hack politicians. Among the most flagrant examples was the appointment of James M. Sullivan, a New York police court lawyer intimate with Bald Jack Rose, the gambler, to the Dominican Republic. Senator Phelan of California who was later commissioned by Secretary Bryan to investigate charges against Mr. Sullivan found that "the candidate was vigorously supported by persons having large financial interests in Santo Domingo with the intention and in the hope of securing pecuniary profit through the incumbency in office of a minister who was friendly and under obligation...." Senator Phelan recommended Mr. Sullivan's resignation or recall.[46]

One of the ablest career men in the service, W. W. Rockhill, Ambassador to Turkey, after almost thirty years' service was permitted to resign to be succeeded by Henry Morgenthau, Chairman of the Democratic Finance Committee and a heavy campaign chest contributor. Another career man, John B. Jackson, Minister to Bulgaria, Rumania, and Serbia, with more than twenty years' service was succeeded by Charles J. Vopicka, a Chicago politician. Jackson thus explains the reason for his retirement: "In reply to my own inquiry I was informed by President Wilson, between his election and his first inauguration, that he approved of the practice which had existed generally (even when Mr. Roosevelt succeeded himself) that all chiefs of mission should submit their resignation to a new President. Accordingly my resignation was in the President's hands on March 4, 1913. I said that I should be glad to continue in the service in which I had been continually for more than twenty years. At that time the Balkan war was going on, and no attention was paid to my resignation until the following August. Then two days after I had notified the State Department by telegraph that peace had been signed at Bucharest, I was informed also by telegraph, that my resignation had been accepted." [47]

Congressman John Jacob Rogers of Massachusetts thus summarized the Bryan appointments: "When President Wilson was inaugurated in 1913 there were forty-one United States ambassadors and ministers. With respect to previous diplomatic experience these were classified as follows:

[46] *Report on the Foreign Service*, National Civil Service Reform League (New York, 1919), 125-7.
[47] *Report on the Foreign Service*, National Civil Service Reform League, 136.

one had been ambassador at a previous post; five had been promoted from minister to ambassador; four had been ministers at a previous post; fourteen had been secretaries in the diplomatic service; three had been consuls; one had been both secretary and consul; thirteen had been appointed without previous diplomatic experience. What has been the history of the last six years? Four of the forty-one are still in the service. Fifty-one men have been appointed ambassador or minister since March, 1913. Only two of the fifty-one so appointed have been secretaries or indeed have had previous diplomatic experience of any kind." [48] It should be noted, however, that nominations to important diplomatic posts have regularly been of a political nature, and in this respect the Wilson administration merely followed Republican precedents.

Statute of February 5, 1915.   Fearing lest the progress made merely by executive order in the development of a career service under Presidents Roosevelt and Taft might be lost, a number of organizations began a campaign to establish greater permanency in the system by means of congressional enactment. The result of this pressure was the law of February 5, 1915.[49] According to its provisions appointments henceforth in both the diplomatic and consular service were to be made to a certain grade or class in either service rather than to a post and the President was authorized to assign or transfer to these classes as the interests of the service required. Consuls general were divided into five classes ranging in salaries from $4,500 to $12,000; consuls in nine classes from $2,000 to $8,000. Diplomatic secretaries, however, were apparently still expected to be chosen only from wealthy families as their remuneration began with $1,200 in class five and reached the maximum of $3,000 in class one.

Perhaps the most important provision of the law was that of Section I which permitted any diplomatic or consular officer to be assigned for duty in the Department of State without loss of grade, class or salary for a period of not more than three years, unless the public interests required further service when one additional year was permitted.

By this law the entire foreign service below the rank of minister was put upon a merit basis providing that the President desired it. The provision for an appointment to a class rather than to a specific post practically necessitated that all positions of importance be filled by career officers. Few candidates for political jobs were desirous of a position which might pay them $1,200 for their services in such a city as Tegucigalpa or Port au Prince.

[48] *Congressional Record,* LVII, Pt. 2 (January 21, 1919), 1826. Cf., however, Charles Seymour, *The Intimate Papers of Colonel House* (New York, 1926), I, 177, for a more favorable view.
[49] 38 *U.S. Statutes at Large,* 805. (Popularly known as the Stone-Flood Bill.)

The career service was strengthened still further when the Act of July 1, 1916 created the position of counselor of embassy or legation and made Class I officers eligible to appointment to this position which ranked next to that of ambassador or minister. The day of the spoilsman was nearing its end.

6

Development
of the Foreign Service
Since World War I

WORLD WAR I was destined to have almost as much influence on the development of the Foreign Service as it did on the development of the Department of State. At the very outbreak of the war the American diplomatic service was asked to take charge of numerous belligerent embassies and legations; assumption of these additional duties in the case of certain posts tripled or quadrupled their work. The inquiries from home for the whereabouts of Americans traveling in Europe completely deluged the clerical forces in the large capitals. In those easy-going days few American travelers possessed passports and those not so supplied found to their dismay that passports had suddenly become an essential requirement. The Paris Embassy issued 4,500 emergency passports in one week following the outbreak of war.[1] The sudden and very considerable expansion of American trade put additional burdens upon the consuls, yet large numbers were ordered to return to Washington to fill important technical positions in the Department of State.

As a result many appointments were made both in the diplomatic and consular service without examinations of any sort, but in all cases it was understood that an examination would be required before the appointment should be regarded as giving the appointee the status of a diplomatic secretary or consul of career.

When the war was over among the pressing problems facing the United States was the necessity of reorganizing the entire machinery for the conduct of our foreign relations to meet the responsibilities entailed by the fundamental changes in the world's system of states and our new preponderance of power and wealth. In a letter dated January 21, 1920, to John Jacob Rogers, a member of Congress from Massachusetts, Secretary of State Robert Lansing stated the situation:

[1] Beckles Willson, *America's Ambassadors to France* (London, 1928), 395.

The machinery of government now provided for dealing with our foreign relations is in need of complete repair and reorganization. As adequate as it may have been when the old order prevailed and the affairs of the world were free from the present perplexities, it has ceased to be responsive to present needs. . . .[2]

After showing the need of reorganization in the Department of State Secretary Lansing turned to the diplomatic service and pointed out the need for higher salaries, the desirability of government owned embassies and legations, and the advantage of bringing the diplomatic and consular services together by establishing an interchangeable system.

Representative Rogers had already introduced three bills during the year 1919 for the reorganization of the diplomatic and consular service but no action on them had been taken. He persisted in his attempts and in 1923 managed to get his bill passed by the House of Representatives. However, due to the legislative jam occurring in the short session, the Senate adjourned before reaching this bill on its calendar. The following year Mr. Rogers was more successful and the important bill bearing his name passed the House on May 1, 1924, by a vote of 134 to 27, and the Senate by unanimous consent on May 15, 1924. It received the approval of President Coolidge on May 24, 1924, and went into effect on July 1, 1924.

The Act of May 24, 1924. The Rogers Bill was not a radical departure in any respect but rather the culmination of a long struggle to take the Foreign Service definitely and permanently out of politics. No longer could the political ward-heeler look to his congressman for a job as consul in some foreign land whose stark realities were in no way disclosed by its euphonious name. Merit alone was to serve as the basis of appointment and promotion, and for the first time in American history the new salary scale provided by the bill permitted a diplomatic secretary to live in a respectable fashion without drawing upon his own private sources.

Henceforth the diplomatic and consular services were to be known as the Foreign Service and the term, Foreign Service officer, was to denote permanent officers below the rank of minister. All appointments were by commission to a class and not to any particular post. All diplomatic secretaries and consuls were divided into nine classes with salaries ranging from $3,000 in Class IX to $9,000 in Class I. Vice consuls of career, consular assistants, interpreters and student interpreters were placed in an unclassified group with salaries from $1,500 to $3,000.

The most important and original feature of the reorganized service was the amalgamation of the diplomatic and consular branches into a single Foreign Service on an interchangeable basis. Until this time a candidate had to choose in advance which service he wished to enter and

[2] *Foreign Service of the United States.* Hearings before the Committee on Foreign Affairs, H.R. 68th Cong., 1st sess., 30-1.

once he started no change was possible. Yet experience might prove to him that he both preferred and was better equipped to work in the branch which he had not entered. The new arrangement made for greater flexibility and permitted the State Department by transferring the officers from one service to the other to determine in which position the officer was the more useful.

Another advantage of the interchangeability feature was the lever afforded to break down a certain degree of snobbery which existed in the Foreign Service. The social status of the two services had always been on different planes due to long continued international practice. As a result many rich men's sons went into the diplomatic service for the social position which it afforded. The possibility that they might have to enter the consular service first and even be kept there or might be transferred from the diplomatic to the consular service took away some of the social glamour and it was hoped would gradually weed out the so-called white-spat brigade.

Hugh Gibson, at that time United States Minister to Poland, in testifying before the House Committee on behalf of the Rogers Bill declared: "You hear very frequently about the boys with the white spats, the tea drinkers, the cookie pushers, and while they are a very small minority they make a noise entirely disproportionate to their numbers. . . . They are a reproach to us and when an American goes into one of our missions abroad and . . . is received by one of these second raters of whom we hear so much, he remembers it for years and he is very properly indignant at it." [3]

The new law also permitted dual commissions to be issued to a Foreign Service officer so that it opened the way to combining diplomatic and consular posts in the smaller capitals. This procedure would make for greater efficiency and at the same time reduce the expense of maintaining two separate establishments.

The Rogers Bill provided specifically for a classified service to which all appointments would be made after examination and a suitable period of probation, and all promotions were to be made on the basis of merit. Provision was made for the Secretary of State to recommend to the President for promotion to the grade of minister any Foreign Service officer who had demonstrated special capacity by reason of efficient service. In cases of such promotion the law provided that the officer should still be entitled to all the benefits of retirement and disability which the act provided.

Foreign Service Retirement Fund.   Strangely enough, until the passage of the Rogers Act no provision had even been made for retirement pay

---

[3] *Hearings, op. cit.,* 40.

or disability allowances for Foreign Service officers. The officers of the Army and Navy were well taken care of in this regard, but the Foreign Service officer with a smaller base pay received no consideration what soever. As a result the Government had to retain officers advanced in years, thus impairing the efficiency of the Foreign Service. Otherwise, after many years in the Service and with no savings possible under the small salary scale which they received, officers must be discharged as unfitted and too old for other work.

In the hearings before the House Committee considering the bill Julius Lay, a former American consul with some thirty years' experience in the service, stated that after he had exhausted his private means by subsidizing Uncle Sam for so many years he was forced to leave the service principally because he had no means for his old age after he should retire. If the Rogers Bill had been in force he declared he would never have left the service. Incidentally, an international bank found Lay's services of sufficient value to pay him several times as much as he had ever received while consul.[4]

The new law created a special fund to be known as the Foreign Service Retirement and Disability Fund. This fund was to be obtained by a contribution of 5 per cent of their base salaries by all Foreign Service officers plus a certain sum to be contributed by the Government. It was estimated that after the system reached its normal basis the Government's contribution would amount to 28 per cent of the amount required. Retirement was automatic at the age of sixty-five with the President authorized to retain an officer on active duty for an additional five years for the interests of the service. Service at posts classified as unhealthful counted for time and a half in reckoning length of service for retirement.

The Foreign Service Personnel Board. The Rogers Act authorized the President to prescribe certain rules and regulations for administering the Foreign Service and President Coolidge by an executive order dated June 7, 1924 (effective after July 1, 1924) proceeded to carry out this provision. A Foreign Service Personnel Board consisting of the Under Secretary of State, two Assistant Secretaries of State, and an Executive Committee composed of three high ranking Foreign Service officers was established to examine into the efficiency records of Foreign Service officers and recommend for promotion on the basis of these records. The Board was also authorized to recommend for transfer into the Foreign Service any officer of the Department of State with at least five years' continuous service whose ability and merit warranted it. This provision it was hoped would level the barrier which existed between the drafting officer and the career officer. The Board could also recommend for pro-

---

[4] *Hearings, op. cit.,* 76.

motion to the position of minister those Foreign Service officers who had demonstrated special capacity.

A Board of Examiners was also named and the type of examination and the essential subjects to be included were specified. Rules for eligibility were laid down and a Foreign Service School was established in the Department of State for the instruction of the successful candidates.

As contemplated by the Act a considerable number of promotions were made very promptly and a new enthusiasm was instilled into the service. Unfortunately the two services were still considered separately by the Personnel Board in making the promotions and the diplomatic branch got more than its proportionate share. Dissatisfaction was openly expressed and Congressman Edwards of Georgia on February 16, 1927, introduced a resolution in the House of Representatives requesting the Secretary of State to furnish the House certain information concerning appointments in the Foreign Service of the United States.[5]

Inequalities in Administering the Rogers Act.   About a month later Lawrence Dennis, First Secretary of the American Legation at Managua, a career officer of independent means, resigned from the service because he claimed that wealth and social position were the determining factors in promotion to desirable posts in the Foreign Service.

Secretary of State Kellogg made a report to the Foreign Affairs Committee of the House on July 26, 1927, conceding that a disproportionate number of promotions had occurred in the diplomatic branch and promised to make an equal number of promotions in the consular branch to equalize the situation. This did not entirely satisfy those interested in the welfare of the reorganized Foreign Service and Senator Harrison of Mississippi on December 17, 1927, introduced a resolution in the Senate similar to that of Representative Edwards requesting an investigation of the administration of the Rogers Act and particularly the work of the Foreign Service Personnel Board. The findings of the Committee on Foreign Relations of the Senate, after a careful investigation was made by a subcommittee of three Senators (Moses, Reed and Harrison), stated that "the application of the Act of May 24, 1924, had been approached in a manner far at variance from the purpose of the legislation."

In the first place the high executives of the State Department who served as members of the Personnel Board were too busy with matters of policy to give adequate attention to the promotion of personnel. In the second place the diplomatic branch exercised the greater influence in the operation of the Rogers Act and secured for themselves the greater benefits. As evidence of this the report pointed out that of the total of 214 promotions in the Foreign Service during the first two and one-half years of the new legislation 63 per cent of all diplomatic officers were advanced while only 37 per cent of the consular officers were so favored.

It was found that the initial injustice in the application of the Act arose from the use of a double list—one diplomatic and one consular—in making promotions, a procedure not contemplated by the Act. The subcommittee also pointed out that those who had served on the Personnel Board were high in the lists of promotions, and recommended that the handling of Foreign Service personnel should be wholly divorced from the personnel itself. The subcommittee also recommended a certain amount of automatic promotion by salary grades within classes and a greater fluidity between the diplomatic and consular branches.[6]

Financial Aids to the Service.   To strengthen the Foreign Service further, in the Appropriation Bill of the Department of State for the fiscal year ending June 30, 1930, provision was made "to furnish the officers and employees in the Foreign Service with living quarters, heat, light, and household equipment in government owned or rented buildings at places where it would be in the public interest to do so." [7] However, the restrictive clause placed the responsibility upon the Secretary of State to decide, whereas an outright allowance for rent, light and heat to every Foreign Service officer stationed abroad was necessary if career men were to be able to live on their salaries. This requirement was met by the Act of June 26, 1930, which provided living quarters including heat, fuel, and light for civilian officers and employees of the government stationed in foreign countries providing they were citizens of the United States.[8] This piece of legislation, which helped materially to take from the shoulders of the suddenly transferred officer the burden of penalties exacted for a cancelled lease of his residence and the quick sale of those of his household effects unsuited for his new post, has been of inestimable value.

The Act of February 23, 1931.   The Moses-Linthicum Act, which became law February 23, 1931, and took effect July 1, 1931, now became the next organic act of the Foreign Service. It was in reality two acts—the first grading and classifying clerks in the Foreign Service, the second an overhauling of the Act of 1924.

As regards clerks,—those receiving from $3,000 to $4,000 were classed as Senior Clerks and those below that level as Junior Clerks. Appointments to the class of Senior Clerks were limited to American citizens and were made by promotions from the ranks of Junior Clerks for efficient service. Post allowances were now made available to clerks where the cost of

[6] *Report of the Senate Committee on Foreign Relations* No. 1069, 70th Cong., 1st sess. (May 3, 1928).
[7] 45 *U.S. Statutes at Large,* 1098.
[8] 46 *U.S. Statutes at Large,* 818.

living made it necessary. Henceforth no clerk not an American citizen could serve in any diplomatic mission.

Both representation and post allowances were authorized and an annual leave of sixty days with pay included. In case the officer returned to the United States the time spent in going and coming was not counted. Provision was also made for sick leave with pay amounting to fifteen days a year.

Elaborate provisions were made for the reorganization of the Board of Foreign Service Personnel so as to make its decisions impartial. No Foreign Service officer below Class I could be assigned for duty in the Division of Foreign Service Personnel. Nor could such officers during such assignment or for three years afterwards be eligible for positions as minister or ambassador. Detailed regulations were also prescribed for the compiling and checking of efficiency records. Automatic salary advances of $100 annually in the four lower classes and of $200 for the four upper were provided to avoid the stagnation which had been noted as a disadvantage under the former system.

A new board of examiners was set up and a more complete organization of the Foreign Service Officers Training School was worked out. A few other administrative changes were made such as the establishment of district accounting and disbursing officers in certain areas and the setting up in the Department of State of the Office of Legal Adviser in place of the Solicitor of the Department of State. Under the Act of 1931 the Foreign Service finally received recognition of its essential value as a highly trained technical force and the machinery was immediately set up by administrative orders, dated June 8, 1931, to make the Act effective. In the words of Assistant Secretary of State Carr "the Foreign Service had finally attained the goal for which Presidents, Secretaries of State, and the businessmen of the country had striven for years, namely a reasonable, adequate provision in the way of pay and allowances for the men who served the United States in a diplomatic or consular capacity in foreign countries." [9]

Serious Effects of the Economic Depression. Unfortunately the severe results of the economic depression began to be felt almost simultaneously with the coming into effect of the Moses-Linthicum Act with resulting hardships in the Foreign Service. Not only were no promotions possible, but the several economy acts of Congress reduced salaries 15 per cent, abolished post and representation allowances, and reduced rental allowances for Foreign Service officers 65 per cent.[10] When this was followed by the depreciation of the dollar in April, 1933, and its subsequent lower

[9] *American Foreign Service Journal,* XI (February, 1934).
[10] Congressional appropriations for rent, heat, and light allowances were as follows: 1931, $664,000; 1932, $1,440,000; 1933, $686,000; 1934, $439,000.

revaluation, the financial position of American officials abroad became unendurable. Those who had private incomes drew upon them to pay their own way and in some cases that of their subordinates. Families were sent home to relatives to lighten the burden, leasing arrangements were cancelled with resulting penalties, life insurance policies were sacrificed, children taken out of school, and even necessary food was not always available.

President Franklin D. Roosevelt immediately requested an appropriation from Congress to help American officials abroad who had suffered because of the depreciated value of the dollar but to no avail. He thereupon in July, 1933, ordered gold sent abroad to a depository so that salary checks might be converted into foreign currency at mint par. This arrangement, however, only helped in some countries while officers in other places remained without relief, even this expedient ceasing in January, 1934, with the revaluation of the dollar.

The Congress was finally prevailed upon to remedy the situation, and in the State Department Appropriation Bill for the fiscal year 1935 a substantially increased rental allowance and post allowances to equalize the cost of living were authorized. A bill was also passed on March 26, 1934, known as the Exchange Bill [11] which provided for the payment of American officials stationed abroad in dollars equivalent to their approximate conversion value before the United States went off the gold standard. The Congress also restored 5 per cent of the salary cut on February 1, 1934, another 5 per cent on July 1 of the same year, and the remaining 5 per cent on July 1, 1935. Departmental orders dated April 15, 1934, and July 3, 1934, classified both posts and officers for the allocation of post allowances, so that before the end of the year 1935 the Foreign Service had practically regained its financial status as contemplated by the Moses-Linthicum Act.

The Foreign Service, however, was still seriously undermanned inasmuch as no examinations had been held since 1932 and every year a certain number of officers were necessarily separated from the service.

In the *Hearings* for the State Department Appropriation Bill for 1936, Assistant Secretary of State Carr pointed out that in spite of new posts being established, as, for example, in Russia, the number of Foreign Service officers had decreased approximately 10 per cent since 1932. Of the 688 authorized, 7 were language officers studying the Chinese, Japanese, and Russian languages and 36 were on duty in the Department, thus leaving only 645 officers to supply 318 diplomatic and consular posts in all parts of the world—that is, about two per post. Since every post must have at least one officer and many required from six to eight, this was inadequate and unsound administration.

[11] 48 *U.S. Statutes at Large*, 466.

Agricultural and Commercial Attachés Consolidated.   Although the need was manifestly great, the Congress as usual was not sympathetic to increased appropriations in this direction, and early in 1939 there were only about 720 officers in the career service. However, on July 1, 1939, President Roosevelt, by the authority of Reorganization Plan II, which had been approved by Congress, transferred the foreign activities and personnel of the Departments of Agriculture and Commerce to the Department of State, thereby adding approximately 113 agricultural and commercial attachés to the Foreign Service of the United States.[12] This consolidation, long sought by Assistant Secretary of State George Messersmith, by establishing one reporting unit for commercial, agricultural, and industrial affairs in each country, eliminated unnecessary duplication and effected a considerable economy in administration. It also improved the morale of the Foreign Service, which had rightly resented the superior facilities afforded the commercial and agricultural attachés compared with those enjoyed by many consular officers whose work often furnished the basic material for the reports of their more affluent colleagues.

Effects of World War II.   At the outbreak of World War II, the Foreign Service of the United States, including noncareer chiefs of mission, career officers, noncareer vice consuls, clerks, and miscellaneous employees, numbered about 4,000 persons. At the close of the war it had more than doubled. Even then it was unable to perform adequately the many duties newly imposed. Among the early war activities of the Foreign Service were the repatriation of thousands of Americans, which meant notification, protection, and often the furnishing of funds and transportation, the representation of belligerent interests,[13] the exchange of war-prisoners, liaison with the Red Cross, and innumerable other duties resulting from war conditions. When the United States became a belligerent, the war requirements entailed stockpiling of strategic materials, blacklisting foreign firms affiliated with Axis powers, control of foreign funds, new visa and passport regulations, and various relief and rehabilitation operations. Propaganda, long eschewed by the Department of State and the Foreign Service, now became a vital part of the national security policy.

Although approximately ninety-five posts located in Axis or Axis-controlled areas were closed between July, 1939, and September, 1943, eighty-eight new posts were established. When it is remembered that over 350 American diplomatic and consular officials abroad were interned for various periods of time, and hundreds were needed for essential work in

[12] *Department of State Press Releases* (May 13, 1939), 395-400. For more detailed analysis, see Department of State Diplomatic Serial No. 3084.

[13] For example, in Berlin as of August, 1940, the American Embassy was representing the interests of Great Britain, Australia, New Zealand, Canada, France, Belgium, Luxembourg, and the Union of South Africa.

the Department of State, and that no Foreign Service examinations were given after 1941, the vital requirements for additional personnel can be appreciated.

The Foreign Service Auxiliary. As early as December, 1940, Mr. Laurence Duggan, an Adviser on Political Relations, urged a comprehensive review of the adequacy of personnel and equipment of the Foreign Service to meet wartime requirements. A subsequent memorandum made such an excellent case that by the middle of 1941 the Foreign Service Auxiliary was established, and it had recruited some 438 officers by October 15, 1943. These officers included young men who were able to serve as noncareer vice consuls, as well as specialists who were able to aid in the more technical wartime activities. The salary scale ranged from $2,000 to $6,500, depending upon age, ability, and experience, and the work ranged from certification of invoices to specialized work in economic analysis. The Foreign Service Auxiliary did such excellent work during the war period that by January 1, 1946, the Auxiliary numbered 976 as against 820 career officers, plus some 2,000 additional clerks.

It should be noted that the regular career officers were not too happy at the rapid development of the Auxiliary Service. A certain resentment was natural when it is remembered that many of these newcomers entered at high levels and with no examination. It was feared that later they might be inducted into the Foreign Service and thereby break down the carefully established career principle. However, the need for specialists to handle newly imposed technical problems had to be met and the Auxiliary Service did meet the test.

The Acts of May 3, 1945, and July 3, 1946. It was long recognized that some of the so-called clerks were performing tasks of such a character that the Moses-Linthicum limitation of a $4,000 maximum salary was both unfair and detrimental to the Service. Furthermore, the existing legislation was too rigid to meet the need for transfer from the State Department to the field, or when necessary between other Departments and State. The temporary law of March 3, 1945, set up a new category of administrative, fiscal, and clerical personnel within the Foreign Service, with a salary scale ranging from $2,600 to $5,600. Qualified Auxiliary officers could be brought into this new classification and obtain permanent status. The act also permitted special tours of duty in the Foreign Service to specialists from other branches of the government or from outside for limited periods of time. Greater flexibility was also obtained by the removal of the per-cent limitations upon the classes of officers under the Rogers Bill.

The Act of July 3, 1946, commonly known as the Foreign Service Manpower Bill, went still further and permitted the appointment, under fairly strict selection requirements, of 250 Foreign Service officers within the next two years. These officers, who were for the most part highly qualified specialists whose experience and training would make them valuable personnel in the Service, were selected with great care and after competitive oral examinations. Inasmuch as the written and oral examinations for entrance into the career service were reinstituted in 1945, at first for the Department personnel and the clerks in the Foreign Service and later for veterans and members of the armed forces, the Foreign Service was on the way to obtaining sufficient personnel to carry on its added responsibilities in the postwar world.

The Foreign Service Act of 1946. It is doubtful whether any legislation pertaining to governmental administration was ever more carefully drawn or prepared by a greater number of experts than the Foreign Service Act of 1946. Not only did members of Congress aid in its preparation, but many officials of the State Department and of the Foreign Service participated actively. The *American Foreign Service Journal* sponsored an essay contest urging all familiar with the Service to submit constructive criticism in the form of papers. Over sixty such contributions were received and the most representative were published during the year 1945. Assistant Secretary of State Julius Holmes reviewed every contribution and directed that the Division of Foreign Service Planning in the Department of State give them particular consideration. To give the names of all those in the Department and in the Foreign Service who made substantial contributions is not feasible here, but mention should be made of Foreign Service Officers Selden Chapin, Monnet B. Davis, Nathaniel P. Davis, Andrew B. Foster, Edmund A. Gullion, Alan N. Steyne, and Carl W. Strom.[14] The Bureau of the Budget was not sympathetic to the Department's bill, but Secretary of State Byrnes was *persona grata* to the Congress, and Congressman Kee and Senator Connally ably sponsored the act, which became law with the President's signature August 13, 1946.

Changes in Classification, Salaries, and Allowances. The Foreign Service Act of 1946 replaced the Rogers Act of 1924 and the Moses-Linthicum Act of 1931—it was in fact a codification of all existing legislation on the subject. One of the most important innovations, particularly from the point of view of the Foreign Service officer, was the creation of the post of career minister. Henceforth a career officer did not jeopardize his future by accepting a position as ambassador or minister. By this legislation not only were able career officers recognized as suitable for the topmost positions, but once promoted, they need not fear lest they "be beheaded with a change of administration." [15] If not named

[14] See particularly Andrew B. Foster, "The Division of Foreign Service Planning," *American Foreign Service Journal,* 11 (August, 1946), and the special issue of September, 1946, *passim.*
[15] See *Report on the Foreign Service, op. cit.,* 58.

a chief of mission, the career minister might serve as Counselor of Embassy or Consul General at the increased salary of $13,500.

The new law increased materially the salaries of all officers. Ambassadors and ministers of Class I were given $25,000 per year; Class II, $20,000; Class III, $17,500; and Class IV, $15,000. When it is remembered that the previous maximum salary of an ambassador was $17,500, a sum established in 1855, the need for a substantial increase is appreciated. However, the new salary scale would have been woefully inadequate if representation allowances had not been increased in an even larger ratio than salaries. Under the new law, although no specific amounts were specified, as much as $25,000 might be allocated to posts such as London and Paris. In addition to these sums for proper representation, allowances were permitted for high cost of living and for the operation and maintenance of a suitable official residence. With the augmented salary and the additional allowances, the Ambassador of the United States in a capital like London might receive as much as $65,000 a year as against $30,000 in the past.

The number of classes of Foreign Service officers was reduced from eleven to six, plus that of career minister. The new salary scale ranged from the minimum of $3,300 in Class VI to the maximum of $13,500 in Class I. These salaries, with the increased allowances for rent, light, and heat and cost of living, plus two new allowances covering unusual expenses incurred by the officer in establishing his residence or for hospitalization for illness or injury incurred in the line of duty, permitted a Foreign Service officer to live in a manner commensurate with his position without possessing a private income.[16]

Reserve and Staff Officers. In recognition of the new requirements of the Service for technically trained experts, many of which had been furnished by the Foreign Service Auxiliary, the Act of 1946 established the Foreign Service Reserve to replace the Auxiliary. These officials were to be appointed either from a governmental agency or from private life on a temporary basis for nonconsecutive tours of duty up to four years at a rank for which they were qualified. They were classified exactly as were Foreign Service officers, except that they were not eligible to become career ministers.

It was understood that these experts would serve in such capacities as mineral attachés, cultural attachés, labor attachés, and information officers. Inasmuch as they were temporary and not more than one hundred and fifty such officers would ever be employed at one time, this innovation would in no way jeopardize the career service. To achieve flexibility, it was permitted that Reserve officers might become Foreign Service offi-

---

[16] By Public Law 160, approved July 6, 1949, all salaries of Foreign Service, Reserve, and Staff officers under $10,000 were increased by $330.

cers by passing such examinations as the Board of Examiners of the Foreign Service might prescribe; or when deemed necessary, the President, with the advice and consent of the Senate might commission such officers as diplomatic or consular officers, or both. By and large, it would seem that the Foreign Service Reserve has proved successful in meeting a need in a manner satisfactory to the good of the Service.

The results of the Moses-Linthicum Act, which aimed to improve the status of the American clerks, were not entirely satisfactory. Although in 1945 approximately 230 of the 1875 employees in this group were serving as vice consuls and doing exactly the same work as vice consuls of career, both their financial compensation and their social status were considerably inferior to that of the career officer.

The Act of 1946 remedied this situation materially. A new classification designated as Foreign Service Staff Officers and Employees covered every American employee from charwoman and janitor to high administrative and fiscal officers. There were twenty-two classes, with salaries ranging from $720 to $10,000 annually. Since they were made eligible for approximately the same type of allowances as Foreign Service officers, the increased compensation and regularized status has improved the morale of this group materially.

The Act also made provision for the retention of alien consular agents and alien clerks and employees. The Secretary of State was given considerable leeway in prescribing schedules of salaries for these persons, although it was prescribed that all as far as possible should receive equal pay for equal work.

Promotions and Retirement.   A fundamental change in the promotion system was inaugurated by the new act. Whereas formerly promotion depended upon recommendation by the Board of Foreign Service Personnel, which included no career officers, and an efficiency rating from a supervisory officer in the field, the new law adopted the Navy system of "promotion up or selection out." Selection boards, including both Foreign Service and Department officers, decided who should be promoted. The composition of these boards changed every year so that the maximum of fairness was attained. As originally administered, officers in Class VI who were not promoted after three years were let out. In Classes V through II, the time allowed was eight years before selection out occurred. By 1950 it was agreed that these periods were too short, and on January 18, 1950, the Board of Foreign Service adopted new regulations. Henceforth, officers of Class VI would not be selected out until they had been unfavorably considered by three consecutive selection boards. Officers in Classes V through II had ten years to make the next grade. However, these officers would go out automatically if three consecutive selection boards rated them as being in the lowest 10 per cent of those eligible for promotion. The A and B Selection Boards of 1950 each contained four Foreign Service officers and two public members, whereas those for 1948 and 1949 each had but one public member.

Although this system seems somewhat harsh, it does eliminate the dead wood and gives opportunity for more rapid advancement to the able officers. Perhaps its principal defect is that the promotion from one class to another will still take approximately six years, even for the outstanding officer. Compared with the rapid promotion possible within the Department of State or from the Department to the top ranks of the Service, it would seem that the career service is unduly penalized. The principal difficulty is the lack of vacancies open to officers eligible for promotion. For example, in the 1948 promotions in Class IV, only 22 promotions were possible out of an eligible list of 187.

The retirement provisions of the 1946 Act are on the whole generous and flexible. A career minister must retire at the age of 65, unless serving as chief of a mission or unless, because of an emergency, the Secretary extends his services. Any Foreign Service officer after twenty years service may retire at the age of 50, but all must retire at 60 unless an emergency exists. The annuities provided are largely based upon the average of the last five years of service and naturally depend upon the length of service and the salary received. For example, a Foreign Service officer whose average salary for the last ten years of service was $10,000 could retire at the age of 60 after thirty years of service at an annuity of $6,000. If he wished his widow to receive a maximum of $2,500 after his death, his maximum annuity would be $4,750.

Miscellaneous Provisions. To keep Foreign Service officers in touch with home conditions, it is required that every such officer shall be assigned for at least three years service in the continental United States during his first fifteen years of service. During this period he might serve in the Department of State or in some other government agency. He might be assigned for instruction or training in some institution of learning or elsewhere. The Act provides for the establishment of a Foreign Service Institute in Washington, which is described elsewhere, to give in-service training.

The administration of the Foreign Service is under the direct control of the Deputy Under Secretary of State for Administration.[17] He is assisted by the Director General of the Foreign Service appointed by the Secretary of State from Class I officers or career ministers of the Foreign Service. An interdepartmental Board of the Foreign Service, consisting of three Assistant Secretaries of State, the Director General of the Foreign Service, and representatives from Agriculture, Commerce, and Labor,

[17] See p. 43 *supra*.

make recommendations to the Secretary of State concerning the functions of the Foreign Service.

Hoover Commission Recommendations.   The Hoover Commission on the Organization of the Executive Branch of the Government in its report on foreign affairs submitted to the Congress on February 18, 1949, not only recommended an internal reorganization of the State Department, but also took up a number of problems of the Foreign Service. The diffusion of command, the cleavage between Foreign Service and Departmental personnel, the discrimination suffered by the staff officers, the faults in recruitment and transfer methods, the failure of the State Department to give sufficient consideration to the reports from the foreign missions all were considered at length and suggestions or recommendations made. One vital recommendation which should always be observed was that the chief of each foreign mission should be the responsible spokesman for the country to which he is assigned.

Unquestionably the most controversial recommendation of the Commission was the consolidation of the Foreign Service and the State Department personnel into a single new Foreign Affairs Service in which all members should have equal status, including compensation and retirement rights. It was recognized that such a move was a very serious innovation, so that, although mandatory, it was recommended that the amalgamation should be carried out over a short period of years. The reasons given for the consolidation stressed the inefficiency of the dual arrangement and the friction due to inequalities of compensation.

Much can be said for such a consolidation; nevertheless, many persons familiar with the two services feared that such a serious loss of morale would result that more harm than good would be accomplished. The need for greater flexibility in transferring officers from one service to the other, which was a vital requirement of the proposed change, had long been appreciated, but it was felt that a less drastic procedure might accomplish the same result.

The recommendations regarding the internal reorganization of the Department were accepted practically without change, and had been put into effect by the end of the year 1949. The consolidated service recommendation was turned over to an Advisory Committee on Personnel which conducted lengthy hearings and sent out an elaborate questionnaire to some 2,200 personnel both in Washington and abroad to get their reactions to the proposed integration of the two services. The Advisory Committee made its recommendations on July 30, 1950, and the Department discussed them at great length. While many of the recommendations were satisfactory, others seemed too drastic and likely to provoke serious opposition and to lower the morale of the service. It was finally decided in the spring of 1951 to attempt a partial integration by assigning more departmental employees abroad and more Foreign Service officers to the Department on a voluntary basis and to liberalize the lateral entry into the Foreign Service category. Other changes were to include a reduction in the number of Foreign Service Staff officers and a redefinition of the status of the Foreign Service Reserve category so as to make it essentially a temporary vehicle for emergencies or special programs. The Department announced that the new personnel program would be put into effect in so far as possible by departmental order beginning April 13, 1951. At the same time it proposed the draft of such legislation as was necessary to make the program effective. The proposed draft is now awaiting action by the Congress.

The Foreign Service Today.   As of January 1, 1951, the Foreign Service of the United States consisted of 16,056 persons. This number included chiefs of mission; career, reserve, and staff officers and employees; consular agents; and alien clerks and employees. Of these the largest single group were the alien employees (11,014), whose duties extended from highly technical legal work performed by an expert to the cleaning of the offices by the charwomen and janitors. The staff officers and employees (3,700), were the second largest group and their work oftentimes was the same as that performed by the career officers of the lower grades. The Foreign Service officers were the third largest group (1,171), and they were followed by the reserve officers (102), and chiefs of mission (69). Perhaps the most noticeable change in the type of official required at the present time as compared with the prewar era is the increase in those trained in economic and technical fields. The embassay and consulate general in a large capital like London or Paris has representatives familiar with almost every phase of human activity. In subsequent chapters we shall attempt to describe what work is done and who is responsible for its doing.

7

Historical Development of Diplomatic Practice

The Origins of Diplomacy. It has been well said that "La diplomatie est aussi ancienne que les peuples eux-mêmes," but diplomatic agents may trace their ancestry still further back, even to divine lineage, the angels or messengers of God. The story is told that King Herod, horrified at the death of his envoy at the hands of the Arabs, called it an execrable deed in the eyes of nations and particularly for the Jews, who had received their sacred laws from God through his angels who are his heralds and his ambassadors. But to begin with secular history, we find the primitive countries of China exchanging diplomatic representatives, with questions of precedence and ceremonial most carefully regulated. The legendary Emperor Yao received envoys from neighboring tribes as early as 2353 B.C.[1] The Laws of Manu for ancient India provide for the appointment by the king of worthy men as ambassadors to carry on political relations with neighboring countries. "Let him also appoint an ambassador who is versed in all sciences, who understands hints, expressions of the face and gestures, who is honest, skillful and of noble family."[2] Egypt in the fourteenth century B.C. engaged in diplomatic correspondence and treaty-making. A treaty signed by Rameses II in 1280 B.C. provided for peace between Egypt and the Hittites, a defensive and offensive alliance, and even for the extradition of political refugees.[3]

Even among primitive savage tribes a certain degree of diplomatic relations existed. Among the aborigines of Southern Australia the tribal chiefs made alliances and sent envoys—on occasion even 'ambassadresses' to treat with neighboring tribes and these envoys were courteously received and never ill treated when on such missions.[4]

[1] Manly O. Hudson and A. H. Feller, *Collection of Diplomatic and Consular Laws and Regulations* (New York, 1933), I. 91.

[2] F. Max Miller, "Laws of Manu," *Sacred Books of the East,* G. Buhler, tr. (Oxford, 1886), XXV, Ch. VII, Sects. 63-68.

[3] *Journal of Egyptian Archaeology*, VI (1920), 179.

[4] Ragnar Numelin, *The Beginnings of Diplomacy* (New York, 1950), 128.

Diplomatic Relations among the Greeks. It was among the Greeks, however, that diplomatic relations became constant and took on a certain stability of form. Although no permanent embassies were maintained, all interstate relations were carried on by means of ambassadors and missions. The fact that there were hundreds of independent states in Greece made permanent embassies a practical impossibility. Nor was it necessary to build up a class of professional diplomats. Most of the distinguished citizens were familiar with the political situation of the times and to that extent well equipped to serve on diplomatic missions.

Important governmental officials were often appointed, sometimes military and naval officers. A Rhodian admiral was sent to Rome to propitiate the Senate. On occasion actors were chosen, sometimes even musicians and poets. The actor Aeschynus served as the diplomatic representative of Athens in Macedonia. The musician Menecles who was the ambassador of the city of Téos pleased the Grossiens exceedingly because in addition to performing his functions as ambassador he gave public recitations on several occasions, accompanying himself with the citharus. The term πρέσβεις is often found in Greek literature referring to ambassadors. The wily Ulysses was peculiarly fitted for such a rôle and served most acceptably. Aristophanes in his comedy, *The Acharnians,* gives an amusing presentation of the Athenians receiving reports from their missions just back from Persia and Thrace.[5]

Certain definite principles of diplomatic practice were widely recognized even at this early period. The inviolability of diplomatic envoys was a fundamental principle of international good conduct. The Athenians and Spartans recognized that they had flagrantly violated this law in the killing of the envoys of the Persian king, Darius. When two Spartan nobles offered their lives in atonement, Xerxes showed his respect for this common law of mankind by refusing the retribution.[6] An ambassador was not subject to local jurisdiction even when he committed an offense in the territory of the foreign state. Thebes declared war upon Thessaly upon the ground that its ambassadors had been arrested and imprisoned, thereby violating the law of nations, even though there was evidence that the Theban envoys were rightly suspected of plotting against the Thessalian Government.

Among the Greeks the right to send ambassadors was inherent in the sovereign powers of the state, and the right to send implied the obligation to receive. The popular Assembly both received and sent diplomatic

[5] B. B. Rogers, *The Acharnians of Aristophanes* (London, 1910), 13-25. Aristophanes slyly intimates that the envoys were so pleased with their work and their salaries that they took eleven years to make a journey for which eleven months would have been ample.

[6] Coleman Phillipson, *The International Law and Customs of Ancient Greece and Rome* (London, 1911), I, 239.

envoys, and oftentimes the subject of the mission was presented publicly by the foreign ambassadors to the representatives of the people. The Greek envoys received their instructions orally or in writing and carried credentials called σύμβολα. Diplomatic representatives were usually accompanied by their suites. Ambassadors were strictly forbidden to accept gifts while on their mission, and Timagoras, an ambassador from Athens to Persia, was condemned to death for accepting presents.[7]

The treatment accorded diplomatic envoys, however, was sufficiently generous. All the members of the diplomatic mission could reclaim both their traveling expenses and their living expenses. Upon the ambassador's return if he had carried out his mission in a satisfactory manner he was often honored by an eulogy publicly proclaimed in the religious festivals and in the theater.

One of the chief functions of diplomats among the Greeks was the conclusion of treaties, particularly treaties of alliance. Such negotiations were conducted in the most formal fashion and solemn oaths were sworn that the obligations of the treaty would be respected.[8]

The right of asylum was a well established principle of international law among the ancients, although statues, tombs, and temples were used instead of embassies. Sometimes an entire city was regarded as a sanctuary, as for example the town of Téos. According to Laurent, the right of asylum is not a sacerdotal privilege; it is rather the voice of humanity, speaking through the mouth of the Delphic priestess.[9] According to Barbeyrac,[10] Aristotle wrote a work concerning ambassadors but unhappily this study has been lost.

Diplomatic Relations among the Romans.   Although Rome particularly in her later period regarded herself somewhat superior to her neighbors and preferred to receive rather than to send ambassadors,[11] nevertheless she accepted for the most part the diplomatic practice of the Greeks. Among the Romans an ambassador was usually called a legatus, less often an orator and sometimes a fecial. The latter term was used for the most part in negotiations looking towards war or peace. The Roman Senate regularly sent at least three ambassadors; very often the number reached ten.

Ambassadors were sometimes chosen by the President of the Senate, sometimes names were chosen by lot and quite often senators were chosen.

[7] Phillipson, *op. cit.*, I, 330, 344.

[8] M. Potiemkine, *Histoire de la Diplomatic* (Paris, no date), I, 30.

[9] F. Laurent, *Histoire du droit des gens et des relations internationales* (Gand, 1850-1870), II, 135.

[10] J. Barbeyrac, *Histoire des anciens traités* (Amsterdam, 1839).

[11] Augustus had engraved on the bronze pillars before his mausoleum his boast that to him were sent embassies from India, the Bastarnians, the Scythians, the distant Sarmatians and Albanians, the Iberians and the Medes.

In any case the one chosen did not have the right to refuse. The expenses of a diplomatic mission were borne by the State.[12]

Cicero in his exact method of statement has well expressed the Roman attitude towards diplomatic inviolability: "The inviolability of ambassadors is protected both by divine and human law; they are sacred and respected so as to be inviolable not only when in an allied country but also whenever they happen to be in forces of the enemy."

The privilege of inviolability extended to the attachés of the ambassador, it included his correspondence and those things essential to the necessary performance of his duties. The principle covered enemy envoys and ambassadors in enemy territory after the outbreak of war. The Romans further maintained that the envoy was inviolable passing through third states either going to or returning from his mission. Any assault upon an ambassador or herald was a violation of *jus gentium.*

The immunity of ambassadors from territorial jurisdiction in both ceremonial and civil matters was fully recognized in Rome. A suit could not be brought against an ambassador because of a contract that he had entered into, in the city or elsewhere, before the surrender of his letters of credence; the diplomatic envoy had the right to be exempt from the jurisdiction of all courts except those of his own country; he possessed the *jus revocandi domum.*[13]

The Senate at Rome considered ambassadors as its guests and received them with a ceremonial of great pomp. They were seated with the senators in the public festivals. Their lodgings were provided for them. The city even offered them at times a money donation. It must be noted, however, that ambassadors had to request permission to be presented before the Senate, and if the Senate refused they no longer possessed diplomatic status. The Illyrian legates in 174 B.C., failing to report promptly, were subsequently denied an audience by the Senate.[14] A distinction also was made between legations coming to establish friendly relations and those coming to break off relations. The latter were not likely to receive as many courtesies of the city.

During the last years of the Roman Empire the bishops became ambassadors. For example, it was the Bishop of Marseilles, Graecus, who as ambassador consented to the cession of Auvergne in order to stave off an overwhelming invasion. The Church was destined to increase its temporal power and play a leading rôle in the diplomacy of the time. One should note that the institution of diplomatic interpreters, the forerunner of our "dragomans" in Oriental countries, was a development of this period.[15]

---

[12] M. Potiemkine, *op. cit.,* I, 50.
[13] R. Redslob, *Histoire des grands principes du droit des gens* (Paris, 1923), 83.
[14] Phillipson, *op. cit.,* I, 316.
[15] Cf. J. Snellman, *De Interpretibus Romanorum* (Leipzig, 1920).

Even a brief consideration of the development of the rights of envoys among the Greeks and Romans indicates that many of the fundamental principles as they exist today had already been well established more than two thousand years ago in this early cradle of European culture. The fundamental difference was that the embassies at that time were temporary rather than permanent. Permanent legations did not exist because they did not fit the needs of the time. But a well established *jus naturale* covered diplomatic practice in antiquity, supplemented by the *jus gentium* and *jus fetiale* of the Romans. The foundations for the diplomatic law of today had been laid.

Diplomacy of the Middle Ages.   It is at the end of the Middle Ages that we find for the first time "diplomacy practiced as an art and taught as a science." Nevertheless, the Papacy and the Catholic Church had made contributions during the Middle Ages which cannot be overlooked. The relations between the Papacy and the Byzantine Empire were so important that the popes maintained more or less permanent ambassadors at the imperial court at Constantinople. These representatives were called *apocrisarii* or *responsales*. One of the earliest of these *apocrisarii* was Julian, Bishop of Cos, accredited by Saint Leo the Great to Emperor Marchian, 453 A.D.[16] The Pope also maintained a permanent *apocrisarius* at the court of the exarch at Ravenna while the archbishop of Ravenna had a special *responsalis* at the papal court. During the later Middle Ages the Popes frequently sent ambassadors on special missions who were called *legati a latere* if cardinals, *legati missi* or *nuntii* if below cardinal rank. They also employed *nuntii apostolici* as resident ambassadors to the Holy Roman Emperor and to various European kings. Diplomatic missions from Venice to the Vatican had already been sent in the ninth century. By 1322 the Pope claimed the right to have resident ambassadors of the Papal See in every quarter of the world. From the reign of Charles V a perpetual nuntius was kept at the Imperial Court in Germany.[17]

The inviolability of the diplomatic envoy was as well recognized in the Middle Ages as in ancient times. Totila, king of Italy in the sixth century, declared that the Goths recognized as fully as the Romans the duty of showing respect to the position of the envoy.[18] The Salic Law and the laws of the Goths and the Saxons imposed a *wergeld* or indemnity for the murder of an ambassador. "The Koran ordains that the envoy manifestly must be well received." [19] When the envoys of Barbarossa

[16] Otto Krauske, *Die Entwickelung der ständigen Diplomatie* (Leipzig, 1885), 8.
[17] R. F. Wright, *Medieval Internationalism* (London, 1930), 94-95.
[18] T. Hodgkin, *Italy and Her Invaders, 476-535 A.D.* (Oxford, 1885), IV, 527.
[19] R. Redslob, *op. cit.*, 145 (quoting Digeste, *De Legationibus*, 50, 7.18); cf. David Jayne Hill, *Diplomacy in the International Development of Europe*, 3 vols (New York, 1906-1914), I, 39.

were seized and imprisoned by the Byzantine Emperor in 1187 at Constantinople, the Chronicler Geoffrey of Vinsauf condemned this act as a violation of the laws sacred among the ancients and even among the barbarians both by custom and by honor.

The procedure and etiquette employed in the diplomatic intercourse of the Byzantine emperors with other rulers during the Middle Ages exhibited a marked ecclesiastical influence. The curious manual dictated by the Emperor Constantine VII in the tenth century entitled *De Ceremoniis* is replete with interesting examples.

Byzantine protocol permitted the Emperor as a mark of special favor to send rare viands reserved normally for his own table to certain favored envoys. However it should be noted that the diplomats were constantly under a close surveillance which restricted considerably their reporting activities. The Byzantine emissaries in order to defray expenses of their delegation were expected to stimulate as large a sale as possible of the products of their country.[20]

Liutprand, Bishop of Cremona, gives a very amusing account of a medieval diplomatic mission. Emperor Otto I sent him on a mission to Byzantium to propose a marriage between the Emperor's son and the daughter of the Byzantine Emperor, Romanus II. The Bishop was imprisoned and treated with every sort of indignity and when finally admitted to an audience the Emperor made certain slurring remarks concerning Otto's soldiers: "The soldiers of thy master do not know how to ride, nor do they know how to fight on foot . . . their gluttony also impedes them, for their God is their belly, their courage but wind, their bravery drunkenness." Liutprand replied that his nation so despised the Romans that by that word they meant "whatever there is of contemptibility, of timidity, of avarice, of luxury, of lying, in a word of viciousness."[21]

Diplomacy as a profession originated at the close of the Middle Ages in the Italian cities which had built up an ever increasing commerce with the East as a result of the Crusades. The immediate result was to enhance the value of diplomacy and increase the prestige of diplomatic agents. In the thirteenth and fourteenth centuries Florence numbered among her diplomats such outstanding citizens as Dante, Petrarch, and Boccaccio. Later Guicciardini and Machiavelli were assigned important missions. In the thirteenth century an ambassador rarely resided at a foreign court for more than one or two months. In the fifteenth century Venice extended the period of an embassy to two years and in the sixteenth to three. The development of the practice of sending permanent missions was rendered the more difficult because of the distrust of permanent representatives.

[20] Regnar Numelin, *Les origines de la Diplomatie* (Paris, 1942), 252-3; also Potiemkine, *op. cit.*, I, 86-93.
[21] Quoted by David Jayne Hill, *op. cit.*, I, 185.

This is not so much to be wondered at when we remember that diplomacy at this time was almost synonymous with treachery and faithlessness. Representatives were received but with suspicion and every precaution was taken to render futile their activities as potential plotters against the safety of the state. Commines, Hotman, Marselaer, and other writers of the sixteenth century placed diplomatic envoys in the same class with spies. Marselaer advocated that when an envoy of an enemy state was received his weapons be taken from him and his clothes be shaken out.[22]

Francesco Sforza, Duke of Milan, had the honor of establishing the earliest permanent embassy in Europe when towards the middle of the fifteenth century he sent Nicodemus as envoy to the Medici in Florence.[23] Thereafter the development of the service as a permanent institution was exceedingly rapid.

Nevertheless Venice was in reality "the school and touchstone of ambassadors." From the beginning of the thirteenth century the Republic began to promulgate a series of laws and decrees for the guidance of her ambassadors. A decree of 1236 forbade ambassadors at the court of Rome from accepting from any source whatever any favors or profits without the consent of the doge and the assembly. An ordinance of 1268 required ambassadors upon their return to surrender all the gifts that they had received.[24] A law of the same year prevented the ambassador from being accompanied by his wife lest she might divulge his affairs. He had to take along his own cook so as not to be poisoned. In 1268 it was decreed that envoys file a written report of their mission within a fortnight of their return. An envoy was not permitted to be absent a single day from his post.

The diplomat's instructions were detailed and exact—how he should act, what he should say and how he should say it. In making an address he must use general terms so as not to commit himself in any way. They were expected to report all that they could learn about the personages of the court, the resources of the country, its financial and military strength.

It might be noted in passing that Italian diplomats often acted as representatives for other countries. For example, Russia under Ivan III made use of Italians who were regarded as masters of diplomacy. One of them, Antonio Volpe, sold his services simultaneously to Russia, Venice, the Vatican and the Golden Hord.[25]

The art of diplomacy developed by Venice and the other Italian cities came into vogue immediately among the monarchs of Western Europe. Louis XI of France, Ferdinand the Catholic of Spain, Henry VII of Eng-

[22] See Krauske, *op. cit.*, 12-25, for interesting examples.
[23] Hill, *op. cit.*, II, 154.
[24] Ernest Nys, *Les Origines du droit international* (Bruxelles, 1894), 298.
[25] Potiemkine, *op. cit.*, I, 152-3; 221.

land established permanent missions at the courts of the neighboring kings. Francis I of France set up a permanent and completely organized diplomatic service. It is claimed that Louis XIV organized his diplomatic service so well that French gradually displaced Latin as the diplomatic language of Europe.

The courts of Rome, France, Spain, Austria, and England regularly received ambassadors while Milan, Mantua, the Swiss cantons, Florence and Naples were assigned resident ministers. The envoy to Constantinople had the rank of ambassador but was designated as *bailo*.

Inviolability of Ambassadors. A very considerable development in diplomatic law is to be noted in this period. The inviolability of the diplomatic representative was recognized in all circumstances. An ambassador conspiring against the safety of the state might be expelled from the country but he could not be put on trial. It is curious to note that in this matter theory was not as far advanced as practice. Conradus Brunus was of the opinion that ambassadors could claim the right of inviolability only so long as they behaved themselves properly and kept within the limits of their ambassadorial functions.[26] Gentilis while favoring the dismissal of an ambassador if found guilty of conspiracy conceded that if injury to the prince had been committed the ambassador must submit himself to the local jurisdiction.[27] Jean Hotman was even more emphatic and declared that "the Ambassador who in the guise of friendship wins the confidence of a prince who is an ally of his master in order to do him an evil turn is to be held inexcusably guilty and may not under any circumstances invoke the diplomatic immunity which might protect him against the penalties imposed upon all those who trouble the peace of a state."[28] It is only with the later treatises of Grotius, Zouche, and Bynkershoek that the theory of diplomatic immunity from criminal jurisdiction is definitely established in theory. "Yet," according to Professor Adair, who has made a profound study of the subject, "throughout the sixteenth and seventeenth centuries no ambassador was ever put to death nor even subjected to any very long imprisonment for crimes committed unless he was a subject of the state to which he had been sent."[29] The recall of the French Ambassador de Noailles, implicated in a plot against Queen Mary of England in 1556; the dismissal of the Spanish Ambassador Mendoza, involved in a plot against Queen Elizabeth in 1583; the action of the Venetian Senate in 1618 in facilitating the flight of the Spanish

[26] Conradus Brunus, *De Legationibus* (Mainz, 1548), IV, 160.

[27] Alberico Gentile, "De Legationibus," *Classics of International Law*, J. B. Scott, ed. (New York, 1924), II, 113.

[28] Jean Hotman, *De la charge et dignité de l'Ambassadeur* (2nd ed., Paris, 1604), f. 67b.

[29] E. R. Adair, *The Extraterritoriality of Ambassadors in the 16th and 17th Centuries* (London, 1929), 64.

Ambassador de Cueva who had organized a conspiracy against the Republic, bear out the statement.[30]

Although in the sixteenth and early seventeenth centuries it was not customary for an ambassador to be accompanied by his wife, incidentally the Spanish Ambassador to the United Provinces in 1649 was called a hermaphrodite delegation for so doing, nevertheless by the beginning of the eighteenth century, Bynkershoek declared that it had become the custom for married ambassadors to take their wives with them.

This development raised the question more pertinently regarding the inviolability of the ambassador's suite. Gentilis took the position that the privileges of the ambassador should be extended to his suite, including his servants. Grotius took the same stand.[31] Zouche was the first to draw a distinction between the diplomatic personnel of the embassy and the servants engaged solely in domestic service. The latter he claimed remained subject to local jurisdiction.[32] However, practice varied in this period as two Venetian cases will show. In 1620 two men were arrested by the Venetian authorities as outlaws, but upon proving that they belonged to the household of the Spanish Ambassador they were released. On the other hand, when in 1643 the secretary to the English resident in Venice carried off a nun from the convent, he was imprisoned for six months and tried.[33]

The affair Matveiev in 1708, when the Russian Ambassador to England was insulted and arrested for debts, aroused a storm of protest in the diplomatic corps. Peter the Great demanded that those responsible should be punished by death. The Government of Queen Anne punished the culprits, although not by death, and sent a special mission to the Czar to express the regrets of the English Government for the unfortunate incident. The English Parliament thereupon passed a law for the protection of the rights of ambassadors and public ministers.[34]

The Right of Asylum. The question as to whether the residence of the ambassador should always be regarded as inviolable was rather difficult because it was joined with the claim of the right of asylum and the so-called *franchise du quartier.* Since the persons of the ambassador and his suite were inviolable the principal reason for insisting upon the inviolability of the embassy was the questionable privilege of protecting refugees or criminals. For this reason Bynkershoek very rationally opposed the inviolability of the embassy. The justice of his position was borne out by the fact that in Madrid and Rome the quarters of ambassadors became

[30] *Ibid.,* 44 ff. Cf. E. Satow, *A Guide to Diplomatic Practice* (2nd edition, London, 1922), I, 254-60.

[31] Grotius, *De Jure Belli ac Pacis* (Oxford, 1925). Vol. II, 447.

[32] Richard Zouche, *Solutio Quaestionis Veteris et Novae* (Oxoniae, 1657), 167-168.

[33] Adair, *op. cit.,* 138, 142.

[34] v. Potiemkine, *op. cit.,* I, 263.

sanctuaries for thieves, and the district a refuge for vagabonds. The conditions finally became so bad that in 1684 the foreign ambassadors at Madrid were notified that the *franchise du quartier* would no longer be recognized and by 1686 the Pope had obtained a renunciation of the *franchise du quartier* from all the important European states except France.

Nevertheless the right of granting asylum persisted and although numerous violations of the right occurred the government whose rights had been violated almost invariably demanded apologies and reparation. A very well known case which occurred in Venice in 1540 will serve as an example. Three Venetians who were accused by their Government of having sold state secrets to the French sought asylum in the French Embassy. When the French Ambassador refused to extradite them on the ground that the diplomatic immunities enjoyed by his residence protected them, the Venetian Government set up two cannons before the embassy gates and threatened to make use of them. The Ambassador thereupon surrendered the traitors, who were hanged forthwith. Francis I was so incensed at this violation of international law that for a period of two months he refused to receive the Venetian Envoy at his court.[35]

A century later when the residence of Lisola, the Imperial Ambassador in England, was broken into by parliamentary troops during the Ambassador's absence, the English Parliament offered compensation and the punishment of the offender.[36] In fact, James I in 1624 had already gone on record as declaring that "The houses of ambassadors are privileged places and they cannot take them out of their houses." [37] During this period it appears that the *droit de culte* and the *droit de chapelle* were quite generally recognized. Except for the incident when Philip II of Spain objected to granting this privilege to the Legation of Elizabeth of England it may be said that everywhere in Western Europe the ambassador could worship as he pleased with his family and servants within his embassy.

Expenses of Embassy.   When temporary missions gave way to permanent embassies the question of entertainment raised another interesting problem. The customary procedure had been for the receiving state to furnish both board and lodging. Philippe de Commynes, Ambassador for Charles VIII of France in the latter part of the fifteenth century declares that all of his expenses were defrayed by Venice while his colleague from Milan was not only given a well furnished house but also three gondolas and an income of one hundred francs a month.[38]

[35] de Flassan, *Histoire générale et raisonné de la diplomatie Française* (Paris, 1811), II, 6.
[36] Adair, *op. cit.*, 217.
[37] *Ibid.*, 211.
[38] *Mémoires de Philippe de Commynes* (Paris, 1843), II, 403, 409.

The expense of such a system was too great to be borne, and early in the seventeenth century the rule was established that ambassadors extraordinary were to be entertained at the king's expense only from the time of their arrival at the court until they had had their first official audience, not more than three or four days later.[39] In fact, Machiavelli, who was Ambassador at the court of France in the sixteenth century, found the expenses of being an envoy exceedingly burdensome. "We beg of you," he wrote, "to send us without delay the funds necessary for the maintenance of our position . . . our fortune and credit do not permit us to live here as do many ambassadors for several weeks at our own expense and without receiving the stipend which your generosity is wont to grant us."[40] Ordinary resident ambassadors had lost their right to entertainment even before this time. Nevertheless, for a century longer exceptional instances required a very elaborate and expensive entertainment, as shown by the case of the first Turkish ambassador who came to Paris in 1720.

Custom required that the envoys of the Sultan be entertained at the king's expense—they and all their retainers for the duration of their visit. The Ambassador Mehemet-Effendi embarked at Constantinople the seventh of October, 1720, and with his suite consisting of some sixty persons was put in quarantine on the island of Maguelonne. He remained in quarantine from the sixteenth of December until the twenty-fifth of January and then he commenced his journey to Paris accompanied by a gentleman courier sent by the king to bid him welcome. A palace was made ready to receive him at Charenton where he rested for eight days before making his solemn entry into Paris. The day of the royal audience the king sent his carriage for the Ambassador and more than thirty thousand troops were drawn up on each side of the line of march from the Ambassador's hotel to the Palace of the Tuileries. Festivities and diversions of all varieties followed the official receptions. When Mehemet-Effendi began his return voyage on the third of August, 1721, he carried away with him a considerable number of handsome gifts. He received a diamond girdle, a collection of arms de luxe, muskets and pistols, clocks, watches, vases of Sèvres, inlaid gold furniture, and some fine Gobelin tapestries that he had particularly admired. It is not hard to understand why the King of France was not overenthusiastic when he learned the news that the Sultan intended to send a ceremonial embassy to Paris.[41]

By the end of the seventeenth century the rule had been well established in Europe that with the exception of the ambassadors of the Czar of Russia, who expected to be entertained at the expense of the monarch

[39] Adair, op. cit., 268.

[40] Machiavel, "Légations et Missions, Légation à la cour de France," Oeuvres complètes, Lettre XIII (Paris, 1837), II, 102.

[41] D'Aubigny, "Un ambassadeur turc à Paris," Revue d'histoire diplomatique, III, 78 ff (1889).

to whom they were accredited, the heads of states should pay the expenses of their ambassadors. In fact, however, the ambassadors found it necessary to contribute heavily from their private fortunes just as they are often compelled to do today.

Problems of Ceremonial and Etiquette. In this early period of permanent missions the problems of ceremonial and etiquette were exceedingly thorny. Before the institution of permanent embassies the envoys had no distinction either of class or of rank. According to Vattel: "In former times public ministers were almost always of the same grade and were called in Latin *legati,* a term which is rendered in French by the word *ambassadeurs.*" [42] During the Middle Ages a diplomatic representative, regardless of sender or of purpose, might be called *legatus, orator, nuntius, ablegatus, commissarius, procurator, mandatarius, agens,* or *ambaxator.*[43] However, with the establishment of permanent missions questions of precedence and ceremonial constantly arose, both during personal visits of ambassadors and on important ceremonial occasions. Although in the words of Vattel, "Nature has established a perfect equality of rights among independent nations, in consequence no one of them may justly claim to be superior to the others," nevertheless inequality of fact existed side by side with equality of law. Russia and Geneva might possess equal rights before the law but they were not equally powerful politically. At the beginning of the fifteenth century Martin de Lodi laid down the principle that the envoy of a great prince should take precedence over the envoy of a lesser, but it was not always easy to determine which was the greater.[44]

In order to regulate this hierarchy among the nations several bases had been proposed,—the form of government, the title of the head of the government, the ancient lineage of the reigning family, the size of the population, the antiquity of independence, the superiority of culture; but the states of Europe could not agree on any basis of primacy. The result was a constant series of disputes over rank among their representatives, sometimes of a rather violent nature. An amusing incident of this sort occurred in 1659. De Thou, the French Ambassador, met the Spanish Ambassador, Don Esteban de Gamarra, on a street in The Hague. Neither carriage would give way to the other, and the diplomats spent the next three hours trying to figure out a plan which would be acceptable to both. Finally it was decided that a fence to the right of Gamarra should be torn down so that he might proceed. In this way both won out, for the Frenchman kept the regular road and the Spaniard had the place to the right.[45]

[42] E. de Vattel, "The Law of Nations," *Classics of International Law,* J. B. Scott, ed. (Washington, 1916), III, 367.
[43] Krauske, *op. cit.,* 152.
[44] Nys, *op. cit.,* 330.
[45] Krauske, *op. cit.,* 208.

One of the most serious of these incidents took place between the Ambassador of France and the Ambassador of Spain in 1661 in London. The occasion was the arrival of the Ambassador from Sweden. When the French Ambassador sought to follow immediately after the Swedish Ambassador the Spanish Ambassador disputed the position with him. In the mêlée which ensued the Spaniards succeeded in killing the horses drawing the French carriage and in dispersing the retinue of the French Ambassador. Louis XIV was so incensed at this insult that he recalled his Ambassador from Madrid and dismissed the Spanish Ambassador at Paris. Not satisfied, he notified the King of Spain that if he did not apologize adequately for this insult and if in the future he did not recognize the precedence of France he would declare war against him. Philip IV of Spain did not wish to recommence the war. He sent a new ambassador who declared at Fontainebleau in the presence of the foreign ambassadors that the Spanish envoys in the future would not dispute the position of the representatives of France.[46]

Classifications Established by the Congress of Vienna.   The question of rank and of precedence of the powers was regulated at the Congress of Vienna in 1815 upon the basis of the rank of the diplomatic agents rather than upon the degree of importance of the states. Even at this Congress a committee worked for two months trying to establish three classes of powers as a means of regulating the position of their diplomatic representatives. But this attempt failed because it could not be decided in which class the great republics should be placed.

The regulations of the Congress of Vienna of 1815 supplemented by an article added by the powers reunited at Aix-la-Chapelle in 1818 established the following classification of diplomatic representatives: the first class included ambassadors, legates *a latere,* that is to say, envoys extraordinary of the Pope chosen from the cardinals and charged with a special mission; and nuncios, that is to say, the envoys of the Pope on permanent mission, chosen from outside the ranks of the cardinals. The second class included envoys extraordinary, ministers plenipotentiary, and the apostolic internuncios, that is to say, the envoys of the Pope of second class. The third class introduced by the Congress of Aix-la-Chapelle comprised ministers resident. The fourth class comprised chargés d'affaires and chargés d'affaires ad interim.[47] The representatives of the first three classes are accredited to sovereigns while the chargés are accredited to ministers of foreign affairs. Article IV of these regulations declares diplo-

---

[46] Ernest Satow, *A Guide to Diplomatic Practice* (2nd ed., London, 1922), II, 26. Cf. Genet, *op. cit.,* I, 311; and Pradier-Fodéré, *op. cit.,* I, 113.

[47] Paul Fauchille, *Traité de droit international public* (Paris, 1921-1926), I, Pt. 3, 42.

matic envoys shall rank within each class in accordance with the official notification of the date of their arrival.[48]

The eight powers signatory of the regulations made at Vienna were Austria, Spain, France, Great Britain, Portugal, Prussia, Russia, and Sweden. Gradually this classification was adopted more or less completely by all the European powers with the exception of Turkey. The United States has adopted these rules in its instructions to its diplomatic officers issued in 1897 and revised in 1941. Today one can say that all civilized states accept this classification, although this does not prevent each state from establishing as it sees fit the hierarchy of its diplomatic corps.[49]

It might be noted that it is only in the twentieth century that states have tended more and more to utilize ambassadors rather than ministers to represent their interests abroad. For example, Great Britain at the beginning of the reign of Queen Victoria sent ambassadors only to Paris, to Saint Petersburg, and to Constantinople. Great Britain raised the legation in Vienna to an embassy in 1860, the one in Berlin in 1862, and in Rome in 1876.

The United States sent no ambassadors until 1893. Today however the United States sends 58 ambassadors and only 13 ministers. When normal relations are resumed with China, Germany, and Japan the number of ambassadors will reach 61. Switzerland is the only important European country today which sends no ambassadors and receives only one—the Ambassador from France.

The Congress of Vienna regulated also to some extent the question of precedence in the signing of treaties by adopting the long-familiar usage of the *alternat*,[50] for the copies to be retained by each state, and permitting the position of other signatories to be decided by lot. Article VII of the regulations states that *"Dans les actes ou traités entres plusieurs puissances qui admettent l'alternat le sort décidera entre les ministres de l'ordre qui devra être suivi dans les signatures."* [51] However, in practice the powers have conformed as regards signatures to the alphabetical order according to the initial letter of the name of each state as written in French. Thus the United States in its French form, États-Unis, regularly precedes France in multilateral agreements.

[48] For text see G. F. de Martens, *Nouveau recueil de Traités de l'Europe* (Göttingen, 1887), II, 449.

[49] For example, a decree of the Council of the Commissars of the People dated May 22/June 4, 1918, provided that "the titles of ambassadors, ministers and other diplomatic representatives are abolished and all representatives of the Russian State accredited to foreign states shall be denominated plenipotentiary representatives of the Russian Socialist Federated Soviet Republic." A. H. Feller and M. O. Hudson, *A Collection of the Diplomatic and Consular Law and Regulations at Various Countries* (Washington, 1933), II, 1195.

[50] That is, giving each state first place for its signature in its own copy of a treaty.

[51] de Martens, *op. cit.*, II, 450-1.

Since the regulations of Vienna, no further official effort to classify diplomatic envoys has been made on an international scale. However, it should be noted that Russia since the fourth of June, 1918, has renounced further participation in the regulations of Vienna by establishing a uniform rank designated as envoys plenipotentiary for all its diplomatic representatives. Nevertheless, to avoid difficulties in the letter of credence the representatives' status in accordance with the Vienna regulations is also given (in parentheses).[52]

We should mention also a fifth class which is called diplomatic agent. This rank of envoy is found as a rule only in states which are not fully sovereign. To Egypt and Morocco a number of powers send diplomatic agents.[53]

The Right of Legation.   Inasmuch as international law rests upon custom as well as upon treaties, it has already been shown that a right of legation has existed from very ancient times. It seems regularly to have been an attribute of sovereign states. Gentilis in his interesting volume "On Embassies" thus presents the historical attestation of the principle: "The right of embassy, Cicero says, is defended by a rampart of human and divine authority, and Caesar and others agree with him. It is in fact according to my interpretation a right that is by reason of a certain divine providence, immutable, of universal application, and admitted and recognized even by barbarous peoples." [54]

Vattel clearly expresses both the law and the reason for it. "Every sovereign state has therefore the right to send and to receive public ministers. For they are the necessary agents in the negotiation of the affairs which sovereigns have with one another, and in the maintenance of the intercourse which sovereigns have the right to keep up." [55] However, the states are not compelled to make use of this right of legation. Its exercise rests upon the mutual consent of the two sovereigns.

The right of sending public ministers is called the active right of legation, while that of receiving is called the passive right of legation. The so-called right of legation has often been specified in treaties. A treaty in 1614 between Sweden and Holland provided for the designation of reciprocal missions between the two signatory parties. The treaty of Belgrade between Russia and Turkey signed in 1739 permitted the Czar to name a minister resident at Constantinople.[56]

In the exercise of the right of legation states have assumed the greatest freedom of action. For example, a single minister may at the same

[52] Fauchille, *op. cit.*, I, Pt. 3, 43.
[53] Satow, *op. cit.*, I, 246.
[54] Alberico Gentili, "De Legationibus," *Classics of International Law,* J. B. Scott, ed. (New York, 1924), II, 58.
[55] Vattel, *op. cit.*, III, 362.
[56] Satow, *op. cit.*, I, 190.

time be in charge of several missions accredited to different governments. In 1825 the Argentine accredited the same minister to both Paris and London. For a brief period the United States accredited a single public minister to Estonia, Latvia, and Lithuania; to Afghanistan and Iran; to Lebanon and Syria; and to Belgium and Luxembourg. The United States still accredits a single minister to India and Nepal, and to Saudi Arabia and Yemen. A state may be represented by the diplomatic representative of another state by agreement with the latter. In 1796 Great Britain and Holland were represented by a single minister in Spain; in 1870 Peru utilized the services of the ministers of the United States in order to be represented in China and Japan. States do not always exchange representatives of the same class. For example, France sends an ambassador to Switzerland and receives a minister.

When the state's interest in another capital are very great it may accredit an ambassador and one or two ministers simultaneously. For example, since World War II the United States has had an ambassador and one or two ministers in both London and Paris.

In the development of diplomatic practice the question arises whether semi-sovereign states and protectorates possess an active right of representation. Although a difference of opinion among authorities exists, it is generally conceded that the extent of the right of representation depends upon the nature of the relations between the superior state and the semisovereign or protected state. For example, Canada exchanged diplomatic representatives with the United States because of important mutual interests before its sovereign status was recognized.

The Codification of the Laws of Diplomacy. This brief sketch of the historical development of diplomatic practice indicates that few principles of international law are more thoroughly grounded in antiquity or have been more consistently recognized in their observance than many of the principles of diplomatic law. Therefore, it is not surprising that the desirability of crystallizing these principles into an international code should have received considerable attention from outstanding authorities in the field. Bluntschli in 1868, Fiore in 1890, Pessoa in 1911, and Phillimore in 1926 have covered the subject adequately in their draft codes. L'Institut de Droit International passed a resolution in 1895 for the codification of the regulations covering diplomatic immunity and in 1929 revised these regulations in order to make them conform to the evolution of international law in these matters. Space prevents more than the most casual consideration of this question, but the recent efforts in this direction deserve at least a passing notice.

The third Pan-American Conference, which met at Rio de Janeiro in 1906 appointed a commission of jurists to prepare a codification of international law in the form of draft conventions covering subjects which seemed ripe for codification. As the commission did not begin work until 1912 it was only after World War I that it was able to function effectively. In 1924 the governing board of the Pan-American Union asked the American Institute of International Law to submit projects of international law to the Committee of Jurists. Thirty projects of public international law were prepared and considered by the committee of jurists at a conference in Rio de Janeiro in 1927. This conference reduced the projects to twelve.[57] The sixth Conference of American States which met at Havana, Cuba, in 1928, debated these projects at great length and accepted seven of them. One of these adopted was a convention on diplomatic officers. It proposed to codify the law of diplomacy under five sections: chiefs of missions, personnel of missions, duties of diplomatic officers, immunities and prerogatives of diplomatic officers, and termination of the diplomatic mission. One of the interesting changes made was a classification of diplomatic officers into two categories, ordinary and extraordinary, the former being permanent representations, the latter on special mission. This convention had been ratified by fourteen states by April 1, 1950. In 1942 the Inter-American Juridical Committee was authorized to "develop and coördinate the work of codifying international law," and in 1945 a resolution of the Mexican Conference on the Problems of War and Peace recommended that the Inter-American Juridical Committee be entrusted with the functions of a central agency for the codification of public international law. The Committee now known as the Inter-American Council of Jurists met in May, 1950, and codification of public and private international law was on the agenda, but no specific action in the field of diplomatic or consular practice was indicated.

Another attempt at codification was under the direction of the League of Nations. In execution of an Assembly resolution of September 22, 1924, the Council of the League appointed a committee of experts which selected eleven subjects for investigation. Seven subjects were picked and a questionnaire sent to various governments to obtain their reactions. After studying the replies the Committee reported that the seven subjects were ripe for codification. Among these subjects we find Diplomatic Privileges and Immunities. At the subsequent session the Committee of Experts prepared a questionnaire upon the "Revision of Classification of Diplomatic Agents." However, neither of these subjects was considered at the first conference for the codification of international law held at The Hague in 1930.

In view of this interest in the subject the faculty of the Harvard Law School undertook to organize a research body to prepare a draft convention on each of the subjects selected as ripe for codification. Committees were formed, and drafts were formulated and discussed at meetings of

[57] For texts of these projects see *American Journal of International Law, Supplement* (January, 1928).

reporters and advisers. The draft on Diplomatic Privileges and Immunities was prepared and published as a supplement to the *American Journal of International Law* in 1932. As a valuable aid to this work the Carnegie Endowment published in 1933 a collection of the diplomatic and consular laws and regulations of various countries under the direction of Manley O. Hudson and A. H. Feller.

Professor Redslob has named the nineteenth century the epoch of science, the twentieth the century of justice. Diplomatic representatives whose primary function is the maintenance of peace will aid materially in the future as they have in the past in making this century an era of justice. Nevertheless, an adequate development of the principles of diplomatic law and their universal acceptance are essential preliminaries to the complete accomplishment of this result. Certainly an early and definitive codification of diplomatic law and practice will accelerate the approach to an era of international justice.

8

Appointment of Diplomatic Officers

The Right of Legation. It is generally conceded by the principal authorities in international law that every sovereign independent state enjoys the right of representation or legation. It is sometimes considered as an active right from the standpoint of sending and a passive right from the standpoint of receiving. Wheaton claims the right of legation is an imperfect right [1] but Oppenheim, Pradier-Fodéré, Fauchille, Satow, Hershey, and others would seem to consider it fundamental. Gentilis declares the right to be "immutable, of universal application, and admitted and recognized by even barbarous peoples." [2] Vattel in his lucid fashion explains the reason: "Nations must necessarily treat and have intercourse with one another in order to advance their interests, to avoid injuring one another and to adjust and terminate their disputes. And since they are all under the indispensable obligation of uniting their efforts to promote their common welfare and safety and of arranging for themselves a means of settling and terminating their disputes ... it follows from the above reasons that each Nation possesses both the right to negotiate and have intercourse with the others, and the reciprocal obligation to lend itself to such intercourse as far as circumstances will permit it to do so." [3]

Inasmuch as heads of states cannot treat with one another directly in a convenient practicable fashion we have already shown the almost immemorial practice of sending diplomatic missions. It was formerly a moot question as to whether semi-sovereign states possessed the right of legation. Heffter conceded it, but Calvo, F. de Martens and Travers-Twiss reserved it to sovereign states. The question is no longer of importance. Even a protectorate today may have diplomatic representation, as shown by the fact that the United States still has a diplomatic agent at Tangier. However, it must be conceded that his dealings with Morocco must be carried on through the French Governor General at Rabat rather than directly with the Sultan at Fez.

[1] Lawrence's *Wheaton* (London, 1864), 374.

[2] Alberico Gentili, "De Legationibus" (Libri Tres, 1594), *Classics of International Law,* J. B. Scott, ed. (New York, 1924), 58.

[3] E. de Vattel, "The Law of Nations," *Classics of International Law,* J. B. Scott, ed. (Washington, 1916), III, 362.

The Vatican's Right of Legation.   The position of the Vatican in this respect is rather an anomalous one. By tradition and long established usage the Pope still sends and receives diplomatic agents, but although his envoys enjoy the privileges and immunities of diplomatic agents they are in reality ecclesiastical rather than international officials.[4] The right of the Holy See to diplomatic representation was not particularly affected by the annexation of the Papal States to the Kingdom of Italy, although some states ceased to send diplomatic representatives. The United States, which had been represented at the Holy See since 1848 by either a chargé d'affaires or a minister resident, ceased to send diplomatic envoys in 1869. President Grant in his message to Congress in 1869 declared that he had been officially informed of the annexation of the Papal States by Italy and the United States had recognized the change in the status of their sovereignty by no longer accrediting a diplomatic agent.

Maurice Francis Egan in his biography states that President Theodore Roosevelt in his earnest desire to settle the religious difficulties in the Philippines, suggested that Egan should go to Rome unofficially to obtain the Pope's reaction to the situation, and that he might be sent later to the Quirinal as ambassador, or if public opinion approved as minister to the Vatican. Egan, however, although a good Catholic, felt that it would be a misfortune to reopen diplomatic relations with the Vatican and nothing further came of it.[5] Instead, William H. Taft, at that time civil Governor of the Philippines, was sent as a special agent of the President to ascertain the attitude of the Vatican on the purchase of the friars' lands by the United States Government. Governor Taft's commission stated specifically that his errand was in no sense diplomatic but purely a business matter.[6]

With the beginning of World War II, President Franklin D. Roosevelt felt that it would be advantageous to renew diplomatic relations with the Vatican, and on December 23, 1939, he appointed Myron C. Taylor, a Protestant, as his personal representative to Pope Pius XII with the rank of Ambassador. President Truman renewed the appointment on May 3, 1946, but when Taylor resigned in 1950 no further representative to the Vatican was immediately accredited. In the fall of 1951, just before Congress recessed, President Truman appointed General Mark Clark as a full-fledged Ambassador to the Vatican. The President was violently criticized on two counts, first that he had timed the appointment so that the Senate could not pass upon it, secondly that it was a move to gain Catholic votes in the next election. The reason given for the appointment was the need for more effective coöperation with the Vatican in the

---

[4] Cf. Amos Hershey, *The Essentials of International Public Law and Organization* (New York, 1927), 165.

[5] Maurice Francis Egan, *Recollections of a Happy Life* (New York, 1924), 198.

[6] See Simeon E. Baldwin's article, "The Mission of Governor Taft to the Vatican," *Yale Law Journal*, XII, I (November, 1902).

defense of the Western World against communism. Subsequently General Clark asked to have his name withdrawn.

It should be noted that a papal legate is usually sent to important states even though not officially received, and as such the Pope has generally sent his legate to Washington. Some presidents have received them strictly informally, but President Theodore Roosevelt seemed to prefer to deal with his old friend, Father Duffy, a simple priest.

When the Fascisti regime once more brought about friendly relations between the Quirinal and the Vatican by the Lateran Treaties of 1929, diplomatic relations between Vatican City and Italy were resumed. At the present time the Holy See maintains diplomatic relations with thirty countries through nuncios and with six by internuncios.

Executive Control of Diplomatic Appointments. In federal systems of government the right of representation logically belongs to the central government. Under the Articles of Confederation (Art. 9) the United States was given the sole and exclusive right of sending and receiving ambassadors and the Constitution of 1789 (Art. II, sect. 2) reads as follows:

He (the President) shall have Power, by and with the Consent of the Senate, to make Treaties, provided two thirds of the Senators present concur; and he shall nominate, and by and with the Advice and Consent of the Senate, shall appoint Ambassadors, other public Ministers and Consuls. . . .

It has become a well established custom in the United States that the President shall have a fairly free hand in nominating diplomatic officers and need not consult the Senate in advance. In 1813 the Senate proposed to confer with President Madison before it confirmed his nomination of a minister to Sweden but he refused on the ground that such a procedure would violate the proper separation of executive and legislative powers.[7]

Senatorial Limitation of the Appointive Power. Once the nomination is made the Senate may clearly reject the appointment if it is so disposed. In 1831 President Jackson appointed Martin Van Buren as Minister to London during the recess of the Senate. When the Senate reconvened it refused to confirm the appointment principally on the ground that while Secretary of State Van Buren had given improper instructions to the United States Minister in London. The Senate's rejection of his appointment did not prevent his subsequent election to the Presidency.[8]

The Senate again opposed President Jackson in refusing to confirm the nomination of Andrew Stevenson, Speaker of the House of Representatives, as Minister to Great Britain, succeeding Van Buren. The post was

[7] John W. Foster, *The Practice of Diplomacy* (New York, 1906), 46.
[8] John W. Foster, *A Century of American Diplomacy* (New York, 1900), 276.

left under a chargé d'affaires for almost two years, and then Stevenson's name was again proposed. Again the Senate was obdurate and tabled the nomination of Stevenson.[9] Jackson was just as stubborn as the Senate and in 1836 he finally obtained the necessary confirmation.

The interpretation made by Attorney General Cushing in 1855 in this connection is often quoted:

The power to appoint diplomatic agents ... is a constitutional function of the President, not derived from, nor limitable by Congress, but requiring only the ultimate concurrence of the Senate; and so it was understood in the early practice of the Government.[10]

In fact the Senate rarely fails to confirm presidential nominations to the diplomatic service even though some of them may be purely and simply political. For instance, the Senate confirmed President Cleveland's appointment of Mr. Van Alen as Minister to Italy where the principal reason for the nomination was a contribution of $50,000 to the Democratic campaign fund. In this case the Civil Service Reform League raised such an uproar that Van Alen declined the appointment.[11]

When Dr. Jacob Gould Schurman, President of Cornell University, was appointed Minister to China in 1921 by President Harding, the nomination was opposed by a number of Republican senators on the ground that he was pro-Japanese. A still larger number of Democratic senators opposed the nomination of George Harvey as Ambassador to Great Britain because of his vitriolic attack on former President Wilson.

When President Coolidge proposed Mr. Morrow's name as Ambassador to Mexico the Senate was in recess but Senators Caraway, Nye, and Frazier were skeptical of Morrow's ability to be disinterested in his service, while Senator James A. Reed of Missouri denounced the appointment violently as a nefarious House of Morgan scheme. Fortunately for the United States the appointment was confirmed. The Senate usually confirms diplomatic appointments very promptly.

During President Franklin D. Roosevelt's long incumbency a number of questionable political appointments were made—for example, two ministers, Daniel Roper and James Cromwell, named to Canada in 1939 and 1940 were thus characterized in a syndicated newspaper column— "one was a political hack whom it was necessary to pry out of the Commerce Department, the other was a political 'fat cat' who had to be suitably but harmlessly removed." The same column praised the appointment of Jay Pierpont Moffat as successor to Cromwell as "both natural and reassuring."

One appointment made by President Roosevelt aroused such a clamor

[9] Sen. Exec. Journal, IV, 516 (March 3, 1836).
[10] 7 Opinions U.S. Attorney General, 193.
[11] See William Dudley Foulke, Fighting the Spoilsmen (New York and London, 1919), 99-103.

of opposition in the press of the country that the nomination was finally withdrawn. This was the appointment of Edward J. Flynn, Chairman of the Democratic National Committee, as Minister to Australia and at the same time personal representative of the President with the rank of Ambassador. Mr. Flynn was wholly inexperienced in the diplomatic field and had received much unfavorable publicity through the alleged use of paving blocks owned by New York City upon his country estate. Although the Senate Foreign Relations Committee approved the nomination, it was feared that the Senate would not accept the committee's recommendations.

President Truman was widely criticized for his appointment of William O'Dwyer as Ambassador to Mexico in the fall of 1950. As Mayor of New York Mr. O'Dwyer had been a party to certain political deals which the Congress proposed to investigate, and it was thought wise to have him out of the country. Nevertheless the Senate controlled by the Democratic party confirmed the appointment by a vote of 42 to 22.

Other appointments of President Truman which the Senate was seemingly a bit loath to confirm were those of Perle Mesta to Luxembourg and Stanton Griffis to Spain.

The Appointment of American Ambassadors.   The principal European powers have regularly exchanged ambassadors ever since the classification of the Congress of Vienna. The United States which limited its rank of envoys to that of minister plenipotentiary until 1893 was oftentimes as a result placed in a humiliating position. In some capitals an ambassador always took precedence over a minister even though the minister might have been waiting in the antechamber for some time previously. This very situation occurred in Berlin when American Minister Bancroft, after a long wait for an audience with the Chancellor had to yield to the British Ambassador, who had just arrived. Bancroft protested so vigorously that afterwards the rule was "first come first served." [12]

As has been noted, the Act of March 1, 1893, provided that the President, when advised of the rank of the foreign representative, might in his discretion direct that the representative of the United States to that government bear the same designation. So that when Great Britain, France, Italy, and Germany forthwith conferred the rank of ambassador upon their representatives in Washington, President Cleveland responded by giving the American envoys in those countries the same title.[13]

When a few years later Mexico accredited an ambassador to Washington the diplomatic corps practically boycotted him on the ground that Mexico was not a sufficiently important state to exercise the privilege of

[12] Eugene Schuyler, *American Diplomacy* (New York, 1895), 113.
[13] See President Cleveland's annual message, Dec. 4, 1893, in *Foreign Relations of the United States*, XII (1893).

sending ambassadors. The underlying reason for their action was because the envoy chosen had served on the court-martial which had condemned the Archduke Maximilian to death.[14]

A clever utilization of the law of 1893 was made by Herbert W. Bowen in order to promote himself. Accredited to Persia as Minister Resident and Consul General in 1899 he began a campaign among his Persian friends to have a minister plenipotentiary sent from Persia to the United States. The plan succeeded and in 1901 a Persian Minister Plenipotentiary was accredited to the United States and Mr. Bowen was forthwith given a similar grade.[15]

Grades in the Diplomatic Service.   The question as to the President's control of grades of diplomatic officers has never been definitely settled. Jefferson was clearly of the opinion that the Senate had no right to negate the grade in advising and consenting to appointments [16] and Attorney General Cushing held that the Act of March 1, 1855, specifying that certain grades be assigned to particular countries to be "recommendatory only and not mandatory." [17] Nevertheless, although authorized by the Constitution, no ambassadors were appointed until the Act of March 1, 1893, gave specific authorization. Furthermore, the Act of March 2, 1909, provided that "hereafter no new ambassadorship shall be created unless the same shall be provided for by an act of Congress." [18]

Following out this policy the Congress specifically authorized the new grades of ambassador to Spain in 1913, to Argentina and Chile in 1914 and to Belgium in 1919.[19] On the other hand, President Wilson appointed an ambassador to Peru in 1919 without any authorization from the Congress other than that found in the appropriation bill for the Department of State.[20] The appointment of an ambassador was approved by a joint resolution of the Senate [21] but it apparently was not acted upon in the House. In similar fashion ministers to Canada and the Irish Free State were appointed in 1927 without other congressional approval than that found in the appropriation bill for the fiscal year ending 1928. In this same bill there is a clear inference that if he desires, the President has the authority to reduce the rank of the representative to Turkey from ambassador to minister with a corresponding reduction in salary.[22] But in raising the Legation in Warsaw to an Embassy in 1930 the Congress

[14] John W. Foster, *The Practice of Diplomacy* (New York, 1906), 27.

[15] Herbert W. Bowen, *Recollections Diplomatic and Undiplomatic* (New York, 1926), 241.

[16] John Bassett Moore, *Digest of International Law* (Washington, 1906), IV, 450.

[17] 7 *Opinions U.S. Attorney General*, 214.

[18] 35 *U.S. Statutes at Large*, 672.

[19] 38 *U.S. Statutes at Large*, 110, 378; 41 *U.S. Statutes at Large*, 291.

[20] 40 *U.S. Statutes at Large*, 1325.

[21] *Congressional Record*, LVII, 4537.

[22] 44 *U.S. Statutes at Large*, 1180.

made a specific authorization by law.[23] In 1935 announcement was made by the Department of State of its intention to raise the American Legation in Peiping to an Embassy following a similar action by Russia and Italy and a proposed similar action by Great Britain and Japan, before any congressional authorization was obtained, and Nelson T. Johnson, a career officer, was sent as Ambassador in June, 1935. Panama, Venezuela, Colombia were raised to embassy status in 1939. Uruguay was raised by presidential approval in 1941; Ecuador, Bolivia, and Paraguay in 1942, the latter two by new letters of credence. Since 1943 all Latin American states exchange ambassadors with the United States.

Appointment of Executive Agents.   Despite discussion to the contrary, numerous precedents attest the fact that the President does possess the power to appoint special diplomatic agents without senatorial confirmation. In a minority report of the Committee of Foreign Relations of the Senate investigating this subject it was found that in the century between 1789 and 1888 the President had appointed 438 persons to conduct negotiations with foreign powers without the advice and consent of the Senate.[24] The following well known examples might be cited: Admiral John Paul Jones commissioned to treat with Algiers in 1792; Joel R. Poinsett, military expert and naturalist who developed the poinsettia from a Mexican flower, named as President Madison's special agent in Southern America from 1810 to 1814; Edmund Roberts sent as special agent to conclude treaties with Cochin-China, Siam and Muscat in 1832; Nicholas P. Trist appointed commissioner to conclude peace with Mexico in 1848; Commodore Perry appointed to conclude a treaty with Japan in 1852; James S. Blount named as special commissioner to the Hawaiian Islands in 1893 with powers paramount to those of the regular minister to investigate and report on the revolution which overthrew the Queen's government; W. W. Rockhill sent as Commissioner of the United States to China in 1900 to aid in the settlement of the Boxer Rebellion indemnities; John Lind appointed by President Wilson in 1913 as confidential agent to Mexico; Colonel House in a somewhat similar capacity to Europe in the First World War period, and particularly Franklin D. Roosevelt's galaxy of personal representatives, Harry Hopkins, Norman Davis, Patrick J. Hurley, Henry Wallace, and Myron C. Taylor. President Truman did not utilize personal agents so regularly although W. Averell Harriman and John Foster Dulles were employed on numerous special missions with considerable success. The fact that the position of Ambassador-at-Large was created in 1949 would seem to diminish somewhat the need for special agents except in period of emergency.[25]

[23] 46 *U.S. Statutes at Large,* 57.
[24] *Senate Document* No. 231, 56th Cong., 2nd sess., VIII, 332.
[25] H. M. Wriston, *Executive Agents in American Relations* (New York, 1929).

Reciprocity of Grades. There is no rule of international law which requires full reciprocity between states in the ranking of their diplomatic representatives, yet for the most part such equality is customary. The state sending a diplomatic representative decides upon the rank and the receiving state may then determine whether it wishes to receive and send a representative of similar standing. We have already noted the refusal of the Government of Portugal to receive a chargé d'affaires from the United States in 1790 so that President Washington raised the rank of his envoy to minister resident. On the other hand, it has not been unknown for states to send envoys of dissimilar rank. Switzerland, for example, has for a long period of time accredited a minister plenipotentiary and envoy extraordinary to France, whereas France has regularly sent an ambassador to Switzerland.

Secretary of State Marcy in a communication to the Chairman of the House Committee on Foreign Affairs in 1856 indicated that a certain degree of flexibility was permitted: "As a general rule no government sends to or at least continues in, another country a minister of a higher grade than that country may reciprocate. This rule, however, is by no means invariable, and for various reasons it seems to be proper to leave it to the President to determine the cases in which exception should be made." [26] John W. Foster, writing in 1906, declared that "the United States has never construed this practice strictly and it sends ministers to not less than eight states which do not maintain regular diplomatic representatives in this country." [27] Lord Phillimore in his draft code of 1926 declares: "A state which sends an ambassador to another state expects to receive an ambassador from that state and so with other ranks. But this is a matter of comity and not of law." [28]

Diplomatic Appointments Subject to Agrément. An outstanding authority in international law has declared that a state possesses complete freedom in its choice of diplomatic envoys: "It may send career diplomats, scholars, soldiers or women, for neither age, religion or sex may be grounds for exclusion." [29] Nevertheless, the receiving state has the unquestioned right to refuse to receive any diplomatic representative who because of his words or actions or character might thereby be incapable of performing in the most efficient manner his official functions.

In order to avoid the unfriendly feeling which might arise through the

[26] Moore, *op. cit.*, IV, 458.
[27] J. W. Foster, *The Practice of Diplomacy* (New York, 1906), 36.
[28] Lord Phillimore, "Proposed Codification of the Law Regarding the Representation of States," *International Law Association, Report of the Thirty-fourth Conference, Session of Vienna, 1926*, 399.
[29] Paul Fauchille, *Traité de droit international public* (Paris, 1926), I, Pt. iii, 36. It should be noted, however, that states generally limit themselves to the choice of their own nationals.

refusal of a state to receive a foreign representative it is customary for the sending state to submit in advance the name of its envoy to the government of the state to whom he is to be accredited. The procedure of determining in advance as to whether the envoy will be *persona grata* is called *agréation* and the approval *agrément.*

As long as the United States appointed no envoy with a higher rank than minister it was not regarded necessary to communicate in advance the names of our foreign representatives. Secretary of State Bayard in referring to the practice declared in 1885 that "no case could be found in the records of the Department of State in which the acceptability of an envoy was inquired or ascertained in advance of his appointment to the mission for which he was chosen, and that there were reasons, growing out of the frequent recurrence of elections and changes of administration in the United States why the practice should not be adopted." [30]

The United States was consistent in this stand in that it neither expected nor asked other governments to consult it before naming their diplomatic representatives. Secretary of State Fish writing in 1870 declared that the United States did not require other governments to ask in advance whether contemplated appointments would or would not be acceptable but when the inquiry was put the State Department was competent to answer frankly, and the next year the French Government asked for the *agrément* for Jules Ferry as Minister to the United States. A few years later when the President of Switzerland expressed some apprehension lest the appointment of a certain person might not be entirely acceptable, the Department agreed with this point of view. [31]

Since the appointment of envoys with the rank of ambassador, the United States has followed the regular custom of ascertaining the disposition of the foreign government in advance. For example, when the American Ambassador to Russia, George T. Marye, was informed by Secretary of State Lansing that David R. Francis was to be his successor, Ambassador Marye was asked to obtain the Russian *agrément* as to Mr. Francis' appointment. [32] The United States decided to follow the same custom in the appointment of ministers so that when John Brinckerhoff Jackson was appointed Minister to Cuba in 1909 Norval Richardson, at that time Chargé d'Affaires, was instructed to obtain the Cuban *agrément.* The procedure employed in this case was to state that the President would like to send Mr. Jackson as minister plenipotentiary if such an appointment would be agreeable. A short outline of Jackson's career was enclosed with the note. The Cuban Government replied that it was most flattered by the appointment of such a distinguished American.

In his letter to Ambassador Myron T. Herrick accepting his resignation

---

[30] Moore, *op. cit.,* IV, 482.
[31] *Ibid.,* IV, 475.
[32] George T. Marye, *Nearing the End in Imperial Russia* (New York, 1929), 463.

Secretary of State Bryan informed Mr. Herrick that William Graves Sharp of Ohio was to be his successor. Ambassador Herrick was asked to secure the *agrément* of the French Government. For his information it was stated that Sharp was serving his third term in Congress and was ranking member of the Committee on Foreign Affairs.[33]

Secretary Bryan found it difficult to pick the right man for the London post because of the financial sacrifice entailed. When finally the press announced that Walter Hinds Page had been chosen, American Chargé d'Affaires Laughlin, not having been notified, had to send a confidential cable to the State Department noting the fact that no *agrément* had been requested. The Department cavalierly replied that it was not yet ready to announce the selection and in due course it would request the *agrément*.[34] When George Kennan was named Ambassador to Russia early in 1952, it was questioned whether the Soviet Government would accord the *agrément*.

The various draft codes prepared either by publicists or by international conferences almost unanimously provide for the *agrément*. Bluntschli in his draft code of 1868 declares: "Les convenances exigent qu'avant de nommer un envoyé auprès d'un état étranger, on notifie à ce poste." [35] Pessoa is even more definite: "No state may accredit its ministers to other states without previous notice to and acquiescence by them." [36] The Convention on Diplomatic Officers adopted by the Pan-American Conference at Havana in 1928, Article VIII, provides: "No state may accredit its diplomatic officers to other states without previous agreement with the latter." [37]

Refusal of the Agrément.   The annals of diplomacy are replete with examples of refusal of the *agrément*. The King of Sardinia in 1792 refused to receive M. de Semonville as Ambassador from France because of his Jacobin proclivities, and in 1820 Sardinia refused to receive the Baron Charles de Martens from Prussia on the ground that his wife was the daughter of a French regicide.[38] A very interesting example occurred in 1832 when the Czar of Russia refused to receive Sir Stratford Canning as Ambassador from Great Britain. The excuse given was that the nomination was made suddenly and without previous notice. The real reason seemed to be the personal objections of the Czar to whom it was alleged

[33] Colonel T. Bentley Mott, *Myron T. Herrick, Friend of France* (New York, 1929), 211.

[34] Emily Bax, *Miss Bax of the Embassy* (New York, 1939), 223-4.

[35] Johann Kaspar Bluntschli, *Le droit international codifié*, Lardy trans. (Paris, 1870), Article 167.

[36] Epistacio Pessoa, *Projecto de Codigo de Directo Internacional Publico* (Rio de Janeiro, 1911), Article 110.

[37] *Sixth International Conference of American States: Final Act* (Habana, 1928), 142.

[38] P. Pradier-Fodéré, *Cours de droit diplomatique* (Paris, 1899), I, 394.

that Canning had been rude when the former was still Grand Duke. It was also suggested that Canning was altogether too familiar with the political relations which had existed for some time between Russia and Turkey to be a desirable emissary. Lord Palmerston endeavored to make an issue of the case but the Czar was adamant in his refusal. As a result, a chargé d'affaires was in charge of the embassy until 1835.[39]

Numerous similar incidents may be cited in American diplomacy. Charles C. Pinckney was refused as Minister to France in 1796 by the French Directory because they were displeased by the recall of James Monroe but as a matter of fact the relations between the two Governments were already exceedingly critical and no American would have been certain of being received. One of America's most famous diplomats to the Far East, Anson Burlingame, was originally sent to Austria but owing to evident opposition to his appointment he was transferred to China before reaching his post. In his case Prince Metternich probably was cognizant of his friendliness towards the Italians and Hungarians.

Perhaps the best known case in American diplomacy is that of A. M. Keiley, who was appointed Minister to Italy in 1885. The Italian Government declared that he was not *persona grata* to the King because he had made a public speech in 1871 in support of resolutions protesting among other things "against the invasion and spoliation of the status of the church by King Victor Emmanuel as a crime against solemn treaties and against the independence of the church on earth. . . ."

Such a stand was justifiable under the circumstances and the United States appointed John B. Stallo of Ohio in Mr. Keiley's place. At the same time Keiley was appointed Minister Plenipotentiary at Vienna. The Austrian Government was no more desirous of receiving Keiley than was Italy and after calling the attention of the American Government to the customary diplomatic practice of the *agrément* declared that the "position of a foreign envoy wedded to a Jewess by civil marriage would be untenable and even impossible in Vienna."

The United States regarded this ground for objection wholly inadmissible; in fact it violated the Constitution of the United States, which guaranteed religious liberty. Secretary of State Bayard while recognizing Austria's right of rejection asked for a reconsideration of the case. The Austrian Government, disclaiming a discussion on religious liberty and diplomatic law extended its grounds of objection somewhat: "Our objections to Mr. Keiley's appointment as minister of the United States to the Imperial Court are founded upon want of political tact evinced on his part on a former occasion, in consequence of which a friendly power declined to receive him; and upon the certainty that his domestic relations

[39] E. Satow, *A Guide to Diplomatic Practice*, 2nd ed. (London, 1922), I, 204-7.

preclude that reception of him by Vienna society which we judge desirable for the representative of the United States, with which power 'we wish to continue the friendly relations existing between the two Governments."

The United States was not satisfied with these additional reasons and since Austria persisted in her attitude Mr. Keiley again resigned and was appointed a judge on the International Tribunal of Egypt where he made an excellent record. President Cleveland in his annual message of December 8, 1885, explained the situation and declared that since the United States could not acquiesce in the reasons advanced he would make no further appointment but would leave the interests of the United States in charge of a chargé d'affaires *ad interim*.[40]

In 1891 former Senator Henry W. Blair was named Minister to China. While en route to his post newspapers gave citations from Senate debates in which Blair compared the coming of Chinese coolies to the United States to the introduction of the yellow fever and referred to the Chinese of San Francisco as "seeds of death" and their quarter there as a "seething, roaring, bloodcurdling curse." The Chinese Government thereupon declared Blair to be *persona non grata* and he was forced to resign his commission. The Chinese later offered to reconsider if the President would try to repeal the Exclusion Law of 1888 but the United States found this position "incongruous and inadmissible." [41]

Among the more recent examples of refusal of the *agrément* might be mentioned the refusal of Mexico to receive James W. Gerard, appointed by President Wilson in 1913, who was regarded as *persona non grata* because of the reputed ill treatment accorded the peons on his mining properties in Mexico.[42] There was also some doubt as to the acceptance of Josephus Daniels as Ambassador to Mexico in 1933 inasmuch as he had been Secretary of the Navy when Vera Cruz had been shelled and taken over by the United States Navy in 1914. Apparently both Roosevelt and Daniels had completely overlooked this incident. Nevertheless, the fact that President Franklin D. Roosevelt, who named Daniels as Ambassador, was Assistant Secretary of the Navy at the time of the Vera Cruz incident made it a little awkward for the Mexican Government to protest on that issue had it been so disposed. The President of the American Chamber of Commerce of Mexico City was said to have informed the Department of State that American business men generally were against the appointment. Also the Mexican Communists staged a demonstration

---

[40] *Foreign Relations of the United States, 1885*, iv. The Keiley incident is covered in J. B. Moore, *Digest of International Law*, IV, 480-3; the correspondence in *Senate Executive Document* No. 4, 49th Cong., 1st sess.

[41] See *Senate Executive Document* No. 98, 52nd Cong., 1st sess. Also see J. W. Foster, *The Practice of Diplomacy* (New York, 1906), 44.

[42] Joseph Sharp, *Let There Be Light* (Leipzig, 1917), 3.

before the American Embassy, going so far as to break several windows as a protest.[43] The Mexican Government, however, found no objection, in fact it granted the *agrément* the day after it was requested. Arthur Bliss Lane, Counselor of the Embassy, declared that this unprecedented rapidity was due to the Mexican Government's desire to forget the Vera Cruz incident.[44]

Although the United States has on various occasions asked for the recall of foreign envoys and at times has even dismissed them summarily, there are very few occasions when the United States has refused the *agrément*. One of the rare cases occurred in 1922 when the United States refused to receive Dr. Hermes as Ambassador from Germany inasmuch as he was at that time under indictment for fraud committed while head of the ministry of *ravitaillement*.[45]

An interesting incident emphasizing the advantage of the *agrément* occurred in connection with the unfortunate Maximilian expedition to Mexico. As a means of securing recognition of his Government in 1865 Maximilian sent a diplomatic envoy to the United States who attempted to present his letter of credence to Secretary Seward through the French Minister at Washington. Secretary Seward returned the letter to the Marquis de Montholon, stating that the President could not receive either the letter or agent since the United States was on friendly terms with the existing republican Government of Mexico. The French Government expressed its embarrassment at this action and declared that Maximilian should have secured the *agrément* of the United States before sending a representative.[46]

The Rôle of Women in Diplomacy. Just as it is generally conceded that neither religion, age, nor social standing are insurmountable barriers to a diplomatic appointment, neither is sex a valid objection to the acceptance of a foreign envoy. Nevertheless, although women have played an important rôle in diplomacy and from time to time have been sent on important special missions very few have been appointed to foreign posts as regularly accredited envoys. With regard to the special mission of the Maréchale de Guébriant, who was sent in the seventeenth century as ambassadress to accompany the Princess Marie Louise de Gonzague to her fiancé, the King of Poland, Wicquefort observed: "One cannot deny but that it hardly accorded with the dignity of a King to be represented by a woman." [47]

[43] *New York Times* (March 29, 1933).
[44] Josephus Daniels, *Shirt Sleeve Diplomat* (Chapel Hill, N.C., 1947), 5-6.
[45] Fauchille, *op. cit.*, I, Part iii, 38.
[46] *Diplomatic Correspondence of the United States, 1865*, Part III.
[47] A. de Wicquefort, *L'ambassadeur et ses fonctions* (London, 1840), Pt. II, 96. For an interesting article on women in diplomacy see Herbert Wright, "Can a Woman Be a Diplomat?" *American Foreign Service Journal* (August, 1940).

The remarkable career of the Chevalier or Chevalière d'Eon de Beaumont can hardly be cited as an example because although this individual was supposed to have served on a diplomatic mission for Louis XV at the Court of Elizabeth of Russia as a woman he or she later served as a Captain of dragoons and Minister Plenipotentiary of France at the British Court as a man. When heavy bets were laid as to the sex of this remarkable person and an action was taken before the King's Bench, the judge and jury declared the chevalier to be a woman; yet to her dying day D'Eon declared herself to be a man and fought many a duel to prove it.[48]

In the twentieth century when women have found it possible to enter almost every trade and profession, diplomacy has been no exception. One of the outstanding women diplomats was Madame Alexandra Kollontay, daughter of a Czarist general, appointed by Soviet Russia first as Minister to Norway, later as Minister to Mexico, and in 1930 as Minister to Sweden where she served continuously until 1945. When in 1943 she was made Ambassador, the Russians claimed that she was the first woman in the world to hold the title of Ambassador. While in Berlin en route to Mexico, in the fall of 1926, Madame Kollontay applied to the American Consul General in Berlin for a visa on her passport to pass through the United States, but by order of Secretary of State Kellogg she was refused on the grounds that she was an outstanding member of the Russian Communist Party. This "little person with light brown graying hair, cut like a page's, troubled gray eyes ... and a persuasive voice in which she speaks half a dozen languages admirably," according to Dorothy Parker, was not to be permitted to expose the United States to the political germs which she undoubtedly carried on her person.

Madame Isabel de Palencia, a very distinguished Spanish feminist, was the Spanish Envoy to Sweden and Chargé d'Affaires to Finland during the Spanish Civil War. Another well known woman diplomat was the Indian Ambassador to Washington, Madame Vijaya Lakshmi Pandit, Nehru's sister. Soviet Russia is currently represented in Bulgaria by a woman, Ambassador Stella Blagóeva.

In the United States although women have for many years been eligible to political positions there seemed to be little desire on their part to enter the diplomatic service until after World War I. One noteworthy exception was the case of Marilla Ricker, a lawyer of New Hampshire, who publicly declared her desire to be appointed minister to Colombia during the second administration of President Cleveland. She is reported to have stated to a reporter, "If Luther McKinney (Minister to Colombia at that time) can fill the place, I can overflow in it." She was not given the appointment.[49]

[48] See Captain J. Buchan Telfer, *The Strange Career of the Chevalier D'Eon de Beaumont* (London, 1885).
[49] Frederick Van Dyne, *Our Foreign Service* (Rochester, 1909), 75.

The first American woman to serve as Minister Plenipotentiary was Mrs. Ruth Bryan Owen, daughter of the Great Commoner, appointed by President Franklin Roosevelt as Minister to Denmark. Mrs. Owen had already served in Congress and her appointment was entirely political. She was gifted with her father's silver tongue and proved to be very popular among the Danes. Inasmuch as the Department of State always sees to it that an experienced career diplomatic officer serves as counselor or first secretary in all embassies and legations, the policy of appointing a certain number of inexperienced politicians as ministers and ambassadors is not as potentially dangerous as it might seem.

The second woman to serve as Minister was Florence Jaffray Harriman, appointed by President Roosevelt as Minister to Norway in 1937. Daisy Harriman, as she was called, was noted for her many public services and she had campaigned vigorously and successfully for President Roosevelt and Governor Lehman in the 1936 election. She learned of her appointment in the newspapers,—there was some delay in according the *agrément*—and the news had leaked out in Norway before the President could officially notify her of her appointment. She was to serve during the Nazi invasion of Norway and Secretary Hull had occasion to congratulate her for her fine work "in the best traditions of our diplomatic service." [50]

President Truman followed his predecessor's example and in 1949 appointed Mrs. Perle Mesta as Minister to Luxembourg. The Senate debated her nomination on the ground of fitness for the post, but her activities as a lavish entertainer in Washington political society had gained her enough friends in the Senate to win approval. Shortly afterwards the President named Mrs. Eugenie Anderson as Ambassador to Denmark, the first American woman to be given the rank of Ambassador. Mrs. Anderson's appointment was wholly political. She had taught musical art and had been an effective Democratic worker in Iowa politics. The chief problem in her case was one of protocol. What would the position of her husband be in diplomatic gatherings? That difficulty, however, would be the concern of the foreign protocol experts so the Senate, with a touch of sly humor, approved the appointment.

The United States appointed the first woman career Foreign Service Officer in 1922 when Miss Lucile Atcherson was appointed as Third Secretary in Berne and later sent to Panama City. She resigned in 1927 to be married. Miss Frances Willis, appointed in 1927, has had up to the present time the longest and most successful career of any American woman in the Foreign Service. Appointed first as Vice Consul to Valparaiso, Chile, she was transferred to the Legation at Santiago in 1931. Her next appointment was as Third Secretary of Legation in Stockholm where for a time during the absence of the minister she served as Chargé

[50] In *Mission to the North* (New York, 1941), Mrs. Harriman has given a vivid picture of her diplomatic mission.

d'Affaires *ad interim*. After service in Brussels, Luxembourg, and Madrid she was transferred to Washington, where she acted as Assistant to Under Secretary Grew and later as Assistant Chief of the Division of Western European Affairs. Returning to the field as First Secretary in the London Embassy, she was named Counselor of Legation at Helsinski in 1951. While at this post she was promoted to Class I, the first woman career officer to be so honored.

For a period the Department discouraged women from taking examinations for the career service, but at the present time they are once more welcomed both as Staff and Foreign Service officers, particularly for work in the field of cultural affairs.

Dual or Multiple Commissions.   It is quite customary for a diplomatic official to be accredited to several states at the same time. For example, a number of states, Austria, Belgium, and Japan among others accredited the same minister to Athens and to Tirana, Albania. Argentina and Cuba sent the same minister to Germany and Austria. Afghanistan, Finland, Greece, Lithuania, and Siam accredited a single envoy to France and Belgium. Austria and Hungary accredited the same envoy extraordinary and minister plenipotentiary to Washington and Mexico City.[51] The United States used to accredit a single envoy to the five republics of Central America and one representative to Greece, Rumania and Serbia. A single American minister was formerly accredited to Esthonia, Latvia, and Lithuania. While the League of Nations was functioning in Geneva various diplomats were accredited both to the League at Geneva and to the Swiss Government at Bern. One of the most unusual instances of multiple representation occurred in 1942, when the United States accredited Anthony Drexel Biddle as Ambassador to the exiled governments of Belgium, the Netherlands, Norway, and Poland, and as Minister to the exiled governments of Czechoslovakia, Greece, Jugoslavia, and Luxembourg.

Plural Diplomatic Representation.   It is much less common for a state to accredit more than one person to a single post on a regular mission. A few rare instances may be cited, however, of more than one diplomatic representative having been accredited to a single post. The *Mémorial diplomatique* of 1881 announced the *agréation* at Washington of a diplomatic mission of three ministers resident from Colombia.[52] During the First World War period the British, appreciating the fact that Ambassador Spring-Rice was not particularly *persona grata* to the State Department nor temperamentally fitted to take charge of all the financial and commercial problems which were bound to arise, sent Lord Northcliffe to be

---

[51] These examples are taken from the 1935 edition of the *Almanach de Gotha*.
[52] Raoul Genet, *Traité de diplomatie et de droit diplomatique* (Paris, 1931), I, 192.

responsible for commercial matters and Lord Reading to be in control of financial questions.[53] In somewhat similar fashion, although for exactly opposite reasons, Ambassador Page, who in the eyes of many Americans had become altogether too popular with the British Foreign Office, was supplemented at London by the more neutral Colonel House.

Since World War II so many technical, economic and social problems must be handled by the larger embassies that several countries maintain not only an ambassador, but also several ministers at an important post. For example the British have an ambassador and three ministers in Washington, Canada has an ambassador and a minister, China has an ambassador and a minister plenipotentiary, a minister, and two minister counselors, and the Netherlands has an ambassador, an envoy extraordinary and minister plentipotentiary, and a minister plenipotentiary.

The United States in 1849 appointed A. Dudley Mann as special agent to Hungary, although we had at that time a minister to Vienna.[54] In the crucial period preceding the War of the Pacific in South America William H. Trescot was commissioned as special envoy with the rank of Minister Plenipotentiary to Chile, Peru, and Bolivia at the same time that the United States had regularly accredited diplomatic representatives in each of these countries.[55] During the very critical Venezuela dispute of 1895-1896, Secretary of State Olney enlisted the services of Henry White to return to London in a semiofficial capacity and assist Ambassador Bayard who was not succeeding as well as the State Department wished. It was hoped that White who had many influential friends in British governmental circles might clarify our position and thereby avert the possibility of a serious conflict.[56] William W. Rockhill was named Commissioner to China with diplomatic privileges and immunities at the time of the Boxer outbreak, although the United States Minister was at the same time in Peking.[57]

Although the United States had no intention of sending more than one ambassador at a time to France in the early period of World War I, because of the difficulties inherent in the situation Ambassador Herrick remained in charge of the Paris Embassy for exactly three months after Ambassador Sharp had arrived. Inasmuch as former Ambassador Bacon was also in Paris at this time the French press congratulated the United States for having three such eminent representatives in Paris at one time.[58] Henry Lane Wilson tells that when he arrived as Minister to Belguim in

[53] Charles Seymour, *The Intimate Papers of Colonel House* (New York, 1926), II, 399; III, 120.

[54] Moore, *op. cit.*, IV, 453.

[55] Moore, *op. cit.*, IV, 454.

[56] Allan Nevins, *Henry White* (New York, 1930), 112.

[57] Moore, *op. cit.*, IV, 456.

[58] Mott, *op. cit.*, 216, 218. See also Beckles Willson, *American Ambassadors to France* (London, 1928).

1905 Mr. Townsend informed him that he had not expected to surrender the post until a fortnight later, intimating that the presence of the new envoy in Brussels might be embarrassing. Although authorized to take charge upon arrival, Wilson decided to visit Paris for two weeks before assuming his official duties.[59]

The United States today has three ambassadors and two ministers plenipotentiary accredited to the United Nations, an ambassador and a minister accredited to Great Britain and the same number to France.

On ceremonial occasions a special mission is sometimes sent and it is quite customary to send a number of delegates possessing diplomatic powers and immunities to important international conferences. At the Peace Conference at Paris the United States was represented by President Wilson, Secretary of State Lansing, former Ambassador White, and General Bliss, not to mention the unofficial coördinating Ambassador-at-Large, Colonel House. At the London Naval Disarmament Conference of 1930 the American delegation included Secretary of State Stimson, Secretary of the Navy Adams, Ambassadors Dawes, Gibson, and Morrow, envoys to Great Britain, Belgium, and Mexico, and Senators Reed and Robinson, as well as the admirals and technical delegates.

Perhaps the rather indefinite language of the provision found in the Havana Convention of 1928 on diplomatic officers may be said to express the law of today on the subject: "Every state may entrust its representation before one or more governments to a single diplomatic officer. Several states may entrust their representation before another to a single diplomatic officer." [60]

[59] Henry Lane Wilson, *Diplomatic Episodes in Mexico, Belgium and Chile* (New York, 1927).
[60] *Sixth International Conference of American States: Final Act*, Article V (Havana, 1928).

9

Reception of Diplomatic Officers

The Letter of Credence. When the diplomatic envoy starts for his post he carries as evidence of his representative character an official document from the head of his state known as a letter of credence, more commonly known by its French name, "lettre de créance." According to Wheaton "every diplomatic agent in order to be received in that character and to enjoy the privileges and honors attached to his rank must be furnished with a letter of credence." [1] On one occasion when Mexico sent a chargé d'affaires to the United States without such identification, Webster informed him that no communication could be carried on between Mexico and the United States except through the American minister to Mexico or until he presented his credentials. [2]

On occasions however where the letter of credence may have been mislaid or delayed it is permissible for the receiving state to transact business informally with the envoy in the capacity of appointed ambassador or minister. In a monarchy the death or abdication of the head of the state requires new credentials to envoys remaining at their posts, but this is not necessary upon the change of administration in a republic where the sovereignty resides in the people and not in an individual. [3]

The letter of credence is addressed to the head of the state to which the diplomatic representative is accredited, and gives his name, his rank, and indicates the general object of his mission. Formerly the language used in the letters of credence was exceedingly verbose and ornate but at the present time the superlatives have given way to a comparatively simple form of address.

The first letter of credence issued in the United States was the one authorizing Benjamin Franklin to represent the new republic at the Court of Louis XVI of France in 1778. After greeting the King of France as Great, Faithful and Beloved Friend and Ally, and expressing appreciation for the assistance given in support of the "Liberties and Independ-

---

[1] Lawrence's *Wheaton, Elements of International Law* (London, 1864), 388.
[2] Daniel Webster, *Works* (Boston, 1890), VI, 445.
[3] Green H. Hackworth, *Digest of International Law* (Washington, 1942), IV, 439-40.

ence of these States," the letter follows almost the same form as that used at the present day.[4]

One of the oddest of these letters was the one commissioning Caleb Cushing as Envoy Extraordinary and Minister Plenipotentiary to the Emperor of China in 1843. It is generally thought that it was prepared by Secretary of State Webster. It merits quotation at least in part because of its charm and originality:

I, John Tyler, President of the United States of America, send you this letter of peace and friendship signed by my own hand.

I hope your health is good. China is a great Empire extending over a great part of the world. The Chinese are numerous. You have millions and millions of subjects. The twenty-six United States are as large as China, though our people are not so numerous. The rising sun looks upon the great mountains and great rivers of China. When he sets, he looks upon rivers and mountains equally large in the United States. Our territories extend from one great ocean to the other; and on the west we are divided from your dominions only by the sea. . . .

Now my words are that the Governments of two such countries should be at peace. It is proper, and according to the will of Heaven, that they should respect each other, and act wisely. I therefore send to you Count Caleb Cushing, one of the wise and learned men of this country. . . .

The Chinese love to trade with our people, and to sell them tea and silk, for which our people pay silver, and sometimes other articles. But if the Chinese and Americans will trade, there should be rules, so that they shall not break your laws nor our laws. Our minister, Caleb Cushing, is authorized to make a treaty to regulate trade. Let it be just. Let there be no unfair advantage on either side. . . . Therefore we doubt not that you will be pleased that our minister of peace, with this letter in his hand, shall come to Peking, and there deliver a treaty with him to regulate affairs of trade,—so that nothing may happen to disturb the peace between China and America.[5]

Duties Preliminary to the Reception. The regular procedure for the newly appointed American diplomatic envoy whose nomination has been confirmed by the Senate is to proceed to Washington to file the prescribed oath of office in the Department of State and to obtain his commission. The commission is a formal document issued under the seal of the United States and signed personally by the President and countersigned by the Secretary of State. It declares that the President inasmuch as he has "special trust and confidence in the integrity, prudence and ability" of the nominee has appointed him ambassador or minister to ———— country and authorizes him to perform the duties of his office and to hold it during the pleasure of the President of the United States. The envoy then confers personally with the Secretary of State and the head of the geographical division which is responsible for diplo-

[4] Text given in John W. Foster, *The Practice of Diplomacy* (Boston and New York, 1906), 51.
[5] Claude M. Fuess, *Life of Caleb Cushing*, 2 vols. (New York, 1923), I, 419.

matic relations with the country to which he is accredited. He inspects
the correspondence on file in the Department and familiarizes himself
with the treaties in force between the United States and the country
to which he has been assigned. He also pays his respects to the President
and to the envoy of the country to which he is accredited. Frequently,
also, the new diplomat, especially if he has been recruited from outside
the career service, consults with the former representative and obtains
from him suggestions as to procedure not to be derived from the official
files.

Before departing, the diplomatic representative is furnished with the
following papers: (1) A sealed letter of credence signed by the President
and addressed to the head of the state to which he is sent; (2) an open
office copy of the letter of credence; (3) diplomatic passports for himself,
his family, and suite; (4) copies of the *Register of the Department of
State* and the *Foreign Service Regulations of the United States*.

The envoy will also receive such general and special instructions as
the Secretary of State may deem necessary for his guidance. He is particularly cautioned against public expression of his views on political
subjects on the eve of his departure or while traveling through a third
country. It is considered advisable for the new envoy to give informal
notice to his predecessor, if he be at his post, or if not, to the chargé
d'affaires, of his expected arrival in order that the usual exemptions of
customs may be extended. This preliminary notice may be given through
the Department, which of course, must be kept fully posted as to his
plans.

Henry Morgenthau tells how after the Senate confirmed his appointment as Ambassador to Turkey he went to Washington to receive his
instructions. The Chief of the Division of Near Eastern Affairs outlined
to him in a series of conversations the duties, rights and privileges of an
ambassador and a brief survey of current relations between Turkey and
the United States. However, the final official instructions from Secretary
of State William Jennings Bryan were as follows: "Ambassador," he said,
"when I made my trip through the Holy Land, I had great difficulty in
finding Mount Beatitude. I wish you would try to persuade the Turkish
Government to grant a concession to some Americans to build a macadam
road up to it, so that other pilgrims may not suffer the inconvenience
which I did in attempting to find it." [6]

Inasmuch as the newly appointed envoy will find upon arrival a mission already established he should request through the representative in
charge a conference with the minister of foreign affairs in order to arrange
for his official reception. At the same time he personally addresses a for-

[6] Henry Morgenthau, *All in a Lifetime* (New York, 1922), 174-5.

mal note to the minister of foreign affairs mentioning his appointment, his rank and requesting the designation of a time and place for presenting his letter of credence.

If the representative is of a rank higher than that of chargé d'affaires, his sealed letter of credence is signed by the President and addressed to the head of the state. As such he must request an audience to present it in person. The open letter of credence is sent to the minister of foreign affairs after a copy has been made for the archives of the mission. If the diplomatic representative is a chargé d'affaires his letter of credence is addressed to the minister of foreign affairs and should be delivered to him in person subsequent to the sending of the office copy.

It is generally customary for the new diplomatic representative to make a brief address upon the occasion of delivering his letter of credence to the head of the state. This is prepared in advance in English and a copy sent to the minister of foreign affairs so that a suitable reply may be prepared. Copies of both the address and the reply must be sent to the Department of State.

Delay in Presentation of the Letter of Credence.   The diplomatic representative must use his best judgment if conditions make it impossible for him to present his letter of credence shortly after his arrival. When Andrew Gregg Curtin, appointed Minister to Russia in 1869, arrived at Hamburg on his way to his post he learned that Prince Gortchakoff, the Russian Chancellor, was staying at Wiesbaden, a short distance away. Minister Curtin visited him and learned that neither the Emperor nor Chancellor would be in St. Petersburg until the end of October. As it was then July and it was impossible to assume his duties until autumn, Curtin received the permission of the Department to spend the summer in Germany. Inasmuch as Mr. Clay was still at his post, the matter was easily arranged. It is interesting to note that Governor Curtin there found his colleagues John Jay, the new Minister to Austria, Elihu B. Washburne, the new Minister to France, and Russell Jones, who was to go as Minister to Belgium.

A much more lengthy delay occurred in the case of Charles Denby, sent as American Minister to China in 1885. Although he entered upon the duties of his post immediately, he was not able to present his letter of credence since the Emperor was still in his minority. It was not until 1891 when the Emperor took over the government that Mr. Denby delivered his letter of credence issued six years before.[7]

A complication arose regarding the presentation of letters of credence after Mussolini's conquest of Ethiopia when Mussolini insisted that the letters of credence of all ambassadors and ministers henceforth be ad-

[7] *Foreign Relations of the United States, 1891,* 376.

dressed to Victor Emmanuel III, King of Italy and Emperor of Ethiopia. As a result, those states which refused to recognize the Italian conquest were represented in Rome by chargés d'affaires. It is alleged that when the United States accredited Ambassador William Phillips to Italy in 1936 the difficulty was surmounted by addressing the letter of credence to Victor Emmanuel III, King of Italy et cetera, et cetera.

The Presentation of the Letter of Credence.   The actual ceremony of presentation is almost as varied as the posts. A very clear picture of the ordinary ceremony is given by Eugene Schuyler, who served as Minister Resident and Consul General to Greece, Rumania, and Serbia and later as Consul General to Egypt:

Etiquette . . . demands that the audience for presenting credentials should take place as early as possible. These audiences are either public or private. In the first the minister is accompanied by the Minister of Foreign Affairs, generally followed by his own secretaries, and goes to the palace in more or less state, according to the customs of the place; for these vary greatly in different capitals. For an ambassador a state carriage is always sent. This is not always the case with the minister in a capital where ambassadors also reside, it being considered desirable to draw distinctions of ceremony between the two. In small countries, where there are no ambassadors, a state carriage is usually sent for the minister, in some cases by an escort. At a formal audience all parties are standing: the minister enters, is introduced to the sovereign by the Minister of Foreign Affairs, addresses a few words to him stating his character, and presents his letters of credence. These the sovereign takes, sometimes goes through the formality of reading them, and replies briefly to the minister. After the formal part of the audience is over, there is generally a friendly conversation of a few moments, and the ceremony ends in much the same way as it began. In some countries it is expected that a formal speech will be made by the minister to the sovereign, and a formal reply made. In such cases the speech is written out in advance and given to the Minister of Foreign Affairs, who returns a copy of the reply before the audience takes place. This is in order to prevent embarrassment, as well as to see that nothing unpleasant be said. In some countries, as in Russia, a minister is nearly always received in private audience. He goes to the palace alone, is met by the Grand Master of Ceremonies, conducted to the Emperor, introduced into his room, and is left alone with him. After a word or two the Emperor requests the minister to be seated; and the conversation is informal.[8]

Early Russian protocol was very rigid regarding the presentation of the letter of credence. Until the Russian envoy had his official audience with the sovereign he could visit no one else. In fact when in 1668 the Russian envoy was invited to exchange visits with the Marquis Saint Luc in Bordeaux he refused on the ground that the Czar's ukase forbade it on pain of death. Nor could the Russian envoy present himself at the same time as other envoys nor even on the same day. Moscovite protocol

---

[8] Eugene Schuyler, *American Diplomacy* (New York, 1895), 136-38; also found in John Bassett Moore, *Digest of International Law* (Washington, 1906), IV, 469-70.

also required that the letter of credence be given only into the hands of the foreign sovereign.[9]

Andrew Curtin when Minister to Russia asked permission to violate the traditional custom in Russia and deliver a brief address at his presentation to the Emperor. Prince Gortchakoff agreed, provided Curtin would furnish an advance copy of his remarks to be given to the Emperor. The address followed the usual type of such speeches emphasizing the traditional friendship and many similarities of the two countries. The Emperor listened with close attention and his reply which was given in excellent English dealt with the topics touched upon by the minister in exactly the same order. The next day Curtin asked Gortchakoff's permission to publish the remarks. Gortchakoff agreed but said they had no copy of the Emperor's reply. Curtin thereupon offered to reproduce the Emperor's speech from memory, which he did. They were sent to the Foreign Office, translated into French, published in the *Journal de St. Petersbourg* and republished in all the important newspapers of Europe. Titian J. Coffey, Minister Curtin's Secretary of Legation, regards the incident as unique in American diplomacy.[10]

At a somewhat earlier period John Quincy Adams found his audience with the Emperor of Russia brief and conventional. The master of ceremonies came to see him the night before to explain the details of the presentation. The next afternoon Mr. Adams went to the Imperial Palace, was conducted to the Emperor's cabinet, which he entered. The Emperor was alone, advanced to meet him and greeted him with the simple statement: "Monsieur, je suis charmé d'avoir le plaisir de vous voir ici." [11]

Washington Irving tells an interesting anecdote concerning the presentation of his friend, John Randolph, to the Emperor of Russia. It had been reported that Randolph knelt as a mark of respect as he came into the Emperor's presence. Randolph's explanation was that as one of his legs was shorter than the other, he approached with a limping gait. Apparently the Emperor thought Randolph was about to kneel as he saluted, for the Emperor made a movement to prevent it, and cried "No, no!" [12]

The presentation as prescribed by the Government of the Union of Soviet Socialist Republics takes place at the Kremlin and is less ceremonious. The ambassador is conducted by the *chef du protocole,* is given a military salute by the Kremlin guards on entering the Kremlin and presents his letter of credence to the President, whose official title is Chairman of the Praesidium of the Supreme Soviet, in the presence of the

[9] For a detailed account of early Russian reception ceremonial see Vladimir Potiemkine *Histoire de la Diplomatie* (Paris, no date), I, 229-36.

[10] Titian J. Coffey, "Curtin as Minister to Russia," in William H. Egle, ed., *Andrew Gregg Curtin* (Philadelphia, 1895), 433-4.

[11] John Quincy Adams, *Memoirs* (Philadelphia, 1875), II, 50.

[12] David J. Hill, *American Authors, Washington Irving* (Boston, 1897), 120.

Secretary of Praesidium of the Supreme Soviet, the Minister of Foreign Affairs, and the Chief of the Political Section of the Ministry of Foreign Affairs charged with the country which the Ambassador represents. A private audience is accorded the envoy afterwards by the President in the presence of the Minister of Foreign Affairs.[13]

Elaborate Receptions in Near East and Far East.   In the Near East the procedure of presentation has always been much more elaborate. Colonel Thomas Skelton Harrison, American diplomatic agent to Egypt in 1897, has given us an excellent and very detailed description of his audience with the Khedive to present his letters of credence. He dressed in his military uniform with epaulets and sword and awaited the Khedive's Grand Master of Ceremonies. The Master of Ceremonies arrived at the agency in a gilded coach with a coachman and groom on the box and two postillions behind. A troop of cavalry preceded and followed the coach, and the streets through which they passed were guarded by foot and mounted police. When they entered the square before the palace a band played "Hail, Columbia" and this was followed by a salvo of twenty-one guns. The route through the palace halls was lined with uniformed and gold laced officials. The Khedive, surrounded by his ministers, met Harrison in the reception room, grasped his hand and then listened to his address. The Khedive read his reply, took his seat on the throne and invited Harrison to sit at his right on a sofa. Servants brought pipes and coffee and all those present partook. The Khedive then accompanied the American envoy to the door, shook hands and waited while Harrison and his secretary backed out of his presence.[14]

Eugene Schuyler gives a very similar picture of his reception a few years earlier: "Everybody says it was a very fine ceremony, but being inside a gilt coach drawn by six horses with an escort of cavalry ... I didn't see very much of it. But there were salutes of cannon from the citadel and the band played *Hail Columbia*.... We made our little speech, then we sat down and smoked jewelled tchibouks about ten feet long ... then coffee in jewelled cups or cupholders and then as I went away a sword was hung over my head...." [15]

One of the most interesting accounts that we have of elaborate audiences is that given by Townsend Harris depicting the first audience during his mission to Japan. He was informed that it would take two months to prepare for the arrival of so great a man as himself to have an audience with the Shogun. He had special uniforms made for his men with the crest of the United States affixed to their tunics. He traveled in state to

[13] For earlier procedure see Sir Ernest Satow, *A Guide to Diplomatic Practice,* 3rd ed. (London, 1932), 143.

[14] Thomas Skelton Harrison, *The Homely Diary of a Diplomat in the East* (New York, 1917), 99.

[15] Eugene Schuyler, *Essays and Memoirs* (New York, 1901), 192.

Yedo escorted by about 350 Japanese of whom eighty were his own servants. Upon reaching the outer walls of the city he was allowed to enter in his *palaquin,* an honor normally restricted to princes. He found a private compound specially prepared for him in Yedo and a drill ground was assigned to him for his daily walk. In preparation for his meeting with the Shogun he gave the Foreign Minister a copy of his intended address and received a copy of the Shogun's answer. The Foreign Minister called for him on the day of his presentation and conducted him to the *palaquin.* He was allowed to remain in his *palaquin* until the last bridge into the Shogun's palace had been reached. Before entering the audience chamber Harris put on new shoes. When the signal was given, the official who accompanied him began to crawl along on his hands and knees. As Harris entered the room, a chamberlain called out in a loud voice, "Embassador Merrican." Mr. Harris proceeded into the room for a distance of about six feet, then stopped and bowed, again proceeded, halted in the middle of the room and bowed again. Finally coming before the Shogun with the feudal lords and relatives of the Shogun prostrate on their faces on either side, he made a short speech as he presented his letters of credence. When this was completed he again bowed. The Shogun began to jerk his head backward over his left shoulder three or four times, at the same time stamping with his right foot. He then replied: "Pleased with the feudal lords and relatives of the Shogun prostrate on their faces likewise pleased with his discourse. Intercourse shall be continued forever." [16] Incidentally, at his second audience in 1859 to present his credentials as Minister Resident Harris found his reception so lacking in cordiality or even in common courtesy that he demanded and obtained a third audience.[17]

Another example of an oriental reception is described by Minister Lloyd Griscom, representative to Persia in 1901. Before entering the Hall of Diamonds, instead of taking off his shoes he put a pair of galoshes over them. The Shah, diamond bedecked, leaning against a piano, received him without any appearance of interest. After listening to Griscom's short speech in French the Shah deigned to make the usual inquiry about the President's health. However, the short conversation was stilted in the extreme and when the Shah asked how one got to America and the Minister replied by a ship across the Atlantic the Shah said he always got seasick and wouldn't go to America. On this unpleasant note the reception ended.[18]

European Reception Ceremonies. Of the European countries Spain has kept perhaps the most elaborate audience ceremonial. The govern-

---

[16] *The Complete Journal of Townsend Harris* (New York, 1930), 395-475.

[17] Payson J. Treat, *Early Relations between the United States and Japan* (Baltimore, 1917), 140.

[18] Lloyd C. Griscom, *Diplomatically Speaking* (New York, 1940), 191-3.

ment furnishes carriages and saddle horses for the ambassador and his suite, even sending spare horses in case of accident. The ornately decorated carriage for the ambassador is drawn by six horses while the less resplendent one for the minister has but two. The ambassador is met in the courtyard by detachments from the garrison regiments and the staircase is lined by halberdiers. He is accompanied by the Introducer of Ambassadors who follows the rules of etiquette very strictly. William Miller Collier, sent as Minister Plenipotentiary to Spain in 1905, declared that the Introducer of Ambassadors called upon him almost every day after his arrival in order fully to discharge his duty of explaining the rules and regulations and requirements relating to the audience. He then goes on to say: "All the courts of Europe have at least one such official, although he is sometimes known as Master of Ceremonies. In Spain there are two. The positions are esteemed great honors and are filled by persons in the diplomatic career of the rank of Minister Plenipotentiary. Everyone must realize how desirable is the existence of such an office, for the rules vary in different courts, and even trained diplomats must be informed as to the local usages. In a court distinguished for the formalities of its etiquette, as is that of Spain, a Master of Ceremonies or Introducer of Ambassadors is an absolute necessity." [19]

Upon entering the throne room the envoy made the usual three bows, *las reverencias,* at the entrance, half way, and near the sovereign, and then made his address. The exit was always made facing the court.[20] Diplomatic etiquette still requires that representation of the same rank shall be received with exactly the same ceremony, shall ride in the same type of carriage with the same number of horses. Collier tells of a diplomat who protested because a certain sovereign did not converse with him as many minutes as he did with other foreign representatives.

Robert Underwood Johnson, sent as Ambassador to Italy in 1920, gives us a full description of his presentation of his letters of credence to King Victor Emmanuel of Italy. He was accompanied by his staff in three royal coaches. The Ambassador rode in the third coach escorted by the Master of the Royal House, who rode backward, facing the Ambassador. The coaches were black but decorated with red and white with two men on the box and three behind dressed in the livery of the court. The Ambassador was greeted by a fanfare of soldiers' trumpets upon arriving at the palace and was conducted to a reception room to await the summons of the King. Immediately after Johnson had made his bows the King shook hands with him and after his formal speech the King chatted

---

[19] William Miller Collier, *At the Court of His Catholic Majesty* (Chicago, 1912), 49.

[20] See Sir Henry Drummond Wolff, *Rambling Recollections* (London, 1908), 390 ff.; Foster, *The Practice of Diplomacy*, 58; and the very elaborate account given by Collier, *op. cit.*, 44-86.

with him very informally. Before the audience was over the Ambassador asked permission to present his staff and after that was over all bowed themselves out.[21]

According to George von L. Meyer, Ambassador to Italy from 1900 to 1905, it was customary for every ambassador to send 500 lire in gratuities to the Royal Stables and lackeys on the occasion of the first presentation.

The reception of a foreign ambassador in imperial Germany was very similar to the ceremonies which we have already described. A minister plenipotentiary went in his own carriage, but the ambassador was honored by having three court carriages sent for him. Andrew D. White, Ambassador to Germany from 1897 to 1902, was somewhat abashed by the procession with its carriages and outriders, the gaping crowds, the presentations of arms and beating of drums and found the ordeal more picturesque than agreeable. However, the reception by the Emperor was simple and kindly, informal conversation taking the place of set speeches.[22]

White in his remarks to the Emperor followed the long established custom of our ambassador to Germany in expressing the gratitude of the United States at the remembrance that Frederick the Great was one of the first of the Continental rulers to recognize the United States.

James W. Gerard, American Ambassador from 1913 to the severance of diplomatic relations between the United States and Germany, also found the presentation ceremony very pretentious. He describes his reception by the Emperor as follows: "... the Emperor, very erect and dressed in the uniform of the Death's Head Hussars, stood by a table. I made a little speech and presented my letters of credence and the letters of recall of my predecessor. The Emperor then unbent from his very correct and impressive attitude and talked with me in a very friendly manner...." [23]

One of the most momentous audiences in American diplomatic annals was the occasion when John Adams presented his credentials to King George III in 1785. Mr. Adams gives a very detailed account of the event including the full text of his speech and the King's reply, both of which on this occasion departed considerably from the routine form.[24]

Walter Hines Page, America's wartime Ambassador to Great Britain, in describing his presentation to King George V notes that the King's Master of Ceremonies called for him with four or five royal coaches so that the entire Embassy staff might accompany him to Buckingham

[21] Robert Underwood Johnson, *Remembered Yesterdays* (Boston, 1923), 520 ff.
[22] *The Autobiography of Andrew D. White* (New York, 1905), 533.
[23] James W. Gerard, *My Four Years in Germany* (New York, 1917), 22.
[24] *Works of John Adams,* 10 vols. (Boston, 1851-65), VIII, 256.

Palace.[25] Sir Edward Grey, the British Secretary of State for Foreign Affairs, stood beside the King throughout the ceremony. After the bows the King shook hands and the short speeches were made. The King in the course of his informal remarks expressed his surprise that a country as great and rich as the United States had not provided a residence for its ambassadors.[26]

General Dawes broke many diplomatic precedents in his short but vivid career as American Ambassador to Great Britain from 1929 to 1932. He undoubtedly established a record when within eighteen hours of his arrival in England he was being taken to the King's summer residence in a landau drawn by four bay horses to present his credentials.[27]

The present procedure at the Court of St. James's is approximately as follows: The ambassador notifies the Secretary of State for Foreign Affairs of his arrival and asks for an audience to present his credentials to the Sovereign. Upon the date fixed the ambassador is accompanied to the palace in a town coach by the Marshal of the Diplomatic Corps with his suite following in other coaches. He is met at the grand entrance by the Equerry-in-Waiting and in the Grand Hall by the Master of the Household. They conduct him to the Bow Room where he meets the Foreign Minister and the Lord-in-Waiting. The ambassador is thereupon conducted into the royal presence by the Lord-in-Waiting and the Marshal of the Diplomatic Corps who thereupon withdraw. Set speeches are not customary. After the audience the Marshal introduces the personnel of the ambassador who presents them to the King. This concludes the ceremony.[28]

Two exceptional instances of courtesy occurred in 1941 when President Franklin D. Roosevelt went to receive the newly appointed British Ambassador, Lord Halifax, on the British battleship on which his Lordship had arrived, and when His Majesty, George VI, hastened to greet the American Ambassador, Mr. Winant, in a railway station in England; the latter was the first time in British history that a king had gone to meet an ambassador.

An interesting incident of diplomatic precedent arose in 1934 on the occasion of the presentation of his credentials by Minister W. W. McDowell of the United States to the Irish Free State. Instead of presenting his letter of credence to the British Governor General, he presented it to Eamon de Valera, President of the Irish Free State. Al-

---

[25] *Foreign Service Regulations of the United States of America* (Washington, 1945), II, 4, provide that the newly appointed diplomatic representative should be accompanied by all Foreign Service officers assigned to the mission in a diplomatic capacity and by all attachés of the mission when presenting his letter of evidence.

[26] Burton J. Hendrick, *Life and Letters of Walter H. Page* (New York, 1923), I, 135.

[27] Paul R. Leach, *That Man Dawes* (Chicago, 1930), 312.

[28] A more complete description may be found in Satow, *op. cit.*, 140-2.

though in some quarters the action was regarded as a snub to Great Britain, Minister McDowell reported that a responsible official of the Free State government had informed the legation that the British authorities had agreed to the presentation of the credentials to the President of the Executive Council.[29]

Early American Reception Ceremonial. The United States has never followed a very elaborate ceremonial in the reception by the President of foreign diplomatic representatives. In the reception accorded by President Washington to Mr. Fauchet, the French Minister Plenipotentiary in 1794, we have the basic outline of present day procedure. Secretary of State Randolph upon receiving a copy of his letter of credence conferred with the President and fixed the time of presentation. At the appointed time the Secretary of State in his carriage accompanied the French Minister and they were shown in by the President's secretary. The President, who was alone, arose and bowed and Secretary Randolph introduced the French Minister, who presented his credentials with a brief speech. They all thereupon sat down, the President opened the sealed credentials and delivered them to Randolph, who read them standing. After a brief exchange of complimentary remarks and some informal conversation the Secretary and Minister withdrew.[30]

President Jefferson, who believed in a greater degree of democratic simplicity than his predecessors, was considerably more informal. In fact, the British Minister, Anthony Merry, quite resented the informality of his presentation. Arriving in his official costume, he found himself at the appointed hour "introduced to a man as President of the United States, not merely in an undress, but actually standing in slippers down at the heels, and both pantaloons, coat and underclothes indicative of utter slovenliness and indifference to appearances and in a state of negligence actually studied." [31] Stratford Canning gives an even more picturesque variant when he declares that President Jefferson received Merry "in his dressing gown, seated on a sofa and catching a slipper after tossing it up on the point of his foot." [32] Henry Adams blames Secretary of State Madison for not warning the British Minister that he would not be expected to wear full dress, but concedes that Jefferson could have received in his bare feet had he so desired.[33]

The procedure under President Monroe is described by Secretary of State John Quincy Adams as follows: "At these audiences the President observes the usual forms practiced by European sovereigns on similar occasions. That is, he receives them standing, dressed in a half military

---

[29] *San Francisco Chronicle* (March 28, 1934).

[30] Moore, *op. cit.*, IV, 465.

[31] John W. Foster, *A Century of American Diplomacy* (New York, 1900), 211.

[32] S. Lane-Poole, *Life of Stratford Canning* (London, 1888), I, 316.

[33] Henry Adams, *History of the United States* (New York, 1898), II, 367.

uniform or a full suit of black. The ministers are in full court dress. He stands in the center of the drawing room and I accompany them, keeping the right hand. On receiving the letter, the President hands it unopened to me. . . . The President has a general answer to the short addresses which the ministers make in delivering these letters, namely, 'that the United States takes a great interest in everything that concerns the happiness of their sovereign,' with very little variation adapted to each particular case. He makes no other conversation." [34]

American Reception of Diplomats at the Present Time. Secretary Bayard writing in 1889 describes the procedure and we find practically no change.[35] However, with the establishment of a ceremonial officer and later a chief of protocol in the Department of State this officer assumed the functions formerly performed by the Secretary of State. The following description of the ceremonies to be observed in connection with the reception of foreign ambassadors by the President was prescribed during the administration by President Hoover:

As soon as practicable after the arrival of the appointed ambassador, an official communication is addressed by him or by the chargé d'affaires to the Secretary of State, requesting that an hour be designated at which the ambassador may pay his respects to the Secretary.

On this occasion the ambassador is usually presented to the Secretary by the chief of protocol. During the course of the visit the ambassador requests an appointment with the President. He leaves with the Secretary a copy of his letters of credence and the text of the remarks which he will deliver when presenting these letters to the President. The ambassador is notified promptly of the time at which the President will receive him. At the hour indicated the chief of protocol (in formal morning dress) and the military or naval aide to the President (in dress uniform) arrive at the ambassador's residence in the President's car. It is customary for the ranking Secretary of the embassy to meet these officials at the door and to accompany them to the drawing room, where the ambassador receives them and presents the other members of his staff. The party then proceeds to the White House in the following order: In the President's car the ambassador is seated at the right of the chief of protocol with the military or naval aide to the President on the folding seat.

In the other cars the members of the staff of the ambassador are seated according to their respective rank. Upon arrival at the White House the ambassador, walking at the right of the chief of protocol, is escorted through the entrance, followed by his staff. A few paces inside the door the President's other aide and four White House aides (in dress uniform) are standing at attention. The President's aide is presented to

[34] J. Q. Adams, *Memoirs*, IV, 314.
[35] Moore, *op. cit.*, IV, 467.

the ambassador, who is then escorted to the Green Room preceded by the aides and followed by his staff. The President's aides then withdraw to notify the President of the ambassador's arrival and to escort the President to the Blue Room, where the reception takes place.

It is customary for the President to take his position at the end of the Blue Room with his aides on either side of him, standing slightly to the rear. The senior White House aide announces to the chief of protocol that the President will be pleased to receive the ambassador. The ambassador, with the chief of protocol at his left, then enters the Blue Room by way of the corridor, preceded by four White House aides. The latter take position uncovered in the Blue Room, on either side of the entrance. The ambassador and the chief of protocol pause just inside the entrance and bow slightly to the President. They next advance to a position about six feet in front of the President. The chief of protocol presents the ambassador in the following manner:

Mr. President, I have the honor to present the Ambassador Extraordinary and Plenipotentiary of _____, His Excellency, Mr. _____.

The ambassador reads his address and the President replies. The ambassador then steps forward, presents his letters of credence to the President, and shakes hands with him. After a few moments of informal conversation the President inquires whether the ambassador will be so kind as to present the members of his staff. The senior White House aide proceeds to the Green Room and escorts the members of the staff to the Blue Room, walking at the left of the Senior Secretary and followed by the other members in the order of their precedence. The ambassador, standing at the President's left, presents the members of his staff, who file past the President one by one and shake hands with him.

After a few moments more of conversation the ambassador takes his leave and again shakes hands with the President. The ambassador and the chief of protocol, preceded by the four White House aides, withdraw to the door, where both turn and bow slightly to the President. The members of the staff follow and also bow slightly to the President upon leaving the room.

The return to the embassy is arranged in the same manner as the arrival.

The chief of protocol and the President's military or naval aide accompany the ambassador to the drawing room of the embassy. After a few moments of conversation they take leave of him and of the members of his staff.

President Franklin D. Roosevelt varied the ceremony to a slight extent in that if he was acquainted with the new ambassador he often dispensed with the reading of the address and its reply. In its place he would suggest to the ambassador that they had certain greetings to exchange which they need not read. Instead, he engaged the envoy in a very informal conversation. The ceremony for a minister plenipotentiary is practically the same as for an ambassador. In receiving the new Minister from Nicaragua, Dr. Don Leon de Bayle, President Roosevelt reduced formalities to a minimum by eliminating the aides and receiving the Minister in his executive offices attired in his regular business suit. President Roosevelt preferred this informal procedure and used it as often as possible.

Language Employed in Presentation.   The foreign envoy in presenting his letter of credence may deliver his speech in either his own language or French, the former being the more usual in oriental countries. The official instructions of the United States specifically state that the presentation address should be "written and spoken in English" but several instances might be cited where the representative seems to have honored them in the breach. T. Jefferson Coolidge, sent as Minister to France in 1892, notes the fact that when presenting his credentials he made with some difficulty a speech in French containing the usual commonplace compliments.[36] General Horace Porter, United States Ambassador to France in 1897, found out that other ambassadors and ministers invariably gave their speeches at the audience of presentation in French. Furthermore, he had received an intimation from the French Foreign Office that President Faure would find it very agreeable if General Porter would follow the established custom. General Porter who could speak French fluently decided that the point was well taken and delivered his address in French submitting at the same time an exact copy in English.[37]

When Ambassador William F. Draper was to be presented to King Humbert of Italy he had carefully memorized his speech of presentation in English. However, he was informed just before leaving his hotel for the audience that King Humbert, having learned that he spoke French, hoped that he would make his address in that language. Mr. Draper could hardly refuse, but he had misgivings as to his ability to remember and translate at the same time. Consequently, all the way to the palace with the crowds cheering, the unfortunate Ambassador spent his time mentally translating his speech so that he might not stumble over an unexpected word.[38]

James B. Angell, sent as Minister to Turkey in 1897, gives a vivid picture of his presentation to the Sultan. In his case he read his speech in English of which preliminary copies in both French and English had already been sent to the Foreign Office. The Turkish Secretary then read a Turkish version of his speech. The Sultan replied in Turkish, which his Secretary translated immediately into English.[39]

[36] Beckles Willson, *America's Ambassadors to France* (London, 1928), 348.
[37] Elsie Porter Mende, *An American Soldier and Diplomat* (New York, 1927), 177.
[38] William F. Draper, *Recollections of a Varied Career* (New York, 1908), 284.
[39] James Burill Angell, *Reminiscences* (New York, 1912), 195.

Procedure after Presentation. On occasions after the formal addresses have been given, the head of the state may engage the diplomatic representative in somewhat lighter conversation, that is, if the envoy is familiar with a language used by the head of the state. Henry Lane Wilson, describing his reception in Chile, found the attempt of President Errazuriz to visit with him after the formal audience a little embarrassing owing to his limited acquaintance with the Spanish language. However, he was able to show his interest and appreciation by such expressions as *si, señor, mucho,* and *poco a poco,* uttered at what appeared to be the appropriate times.[40]

In European courts, following the delivery of the letter of credence, the ambassador was quite often introduced to the royal family. Andrew D. White mentions the fact that after his reception by the Emperor of Germany he presented his embassy secretaries and attachés and was then conducted into the presence of the Empress.[41] John W. Foster relates that after his audience with the Emperor Alexander II he was received by the Czarevitch and Czarena. After the audience was over he had difficulty in finding the proper knob of the door, owing to the necessity of making his exit backwards. The Czarevitch, noticing his embarrassment, shouted out in English, "Mr. Foster, take the other knob." [42] According to William M. Collier, American Minister Plenipotentiary to Spain, after the audience with the King was over he was received by the Queen Mother and her ladies in waiting. He was also expected to make a call immediately upon the Prime Minister and Minister of State, but in a frock coat rather than in full dress.[43]

Once accredited through the presentation of his credentials, the diplomatic representative is expected to call upon his colleagues and to enter actively upon the performance of his functions. According to the official instructions to American diplomatic officers "the official duties of a diplomatic representative begin on the day of his formal reception by the chief of state. . . ."

Nationality as an Obstacle to Reception. Although there are exceptions to the rule, it is a generally accepted policy that a state will not receive one of its own citizens as a foreign ambassador or minister. When in 1928 the Lithuanian Government requested the *agrément* for a naturalized American citizen as minister to Washington, Secretary of State Kellogg requested the American Minister at Riga to explain that it was the established policy of the United States not to receive American citizens as diplomatic representatives of foreign governments. Again in 1938 Chief

[40] Henry Lane Wilson, *Diplomatic Episodes in Mexico, Belgium and Chile* (New York, 1927), 31.
[41] *The Autobiography of Andrew D. White, op. cit.,* 533.
[42] John W. Foster, *The Practice of Diplomacy* (New York, 1906), 60.
[43] Collier, *op. cit.,* 59-61.

of Protocol Summerlin declared that the United States "could not agree to the appointment of an American citizen as a foreign Ambassador or Minister accredited to this government."[44]

A famous exception to this rule was the acceptance of Anson Burlingame, former United States Minister to China, as a representative of China heading a mission to the principal powers including the United States. The so-called Burlingame Treaty of 1868 was the result of this mission.

A more recent and less excusable exception was made in 1945 when Dr. Oskar Lange, a naturalized American citizen of Polish origin, was named as the first Ambassador of the Provisional Government of Poland to the United States. The United States Ambassador to Warsaw had recommended to the Department of State that the *agrément* be refused both because of Lange's American nationality and also because his known Communist affiliations would not make him acceptable to the Polish-American community in the United States. It was discovered later that Stalin had inquired of Harry Hopkins whether the United States would object to Lange holding an important part in the Polish Government and that Joseph E. Davies, one-time Ambassador to Moscow, had supported Lange's appointment.[45]

---

[44] Green H. Hackworth, *Digest of International Law* (Washington, 1942), IV, 452-3.

[45] Arthur Bliss Lane, *I Saw Poland Betrayed* (New York, 1948), 132-3.

10

Diplomatic Duties—I

POLITICAL FUNCTIONS RELATING TO THE HOME GOVERNMENT

The Envoy and His Government.   The diplomatic representative today is universally regarded as holding a post of dignity and honor in the service of his country. No longer can one say as did Callières: "on appelle un ambassadeur un honorable espion." [1] The position of an ambassador or minister is also a most difficult one and requires ability and probity of the highest order. Unfortunately the idea is still prevalent that diplomacy is only a synonym for intrigue and that a diplomat must deceive to succeed. Even Machiavelli, an absolute realist, knew better than that as shown by the instructions to the French ambassador accredited to Charles V, which advised him to make every effort so as not to be regarded as a man who thought one thing while he said another. Jules Cambon, a very able ambassador in his time, declared that the quality most essential in a diplomatic agent is moral integrity. "His tested trustworthiness must inspire both in the government to which he is accredited and in his own government such confidence that his word will never be suspected." [2]

Present Importance of the Diplomatic Service.   The idea has also become current that since new means of rapid communication have been discovered and the most distant post can be reached immediately by cable or radio, the foreign representative is merely an automaton carrying out the will of the foreign office. The situation is quite the reverse. The new inventions have made more complex and complicated the problems of international intercourse and the need for men of the highest ability to represent their country abroad has never been greater.

Secretary of States Hughes had very strong opinions on this point. "It is perfectly idle to believe that we can get along without diplomatic representatives because we have increased facility in communication.

[1] F. de Callières, *De la manière de négocier avec les souverains* (Paris and Amsterdam, 1716), 41.

[2] Jules Cambon, *Le Diplomate* (Paris, 1926), 13.

We need the man. We cannot rely on paper; we cannot rely on direct messages. We need the man in the personal contact with other men transacting the business of their government." [3] Jules Jusserand, formerly French Ambassador to the United States, was equally emphatic: "Experience has already shown and will more and more show that no invention, no telephone, no aeroplane, no wireless, will ever replace the knowledge of a country and the understanding of a people's dispositions. The importance of persuading a prince and his minister has diminished; that of understanding a nation has increased. . . ." [4]

Relations between the Diplomat and the Foreign Office.   The foreign office must depend almost entirely upon the information which it receives from its foreign representatives for its guidance. Its foreign policy must be constructed upon their reports. Therefore, the most complete understanding should exist between the two and the foreign office must have the utmost confidence in the ability of its representatives. Without this relationship it is manifestly impossible for the foreign office to utilize effectively the services of its officers in the field. According to Maurice Francis Egan, United States Minister to Denmark and a man of remarkable ability, "the diplomatists were much wiser than their governments— for the reason that given even ordinary ability and powers of observation, the man on the spot is likely to be much wiser than the bureaucrats of the Foreign Offices who are swayed very often by partisanship or public opinion at home." [5]

This, however, is hardly a fair presentation of the situation because the officer in the foreign office may have had just as much experience as the officer in the field and he has the advantage of reports from many other sources and places to give him a somewhat broader and more objective viewpoint. Unfortunately, the foreign office has on occasions been inclined to justify Mr. Egan's criticism and to regard itself as the sole fount of wisdom in foreign affairs. The envoy feels that all too often the foreign office seems to disregard completely the recommendations which come from its agents abroad. This makes for a lack of confidence on the part of the representative which quickly shows itself in his work. An extreme case is cited by Bruce Lockhart in his interesting account of his work as a British agent. The Brazilian Minister to Russia claimed that success in diplomacy came to him who did least. When he entered the service he was full of zeal and while at his first post as secretary in London he worked strenuously to prepare an elaborate report on the Brazilian coffee trade

[3] *Foreign Service of the United States, Hearings before the House Committee on Foreign Affairs*, 68th Cong., 1st sess. (Washington, 1924), 13. See also Royal Cortissoz, *The Life of Whitelaw Reid* (New York, 1921), II, 344, for a somewhat similar viewpoint.

[4] J. J. Jusserand, *The School for Ambassadors* (New York and London, 1925), 59.

[5] Maurice Francis Egan, *Recollections of a Happy Life* (New York, 1924), 239.

with England upon which he based certain recommendations. His recompense was a reduction in rank and a less important post in the Balkans. When later he was transferred to Berlin he again became zealous and furnished his Government with an admirable report on technical education in Germany. Once more he suffered reduction in rank. From then on he did nothing to remind his Government of his existence and his promotion was steady and rapid.[6] William F. Draper, American Ambassador to Italy, gives a somewhat similar opinion. In his autobiography he writes: "I learned later that initiative in a diplomat is not a desirable quality; that in large matters an ambassador is expected to be what some one has called a clerk at the end of a wire; and that in small ones he is liked better if he uses his own judgment without bothering the Department with detail." [7] The master diplomat, Talleyrand, in giving advice to young diplomats invariably cautioned, "Surtout pas trop de zèle."

In the United States where appointments to important ambassadorial posts are quite often based upon political services rather than upon proper qualification, perhaps there is some excuse for this lack of confidence. When William G. Sharp, a small-town newspaper owner, was appointed Ambassador to France to relieve Myron T. Herrick in the critical period of World War I, he knew no French, little of France, and had had no experience whatsoever with diplomatic matters except for his service as member of the Congressional Committee on Foreign Affairs. Even Mr. Morgenthau, a man thoroughly conversant with world affairs, regretted that a new ambassador has only a month to become acquainted with the duties of his post and to receive his instructions.[8]

Perhaps another excuse for the failure of ministries of foreign affairs to accept recommendations of their diplomatic representatives is the fact that in democratic governments the parliamentary bodies must oftentimes be consulted or at least pass upon the proposals. If the matter requires secrecy the best solution sometimes is to drop the whole affair. On the other hand, an able diplomat confident that he is right can sometimes overrule the policy of the foreign office. Ambassador Page by a threat of resignation was largely instrumental in compelling the United States Department of State to relinquish its attempt to persuade Great Britain to accept the Declaration of London after the outbreak of war.[9]

It is not unusual for the foreign office to ignore outspoken convictions of their envoy which actually contravene the avowed foreign policy of the appointing country. Making speeches innocuous to all parties concerned is one of the most exacting yet important duties of a diplomat, but

[6] R. H. Bruce Lockhart, *British Agent* (New York and London, 1933), 279.

[7] W. F. Draper, *Recollections of a Varied Career* (New York, 1908), 281.

[8] Henry Morgenthau, *All in a Life-Time* (New York and London, 1922), 174.

[9] Burton J. Hendrick, *Life and Letters of Walter H. Page* (New York, 1923), III, 187.

the danger inherent in such casual commitments is apparent. Shortly after the war when our Ambassador to France, Myron T. Herrick, was asked to dedicate a memorial to French and American soldiers, who had fallen at the last great battle of Champagne, he took the occasion to criticize the prevailing American attitude towards reparations and to declare that the obligation of the American people did not cease with the Armistice. Several American newspapers thereupon announced that the Ambassador had been disavowed by the State Department, others declared that his recall would be demanded. Secretary of State Hughes merely explained that the views expressed by Herrick were his own and that the speech did not mean any change in the attitude of the American Government.[10]

If a diplomatic representative objects seriously to the policy of his home government he should resign. The Japanese Envoy to France in 1938, Ambassador Sugimura, opposed the Japanese Government's policy of alliance with Germany and the extension of military operations to South China. Ambassador Sugimura requested a furlough which was granted. The American career diplomat, Hugh Wilson, declares that an envoy is like an attorney; he does his best to persuade his government to follow a given course. If he fails and the course is flagrantly against his conscience he must resign. If he remains he must do his best to carry out his government's policy.[11]

The Function of Negotiation.   The duties of a diplomatic agent have often been summarized by these three words: to negotiate, to observe, and to protect. But before a diplomat is in a position to do any of these things properly he should be familiar with the treaties between the two countries, the correspondence of his predecessors, in fact, with all documentary material essential to a complete understanding of his position. He must familiarize himself with the written instructions from his government to previous diplomatic officers, as well as remember at all times the special instructions to himself.

The first and most important duty of a diplomatic representative is to maintain friendly relations with the country to which he is accredited. The maintenance of peace is a vital requirement and he should bend every effort to achieve it. Charles de Martens in his *Diplomatic Guide* emphasizes the importance of this task: "The public minister must never lose sight of the fact that it is his duty at all times to act as a minister of peace; the maintenance of friendly relations must be the constant object of his efforts ... if a misunderstanding of any sort exists between the two governments he must strive to dissipate the clouds, remove prejudices, justify his government against any accusations which may be brought against it and make any necessary complaints with the greatest possible

10 T. Bentley Mott, *Myron T. Herrick, Friend of France* (New York, 1929), 270-3.
11 Hugh Wilson, *Education of a Diplomat* (New York, 1938), 57.

moderation." [12] Or, to quote the very apt phrase of Choiseul: "La véritable finesse est la vérité dite quelquefois avec force toujours avec grace." Perhaps however it should be added that a clumsy lie—*mentir bêtement*—is the unforgivable sin in diplomacy.

In carrying on the duties of his mission the envoy must always support the foreign policy of his country even though it may not be pleasing to the government to which he is accredited. But in maintaining the dignity of his country, he must make every effort to justify its position. "He must join suppleness of negotiation to vigor of objectives. His motto should be the one expressed by the Baron de Martens: *'Fortiter in re, suaviter in modo.'* "

One of the outstanding examples in American diplomacy of a foreign representative exercising his influence in the maintenance of friendly relations under the most trying circumstances is the remarkable work of Charles Francis Adams, American Minister to Great Britain during the Civil War. Again and again by his calm and judicious presentation of the position of the North he was able to avert a rupture. Some of Secretary Seward's instructions were so bellicose and threatening that if delivered verbatim they would have brought about war "before the carriage of the American Minister had rattled out of Downing Street." [13] It was fortunate that Lord Lyons, British Minister at Washington, was equally desirous of keeping the peace, a statesman who has been called "one of the peace-makers of the world." In fact, Lyons in a personal letter to the Governor General of Canada declared: "My mind is almost unremittingly employed in devising means to maintain the peace." [14]

During the First World War when Great Britain was guilty of innumerable violations of American neutrality, the superb diplomatic ability of Ambassador Page helped to keep the United States from becoming seriously involved. An excellent example of his clever technique occurred in the case of the *Dacia*. Appreciating the fact that if the vessel were to be seized by the British it would add fuel to the already inflamed state of Anglo-American commercial relations, he arranged that the French, rather than the British, should seize this vessel; although the result was exactly the same the psychology of the situation was quite different, and what had been a serious threat to friendly relations by the British was taken as a normal belligerent action on the part of the French.

A more recent example of success in a difficult position was afforded by the conduct of Ambassador John W. Davis, who was the American representative at London after the Senate of the United States refused to

[12] Charles de Martens, *Guide diplomatique* (Leipzig, 1866), I, 169.

[13] See particularly the Despatch No. 10 of May 21, 1861, *U.S. Messages and Documents 1861-1862*, 88. The whole period is exhaustively treated in E. D. Adams, *Great Britain and the American Civil War*, 2 vols. (New York, 1925).

[14] R. B. Mowat, *The Diplomatic Relations of Great Britain and the United States* (New York and London, 1925), 168, 171.

ratify the Treaty of Versailles. "According to associates of that period he succeeded to a remarkable degree, preserving his own dignity and that of the government he represented while never faltering in his devotion to the invalid in the White House." [15]

Observation and the Preparation of Reports.   A diplomat must observe with an intelligent and unprejudiced viewpoint everything that takes place about him and report fully and accurately whatever might interest his government at home. The *Foreign Service Regulations of the United States* emphasize the fact that the submission of political reports is a duty which rests primarily upon diplomatic officers. In preparing political reports the diplomatic representative must have in view certain objectives such as giving the Department of State a general idea of the political situation in the country with particular reference to the relations of the United States with that country and at the same time furnish conclusions useful to the Department in formulating its policy. The diplomatic representative must also furnish information regarding all negotiations and report any action taken in the furtherance of American interests or the protection of American nationals.[16]

Necessarily the subjects of these reports will be exceedingly varied. Political questions will naturally take first place and the foreign office has a right to expect a full and unbiased account of all political questions which might in any way affect the relations between the two countries. Particular emphasis should be placed upon the attitude of the press and public opinion abroad as it relates to American foreign policy. Nor is it sufficient to relate the bare facts. A good diplomat should attempt to interpret the facts to the best of his ability. Baron Szilassy, a career diplomat, has well expressed this idea: "There are some diplomats who believe that their task is accomplished when they have enumerated the facts exactly, reported their conversations faithfully; they never give an opinion without being invited to do so. We do not agree with this method of approach, and believe on the contrary that if it is important to give a detailed account of interesting events it is even more important to evaluate them justly, and a government has the right to demand this of a man of judgment and experience." [17]

But in addition to the facts and their interpretation the envoy must describe the public men with whom he deals, evaluate their abilities and

[15] T. A. Huntley, *John W. Davis* (New York, 1924), 117.

As an illuminating instance of an ambassador's failure to prevent war one might cite the case of British Ambassador Sir Neville Henderson, in his relations with Hitler and von Ribbentrop. He frankly entitled his account of the affair, *Failure of a Mission.*

[16] *Foreign Service Regulations of the United States of America* (Washington, 1945), VI, 1, Note 22.

[17] J. de Szilassy, *Traité pratique de diplomatie moderne* (Paris, 1928), 160.

influence. He should give a clear picture of the diplomatic scene, the relative merits of his colleagues and their respective influence and importance. In some cases even gossip and trivialities are of value in diplomatic reports. The Kaiser was so incensed at von Donnersmarck, his envoy at Copenhagen, because he was unwilling to report frivolities that he was sent back from Denmark to Weimar.[18]

The *United States Regulations* suggest that it is very helpful if diplomatic officers prepare a *Who's Who* of important persons in different countries and their attitude towards the United States. The resources of the country, its foreign and domestic commerce, its military and naval developments are all grist for the diplomat's mill. In these days when political events are so largely conditioned by economic phenomena the diplomatic representative must let no financial or economic trend escape his attention. The American Ambassador to Russia at the time of the Bolshevik Revolution, David R. Francis, declared that his experience strengthened his opinion that friendly diplomatic relations could be engendered and fostered and promoted by close commercial relations. He felt that the ordinary policy of leaving commercial matters entirely to the consular service was a mistake and he devoted much time and thought to cultivating direct commercial relations between the United States and Russia.[19]

President Theodore Roosevelt wanted information on every possible subject from his diplomatic representatives abroad and every important matter had to be reported with the greatest detail. In fact, certain legations found their principal work was the compiling of reports upon sociological, economic, and financial matters.[20] Ambassador Page while in London regarded it as his duty to collect information and impressions, to discover what important people thought of the United States and its policies and to send forward all such data to Washington. He called himself "a listening post on the front of diplomacy." [21]

The older writers on diplomacy paid a great deal of attention to the form and content of these *dépêches*. Meisel in his excellent work entitled *Cours de style diplomatique* has given very careful consideration to this subject: "The public minister will relate simply and naturally all the information that he obtains during the course of a negotiation and whether he is making a report essentially historical or whether he is merely expressing his opinion, he will avoid all recondite expressions and all rhetorical efforts, remembering well that it is not his function to persuade but rather to make a clear exposition of the matter . . . he will choose the clearest expressions and the most exact to express his ideas,

---

[18] Egan, *op. cit.*, 247.
[19] David R. Francis, *Russia from the American Embassy* (New York, 1921), 25.
[20] Egan, *op. cit.*, 223, 235.
[21] Hendrick, *op. cit.*, I, 361.

and to retrace the facts as they have occurred; clarity is much to be preferred to prolixity." [22]

In every case where the report contains the translation of a document or a newspaper article or political discourse the envoy will do well to enclose a copy in the original language. Despatches are ordinarily in the form of telegrams or letters. The envoy must decide which form should be used. Usually the majority of reports will be regular despatches prepared to catch the mail boat or mail train but when emergencies arise the diplomat should not hesitate to use the telegraph. On occasions a brief résumé of the situation can be telegraphed and fuller details reserved for letters following. Sometimes the envoy uses telegrams when he feels that his written communications do not receive the proper attention at the foreign office. Upon occasions the envoy has even been compelled to make use of a foreign press correspondent whose despatches to his newspaper would most certainly be read by the foreign minister before the official telegrams of the envoy.

With the recent great expansion of the interest of the United States in world affairs there has come an increasing demand on the part of the Washington agencies for the services of the reporting facilities of Foreign Service officers. In order to provide a more flexible and adequate reporting service an Executive Order was issued June 4, 1951, which requires reporting to be of "substantial" interest to the United States. By comparing the needs of Washington agencies with the facilities of the various posts reporting machinery it is hoped to meet informational requirements at home with a minimum of waste effort abroad.

Lack of Coöperation between Foreign Offices and Envoys.   It seems to be a common feeling on the part of ambassadors and ministers that the foreign offices pay too little attention to their despatches. Robert Underwood Johnson while Ambassador to Italy, although he endeavored to send the Department only the most significant information, complained that hardly ever did he receive even the response of acknowledgment.[23] Miles Poindexter, former American Ambassador to Peru, once told the writer that if the State Department had paid the slightest attention to his despatches the United States would never have proposed a plebiscite as a means of settling the Tacna Arica dispute. Ambassador Page became so incensed at the little attention paid to his telegrams that he threatened to send a despatch saying that an earthquake had swallowed up the Thames, that a suffragette had kissed the King, and that the statue of Cromwell had made an assault against the House of Lords, to see if anybody would decipher it.[24]

[22] August Heinrich Meisel, *Cours de style diplomatique* (Paris, 1826), II, 301.
[23] Robert Underwood Johnson, *Remembered Yesterdays* (Boston, 1923), 556.
[24] Hendrick, *op. cit.*, I, 239.

On the other hand, the diplomatic representative is not always kept fully informed of important developments or events which are vital to the proper performance of his duties. A famous instance of this sort occurred in connection with William Trescot's attempt to bring about a fair settlement of the War of the Pacific. When Secretary Frelinghuysen succeeded Secretary Blaine, a change of policy was inaugurated but Mr. Trescot was not informed. It was only from the Chilean foreign minister that he learned that new instructions had been issued and they were already in the hands of the Chilean Government. His surprise and chagrin may easily be imagined.[25] Ambassador Francis tells that on one occasion when he made an address to the Russian people upon his own responsibility he learned of the State Department's approval two months later through a newspaper clipping sent to him by Mr. Morris, the American Minister to Sweden.[26]

The officer in the field is always at a disadvantage when he questions in the slightest degree the omniscience or the justice of any action of the Department. When Foreign Service Officer Beaulac sent in a second request for leave pointing out that he had been on the job for eighteen months including most Sundays and holidays with a single week-end away from his post, the Department replied it had no record of the week-end leave and would he kindly report the exact dates and henceforth notify the Department promptly when he did go on leave.[27]

Maintaining the Secrecy of Despatches. The question of preserving the secrecy of the despatch is sometimes an important element and the envoy must decide how the despatch should be sent to meet most satisfactorily the situation which he faces. Even when sent in code if the message goes via foreign cables the envoy cannot be sure that it will not be copied and deciphered by experts trained in this work. It was the Japanese claim that due to the activities of the "American Black Chamber" which decoded all cables sent by Washington embassies to their governments Charles Evans Hughes knew in advance that the Japanese delegation to the Washington Conference of 1922 had been instructed to yield on the famous 5-5-3 ratio.[28]

During World War I even the most elaborate codes and ciphers were penetrated by enemy experts. According to Major H. O. Yardley, American cryptographer during the war, Great Britain was able to read every code telegram that was transmitted over her cables.[29] The United States again broke the Japanese code before Pearl Harbor and knew in advance

25 Graham H. Stuart, *Latin America and the United States* (New York, 1943), 433.
26 Francis, *op. cit.*, 232.
27 Willard L. Beaulac, *Career Ambassador* (New York, 1951), 66.
28 Drew Pearson, and Robert S. Allen, "The Washington Merry Go Round," *San Francisco Chronicle* (November 18, 1934).
29 Herbert O. Yardley, *The American Black Chamber* (New York, 1931), 219.

the terms of the proposals presented by the two Japanese Envoys in Washington.

Even in peace time the problem of maintaining the secrecy of diplomatic communications sometimes arises. On one occasion when the Sultan of Turkey wished to get an answer to a message which he had sent indirectly to a former American Minister to Turkey he asked that the answer be sent in a letter to the chief dragoman of the American Legation who would deliver it to the Sultan through the hands of a special court chamberlain.[30] Even in the United States there have been occasions when the diplomatic representative has been invited to write a private letter to the Secretary of State lest his official despatches be read by persons who were not sufficiently discreet.[31] Henry Lane Wilson while Minister to Chile during the Spanish-American War worked out a code system to be used between the diplomatic and consular offices in South America which was of great value in maintaining surveillance of ships of all nationalities entering South American ports.[32]

Relations with the Press. It goes without saying that a diplomat should always be on the friendliest relations possible with the foreign correspondents of the newspapers of his own country. They can be of inestimable use to him and their ill will can do him considerable harm. Henry Lane Wilson goes so far as to recommend that newspapers choose their foreign correspondents very carefully so that they may not misinterpret the acts of a minister and thereby lower his prestige with the government to which he is accredited and at the same time impair his usefulness.[33] In fact, diplomats have been known to speak of press correspondents as their "colleagues of the press." The United States *Instructions* emphasize the fact that "good relations with press correspondents, and especially with those representing the American press are of the greatest importance in that they are close followers of the political situation and are often able to put inquiries and obtain information which could not be obtained discreetly by the diplomatic mission."[34]

As regards the press of the country to which he is accredited the envoy must necessarily exercise the greatest discretion. Sometimes it is advisable to give interviews; on occasions the representative must object to the implication of statements which reflect upon his country's foreign policy or he may deny outright misstatements of fact. Usually, however, the

[30] Cortissoz, *op. cit.,* II, 158.

[31] Herbert W. Bowen, *Recollections Diplomatic and Undiplomatic* (New York, 1926), 243.

[32] Henry Lane Wilson, *Diplomatic Episodes in Mexico, Belgium and Chile* (New York, 1927), 50.

[33] Wilson, *op. cit.,* 186.

[34] *Instructions, op. cit.,* VIII, 6-b.

diplomat finds it advisable to pass over in silence attacks in the press unless they are so violent as absolutely to require his attention.

Sometimes a diplomatic representative seems to have no realization of the position of the press in the country to which he is sent. An excellent example of this is cited by Poultney Bigelow. The German Ambassador to the United States, Dr. von Holleben, came to him and in all seriousness asked for his assistance to purchase the good will or at least the silence of the *New York Herald* in regard to the Emperor of Germany.

He seemed much astonished to learn that the private income of the proprietor of the *Herald* was probably greater than that of William II and was somewhat offended that Bigelow regarded the proposal as a joke.[35] George Seldes, a well known American newspaperman, found that the American press in Mexico City during the Calles administration was antigovernment, therefore all the news was colored by this sentiment. He felt that if the newly appointed American Ambassador, Mr. Morrow, was to succeed in his policy of good will, the newspaper attitude would have to be changed accordingly.[36]

Ambassador William E. Dodd while representing the United States in Germany during the Hitler regime thought very highly of the press representatives. They were realistic and honest in their approach to foreign affairs and he respected and used their information. On one occasion a correspondent of the Associated Press saved the American ambassador in a European capital from a most embarrassing situation by informing him of the death of President McKinley just ten minutes before the doyen of the diplomatic corps came to offer his condolences. The despatch from the State Department giving the information arrived several hours later.

At times the diplomatic envoy must parry all requests of correspondents for information. Sir Ronald Lindsay, British Ambassador to the United States, when calling to discuss with Secretary Hull the bombing of United States and British gunboats by the Japanese evaded all questions of the reporters. When one finally wanted to know if the Ambassador could think of any other question that they might ask, the Ambassador replied in the negative and then smiling asked if they could think of any more evasive answers that he might have given.

Information Services. Since World War II the United States has established in most foreign capitals press attachés whose duty it is to keep in close touch with the local press, furnish press releases, and prepare summaries of the pertinent news in the press of the country. But in addi-

[35] Poultney Bigelow, *Prussian Memories, 1864-1914* (New York and London, 1915), 140.
[36] George Seldes, *You Can't Print That* (New York, 1929), 348.

tion to the customary informational press activities the United States has seen the need to employ additional means to publicize its foreign policy and to combat the sinister propaganda which has been such a successful adjunct of Soviet aggression. The present information program of the United States currently known as a "Campaign of Truth" utilizes the informational sources of press, radio, and motion pictures as well as the exchange of persons. It utilizes the services of 147 Information Centers in sixty different countries. The United States Information and Education Service program as it is called requires a larger budget and more personnel than any other function of our Foreign Service activities. Of the 269 Foreign Service missions maintained by the United States abroad 156 perform special informational activities in addition to other duties.

The press activities of the United States Information and Education Service includes the distribution throughout the world of news materials, feature articles, booklets and other publications. Pictures and posters are sent to some 10,000 foreign newspapers and periodicals. The weekly *Air Bulletin* with its digest of United States news and the *Press Features* with special articles, both published in the United States, have a world wide circulation. Documentary films presenting every phase of American life with captions and texts in thirty-four different languages are shown in United States Information Centers and also in traveling motor vehicles.

The Voice of America is broadcast in some forty-four languages every hour of the day and night and it now reaches practically every part of the world. Transcriptions are made and distributed by the Information Officers and heard by hundreds of thousands of listeners. The libraries of the United States maintained abroad and the exchange of professors and students are long range procedures which are increasingly productive of reciprocal appreciation and understanding.[37]

The Cultural Attaché.   The so-called "cultural attaché" is a vital part of this program of understanding. Unfortunately this term has been discarded for the broader and more nondescript title "public affairs officer." This term might include an information officer or press attaché or a cultural relations specialist. The informational and cultural services are sometimes combined but there is a vast field for the cultural attaché far removed from the normal functions of the press attaché. He must be grounded in the literature, music, and art of his own country and of the country of his post. He must be conversant with the social and natural sciences and be at least familiar with medical and engineering developments. All phases of education, the schools, the colleges and universities, the techniques of teaching, the methods of research and the library

[37] See the excellent article "The New Arm of Diplomacy" by Richard L. Brecker, in *Foreign Service Journal* (August, 1951), 23-9.

facilities both at home and abroad are a part of his domain. But above all he must be interested vitally in the basic well being of the people and achieve understanding and mutual appreciation on both the social and intellectual level.[38]

The outstanding success of Cultural Officer E. Wilder Spaulding in Vienna shows the great possibilities of this type of diplomacy. By their many and varied contacts Dr. and Mrs. Spaulding were able not only to bring home to the Austrians an appreciation and understanding of the position of the United States in the occupation of Austria but to bring about a more friendly attitude towards the occupying forces.

The Making of Speeches. The foreign envoy is constantly called upon to make addresses and upon such occasions he must be very careful to avoid mentioning political issues which are being discussed either at home or abroad. The *Foreign Service Regulations* of the United States recommend that a Foreign Service officer should as far as possible avoid making public speeches but when he finds this impossible he must transmit a copy of his address by despatch to the Department of State.[39] However, a diplomat can often do much to enhance his country's prestige and to explain its position by public appearances. General Horace Porter, Ambassador to France from 1897 to 1905, could speak fluent French and never passed up an opportunity to express the good will of the United States towards France in public addresses. According to his daughter, General Porter not only disregarded the stereotyped instructions of the State Department discouraging speech-making on the part of diplomats but in fact spared no pains in making the most of his chances.[40] Prince Lichnowsky, the German Ambassador to Britain before World War I was so successful in creating good feeling between the two countries that his French colleague was instructed to counteract his "propaganda" by appearing more frequently at public functions.[41]

At the Court of St. James's where no language barrier exists, the American ambassador is under constant pressure to make public addresses. Ambassador John Hay is said to have spent the greater part of his time in declining invitations to dine and speak, whereas his successor, Joseph Choate, a remarkably effective after dinner speaker, became "a British lecturer at large." Every American ambassador makes his first public address in Great Britain before the Pilgrims Society and Ambassador John W. Davis unquestionably enhanced his own reputation and the prestige of the United States by his brilliant address before this body.

[38] See the well written essay *The Cultural Attaché* by Howard Lee Nostrand, Hazen pamphlet No. 17 (New Haven, Conn.); also Merrill Cody's "The Work of the Cultural Relations Attaché," *Department of State Bulletin* (April 1, 1945), 574.

[39] *Regulations, op. cit.* (October, 1945), 1-14.

[40] Elsie Porter Mende, *An American Soldier and Diplomat* (New York, 1927), 233.

[41] Prince Lichnowsky, *Heading for the Abyss* (New York, 1928), 39.

On the other hand George Harvey, a caustic, witty, but politically minded Ambassador, was constantly criticized for allusions in his public addresses. Determined to make one speech which could not be criticized he chose as his subject "Women's Souls" and facetiously tried to prove they had none. Unfortunately his British audience seemed to lack a sense of humor and this address received the most bitter criticism of all. More recently the American Minister to Canada, James H. R. Cromwell, was officially criticized for an address violating his instructions and the neutrality policy of the United States. His resignation was accepted shortly afterwards.

One of the most famous public addresses by an American diplomat to outline United States foreign policy was made by Ambassador Joseph Grew before the America-Japan Society in Tokyo in the fall of 1939. This speech "direct from the horse's mouth" warned the Japanese Government that the United States well understood "Japan's new Order in East Asia" and objected strongly to it. It had a profound repercussion throughout Japan.

Rarely have public addresses by an ambassador abroad been utilized more effectively in support of his country's foreign policy than those made by United States Ambassador James Clement Dunn in Italy in his successful efforts to combat communism after World War II. He explained in countless prepared and extemporaneous speeches delivered in Italy before large public audiences and small groups of influential persons the motives of friendship and humanity that underlay the policy of the American people in setting up the various relief programs. He visited factories and farm areas and talked to artisans and farmers. He met American supply ships and from their decks spoke to the people crowding the docks. He visited towns where housing projects had been constructed with American funds and participated in the ceremonies. In some hill towns of the Abruzzi, accompanied by Mrs. Dunn, he was invited to hand over the keys of the completed apartments in ceremonies where the entire population of the area participated. From these areas no Communist senators or deputies were sent to the Italian Parliament.

The Protection of Nationals.   One of the duties which all governments require of their diplomatic representatives in foreign lands is the protection of nationals whose rights have been abused by local authorities. De Garden in his classic *Traité complet de diplomatie* declares that certainly one of the most honorable and most useful functions of the minister is to defend carefully and favor the interests of his fellow citizens in the country to which he is accredited. "But the foreign envoy must not furnish his assistance and his support to his nationals except after they have had recourse in vain through regular channels to the local authorities to obtain justice. The public minister must also use prudence, tact and moderation in the questions that he is called upon to settle." [42] The United States in its *Regulations* makes it an essential requirement in all cases that the right of a citizen to claim protection is founded upon the correlative right of the United States to claim his allegiance and support. The instructions also require a careful examination into the applicant's grievances. If the complaints are well founded the diplomatic representative should interpose firmly but with courtesy and moderation with the appropriate authorities and report the case to the Department of State for its further action if any be required. [43]

At times the diplomatic representative protects a national at great danger to his own safety. The American Minister to Nicaragua in 1853, Solon Borland, in order to save an American accused of murder from mob violence seized a rifle from a bystander and although hit by a broken bottle held the crowd at bay. That night when a group of armed men threatened to seize the prisoner, Minister Borland again was able to protect him.

In a famous case of protection of a naturalized American citizen in Morocco when President Theodore Roosevelt interposed personally with a much quoted instruction sent to the American consul in Tangier "Perdicaris alive or Raisuli dead" it was subsequently ascertained that at the time of the ultimatum Perdicaris was a Greek subject rather than an American citizen.

An extreme case of protection occurred during the Boer War when Secretary of State Hay requested Ambassador Choate in London to attempt to secure the release of Americans who had served against the British in the Boer War even though such individuals had forfeited all rights of protection.

A naturalized American named Van Jennings, while in the United States, published attacks against President Estrada Cabrera of Guatemala. When subsequently he returned to Guatemala he was arrested and tried for conspiracy against the President's life. He appealed to the American Chargé d'Affaires, Hugh Wilson. The latter went to the President and obtained his promise to pardon Van Jennings after his condemnation providing Mr. Wilson would see to it that Van Jennings would leave on the first ship. When Van Jennings was pardoned Wilson met him at the prison door and had the American Military attaché escort him to the port and place him on board the American vessel in the harbor. [44]

An interesting case of protection occurred during the German occupation of Paris in World War II. An American woman, Mrs. Etta Shiber, disappeared from her apartment in Paris. Foreign Service Officer Edwin A. Plitt of the American Embassy investigated and found that she had

---

[42] Paul Fauchille, *Traité de droit international public* (Paris, 1926), I, Part iii, 53.
[43] *Regulations, op. cit.* (May, 1945), XXI, 4.
[44] Hugh Wilson, *Education of a Diplomat* (New York, 1938), 52.

left with two Germans. He made a personal search and when the trail led to the *Cherche-Midi* prison he entered by a ruse and talked the commandant into bringing out the files. Whether intentionally or not he was permitted to note that Mrs. Shiber's name appeared, so he made a formal demand for her release. Ten days later she was released but when contrary to instructions she returned to her apartment she was again arrested and put on trial for assisting in the escape of British soldiers in the occupied zone. Plitt obtained a lawyer for her defence and was then astounded to learn that she claimed her activities had been according to instructions from Mr. Plitt of the American Embassy. At first the Germans demanded Plitt's recall but when the accusation was shown to be false Mrs. Shiber was condemned to life imprisonment. The Department of State later exchanged a German spy Johanna Hoffman under sentence in the United States for Mrs. Shiber.

In the period of the so-called cold war with communism the United States has often been called upon to protect American nationals in countries 'behind the iron curtain.' The case of Robert A. Vogeler, an American official of the International Telephone and Telegraph Company who was arrested in Hungary, became a *cause célèbre*. He was seized and after months of harsh treatment forced to sign a false confession of spying and sentenced to fifteen years imprisonment. The United States diplomatic representatives in Budapest and Vienna made the strongest representations but to no avail. It was only after a campaign of pitiless publicity in the press of the United States, largely procured through the efforts of his wife, that Vogeler was released after seventeen months of imprisonment, and then only by the payment by the United States of what was equivalent to a very substantial ransom. The United States, which in reprisal had closed Hungarian Consulates in Cleveland and New York and banned American travel in Hungary, agreed to permit the Consulates to reopen, to permit Americans to travel in Hungary and in addition to restore some $70,000,000 worth of Hungarian property held in the American zone of Germany.

The case of William N. Oatis, Associated Press correspondent, seized upon equally flimsy accusations in Czechoslovakia, may become an even more notable case. He was not permitted to talk with any representative of the United States Embassy and was condemned to ten years imprisonment by a Czechoslovak court in violation of the most elementary rules of justice. The United States protested vigorously and banned Czech air flights over Western Germany in retaliation, but Oatis still remains incarcerated in Czechoslovakia.

International Claims.   The annals of diplomacy are full of interesting cases which fall under the heading of protection of the property of nationals. According to John W. Foster, "No other branch of international relations presents to the American diplomatic representative such a fruitful source of embarrassment as the private claims of his countrymen against the government to which he is accredited." [45] Although very successful in arranging for the settlement of claims, Josephus Daniels declared that claims were the most bothersome part of diplomacy in Mexico and cited the case of one consular officer who resigned because he was "tired of being a debt collector." [46] The more important cases of this sort are referred to claims commissions or arbitration tribunals.[47] In this connection an interesting incident arose when Secretary of State Hay asked Ambassador Choate, then representing the United States in London, to serve as counsel for the United States before the tribunal to which the Alaska Boundary case was to be referred. Choate refused on the ground that it was incompatible with his position as Ambassador to take an active part in the procedure, but agreed to give any other assistance in his power. The State Department was not particularly pleased at his refusal.[48] In the famous Venezuela Claims case the American Minister, Herbert W. Bowen, was given plenary powers to represent Venezuela by President Castro authorizing him to effect a settlement of the claim with the diplomatic representatives at Washington of the claimant powers, or the preliminaries of such claims as were to be submitted to The Hague for arbitration. Mr. Bowen proceeded to Washington and settled some of the claims and had the rest referred to The Hague Tribunal.[49]

The instructions to American diplomatic officers do not permit the envoy to intervene without specific authority if the claim is founded on contract. Even in cases of tort unless the necessity is urgent it is expected that the diplomatic agent will communicate with the Department of State before acting. Aliens preferring claims against the United States must present them through their governments' diplomatic representatives in Washington.

Sometimes, it must be confessed, a stronger power will flagrantly abuse the right of protecting its nationals in its dealing with a weaker one. The Government of Haiti arrested a certain Luders, born of a German father and a Haitian mother. He sought aid from the German Legation. The German Chargé d'Affaires demanded that he be liberated, that an indemnity be paid and the officials who arrested him be punished. Inasmuch as the matter was pending and Luders was Haitian according to local law, the Government of Haiti insisted that justice be permitted to take

[45] John W. Foster, *The Practice of Diplomacy* (New York, 1906), 359.

[46] Josephus Daniels, *Shirtsleeve Diplomat* (Chapel Hill, N.C., 1947).

[47] For extensive treatment of this subject see J. B. Moore, *Digest of International Law* (Washington, 1906), VI, Ch. 21, "Arbitrations," *passim;* C. C. Hyde, *International Law* (Boston, 1922), I, 472-538.

[48] E. S. Martin, *Life of Joseph H. Choate* (New York, 1920), II, 220-2; see also W. R. Thayer, *Life and Letters of John Hay* (New York, 1915), II, 212.

[49] Bowen, *op. cit.*, 257-73.

its course. Thereupon Germany broke off diplomatic relations, sent two warships to Port-au-Prince, asked an indemnity of $30,000 and an apology, and if this were not forthcoming, the city would be bombarded. Haiti could do nothing other than agree to the odious conditions which had been imposed.[50]

While he was American Minister to China, Paul S. Reinsch had occasion to demand a substantial indemnity for a young American teacher who was murdered while ascending the Yangtse river in a small boat with two companions who were also seriously wounded. Since it was alleged that the Chinese assailants wore uniforms, the Chinese Government finally agreed to pay $25,000 as indemnity. A little later an American driving his car recklessly killed an old Chinese woman in the streets of Peking. The American Minister had the American driver pay $300 to the woman's relatives.[51] The Chinese Minister of Foreign Affairs did not fail to call Minister Reinsch's attention to the relative value of the two lives.

Protection of Individual Rights.   The Mexican Government, disgruntled because foreign representatives had been too officious in their protection of foreign property and foreign nationals in Mexico, decreed that foreign proprietors agree not to invoke the diplomatic protection of their Government, but consent to submit themselves as Mexicans to Mexican laws in all difficulties which might arise concerning their property. This was such a manifest denial of the rights of protection guaranteed by international law that the United States refused recognition of the Mexican Government until it was modified.[52]

The American diplomatic and consular representatives are constantly finding it necessary to protect American citizens who carelessly or thoughtlessly violate laws or regulations of foreign countries. A young American voyaging in the Mediterranean in his cabin cruiser got into waters listed by the Turks as naval reserves. He anchored, went on shore and raced up and down for exercise. He was seized, found to be without a passport upon him and thrown into jail as a spy. The American Embassy found out from *Who's Who* that his father was a prominent and wealthy American. The attention of the Turkish Government was called to the undesirable publicity and even ridicule with which the affair would be treated in the American press if the Turkish authorities had made a mistake, as they undoubtedly had. The Turkish Government, finding no incriminating documents and appreciating the point made by the American Embassy, released the young man.

Formerly the diplomatic representatives of the United States were

[50] *Revue générale de droit international public,* V, 103-16.
[51] Paul S. Reinsch, *An American Diplomat in China* (New York, 1922), 166-7.
[52] Stuart, *op. cit.,* 168-71.

constantly importuned by naturalized American citizens who having returned to the country of their birth had been inducted into military service. Before the Act of 1868, giving naturalized citizens abroad the same
protection as native citizens, a naturalized citizen was not regularly
protected against military service in his native country. Mr. Wheaton,
when Minister to Prussia, made that abundantly clear in the case of Mr.
Knoche, a naturalized American citizen forced into the Prussian army.[53]
Subsequently the United States made an effort even in these cases and
often was successful. John Bigelow cites several instances where he was
successful in France.[54] Andrew D. White got into one of his few disputes
with Bismarck over the case of a young Hebrew who had been arrested
in Alsace-Lorraine for trying to evade his military service.[55] The United
States was finally compelled to adopt the policy long followed by Great
Britain and, except in unusual instances, refuse protection as regards
military service to naturalized citizens returning to their native country.

Services Rendered to Nationals. In addition to protection, a diplomat
is called upon to render all sorts of services to his nationals some of which
he finds exceedingly tiresome. Certain duties such as issuing of passports,
solemnizing of marriages, aiding destitute nationals, are oftentimes specifically required of the diplomatic representative. But these are a very
small part of the services which he renders to his fellow citizens. Walter
H. Page gives an amusing picture of the scope of these duties while he was
Ambassador in London during the war years: "There are a dozen other
kinds of activities such as American marriages which they always want
the ambassador to attend; getting them out of jail when they are jugged;
looking after the American insane; helping Americans move the bones of
their ancestors; interpreting the income-tax law; receiving medals for
Americans; hearing American fiddlers, pianists, players; sitting for American sculptors and photographers, writing letters of introduction, getting
tickets to the House Gallery; getting seats in the Abbey; getting tickets to
the races, the art galleries, the House of Lords; ... people who present
books, women who wish to go to court ..." [56] One American father whose
son collected cigar bands wrote to Myron T. Herrick, the Ambassador of
the United States to France, asking him to send bands from cigars that had
been smoked by Foch, Poincaré, Briand, and Clemenceau. Herrick wrote
a personal reply expressing his regret at not being able to comply with
the request since Foch smoked a pipe, Poincaré cigarettes, Briand's cigars
were without bands and Clemenceau chewed tobacco.[57] However, perhaps the most surprising request ever made to an American ambassador

[53] Moore, *op. cit.*, III, 564.
[54] John Bigelow, *Retrospections of an Active Life* (New York, 1909), 406.
[55] *The Autobiography of Andrew D. White* (New York, 1905), 592-5.
[56] Hendrick, *op. cit.*, I, 160.
[57] T. Bentley Mott, *Myron T. Herrick, Friend of France* (New York, 1929), 148.

occurred upon the death of Queen Victoria when an enterprising American requested the Ambassador to obtain permission for him to embalm her body.

The Italian diplomat, Daniele Varé, famous both as an envoy and as a writer, tells how he was able at the same time to render a service to the Italian nation and please a number of Danish friends at his post. An Italian florist in Copenhagen had imported 2,000 lire worth of flowers from San Remo. New regulations issued by the Danish Government forbade the export of Danish kroner except with the consent of the Government and in this case even if consent should be given the flowers would be dead by the time proper arrangements could be made. When the florist came to Varé for help he solved the problem promptly by buying the entire consignment himself and distributing them to his Danish friends in the capital.

Presentation of American Women at European Courts. The duty of presenting American women at the courts of European royalty has always been a very thorny problem for American ambassadors to monarchical posts. According to long established custom it is the policy of the Department of State not to take any part in matters concerning the presentation of American citizens at foreign courts so the matter is left entirely to the discretion of the ambassadors and ministers. Inasmuch as the number to be presented is strictly limited and the number desirous of meeting royalty is very great, the position of the diplomat is an unhappy one. Political influence must be taken into consideration as much as social standing.

John Quincy Adams while Minister to Russia laid down very strict rules regarding court presentations and was caustic in his remarks concerning them. "The ambition of young Americans," he declared, "to crowd themselves upon European courts and into the company of nobility is a very ridiculous and not a very proud feature of their character. There is nothing in my estimation of things meaner than courting society when if admitted it is only to be despised. Yet such is this vicious appetite for great acquaintance and so little delicacy has it that an American minister abroad can preserve himself from sharing in the scramble which it excites only by adopting such rules as these." [58]

Secretary of State Seward in his instructions to Mr. Dayton, the American Minister to France in 1862, showed considerable resentment at the actions of certain Americans who were causing embarrassment to the American representative by their personal pretensions. Secretary Seward advised him that he should "rather introduce nobody, however justly distinguished, than let a question of fashion or ceremony appear in the

---

[58] C. F. Adams, *Memoirs of John Q. Adams*, II, 305.

records of the important period in which we are acting for the highest interests of our country and of humanity." [59]

Elihu B. Washburne, Minister to France during the period of the Franco-Prussian War, seemed to have appreciated the opportunity to present American ladies to the Empress. At his first presentation he introduced twenty-eight American ladies, more than any other nationality. He confessed that his electioneering experiences in nine congressional campaigns stood him in good part in remembering names. [60]

Arthur Sherburne Hardy, American Minister to Athens, tells that "it was in Greece that we began to encounter those perplexities growing out of the ambition of one's nationals to bask in the sun of royalty. . . . Armed with one of those letters from the State Department bespeaking for the bearer special courtesies and privileges, the American applicant presents his claim for an audience with the same easy assurance with which he adds to his belt the scalp of any notable object double-starred by Baedeker." [61]

Even the dress to be worn afforded complications. It is said that Ella Wheeler Wilcox wanted to be presented with a head dress of water lilies instead of three feathers and a veil, and made a touching but unavailing appeal to the Lord Chamberlain.

When Joseph P. Kennedy was named Ambassador to Great Britain in 1938 the problem had become so acute that he determined to do something about it. He conferred with the State Department, with his friend Senator Henry Cabot Lodge, Jr., with President Franklin D. Roosevelt, and with the court officials of Buckingham Palace. He pointed out that he had three hundred applications on his desk and the maximum number that he could recommend for presentation was about thirty and that was more than all other states together requested. One applicant had endorsements from five senators, thirteen representatives and five governors and was coming over merely to be presented. In reply to a letter from Senator Lodge to support a Boston girl's request for presentation Ambassador Kennedy declared that henceforth the only Americans to be presented at Buckingham Palace would come from the immediate families of American officials or from Americans living in Great Britain for business or professional reasons. This would cut the number to about a half dozen a year conforming to the custom of other countries and would relieve the pressure put upon the ambassador.

Diplomatic Assistance to Scholars. American diplomatic representatives can be and usually are of great assistance to scholars, scientists, archaeologists, and other investigators who need diplomatic support to

---

[59] Moore, *op. cit.*, IV, 571.
[60] E. B. Washburne, *Recollections of a Minister to France* (New York, 1899), I, 36.
[61] Arthur Sherburne Hardy, *Things Remembered* (New York, 1923), 123.

carry on their research projects. A research student may not work in the famous *Bibliothèque Nationale* in Paris without a letter of recommendation from his diplomatic representative. Poultney Bigelow points out that neither Prescott nor Washington Irving could have prosecuted their researches in the Spanish archives without diplomatic assistance. He gives James Russell Lowell, American Minister to Great Britain, credit for opening up the English archives to him.[62] The author when making a study of the international city of Tangier received most valuable assistance from Norman Armour, then Counselor at the Paris Embassy, and through his assistance was enabled to check certain confidential documents in the French Foreign Office archives. The subsequent work in Morocco would have been wholly impossible without the constant aid and coöperation of Maxwell Blake, the American diplomatic agent.

In certain areas of the world where archaeological investigators are interested or in countries where scientists are desirous of making surveys the coöperation of the diplomatic representative is an absolute requirement for success. Lloyd Griscom, while Secretary of Embassy in Constantinople, was constantly approached by archaeologists who wished permission to excavate in various parts of the Turkish Empire. One who had spent his life collecting references to the Golden Calf was now determined to find it.[63]

Diplomats Improve Commercial Relations.   American diplomatic representatives are instructed to give a certain amount of assistance to legitimate American commercial interests. In extending such aid the envoy is cautioned to avoid discrimination between competing American interests and to see to it that such assistance is consistent with his other duties and with his diplomatic character. Such assistance normally may include aid in the establishment of contacts, the giving of information and the making of judicious suggestions, but officers must carefully avoid acting as intermediaries or participating in private business transactions or taking responsibility for decisions of the private American interests concerned.

One of the reasons for the recognition of Soviet Russia in 1933 was the need to improve commercial relations between the United States and Russia. Ambassador Joseph Davies, ably assisted by Foreign Service Officers Loy Henderson, George Kennan, and Elbridge Durbrow, after strenuous efforts, succeeded finally in obtaining a trade agreement which raised by one-third the commitment of the Soviet Union for purchases of American goods.[64] Unfortunately, the outbreak of the war in Europe soon afterwards prevented the hoped for results.

[62] Bigelow, *op. cit.*, 164.
[63] Lloyd Griscom, *Diplomatically Speaking* (New York, 1940), 158.
[64] Joseph E. Davies, *Mission to Moscow* (New York, 1941), 176-8.

When George Messersmith was Ambassador to Cuba in 1942 he worked out an arrangement for the purchase of Cuba's entire sugar crop at a price mutually satisfactory and advantageous. The arrangement proved to be so sound and equitable that it was renewed for the two following years. When in 1946 and 1947 the Argentine Government was nationalizing all foreign owned industries, Ambassador Messersmith was able to prevent the Argentine Government from taking over the packing industry and the cement industry in which American capital was heavily invested by showing President Perón that such action would have a disastrous effect upon the already weakened financial structure of the country.

It is alleged that the reason that Emperor Haile Selassie purchased most of his silverware, furniture, and other household equipment in the United States was because his friend, the American Minister, recommended American products so effectively.

Extradition of Fugitives. The United States has treaties with most foreign countries for the extradition of fugitive criminals upon the demand of the state from which the fugitive has fled. Without such a treaty the United States does not regularly either surrender or request the surrender of a fugitive. When a case arises the President of the United States through the Secretary of State instructs the diplomatic representative to request the provisional arrest of the fugitive pending the receipt of the formal extradition papers. Such requests are regularly addressed to the foreign office of the state to which the criminal has fled. As a general rule the function of the diplomatic representative is of purely routine nature. However, there have been occasions where the American representative has had an excellent opportunity to use his ingenuity to bring about the extradition of a fugitive from justice.

One of the best examples of diplomatic finesse occurred in the case of Samuel Insull. It will be remembered that Mr. Insull, having been accused of and indicted for the crimes of embezzlement and larceny in connection with the Middle West Utility Company and the Mississippi Valley Utility Corporation, had fled to France. On October 7, 1932, the Department of State cabled the American Embassy in Paris requesting the provisional arrest and detention of Samuel Insull with a view to his extradition. When the embassy made the request it was informed unofficially that Mr. Insull had left for Italy on October 4. A few days later the State Department learned that Insull had been arrested in Athens and was being detained upon a technical inquiry into his identity and purpose in Greece but unless a request for extradition was made he would be released within twenty-four hours. Unfortunately although an extradition treaty with Greece had been signed and approved, ratifications had not been exchanged so the Greek Government could not extradite him nor keep him in custody. Venizelos, however, agreed to detain Insull in Greece until the extradition treaty was ratified. In the meantime the United States instructed the American Legation to take up Insull's passport but he refused to surrender it. On November 1, the exchange of ratifications occurred and on November 4, Insull was again arrested and provisionally detained. A new delay occurred due to the failure of the Governor of Illinois to make the request to the Department of State for a writ of extradition. As a result, the Greek Government became somewhat uncertain as to the intentions of the American Government, and it required very delicate diplomatic action to have Insull kept in custody.

The writ of extradition was finally applied for on November 15, and issued by President Hoover the same day. A certified copy of the papers was sent to the American Legation together with the extradition warrant. However, when the case was brought before the Athens Court of Appeals it was held that the charges were unproved and the request for extradition was denied. The United States thereupon cancelled Insull's passport and prepared to bring new charges. In the meantime Insull applied for Greek citizenship and declared his intention of exploiting Greek lignite mines and Macedonian coal mines. On August 26, 1933, a second request for extradition was made and Insull was again taken into custody. According to press reports the United States Legation submitted twenty-four volumes in Greek and English to support the extradition requests.[65] Again the Greek Court of Appeals refused extradition on the ground that proof of criminal intent was lacking. The United States thereupon in an exceedingly caustic note denounced the extradition treaty inasmuch as no further action under the treaty would be advisable.

It was now up to American Minister MacVeagh to obtain the expulsion of Insull without in any way committing his government or indicating that the United States had any further official interest in the matter. Minister MacVeagh knew that Greek law provided the means for expelling an alien by executive order for reasons of public interest upon the recommendation of the cabinet. The American Minister in a very discreet manner let the Premier know that the continued presence of Mr. Insull in Greece could not help but be an impediment to the desired cordial relations between the two countries. When the Greek Government replied that it would like to expel the fugitive but could not send him away legally to any other country the American Minister promised that either the cancellation of Insull's passport would be rescinded or he would be furnished with valid travel documents. Apparently the suggestions of the American representative were not disregarded, for a few weeks later the Greek Government notified Insull that he would have to leave Greece at the end of the month. Mr. Insull thereupon fled ingloriously to Turkey, but

65 *New York Times* (September 20, 1933).

his race was run. Due to the hurried ratification of an extradition treaty between the United States and Turkey, Robert P. Skinner, American Ambassador at Ankara, took the fugitive into custody. Diplomacy had succeeded where legal methods had failed.

In this case an additional duty devolved upon the American Embassy. To make certain of Mr. Insull's return to the United States, Burton Y. Berry, Third Secretary of the American Embassy, took custody of Insull for the Turkish Government and delivered him personally in Chicago into the hands of the United States Marshal for the Northern District of Illinois.

Another interesting example of clever diplomatic technique occurred earlier in connection with a case of irregular extradition. The Spanish authorities in Cuba, learning that a Cuban who had committed a murder in Havana was living in Florida, kidnapped him and brought him back to Cuba without the knowledge or consent of the United States. When Secretary of State Blaine learned of this highhanded procedure he cabled the American representative in Madrid, General Grubb, to have the fugitive returned to the United States. General Grubb's protest that the procedure was "illegal" seemed to have no effect on the Spanish Minister of Foreign Affairs.

At the suggestion of Secretary Blaine, General Grubb visited the Spanish Minister again the following day but this time declared the procedure was "irregular" since extradition was provided for just such cases. Since irregular methods are open to the suspicion of being unfriendly and a delicate situation already existed in Cuba, a friendly relationship between the two powers was particularly desirable. The American Envoy suggested thereupon that the execution be stayed, the criminal be returned to the United States and that a requisition for the return of the criminal be presented immediately to the United States through the Spanish diplomatic representative. The Spanish Minister yielded to the argument and a diplomatic conclusion to the incident was satisfactorily arranged.[66]

[66] Bowen, *op. cit.*, 164.

11

Diplomatic Duties—II

POLITICAL FUNCTIONS RELATING TO FOREIGN STATES

Relations with the Government to Which Envoy Is Accredited.   In all of his relations with the government to which he has been accredited the envoy must bear in mind constantly that the principal object of his mission is the maintenance of cordial relations between the two states. Therefore, the tone of all notes and communications to the foreign government must be courteous and all irritating or provoking expressions carefully avoided. An outstanding illustration of this requirement occurred early in American history when the British Minister, Francis James Jackson, took a very haughty tone in dealing with the American Secretary of State. He even went so far as to accuse the President and Secretary of State of deliberately formulating an agreement with his predecessor with full knowledge that this was contrary to the British Minister's instructions. Secretary of State Robert Smith, after denying the allegation, categorically informed Mr. Jackson that "such insinuations are inadmissible in the intercourse of a foreign minister with a government that understands what it owes itself." [1] When Jackson repeated his unwarranted assertions, the President dismissed him and published the correspondence.

It not infrequently happens that the original form of such notes is of an undiplomatic nature, and it is then the practice of some embassies to smooth down any uneven language before transmitting the document. One such occasion arose during the early part of World War I when Secretary Bryan was absent from the State Department and Mr. Lansing prepared a long communication to Ambassador Page in London which, before being sent, was shown to the British Ambassador to the United States, Sir Cecil Spring-Rice. The British representative declared that had the despatch gone as written it would have been tantamount to a declaration of war and that if, by any chance, the newspapers had got hold of it, as so often happened during the days of State Department disorganization, panic might have occurred. Despite the ameliorating

---

[1] Beckles Willson, *Friendly Relations* (Boston, 1934), 69-74.

influences of Colonel House and President Wilson, however, the note as actually sent was sufficiently caustic to inspire Sir Edward Grey, Foreign Secretary, to comment: "This reads as though they thought that they are still talking to George the Third." [2]

The sincerity of the foreign government must never be called into question. "Facts may be denied, deductions examined, disproved, and condemned, without just cause of offense; but no impeachment of the integrity of the government in its reliance on the correctness of its own views, can be permitted without a total forgetfulness of self-respect." [3] This was written before the civilized world had to deal with the churlish boors of Soviet Russia.

Character and Form of Negotiations. As to their character, these negotiations may be official, semiofficial, or confidential. A negotiation is official when it is made in the name of the government and the agent assumes the responsibility for it. A semiofficial negotiation on the contrary imposes no responsibility upon the government; it informs without pledging. Relations with the *de facto* instead of with the *de jure* government of a state are sometimes spoken of as semiofficial. Confidential negotiations are, as the word implies, those which are carried on wholly outside of official reports and must remain secret between the parties concerned.[4]

As to form—the relations between the agent and the government to which he is accredited are written, oral, or mixed; and it may be said that as far as possible the envoy should carry on political negotiations orally. Rayneval gives it as a general rule that a public minister must be very reserved in his written communications lest he place himself in a compromising situation which must later be disavowed.[5] Ordinarily a diplomatic agent should not communicate the text of the instructions that he receives unless specifically ordered to do so. He can impart the sense of his instructions by word of mouth with equal force and much less risk. However, when in 1825 the Russian and Austrian Ambassadors informed George Canning, Secretary of State for Foreign Affairs of Great Britain, that they could read the despatches from their Governments to him but were prohibited from giving him copies, he refused to listen to the reading of a despatch unless he was allowed to retain a copy of it. Otherwise they could limit themselves to verbal communications. It is interesting to note that some five years earlier when Stratford Canning was Minister to the United States he was instructed by Lord Castlereagh, Secretary of

[2] Burton J. Hendrick, *The Life and Letters of Walter H. Page* (New York, 1925), I, 378-91. See also Stephen Gwynn, *The Letters and Friendships of Sir Cecil Spring-Rice* (Boston and New York, 1929), II, 233.

[3] John Bassett Moore, *Digest of International Law* (Washington, 1906), IV, 707.

[4] Raoul Genet, *Traité de diplomatie et de droit diplomatique* (Paris, 1931), II, 380.

[5] Baron Gérard de Rayneval, *Institutions du droit de la nature et des gens* (Paris, 1832), 373.

State for Foreign Affairs, to transact his business with the American Government as far as possible by personal intercourse with the Secretary of State, rather than by writing notes, in order to avoid diplomatic controversy.[6] Dwight Morrow, according to his biographer, Harold Nicolson, conducted practically all his negotiations with Mexico orally.

After Morrow had resigned his post the Mexican Minister of Foreign Affairs, Mr. Genaro Estrada, complimented him upon his mastery of the art of negotiation. The American Ambassador "departed from all the traditional formulas of useless, and at times dangerous academic discussions by means of notes, a practice which is wont to result in ill feeling and mortifying impasses, in favor of direct oral discussions in terms of constant friendliness." [7]

Forms of Correspondence. According to Baron de Szilassy, the correspondence between the envoy and the minister of foreign affairs, following universal usage, is carried on in the four following forms:

1. The note or official letter which bears regularly the signature of the one who sends it and is addressed to the minister or to the one to whom it is sent personally; it is the official document par excellence; and is usually in the first person, though sometimes in the third;
2. The *note verbale* which originates in the chancellery, which is drafted in the third person and is never signed;
3. The *mémoire, aide-mémoire,* or memorandum, a document which has for its purpose to fix certain points in the memory of the interlocutor; the *mémoire* is concise, absolutely impersonal, relates facts only and never bears a signature;
4. Private letters which vary in form according to the subject, the end in view and the degree of intimacy of the correspondents.[8]

Mention should also be made of collective or identic notes utilized by the powers in making joint representation to a government in regard to a particular matter. Turkey and China have often been recipients of such communications.

Oral interviews between the envoy and the minister of foreign affairs take place generally at the bureau of the ministry at an official reception at the hour fixed by the minister. "The oral forms of diplomatic negotiation clearly cannot be enclosed within the frame of a rigorous classification. Only the experience and the practice of the agent . . . can guide him in the delicate and difficult art of oral reports." [9]

If the affair is very complicated and easily susceptible of misunderstanding the envoy may complete his verbal overture by leaving in the

---

[6] Willson, *op. cit.*, 109.

[7] *U.S. Press Releases* (Oct. 4, 1930), 219.

[8] J. de Szilassy, *Traité pratique de diplomatie moderne* (Paris, 1928), 66; see also E. Satow, *Diplomatic Practice* (London, 1932), 56-71.

[9] Genet, *op. cit.*, II, 385.

hands of the minister of foreign affairs a short memoradum on the subject. This procedure is designated by the term *mixed relations.*

Ceremonial Communications. Among those functions which sometimes fall to the lot of the diplomatic envoy is the drafting of ceremonial letters which are exchanged between the heads of state on the occasion of certain important events: the accession to the throne, the election of a president, the birth of an heir to the throne, the death of the head of the state, a royal marriage,—all these ceremonial occasions require letters of felicitation or condolence. The Bureau of Protocol in the Ministry of Foreign Affairs is responsible for the drafting of these communications, but sometimes when the occasion requires, the envoy must do it for himself.

On many occasions American diplomats have had to serve in this capacity. Arthur Sherburne Hardy, a career diplomat of the United States, relates that in his day "the death of a princess or the celebration of a royal birthday was passed over in official silence by the Department of State. It was embarrassing when telegrams of condolence or of felicitations were pouring in from the foreign offices of colleagues to maintain an isolated and apparently indifferent taciturnity. Silence was no longer golden nor was the expression of a merely personal feeling conveyed by the inscription of one's name in the visitors' book of the Palace quite sufficient. It was therefore my practice to feign an official outburst of sorrow or joy appropriate to the event and to fabricate messages unknown to the cable." [10]

In some countries a function called signing the books takes place on national holidays, on birthdays, or upon the decease of members of the royal family. In France the book is signed at the Elysée and cards left for the prime minister and minister of foreign affairs. In Rome it is done after one has been at court and also on birthdays of members of the King's household. In London the books are kept for "inscription on the King and Queen" and serve as a substitute for leaving cards. Signing of the visitors' book also takes place in embassies and legations in matters of condolence or congratulations as the case may be.

Relations with Officials. In addition to his relations with the foreign minister the envoy must carry on friendly relations with the subordinates in the foreign office and with numerous other officials of the government. Much of his influence will depend upon the position which he makes for himself in this governmental hierarchy. If he fits himself into the structure he will find not only his sources of information augmented but his influence in improving friendly relations increased manyfold. For a considerable period of time the United States was unfortunate in its choice of

[10] Arthur Sherburne Hardy, *Things Remembered* (New York, 1923), 146.

ambassadors to Mexico. They stood aloof and seemed wholly unable to meet the Mexican Government officials on a common ground. Then President Coolidge in 1927 by a happy inspiration chose Dwight Morrow as Ambassador to Mexico. The atmosphere cleared as if by magic and relations between the two countries were quickly placed upon a sound basis of mutual coöperation and friendship.

Josephus Daniels carried on the Morrow tradition and by his selflessness and tact made himself respected and loved by all Mexican officials who came into contact with him. Lord Bryce was equally successful in his sojourn in Washington as British Ambassador to the United States.

Interference in Internal Affairs. One of the fundamental rules of diplomatic practice stipulates that a public minister must not interfere in the internal affairs of the state to which he is accredited. In the instructions to American diplomatic officers they are expressly forbidden to participate in any manner in the political concerns of the country of their residence; and they are directed especially to refrain from public expressions of opinion upon local political or other questions arising within their jurisdiction.[11]

Nevertheless, actual cases of interference in the internal affairs of the states to which the envoys are accredited are very numerous. In France, for example, the papal nuncios on several occasions have corresponded directly with the national clergy and have encouraged resistance to the national laws.[12] Monsieur de Reus, Dutch Minister at Caracas in 1908, was deprived of all official authority by the Venezuelan Government for having addressed to the publication of an organization of students of the Public School of Commerce a letter in which he expressed himself with a certain severity towards the government in power. This strictly private letter was brought to the attention of President Castro and it required no more than this for the Dutch Minister to receive his passports together with a note of condemnation.[13]

There is also the unfortunate case of Lord Sackville-West, British Minister to the United States, who was the victim of a political plot. He had received what purported to be a private letter asking him to name the candidate for the presidency of the United States whose election in 1888 seemed the most favorable for the maintenance of friendly relations between Great Britain and the United States. He replied frankly, and his reply was divulged by his correspondent. The United States asked for his resignation immediately.[14]

[11] *Foreign Service Regulations of the United States* (Washington, October, 1945), I, 15.
[12] Paul Fauchille, *Traité de droit international public* (Paris, 1926), I, Pt. iii, 54.
[13] Genet, *op. cit.*, II, 393, 465.
[14] Moore, *op. cit.*, IV, 536-48.

There are occasions when the envoy seems justified in intervening in a matter of foreign policy when its continuance would manifestly jeopardize the existing friendly relations. Yet even in such cases the results are rarely satisfactory. In 1924 the Congress of the United States voted an immigration law which abrogated the Gentleman's Agreement of 1907-08 with Japan. During the debate in the Congress, Japanese Ambassador Hanihara wrote a letter to Secretary of State Hughes in which he spoke of grave consequences which might follow the acceptance of this measure. The letter raised a tempest in the Senate, which regarded it as a veiled threat. The action of the Ambassador only rendered the more certain a favorable vote upon this measure.

In times of extreme emergency such diplomatic action is not uncommon and the State Department approved the very drastic policy of United States Ambassador David Francis, who in 1918 issued an impassioned appeal to the Russian people to disregard the Brest-Litovsk Treaty and to repel the Germans. The German Minister of Foreign Affairs demanded that Francis be removed, but the Bolshevik Government replied that he had said no more than President Wilson had said to the Bolshevik Congress.[15] In fact, his chief, President Wilson, followed almost the identical policy in appealing to the Italian people over the head of their Government in the Fiume question. When Lord Chilston, Dean of the Diplomatic Corps in Moscow in 1938, proposed a joint protest to the Soviet Foreign Office because the Soviet authorities not only examined the personal effects which returning diplomats took out of Russia, but also exacted a tax for the service, he requested the support of Ambassador Davies of the United States. When Davies and others of the Diplomatic Corps refused to support the *démarche* the matter was dropped.[16]

Relations with Colleagues of the Diplomatic Corps. The Diplomatic Corps comprises all the heads of missions with their attachés and secretaries. The oldest representative in length of service at the post who is of the highest category is the *doyen du corps.* He is the mouthpiece of his colleagues on public occasions and defender of their privileges at the capital where they are accredited. However, he may only represent his colleagues after having consulted them and secured their approval.

Maurice Francis Egan, formerly American Minister to Denmark, declares that the normal relationship of the envoy to the Diplomatic Corps is somewhat of a family relationship. "In any foreign city, it is as a group rather isolated. There are certain social conventions which hedge it about, and while one may choose one's friends and associates as one pleases, the corps in itself is very critical as to the fitness of these friends and associates; the instructions from every foreign office are always to the

[15] David R. Francis, *Russia from the American Embassy* (New York, 1921), 232.
[16] Joseph E. Davies, *Mission to Moscow* (New York, 1941), 322-4.

effect that an envoy and his wife are expected to cultivate the good will of their colleagues." [17]

The late Rudolph Holsti, former Minister of Foreign Affairs in Finland, and an experienced diplomat assured the writer that the isolation of the Diplomatic Corps is undoubtedly more due to local circumstances than to a desire of the diplomats to separate themselves from "la haute société." If in a capital there are very few families wealthy enough to entertain diplomats and, if in addition, comparatively few people of the local population speak French, English, Spanish, or German, the Diplomatic Corps is bound by unavoidable circumstances to cultivate informal relations chiefly among themselves.

In posts where the civilization of the country is alien to Western standards, diplomats see each other constantly. According to Paul Reinsch, one-time Minister of the United States to China, the Diplomatic Corps in Peking met frequently and had more comprehensive and complicated business than falls to such a body in other capitals. The system of extraterritoriality of its very nature required that local legislation be watched carefully lest the established rights of the foreign envoys be in any way curtailed.[18] Hugh Wilson declares that in Peking the Corps was formerly like a great club and he also notes that in most small posts the diplomatic body gets well acquainted. But he goes on to say that in the large cities of western Europe the contrary is the case; "the Corps is widely scattered, meets officially only once or twice a year and mingles more with the society of the city itself and less with its colleagues." [19]

Negotiation of Treaties.   Formerly the making of political treaties was an important function in a diplomat's work, but today if the treaty be a very important political document the State Department guides every step or a special commission is sent to negotiate the treaty. One can hardly imagine treaties as important as those signed by Caleb Cushing with China, or by Commodore Perry or Townsend Harris with Japan, or even the very irregular treaty of Guadalupe Hidalgo negotiated by Nicholas Trist after his recall, signed by a single diplomatic agent on his own responsibility today. The negotiation and signing of the Treaty of Trianon with Hungary by the United States Ambassador to France, Hugh Wallace, in 1920, and of the American Treaty of Lausanne with Turkey by the United States Minister to Switzerland, Joseph Clark Grew, in 1923 might be regarded as exceptional examples. Mr. Wallace's rôle was due to the departure of the American Peace Commission. Mr. Grew was a career diplomat of long experience who had just acted as observer during the negotiations of the Allies at Lausanne. And even in this case, Minister

---

[17] Maurice F. Egan, *Recollections of a Happy Life* (New York, 1924), 250.
[18] Paul Reinsch, *An American Diplomat in China* (Garden City, N.Y., 1922).
[19] Hugh Wilson, *Education of a Diplomat* (New York, 1938), 123.

Grew was in constant touch with Secretary Hughes and the Near East Division of the State Department. On the other hand, with the increase of nonpolitical treaties, the diplomat is often called upon to work out bilateral agreements on various social, economic, and technical matters.

The United States gives very specific instructions to its diplomatic representatives with respect to the negotiation of bilateral treaties.[20] If a treaty is to be negotiated by an American diplomatic agent he is furnished with the full power of the President authorizing him to negotiate, conclude and sign the contemplated agreement. If the proposal originates with the United States its envoy is furnished a tentative draft of the proposed treaty to be submitted to the other government for its consideration. Any modifications or counter proposals must be submitted by the representative to the Department of State. If the proposal originates with the other government, the envoy forwards the draft to the Department and awaits instructions. The diplomatic representative will only sign a treaty when so advised by the Department.

When signing has been agreed upon two originals are prepared for each government. The principle of the *alternat* is carefully observed. When English and another language are employed the text in both languages is printed in parallel columns of the same page or on opposite pages of the same sheet. Each government retains the original in which its language appears in the left-hand column or page. In the same way each government retains the original where the name of the country and its plenipotentiary appear above that of the other. Before signing, the diplomatic representative must be certain that the texts in both languages in the treaty conform exactly to those of the drafts, that the idea conveyed by the foreign text accords with that of the English text, and that the punctuation is the same. In multilateral agreements when several languages are employed as for example at the Latin American conferences where English, Spanish, and Portuguese are all official languages, a fourth text, in French, may be prepared to serve as the authentic interpretation in case of litigation. This is the text which, in diplomatic language, *fait foi.*

Full powers may be either exhibited or exchanged by the plenipotentiaries at the time of signature as the foreign government may prefer. At Washington the custom is merely to exhibit them.

After the treaty is signed the diplomatic representative should forward the original to the Secretary of State. Since all treaties signed on the part of the United States must be approved by the Senate before ratification, the United States prefers that the treaty provide that exchange of ratifications shall be effected "as soon as possible," rather than within a specified time. Exchange of ratifications is effected by a mutual ex-

---

[20] *Regulations, op. cit.,* XI.

change of ratified copies by plenipotentiaries of the two governments. A protocol signed in duplicate by both plenipotentiaries in the alternat form attests the exchange. The American agent should then immediately cable the date of exchange and the date of the instrument of ratification of the foreign government so that the treaty may be promptly proclaimed by the President. The instrument of ratification of the foreign government and a copy of the signed protocol are forwarded by the first following mail.[21]

Participation in International Conferences. The development of the international conference has increased the opportunity of the diplomatic representative to meet with his colleagues from other capitals in drawing up multipartite international conventions on a great variety of subjects. In the various conferences on the limitation of armament in the period following World War I, numerous diplomats participated as delegates. At the Washington Conference for the Limitation of Armament held in 1921, Belgium, Great Britain, France, Italy, Japan, China, the Netherlands, and Portugal were all represented by their diplomatic envoys at Washington as well as by additional plenipotentiaries. The United States has also utilized diplomatic envoys to serve as unofficial observers at a number of international conferences. Joseph Clark Grew was utilized by President Wilson to organize data for the delegates at the Peace Conference in Paris and became later supervisor-director of the secretarial staff at the Peace Conference. He served with Ambassador Child at the first Lausanne Conference as an unofficial observer when the Allies were endeavoring to make peace with Turkey and he headed the American delegation at the second Lausanne Conference to negotiate and sign a treaty of amity and commerce with Turkey on the part of the United States.

Richard Washburn Child declared that he attended the Conference of Genoa "not as a member of the conference officially or unofficially but merely as ambassador to Italy interested in the international conference attended by more nations than any other in history." [22]

Ambassador Hugh Gibson was constantly utilized by Presidents Coolidge and Hoover to attend international conferences as a representative of the United States. He served as chairman of the American delegation at the Conference for the Supervision of International Trade in Arms. He attended the various sessions of the Preparatory Commission for the Geneva Disarmament Conference and then served as a delegate when the General Conference was called. This was said to be the first occasion since the Peace Conference when an American representative other than an "unofficial observer" attended an international conference in Europe.

---

[21] For a brief but comprehensive account of the procedure of treaty-making see Elmer Plischke, *Conduct of American Diplomacy* (New York, 1950), 267-301.

[22] Richard Washburn Child, *A Diplomat Looks at Europe* (New York, 1925), 4.

Gibson acted as chairman of the American delegation at the Limitation of Naval Armaments Conference in Geneva in 1927 and as a delegate to the London Naval Conference of 1930. He also served as observer at the conference of experts for a moratorium on international debts in London in 1931.

Former Assistant Secretary of State, Dean Rusk, has pointed out that the growth of international conferences,—there are now about six thousand meetings of international organizations somewhere in the world throughout the year,—has brought into existence a new sort of diplomacy which he designates as parliamentary diplomacy. Whereas formerly most questions between states could be settled bilaterally now most problems are multilateral and a state even though as important as the United States is only one member of a number of organizations in which three score states have interests and votes. In this parliamentary diplomacy there is unlimited pressure to compromise, but both the mechanics and politics of compromise are difficult. The fact that the United States today is usually expected to take the initiative and assume much of the responsibility makes the lot of the American envoy a delicate one. Fortunately this conference diplomacy has developed experts, and the United States, ably represented by men like Dean Acheson, John Foster Dulles, W. Averell Harriman, and Philip C. Jessup, has played a rôle not without honor.

Protection of Citizens of Third Powers. Among the functions which a diplomatic representative is sometimes called upon to perform is the protection of citizens of third powers. Usually this is a purely temporary arrangement where the nationals' government has no diplomatic representative, but there have been occasions when the arrangement has continued over a fairly long period of time. For example, John W. Foster, United States Minister to Mexico after the downfall of Maximilian, unofficially exercised his good offices with the Mexican Government for eight different European countries. The British residents regarded him as their *de facto* Minister, and the London Foreign Office frequently expressed its appreciation for his services.[23]

The United States has from time to time permitted its diplomatic representatives at the request of friendly powers and with the consent of the jurisdictional government to represent these powers at such places as the powers requesting have no diplomatic representation. This authority is restricted to the granting of services or good offices of the representative to meet what is ordinarily a temporary exigency of the friendly government. These services are performed after the consent of the jurisdictional government has been obtained and under instructions from the Department of State. In performing such offices the diplomatic officer serves as

[23] John W. Foster, *Diplomatic Memoirs* (New York, 1909), I, 31.

the agent of the foreign government, responsible to it for the duties which may be performed and that government alone is responsible for his acts. By a Constitutional provision he is prohibited from becoming a diplomatic or consular officer of the foreign government.

In 1854 at the request of a Mexican citizen in Peru for protection, the American Minister, J. Randolph Clay, inquired how far United States representatives should extend their good offices in behalf of foreigners whose governments had no diplomatic or consular representation. Secretary of State Marcy replied: "Any good offices which a minister may undertake must be entirely of a personal character, or such as may be demanded by humanity or the pressing urgency of the case...." [24] When in 1874 the German Consul at Guatemala left before his successor arrived he asked the American Minister to watch over the interests of German subjects. Minister Williamson consented and the Department approved his action. [25]

The United States for a number of years authorized its diplomatic representatives to use their good offices in behalf of Swiss citizens in countries where the Swiss Government was not represented. Such services included the presentation of claims, the protection of Swiss citizens from violence, and the use of good offices in behalf of Swiss citizens called for military service abroad. [26]

One of the most interesting examples of American protection of foreign interests in times of peace occurred in Iran from 1921 to 1927 when the United States assumed the protection of the interests of the Netherlands Government. For a period this also included consular work as well as diplomatic. When a question of enforcement of claims arose the situation became so complicated that the Netherlands Government found it advisable to name both a minister and an honorary consul. [27]

Care of Foreign Legations. The commonest examples of such good offices occur in periods of severed diplomatic relations or war. In such cases the diplomatic envoy is asked to protect in the state to which he is accredited the interests of nationals of the power whose diplomatic representative has been withdrawn. Under such circumstances the neutral diplomatic officer may be expected to aid in facilitating the departure of the diplomatic and consular representatives of the belligerent state and its nationals domiciled in the country to which he is accredited. Quite commonly he takes over the embassy or legation, guards its archives and performs such functions as are essentially protective in character.

[24] Moore, *op. cit.,* IV, 585.
[25] *Ibid.,* 588-9.
[26] Moore, *op. cit.,* IV, 585.
[27] The whole question of the protection of foreign interests both in peace and war is covered in a scholarly manner by William McHenry Franklin in his monograph, *Protection of Foreign Interests* (Washington, D.C., 1946).

At the outbreak of the Franco-Prussian War in 1870 the American Minister to Paris, Elihu B. Washburne, was the only representative of a great power who remained in Paris. At the request of the German Ambassador to Paris and with the authorization of the State Department he took over the German Embassy and raised the American flag over it. He agreed to protect the interests of the subjects of the North German Confederation and of the South German States. There were about 30,000 Germans in Paris and as the French refused to allow those of military age to depart and as feeling ran high against all Germans his problem of repatriating some and protecting others was not an easy one. He distributed money sent by Germans to their interned relatives and friends and he served as a means of communication between Germany and France. According to Minister Washburne, "When Bismarck wished to send a memorandum to the French Government he would address it to Count Bernstorff, the German Ambassador in London, who communicated it to Mr. Motley, United States Minister in London, who in turn sent it to Mr. Washburne, who turned it over to the French Minister of Foreign Affairs." [28]

Before the entrance of the United States into World War I American diplomatic representatives in Europe were called upon to represent many of the belligerent powers at the various capitals.[29] Ambassador Gerard in Berlin for example took over the British, Japanese, Serbian, and Rumanian interests. He was also instrumental in aiding the Russian Ambassador to leave Berlin by sending him the American Embassy's chauffeur and footman. The representation of British interests involved our Embassy in a number of complex and delicate problems and imposed upon the staff a vast amount of arduous and exhausting labor. The responsibilities assumed included the inspection of prison camps, the keeping of records of all British civilians and prisoners of war in Germany, the relief of interned civilians—a member of the Embassy went twice a week to the great civilian internment camp at Ruhleben where 5,000 British were interned—the administration of funds involving millions of dollars and the carrying on of diplomatic negotiations between the two Governments. It has been said that never before in history has an equal or even comparable amount of labor and effort been exerted by the representatives of a neutral government in caring for the interests of one belligerent in the territory of another belligerent.[30]

---

[28] Elihu B. Washburne, *Recollections of a Minister to France* (New York, 1889), I, 39-54, 96.

[29] For a complete account of the activities of the American Legation in Belgium during the early years of the World War see Hugh Gibson, *A Journal from Our American Legation in Belgium* (New York, 1917).

[30] *House of Representatives Report*, No. 695, 65th Cong., 2nd sess., 2. See also James W. Gerard, *My Four Years in Germany* (New York, 1917), and *Face to Face with Kaiserism* (New York, 1918).

In somewhat similar fashion Ambassador Myron T. Herrick in France took over the German, Austro-Hungarian, and Turkish interests in Paris. He, too, despite a greatly augmented staff had considerable additional labor imposed by the necessity of visiting and inspecting detention camps, hospitals, and prisoners.[31] He wrote to his son on November 4, 1914, that he had sent 2,300 interns through the lines to Switzerland on a single day with more to follow.[32] When the French Government moved to Bordeaux, Herrick decided to remain in Paris contrary to the regular rule because President Wilson appreciated the fact that Herrick would be of greater service in Paris. The result was still more work for the Embassy since he was now requested to take over the interests of Great Britain, Japan, Serbia, and others. Herrick remarked that with so many "interests" concentrated in his hands, Mr. Kellogg intimated that the Attorney General might try to dissolve him on the ground of being a trust.[33]

Ambassador to France William C. Bullitt played a somewhat similar rôle in World War II when at the request of the French Government he remained in Paris instead of accompanying the French Government to Bordeaux. For a short period he served as acting Mayor of Paris in charge of all municipal administration, including police and fire services. It was he who arranged for the peaceful occupation of the city by the Germans and obtained a promise from the German General in command that all embassies and legations which had been left in Bullitt's charge should be given protection.

An interesting case of protection arose in 1942 when the Swiss Minister in Tokyo who was protecting American interests tried to have shipments of office equipment which had been consigned to the American Embassy at Tokyo and the American Consulate at Mukden, released by the Japanese customs authorities who had had them since the outbreak of the war with the United States. At first the Japanese offered to buy the supplies but when this was refused they allowed the Swiss Minister to buy them and place the value in a blocked account to the credit of the United States.[34] It should be noted that in spite of Swiss protests the Japanese violated the archives of the American Embassy at Peiping and the consular archives at Canton, Swatow, Shanghai, Hanoi, and Saigon.[35]

In World War II when neutral states were few the Swiss Government protected the interests of twenty-six belligerent powers in one or more of the other belligerent states, Sweden the interests of sixteen and Spain the interests of five. Japan and Rumania were the only two belligerents that used the services of all three neutrals.

[31] There were more than 100,000 Germans in France to be cared for. See Lee Meriwether, *The War Diary of a Diplomat* (New York, 1919), 170.
[32] T. Bentley Mott, *Myron T. Herrick, Friend of France* (New York, 1929), 193.
[33] Mott, *op. cit.*, 157.
[34] Franklin, *op. cit.*, 183-4.
[35] *Ibid.*, 186.

Stopping a Revolution. The diplomat must not only be prepared to preserve peace between his own country and the country to which he is accredited but he may use his good offices effectively to prevent revolutionary bloodshed in the country of his post. An excellent illustration of this procedure occurred in connection with a revolution in Guatemala in 1944. Before daylight one morning United States Chargé d'Affaires Affeld was awakened by the sound of machine gun fire in the vicinity of the American Embassy. Before he could finish dressing the chief of the American Military Mission in Guatemala phoned that a revolution had broken out. It was soon learned that the attack was upon the Government forts and that the revolutionaries intended to oust the President and his cabinet.

While Chargé Affeld was sending a telegram to the United States announcing the situation, the President of Guatemala phoned requesting aid from the American Mission. He was informed that the United States would not interfere in any respect in Guatemala internal affairs. Subsequently two members of the revolutionary Junta requested permission to use United States Embassy facilities to communicate to the Government its terms of surrender. Chargé Affeld agreed that the Embassy telephone might be used but the Embassy could not be a place of asylum. The revolutionary leaders therefore telephoned their terms. The President asked for time to discuss the matter and a place of meeting. The revolutionaries agreed providing the meeting would be in the American Embassy and with a minimum of delay. The United States Military Attaché phoned the President, who said the two representatives were on their way. When the two arrived Chargé Affeld permitted them to use an Embassy room for conferences. The Government representatives could not make a final decision and returned to the Palace to get the President's answer. Before a satisfactory agreement regarding guarantees of protection for the resigning government officials was obtained the entire diplomatic corps under the chairmanship of the Papal Nuncio, dean of the corps, met in the United States Embassy with the representatives of the Government and the revolutionary faction. When they had worked out an acceptable basis of surrender, the members of the diplomatic corps affixed their signatures as witnesses and the revolution was over and a new government installed.

Maintaining Cordial Relations. The envoy has important obligations to the country of his post as well as to his own government and sometimes a diplomat can serve both at the same time. While he was Minister to Haiti, Norman Armour, learning that President Franklin D. Roosevelt was making a trip through the Caribbean, requested that he stop off at Haiti, thus returning the visit previously made by President Vincent. The Haitian Government, taking it for granted that the President would accept, made elaborate plans for his reception even to fixing up a special barge to make it easy for him to descend from the cruiser.

At the last moment Minister Armour was notified that President Roosevelt would be unable to land, but would receive President Vincent on board. This provoked such a crisis in Port-au-Prince that President Vincent said he would have to resign. Minister Armour sent a strong despatch to Washington urging reconsideration and pointing out the serious consequences of a refusal. When no answer was received, Armour, although sick in bed with *dengue* fever, had a plane retained and the night before the President was to arrive he got up and flew to the port of proposed debarcation. He was so ill that he fainted in going aboard the President's vessel.

President Roosevelt was so impressed that he landed as had originally been arranged, made an excellent address, and promised to withdraw the American marines several months before the term prescribed by a joint agreement.

Exceptional Cases.   The life of a diplomat is a varied one and the unusual is always cropping up. As a striking example Career Minister Walter J. Donnelly, who had specialized in Latin American affairs and had over twenty years of outstanding success in this field, was suddenly transferred to Vienna to act in the dual capacity of Minister and High Commissioner in occupied Austria. Donnelly who spoke Spanish and Portuguese fluently and had served only in Central and South American posts found himself in a German-speaking state where every political and economic problem was new to him. He found that he was expected to effect a transition from military to civilian occupation and do it quickly. Fortunately, the headquarters of the American Army had previously been moved to Salzburg and Counselor of Embassy Walter C. Dowling had already made an excellent beginning. By taking over one function at a time instead of all at a specified time the transition was made smoothly and effectively. Within six weeks' time the whole turnover was completed including a merging of the High Commission's economic staff and the United States Information Service with the legation staff. The result proved to be a model for occupation procedure and Foreign Service Officer Donnelly was rewarded by being raised in rank to an Ambassador.

Inasmuch as Vienna was practically the only place where East and West met on a fairly friendly basis it was the hottest spot from the point of view of East-West trade. Since the USSR was attempting the economic penetration of Austria and had flagrantly violated the Potsdam agreements in seizing a large number of Austrian industrial enterprises by claiming them to be German assets, it was the province of the American economic experts to aid Austrian countermeasures to weaken those industries and to strengthen in every way possible the Austrian position.

Foreign Service Officer Clinton L. Olson was responsible for reporting on and taking countermeasures against Soviet and satellite penetration into Austria. He had to control East-West shipments, screen U.S. export license applications for shipment to Austria for materials of strategic importance and was successful in stopping millions of dollars worth of munitions and munitions-making machines sold to the Soviets by Germans.

A very clever diplomatic coup was put over by Ambassador Ellis O. Briggs while representing the United States in Communist-controlled Czechoslovakia. When he learned that the Communists intended to ignore the hundredth anniversary of the great liberal Czech statesman Masaryk's birth he decided to circumvent them. He arranged to name the USIE library in Prague the Masaryk Library. He had a commemoration plaque made and when the anniversary day arrived he made a speech and had the plaque posted in spite of Communist opposition. A large crowd was present and the whole affair was made a great sensation.

Quick action on the part of Ambassador Robert Butler averted a riot and bloodshed in Havana, Cuba, on one occasion when some American sailors on shore leave desecrated a monument of Cuba's national hero José Marti. He sent his regrets immediately to the Foreign Office and asked permission to lay a wreath at the foot of the statue and to express publicly his profound admiration for the Cuban patriot and his deep humiliation for the inexcusable performance of his countrymen.

Ambassador John G. Winant was requested on one occasion by Mr. Bevan to try and persuade coal miners on strike in Durham to return to work. In a short speech of great sincerity and simplicity he was able to get the men back in the mines immediately.

Unfortunately for the diplomat the most important of his duties, the maintenance of cordial relations, is an intangible matter. No definite procedure can be outlined—the envoy must depend almost entirely upon his own wisdom and judgment. And if he is particularly successful in a delicate negotiation by the very nature of the case the details must remain secret or he may never be successful again. Therefore, as Jules Cambon has aptly remarked: *"Les diplomates ne sont pas comme les militaires les enfants gatés des historiens";* nevertheless, measured in terms of real value to their country, their influence is perhaps of even greater importance, inasmuch as it is exerted regularly and effectively in the maintenance of peace.

Dangers in Performance of Duties. The public unfortunately does not always realize that a diplomat may have to undergo hardships and face serious dangers in the accomplishment of his mission. Early in World War II Walton Butterworth, First Secretary of the Embassy at Lisbon and Madrid, was in charge of economic warfare activities in that area. In the course of one of his trips his plane made a forced landing on the water and broke apart. He broke the window in which the passengers were trapped, pushed them out, followed them and helped them onto the wing which was floating. When they were all finally rescued Butterworth was taken ashore carrying his briefcase containing his secret papers in his hands.

During the Nazi blitzkrieg when London was being bombed almost nightly, American Ambassador John G. Winant remained at his post in spite of the fact that over a million Britishers, some holding high governmental positions, were evacuated because of the great danger.

Robert B. Macatee, First Secretary of the Legation and Consul to Belgrade in the spring of 1941 was directed by Minister Arthur Bliss Lane to follow the Yugoslav Government in its flight from the Germans. With several newspaper correspondents he drove to Uzice and found the place thronged with refugees and no hotel space available. With no gas to be had he was lucky in finding an abandoned gasoline drum from which he was able to dip out gasoline with a can. With bombs bursting round about constantly Macatee and the newspapermen drove through rain and snow to Serajevo taking twenty-four hours to travel 150 miles. Cold and wet they had to sleep in their car. They were thereupon evacuated again leaving under machine-gun fire. When they reached Perast they learned that the Government had capitulated so it meant driving all the way back to Belgrade now occupied by the Germans.

Foreign Service Officer Thomas W. Wasson was stationed at Dakar in the early part of World War II when the British bombarded the port. He rode about on his bicycle to get the most accurate information to telegraph to his Government. Subsequently while Consul General at Jerusalem he attended a meeting at the French Consulate General of the Commission engaged in establishing a truce for Palestine. While returning to the American Consulate he was mortally wounded by a sniper's bullet. The assailant was never discovered but it was suspected that he might have been a member of the terrorist Stern Gang which also murdered Count Bernadotte, the Swedish philanthropist who had spent his life in aiding the oppressed. On October 12, 1949, Wasson was awarded posthumously one of the first medals ever given by the Department of State for outstandingly meritorious service.

A unique case occurred in Bogotá, Colombia, in 1935, when illiterate tenant farmers thinking that the German Minister Dr. Otto von Hertig was a trespasser attacked him while walking with his son on the outskirts of Bogotá. He was clubbed into insensibility and his hands were fractured. His young son ran away and obtained help. The Foreign Minister of Colombia and other high officials visited Frau von Hertig at the Legation and expressed their personal and official regrets.

12

Diplomatic Duties—III

SOCIAL FUNCTIONS

SOCIAL FUNCTIONS ARE necessarily a very important part of diplomatic life and the envoy's success or failure is sometimes dependent upon his ability to utilize effectively and intelligently the many social contacts which they afford. The American official instructions state that the diplomatic representative should omit no occasion to maintain the most friendly personal and social relations with the members of the government and of the diplomatic corps at the place of his residence. Napoléon I, in his instructions to his Ambassador in Warsaw, declared that a successful diplomat must *"Tenez bonne table et soignez les femmes."* A more modern definition of the accomplished diplomat is one who makes people feel at home when he wishes they were.

Official Calls.   The newly appointed diplomatic representative is supposed to make the first call on all of his colleagues of the same rank as himself and hold himself in readiness to respond to the requests of those of lower rank for appointments to pay their respects. The official calls take up considerable time in the larger capitals, but the clever envoy can utilize them to form an approximate idea of the milieu in which he is to function. The establishment of cordial relations with the other members of the diplomatic corps is oftentimes as important to the diplomat's political as it is to his social success.

In making the first official calls on his colleagues the ambassador begins with the dean of the diplomatic corps and then follows with the others in the order of their seniority at the post.[1] The new diplomatic representative writes to each colleague asking what would be a convenient hour for the presentation of his respects. After visiting all the ambassadors in turn the newcomer should be available to the various ministers so that they may pay their respects. Robert Underwood Johnson, former American Ambassador to Italy, points out that a clear line of distinction is drawn

[1] Ministers of a country which has just been accorded recognition are expected to call upon the representatives of the recognizing powers.

between embassies and legations in this social function. The minister makes the overture and must be personally received, but on returning his call the ambassador may either leave his card in person or go in for an interview. Mr. Johnson made it his custom to extend the full courtesy of a call, believing this additional consideration was appreciated and was of use to him in future relations with the ministers then in Rome.[2]

As a rule the diplomatic corps makes every effort to smooth the pathway of diplomacy for the neophyte. Andrew D. White, former American Ambassador to Germany, noticed particularly the cordiality of his colleagues and of the ruling family. They all tried to begin a conversation agreeable to the newcomer. One would start a discussion on American shipping, another on American art, another on scenery in Colorado, another on American dentists, with Niagara to fall back upon if all other subjects failed.[3]

The Wife of the Ambassador.   In the case of monarchies the ambassador's wife is also presented at court very soon after her husband's presentation, but in a much less ceremonious fashion. She makes the prescribed three curtseys in entering the queen's presence, but after that the audience is usually quite informal. Inasmuch as royalty terminates all interviews, oftentimes by an indirect signal, the visitor must be on the watch for it. The story is told that Lord Russell casually asked Prince Bismarck how he was able to keep bores from monopolizing his valuable time. He replied that he and the Princess had contrived an excellent method: whenever a person stayed too long, she would call to the Prince that he must come and take his medicine. Hardly had he finished describing the technique when, to the discomfiture of both guest and host, the Princess strolled into the room and remarked that the Prince's medicine was waiting.

After her visits to the court the ambassadress, as she is sometimes called, must also make a round of official calls. Mrs. Child, wife of a former Ambassador to Italy, thus describes the Italian procedure: "First of all I called upon the wife of the minister of foreign affairs and then in order of precedence upon the wives of the other ambassadors. The hours of all these visits were arranged by an interchange of formal notes as they were not an empty matter of leaving cards but were to serve the useful purpose of our becoming known to one another. Each of these calls was then returned, also by appointment."[4]

The rôle played by the diplomatic representative's wife is a very important one and according to the late Ambassador Walter H. Page, the ambassador's wife in London is almost as important as the ambassador

---

[2] Robert Underwood Johnson, *Remembered Yesterdays* (Boston, 1923), 543.
[3] *The Autobiography of Andrew D. White* (New York, 1905), 533.
[4] Maude Parker Child, *The Social Side of Diplomatic Life* (Indianapolis, 1925), 36.

himself. Henry James is supposed to have said that when Whitelaw Reid was Ambassador to London the United States Embassy was *the Embassy* of London due to Mrs. Reid's charm and social ability. There have been instances like that of the celebrated Princess Lieven where the lady in her famous salons in London and Paris unofficially wielded far more influence than her husband in his chancery. Satow declares that if a diplomatist suggested for appointment is married, the social gifts, character, religion, past history or original nationality of his wife may be an important factor in the determination of his appointment.[5] Bismarck expected any German diplomat to resign who married an American and when he offered the Embassy at London to the Count von Hatzfelt, it was on condition that he divorce his American wife. The Count refused but at his wife's insistence he agreed to a legal separation. Although Hatzfelt served his country as a bachelor in London, he lived openly with his wife on their country estate. When his diplomatic career was over he remarried the Countess.[6]

The older authorities were not so certain as to the usefulness of ambassadors' wives. Charnoy in his volume *L'idée du parfait ambassadeur* even questions whether an ambassador should take his wife with him to a foreign post. "The frailty and inconstancy attributed to the majority of women, their tendency to talk too much, the luxury and expense entailed by the lavish establishment which they require, raise the question as to whether it would not be better to leave them at home." On the other hand the same author shows us that it is possible for a wife to aid the ambassador greatly in his domestic affairs which the stress of official duties may otherwise cause him to neglect. She may even contribute to the intellectual and social brilliance of the embassy by attracting people of distinction through her personality and charm.[7]

Pradier-Fodéré writing at a considerably later period concedes that the wife of a diplomat can aid in a very important way her husband's social prestige, and indirectly his value to his government. "All men in political life need a salon, particularly a woman's salon because at such a place engagements are of less importance and interviews less compromising. To visit an ambassador may be considered a démarche, to visit his wife is merely an act of courtesy. In this way an interview may be had very simply, the wife may serve as go between and without the slightest responsibility each may make his proposition and reply...."[8]

Ambassador Page gives an excellent example of such an occasion. A certain woman, well known for her activities in behalf of Anglo-

---

[5] Ernest Satow, *A Guide to Diplomatic Practice*, 3rd ed. (London, 1932), 119.

[6] Anonymous, *Intimacies of Court and Society by the Widow of an American Diplomat* (New York, 1912), 181.

[7] Rousseau de Charnoy, *L'idée du parfait ambassadeur*, L. Delavaud, ed. (Paris, 1912), 29.

[8] P. Pradier-Fodéré, *Cours de droit diplomatique* (Paris, 1899), I, 389-90.

American friendship, called upon Mrs. Page and in the course of the visit informed her that unless the activities of certain British commercial interests were checked a serious situation might arise between Great Britain and the United States. Mrs. Page made a memorandum and gave it to the Ambassador. Ambassador Page sent it to President Wilson, who thereupon took steps to put an end to the Cowdray machinations.[9]

Madame Jusserand, wife of the French Ambassador in Washington for so many years, was noted for her tact and finesse in meeting any sort of problem. Maurice Francis Egan goes so far as to declare that no diplomatic lady at any capital ever achieved a greater position than did Madame Jusserand at Washington.[10]

Sometimes, however, wives of diplomats are likely to act in a very undiplomatic fashion. Norval Richardson, formerly Secretary at the American Embassy in Rome, tells that when in 1915 the first Italian soldiers were leaving for the front he was sent by the American Ambassador to warn his wife that it was Italy, not the United States, that had declared war. As Richardson had feared, his wife was found waving the American flag and throwing roses at the soldiers. When he informed her that the United States was still neutral she gave him a scornful look and replied: "The ambassador may pretend to be neutral—the United States may be neutral—but I want the whole world to know that I am not." Thereupon she waved the flag with renewed enthusiasm as she shouted, "Viva Italia!" [11]

Social Life. It has already been made clear how important is the social life of the foreign representative. Szilassy gives some excellent advice on this subject. In the first place the envoy must establish cordial relations with his countrymen residing in the country to which he is accredited. As a general rule the envoy should be particularly careful to treat his compatriots on a basis of complete equality. Periodically he should entertain at luncheon or dinner those whom he considers to be worthy of this consideration and he will also do well to invite at least once a year the entire colony. It goes without saying that he must entertain outstanding notables from home and his colleagues at other posts when they pass through the capital where he is stationed. At his first official reception or *recievimento* General Porter, American Minister to France, invited not only all the high dignitaries on the list furnished by the Protocol, but in addition some two hundred Americans of note then resident in Paris, making a total of about fifteen hundred. Ambassador Myron T. Herrick regularly invited the entire American colony in Paris to his Fourth of July receptions, where an excellent buffet with champagne was served to all.

[9] Burton J. Hendrick, *Life and Letters of Walter H. Page* (New York, 1923), I, 190.
[10] Maurice Francis Egan, *Recollections of a Happy Life* (New York, 1924), 195.
[11] Norval Richardson, *My Diplomatic Education* (New York. 1929), 150.

The envoy must also entertain for various groups of people in the country to which he is accredited, such as members of the government, high military authorities, the chief judges, eminent ministers of the clergy, leaders of learned societies, outstanding industrialists interested in his country's trade, professional people of influence, and always in such a way as to avoid any jealousies or animosities.

Besides entertaining he must make calls in return, accept invitations to dinner, frequent certain salons and make himself an integral part of the life of the capital. It was Ambassador Dawes who when returning from a prolonged official reception was asked why he limped; he replied, "Diplomacy is not too hard on the brain, but it's hell on the feet." [12] When Ambassador Fletcher heard this anecdote he is said to have remarked, "It depends upon which end you make use of most."

General Porter, United States Minister to France, regarded most of the official dinners as brilliant but dull, due probably to the stereotyped seating arrangements which were made on a basis of protocol rather than the particular interests of the guests. Attempts are sometimes made by independent-minded hostesses to seat guests solely for their possible enjoyment, but the results are usually disastrous. A certain American hostess who disregarded completely her secretary's advice and kept her husband ignorant of her intentions, so angered the most important guests by placing them in the wrong places at the table that they refused to remain for the dinner. From her point of view they acted like "overgrown babies" but it put an end to her husband's diplomatic career.[13] On one occasion United States Ambassador Irwin B. Laughlin remained away from a dinner to the diplomatic corps given by President Zamora of Spain because the Speaker of the Cortes was given precedence over the Ambassadors in the seating arrangements.

Paul Reinsch, while Minister to China, did not adhere to rank in seating his guests at informal dinners if it made conversation impossible. He, however, always explained the reason for the arrangement to any guest who might have been prejudiced thereby. Upon very formal occasions he followed rank and let conversation take care of itself.[14]

Arthur Sherburne Hardy tells of a certain Russian ambassador who was insulted by the fact that a lady-in-waiting of the Queen was given precedence over his wife. He showed his displeasure during the course of the dinner, but he made it even clearer as he left. Giving his arm to his wife and bowing to his hostess he remarked, "*Quand on ne sait pas donner un diner on ne dérange pas les gens.*" [15]

In entertaining the diplomat must avoid extremes. Opulent extrava-

[12] Paul R. Leach, *That Man Dawes* (Chicago, 1930), 325.

[13] Maude Parker Child, *The Social Side of Diplomatic Life* (Indianapolis, 1925), 55-7.

[14] Paul Reinsch, *An American Diplomat in China* (Garden City, N.Y., 1922), 233-4.

[15] Arthur Sherburne Hardy, *Things Remembered* (New York, 1923), 233.

gance is as out of place as parsimonious frugality. Ambassador William C. Bullitt received much notoriety for his lavish manner of entertaining. A party given in snow-covered Moscow was named after Stravinsky's *Sacré du Printemps.* To fit the name, blooming tulips were flown from Holland, a tablecloth of growing grass was fabricated, and the dining room was ornamented with young animals in glass cages. Subsequently, while Ambassador in Paris, in order that he might have the best chef in Europe provide the confections for his spring ball, Bullitt borrowed the renowned chef of Admiral Horthy of Hungary and had him flown to Paris for the event.

In spite of the fact that the social side of diplomatic life can be boring in the extreme it oftentimes furnishes opportunities for making very important contacts and getting information of considerable value. Even Ambassador Walter H. Page, who could hardly be accused of social butterfly tendencies, enjoyed heartily the social season in London and conceded that he heard more gossip, got more points of view, saw more people and got closer to his colleagues than at any other time of the year.[16]

Diplomatic Uniforms.   Before concluding this subject of social functions a word must be said regarding diplomatic costumes. Diplomatic ceremonial occasions have always been noted for the brilliant and elaborate costumes and dress worn by the foreign representatives. Although the United States for over a century appointed no representative higher than a minister plenipotentiary, no objection was raised in the early days of American diplomacy to the wearing of an elaborate diplomatic uniform. Benjamin Franklin is alleged to have appeared at the court of Louis XVI wigless and carrying a crabapple cane, but subsequently he wore a blue court dress embroidered with gold and his scanty locks were covered by a wig. A State Department circular of 1817 prescribed a costume consisting of a blue coat lined with white silk, a gold embroidered cape, white cassimere breeches with gold knee buckles, white silk stockings and gold or gilt shoe buckles. A three-cornered hat with a black cockade and a sword completed the costume.

Secretary of State Van Buren during the super-democratic administration of President Jackson suggested that a black coat with a gold star on each side of the collar "the underclothes to be black, blue or white at the option of the wearer," a three-cornered hat and a sword with a white scabbard would be cheap and adapted to the simplicity of our institutions.[17]

Secretary Marcy in a famous circular dated June 1, 1853, urged the

[16] Burton J. Hendrick, *Life and Letters of Walter H. Page* (New York, 1922-25), III, 47.
[17] Moore, *op. cit.,* IV, 761.

American diplomat to show his sense of devotion to republican institutions by appearing at court in the simple dress of an American citizen. If occasions arose when such a costume seemed inadvisable the envoy was expected to wear a costume with the minimum of elegance to suit the occasion.[18] Townsend Harris on his mission to Japan in 1857 completely disregarded the suggestion and arrayed himself and his cohorts in finery almost Oriental in its lavishness.

Inasmuch as the ordinary evening dress of an American citizen was exactly the same as the regular habiliments of waiters and servants, to many Europeans the regulation seemed ridiculous in the extreme. The American Minister to Great Britain, Mr. Buchanan, stayed away from the opening of Parliament in 1854 because no one was admitted unless in full court dress. Buchanan finally compromised by wearing a sword with his evening suit of black to the Queen's levee, a costume which was recognized as appropriate.

At the same time the American Minister at Paris, Mr. Mason, decided that a uniform of simple character was desirable for ceremonial functions, but the Secretary of the Legation, Mr. Sanford, who, as Chargé d'Affaires, had worn a regulation American evening dress suit, resigned in high dudgeon at his superior's willingness to wear a "diplomatic livery." In Stockholm the King was willing to receive Minister Shroeder in plain dress for diplomatic business but court occasions required court dress. Minister Vroom at Berlin was informed that the Emperor would consider an appearance before him without court regalia as disrespectful so he adopted a fairly elegant costume. The American Minister at Vienna wore his uniform as a colonel.

The matter caused so much discussion that the Senate took up the question and debated it at length. The result was a joint resolution of the Congress passed March 27, 1867, which "prohibited persons in the diplomatic service of the United States from wearing any uniform or official costume not previously authorized by Congress." Inasmuch as Congress had already permitted Army and Navy officers to wear their uniforms, diplomatic envoys who had served in the fighting services could wear their dress uniforms.[19]

The question of dress came up with Mr. Washburne, American Minister to France, on the occasion of the opening of the new Corps Législatif, November 29, 1869, which was regarded as one of the most colorful of French ceremonial occasions. Washburne noted the situation in his memoirs: "The diplomatic corps was present in full numbers, and all glittering in uniform and tinsel except myself. Congress had very wisely

[18] *Ibid.*, 762.

[19] This subject is elaborately covered in *Senate Executive Document* No. 31, 36th Cong., 1st sess. (April 2, 1860), and in John Bassett Moore, *Digest of International Law*, IV, 761-3. See also Eugene Schuyler, *American Diplomacy* (New York, 1895), 139-45, and John W. Foster, *The Practice of Diplomacy* (New York, 1906), 130-41.

prohibited its diplomats from indulging in the nonsense and flummery of court dress. I did not see but that, in my plain suit of black, I got along as well as any of the others." [20]

Other American representatives, however, have felt otherwise about the regulation. Eugene Schuyler, finding himself the only black-coated person at the ceremony when the Grand Duke Alexis of Russia took the oath of allegiance, felt very awkward and found the law requiring an American representative to appear in the costume of a waiter foolish and ridiculous.[21]

Ambassador Choate is said to have remarked to Whitelaw Reid while they were standing in court queue: "At a court this republican simplicity dodge of ours about plain clothes is the most impertinent piece of swagger in the world . . . not one human being in the room fails to notice the conspicuous character of their dress or to know that they are the modest and retiring American ambassador." [22]

George Horton, for many years Consul General of the United States, tells of a touchy, pompous American minister who was approached by a lady at a social function with the query, "I beg pardon, but are you the butler?" "No, madame," he snapped at her, "are you the chambermaid?" [23]

The Foreign Service Regulations of the United States simply state that Foreign Service officers and employees are forbidden to wear any uniform other than one authorized by the Congress.[24] Nevertheless, the American foreign envoy has been permitted a certain degree of latitude in his attire. Secretary Olney in 1896 instructed Mr. Breckinridge, American Minister to Russia, that he might conform to local requirements and wear the prescribed costume appropriate to the occasion. Three years later Assistant Secretary of State Adee, noted the distinction which the Department of State made between a uniform and a court dress conforming to local custom. The latter was regarded as not obnoxious to the statutory prohibition.[25] A diplomatic envoy affiliated with a recognized military or naval organization is permitted to wear the uniform of that group.

At the present time the Court of St. James's is one of the few diplomatic posts where some sort of court costume is *de rigueur*. Ambassador Walter H. Page notes the fact that at a King's levee "if you are not entitled to wear a uniform you have a dark suit, knee breeches, and a funny little sword." George Harvey was much ridiculed in the American press for wearing court dress on ceremonial occasions. Ambassador Dawes, who

---

[20] Elihu B. Washburne, *Recollections of a Minister to France* (New York, 1889), I, 20.
[21] Eugene Schuyler, *Essays and Memoirs* (New York. 1901), 34.
[22] Royal Cortissoz, *Life of Whitelaw Reid* (New York, 1921), II, 351.
[23] George Horton, *Recollections Grave and Gay* (Indianapolis, 1927), 74.
[24] *Regulations* (February, 1946), I, 27.
[25] Moore, *op. cit.*, IV, 772.

seemed possessed with the idea that to be himself he had to be different from everyone else, appeared at court in plain evening clothes, instead of knee breeches. A special dispensation is said to have been made for him in the matter of dress, but not at his solicitation.[26]

Ambassador John G. Winant confessed his lack of qualifications as to ceremonial attire. He declared that the first time that he wore a tall hat and a tail coat at a tea in Buckingham Palace everybody wore a straw hat and a short coat; when later he wore a short coat and straw hat everyone else had a tall hat and tail coat. Ambassador Gerard, who served in Germany just before World War I, declared that he had given up the fancy diplomatic uniform which some of his predecessors had designed, for the "democratic, if unattractive, dress suit" because congressmen and newspapermen while not objecting to uniforms being worn by the Army and Navy, police and postmen, were prejudiced against the usual diplomatic uniform.[27]

The American regulations regarding diplomatic uniforms are now so well known that although the American representative may be somewhat conspicuous in his simple black evening dress—"a crow in a flock of parrots"—nevertheless he is wearing the costume specified and need not worry further about it. Andrew D. White, whose diplomatic career was long and distinguished, was inclined to regard the whole question as of little importance. In his autobiography he frankly confesses that "having never worn anything save plain evening dress at any court to which I have been accredited, or at any function which I have attended, I have never been able to discover the slightest disadvantage to my country or myself from that fact." [28] Perhaps one may agree with Talleyrand who when he saw Castlereagh at Vienna wearing his ordinary dress-coat with the Order of the Garter among the resplendently attired ambassadors bedecked with insignia and decorations exclaimed: "Ma foi! C'est distingué."

Decorations, Presents, and Honors. Governments have long recognized the fact that foreign governments might attempt to influence their envoys by presents and decorations and have therefore frowned upon the acceptance of such forms. Queen Elizabeth of England went so far as to send to prison two of her Envoys, Anthony Sherly and Nicholas Clifford, for having accepted without her permission the order of Saint Michel from King Henry IV of France.[29] The Constitution of the United States specifically forbids any employee of the Federal Government from accepting any presents, offices or titles of any kind from any foreign state without the consent of Congress. John Quincy Adams, after having refused

---

[26] Paul R. Leach, *That Man Dawes* (Chicago, 1930), 316.
[27] James W. Gerard, *My Four Years in Germany* (New York, 1917), 22.
[28] *Autobiography of Andrew D. White* (New York, 1905), II, 371.
[29] Vladimir Potiemkine, *Histoire de la Diplomatie* (Paris, no date), I, 170.

the usual present for ministers valued at four hundred pounds sterling given by the British Government at the termination of his mission, expressed his approval of the American practice first because of the possibilities of corruption and secondly because the United States would not reciprocate. "For American ministers to be receiving gifts from foreign powers whose diplomatic agents in America never receive anything in return would exhibit them rather as beggars receiving alms from opulent princes than as the independent representatives of a high minded and virtuous republic." [30]

The *Regulations* prohibit Foreign Service officers "from accepting under any circumstances any present, decoration, medal, or testimonial that may be tendered to them by any foreign sovereign, head of state, or foreign government." [31] Nevertheless, if presents or testimonials are tendered in acknowledgment of services, the envoy may apply to Congress for permission to accept them.

The Congress of the United States has been very loath to grant the necessary permission and it was not until 1856 that several naval officers were permitted by a special act of Congress to receive gold medals for exceptional service. In December, 1874, for example, the Germans wished to give the American Minister to France, Elihu Washburne, some testimonial in recognition of his services to Germany during the Franco-Prussian War. Congress would not permit him to receive such a gift, so Washburne received the appreciation expressed in a letter from the Emperor. After his term of office, however, Emperor William caused a full-length portrait to be painted for Washburne and sent it to the German Consul at Southampton to be presented to the Minister on his way home when he was out of office. Similar portraits were received by Washburne from Bismarck, Thiers, Gambetta, and Lord Lyons, the British Ambassador at Paris.

By an act approved January 31, 1881, Congress authorized eight American officials of whom all but two were Army or Navy officers to accept decorations from various governments and sovereigns. The act further provided that "any present, decoration, or other thing which shall be offered or presented by any foreign government to any officer of the United States, civil, naval, or military, shall be tendered through the Department of State and not to the individual in person, but such present, decoration or other thing, shall not be delivered by the Department of State unless so authorized by act of Congress." [32]

Prior to 1918 the Department of State had recommended to Congress some two hundred cases, so few of which were approved that the Department finally adopted the policy of merely submitting such cases to Con-

[30] John Quincy Adams, *Memoirs* (Philadelphia, 1875), III, 527.
[31] *Regulations, op. cit.*, XV, 4.
[32] 21 *U.S. Statutes at Large*, 603.

gress through the President without recommendation. The war, however, brought about a new situation and by an act of Congress of July 9, 1918,[33] officers of the Army and Navy were permitted to accept decorations from allied powers similar to those conferred by the Government of the United States upon its own members. The United States reciprocated in that numerous foreign officers were honored by being awarded the distinguished service medal of the United States.

An interesting case was put to Congress in 1918 when the British Government presented a piece of silver plate to each of the twenty-two members of the American Embassy in Berlin in grateful recognition of the work which they had done in protecting British interests for over two years or until the United States entered the war.[34] The gifts consisted of cups, centerpieces, inkstands and picture frames and ranged in value from about $15 to $100. In his letter to the chairman of the House Committee on Foreign Affairs Secretary of State Lansing indorsed the bill as an exceptional case because of existing conditions and the humane, meritorious and laborious services rendered by the staff of the Embassy at Berlin in looking after British prisoners of war and otherwise representing British interests in Germany. He also felt that we should recognize the spirit of gratitude which induced the British Government to offer this plate and that it would be an act of international comity to permit its acceptance. The Congress after debate consented.

In the same way the British Government wished to show its gratitude to Ambassador Herrick in France for the protection accorded after the French Government and British Embassy had left Paris early in the war, and sent on to his home in Cleveland a piece of old English silver plate. The French Government bestowed upon Mr. Herrick the Grand Cross of the Legion of Honor, its highest distinction,[35] and the city of Paris bestowed upon him a gold medal.[36] As Herrick had already returned to private life, no action of Congress was necessary.

In fact, many an American representative unable to accept a token of appreciation from a foreign government while in office has with perfect propriety received the gift or decoration after retiring from public service. When Benjamin Franklin resigned as Minister to France in 1785, the King, in honor of his remarkable services and as a token of his personal affection for Franklin, presented him with his portrait circled twice with 408 diamonds. Governor Andrew Gregg Curtin, former American Minister to Russia, was unable to accept the portrait of the Emperor at the close of his mission, but later the Emperor's portrait as well as one of Prince Gortschakoff were forwarded to America and hung in Governor Curtin's

---

[33] 40 U.S. Statutes at Large, 872.
[34] 40 U.S. Statutes at Large, 1326.
[35] T. Bentley Mott, Myron T. Herrick, Friend of France (New York, 1929), 230.
[36] Mott, op. cit., 253.

home.[37] In the same way, the Grand Cordon of SS. Maurice and Lazare was received by Ambassador Draper from the King of Italy after his resignation.[38] At the close of his mission to France in 1905 Ambassador Porter had conferred upon him the Grand Cross of the Legion of Honor. The French Government offered to bestow at the same time a similar honor upon Secretary of State Hay. An act of Congress was necessary in the second instance, and a resolution to this effect was introduced. However, when strong senatorial objection was manifested Secretary Hay requested that the resolution be withdrawn.[39] Former Foreign Minister Holsti of Finland informed the author that when he presented a decoration to Joseph Grew, the Secretary General of the American Peace Delegation at Versailles, the latter asked that the decoration be deposited in his name in the State Department, which would turn it over to him when he left the Foreign Service. An executive order, March 19, 1937, however, forbade this practice and Secretary Hull in an instruction dated March 10, 1938, declared that the Department of State must decline to accept decorations or presents for deposit on behalf of American diplomatic and consular officers when tendered by a foreign embassy or legation in Washington. It should be noted that Acting Secretary of State Sumner Welles in an instruction dated December 13, 1938, to the United States Embassy in Chile declared that "the prohibition against the acceptance of foreign decorations was held not to apply to wives of officers of the United States." [40]

The *Foreign Service Regulations of the United States* specifically forbid Foreign Service officers from transmitting gifts from foreign citizens, subject or organizations to the President of the United States. However, a delicate problem sometimes arises when a foreign potentate wishes to bestow a present upon the President. Such acts are normal in oriental countries and a refusal of acceptance would be regarded as a serious discourtesy. An amusing incident occurred in connection with the arrival of the first Cambodian minister to the United States. The American Minister at Saigon, Donald Heath, telegraphed to the American Chargé at Pnompenh that Saigon newspapers carried a White House announcement that the King of Cambodia was sending a white elephant to President Truman. Chargé Don Cattell investigated and replied that the King said he could not have made such a promise since white elephants were nonexistent, but nevertheless he would gladly send an elephant to the President. President Truman, although not partial to elephants, could not refuse to accept the gift and the diplomatic corps thereupon had a real

[37] William H. Egle, ed., *Andrew Gregg Curtin: His Life and Services* (New York, 1896), 65-8.
[38] William F. Draper, *Recollections of a Varied Career* (New York, 1908), 330.
[39] Elsie Porter Mende, *An American Soldier and Diplomat* (New York, 1927), 289.
[40] See Hackworth, *op. cit.*, IV, 475-84.

problem in securing suitable transportation. After months of negotiation regarding trucks, boats, food for the elephant, a mahout to accompany him, the elephant was shipped from Singapore. When it died en route the King of Cambodia sent his regrets and promised to send a more transportable present the next time.

American diplomatic representatives have had honors conferred upon them of a different character which clearly do not come within the Constitutional prohibition. For example, American diplomatic representatives to Great Britain, Lowell, Choate, and Page, were chosen as presidents of the Birmingham and Midland Institute, an unofficial but very outstanding honor. Ambassador Choate was the first non-British subject ever to be made an honorary bencher of the Honorable Society of the Middle Temple. Ambassador Davis was later given the same recognition. Ambassador Davis was also made Senior Warden of the Grand Lodge of Freemasons of England, a unique distinction never before conferred upon a foreigner.[41]

When Whitelaw Reid was Ambassador to Great Britain Mr. Gladstone inquired as to what honors the United States conferred upon its citizens as a reward for distinguished public service. Reid was at first somewhat at a loss to reply. He finally answered: "There are only three things we can do. If they live at the North, we can invite them to lecture; if they live at the South, we can call them Colonel or General; wherever they live, if they can get votes enough we can send them to Congress and let them take the consequences."[42]

[41] Theodore H. Huntley, *John W. Davis* (New York, 1924), 117.
[42] Cortissoz, *op. cit.*, II, 334.

13

Diplomatic Rights and Privileges

Legal Basis of Diplomatic Privileges. We have already seen in a previous chapter that diplomatic privileges and immunities are among the oldest examples of customary international law. Both in ancient times and in the dark ages the sacred and inviolable character of the ambassador was everywhere recognized. In fact, so well have these principles been established that states have not always regarded it as necessary to reassert them in conventional law. Nevertheless treaties dating back as far as the seventeenth century have certain provisions relating to diplomatic privileges and immunities. For example, a treaty of peace, friendship, and commerce concluded between James I of England and Michael Romanov, Grand Duke of Russia in 1623, provided for certain diplomatic privileges and immunities.[1] Subsequent treaties between Great Britain and Denmark in 1670,[2] Great Britain and Portugal [3] in 1809, and Great Britain and Turkey also in 1809 [4] have somewhat similar provisions.

A number of states have also passed municipal laws providing that any act against a diplomatic agent was punishable as a criminal offense. According to Wicquefort, the Netherlands in 1651 promulgated a law which forbade anyone from offending, damaging or injuring by words, by act or by appearance ambassadors, ministers, or other diplomatic agents of kings, princes, republics, or anyone else having the quality of public minister.[5]

England in 1708 voted the Act of 7 Anne for the protection of the privileges of ambassadors and other envoys of princes and of foreign states.[6] The laws of the United States declare that every person who "assaults, strikes, wounds, imprisons, or in any other manner offers violence to the person of a public minister in violation of the law of nations shall

[1] J. Dumont, *Corps universel diplomatique du droit des gens* (Amsterdam, 1726-31), V, Pt. II, 436.
[2] *Ibid.*, VII, Pt. I, 132.
[3] Sir E. Hertslet, *Commercial Treaties*, 30 vols. (London, 1820-1925), II, 27.
[4] *Ibid.*, II, 371.
[5] A. de Wicquefort, *L'ambassadeur et ses fonctions* (London, 1840), I, Sect. 2.
[6] *British and Foreign State Papers*, I, 993.

be imprisoned for not more than three years and fined at the discretion of the court." [7]

Certain states, particularly those which have codes based upon the Napoleonic Code, have accepted the principle that diplomatic immunities are regulated by international law and consequently have not sought to regulate the question by municipal legislation. A law of Haiti states that diplomatic agents are governed by international law, the customs of states and by political treaties. [8]

Status While en Route through Third States. Inasmuch as a diplomatic agent proceeding to his post often finds it necessary to cross the territory of a third state, certain principles have been advanced as to his status, although authorities still differ as to just how far his privileges and immunities extend. Most of the classic writers, including Grotius, Bynkershoek, Gentilis, and Zouche, were inclined to restrict an ambassador's privileges to the state to which he was accredited. As Gentilis puts it, "from their very name, the function of ambassadors is limited to those to whom they are sent. Among others they are not entitled to the rights of embassy." [9] More recently Baron Heyking takes the same position: "In the absence of a special arrangement to the contrary . . . the state which permits passage enjoys with regard to the ambassador all the rights which it may possess against a private person." [10]

The weight of modern authority, however, is inclined to grant the envoy a right of innocent passage "through all states friendly to his own country and to the honors and protection which nations reciprocally owe to each other's diplomatic agents . . . and any insult or injury to him is regarded as an insult or injury both to the state which sends him and that to which he is sent." [11] Wheaton, Wharton, Rivier, Satow, Pradier-Fodéré, Fauchille, and Genet take this view. The Superior Court of New York in 1839 and again in 1889 set aside summons against diplomatic envoys passing through on the way to their posts. [12] When a head tax was imposed upon the Japanese Chargé d'Affaires in Mexico by administrative officials of the United States as he was returning to his country via El Paso and San Francisco, the Secretary of Commerce and Labor of the United States declared that "the action of administrative officers in

---

[7] *Revised Statutes of the United States*, par. 4062.

[8] See Sir Cecil Hurst, "Les immunités diplomatiques," Académie de Droit International, *Recueil des Cours*, XII, 137.

[9] Alberico Gentili, "De Legationibus" (Libri Tres), *Classics of International Law*, No. 12 (Oxford, 1924), II, 62.

[10] A. Heyking, "L'Exterritorialité," Académie de Droit International, *Recueil des Cours*, VII, 266.

[11] H. W. Halleck, *International Law*, 2 vols. (London, 1908), I, 389.

[12] Manley O. Hudson, *Cases and Other Material on International Law* (St. Paul, 1929), 854; James Brown Scott, *Cases on International Law*, 2nd ed. (St. Paul, 1922), 293.

collecting a head tax on account of the diplomatic and consular officers of foreign countries seeking admission into the United States was in error." [13] Finally the Convention on Diplomatic Officers adopted by the American states at Havana in 1928 provides:

> Persons belonging to the mission shall also enjoy the same immunities and prerogatives in the States which they cross to arrive at their post or to return to their own country, or in a State where they may casually be during the exercise of their functions and to whose Government they have made known their position.[14]

An interesting case of opposition to the passage through an intervening state of an American diplomatic representative occurred in France during the régime of Emperor Napoleon III. Pierre Soulé, the American Minister to Madrid, after attending a conference at Ostend arrived at Calais intending to return to his post via Paris. He was stopped there by a ministerial order and refused permission to proceed without the Government's knowledge. Mr. Mason, American Minister to France, protested and the French Minister of Foreign Affairs declared the French Government had no intention of preventing an American envoy from crossing French territory to go to his post and if Minister Soulé were going directly to Madrid the route of France was open; if he intended to stop over in Paris, however, that privilege was not accorded. The United States was satisfied with the recognition of the right of its envoy to traverse France, but Soulé went back by way of Great Britain and Portugal. The reason for Napoleon's answer seems to have been that Soulé, a naturalized American of French birth, had made speeches against the government of Louis Napoleon and had fought a duel with the French Ambassador at Madrid.[15]

We have already mentioned the case of Madame Kollontay, the Russian Ambassador to Mexico, who was refused innocent passage through the United States in 1926 by Secretary Kellogg because the United States at that time did not entertain diplomatic relations with the Soviet Government.[16]

The question has been raised as to whether a diplomatic agent may claim the same privileges and immunities from a third state if he is temporarily sojourning there for no reason connected with his official duties. In this instance it would appear that such privileges as might be accorded would be by comity rather than by law. For example, when divorce proceedings were instituted in Paris in 1910 against the secretary of the United States Legation at Brussels, although the Paris court declared

[13] *Foreign Relations of the United States, 1903,* 664.
[14] *Sixth International Conference of American States: Final Act* (Habana, 1928), Article 23, "Convention on Diplomatic Officers."
[15] John Bassett Moore, *Digest of International Law* (Washington, 1906), IV, 557.
[16] *Department of State Press Release* (Washington, November 5, 1926).

itself incompetent because the defendant had never been domiciled in France, nevertheless the court held that envoys could not claim immunity when a sojourn in third states had no connection with their official duties.[17]

In similar fashion the New York Superior Court in 1924 in the case of Carbone *v.* Carbone held that there was a clear distinction between immunity from civil process and immunity from arrest. The country of passage is only obligated not to restrain him from discharging his diplomatic function by restricting his personal liberty. Therefore a warrant for the arrest of the Panamanian attaché to Italy was annulled, but a motion to vacate the service of summons was denied.[18]

The instructions to American diplomatic officers note the fact that transit free of customs dues is usually conceded by a third state through whose territory a diplomatic representative passes on his way to or from his post. However, it is conceded that the status of the envoy in the third state "lacks the extra-territorial element of immunity belonging to him in the country to which he is accredited." [19]

The Counselor of the Italian Embassy in Japan was given the free entry of his baggage and effects without examination upon his arrival in San Francisco in 1909, and the Treasury Department in 1936 authorized the customs officers in New York to extend free entry privileges to the wife of the Brazilian Minister in Warsaw arriving in transit at that port.[20]

Perhaps it should be noted that an envoy when planning to travel through states to which he is not accredited receives as a matter of courtesy at the same time as the visas a letter of *laisser-passer* to all customs authorities.

Passage through Third States in Time of War. In time of war the question of innocent passage is somewhat more complex. Early in 1866 Charles A. Washburn, American Minister to Paraguay, was prevented by Brazil and Argentina, who were at the time at war with Paraguay from passing up the Parana River to reach his post at Asuncion. Secretary Seward protested vigorously to both Argentina and Brazil and they finally gave the necessary orders although under protest. A year later when an American naval vessel was sent to convey Minister Washburn and his family back to the United States, permission was again refused and it was only when Mr. Webb, the American Minister to Brazil, threatened to ask for his passport that the American public vessel was permitted to carry out the mission.[21]

At the outbreak of World War I when Mr. Dumba, Austrian Ambas-

[17] *Journal de Droit International, Clunet* (1910), 529.

[18] Edwin DeWitt Dickinson, *Cases on the Law of Nations* (New York, 1929), 585.

[19] *Instructions to Diplomatic Officers of the United States* (Washington, 1927), VII, 13.

[20] Green H. Hackworth, *Digest of International Law* (Washington, 1942), IV, 589.

[21] Graham H. Stuart, *Latin America and the United States* (New York, 1943), 468.

sador to the United States, and Captains Boy-Ed and von Papen, German
naval and military attachés, were recalled at the request of the United
States they were granted safe conducts by the Allied Powers at the
request of the United States. In the same way, when the United States
entered the war, Count Bernstorff, German Ambassador to the United
States, was granted safe conduct by the Allies for his return to Germany
at the request of the United States.[22] On the other hand, when Count
Tarnowski was appointed to succeed Dumba as Ambassador to Washington, the British Government refused him a safe conduct on the ground
that his predecessor had plotted against the Allies. The United States
protested on the ground that sovereign states possessed an inalienable
right to exchange ambassadors and that third states, even in time of war,
were not justified in denying it. The United States won its contention.[23]

The British Government issued an *aide-mémoire* in 1939, stating that it
was the practice of the British Government to refrain from removing from
neutral ships or detaining the following categories of persons: heads of
diplomatic missions accredited to neutral states and their families and
servants accompanying them; diplomatic or commercial counselors, secretaries, attachés; military, naval, and air attachés; career consuls and vice
consuls.[24]

The Beginning of Diplomatic Privileges. Authorities still differ as to
the exact time when diplomatic privileges and immunities begin. Some
claim that they begin once the person nominated has been accepted by
the receiving state. Others would wait until the formal reception was held
by the receiving state. Still others date the operation from the moment the
envoy enters the territory of the receiving state. The latter view would
seem to be the most reasonable and it has been sanctioned both by law
and by treaty. The Panamanian law of 1925 (Article 44) declares that
"the inviolability of diplomatic agents and their exemption from local
jurisdiction commences from the moment of entry at the frontiers of the
state. . . ." [25] Paraguay follows the same rule. The Havana Convention on
Diplomatic Officers of 1928 declares: "Diplomatic officers enter upon the
enjoyment of their immunity from the moment they pass the frontier of
the State where they are going to serve and make known their position." [26]

Exemption from Customs Duties. Among the privileges generally
accorded to a diplomatic envoy by comity rather than by law is that of
exemption from customs duties. Vattel did not feel that a public minister

[22] J. W. Garner, *International Law and the World War* (London, 1920), I, 45.
[23] Charles G. Fenwick, *International Law,* 2nd ed. (New York, 1934), 378.
[24] Hackworth, *op. cit.,* IV, 465.
[25] A. H. Feller and Manley O. Hudson, *Diplomatic and Consular Laws and Regulations* (Washington, 1933), II, 942.
[26] *Sixth International Conference of American States, op. cit.,* Article 22.

deserved any consideration of this sort inasmuch as the payment of duties in no way interfered with the performance of his official functions. Even Vattel, however, conceded that "the independence of the ambassador exempts him from all personal or capitation taxes and other assessments of that character." [27] Nevertheless, at the present time it is a common usage of international intercourse that a diplomat be given the privilege of importing without the payment of duties all articles for his official or personal use and at the same time he is exempt from income or other personal and sumptuary taxes. The application of this privilege varies in different countries, and in some is restricted to the chief of the mission. It is the duty of the representative to acquaint himself with the formalities and limitations prescribed in such case by the local law or regulations and to conform therewith. The privilege is one of usage and tradition, rather than of inherent right. The practice of the Government of the United States is to accord such privileges to chiefs of missions, and on a reciprocal basis to members of their staffs.

Supplies for the official use of foreign embassies and legations such as office furniture may be entered free of duty but upon a reciprocity basis. Materials to be used in the construction of embassy or legation buildings are exempt from customs duties. The United States customs regulations of 1937 include the free entry of automobiles for the use of diplomats and their families and permit their subsequent sale without any claims being made.[28]

The laws of the following countries specifically provide for the exemption of diplomatic envoys from tariff duties: Austria, Belgium, France, Germany, Great Britain, Italy, the Netherlands, the Union of Soviet Socialist Republics, Spain, and the United States.[29] It should be noted that such privileges are regularly upon a reciprocity basis. Some states limit the exemption to the heads of mission alone. Others extend the exemption to members of the mission personnel. Some states grant exemption only during the first year of residence. Great Britain limits the amount of wines, spirits, and tobacco while Italy restricts the number of cigars and cigarettes which may be entered free of duty.

If by chance the customs agents suspect some irregularity they may insist upon an inspection of the luggage. A case of this kind occurred in 1905 when the American Ambassador to Italy, Henry White, returning to his post from a vacation in Austria, was held up on the Italian frontier and his baggage carefully inspected.[30]

It goes without saying that a diplomatic agent ought not to take ad-

[27] E. de Vattel, "Law of Nations," *Classics of International Law* (Washington, 1916), III, 385.
[28] *Foreign Service Regulations of the United States* (Washington, February, 1946), III, 5.
[29] Feller and Hudson, *op. cit., passim.*
[30] *Revue générale de droit international public* (Paris, 1906), XIII, 205.

vantage of these privileges. According to Callières, "There are a number of ministers who abuse the right of customs exemption which they possess in various countries, both as regards provisions and in the case of merchandise necessary for the maintenance of their establishment. These representatives go so far as to enter a large amount of provisions for the merchants from whom they exact tribute by lending to them their name in order to defraud the sovereign."[31] Genet states that large quantities of narcotics of German origin have been introduced into France under the protection of the legation of an Oriental country.[32]

Embassy Importations in the United States. During the era of prohibition in the United States a number of interesting incidents occurred with regard to "embassy liquor" as it was called. Inasmuch as in spite of the Volstead Act diplomats were privileged to have their liquor protected from seizure and confiscation, liquor shipments to embassies and legations occurred regularly. The normal procedure of foreign representatives was to notify the Department of State when a shipment of liquor was due and to request free entry. The State Department referred the request to the Treasury Department which granted the permission. Upon arrival of the shipment an attaché of the embassy or legation would go to the port of entry, present his credentials, identify the shipment and have it transported to the official residence.

The police, however, were overzealous at times and upon a number of occasions detained or arrested drivers of trucks carrying "embassy liquor." Matters were brought to a head when on March 15, 1929, the Washington police seized a truckload of sixty cases of whiskies, wines and other intoxicating beverages consigned to the Siamese Legation, in spite of the fact that the Third Secretary of the Legation was riding with the truck driver. Although the liquor was subsequently delivered and none was kept for evidence, the driver and his helper were held under bond and the truck confiscated.

In order to prevent further incidents of this sort, on March 22, 1929, the Treasury Department issued an order granting complete immunity for the importation into the United States and the transportation to the diplomatic mission to which it was consigned of all "embassy liquor." The only restrictions were that all liquor should be imported through Baltimore and that due notification be given the United States authorities so that a Treasury Department order identifying the shipment might be delivered to the diplomat. Any infraction of the diplomat's immunity by a peace officer of the United States would make the latter liable to a severe penalty.[33]

[31] F. de Callières, *De la manière de négocier avec les souverains* (Paris, 1716), 163.
[32] Raoul Genet, *Traité de diplomatie et de droit diplomatique* (Paris, 1931), I, 437.
[33] *New York Times* (March 23, 1929).

When the Japanese Chargé d'Affaires in 1924 requested that the free passage through the United States of a case of Japanese sakè for the personal use of the Japanese Minister at Mexico City be arranged, Under Secretary Grew declared that such transportation would be a violation of the laws of the United States.[34]

American diplomats returning from their posts were not able to plead diplomatic immunity as a basis of nonpayment of duties on liquor after the end of prohibition, even though the liquor was claimed to be remnants of the embassy stock. According to Washington correspondents, Walter E. Edge, Ambassador to France, and Frederic M. Sackett, Ambassador to Germany, had unused stocks amounting to 900 and 400 bottles, respectively. Secretary of the Treasury Morgenthau, a Democrat, saw no reason to postpone the operation of customs regulations in order to accommodate two wealthy Republican ex-diplomats.

Exemption from Taxes. Although there is not as much uniformity in the exemption from other taxes, an examination of the laws of the various countries indicates that the diplomatic agent is usually exempt from the payment of income taxes or any tax upon property owned or used for the purposes of the mission. Taxes on automobiles and licenses for their use are generally included in the exemptions, while stamp taxes as a rule must be paid.

As an act of international courtesy and on a reciprocal basis the District of Columbia issues free of charge special diplomatic license plates for the automobiles of diplomats and members of their families in Washington.

According to a ruling made by Assistant Secretary of State Messersmith in 1937, diplomatic officers residing in the United States are entitled to exemption from sales taxes such as those imposed on gasoline, automobile tires and inner tubes if they are purchased from the producer or manufacturer for their personal or official use. Reciprocal treatment is of course expected. The exemption from state sales taxes in the United States is also customary.

When in 1932 the authorities in Tokyo made certain assessments against the American Embassy in connection with improvements on streets bordering the Embassy property the Department authorized the payment but at the same time the American Ambassador was instructed to inform the Foreign Office that the Japanese Embassy in Washington was exempt from the payment of similar assessments.[35]

A clear distinction should be noted between taxes and assessments or charges. It is not to be expected that a state where the government controls water, gas, and electricity will furnish these utilities to the foreign envoy

[34] Hackworth, *op. cit.*, IV, 600-1.
[35] Hackworth, *op. cit.*, IV, 574, 580.

free of charge. In the same way, any property owned by the diplomatic envoy or members of his family not used for residence or purposes connected with the mission need not be exempt from taxation. According to the laws of the United States, ministers and ambassadors accredited to the United States are exempt from payment of the Federal income tax upon their salaries or upon income derived from investments in the United States. The income derived from any business carried on by them would be taxable. Property in the District of Columbia owned by foreign governments for embassy and legation purposes is exempt from general and special taxes and assessments. Property owned by an ambassador or minister and used for mission purposes is exempt from general taxes but not from special assessments or improvements. The payment of water assessments is required in all cases as this is not regarded as a tax but the sale of a commodity.[36]

Right of Chapel. Another privilege or prerogative of comity rather than law is the right of private religious worship, or the *droit de chapelle.* This privilege included the right of constructing a chapel for the diplomatic mission and making use of it; of maintaining an ecclesiastic in it in charge of the religious service and permission for other persons, particularly the fellow citizens of the envoy, to take part in the religious services.[37] Certain restrictions were sometimes imposed. The tolling of bells was not usually permitted; the state might require that the exterior of the chapel should not indicate its use; and the ceremony might be required to be carried on in the language of the diplomat. For example, in 1846, the Vatican informed the diplomatic agent for Prussia that services in the legation chapel might not be carried on in Italian.[38] In its treaties with Latin American states the United States formerly was accustomed to insert a clause regarding religious freedom and in the treaty with Venezuela of January 20, 1836, it was provided that citizens of the United States should not be disturbed in the proper exercise of their religion in private houses or in the chapels appropriated for that purpose.[39] The British Legation in Madrid formerly hired rooms for chapel attendance in a private home outside the Legation, but no sign directing worshippers to it was permitted on the outside of the chapel. The American colony regularly attended here.[40]

This privilege has no longer the same importance today as formerly when a spirit of religious intolerance existed and all profession except that of the state religion was prohibited.

[36] *Circular Instructions, Department of State* Serial No. 766 (November 9, 1928).
[37] P. Pradier-Fodéré, *Cours de droit diplomatique* (Paris, 1890), II, 267.
[38] F. von Holtzendorff, *Handbuch des Völkerrechts* (Leipzig, 1885-89), III, 659.
[39] *U.S. Statutes at Large,* 472.
[40] John W. Foster, *Diplomatic Memoirs* (New York, 1909), I, 289,

Ceremonial Privileges. The diplomatic representative has certain rights of ceremonial which may be briefly mentioned. He may place the national coat of arms above the principal entrance of his residence and he may fly his national flag upon occasions of special ceremony. A diplomatic official is usually entitled to a salute when a naval contingent of his country is in port. The number of guns fired apparently depends upon the regulations in force. The United States and Great Britain authorize a salute of nineteen guns for an ambassador, while the French give him seventeen; in the case of an envoy extraordinary and minister plenipotentiary the British authorize a salute of seventeen guns, the Americans fifteen and the French thirteen. The British minister resident receives fifteen, the American thirteen and the French eleven. The chargés d'affaires of Great Britain, the United States and France get respectively thirteen, eleven, and nine.[41] According to American practice the salute is usually fired while the diplomatic representative is being conveyed from the vessel to the shore. He stands facing the vessel and at the end of the salute he raises his hat in acknowledgment, or he may keep his hat in his hand throughout the salute.

Right to Title. Another prerogative of ambassadors is the right to the title of *Excellency.* This honorary title dates from the Treaty of Westphalia and according to Callières it is limited strictly to ambassadors. In practice, however, the title is quite commonly extended to ministers. The British, French, and Spanish Governments still authorize its use, but the United States makes no mention of it in its instructions to diplomatic officers.

The Diplomatic List. In many countries it is customary to publish a diplomatic list in which are inscribed all those persons who are recognized as having the right to the benefit of diplomatic privileges and immunities. Sometimes the chiefs of protocol keep a much more extensive list of the members of missions which serves as a list for official dinners and ceremonial functions. In Washington formerly a number of lawyers who acted as counselors for certain legations had their names inserted in the *Diplomatic List* in order to obtain invitations to the receptions at the White House. Secretary of State Root discontinued the practice by ruling that an American citizen could not be clothed with a diplomatic character in a foreign legation in Washington. The *Diplomatic List* is now published by the Department of State every month and is restricted rigidly to the names, addresses and telephone numbers of the members of the foreign

[41] *Instructions, op. cit.,* IV, 6; *King's Regulations and Admiralty Instructions,* Article 66; *Décret du 18 février, 1928,* Chap. II, Sect. III, *Journal Officiel du 2 juin, 1928,* 6085.

missions and their families. A similar supplemental list contains the names of the domestics of each embassy.

A number of states also issue diplomatic identity cards through their protocol officers to all diplomatic representatives and their wives and children. Turkey, for instance, issues such a card which guarantees to the holder full diplomatic immunity and the right to travel freely in the Turkish Republic.[42] When in 1937 the Dominican Republic requested the Department of State to issue identification cards to its subordinate employees the Department responded that the possession of identification cards was not a statutory requirement in the United States. However as a courtesy the United States issues upon request diplomatic identification cards gratuitously to accredited diplomatic officials. Special automobile license plates are also quite regularly issued to foreign envoys which by indicating the identity of the car warns off the overzealous sheriff in case of speeding. In Lima, Peru, where certain streets were for one-way traffic, the diplomat could travel in the opposite direction; he was also exempt from tolls on the highways which regularly collected them.

Although diplomatic privileges extend regularly to all the members of the envoy's staff, a rather curious clause of limitation is found in the Austro-Russian treaty of 1922. According to this provision complete diplomatic privileges are accorded to chiefs of mission and to seven other members of the legation, but the functionaries above that number are not immune even from arrest.[43]

The United States is inclined to a very liberal interpretation of foreign diplomatic lists which are submitted. All attachés including acting commerical attachés are acceptable; student interpreters and language attachés are specifically included. The Department of State has also sanctioned the inclusion in the list of employees of foreign embassies and legations the names of native physicians whose duty it was to minister solely to the medical needs of the chief and staff of the mission. Although the United States has no such post as physician to an embassy it authorized on one occasion the Ambassador in Tokyo to permit a doctor to assume the honorary title of "Physician to the American Embassy at Tokyo." It should be noted that the United States as a rule does not permit the inclusion in the *Diplomatic List* of the names of foreign diplomatic officers who have only honorary status.[44]

[42] Feller and Hudson, *op. cit.*, II, 1190.
[43] Francis Deák, "Classification, immunités, et privilèges des agents diplomatiques," *Revue de droit international et législation comparée* (1928), 193.
[44] Hackworth, *op. cit.*, IV, 433-4.

14

Diplomatic Immunities

Inviolability of Person. The inviolability of the person of the diplomatic agent is the fundamental principle from whence flow all other immunities. In order to obtain this absolute security the state must not only abstain itself from any act which infringes upon the rights of the diplomatic agent, but it must prevent the commission of such acts and punish any individuals who may have committed such an offense. According to Vattel, anyone "who did violence to an ambassador or to any other public minister not only committed an injury to the sovereign whom the minister represented but he attacks the common safety and welfare of all nations. . . ." [1]

The right of inviolability embraces all classes of public ministers—the chargé d'affaires enjoys this immunity as fully as does the ambassador. It extends to all the persons who either officially or unofficially are connected with the diplomatic mission, regardless of their nationality. Furthermore, the diplomatic agent should enjoy a greater degree of protection than the ordinary citizen of the country to which he is sent. For example, in 1912 a reporter of an important Cuban newspaper assaulted Hugh Gibson, Chargé d'Affaires of the United States in Havana. The assailant was arrested but the judge released him with the remark that it made no difference to him whether the victim was the minister of the United States or a Cuban of the lowest class. The United States Government protested vigorously at this interpretation of international law and demanded satisfaction. The reporter was finally taken into custody again and given a sentence of two and one-half years in jail. [2]

The long established inviolability of person of all diplomatic officials no longer holds in the police states "behind the iron curtain." The national employees of foreign embassies and legations in Communist-dominated states have no rights which these governments are willing to respect. The case of Michael Shipkov, a translator who worked in the United States

---

[1] E. de Vattel, "The Law of Nations," *Classics of International Law* (Washington, 1916), III, 371.
[2] *Foreign Relations of the United States, 1912,* 268. See also *National Cyclopedia of American Biography*, Current, Vol. A, 420.

Legation in Sofia, Bulgaria, is an excellent illustration. Mr. Shipkov was arrested by Communist secret police on August 20, 1949, as he left his work at the Legation. He was taken to a prison where after thirty-two hours of torture he broke down, confessed to acts that he had never perpetrated and even agreed to return and spy for the Communist police in the American Legation. Instead he returned and prepared an 8,000 word affidavit describing the methods of torture used to extort his confession. The United States attempted to obtain passports for Shipkov and his family to leave the country. The request was refused and Shipkov was again arrested and indicted for treason. His fate remains unknown. When another translator, Ivan Seculov, was arrested and was reported a suicide three days later and other employees resigned or disappeared the United States severed diplomatic relations with Bulgaria.[3]

The Assassination of Diplomats. In modern times the murder of a diplomat is rather a rare occurrence and when it does occur the government to which he is accredited is held strictly accountable. One of the famous instances was the murder of the German Minister to China, Baron von Kettler, by soldiers of the regular Chinese army during the Boxer uprising. The fact that he was on his way to the Tsung-li-yamen on an official errand made the offense the more serious. China was compelled to dispatch to Berlin an expiatory commission headed by an imperial prince to express the regrets of the Emperor of China and of the Chinese Government for the murder of the German Envoy. China was also compelled to erect in the place where the murder was committed a commemoration monument suitable to the rank of the deceased and bearing an inscription in Latin, German, and Chinese expressing the regrets of the Emperor of China for the murder.[4]

Another murder of a German diplomatic agent occurred in 1918 when Count Wilhelm Mirbach, the first German Ambassador to the Bolshevik Government, was assassinated in his office in the embassy by two Russians from the Left Social Revolutionary Party. The murderers also shot at the attachés and then threw a hand grenade to make certain that as much destruction as possible had been accomplished. Marie Spiridonova, Social Revolutionary leader, boasted that she had been the organizer of the plot to assassinate Mirbach in order to annul the Brest-Litovsk Treaty.[5] It was reported that the Bolsheviks shot some two hundred members of the Social Revolutionary Party for participation in the murder plot.

[3] *Department of State Bulletin* (March 13, 1950), XXII, 387-96.

[4] See Payson J. Treat, *The Far East* (New York, 1928), 346, 356, 424; also John Bassett Moore, *Digest of International Law* (Washington, 1906), V, 514-15. For an account of the reception of the expiatory mission of Prince Tschun see *Foreign Relations of the United States, 1901*, 187.

[5] Louis Fischer, *The Soviet in World Affairs* (London, 1930), I, 121.

An assassination under somewhat different circumstances occurred in 1923 when Mechilav Vorovsky, the Soviet unofficial observer to the Lausanne Conference, was murdered by a White Russian whose relatives, it was claimed, had been killed by the Soviets. In this case the Swiss Government did not regard itself responsible inasmuch as Vorovsky had not been invited to the Conference and when he appeared was definitely excluded. Nevertheless, when he was threatened by Swiss Fascists the Federal Government gave him police protection. The murderer was promptly arrested and confessed that this was merely a part of a plot of the old Russian Red Cross to kill Bolshevik leaders. In spite of his guilt, Conradi, the assassin, was acquitted by a Swiss jury. The Soviet Government protested violently, but Switzerland refused to act further. The Soviet Government thereupon instructed its representatives abroad to refuse passport visas to Swiss citizens desirous of entering Russia and later established a boycott on Swiss products.[6]

Another example of the murder of a public envoy occurred in 1927 when Peter Vorkoff, Soviet Minister at Warsaw, was assassinated by a Russian monarchist, Korenko. Marshal Pilsudski and all the members of the Polish cabinet expressed their profound regret and the Polish Government offered an indemnity to the widow. It also agreed to permit the Soviet Government to participate in an inquiry at Warsaw. Korenko was sentenced to fifteen years imprisonment and was later beaten in jail by Communists.

Redress for Offenses to Diplomats. The great majority of states have very strict laws punishing offenses against the person of a diplomat. We have already noted the laws of Holland and the United States on this subject. The French law of 1881 punishes any offense committed against ambassadors, ministers plenipotentiary, envoys, chargés d'affaires, or other diplomatic agents accredited to the government of the Republic with a week to a year's imprisonment and with a fine of 50 to 2,000 francs or either of the two penalties. This law was amended in 1893 to provide prosecution only at the instance of the injured party.[7] Austria and Italy regard ordinary offenses as aggravated when perpetrated against the person of a foreign envoy.

On January 17, 1932, the Ethiopian police and members of a crowd attacked American Minister Addison Southard and his chauffeur. The Department of State instructed him to seek an audience with the Emperor and to tell him that the United States expected that prompt action would be taken to punish the guilty parties and effective steps taken to prevent similar occurrences. The police involved were subsequently found guilty,

6 *New York Times* (May 11, November 17, 22, 1923).

7 A. H. Feller, and Manley O. Hudson, *Diplomatic and Consular Laws and Regulations* (Washington, 1933), I, 537.

fined and sentenced to a year in prison and the sentence publicly announced at the place of attack.[8]

Nationals Serving in Diplomatic Capacity.   The prerogatives of a diplomatic agent extend regularly to all the officials of the mission, although a state may refuse to grant immunity to one of its own nationals serving as secretary, except upon its own terms.[9] Some states refuse to receive their own nationals in any diplomatic capacity. When in 1886 the Government of Honduras appointed Jacob Baiz, an American citizen, as Chargé d'Affaires of the Republic to the Government of the United States, the Secretary of State refused to receive him on the ground that the privileges and immunities of a foreign minister made it inconvenient that a citizen of the country should enjoy such an anomalous position.[10] Ever since 1906 the United States, while not objecting to the employment of American citizens as counselors by foreign embassies and legations, has consistently refused to allow their names to be published in the Diplomatic List, nor are such persons exempt from suits. The Havana Convention of 1928 declares that "States are free in the selection of their diplomatic officers; but they may not invest with such functions the nationals of a state in which the mission must function without its consent." [11]

Immunity of Family and Official Personnel.   Diplomatic inviolability extends to the agent's wife and family and usually to his servants although there is some conflict of authority in the latter case. In the case of the family, the immunity would seem to be absolute. The son of a member of the Chinese Legation in Washington in 1922, even though suffering from a contagious disease, was permitted to enter in spite of a decision of the immigration officials to the contrary.[12] A servant of the Minister of Bavaria to Great Britain was recognized as having the right to exemption, whereas the physician of the same Minister was refused exemption because he was not able to establish his appointment as bona fide.[13] A sound basis for the determination of status would seem to be one based upon the doctrine *ne impediatur legatio.* If the servant is charged in the slightest degree with functions pertaining to the official work of the diplomat, he should be granted immunity. For example, a chauffeur regularly engaged in driving the envoy from his home to the chancery would be clearly

[8] Hackworth, *op. cit.,* IV, 509-10.
[9] C. C. Hyde, *International Law Chiefly as Interpreted and Applied by the United States* (Boston, 1922), I, 754.
[10] Moore, *op. cit.,* IV, 650.
[11] *Sixth International Conference of American States: Final Act* (Habana, 1928), Convention on Diplomatic Officers, Article VII.
[12] 285 *Federal,* 396.
[13] Francis Deák, "Classification, immunités, et privilèges des agents diplomatiques," *Revue de droit international et législation comparée* (The Hague, 1928), 533.

privileged while a groom whose duties consisted in tending the ambassador's riding horses might not be accorded immunity. Workmen occasionally employed about the grounds would have no right to claim diplomatic immunity.

An interesting incident in this connection occurred in 1930 when a certain Jules Chaumonet, who claimed to be a butler of the French Embassy, was arrested for reckless driving. He had struck a taxicab driver with his automobile and had seriously injured him. Inasmuch as Chaumonet's name appeared neither on the Department of State Diplomatic List nor on the list filed with the United States marshal for the District of Columbia, he could not claim immunity according to the laws of the United States. His only possibility of securing release through diplomatic privilege lay in a request from the French Embassy on the basis of an error in the Diplomatic List or that the State Department might grant his immunity as a matter of comity.[14]

Treatment Accorded Nonofficial Personnel. In practice there would seem to be three forms of treatment accorded nonofficial personnel. Great Britain and the United States accord substantially the same privileges and immunities as obtain for diplomatic officers. The official instructions declare: "The personal immunity of a diplomatic representative extends to his household. . . . Generally his servants share therein, but this does not always apply where they are citizens and subjects of the country of sojourn." [15] Other states, as for example, Belgium and Italy, grant no privileged standing to the nonofficial personnel. Finally, a number of states—Germany, Poland, and Hungary—grant diplomatic immunities to servants, providing they have the same nationality as the diplomatic representatives.[16] The Havana Convention of 1928 seems to avoid the issue directly by granting immunity specifically only to the entire official personnel of the mission and to members of the respective families under the same roof.

In the case of Carrera *v.* Carrera, which was decided by a Federal District Court of the United States and upheld upon appeal, it was held that a domestic servant in the Czechoslovakian Embassy who was suing her husband, also a servant in the same Embassy, for separate maintenance and custody of their child could not maintain the suit inasmuch as the Czechoslovakian ambassador had requested that the suit be dismissed on the basis of the diplomatic immunity of the defendant. In this

---

[14] *Cumulative Digest of International Law and Relations* (Washington, November 6, 1930).

[15] *Foreign Service Regulations of the United States* (January, 1941), III, 1.

[16] Cf. "Report of the Council of the League of Nations on the Questions Which Appear Ripe for Codification," *League of Nations Publication* C. 196. M. 70 (1927), V, 83.

case the defendant's name appeared on the so-called White List of employees of the Embassy of nondiplomatic rank.[17]

Couriers, Correspondence and Communication. It is essential that the correspondence of diplomatic representatives be absolutely inviolable for the satisfactory functioning of the mission. Fauchille declares that the minister must possess "absolute liberty to correspond with his government, to send and receive letters and despatches whether by special couriers provided with papers stating their position or by the facilities of the local post." [18]

In times of peace there are rarely any violations of this fundamental right. A few instances, however, may be cited. The Spanish customs officers at Irun seized in 1893 the pouch and correspondence of the courier of the French Embassy at Madrid and detained him for twenty-four hours. Upon the strong protest of the French Government the Spanish Government dismissed the overzealous official.[19] In 1908 while the United States and Venezuela were engaged in a heated correspondence which ultimately resulted in the rupture of diplomatic negotiations the Venezuelan post office opened the pouches containing the official diplomatic correspondence from the United States. In 1921 the Danzig officials demanded to know the contents of the letters and documents which were being dispatched by a Polish courier to Warsaw. When the officer refused he was obliged to interrupt his journey. The Polish Government registered a strong protest with the Danzig Senate against this violation of diplomatic immunity. On June 19, 1918, Secretary of State Lansing expressed his regret to the Minister of Ecuador in Washington that two envelopes—one to the Minister and the other to the President of Ecuador had been censored by United States functionaries and declared that disciplinary action had been requested to prevent the recurrence of such an incident.[20]

In the same way messengers and couriers who carry official despatches possess the right of inviolability. They should be exempt from every form of visit and search in passing through friendly countries. The instructions to diplomatic officers of the United States state that couriers and bearers of despatches employed by a diplomatic representative in the service of his government are privileged persons as far as is necessary for their particular service whether in the state to which the representative is accredited or in the territory of a third state with which the government they serve is at peace.[21]

[17] 174 F (2nd) 496; U.S. Court of Appeals (Washington, Feb. 28, 1949).
[18] Paul Fauchille, *Traité de droit international public* (Paris, 1926), I, Pt. iii, 66.
[19] *Revue générale de droit international public* (Paris, 1894), 1, 60,
[20] Hackworth, *op. cit.*, IV, 618.
[21] *Regulations, op. cit.* (Jan. 1941), III, 1, note 5,

Communications in Time of War Inviolable. It is in times of war that the real problem of free communication arises. The United States has consistently taken the stand that so long as the United States is neutral it has a right to communicate with its diplomatic representatives even if the foreign capital is in a state of siege. Secretary Fish forcibly expressed the American doctrine when the Argentine military commander besieging Asuncion refused to permit a messenger to communicate with the United States Minister to Paraguay, Mr. Washburn. He considered the action as especially unfriendly to the United States and wholly without substantial reasons and he was aware of no instance where a belligerent measure designed to prevent commercial intercourse with the enemy had been invoked to prevent the government of a friendly state from communicating with its diplomatic agent in the blockaded areas.[22]

A somewhat similar situation arose during the siege of Paris by the Germans in 1870. The United States again protested vigorously and successfully when the German authorities refused to allow Mr. Washburne, the American Minister in Paris, to send a message to London with diplomatic despatches unless the contents of the pouch were unsealed.

The practice of the United States has coincided with this expression of policy. During the Civil War General McClellan was directed to instruct General Wool and other commanding officers in cases where packages or parcels addressed to a foreign minister or government fell into their hands to transmit them unopened to the Department of State.[23] Instructions to naval officers required such articles to be consigned unopened to the proper naval, diplomatic or consular officer. On January 5, 1918, the Department of State issued regulations permitting uncensored correspondence when under official seal between embassies and legations in the United States and their respective governments and between embassies and legations in the United States and embassies and legations of the same Power in other countries.[24]

Violation of Neutral Diplomatic Rights. During World War I numerous violations of neutral diplomatic rights occurred, particularly in the delay of messages or refusal to permit the passage of cipher messages by way of cables controlled by the belligerents. On August 27, 1914, Ambassador Page at London informed the Secretary of State that British censorship regulations provided that only messages passing between diplomatic missions and the Government at Washington could go in cipher. All others had to be open.[25] Subsequently a telegram from Minister Reinsch in Peking to the Consul General at Hong Kong was held, although later

[22] Moore, *op. cit.*, IV, 696.
[23] *Ibid.*, 711.
[24] Hackworth, *op. cit.*, IV, 629.
[25] *Department of State—Diplomatic Correspondence with Belligerent Governments Relating to Neutral Rights and Duties*, II, 72.

it was allowed to pass. Ambassador Thomas Nelson Page at Rome complained that the French were delaying or intercepting official telegrams from the American Consul General at Genoa to the Embassy.[26]

In order to protect the diplomatic pouch service the United States at the outbreak of the war attempted to establish uniform regulations for transmission of American diplomatic correspondence in belligerent territory and suggested the following regulations:

1. All correspondence between American diplomatic and consular officers to be inviolable if under seal of office.
2. No private correspondence to be forwarded by diplomatic and consular officers under official seal.
3. Official correspondence between American diplomatic officers residing in different countries not to be opened or molested if under seal of office.
4. Official correspondence under seal of office between the State Department and American officers abroad not to be opened or molested.
5. Pouches under seal passing between American diplomatic missions under mail or courier not to be opened or molested.[27]

On the whole these regulations were accepted and observed by the belligerents although a few exceptions occurred. For example, it was claimed that the entire mails, including presumably American diplomatic and consular pouches, were removed by British authorities on December 23, 1915, from the Dutch steamer *Nieuw Amsterdam*.[28]

One of the very interesting incidents pertaining to the transmission of diplomatic correspondence during war times occurred in Argentina. The German Chargé d'Affaires at Buenos Aires dispatched through the pouch of the Swedish Legation several exceedingly incriminating documents, including the famous note suggesting that two small Argentine vessels be spared or sunk without a trace (*spurlos versenkt*). It would seem as though the Swedish Minister, Baron Lowen, in sending these despatches as a part of his own diplomatic correspondence when they were addressed to the Foreign Office at Berlin was engaged in a highly reprehensible form of unneutral service. Even though he might have been ignorant of the content of the despatches, he, a neutral, was rendering a definite service to the belligerent German Government.

The proper procedure seems to have been followed by Dr. Henry Van Dyke, American Minister at The Hague. He was asked by the Imperial Austro-Hungarian Legation to transmit a message in the American diplomatic code to the American Minister in Brussels to be delivered to the Austro-Hungarian Legation, which was still in Belgium. When he found that a part of the despatch was written in the Viennese numerical cipher which he could not read he refused to transmit the despatch on the

26 *Ibid.*, II, 82.
27 *Ibid.*, II, 67.
28 *Ibid.*, III, 145.

ground that his instructions explicitly forbade sending a message in two codes.[29]

In November, 1939, the Department of State, through the Embassy in London, requested that the British Foreign Office instruct British censorship officials to desist from further interference with American diplomatic and consular mails. The British replied that although authentic diplomatic and consular mail was exempt from examination; nevertheless, discretion has to be left to the examiners to determine its character, hence no such general instructions could be issued.[30]

Reputation of Diplomats. The public minister should be protected against any defamation of his reputation. The liberty of the press in this case is restricted by international law. When an article in the *New York Journal and Patriotic Register* of September 13, 1794, entitled *The British Solomon,* libeled the British Minister, the Attorney General of the United States declared that the law of libel which protected the citizen was in the case of a foreign minister "strengthened by the law of nations, which secures the minister a peculiar protection not only from violence but also from insult." [31]

When in 1856 the editor of a newspaper under the control of the Peruvian Government published an article offensive to the diplomatic corps he was dismissed and the Government saw to it that its disapproval was published in the same newspaper.[32]

During World War I the Swiss Government was constantly struggling to prevent the publication of articles in the press and the circulation of petitions among the people derogatory to the German minister with a view to forcing his recall. A regulation with severe penalties attached was finally promulgated by the Swiss Federal Council in order to maintain a strict neutrality.

Immunity of Residence. It is almost an axiom of diplomatic practice that the official residence of the diplomatic officer and the chancery of the embassy or legation should be exempt from local jurisdiction. Vattel explains the principle thus: "The independence of the ambassador would be very imperfect and his safety very uncertain if the edifice in which he lived did not enjoy a complete immunity and if it were not inaccessible to the regular officers of justice." [33] The Havana Convention of 1928 has this provision: "No judicial or administrative functionary or official of the State to which the diplomatic officer is accredited may enter the

[29] David Jayne Hill, "The Luxburg Secret Correspondence," *American Journal of International Law,* XII, 135 (January, 1918).
[30] Hackworth, *op. cit.,* IV, 631-2.
[31] Moore, *op. cit.,* IV, 629.
[32] Deák, *op. cit.,* 538.
[33] E. de Vattel, *op. cit.,* Bk. IV, Chap. IX, Sect. 117.

domicile of the latter or of the mission without his consent." [34] The *Foreign Service Regulations of the United States,* III, 1, specifically provide that "Premises which are occupied by a diplomatic representative and members of his staff either as offices or residences, the goods contained therein, and the records and archives of the mission are inviolable. They cannot be entered, searched, or detained by the local authorities even under due process of law."

One of the often quoted instances of violation of this rule occurred in 1827 when the coachman of Mr. Gallatin, the United States Minister to Great Britain, was arrested in the Legation stable on a charge of assault. Mr. Gallatin had already dismissed the servant, but he objected to the unauthorized action of the police in failing to respect the inviolability of the Legation. Although the British Government was not convinced that a violation of the law had occurred, assurance was given that in the future measures would be taken to inform the minister before executing a warrant in order that he might not be inconvenienced. [35]

A somewhat unusual example occurred during the occupation of Paris by the Germans in 1871. The home of the American Minister, Mr. Washburne, was invaded by members of the French National Guard. Although Mr. Washburne was not occupying the house at the time, the German military authorities took this as an offense against their own Government inasmuch as the American minister was protecting their interests. Thus we have Germany protesting against the violation of American diplomatic immunity. The French Government expressed indignation and regret at the occurrence but was unable to find the guilty parties. [36]

On occasions when public feeling is aroused against a certain state a mob is likely to attempt to wreak its vengeance upon the diplomatic property of that country in the capital of the injured state.

When the foreign policies of two countries clash or when some untoward event arouses public opinion it is essential that the governments concerned furnish every protection against mob violence to the diplomatic premises of the unpopular state. For example, when the United States handed down its award in the Tacna-Arica dispute, the Government of Peru threw a military guard around the American Embassy to protect Ambassador Pointexter and the American mission from injury at the hands of incensed Peruvians.

If it is suspected that the premises of the diplomatic mission are being used for subversive propaganda against the safety of the state does the immunity still hold? In 1927 the Chinese Government at Peking, suspect-

[34] *Sixth International Conference of American States, op. cit.,* Article 16.
[35] Sir Ernest Satow, *A Guide to Diplomatic Practice,* 2nd ed. (London, 1922), I, 295-300.
[36] Elihu B. Washburne, *Recollections of a Minister to France* (New York, 1889), II, 133-5.

ing the Soviet Embassy of aiding the Chinese communist movement, broke into the Embassy and seized a quantity of arms, munitions, and documents. When the Soviet Ministry of Foreign Affairs protested and demanded restitution, the Peking Government replied that the results of the search fully justified the violation of diplomatic immunity. Diplomatic relations between the two Governments were severed soon afterwards.[37]

A rather amusing incident is told of a Berlin landlord who, angered at the large number of visitors who came daily to the passport bureau of the Rumanian Legation, gave the Rumanian mission a notice of twenty-four hours to vacate the premises. When the minister refused to move, the proprietor had a wall built closing the entrance to the chancery. The Rumanian Minister protested to the German Foreign Office, but when no immediate relief was obtained he called in masons and had them tear down the wall. When the proprietor had it rebuilt the German Foreign Office intervened and placed a guard of police at the Legation to permit freedom of entry. The landlord then offered the edifice to the German Ministry of Social Welfare to be used for the housing of the poor. But the Rumanian successfully stood upon his diplomatic rights.[38]

During the Bolshevist Revolution of 1918, Norman Armour, Second Secretary of the American Embassy, was left in charge of the American mission at Vologda by Ambassador Francis. When he was ordered to proceed to Moscow by the head of the Extraordinary Revolutionary Committee he refused. A train was prepared and when Armour again refused, troops entered the embassy during the night and compelled the American mission to depart.[39]

The regulations of the Union of Soviet Socialist Republics are very strict on this subject and state that premises occupied by diplomatic missions and their families are inviolable. "Searches and seizures on these premises may be effected only on the request or with the consent of the diplomatic representative. . . ." [40] Nevertheless, acting under orders of the Bolshevist Government, Russian troops in August, 1918, broke into the Embassy of Great Britain at Petrograd and destroyed the archives and documents.[41] Russia suffered in a similar manner in 1923 when agents of the Italian police entered into the offices of the Russian mission in Genoa with the aid of a locksmith and searched it.[42]

Protection Against Picketing. In recent years when it has become popular to express distaste for the domestic or foreign policy of a state

---

[37] V. Yoshitomi, "L'affaire de la perquisition de l'ambassade sovietique à Pékin," *Revue générale de droit international public,* XXXV (1928), 184.
[38] Fauchille, *op. cit.,* I, Pt. iii, 73.
[39] David R. Francis, *Russia from the American Embassy* (New York, 1921), 289.
[40] Feller and Hudson, *op. cit.,* II, 1219.
[41] Fauchille, *op. cit.,* I, Pt. iii, 75.
[42] *Ibid.,* 73.

by displaying offensive placards or marching with banners with critical devices thereon in the vicinity of its embassy or legation, or picketing its embassy or legation, the question has arisen as to whether such actions are not an infringement upon the freedom of international intercourse. For example in October, 1937, Chinese patriots attempted to picket the Japanese Embassy in Washington and in the following year veterans of the Abraham Lincoln Brigade flew over the Italian Embassy trailing a streamer bearing the legend: "Quarantine the Aggressor." On another occasion District of Columbia police took away a banner from pickets in front of the Italian Embassy bearing the device: "Mussolini Murders Babies."

Even though the right of freedom of speech and of assembly is a constitutional right in democratic countries public demonstrations of an offensive character tend to arouse resentments both at home and abroad and are a disturbance of the peace and dignity of the foreign mission. For this reason protection against crowds or mobs expressing contempt or disapprobation of the mission or its members or even against picketing seems to be a desirable requirement.

A joint resolution of the Congress of the United States passed February 15, 1938, makes it unlawful to display within 500 feet of an embassy, legation, or consulate in the District of Columbia any flag, banner, placard, or device designed to intimidate, coerce, or bring into public odium any foreign government, party or organization, or any diplomatic or consular representative or to congregate within 500 feet of any embassy, legation, or consulate and refuse to disperse after being ordered to do so by the police authorities. This resolution was upheld by the United States Court of Appeals for the District of Columbia.[43]

Asylum. The problem of the immunity of the residence becomes much more complicated when involved with the question of asylum. Although the right of asylum is still recognized in certain parts of the world, particularly in Latin American countries where revolutionary activities are not uncommon, there is a growing sentiment against granting it under any conditions. Even where the right still exists it may be granted only to political refugees and at a time of urgent necessity as the sole method available to protect the life of the person seeking asylum. According to Sir Cecil Hurst, "the right of asylum is only a temporary protection against injustice and arbitrary acts." [44]

The Latin American Republics signed a convention relative to asylum at Havana in 1928 which indicates their present stand on the subject. According to Article I it is not permissible for states to grant asylum to

[43] Hackworth, *op. cit.,* IV, 511.

[44] Sir Cecil Hurst, "Les immunités diplomatiques," Académie de Droit International, *Recueil des Cours,* XII, 218.

persons accused or condemned for common crimes or to deserters from the Army or Navy. By Article II asylum to political refugees is governed by the following rules:

1. Asylum may not be granted except in urgent cases and for the period of time strictly indispensable for the person seeking it to ensure his safety in some other way.
2. Immediately upon granting asylum the diplomatic agent must report the fact to the Minister of Foreign Relations of the refugee's state.
3. The government may require that the refugee be sent out of the state within the shortest time possible but it must accord the necessary guarantees for the inviolability of his person.
4. Refugees shall not be landed in national territory nor in places immediately adjacent.
5. While enjoying asylum refugees may not be allowed to perform acts contrary to public peace.[45]

The United States signed this convention with the reservation that it did not recognize or subscribe to the so-called right of asylum as a part of international law. In its instructions to its diplomatic officials the United States clearly indicates that it neither favors nor encourages the right of asylum. While conceding that in some countries where revolutions are frequent and instability of government exists the practice has become established, the United States impresses upon its representatives that they should refuse to grant asylum except in cases of urgent necessity where imminence of danger from mob violence exists. This "involuntary refuge" must last only during the period of active danger and refuge must be refused to persons fleeing from the legitimate agents of the local government.[46]

When in 1905 Mr. Powell, Minister of the United States to Haiti, granted asylum to an American citizen named Cameau, who alleged that he was in danger of being arrested, the American Envoy was severely criticized by the State Department on the ground that mere allegations were not sufficient but that actual proof was required that the refugee's life was in imminent jeopardy.[47]

Numerous examples of the granting of asylum might be cited, particularly in Latin American countries. Several instances which occurred in Peru in the year 1865 were carefully considered by the entire diplomatic body. The first, which took place in May, concerned the protection accorded by the American Minister, Mr. Robinson, to General Canseco, who sought asylum in the American Legation. When certain difficulties arose, the diplomatic corps agreed that asylum should be granted with the greatest reserve and then only for sufficient time to permit the refu-

[45] *Report of the United States Delegates to the Sixth International Conference of American States* (Washington, 1928), 225.
[46] *Regulations, op. cit.,* III, 4, note 1.
[47] *Foreign Relations of the United States, 1905,* 553.

gee to secure other means of protection. Following the revolution of November of the same year, four ministers of the Pezet administration sought refuge in the French Legation. When the Peruvian Government demanded their surrender the French Chargé refused and was sustained by his Government. Another meeting of the diplomatic corps took place at the request of the Peruvian Foreign Minister who sought the abolition of the right of asylum. He was supported by the new American Minister, Mr. Hovey, who cited Wheaton, Woolsey, and Polson to support his stand. The other ministers of Latin American states would not agree to its complete elimination and no definite action was ever taken.[48]

One of the cases which had rather serious consequences occurred in Chile in 1891 in the revolution against President Balmaceda. When the Congressionalist forces were victorious, Balmaceda, fearing mob violence, sought refuge in the Argentine Legation. His family and a number of Government officials sought asylum in the American Legation. The Chilean Government protested against the protection afforded by Mr. Egan, the American Minister, but he refused to surrender the fugitives until they were given safe-conducts.[49] As a result of the animosity engendered by this protection afforded by the American Legation to the defeated faction, an attack was made upon the officers and men of an American warship during shore leave in Valparaiso a few months afterwards.

The intervention of the United States marines in Haiti in 1915 was partly due to the violation of the right of asylum by the Haitians. President Guillaume Sam, after putting to death a large number of influential Haitians, fled for refuge into the French Legation. The infuriated populace, bent on his destruction, broke into the Legation, dragged him out and cut him to pieces. Admiral Caperton landed the marines to protect the Legation and restore order and there they remained for about twenty years.

During the Spanish Civil War, Latin American embassies in Madrid provided sanctuary for many Spanish Loyalists who had fled from Franco forces. When General Franco was victorious and established the Falangista government in power he demanded the return of seventeen Loyalists harbored in the Chilean Embassy. When the Chileans succeeded in spiriting them to safety Franco severed diplomatic relations with Chile.

Perhaps the most famous of all cases of asylum is that of the Peruvian leader of the Aprista Party, Haya de la Torre, who on January 3, 1949, sought and was granted asylum in the Colombian Embassy in Lima. Subsequently, the Colombian Ambassador informed the Peruvian Min-

---

[48] The debate in detail may be found in P. Pradier-Fodéré, Cours de droit diplomatique (Paris, 1899), II, 93-105.
[49] Graham H. Stuart, Latin America and the United States (New York, 1943), 441.

ister of Foreign Affairs that it regarded Haya de la Torre as a political refugee and requested a safe-conduct so that he might leave the country. The Peruvian Government refused and finally after months of diplomatic negotiations the matter was taken to the World Court by the Colombian Government. On November 20, 1950, almost two years after the Peruvian politico had entered the Colombian Embassy, the Court ruled that Colombia's qualification of Haya de la Torre as a political offender was not binding on Peru, but neither had Peru proved that he was not a political refugee. Furthermore, since diplomatic asylum should only be granted under conditions of urgency and these had not been proved to exist, Peru was not required to grant a safe-conduct. Since the Court had not stated that Colombia must release the prisoner a new action was brought to determine whether he must be handed over to the Peruvian authorities. On June 13, 1951, the Court in a sibylline decision declared that asylum must cease immediately because it was granted irregularly. Nevertheless, Colombia was not compelled to surrender Haya de la Torre and he is still the guest of the Colombian Embassy.[50]

The problem is not entirely limited to Latin America. As late as 1895 in Turkey a former grand-vizier found it advisable to seek refuge with his son in the British Embassy at Constantinople. The Sultan demanded his immediate surrender, but the British Ambassador, supported by the entire diplomatic corps, refused to compel the two refugees to leave. The Sultan finally gave formal assurances in writing that his former official was free to live in any part of the Turkish capital without fear of molestation. Relying upon these promises Saïd Pasha left the Embassy accompanied by one of the dragomen. At the same time the British Ambassador notified the Turkish Minister of Foreign Affairs that the grand-vizier had left of his own accord, relying upon the assurances given which he trusted would be carried out.[51]

A curious case of asylum occurred in 1926 when the Estonian Envoy to Moscow, A. A. Birk, disappeared from his legation and after making certain accusations against both Estonian and Soviet authorities asked the Norwegian Envoy, Mr. Urbye, to extend to him the full rights of asylum. The question was ultimately settled by the dismissal of the Estonian Minister and the appointment of a substitute.

Even the United States Department of State in 1911, at the request of the American Chargé d'Affaires in Peking that he be permitted to offer asylum to the Emperor and Empress Dowager of China, authorized that a temporary refuge be afforded where he felt that it was necessary to preserve innocent human life.[52]

[50] *American Journal of International Law*, 45, 755-62 (October, 1951).
[51] *Revue générale de droit international public* (Paris, 1896), III, 375.
[52] *Foreign Relations of the United States, 1912*, 174.

Inviolability of Archives. The inviolability of the diplomatic domicile and offices includes the archives of the mission. Not only are they the property of the mission but their importance and confidential character gives added reason for their protection. The question could hardly arise except in cases of severance of diplomatic relations. Even at such a time the departing envoy is usually able to turn over the building and archives to a neutral colleague. When Italy took over the Austro-Hungarian Embassy in 1916 every precaution was taken for the protection of the archives. In fact, a period of two months time was allowed for their transfer which was supervised by the Spanish Embassy under the protection of the Italian police.[53]

When the Czarist government was overthrown by the Bolsheviks the question of the Russian archives in the various countries raised an interesting problem. When consulted on the subject the eminent Swiss authority, O. Nippold, declared: "Normally the inviolability of foreign ministers extends to the archives which are equally inviolable. Local authorities can neither examine them nor seize them. If a diplomatic mission terminates, either the personnel of the legation or that of a friendly power should affix the seals; as a last resort only if the personnel is absent should this task be assumed by the local authorities.[54] The Swiss Government thereupon put under sequestration in Berne both the Russian Legation and its archives.

We have already noted that the principle of diplomatic inviolability extended to all members of a diplomatic mission including attachés, secretaries, interpreters, the family and servants. To this number should be added the representatives sent on special missions for important ceremonial or other occasions. Envoys to important international conferences and congresses are also regularly accorded the same privileges and immunities enjoyed by diplomats.

Immunity of Officials of International Organizations. The development of international organization and adjudication has extended still further the scope of diplomatic immunities. The Covenant of the League of Nations provided that representatives of the Members of the League and all League officials engaged upon League business should enjoy diplomatic privileges and immunities. The League Covenant also provided that buildings and other property occupied by the League or its officials should be inviolable. The Swiss Federal Council by a special modus vivendi of 1926 granted full diplomatic privileges and immunities to all League officials and inviolability to all of its buildings, archives, and properties.

[53] *Revue générale de droit international public* (Paris, 1917), XXIV, 244.
[54] *Revue de droit international, Clunet,* XLV, 1134.

The Netherlands, by an agreement signed in 1928, did the same for the judges and property of the World Court.

A similar agreement was negotiated by an exchange of notes on June 26, 1946, between the International Court of Justice and the Netherlands Government, whereby both judges and staff officials of the Court were granted diplomatic privileges and immunities.

On February 13, 1946, the General Assembly of the United Nations adopted a General Convention on the privileges and immunities of the United Nations.[55] When it was definitely decided to establish the permanent headquarters of the United Nations in New York City it was necessary to make an agreement with the United States. Such an agreement was signed by Secretary of State Marshall and Secretary General Trygve Lie at Lake Success on June 26, 1947, giving members of the various diplomatic missions to the United Nations full right to diplomatic immunities. It is specified in the Convention that the United Nations will coöperate in the proper administration of justice and in the observance of police regulations. The agreement entered into effect by an exchange of notes November 21, 1947.[56]

In practice it would appear that in a number of instances when representatives of the United Nations have violated speed laws they have permitted themselves to be fined without claiming diplomatic immunity. For example, Dr. José Arce, Ambassador of Argentina and chief representative of Argentina to the General Assembly, refused to request immunity and paid a fine of $15 for speeding in Irvington-on-Hudson.

A test case was made in New Rochelle, New York, when the chauffeur of Secretary General Trygve Lie was charged with speeding on the Hutchinson River Parkway while operating a car owned by the United Nations and occupied by Lie en route to an official conference of the United Nations. On this occasion legal counsel for the United Nations challenged the Court's jurisdiction on the ground that the defendant at the time of the alleged offense was performing his official functions and therefore entitled to immunity. The Court ruled however that the defendant was not entitled to immunity as a matter of law without a trial of the issue of fact and was therefore compelled to plead to the information before the Court.

The Secretary General thereupon requested that the Legal Adviser of the State Department give his opinion. The Legal Adviser, Mr. Fahy, replied that in his opinion the employee was entitled to the immunity claimed. Unquestionably this opinion could have been accepted by the Court, but when the Secretary General after noting the opinion declared

[55] *Journal of the General Assembly*, No. 34, 687-93.
[56] For text and exchange of notes see *Yearbook of the United Nations* (New York, 1949), 199-204.

that he didn't wish to press the principle of immunity and offered to pay the fine the principle at stake remained unsettled. However there is little doubt but that in such cases the policy of the State Department would be conclusive upon the Court.[57]

An interesting case where diplomatic immunity was refused occurred when a Soviet national by the name of Gubitchev, employed as a member of the Headquarters Planning Office of the United Nations Secretariat, was indicted in New York for violation of the espionage laws of the United States. A motion to dismiss the indictment was refused on the ground that although Gubitchev was an officer of the Soviet diplomatic service and had a diplomatic passport and a diplomatic visa, he had never been received by the United Nations as a diplomatic emissary nor had his name been included in the list of members of the United Nations entitled to diplomatic immunities. Under these circumstances he had received no immunity preventing his prosecution on this indictment.[58]

Jurisdictional Immunity.   It has been said that immunity from local jurisdiction is the most important privilege which a diplomat enjoys.[59] The famous Diplomatic Privileges Act, otherwise known as the Act of 7 Anne, was passed in 1708 as a result of the violent arrest and seizure of Mattweof, Ambassador of Peter the Great. This act declared that "all writs and processes that shall at any time hereafter be sued forth or prosecuted whereby the person of an ambassador or other publick minister . . . may be arrested or imprisoned, or his or their chattels may be distrained, seized or attached, shall be deemed and adjudged to be utterly null and void. . . ." [60] The British courts in numerous subsequent cases upheld this law as declaratory of international law on the subject.[61]

Almost all the great publicists, classic and modern, accept this principle: Grotius, Bynkershoek, Vattel, Bluntschli, Calvo, Wheaton, Hall, Pradier-Fodéré, Fauchille, Satow, and Genet. This immunity of jurisdiction so universally admitted covers both criminal and civil cases. The first paragraph of the section devoted to immunities in the instructions to American diplomatic officers states that "A diplomatic representative possesses immunity from the criminal and civil jurisdiction of the country of his sojourn and cannot be sued, arrested or punished by the laws of that country. . . . It is not to be supposed that any representative of this country would intentionally avail himself of this right to evade just obli-

[57] The incident is discussed at length by Lawrence Preuss in *American Journal of International Law*, XLI (July, 1947), 555-78.

[58] *American Journal of International Law*, XLIV (July, 1950), 586-90.

[59] Deák, *op. cit.*, 201.

[60] *British and Foreign State Papers*, I, 903; E. D. Dickinson, *Cases and Other Readings on the Law of Nations* (New York, 1929), 562.

[61] See Barbuits Case (1735) 25 *Eng. Rep.* 777; Triquet *v.* Bath (1764) 3 Burr. 1478.

gations." [62] The Revised Statutes of the United States provide that any judicial process whereby the person of any public minister is arrested or imprisoned is declared to be void.[63]

Immunity from Criminal Jurisdiction. Sir Cecil Hurst has declared that no instance has been cited where a diplomatic agent has been subjected to the criminal jurisdiction of the country to which he was accredited without his consent.[64] An extreme instance of jurisdictional immunity occurred in London in 1916 when the body of the First Secretary of the Italian Embassy was found in a hotel bedroom. As he had been shot, it was the duty of the coroner to hold an inquest into the cause of the death. Nevertheless, when the Italian Ambassador objected, the British authorities withdrew jurisdiction, conceding that the diplomatic exemption from civil or criminal process excludes the jurisdiction over the dead body of any member of an ambassador's suite.[65]

It should be noted, however, that although the diplomatic agent cannot be tried by the local courts, nevertheless he can be recalled or dismissed and punished by his home government upon his return.

When in 1868 Secretary of State Seward learned that two official members of the Prussian Legation had been guilty as principal and second of violating the law of the District of Columbia against dueling, he brought the matter to the attention of the German minister. Since the persons in question were "protected by the law of nations from judicial prosecution for a violation of the statute . . .", the matter was brought to the attention of their Government that they might "in a proper manner be made sensible of its displeasure." [66]

If a public minister should conspire against the safety of the state he may be restrained temporarily and expelled at the earliest possible moment but no punishment may be inflicted upon him by the injured state. Numerous historical cases might be cited in substantiation of this customary procedure. A much quoted early case occurred in 1584. Evidence showed that Mendoza, the Spanish Ambassador to England, had conspired to introduce foreign troops and dethrone Queen Elizabeth. The English Government, following the opinions of Gentilis and Hotman, who declared that an ambassador though a conspirator, could not be put to death, but should be sent home for punishment, ordered him to depart and sent a commission to Spain to bring a complaint against him.[67] The British Ambassador to Spain during the revolutionary activities of 1848,

---

[62] *Instructions, op. cit.,* VII, 1.
[63] *Revised Statutes of the United States,* Sects. 4063, 4064.
[64] Hurst, *op. cit.,* 92.
[65] Satow, *op. cit.,* 2nd ed. (London, 1922), I, 260.
[66] Moore, *op. cit.,* IV, 634.
[67] Sir Robert Phillimore, *Commentaries on International Law,* 3rd ed. (London, 1879-1889), II, 206.

Henry Bulwer, was given forty-eight hours to leave on the ground that he was guilty of complicity in the revolt. In this case the real reason was the interference by Bulwer in Spanish political affairs in accordance with instructions from the British Foreign Minister. Since the Spanish Government made no serious effort to justify their charges Lord Palmerston responded by dismissing the Spanish Minister in London.[68]

A number of such incidents occurred in the United States preceding its entrance into World War I. Constantin Dumba, the Austro-Hungarian Minister at Washington, admitted that he proposed to his Government plans to instigate strikes in American manufacturing plants engaged in the production of munitions of war and used an American citizen with an American passport to carry these official despatches to his Government. The Government of the United States immediately requested his recall.[69]

The cases of Captain Boy-Ed, Naval Attaché, and Captain von Papen, Military Attaché, of the Imperial German Embassy at Washington, were more serious. They were guilty of numerous violations of American laws and of their obligations as diplomatic officials. Captain Boy-Ed was engaged in efforts to provide German warships at sea with coal and other supplies in violation of American laws. Captain von Papen furnished funds to various individuals with instructions to blow up certain factories and bridges and also directed the manufacture of incendiary bombs and their placement on Allied vessels.[70] In these cases the United States was compelled to address the German Ambassador on two successive occasions with requests that they be recalled.

In the case of Wolf von Igel, secretary to the German military attaché, who was arrested in 1916 and his papers seized on the grounds that he was conspiring against the safety of the United States, the United States questioned the German Ambassador's claim of immunity on the ground that the crimes were so grave and were committed before his name had been notified to the Department of State as an attaché of the German Embassy. Both states maintained their positions but when diplomatic relations were severed in 1917 his bond was cancelled and he returned to Germany on parole. Since he never returned the case was dismissed in 1927.[71]

In the case of an American assistant military attaché who killed two persons in Switzerland through alleged reckless driving the Swiss Government thought under the circumstances the Department of State might agree to a renunciation of the attaché's immunity. However it did not

---

[68] W. E. Hall, *A Treatise on International Law*, 4th ed. (Oxford, 1895), 316.

[69] "Diplomatic Correspondence between United States and Belligerent Governments," *American Journal of International Law, Supplement*, X, 361 (1916).

[70] *Report from Committee on Foreign Affairs to House of Representatives*, No. 1, 65th Cong., 1st sess., 5-9.

[71] Hackworth, *op. cit.*, IV, 517-19.

press the request but made the United States responsible for holding the accused to trial. A military court martial was held by the American authorities and the attaché was acquitted.[72]

Immunity from Police Jurisdiction. A diplomatic agent is free from local police jurisdiction but the government to which he is accredited has a right to expect that he will obey such municipal regulations as speed laws, sanitary measures, measures for fire protection and game laws. Since the advent of the automobile, diplomatic officers have been frequently arrested for speeding by county sheriffs and constables wholly unacquainted with the law of diplomatic immunity. A secretary of the British Legation was arrested in 1904 at Lenox, Massachusetts, for driving at an unlawful speed. Taken before the local magistrate, the secretary claimed exemption through his diplomatic status, but the magistrate refused to recognize such a plea and imposed a fine. The State Department took up the case with the Governor of Massachusetts. When the magistrate explained that he was ignorant of international law and apologized, the incident was closed.[73]

The situation in Washington, D. C., where both diplomats and congressmen assume diplomatic privileges and immunities is particularly unfortunate. On one day in 1926 the District Commissioners transmitted to Secretary Kellogg the case of the Second Secretary of the Belgian Embassy caught speeding through traffic on Massachusetts Avenue at fifty-five miles an hour and that of an attaché of the Ecuadorean Legation who, having had his attention called to a violation of the parking ordinance, replied to the policeman, "If I choose to leave my car in the middle of Sixteenth Street it would be none of your damn business," and pushed the officer from the running board. The State Department threatened to suggest the withdrawal of offending diplomats if violations continued.

A case which attracted much publicity occurred in Elkton, Maryland, when the town officer arrested Ghaffar Khan Djalal, Minister from Iran, for speeding and reckless driving. When both the envoy and his wife resisted, the former was taken into custody, handcuffed and brought before a local justice of the peace. The charge was dismissed, but the costs were assessed against the chauffeur. A formal protest was lodged with the Department of State by the irate plenipotentiary and he ultimately received expressions of regret from Secretary Hull and the Governor of Maryland. The police officer was dismissed for his violation of diplomatic immunity.

When one of the American diplomatic secretaries in Tokyo was arrested on a Japanese train for gambling, a grave offense under Japanese

---

[72] *Ibid.*, 519-20.
[73] Frederic Van Dyne, *Our Foreign Service* (Rochester, 1909), 79.

law, he escaped punishment by pleading diplomatic immunity, but he did not escape the wrath of the American Ambassador who saw to it that he was soon transferred back to Washington.

An interesting case which would seem to be an exception to the general rule occurred a few years ago in Paris. Ferdinand Belin, a secretary of the United States Embassy in Paris, was condemned to pay an indemnity for having injured two people with his automobile. The Paris court rejected the claim of diplomatic immunity on the ground that "diplomatic immunities have been created in the interest of governments and not for their agents and do not extend to the private affairs of the latter." [74] Since Belin's official functions had ceased prior to the commencement of the suit, the plea of immunity was rejected also upon the ground that immunity did not extend beyond the time of the diplomat's mission.

Immunity from Civil Jurisdiction. A public minister's freedom from civil jurisdiction is complete in so far as it is necessary for him to be free to perform his official duties. He may not even be sued for debts and his furniture and other personal property is exempt from seizure through judicial procedure. When some years ago the owner of "Stewart Castle" in Washington attempted in vain to secure payment for damages incurred during the incumbency of the Chinese Legation, he presented his claim to the Department of State. After investigating the claim, the American Minister at Peking was authorized to bring the matter to the attention of the Chinese Government and a settlement was effected.[75]

Certain exceptions, however, are sometimes claimed. For example, if a public minister engages in commerce or professional affairs, are these transactions subject to local jurisdiction? Although the consensus grants a complete immunity from civil actions under all circumstances, Hershey [76] and a few other authorities permit such exceptions and the Italian courts have so decided in two such instances.

The British and American courts have consistently ruled against any kind of a civil process against a public minister. French courts have followed the same course. In fact, in a judgment of the Cour de Paris in 1876 (S.77.2.17), it was held that diplomatic agents are exempt from civil jurisdiction even as to acts committed in a private capacity. Even a French citizen, the agent of a foreign state, enjoys diplomatic immunities in France.[77]

---

[74] Deák, *op. cit.*, 204.

[75] Van Dyne, *op. cit.*, 80.

[76] Amos Hershey, *Essentials of International Public Law and Organization* (New York, 1927), 406.

[77] For summary of American, British, and French cases see *American Journal of International Law, Supplement*, XXVI, 100-2.

The Convention of Havana of 1928 is very explicit upon this point:

Diplomatic officers are exempt from all civil or criminal jurisdiction of the state to which they are accredited; they may not, except in the case when duly authorized by their government, waive immunity, be prosecuted or tried unless it be by the courts of their own country.[78]

The implication in this convention is that if the government of the diplomatic agent gives its permission the envoy may renounce his immunity. But in order to renounce this privilege it is necessary that the government give its express consent to submit to the local authority. In the case of a murder committed in Belgium by the son of the Chilean Chargé d'Affaires the Belgian Government refused to prosecute even after the father had renounced immunity of jurisdiction for his son until the Chilean Government gave formal notice that it would consent for the murderer to be tried in Belgium.[79] If, however, the envoy begins an action himself before the local jurisdiction he must submit to the consequences of his action even to the extent of being condemned to pay the costs if the suit should fail.

In 1939 when an attachment of property in possession of the Costa Rican Minister in Washington was contemplated the Legal Adviser of the State Department, Green Hackworth, notified the United States Marshal that neither writs nor processes in either criminal or civil actions requiring the presence in court of ambassadors or ministers could be properly served on diplomatic representatives.[80]

Exemption from Giving Testimony. The immunity of a diplomatic agent permits his refusal to testify in court even though his evidence is essential to secure conviction. The American instructions declare explicitly that he cannot waive his privilege, except by the consent of his Government, for it belongs to his office, not to himself. When a case of homicide occurred in Washington in 1856 in the presence of the Dutch Minister, Mr. Dubois, inasmuch as his testimony was regarded as essential was asked to appear and testify. When he declined the United States, conceding his right to refuse to appear, brought the matter to the attention of his Government, since the circumstances of the case appealed strongly to the universal sense of justice. The Netherlands Government agreed to Dubois giving his declaration under oath but such procedure could not be admitted as evidence in American law.[81] According to Calvo,[82] Oppenheim,[83] and Foster,[84] the Dutch Minister became *persona*

[78] *Sixth International Conference of American States, op. cit.,* Article 19.
[79] *Revue générale de droit international public* (Paris, 1907), XIV, 159.
[80] Hackworth, *op. cit.,* IV, 534.
[81] *Senate Executive Document* No. 21, 34th Cong., 3rd sess.
[82] Charles Calvo, *Le droit international théorique et pratique,* 4th ed., 6 vols. (Paris, 1896), III, 319, Par. 1520 n.
[83] L. Oppenheim, *International Law,* 2 vols. (New York, 1912), I, 465.
[84] John W. Foster, *The Practice of Diplomacy* (New York, 1906), 161.

non grata and his recall was requested. Satow, however, declares this not to be true, that his recall was at his own request, and that when Dubois left, the President declared that his conduct in the United States had met the approbation of this Government.[85]

On the contrary, the Venezuelan Minister at Washington who had been present at the assassination of President Garfield asked permission of his Government to waive his immunity and he testified against the assassin.[86] In similar fashion Mr. Iddings, Secretary of the American Embassy at Rome, was permitted to give testimony against a pickpocket. In this case the deposition was taken at the embassy by the judge before whom the case was pending.[87]

In 1902, when the son of the United States Minister to Guatemala shot and killed another American in Guatemala City, Secretary Hay at the request of the Guatemalan Government instructed the American Secretary of Legation who had witnessed the shooting to waive his diplomatic immunity and testify before the Guatemalan courts. Incidentally, the accused might have claimed exemption as a member of the diplomat's family. The Minister, however, cabled the State Department that his son was in business for himself and not connected with the Legation in any way to be entitled to immunity. He was tried and acquitted in the Guatemalan courts.[88]

The Belgian Foreign Office in 1928 requested that a clerk in the American Embassy in Brussels be permitted to testify in court as a witness to an accident. The State Department granted this request providing the interests of the mission were not concerned and that the Belgian Government would reciprocate in a similar case in the United States.[89]

Duration of Immunities. As to the duration of immunities, it would seem as though an envoy should enjoy diplomatic immunities from the moment when the *agrément* has been secured from the government to which he has been accredited. The privilege should continue during the entire period of his mission as well as to include time sufficient for him to return to his country. During a trial before an American tribunal the judge aptly expressed the principle in force: "The diplomatic agent has the right to immunities 'eundo, morando et redeundo.'"[90]

Ordinarily a reasonable length of time ensues before the diplomat's immunity from local jurisdiction ceases. However in 1906 when France broke off diplomatic relations with Venezuela and entrusted its interests to the United States, the Venezuelan Government held that the French

[85] Satow, *op. cit.*, 2nd ed. (London, 1922), 282 note.
[86] Moore, *op. cit.*, IV, 644.
[87] *Foreign Relations of the United States, 1901*, 302.
[88] Van Dyne, *op. cit.*, 82.
[89] Hackworth, *op. cit.*, IV, 554.
[90] James Brown Scott, *Cases in International Law* (St. Paul, Minn., 1922), 291.

Minister became subject to local law immediately upon the cessation of his mission. He was then practically expelled from Venezuela in spite of a protest by the resident diplomatic corps. The United States concurred in the position taken by the powers.[91]

The Pan American Convention of 1928 on diplomatic officers follows the general rule:

Diplomatic officers enter upon the enjoyment of their immunity from the moment they pass the frontier of the state where they are going to serve and make known their position. The immunities shall continue during the period that the mission may be suspended, and even after it shall be terminated, for the time necessary for the officer to be able to withdraw with the mission.[92]

Restrictions on diplomats in a police state. The position of a diplomat in a police state is difficult even when the ordinary immunities are granted. Soviet Russia makes the life of a foreign diplomat particularly unpleasant but even in Czarist Russia the situation was not too satisfactory. In a dispatch to the Department of State dated January 28, 1852, American Minister Neill S. Brown complained that official communications were opened and inspected as a matter of course, ministers were spied upon and their servants forced to disclose what went on in the legations. No courtesy or liberality was shown by the Government in furnishing information of any value—"secrecy and mystery characterize everything." A year later he was still unable to obtain accurate information and the "rigor of the police" was so great that he felt his every movement was closely watched by eyes that he never saw.

Ambassador Walter Bedell Smith, who quotes these dispatches, found a century later that the situation had changed little and if anything for the worse. He was constantly followed by secret service agents and neither he nor his staff were able to establish normal relations with the Soviet officials or civilians of Moscow. The secret police or MVD dominated the life of the people and the actions of the officials. The Foreign Office itself could not issue an entry visa to a diplomatic attaché without the approval of the Lubianka.

To live modestly a huge expenditure was necessary because of the high artificial exchange rate fixed for the Russian ruble. Even then it was necessary to import personally items of everyday need which the poorest American citizen takes for granted and these imports were drastically restricted. Materials to repair the Embassy or chancery buildings were never available although the buildings were in a rundown condition. The housing situation for members of the staff was inexcusably bad. The American Ambassador had to read daily in the official newspapers and hear over the government radio vicious lies concocted to stimulate

[91] Hackworth, *op. cit.*, IV, 457.
[92] *Sixth International Conference of American States, op. cit.*, Article 22.

popular hostility against his country. The position of the foreign diplomat in a regime "nailed in place by bayonets" and held together by force and propaganda is not a pleasant one.[93]

Subsequent to Ambassador Smith's return still more rigid restrictions were imposed upon foreign envoys. By an order issued in January, 1952, the Soviet Government put twenty-two cities on the restricted list—that is 80 per cent of the major cities with a population of 100,000 or more—in fact every city with a substantial industrial development. Under these restrictions the foreign diplomat could travel only about twenty-five miles around Moscow and the only unrestricted cities of importance left were Leningrad, Stalingrad, and Odessa. In March, 1952, the United States retaliated by restricting the movements of Soviet diplomats.

[93] See Walter Bedell Smith, *My Three Years in Moscow* (Philadelphia, 1950) for an exceedingly well written account of the restrictions upon diplomats in Soviet Russia.

15

Termination of Diplomatic Missions

Method of Termination. Ordinarily a diplomatic mission terminates by the resignation, recall or dismissal of the diplomatic envoy. This, of course, excludes missions sent for special purposes which end with the fulfillment of their objectives and also missions where the letters of credence are issued for a specific time only. In the monarchical system of Europe the authority of a public minister expires normally upon the death, abdication or deposition of his sovereign, and he must have a new letter of credence to continue his functions. This is not at present, however, the case with republics where the executive power is permanent and continuous. According to Attorney General Cushing, "in the United States it is clear that commissions do not expire merely by the death or other change in the person of the President. Nor has it been customary to receive or require new credentials to ministers at every new election of the supreme executive chief of the American Republic." [1] However, at the resignation of President Thiers of France in 1873, the larger European states on the Continent insisted that new credentials be sent while Great Britain did not.[2] In the case of Great Britain after the death of George V and the abdication of Edward VIII new credentials were received by British ambassadors only after a considerable lapse of time. These were given to the ministers of foreign affairs without any ceremonies thus avoiding any loss of precedence in the diplomatic list by the diplomats in question. It should perhaps be noted that in the case of a chargé d'affaires who is accredited to the minister for foreign affairs the death of the sovereign does not affect his position.

Resignation of Noncareer Diplomats. The question with regard to automatic resignation of American ambassadors and ministers upon the change of presidents has never been definitely settled. The official instructions are silent on the subject. However, there seems to be little doubt but that by custom and practice all political appointees to ambassadorial

[1] 7 *Opinions U.S. Attorney General*, 590.
[2] Jules Valfrey, *La diplomatie française au 17ième siècle* (Paris, 1881), II, 190.

and ministerial posts regularly offer their resignations upon a change of administration and such resignations are usually accepted. Although President Theodore Roosevelt was a vigorous opponent of the spoils system, even he asked for the resignation of all the ambassadors and ministers and accepted a considerable number of them.[3]

John B. Jackson, who had been in the foreign service since 1890, upon the election of President Wilson inquired as to whether he should resign. He was informed by President Wilson that he approved the practice which had generally existed that all chiefs of mission should submit their resignations to a new President. Although Jackson indicated that he would be glad to continue in the service in which he had been continuously for more than twenty years, a successor was appointed purely on a political basis.[4]

According to John W. Foster, a career diplomat, by practice if not by law, "ambassadors and ministers are expected to tender their resignations on a change of the home government, and the resignations usually reach Washington in time to be in the hands of the new Secretary of State when or very soon after he assumes office." If the diplomatic representative fails to tender his resignation, he is informed of the appointment of his successor and if even then he does not resign he is recalled summarily.[5]

There have been occasions when the resignation of a diplomatic representative has not been accepted, even though he was the political appointee of a different administration. Perhaps the outstanding example is the case of Maurice Francis Egan, the so-called unofficial diplomatic adviser of three presidents. Egan was offered diplomatic posts by both Cleveland and McKinley and was appointed Minister to Denmark in 1907 by President Roosevelt. There he remained throughout the administration of Taft, through the first Wilson administration and until President Wilson's second term was half over, illness ending his service. This twelve year term is the longest that any noncareer American diplomat has ever served at a single post. Incidentally, Egan was offered the ambassadorship to Japan by Roosevelt and that of Vienna by both Taft and Wilson, but he preferred to remain at Copenhagen.

Andrew D. White, appointed Minister to Germany by a Republican President, had the rare experience of having his resignation accepted by the succeeding Republican President in 1881; whereas, while as Minister to Russia under appointment by President Harrison, another Republican, he was invited by President Cleveland, a Democrat, to continue in office.

[3] Allan Nevins, *Henry White* (New York, 1930), 236.

[4] "Report on the Foreign Service," *National Civil Service Reform League* (New York, 1919), 136.

[5] John W. Foster, *The Practice of Diplomacy* (New York, 1906), 175.

Touched by the cordial letter of President Cleveland, White stayed on at his post for a year longer.

Henry Wheaton, one of our earliest career diplomats, after serving eight years as Chargé d'Affaires in Copenhagen, and eleven years as Chargé d'Affaires and Minister to Berlin under Presidents John Quincy Adams, Andrew Jackson, Martin Van Buren, William Henry Harrison, and John Tyler, was asked to resign by President James K. Polk. The Prussian Minister, Humboldt, wrote to him in 1846 that the King lamented his removal and could not understand the motives of a government in dispensing with such a minister.[6]

After the election of Woodrow Wilson in 1912, Mr. Herrick, American Ambassador to France, sent in his resignation according to the usual custom, but it was not immediately acted upon. Although Herrick knew that William F. McCombs, Wilson's campaign manager, was slated for the post, it appeared that McCombs could not make up his mind to accept. In fact he went over to Paris and discussed the matter with Herrick and finally decided he could not afford the necessary expense entailed. So it was not until over a year after Wilson's inauguration that Mr. Sharp was named Ambassador to France and Herrick so notified. However, owing to the outbreak of the war, Herrick was asked to remain at his post even after Sharp's arrival and he did not leave until November, 1914.[7]

President Franklin D. Roosevelt who remained in office three full terms and was reëlected for a fourth, rarely allowed politically appointed ambassadors to remain in office for more than one presidential term. For example, in London, Robert W. Bingham served during President Roosevelt's first term, Joseph P. Kennedy during his second, and John G. Winant during the third. In France, Jesse I. Straus, William C. Bullitt, and Admiral William D. Leahy each held office for approximately one presidential term. In Soviet Russia the conditions were so unsatisfactory that no ambassador wished to remain even for one term and as a result during Roosevelt's three terms five ambassadors served: William Bullitt, Joseph E. Davies, Laurence Steinhardt, Admiral William H. Standley, and W. Averell Harriman.

Resignation of Career Diplomats. With the establishment of a career diplomatic service in the United States and the appointment of an ever increasing number of Foreign Service officers to the posts of minister and ambassador, the question arose as to whether they too were expected to offer their resignations. John Van Antwerp MacMurray, a career officer of some thirty years experience, insisted that it was not necessary. According to MacMurray the question first arose when President Wilson

[6] *National Cyclopedia of American Biography* (New York, 1908), I, 274.
[7] T. Bentley Mott, *Myron T. Herrick, Friend of France* (New York, 1929), 218-21.

came into office, inasmuch as about a dozen career men had already been permitted to be chiefs of mission. Having communicated among themselves, they decided not to send in their resignations on the ground that it would be inappropriate in those who had devoted themselves to the service in a wholly nonpartisan manner. Furthermore, it was unnecessary since the President could displace any officer by the mere appointment of a successor. This precedent was followed by the career men during the administrations of Harding and Coolidge. Unfortunately, at the beginning of the Hoover administration the question was raised at a press conference and Secretary Kellogg, taken off his guard, declared that the career men would follow the custom of submitting their resignations. As a result, a number of service men felt obliged to submit their resignations.[8]

President Hoover not only refused to accept the resignations of those career men who submitted them, but increased the number of chiefs of mission drawn from the career service. President Franklin D. Roosevelt, in spite of the fact that a Democratic administration now succeeded a Republican, nevertheless recognized the advantages of the career service. He appointed Alexander Weddell and subsequently Norman Armour as Ambassadors to Argentina, both outstanding career men. He sent experienced diplomat Hugh Gibson, a good friend of Herbert Hoover, as Ambassador to Brazil and Sumner Welles and later Jefferson Caffery, both trained diplomats, to handle the serious situation in Cuba. He retained career diplomats Minister Nelson T. Johnson in China and Ambassador Joseph C. Grew in Japan and sent Foreign Service Officer Robert P. Skinner as Ambassador to Turkey.

Under the Truman administrations the question ceased to be so important as a result of the Foreign Service Act of 1946. This law by establishing the position of career minister permitted Foreign Service officers to accept positions either as ambassador or minister without losing their status of career minister in the Foreign Service. Although President Truman made a considerable number of purely political appointments, as for example, Stanton Griffis to Poland, William D. Pawley to Peru, Richard C. Patterson, Jr., to Guatemala, William O'Dwyer to Mexico, and Perle Mesta to Luxembourg, more than half of the posts of ambassadors and ministers were career officers during his two administrations.

Resignation Impelled by Expense of Office.   Although a change in the politics of the administration has been the reason for the greatest number of resignations in the American diplomatic service, the heavy personal expense entailed has also been an important cause. Inasmuch as at most of the important capitals an ambassador must spend several times his

---

[8] J. V. A. MacMurray, "Should Career Men Now Chiefs of Mission Offer Their Resignations to Incoming President?" *American Foreign Service Journal*, X, 79 (February, 1933).

salary, many excellent American diplomats have been forced to resign. Even before the Constitution was formulated, Thomas Jefferson on a special mission to Paris complained of meager salary that compelled him to live by a rigid economy bordering on meanness. In a congressional investigation held in 1924 John W. Davis declared that, living very unostentatiously in the period directly after the war, he was forced to expend between fifty and sixty thousand dollars, roughly three times his salary. Page, who preceded Davis, had a difficult time financially and finally had to resign because of it. It was said that President Wilson, realizing that from his private income Ambassador Page was unable to maintain his position at St. James's, asked mutual friends to defray the expenses in excess of the Government allowances.[9] Harvey, who succeeded him, was able to endure the financial strain for less than two years. Yet these were all wealthy men.

Career men frequently have had to resign when promoted to more expensive posts. John R. Carter, when promoted from Minister to Rumania to Ambassador to Argentina in 1910, was unable to accept the more expensive post and was compelled to resign from the service.[10] John W. Dulles in 1926 resigned from the Foreign Service because of "the financial burden involved in the acceptance of higher positions in the diplomatic service." [11] After eighteen years in the Service Francis White, Minister to Czechoslovakia, resigned because he was unable to continue the additional expense beyond his salary.[12]

This situation has been remedied to a considerable extent by the Foreign Service Act of 1946, which raised ambassadors' salaries from $17,500 to a maximum of $25,000 and also increased representation allowances to as much as $25,000. This act by allocating additional sums for high cost of living posts and for the maintenance of suitable official residences has made it possible for an American without a substantial private income to accept an ambassadorial post abroad and to maintain it adequately.

An American diplomatic officer has the right to resign at any time and his resignation should always be tendered to the President. If he is at his post the resignation regularly takes effect when the officer is relieved by his successor. In any case a diplomatic officer's official functions do not cease until he has received notification of the appointment of his successor, either by specific instructions from the Department of State or by the exhibition of his successor's commission.

Disagreement in Policy. Upon certain occasions a diplomatic envoy finds it necessary to resign because he feels it impossible to carry out the

[9] Nicholas Roosevelt, "Diplomacy in Rags," *Christian Science Monitor* (February 21, 1934).

[10] *Report on the Foreign Service* (New York, 1919), December 8, 1933, 135.

[11] *New York Times* (September 27, 1926).

[12] *New York Times* (December 8, 1933).

policies as laid down by the Department of State. An outstanding example occurred during the period when General Cass was Minister to France and Webster was Secretary of State. Cass resigned when the Government, by concluding the Webster-Ashburton Treaty, took a stand directly opposed to that which he had taken in regard to the Quintuple Alliance and for which he had been commended. He maintained that such official approval and yet evident renunciation of his actions by the counter policy immediately adopted made it impossible for him to retain his position with self-respect.[13]

Henry Lane Wilson, appointed Ambassador to Mexico during the Taft administration, took exception to Secretary Bryan's conduct with reference to the Embassy in Mexico and tendered his resignation twice quite forcibly. However, it was not accepted until Ambassador Wilson was summoned to Washington and prepared a memorandum recommending the recognition of Huerta as President of Mexico. President Wilson thereupon accepted his resignation and gave as his reasons when asked by the press, that the course which Ambassador Wilson thought it his duty to pursue did not conform with the policy of the administration.[14]

Major General Patrick J. Hurley, who had been sent to China as Ambassador in the fall of 1944, was unable to see eye to eye with the State Department's policy with regard to Chinese Communists. He felt that the former Roosevelt policy in the Far East was being sabotaged both by the State Department and the career Foreign Service officers. When he returned to Washington to make his charges personally and failed to convince President Truman and Secretary of State Byrnes, his resignation was accepted.

In the case of Ambassador Arthur Bliss Lane, a career Foreign Service Officer who resigned after more than thirty years of service, the reason was to bring to the attention of the American people the tragic plight of Poland under Soviet domination. He felt that the State Department had not taken a sufficiently strong stand and after the fraudulent and governmental controlled elections in January, 1947, in flagrant violation of the Yalta and Potsdam commitments, he asked to retire.[15]

Recall by the Home Government. A diplomatic representative is always subject to recall by his government either at its own volition or at the request of the foreign government. If he is to be recalled permanently by his own government the ordinary procedure is to give him the opportunity first to resign. An example of this which caused considerable flurry in American history occurred when President Taft requested the resignation of Henry White, at that time Ambassador to France. White had

---

[13] W. T. Young, *Life and Public Service of Lewis Cass* (Detroit, 1852), 171.
[14] *Report on the Foreign Service, op. cit.*, 141.
[15] Arthur Bliss Lane, *I Saw Poland Betrayed* (Indianapolis, 1948).

been in the diplomatic service of his country some thirty years and Roosevelt regarded him as the best man in the United States diplomatic service; in fact, Roosevelt had said as much to Taft and the latter had signified his intention of retaining him. However, it seems that when Taft had visited London on his honeymoon some twenty-five years earlier he had requested that White, then secretary of the legation, procure seats for an important parliamentary debate. When White was not able to obtain them he sent instead some tickets to view the royal mews. Mr. Taft apparently resented this act and never forgot what he regarded as an uncalled-for slight.[16] It might be noted that White had also been asked to resign at the beginning of the second Cleveland administration because Cleveland's friend, Daniel Lamont, the new Secretary of War, felt that White had slighted him by failing to call upon him during a visit to London.[17]

If a diplomatic representative fails to accept the more gracious method of resignation he is subject to summary recall. During one period in American history when the so-called "Tenure of Office Act" was in effect, a diplomat who retained the support of the Senate could not be recalled. When Secretary of State Seward asked for the resignation of Cassius M. Clay, Minister to Russia, Clay agreed to resign but his resignation would only take effect upon the arrival of his successor. The Senate refused to approve a successor and Clay, who hated and despised Seward very cordially, remained in office three years after his resignation had been asked.[18]

John Lothrop Motley was not so successful in his refusal to resign his position as Minister to Great Britain in 1870. Motley had been constantly violating his instructions with regard to his method of presenting the Alabama claims, preferring the belligerent attitude of his friend, Senator Sumner, to the more diplomatic attitude demanded by President Grant and Secretary Fish. When Sumner wrecked the annexation treaty of Santo Domingo in the Senate, Grant immediately asked for the resignation of Motley. Motley refused to resign. The next day the press announced the appointment of General Schenk and his confirmation by the Senate. Again Motley refused to resign and it was not until several months later when President Grant ordered him to put the Legation in the hands of Secretary Moran and to return that he acceded. He regarded his recall as an indignity to which no public minister of the United States had ever before been subjected.[19]

Another example of a minister recalled by the United States is that of

---

[16] Nevins, *op. cit.*, 299.
[17] Nevins, *op. cit.*, 73.
[18] *The Life of Cassius Marcellus Clay* (Cincinnati, Ohio, 1886), 407.
[19] Royal Cortissoz, *The Life of Whitelaw Reid* (New York, 1921), I, 189; Beckles Willson, *America's Ambassadors to England* (London, 1928), 354.

Herbert W. Bowen, Minister to Venezuela from 1901 to 1905. In his case certain facts came to his attention regarding the business activities of his predecessor, Francis B. Loomis, who had been recalled at the request of the Government of Venezuela. In an interview with the press he gave out some information which President Roosevelt felt to be strictly confidential. Bowen was first offered a transfer, but when he refused he was recalled and dismissed.[20]

The most striking example of summary recall by the home Government in the annals of American diplomacy occurred in 1906 when Bellamy Storer, United States Ambassador to Austria, was recalled by President Roosevelt without the formality of sending a letter of recall. According to the correspondence subsequently published in full, Mrs. Storer had made use of the embassy position to secure a cardinalship for Archbishop Ireland. President Roosevelt had notified Ambassador Storer that his wife must cease her activities and when he failed to carry out his instructions he was recalled by cable and the secretary appointed chargé d'affaires.

An inexplicable and seemingly inexcusable example of recall by the home Government occurred in Argentina in 1947 when United States Ambassador George Messersmith was recalled by the State Department from Buenos Aires and requested to resign. An outstanding career diplomat who had served the United States effectively for thirty-three years, Messersmith had sought to retire while serving as Ambassador to Mexico but he had been requested urgently to take the difficult Argentine assignment by both President Truman and Secretary Byrnes. He was instructed to combat Nazi influences but at the same time to improve relations with Perón, dictator of Argentina, who had forced the recall of United States Ambassador Spruille Braden for attempting to influence the voters against his election as President. Ambassador Messersmith was highly successful in his mission and received the President's commendation. Suddenly and without previous warning when General Marshall became Secretary of State, Ambassador Messersmith was recalled and his resignation requested without being informed of the reasons for the drastic action. Incidentally Messersmith was immediately offered a position in Mexico City in private industry at a salary considerably higher than he had received as Ambassador.

Recall Requested by the Foreign Government.   A frequent mode of terminating an envoy's mission is by recall at the instance of the government to which the diplomatic representative is accredited. It is generally conceded that if the agent has made himself *persona non grata,* or if he has rendered the relations between the two governments strained, or if he has committed some act which makes his further residence at the

[20] Herbert W. Bowen, *Recollections Diplomatic and Undiplomatic* (New York, 1926), 295-309.

capital difficult, the state to which the envoy is accredited may justly request his recall. Although there is no legal obligation involved, it is customary for the sending state to grant such a request promptly providing the request has been made in good faith and with sufficient reason. It is expected that the reasons for the recall should be given. If the sending state feels that the envoy has merely carried out his instructions and the recall is due to the objections of the receiving state to the policy of the sending state, it may refuse to comply. The receiving state may then dismiss the envoy. On some occasions of this sort the sending state recalls its ambassador or minister and leaves the post in the hands of a chargé d'affaires as a mark of its displeasure.

Numerous examples have occurred when American envoys have been recalled at the request of the foreign government. One of the earliest examples was the case of Gouverneur Morris, appointed Minister to France by President Washington in 1792. Although a supporter of the Revolution in his own country, Morris was essentially an aristocrat and was unable to endure dispassionately the violent excesses of the French Revolution. He expressed openly his feeling that the new constitutional developments would fail and he made an attempt to secure the escape of Louis XVI from Paris and almost succeeded. On numerous occasions Morris offered asylum to refugees who had good reason to fear death at the hands of the mob. The Government of the Republic, to whom Morris had never been overly sympathetic, asked for his recall directly after the United States had requested the recall of Citizen Genêt. Washington was forced to comply, even though he approved heartily of Morris' work as Minister.[21]

While Mr. Buchanan was Secretary of State he had occasion to recall the American Chargé d'Affaires at the request of the Peruvian Government for his decidedly undiplomatic conduct. In a communication to Mr. Jewett Secretary Buchanan informed him that the President regretted that he seemed to be on such unfriendly terms with the Peruvian Government:

It is a primary duty of a diplomatic agent to cultivate the good will of the authorities of the country to which he is accredited. Without this his usefulness must be very much impaired. It is impossible that you can reform either the morals or the politics of Peru, and as this is no part of your mission prudence requires that you should not condemn them in public conversation. . . . It is of great importance that the duties of neutrality and friendship should be faithfully performed by that government to the United States and these cannot be successfully enforced by the agency of a minister against whom the Peruvian authorities have conceived so strong a prejudice, whether well or ill founded, as to induce them to make the reiterated request for his recall.[22]

---

[21] Beckles Willson, *America's Ambassadors to France* (London, 1928), 48-61; see also John Bassett Moore, *Digest of International Law* (Washington, 1906), IV, 488-96.
[22] Moore, *op. cit.*, IV, 492-95.

A very interesting example of the refusal of the United States to recall an envoy at the request of the accrediting country occurred in the case of Mr. Wise, Minister Plenipotentiary to Brazil in 1846. Wise had occasion to protest vigorously the action of the Brazilian Government in seizing and impressing an American naval officer. As a result of an acrimonious correspondence the Emperor of Brazil refused to receive Minister Wise, even when he asked to present a letter from the President congratulating the Emperor upon the birth of a princess. Since the United States supported fully Wise's action, it refused to recall him, although the Brazilian Government requested it several times and Wise himself had asked for it. The United States finally appointed a new envoy while still sustaining the conduct of Wise, who departed without asking for an audience to present his letter of recall.[23]

The Recall of Foreign Envoys by the United States.   The United States seems to hold the record among states for the number of occasions when it has requested the recall of foreign representatives. Beginning with the request for the recall of Citizen Genêt from France, a large number of instances have occurred when the United States has felt it advisable to request the recall of foreign representatives accredited to the United States. One of the serious cases was that of Russian Minister Catacazy, accredited to the United States during the administration of President Grant. In the instructions to United States Minister Curtin at St. Petersburg, Secretary Fish declared that the Russian Envoy had interfered officiously in matters of legislation, he had used the press to influence pending questions and to denounce measures and individuals, he had used abusive and vituperative language towards many persons in public positions, including the President, and had attempted to defeat certain diplomatic efforts between the United States and Great Britain. In this case the recall was delayed until the pending visit of Grand Duke Alexis had taken place.[24]

Perhaps the most striking instance occurred just preceding the Spanish-American War when a New York newspaper published a private letter written by Dupuy de Lome, the Spanish Minister at Washington, to a friend in Cuba in which he characterized President McKinley as a "weak ... would-be politician who tries to leave a door open behind himself while keeping on good terms with the gringoes of his party." This letter had been purloined from the mails and printed to increase the friction already existing between the two countries. Although this was a very questionable piece of journalism, the Spanish representative was guilty of exceedingly undiplomatic conduct. The United States immediately re-

[23] Graham H. Stuart, *Latin America and the United States* (New York, 1943), 459-64.
[24] Moore, *op. cit.*, IV, 501-3.

quested his recall. He did not await action by the Spanish Government but handed in his resignation.[25]

A more recent example which we have cited elsewhere was the request for the recall of Dr. Constantin Dumba, the Austro-Hungarian Ambassador at Washington, who was violating his official position by proposing plans to his Government for instigating strikes in American munitions factories. He was also guilty of using an American citizen with an American passport to carry official despatches to the Austro-Hungarian Government. The United States requested his recall on the ground that he had been guilty of improper conduct.[26]

Dismissal of Public Ministers.   According to Hershey, the dismissal of a minister should only occur as a last resort, as for example, just before the outbreak of hostilities, or if reparation has been refused for a serious injury or if the minister has been guilty of conduct which cannot further be condoned, or if he has seriously interfered in domestic affairs.[27]

Although not so many instances of dismissal as of recall are to be found, important examples have occurred. The cases of the Marquis Yrujo, Spanish Envoy to the United States in 1805, and of F. J. Jackson, British Minister in 1809, were both cases of request for recall which, because of unnecessary delay upon the part of the home governments, became outright or virtual dismissals upon the part of the United States.[28]

Jackson's repeated allegations that both President Madison and Secretary of State Smith had deliberately signed an agreement with the previous British Minister in violation of his instructions was a flagrant violation of normal diplomatic courtesy. The British historian Beckles Willson declares Jackson stands "condemned at the bar of history" and broke "all records for the speed and completeness with which he had become *'persona non grata.'* [29]

In the unfortunate case of Lord Sackville-West, mentioned earlier, the British Government refused to recall its Envoy, but suggested that he be instantly dismissed as this procedure would not end his diplomatic career. Lord Sackville-West had been requested during the presidential campaign of 1888 by a Mr. Murchison, presumably a former British subject, to advise him as to the candidate most likely to favor British interests. As the campaign seemed to be waged on the Irish question and on enmity to England as much as on domestic matters, the letter seeking advice was

[25] *Foreign Relations of the United States, 1898*, 1007-1016.

[26] "Diplomatic Correspondence between the United States and Belligerent Governments—Neutral Rights and Commerce," *American Journal of International Law, Special Supplement*, X, 361.

[27] Amos Hershey, *International Public Law and Organization* (New York, 1927), 399.

[28] Moore, *op. cit.*, IV, 508-30.

[29] Beckles Willson, *Friendly Relations* (Boston, 1934), 73-5.

quite understandable. The British Envoy, not suspecting a trap, wrote a very innocuous reply intimating that President Cleveland would probably follow a conciliatory policy and he enclosed a press clipping from the *New York Times* which gave certain reasons for supporting Cleveland. The whole matter was a despicable trick arranged by a Republican to discredit President Cleveland with the Irish party. Upon publication of the Sackville reply the press took up the hue and cry of interference in domestic politics and Secretary Bayard in the interests of President Cleveland's election asked for Lord Sackville's recall. The matter was such a tempest in a teapot that Lord Salisbury wished time to look into the matter. The political crisis demanded immediate action, however, and Lord Sackville was sent his passports.[30]

A *London Times* editorial on the subject indicated the attitude of British public opinion:

A more ridiculous spectacle has rarely been witnessed in any civilized country than the flurried and unmannerly haste with which the government of President Cleveland has endeavored to put a slight upon this country, obviously for electioneering purposes, before Her Majesty's ministers could deal, one way or the other, with the alleged indiscretion of the British representative at Washington.[31]

The publication by the United States of the infamous *spurlos versenkt* correspondence of Count Luxburg, Minister of the Imperial German Government at Buenos Aires, sent to Germany via the Swedish Legation, caused his summary dismissal at the hands of the Argentine Government. In this case the German Government disavowed their representative and expressed regret at the incident. When more serious violations of the obligations of his diplomatic position were discovered, Luxburg was interned, but later granted a safe conduct by the Allies to return to Germany.[32]

Termination of Mission by War. A regular preliminary to war is the termination of diplomatic relations between the countries concerned. Quite often this occurs some little time before the opening of hostilities, but sometimes the declaration of war coincides with the diplomatic rupture. The well accepted rule of international law prescribes that immediately upon a declaration of war the enemy diplomatic agents, the members of their staff, and their families be given passports and safe conducts to the frontiers. If popular opinion has been aroused the belligerents must see to it that special measures are taken to protect the envoy until he shall have crossed the frontier. The French Government provided a special train for the German Ambassador in 1914 and pur-

[30] Beckles Willson, *Friendly Relations* (Boston, 1934), 252-9; *Foreign Relations of the United States, 1888*, II, 1667-1718; *British and Foreign State Papers*, LXXXI, 479.
[31] John W. Foster, *op. cit.*, 189.
[32] *American Journal of International Law, 1918*, XII, 135-40.

posely kept secret the exact hour of its departure. The various Allied representatives at Vienna were all given special facilities and protection until they crossed the frontier.

The British Embassy in Berlin was threatened by mob violence when it became known that Great Britain had joined France against Germany. A phone call from Sir Edward Goschen, the British Ambassador, to the German Foreign Office brought a force of mounted police and an apology from the German Foreign Minister. A special train was prepared and a colonel of the German guards accompanied the train to the Dutch frontier. The French Ambassador, M. Cambon, did not receive such considerate treatment. He was handed his passports and compelled to depart by way of Copenhagen in spite of his request to go by a shorter route. The trip was long and unpleasant in the extreme. The Russian Ambassador to Germany received similar treatment.[33]

The United States sent the German Ambassador, Count von Bernstorff, his passports at the same time that he was notified that diplomatic relations between the United States and Germany were severed. Following this, the United States secured a safe conduct for the German Ambassador and his suite from the British and French Governments. Arrangements were made for his passage on the Scandinavian-American S. S. *Frederick VIII*. He was escorted from Washington to the boat by official representatives of the State Department and guarded by a special detail of Secret Service officers. He received numerous telegrams, gifts, and huge quantities of flowers at his departure.

Ambassador James W. Gerard was not so fortunate in Berlin. His passports were withheld for more than a week, and during this period he was kept without telegraph or telephone service and was not even permitted to receive his mail.[34] Apparently a false report had been received as to the treatment which had been accorded the German Ambassador in the United States.

Diplomatic Exchange in World War II.   The problem of the exchange of diplomats of enemy belligerents was much more complicated in the Second World War because of the mutual distrust and the large number of countries at war.

For example at the outbreak of war in 1939, the British and French Embassies were not permitted to cross the German frontier until the German Embassies had crossed the corresponding frontiers of France and England. The United States was very liberal in its treatment of the Axis diplomats. For example the members of the German Embassy staff were allowed to remain in their private houses until they could take care

[33] James W. Garner, *International Law and the World War* (London, 1920), I, 39-43.
[34] James W. Gerard, *My Four Years in Germany* (New York, 1917), 383.

of their personal affairs and pack up their belongings. They were given police protection in going between their homes and the chancery. They always had free access to representatives of the Swiss Legation, which had assumed representation of German interests. Later they were housed at the Green Brier Hotel at White Sulphur Springs in West Virginia. The Italian, Bulgarian, and Rumanian missions remained in their homes in Washington, D. C., until the middle of January, 1942, when they too were assembled at White Sulphur Springs. The United States Government assumed all expenses attached to their detention.

The United States chartered the Swedish steamship *Drottningholm* to serve as an exchange vessel and arranged that it should travel under the safe conduct of the various belligerent governments. The Swiss and Portuguese Governments agreed to serve as guarantors for the compliance of the various exchange agreements for the Axis and American officials. Lisbon served as the point of exchange in Europe. On May 7, 1942, the S. S. *Drottningholm* sailed for Lisbon with the diplomatic personnel of the German, Italian, Hungarian, Rumanian, and Bulgarian Embassies and Legations. On its return trip it carried American diplomatic officials who had been given safe conduct from the various Axis capitals.

In departing from the United States the diplomats could take all their personal effects. In the case of the representatives of Vichy France who were not repatriated until early in 1944, a problem arose regarding the taking away of large quantities of rationed food which were far greater than amounts justified as supplementary rations during the voyage. It was finally agreed to permit the food to go as a humanitarian measure. Ambassador Henry-Haye was even permitted to take six cases of vitamins which had been stored in New York since 1941 upon his promise to distribute them to the children of France.

The Japanese Government was not as generous with American Ambassador Grew and his staff as the United States was with the Japanese Embassy in Washington. The Japanese were first sent to the luxurious Homestead Hotel in Hot Springs, Virginia, and later transferred to the equally spacious Green Brier Hotel in White Sulphur Springs, West Virginia. In Tokyo during the first three weeks after war had been declared, the American Ambassador and his staff were confined strictly to their compound and all telephone communications and all radios were seized. The police entered at will both chancery and private apartments and at times peered through the windows. For several days after the Swiss Minister took charge of American interests he was not allowed to visit the Embassy. In similar fashion the Japanese troops occupied the premises of the American Legation at Bangkok and Minister Peck and his staff were confined to the Legation. Here, too, telephone communications were cut and radios confiscated. An interminable delay occurred before negotiations were completed for the exchange. As finally arranged, the exchange point was Lourenço Marques in Portuguese East Africa. The United States chartered the Swedish motorship *Gripsholm* but the Japanese did not grant a safe conduct to the vessel until June 16, 1942. Two days later it left New York for Lourenço Marques with the diplomatic staff of Japan and Thailand aboard. The Japanese used one of their own vessels, the *Asama Maru*, as the exchange ship.

Ambassador Grew in his diary declares that the entire Embassy staff were treated as criminal prisoners and throughout the internment period were subjected to repeated indignities and humiliations by the police. They could not leave the Embassy except for medical reasons. Perhaps the most trying period of all was the last seven days when with many hundreds of other Americans the Embassy staff on board the *Asama Maru* stood at anchor off Yokohama until the exchange negotiations were finally completed. This was a full week after the *Gripsholm* had left New York. The diplomatic staff did not reach New York until the end of August, 1942.[35]

Neutral Envoys in Belligerent States. It is not generally expected that the outbreak of war should terminate the mission of neutral envoys, even though the capital may be invested or captured. In occupied territory the diplomatic representative is inviolable so long as he maintains a strictly neutral attitude, although his privileges and immunities are subject in practice to the military necessities of the invader. We have already discussed the position of Minister Washburne in Paris in 1870 and Ambassador Herrick in 1914.

When the German Army occupied Bucharest in 1917, the German Government requested the diplomatic representatives of neutral powers to leave on the ground that the Rumanian Government had left and the country was under German military administration. The chargés d'affaires of the neutral countries left Bucharest as suggested in a special train provided by the German Government.[36]

On the other hand, although most of the diplomatic representatives left Brussels after the occupation of Belgium by Germany in 1914, a few envoys, including Brand Whitlock, Minister of the United States, and the Marquis de Villalobar, Minister of Spain, were permitted to remain and enjoyed their regular diplomatic privileges and immunities. Hugh Gibson, at that time First Secretary of the American Legation, tells that when the German Chief of the Political Department asked the Marquis Villalobar what his position would be when the Belgian Government would be driven completely out of the country, Villalobar replied, "My situation will be the same as yours. We are both representatives of our country

[35] Joseph C. Grew, *Ten Years in Japan* (New York, 1944).
[36] Sir Cecil Hurst, "Les immunités diplomatiques," Académie de Droit International, *Recueil des Cours* (Paris, 1927), II, 232.

in a country not our own." [37] Whitlock remained until just before the United States entered the war on the side of the Allies.[38]

Germany demanded in 1940 that after the occupation of Norway, Holland, and Belgium, the neutral states should immediately recall their ministers to these countries. When some neutral countries refused to recognize the partition of Poland between Germany and Russia in 1939, both powers demanded in 1940 that the Polish legations still in function in some European capitals should be expelled. The same procedure was extended in 1941 by Germany to Yugoslavian and Greek representation.

We have already discussed the rôle played by United States Ambassador Bullitt in Paris when the German armies entered the city.

Effect of a Revolution. During the course of a revolution the diplomatic representative is expected to remain at the capital and keep his government accurately informed as to the progress of the revolt. In some Latin American states the United States embassy or legation has served as a sort of center of noncombatant activity. During the period of revolutionary activity in Mexico in 1913-1914, the United States Ambassador Henry Lane Wilson, although invited by the Mexican Government to remove the Embassy to Tacubaya for safety, refused on the ground that it was his duty to protect American property and the American colony in the capital.[39]

It is impossible to state exactly the status of a diplomatic mission when a successful revolution overturns the established government and sets up a new one in its place. The customary procedure is for the diplomatic envoy to remain with his mission suspended rather than terminated until his government decides whether to recognize the new government. During this period he continues to enjoy his diplomatic privileges and immunities, but maintains no formal relations with the *de facto* government.

In the case of the revolution in Portugal in 1910, the British Government delayed official recognition until guarantees had been given and an election had confirmed the stability of the new republic. The British diplomatic mission merely suspended its activities during this period.

Just one week after the Russian Revolution began in March, 1917, David R. Francis, the United States Ambassador to Russia, recommended immediate recognition of the Provisional Government of Prince Lvoff. The State Department agreed and recognition was granted on March 22, the first by any of the foreign governments represented at St. Petersburg.[40] When the Lenin-Trotsky Bolshevik Government came into power

[37] Hugh Gibson, *A Journal from Our Legation in Belgium* (New York, 1917), 271.
[38] For the complete story of the activities of the United States Legation during the war period see Brand Whitlock, *Belgium*, 2 vols. (New York, 1919).
[39] Henry Lane Wilson, *Diplomatic Episodes in Mexico, Belgium and Chile* (New York, 1927), 260.
[40] David R. Francis, *Russia from the American Embassy* (New York, 1921), 91-3.

in November at first it made no request for recognition, nor did Ambassador Francis wish to accord it. He even refused to associate himself with a joint request for protection made by the British, French, and American military attachés lest it be regarded as indirect recognition.

Subsequently the Bolsheviks reversed their stand and made every effort to secure recognition. When it was not accorded, the various diplomatic representatives who met daily in the American Embassy decided at the end of February, 1918, to leave Petrograd. Francis went to Vologda where he was later joined by several other envoys. From March 4, 1918, Francis designated Vologda as "the diplomatic capital of Russia" and such it remained for the next six months. In a letter to his son dated March 19, 1918, Ambassador Francis declared that he had never recognized the Bolshevik Government, but that he had established a quasi-business or working arrangement with it. Although the Bolshevik Government on July 23 arranged for a special train to bring the diplomats to Moscow, they refused and insisted upon going to Archangel. Francis remained at Archangel until November 6, 1918, when he was recalled.[41]

Termination as Designated by Pan American Conference. The Sixth Pan American Conference held at Havana February 20, 1928, devoted one entire section to the termination of the diplomatic mission, and it perhaps deserves quotation in full:

The mission of the diplomatic officer ends:
1. By the official notification of the officer's Government to the other Government that the officer has terminated his functions;
2. By the expiration of the period fixed for the completion of the mission;
3. By the solution of the matter, if the mission has been created for a particular question;
4. By the delivery of passports to the officer by the Government to which he is accredited;
5. By the request for his passports made by the diplomatic officer to the Government to which he is accredited.

In the above mentioned cases, a reasonable period shall be given the diplomatic officer, the official personnel of the mission, and their respective families to quit the territory of the State; and it shall be the duty of the Government to which the officer was accredited to see that during this time none of them is molested nor injured in his person or property.

Neither the death [42] or resignation of the head of the State nor the change of government or political regime of either of the two countries shall terminate the mission of the diplomatic officers.[43]

[41] *Ibid.*, 234-65.

[42] In the case of an envoy accredited to a sovereign, the death of the latter formerly necessitated the recommissioning of the envoy to the new head of the foreign state. General John W. Foster, for instance, was issued new credentials when Alexander II died during Foster's ministry there. See John W. Foster, *Diplomatic Memoirs* (New York, 1909), II, 247.

*[43] *Sixth International Conference of American States: Final Act* (Habana, 1928), Article 25, "Convention on Diplomatic Officers."

Procedure in Quitting Post. If the diplomatic envoy is leaving a post permanently the established custom requires him to request a farewell audience with the head of the state in order to present his letter of recall. This, as in the case of submitting his credentials, is done by sending a copy of his recall to the head of the state through the minister of foreign affairs, and requesting an audience. The audience is usually private, the envoy presents his letter of recall and receives a recredential or *lettre de récréance,* in which the head of the state expresses his regret at the departure of the envoy as well as appreciation of his work. No farewell audience occurs if the mission terminates with a breach of diplomatic relations between the two countries. In the case of Ambassador to Germany, James W. Gerard, who had practically been ostracized by the Kaiser for the year prior to American entrance into the war on the ground that he would not receive the ambassador of a country which furnished munitions to the enemies of Germany, the farewell audience was given by the Chancellor and the Foreign Secretary.[44]

When Ambassador Andrew D. White resigned his post on his seventieth birthday he delayed his departure from Berlin because the Emperor was absent. In his case the special audience included his wife and took place at a private luncheon with the Emperor and Empress. The Emperor presented him with the "Great Gold Medal for Art and Science" and sent him the same day a porcelain vase with his portrait.[45]

The generally accepted procedure for the ambassador or minister accredited to the President of the United States has been to present the letter of recall at a formal audience at the White House. A minister with a letter of recall would take leave of the President at the White House but without a letter of recall he would take leave of the President at the Executive Office with an appropriate member of the Department of State present. In practice the letter of recall is usually presented by the ambassador or minister's successor when he presents his letter of credence and the ambassador's farewell call on the President is usually an informal one. Since 1937 it has been the practice in the Department of State to file the letters of recall of a retiring ambassador or minister with the letters of credence of the new representative without replying to the former.

[44] Gerard, *op. cit.,* 321, 385.
[45] *Autobiography of Andrew D. White* (New York, 1905), II, 212. For a description of Ambassador Marye's farewell audience with the Czar see George T. Marye, *Nearing the End in Imperial Russia* (New York, 1929), 469 ff.

16

Historical Development of Consular Practice

CONSULAR PRACTICE like diplomatic practice has its roots buried deep in the dark earth of antiquity. In fact, permanent consulates quite similar to our present institutions precede by many centuries the establishment of permanent embassies. In the earliest examples which are to be found of an institution protective of commerce the judicial function is paramount. Certain countries have permitted foreign merchants domiciled within their territories to choose magistrates who might judge disputes between their countrymen living abroad, in accordance with their own national laws.

The Greek Proxenoi. Herodotus relates how the Egyptians six centuries before Christ granted to the Greeks who were established at Naucratis the right to choose among themselves a magistrate who should apply to them the laws of the mother country.[1] These magistrates were called προστάτης.

In Greece where the foreigner was deprived of all political rights it was customary to require domiciled aliens, *métèques,* to choose a protector or prostates who served as their intermediary in judicial and political relationships with the state.[2] However, among the Greeks we find another institution, προξενία, which is much more similar to the present consular institution. The proxenus was for the foreign state what the prostates was for the foreign individual. The arrangement of proxenus constituted a veritable contract between an independent state and a particular citizen of another state. By this contract the proxenus became the official protector or prostates of the government which commissioned him.[3] In fact, in modern Greece the term *proxenus* is equivalent to our word *consul.*

---

[1] Alex de Milnitz, *Manuel des Consuls* (London, 1837), I, 9.
[2] See M. Clerc, *Les Métèques athéniens* (Paris, 1893).
[3] See A. Schaube, "La Proxénie au Moyen-Age," *Revue de droit international et législation comparée,* XXVIII, 531 (1896).

Proxenoi were appointed by the foreign government from citizens of the country where protection was desired. Thus the proxenus had an official status as regards the government he represented but no special status in his own country. The proxenus was accustomed to have the decree of his nomination engraved upon marble with bronze hands as emblems of alliance, or with fishes as symbols of travel and maritime intercourse.

The duties of the proxenus were manifold. He protected the nationals of the government he represented and acted for them before the assemblies and the courts. He served as witness when they made their wills and he determined the succession of deceased foreigners without heirs. He facilitated the sale of cargoes and he obtained security for the loans of his protégés.[4]

The proxenus received foreign ambassadors and other diplomatic officials and procured admission for them to the assemblies, temples and theaters. He served in the making of treaties. He was often chosen as arbitrator in disputes between the government which he represented and his own government. At times he intervened to prevent war. Quite often his own country sent him as ambassador to the country which he represented. Callias, the proxenus of Sparta in Athens, was sent several times to Sparta by Athens as Ambassador.

Although it is not known whether the proxenoi received payment for their services they did enjoy many privileges. In a war between their own state and the state they represented their persons and property were protected. They had the right of free import and export of all merchandise. They were given exemption from certain taxes and the majority of imposts. They had the right of access to public assemblies. They had the right to have their personal affairs judged out of turn. They had the right to acquire and possess real estate. They could use a special seal in their official duties. Also they could place over the doors of their houses the arms of the city which they represented.[5]

Outstanding Greeks served in the capacity of proxenoi. Pindar represented Athens at Thebes, Thucydides at Pharsalis, Alcibiades and Cimon represented Sparta at Athens, and Demosthenes served as proxenus for Thebes in the same city. "There is evidence that this institution was common to more than seventy-eight Greek states, cities or confederations."[6]

"By way of summary," states the eminent authority Monceaux, "as

---

[4] For an excellent brief account see Coleman Phillipson, *The International Law and Customs of Ancient Greece and Rome* (London, 1911), I, 147-56. See also Paul Monceaux, *Les Proxénies grecques* (Paris, 1886) and C. Tissot, *Des Proxénies grecques et de leur analogie avec les institutions consulaires modernes* (Dijon, 1868).

[5] D. B. Warden, *On the Origin, Nature, Progress and Influence of Consular Establishments* (Paris, 1813), 36.

[6] Paul Leroy, *Des consulats, des légations et des ambassades* (Paris, 1876), 84.

permanent intermediaries between two cities, as patrons of a foreign city before the tribunals and assemblies of their home country, as diplomats and negotiators of treaties, as arbitrators between states, the proxenoi played a very considerable rôle in the international life of ancient Greece." [7]

Kindred Institutions among the Romans. The Romans never looked with the same favor upon commerce as did the Greeks, and when they became masters of the Hellenic world the institution of proxenia had already gone into decline. Nevertheless in the institution of patronage among the Romans we see a certain resemblance to the Greek proxenia. The principal difference was that in the case of the Roman patronat the patron or protector was usually a Roman patrician who was willing to act in this capacity towards a foreign city which owed allegiance to Rome. Sometimes the patrons were chosen by the foreign communities, sometimes the conquerors were named by the Roman senate as protectors of the vanquished. Cicero has clearly stated the situation: "Justice has always been respected to such an extent with us that the very persons who received the surrender of cities or conquered nations became their patrons in accordance with the custom of our fathers." [8] The decrees conferring the patronat were engraved upon plaques of bronze or marble which were called *tessera hospitalis.* Some of the most influential Romans served as patrons of foreign peoples. Cicero was patron of Syracuse, Caesar of Chios, Cato of Cyprus and Cappadocia, Pliny the Younger of Betica. [9]

Another institution existed among the Romans which perhaps might be compared to our present day consular establishment. It was the *praetor peregrinus.* Foreigners in Rome were called peregrines and the *praetor peregrinus* was the magistrate charged with settling their disputes in accordance with the principles of *jus gentium.* The *praetor peregrinus* had the same rank as the *praetor urbanus.* Although his principal function was to interpret the law between foreigners or between Roman citizens and foreigners he served sometimes as ambassador and performed certain international judicial functions. [10] The law applied by the *praetor peregrinus* to the foreigner was based partly upon their national laws and partly upon the *jus gentium.*

It is also to the Romans that we are indebted for the word *consul.* As employed by the Romans, the word consul referred to one of the two principal magistrates of the Roman republic. The term was later adopted

[7] C. V. Daremberg, et E. Saglio, eds., *Dictionnaire des antiquités grecques et romaines* (Paris, 1884), 740.

[8] Cicero, *De Officiis,* I, 38.

[9] A. M. Candioti, *Historia de la institución consular en la antigüedad y en la edad media* (Buenos Aires, 1925), 85.

[10] Phillipson, *op. cit.,* I, 269.

both by emperors and kings. It finally became so popularly used that it lost its standing with monarchs and the term came to be used to designate the chief magistrates in the cities of Southern Europe; for example, Provence and Languedoc of Southern France in the year 1000 A.D. and some of the Italian cities at the same period were ruled by magistrates who were given the title of "consuls." [11] It is also during the Middle Ages that we encounter the term *judge-consul* or *merchant-consul*, a magistrate competent to pass upon commercial disputes. It is at this period also that we find the term overseas consul—*consul in partibus ultra marinis*—to designate the official sent by an independent city to the port of a foreign country to protect the commerce and decide the disputes of its nationals.[12]

Establishment of the Consular Regime.   After the fall of the Roman Empire we find a law of the Visigoths of the fifth century which set up a sort of foreigners' court which was authorized to exercise jurisdiction over foreigners in accordance with their own national laws. These foreigners who served as judges were named *telonarii*.[13]

According to Pardessus this law of the Visigoths is thought to be one of the most ancient examples of the jurisdiction accorded to consuls that a nation exercised over its nationals residing abroad.[14] We should also note in passing that the Chinese possessed tribunals of commerce in the eighth century and the Arabs in the ninth century, so that it might well be disputed as to which nation has the honor of setting up the first consulates.[15] It was only when the crusades created the great development of commerce between the cities of the Mediterranean and the Near East, however, that the real consular regime began. In fact, Milnitz declares that the development of the consular institution abroad can be classed among the most remarkable and most useful effects that these armed pilgrimages produced upon the conditions of maritime commerce of Europe.[16]

Before continuing this sketch of the historical development of the consular institution we should note the outstanding maritime codes of the Middle Ages.

The Maritime Codes of the Middle Ages.   Unfortunately the oldest and one of the most famous of these codes, the Lex Rhodia, has come down to us in considerably abbreviated form. References to the law of

[11] Sir Geoffrey Butler, and Simon Maccoby, *The Development of International Law* (London, 1928), 83.

[12] de Milnitz, *op. cit.*, I, 3-6.

[13] Candioti, *op. cit.*, 99-101.

[14] J. M. Pardessus, *Collections des lois maritimes antérieures au XVIIIᵉ siècle* (Paris, 1828-1845), I, 153.

[15] M. Capello, "Les Consulats et les Bailages de la République de Venise," *Revue de droit international et législation comparée,* XXIX, 161 (1897).

[16] de Milnitz, *op. cit.*, II, 13. See also Warden, *op. cit.*, 50-1.

jettison, undoubtedly the Rhodian law of *jactu,* were made by both Cicero and Sallust.[17] The texts that we have were probably put together from earlier treatises and local customs somewhere between 600 and 800 A.D.[18]

The first code that specifically covers the work of consuls is the one known as the Tables of Amalfi and probably dates from the eleventh century although some authorities date it as late as the fifteenth.[19] According to the rules laid down in this code captains departing and returning must first visit the consuls and the consuls are empowered to punish sailors who have not carried out the terms of the contract with the owners.

Another famous collection of maritime customs is the *Rôles* or Judgments of Oléron, whose exact date is also unknown although the various texts which are found in Great Britain in a collection designated the *Black Book of the Admiralty* are of the fourteenth century.[20] Pardessus and Milnitz agree that the *Rôles d'Oléron* are of French origin and Twiss thinks that they were the result of legal privileges granted by the Dukes of Guienne to the Commune of Oléron in the twelfth century. The judgments are largely concerned with relations between the master of the ship and his crew and no mention is made of magistrate or consul.

The Consolato del Mare. Of all the compilations of maritime usages, however, the *Consolato del Mare* is the most famous. Although the date and place of this compilation are uncertain, the authorities for the most part attribute the *Consolato* to Barcelona and they believe that it was originally drafted in the fourteenth century. There are several editions of this manuscript. One edition published in 1494 in Barcelona is regarded as the first edition and an excellent copy of this edition is to be found in the *Bibliothèque Nationale de Paris.* There are also in the *Bibliothèque Nationale* in Paris two manuscripts of the *Consolato* written in Catalonian on fourteenth-century paper.[21]

Milnitz characterizes the *Consolato* in these words: "The *Consolato del Mare* although drawn up in a crude and somewhat jumbled fashion is really a remarkable production; whatever its imperfections may be, one cannot fail to appreciate the wisdom of the regulations which it lays down and which have become the basis of the maritime legislation of Europe today.... The *Consolato* is more extensive than the *Rôles* of Oléron and furnished the navigators of the Mediterranean a résumé of

---

[17] *Ibid.,* I, 17-18.

[18] See the excellent study by Walter Ashburner, *The Rhodian Sea Law* (Oxford, 1909). The text may also be found in Pardessus, *op. cit.*

[19] Candioti, *op. cit.,* 237-40.

[20] Travers Twiss, ed., *The Black Book of the Admiralty* (London, 1871-1876), 4 vols., I, II, III.

[21] For an excellent commentary on the origin of the *Consolato* see *The Black Book of the Admiralty, op. cit.,* III, xxv-lix, etc.

the laws that each one was accustomed to obey in his own country; it was more complete than any one of these isolated laws, since it borrowed from each of them what the others lacked, and withal it furnished such an excellent codification that solely by the authority of its common sense and wisdom it served as guide in the tribunals of commerce." [22]

The most interesting commentary on the *Consolato*, however, comes from a contemporary observer, Jerome Paul, the chaplain of Pope Alexander III, who wrote an account of the city of Barcelona in 1491 A.D. "There are at Barcelona laws as to buildings and as to commerce, and judgment is rendered according to them on principles of equity, and summarily by two magistrates who are called consuls; and hence the laws are called consular laws; the use of which laws prevails at this time not merely in that city but in almost every maritime city, the controversies of mariners and of merchants are settled by these laws, or by laws derived from them, with the greatest authority; and as formerly men spoke of the Laws of Rhodes, now everyone speaks of the Laws of Barcelona." [23]

In some editions of the *Consolato* the compilation begins with forty-two chapters relative to the election of consular judges and the method of procedure before them. It is thought that this preliminary code was drawn up by King Peter III for the city of Valencia. These regulations are not a part of the *Consolato* proper, but rather an injunction requiring the observance of the rules which follow.[24] The *Consolato* is a complete codification of maritime law of this period and it is here that are found the principles of neutrality such as: a neutral flag does not protect enemy cargo but neutral cargo is free under an enemy flag. Curiously, the word consul is used only once in the *Consolato* proper, in chapter LXXV.

Germanic Maritime Law.   In concluding this sketch of medieval sea law largely the product of the Latin countries, one should not overlook completely the contributions of the Germanic peoples. Perhaps the most famous of these compilations is known by the title of Maritime Law of Wisby, a city situated in the Baltic upon the island of Gothland. This code dates from the fourteenth century; the first edition seems to be the copy made in 1505 in Copenhagen.[25] This compilation has many similarities to the Codes of Lübeck and undoubtedly the two together with the *Consolato del Mare* served as a basis for the laws of that famous commercial organization of the Middle Ages, the Hanseatic League.[26]

This powerful commercial organization, which controlled the maritime

---

[22] de Milnitz, *op. cit.*, I, 99-100.

[23] *The Black Book of the Admiralty, op. cit.*, III, lviii.

[24] de Milnitz, *op. cit.*, I, 100. For text see Pardessus, *op. cit.*, V, 374.

[25] de Milnitz, *op. cit.*, I, 78.

[26] A treaty of 1438 between King Henry VI of England and the consuls of the Teutonic Hanse provided that henceforth the laws and ordinances of the *Consolato* should be observed in matters pertaining to consular jurisdiction at Hanseatic ports.

trade of all Northern and Western Europe from the thirteenth to the sixteenth century, maintained consulates in nearly one hundred different cities of Northern and Western Europe. Although instead of choosing noblemen as was the custom of the Mediterranean cities, the Hanseatic merchants chose consuls or aldermen from their own numbers, nevertheless the functions and duties were approximately the same. In fact, Candioti has proved that the claim oftentimes made that the Hanseatic League employed the institution of aldermen in all parts of Europe except Portugal is inaccurate. He has proof that they had set up foreign consulates in Seville and Sicily as well as in Portugal.[27]

Mediterranean Commerce and Consular Establishments. Merchants of the Mediterranean cities of Venice, Pisa, Genoa, Amalfi, Marseilles and Barcelona who had adopted the *Consolato del Mare* to settle their commercial differences were wont to travel to Egypt, Palestine, and Syria. They set up factories and mercantile establishments there in order to facilitate their commercial operations. These trading establishments occupied a special quarter in each city and they were generally exempt from local taxes. The merchants were not willing to be tried in accordance with the laws of the Saracens. It was therefore necessary for these merchants to have their disputes judged by a magistrate familiar with their national laws. They also had need of a representation accredited to the Mussulman Government through whom they might present their petitions for redress the more effectively and thereby obtain justice. This magistrate chosen from among the merchants of a single city was called baile or consul. His jurisdiction was obtained from the Mussulman princes under the form of a treaty or capitulation.

The authorities have never been able to agree upon the exact date of the first consular establishment. Milnitz finds that the earliest date of the institution in the Middle Ages is anterior to the tenth century and the merchants of Pisa were the first to obtain these privileges in the Levant.[28] Pawinski also declares that the consuls of Pisa were the first representatives of this new institution and gives the date as 1087.[29] Fauchille states that the Greek Emperor in Constantinople accorded the Venetians the right of sending magistrates to judge their citizens in both civil and criminal matters in 1060.[30] Perhaps we may say with de Laigue that French, Pisans and Venetians benefited concurrently from the same advantages and by many years were the first to make use of consuls.

---

[27] Candioti, *op. cit.*, 203-6. See also Worms, *Histoire commerciale de la Ligue hanséatique* (Paris, 1864).

[28] de Milnitz, *op. cit.*, I, 162.

[29] A. Pawinski, *Zur Entstehungsgeschichte des Consulats in den Communen nord und mittel-italiens* (Göttingen, 1867), 37.

[30] Paul Fauchille, *Traité de droit international public* (Paris, 1921-1926), I, Pt. 3, 112.

The functions and duties of consuls in this early period as laid down by the regulations of Barcelona in 1266 gave them "full jurisdiction to order, govern, cite, regulate, punish and take any other action with respect to persons who voyage from our shores to places across the sea and establish their residence in those ports ..." [31]

Don Antonio de Capmany gives an interesting picture of the organization and powers of consuls as established by King Peter IV of Aragon by his patent of 1347, conceding to the city of Barcelona the right to establish a consular tribunal.

There were two consuls, a military consul and a merchant consul who presided over the college of merchants, an organization of merchants registered in the city. The consuls were accorded honors equivalent to those entitled to the title "the magnificent" and when they made a formal public appearance they were preceded by two mace bearers who carried maces of silver that were lowered before no one. They were placed under the jurisdiction of the Barcelona municipal council.

The two consuls exercised jurisdiction in the first instance in accordance with forms established by the *Consolato del Mare*. They enjoyed the right of making regulations supplementary to the *Consolato del Mare*. A decree of Pierre IV attributed to them exclusive and final jurisdiction over all maritime and commercial questions and their judgments were to be considered as if rendered in person by the King. They had the right of imposing fines and other civil penalties upon bankers who violated the laws established to protect the credit. They had jurisdiction in matters relating to bills of exchange, corporations, associations and contracts of every sort involving business matters.

The consuls could also together with the municipal council suspend in case of fraud brokers and members of the stock exchange.[32]

An equally interesting although somewhat different account is given by Schaube. Certain well known citizens of Narbonne in 1278 chose as consul at Pisa the notable Pisan Ugolino. He had three principal functions: first *hospes,* second *defensor,* and last *judex.*

As *hospes* "he was obliged to assure to all the citizens of Narbonne who might come to Pisa the necessary shelter for themselves and at the same time facilitate the disposition of their merchandise. ..."

As *defensor* "he was called upon to protect the rights, the privileges and the liberties of the citizens of Narbonne living in Pisa, and at the same time to defend every citizen of Narbonne individually against injustice and violence. ..."

As *judex* "he must watch over the citizens of Narbonne residing in Pisa and had both the right and duty of maintaining order and justice among them." [33]

[31] Candioti, *op. cit.,* 319.
[32] de Milnitz, *op. cit.,* I, 170 ff.
[33] Schaube, *op. cit.,* 529.

The Development of the Consular Institution. The development of the consular institution was quite rapid. The city of Amalfi sent a consul to Naples in 1190 and Marseilles obtained in 1226 the right to have consuls in the Duchy of Savoy with jurisdiction over their compatriots. Genoa created two *consules maritimi* in 1250 to judge foreigners and settle maritime disputes. The Genoese obtained from King Ferdinand of Castille in 1251 the right of having consuls at Seville who could judge not only the differences between their nationals but also the disputes between the Genoese and the citizens of Seville. In the thirteenth century Venice had consuls in more than thirty cities including Montpellier, Tunis, Alexandria, Cairo, and Damascus.[34] In 1265 the Venetians were accorded the right of appointing a bailo to Constantinople who later became consul general. As consul general of the establishment he exercised all the rights of a lord in the Venetian quarter.[35] When Florence in 1423 sent an embassy to Egypt to obtain a commercial capitulation the ambassadors were instructed to insist that the Florentine consul receive the same privileges and honors accorded to the consuls of the most favored nations.

The English merchants trading with Prussia and the Hanseatic towns as early as 1391 had confirmed by the crown the appointment of a "governor" whose duty it was to settle disputes between English merchants and to protect their interests in dealing with foreigners. Similar "governors" were later set up in Holland, Norway, Denmark, and Sweden.[36]

To Richard III of England goes the honor of having the first consul by royal authority in England. The letters patent were issued in the year of 1485 to a certain Laurent Strozzi and their provisions are worthy of citation:

For Laurence Strozzi

To all and singular to whom these Presents shall come, Greeting. Whereas certain merchants and others of this our Kingdom intend, God willing, to visit certain foreign countries particularly Italy with their own vessels or transported in others . . . and inasmuch as it has been found advantageous among the states to appoint a particular magistrate by whose judgment and finding the differences and disputes which may arise among our merchants and others while exercising their trades in these foreign lands may be able to be investigated and settled . . . and since the outstanding fidelity and probity of the Florentine merchant, Laurence Strozzi, has been brought to our attention . . . we do establish, ordain and name the aforesaid Laurence as far as is within our power the jurisdiction of hearing and judging the disputes, litigations and controversies which may arise between our subjects in those parts. . . .[37]

[34] Capello, *op. cit.*, 173.
[35] *Ibid.*, 176 ff.
[36] Butler and Maccoby, *op. cit.*, 212.
[37] The original Latin copy of this letter patent is found in Thomas Rymer, *Foedera, Conventions, Literae*, etc., 20 vols. (London, 1726-1735), XII, 270.

Russia was one of the last among the European powers to set up a consular system. Peter the Great sent the first consular agent to Holland, a second to Bordeaux, and a third to Cadiz in 1723. The latter carried not only the consular letters patent but also letters of credence addressed to the Central Government.[38] Austria did not appoint consuls in Europe until 1752 but she had sent consuls to the Levant before this time.

Emphasis should be placed upon the fact that the general practice during the Middle Ages was to name a notable citizen of the city where representation was desired as consul of the city desiring protection. It is only in the sixteenth century that the custom began of naming nationals as consular representatives in foreign lands. The extent of consular powers even in the seventeenth century was quite variable. For example, the consuls at Venice had no jurisdiction over their nationals, while those at Florence and London had the right to settle all the disputes which might arise among their nationals.[39] The powers of consuls in the Near East were naturally very much broader in extent than those of consuls in Europe because the need of protection for Christian merchants and sailors was much greater.

Consular Development in the Middle Ages.   A summary of the duties and functions of consuls of the Middle Ages and of the beginning of modern times indicates a very extensive jurisdiction. The consul had to protect his nationals and act in their defense; he was expected to give them assistance and advice; it was his duty to prevent frauds and to see to it that treaties were properly executed; he must protect the deposits consigned and take the necessary measures in case of accident or shipwreck; he had to settle disputes arising between his nationals and to fix the penalties when the local authorities permitted it; it was his duty to rule upon inheritances and to protect the national religion. The consul obtained the authority to exercise these functions through letters patent or charters of privilege issued by the country in which he exercised his profession. The letters patent finally came to be called exequaturs, bérats in the Levant. Inasmuch as consular jurisdiction was an infringement upon territorial sovereignty consular rights for the most part had to be obtained by treaties.

In the Near East where consular rights were of the greatest importance, the European powers were quick to see the need for treaties. The Italian cities signed treaties of commerce with the Ottoman Empire in the fifteenth century, a few of which bore the name of capitulations. France, however, was the first of the great powers to sign capitulations with Turkey. Francis I in 1535 signed with the Sultan of Turkey a treaty of

[38] F. Borel, *De l'origine et des fonctions des consuls* (Leipzig, 1831), 18.
[39] P. E. Reynaud, *Des ambassadeurs chez les Romains, des consulats* (Paris, 1874), 154.

commerce and friendship which provided that their subjects could respectively buy, sell, exchange, convey and transport by land and by sea from one country to the other all sorts of merchandise and that a bailo or consul "might hear, judge and conclude all trials, lawsuits and disputes both criminal and civil which might arise between merchants and other subjects of the King." [40] The provisions of this treaty have served as a foundation for subsequent consular jurisprudence in the Levant.

Although the wars of the fifteenth century arrested the development of the consular institution, at the end of the sixteenth century it began to flourish again. To the extent that commercial relations acquired greater importance it was natural that the states should adopt an institution which had already proved itself so useful. But with the development of monarchical authority the power of nominating consuls was taken over by the state. The consul ceased to be the representative of a group of merchants in a strange city. He was now commissioned by the government and became an official representative of the state. The result in Europe was that consuls lost to some extent their rights of jurisdiction over their nationals. The sovereign states no longer wished to surrender the prerogative of dispensing justice in their own territories.

The establishment of permanent embassies at this period tended to diminish the powers of the consuls inasmuch as consuls were no longer required to perform diplomatic functions. Little by little as the consuls lost their judicial powers their duties in relation to commerce increased and their principal functions became the protection and safeguarding of their country's commercial and industrial interests and a similar duty for their nationals. It was only in the Levant and the Far East that the consuls retained their judicial attributes.

During the seventeenth and eighteenth centuries the development of the consular service was constant although not so rapid as in the second half of the nineteenth century. The improvement in communication facilities and the remarkable increase in commercial activities during this period exerted a profound influence upon the extension of the consular service. Chateaubriand while discussing the Congress of Verona remarked that the time of the ambassadors had passed and that that of the consuls had returned. The valuable services of Theodore Rouston, French Consul in Tunis, who not only won railroad concessions from the Bey but finally brought about the French protectorate over Tunis in 1882, showed the great possibilities afforded to the consular service.

The Present Situation.   It is in the seventeenth century that we have the beginning of national legislation to regulate the organization and jurisdiction of consular establishments. France disputes with the Nether-

[40] G. Noradounghian, *Recueil d'actes internationaux de l'Empire Ottoman* (Paris, 1897), I, 83.

lands the honor of being the first state to set up systematic legislative provisions relating to consuls. It was the ministry of Colbert which gave to France the famous marine Ordinance of 1681, an important part of which was devoted to consulates. This remarkable ordinance, which is still in force except for those provisions which have been formally repealed, treats both of consular organization and its judicial and extra judicial functions. Important modifications were made in the Ordinance of 1681 by the Edict of 1778 and the Ordinances of 1781, and in 1833 a general codification was made by a series of important decrees. The present organization and powers of the French consular service are based upon this legislation slightly modified by a few more recent ordinances and decrees, particularly the four decrees of 1920.[41]

The first general consular regulations adopted by the States General of the Netherlands actually antedate by several years both the instructions and the great *Ordinance* of Colbert. The Dutch regulations applicable to consuls resident in Spain, France, and Italy were issued in 1658. These were modified by successive enactments leading up to the fundamental regulations of 1871 which, with minor changes, still stand.[42]

The Emperor of the Holy Roman Empire did not appoint consuls and the first German consular regulations seem to have been issued by Prussia in 1796. The Confederation enacted a law regarding the organization of consulates in 1867, which was completed by the instructions of 1871 and 1873. These regulations are for the most part still in force.[43] Great Britain, which sent her first consul to Italy in 1410, enacted no legislation regarding consuls until the nineteenth century and the first general instructions for consuls were issued in 1846. Present consular practice is based upon revisions of these instructions.[44]

Consular practice of the Italian cities during the Middle Ages was based almost entirely upon treaties. Modern Italian consular law is a development of the Sardinian system first issued in 1815 and replaced by the regulations of 1835. The present practice is governed by the laws of 1858 and 1866 with certain minor modifications.[45]

The United States elected its first consul in France in 1780 while still governed by the Continental Congress. However, the first legislation upon the subject was enacted in 1792 and this act, with slight amendments, held until 1856. Subsequent changes were made by executive

---

[41] F. De Cussy, *Règlements consulaires des principaux états maritimes de l'Europe et de l'Amérique* (Paris et Leipzig, 1851), 149 ff.; or A. H. Feller, and M. O. Hudson, *A Collection of the Diplomatic and Consular Laws and Regulations at Various Countries* (Washington, 1933), I, 513 ff.

[42] Feller and Hudson, *op. cit.*, I, 854-85.

[43] *Ibid.*, I, 547-73.

[44] *Ibid.*, I, 167-218.

[45] Ibid., I, 685-717.

orders until the service was reorganized by the Act of 1906. In 1924 the diplomatic and consular services were consolidated and important changes were made by the laws of 1931 and 1946.

The Consular System Today. Although national legislation has had some influence upon the development of consular law, consular practice today just as it did in the Middle Ages rests largely upon consular treaties and conventions. The world is bound by a close network of these agreements in which every phase of consular practice and immunity is covered. Even the smallest and most backward states have been anxious to regulate their commercial relations with their neighbors by means of consular conventions or general treaties of commerce. It should be noted that the vast majority of such treaties are bipartite in character. Some of these agreements are devoted entirely to consuls while others of a broader character such as treaties of commerce, navigation, peace, friendship and so forth usually contain provisions regarding consular privileges and immunities.

It is practically impossible at the present time to give an exact figure regarding the number of consuls sent and received by the states of the world due to the practice of many countries of granting dual commissions to their foreign service officials to permit their serving either in a diplomatic or consular capacity. In 1931, figures obtained from official sources indicated Great Britain sent 1,075 consuls and received 1,605, France sent 851 and received 1,566, the United States sent 870 and received 1,435. The total number of consular officials sent and received by all the states of the world was listed as 34,523.[46]

To obtain some sort of comparison with the present situation, twenty years later, the following figures may be of some interest. In the year 1951 the total number of foreign representatives diplomatic and consular residing in Washington numbered 2,581 whereas at the same time the United States had sent abroad 3,169 Americans in either a diplomatic or consular capacity. More specifically, the United States in 1951 sent to Great Britain, Northern Ireland, and the British possessions overseas (excluding the self-governing dominions) 174 officers with consular commissions of whom 19 of the 40 stationed in London had dual commissions. At the same time Great Britain had 70 regular consular officers in the United States and 2 honorary consuls. For the same period the United States had 72 officers with consular commissions in continental France of whom 27 of the 45 stationed in Paris were Foreign Service officers with both diplomatic and consular status. On the other hand, France had only 52 consular representatives in the United States in 1951

---

[46] *Annuaire du corps diplomatique et consulaire* (Geneva, 1931).

of whom 27 were honorary. The United States at the present time has unquestionably the largest diplomatic and consular corps of any country in the world.[47]

The Codification of Consular Law.   Various attempts have been made to codify consular law and with perhaps a greater degree of success than has been attained in diplomatic law. Bluntschli in 1868, Field in 1876, and Fiore in 1890 prepared comprehensive codes covering the rights, powers, duties, and privileges of consuls.[48] The Institute of International Law in 1896 and the American Institute of International Law in 1925 worked out brief codes largely confined to the privileges and immunities of consuls. The Committee set up by the League of Nations to consider those subjects on international law which appeared ready for codification included the legal position and functions of consuls. The subcommittee which reported on this subject declared that the regulation of the legal status of consuls by international agreement was not only desirable but indispensable from every point of view. A brief code covering certain essential prerogatives and privileges was appended. The Inter-American Commission of Jurists meeting at Rio de Janeiro in 1927 prepared a rather complete draft code covering all phases of consular activity which was adopted as a convention at the Sixth Pan-American Conference which met in Havana in January, 1928. Twenty of the republics of the Western Hemisphere signed this consular convention and eleven had ratified it by April 1, 1950.

Perhaps the most elaborate code of consular procedure and practice is the one prepared by a Research Group in International Law directed by Manley O. Hudson, of the Harvard Law School. This carefully drawn code is the joint work of some fifteen American authorities in the field of international law and covers very adequately and systematically the legal position and functions of consuls.

From these various codes it is possible to settle perhaps the very thorny question regarding the legal position of consuls in international law. The consensus seems to be that while a consul is not a public minister and does not possess a representative character, nevertheless the consul must possess the legal status indispensable for the discharge of his duties. He must possess therefore as a minimum such immunities as cover the inviolability

---

[47] *Department of State, Justice, Commerce, and the Judiciary Appropriations for 1952*—Hearings 82nd Cong. 1st sess. 1016-21. A complete listing of all consular representatives sent abroad by the United States is found in the *Foreign Service List*, published three times a year by the Department of State. Similarly the consular representatives of foreign nations in the United States are found in *Foreign Consular Offices in the United States*, published annually by the Department of State.

[48] J. C. Bluntschli, *Le droit international codifié*, 4th ed. (Paris, 1884); D. D. Field, *Outlines of an International Code* (New York, 1876), 58-77; Pasquale Fiore, *International Law Codified* (New York, 1918).

of consular archives and exemption from such restraint as might interfere with the proper performance of official duties. It is to be hoped that such rights may soon be recognized universally as proper prerogatives for the adequate protection of consular representatives. Such recognition would be only a fitting acknowledgment of the invaluable assistance which the consular system has rendered to the development of commerce between nations.

17

Consuls—Classification and Appointment

Consular Conventions. We have already noted that the world is bound up today with a fine network of treaties, a large number of which are devoted to commercial relationships between states. The majority of these treaties of commerce and navigation are bilateral agreements in which specific provision is made for the reciprocal establishment of consulates and for most favored nation treatment as to consular privileges and immunities. Within the last century a number of treaties have been signed whose provisions are related entirely to consular establishments and in recent times the so-called consular convention is becoming ever more popular.

The earliest treaties of this sort, 3 in number, were made between France and the Ottoman Porte in the sixteenth century. During the seventeenth century there were 10 such treaties signed, of which 4 were between European countries. The eighteenth century witnessed the number increase to 27. According to Phillimore, in the first seventy years of the nineteenth century, 95 such treaties were signed,[1] and Hall finds 52 in the next twenty years.[2] Between the years 1890 and 1900 there were 87 treaties of commerce and navigation negotiated, of which 28 were specifically consular conventions.[3] Using these figures as a basis, a conservative estimate would give us over 200 treaties with provisions covering consular regulations signed during the nineteenth century. During the twentieth century a very rapid increase has taken place and Feller and Hudson list over 900 such treaties as having been signed by 1933.[4]

Contemporary consular conventions almost invariably provide for full

[1] Sir Robert Phillimore, *Commentaries upon International Law,* 3rd ed. (London, 1882), II, 280 ff.

[2] W. E. Hall, *International Law,* 4th ed. (London, 1895), 337.

[3] *United States Department of State, Catalogue of Treaties 1814-1918* (Washington, 1919).

[4] A. H. Feller and Manley O. Hudson, *Diplomatic and Consular Laws and Regulations* (Washington, 1933), II, Appendix.

reciprocity and most favored nation treatment as regards the establishment of consulates. They permit the enjoyment of certain consular privileges and immunities and provide for the exercise of consular functions. The widespread tendency to conventionalize consular regulations has tended naturally to standardize them, and for this reason a well established consular law may be said to exist today.

One of the most recent examples of a consular convention to which the United States is a party was signed in 1948 between the United States and Costa Rica and went into effect in March, 1950. It provides most favored nation treatment and declares that the consular officer "shall be entitled to the high consideration of all officials national or local with whom he has official intercourse." ... Somewhat of an innovation is the permission for the consular representative to exercise diplomatic functions, if reciprocally agreed upon, simultaneously with his consular functions.[5]

Modern Practice. It is a generally conceded principle of international law that states may maintain consuls in the commercial centers of friendly powers with whom they carry on normal diplomatic relations.[6] Even if this principle were questioned, the interchange of commodities and the intercourse between states has developed to such an extent that enlightened self-interest would require a state to accept the practice. No state today in the civilized world refuses to receive consular representatives from a friendly state. There are practically no fully sovereign states which do not send as well as receive consuls.

In 1951 the United States maintained consular representation in 101 different states or colonial possessions of which by far the largest number were in the British Empire. Since all Foreign Service officers have dual commissions and many in the foreign capitals were interchangeable as diplomatic or consular officers it is almost impossible to state the exact number of American consular officers. Great Britain with 66 consular officers in the United States has the largest number of career consular officers of any foreign state. Mexico with 94 has the largest total of consular officers, but more than half of these are honorary consuls or vice consuls. Some seventy-two states maintain consular establishments in the United States at the present time. In the case of Czechoslovakia, Hungary, Rumania, and the U.S.S.R. all protection of nationals is carried on from the embassies in Washington. Poland for the present is conducting the consular relations of Bulgaria in the United States.

The United States, during the time when it had no diplomatic relations with Soviet Russia, utilized the services of Turkish consulates in Russia for the exercise of certain American legal and notarial formalities. Al-

[5] *Treaties and International Acts of the United States,* No. 2045.

[6] Although, as many authorities declare, states are not obliged to receive consuls, the custom is so well established that the affirmative statement seems justified.

though the international city of Tangier does not send consuls, it receives consuls from most of the important powers and the foreign consuls practically constitute the city government.

Classification of Consuls.   Only states can send consuls and as a general rule only nationals may serve as professional consuls or *consuls de carrière.* The United States, Great Britain, and France as a rule appoint only nationals to consular posts.

Career consuls or *consules missi* are public officials of the sending state who are not permitted to engage in private business of any kind and as public functionaries they enjoy certain prescribed privileges and immunities. Commercial consuls or *consules electi* are chosen by a state from its own citizens engaged in business in a foreign country or even at times from foreign nationals. These so-called honorary consuls may not claim the same privileges and immunities as the professional consuls, but social distinctions are rarely made. The United States has ruled that a career vice consul outranks an honorary vice consul even though the commission of the latter antedates that of the former.

A state is unrestricted in its choice of consular representatives and the receiving state has an equal right to refuse to receive an unsatisfactory appointee.

According to the Constitution of the United States the President with and by the consent of the Senate appoints consuls general, consuls, vice consuls of career and language officers.[7] According to the laws and regulations now in force in the United States, consular officers comprise (1) Foreign Service officers assigned to duty as consuls general, consuls, vice consuls and language officers; and (2) noncareer officers such as vice consuls not of career and consular agents. These latter are appointed by the Secretary of State.

The general term consular officer includes consuls general, consuls, vice consuls, interpreters in consular offices, student interpreters, and consular agents. The word consul is also used in a general sense to denote a consular officer exercising the functions of consul general, consul, or vice consul. With respect to rank and duties consuls are usually divided into five classes: consuls general, consuls, vice consuls of career, vice consuls not of career, and consular agents.

Consuls General.   Consuls general are usually consuls with supervisory powers over one large consular district or several smaller districts. For example, the American Consul General in Barcelona exercises supervisory jurisdiction over all of Spain and the Canary Islands. The Consulate General at Lisbon takes care of the Azores and Madeira as well as Portugal. The provinces of Manitoba, Saskatchewan, and Alberta are under the

---

[7] United States Constitution, Article II, Sect. 2.

jurisdiction of the Consulate General at Winnipeg.[8] The United States possessed in November, 1946, before the Iron Curtain was lowered, twenty consulates general and twenty-eight consolidated missions which exercised supervisory powers. There are certain posts, however, which are ranked as consulates general where no supervisory powers are exercised. For instance, the post of Geneva, Switzerland, was a semidiplomatic post when the League of Nations was functioning and as such was ranked as a consulate general. Other posts are so important that even within the same state they are classed as consulates general. Liverpool and Southampton are such examples.

Consuls general are the immediate superior officers of the consular officials within their respective jurisdictions. They exercise their supervisory powers usually by correspondence, although permission may be granted in appropriate circumstances for them to visit the consular offices in their jurisdiction for the purposes of inspection and report. With the exception of accounts, a consular officer regularly transmits all of his correspondence with the Department of State under open cover through the consul general in charge of his district.

Where there is no consul general with supervisory powers, the diplomatic representative exercises a general supervision over consular officers within his jurisdiction. Diplomatic and consular missions are expected to keep each other informed on all essential matters, and to maintain an attitude and practice of mutual helpfulness. By an executive order of April 4, 1924, President Coolidge instructed representatives of the United States in foreign cities to meet in conference at least fortnightly under the chief diplomatic officer, or if there was none, under the ranking consular officer. Any political information which comes to the attention of a consul is transmitted to the diplomatic representative through the supervising consul.

Vice Consuls. Vice consuls are divided into two categories: vice consuls of career and those not of career. American vice consuls of career are Foreign Service officers commissioned by the President as vice consuls. They are regularly given a diplomatic as well as a consular commission and are subject to transfer at any time into the diplomatic service. Vice consuls not of career are commissioned by the Secretary of State as occasion may require, usually from the clerks at the consular offices. They receive compensation as clerks and are not eligible to appointment as Foreign Service officers without passing the prescribed examinations. Both career and noncareer vice consuls must be American citizens and

[8] *Foreign Service Regulations of the United States* (November, 1946), 101-526; 101-561. Originally compiled in 1896 but now revised and published in loose-leaf form, each page dated; henceforth cited as *Regulations* with the date appearing at the bottom of the page. They are ultimately to be published in loose-leaf form in four volumes under the title *Foreign Service Manual*.

may not engage in private trade. Since 1946 noncareer vice consuls are regularly classified as Foreign Service Staff officers.

Consular Agents.   In addition to these officers it is necessary sometimes to appoint an official known as a consular agent in an out-of-the-way place where the duties are not sufficient to warrant the appointment of a full time vice consul. Such consular agents are appointed by the Secretary of State usually upon the nomination of the principal consular officer. Although wherever practicable American citizens only are appointed as consular agents, in some places it is necessary to appoint a national of another state.

There have been occasions when a foreigner has been so eager to serve as a consular representative of a foreign nation at a small post in his home country that he has become a citizen of the country which he wished to represent. An excellent example is the case of Simon Damiani, a Corsican who came to the United States, was naturalized and then returned to his native land and became the American Consular Agent in Bastia. He served there in this capacity for more than thirty years and brought up his children as Americans, although none of them had ever been in the United States or could speak a word of English.[9]

Ralph Nevill, who served as secretary to Sir Henry Drummond Wolff, British Minister to Persia, tells of meeting an English consular officer in a port on the Black Sea who had an English name but a decidedly Levantine appearance. When Nevill asked why the servant, who wore a makeshift European uniform, did not wear the picturesque costume of the region, the consul replied that it would be prettier but that he liked to see someone about in a dress reminding him of home. Home was England, which he had never seen.[10]

Consular agents receive their compensation through fees collected by them, but no consular agent may collect more than $1,000 a year for his services. Consequently, contrary to the rule for all other consular officers, a consular agent is permitted to engage in a trade or profession. As of January 1, 1951, there were about thirty consular agents in such small posts as Camaguey, Cuba; Christchurch, New Zealand; Tela, Honduras; Iquitos, Peru; Manaos, Brazil; and Port Limmon, Costa Rica.

Language Officers.   Language officers are Foreign Service officers who are assigned to certain countries, particularly in the Far East and Near East, where they may study and perfect themselves in prescribed foreign languages. Once they have passed the required examinations they are eligible for advancement in the service on the same basis as other Foreign Service officers.

[9] See Lee Meriwether, *The War Diary of a Diplomat* (New York, 1919), 24, 36.
[10] Ralph Nevill, *Unconventional Memories* (New York, 1923), 123.

Inspectors. Foreign Service inspectors are Foreign Service officers who have had considerable training and experience and who are detailed to visit and report on the work of diplomatic and consular offices. All consular offices of the United States by law are supposed to be inspected at least once in every two years. The inspectors' suggestions and directions must be followed and in urgent cases the inspector may suspend the principal consular officer and administer the office temporarily.[11]

As of 1951 the regular Corps of Inspectors consisted of twelve high ranking Foreign Service officers, and because of complex administrative problems which have developed there are also four "administration inspectors" chosen from the Foreign Service Staff officers. The normal assignment of an inspector requires nine months in the field and three months in Washington. For the fiscal year 1951, one hundred and fourteen inspections were contemplated.

Upon occasions Foreign Service inspectors are given special missions. When the press criticized the manner in which our Foreign Service officers evacuated Americans from Seoul after the invasion in June, 1950, Inspector Wilson C. Flake was sent out to investigate. He found that approximately 1,800 Americans had been evacuated within sixty hours without anyone getting hurt. The accusation that high ranking officers came out with packing cases of effects while others came with only the clothes they wore was false. The packing cases it was learned contained emergency rations, blankets and sheets. Another complaint that top officials came out on the first airplanes was equally false. The only clerk who came out in the last plane explained that he was afraid of planes—stayed off as long as he could and was compelled to get on the last one.

Consular Commission. Every American Foreign Service officer, whether he be assigned to the diplomatic or consular service, must take a prescribed oath of office and file with the Department of State a bond equivalent to one year's salary. Formerly only consular officers were required to file a bond because of their responsibility in handling public moneys, but since interchangeability was inaugurated by the Rogers Bill, all appointments are to the Foreign Service.

As an official authorization from the home government that he is empowered to perform his official duties, a consul receives from his government a commission, sometimes called letters patent or *lettres de provision*. The commission is signed by the head of the state and gives the name, rank and authority of the consular official. In the United States the commission is signed by the President, countersigned by the Secretary of State and carries the seal of the United States. The Convention on Consular Agents adopted at Havana February 20, 1928, provides that the

[11] *Foreign Service Manual* (August, 1951), 130-135.

commission shall contain "the name, the category and the authority of the appointee." [12]

The consular officer does not receive the commission directly but it is sent by the Secretary of State to the American diplomatic representative in the country where the post is located. Upon receipt of the consul's commission the diplomatic envoy applies to the foreign office of the country to which he is accredited for an exequatur, an official document issued by the receiving state which authorizes the consul to perform his functions.

Nature and Form of the Exequatur.   The exequatur is in fact an executive order of the foreign government which recognizes the official character of the consular officer and grants him the privileges or immunities conferred upon his office by treaty, law or custom and permits him to exercise his official duties. In the United States exequaturs are signed by the President, countersigned by the Secretary of State, and bear the seal of the United States; they are issued only to foreign consuls who come with regular commissions signed by the chief executive of the appointing state. Subordinate officers receive a certificate of recognition signed by the Secretary of State.[13]

The form of the exequatur varies; usually it is a distinct document, as in the United States; sometimes it is merely the word *exequatur* written upon the commission, as in Hungary, again it is a notice in the official government organ, as in Germany. Sometimes no exequatur is issued to a vice consul. "The true nature of the exequatur is that of a contract between the foreign state and the sending state and its object is to permit the consul to take advantage of its service and use it in the interest of both states." [14]

All current treaties and conventions provide for the deliverance of the exequatur without payment and it is the rule today even in the absence of a treaty. In Turkey, however, it was formerly an expensive procedure to obtain an exequatur or *berát*, as it was called.

Once the exequatur is granted the local authorities are instructed by the receiving government to recognize the official status of the consular official and see to it that he enjoys such privileges and immunities as he may be entitled to under the law. A new exequatur is not required by a change of government. Conditions are rarely imposed in the exequatur, but when they occur the United States refuses acceptance.

Refusal of Exequatur.   The receiving government possesses an unqualified right to refuse an exequatur to a foreign consul, nor does it have

[12] *Sixth International Conference of American States: Final Act* (Habana, 1928), Article 4, "Convention on Consular Agents."
[13] John Bassett Moore, *Digest of International Law* (Washington, 1906), V, 14.
[14] E. C. Stowell, *Le Consul* (Paris, 1900), 208 ff.

to give the reasons for its action.[15] According to Secretary of State Blaine, however, "the undoubted right of withholding an exequatur is ... an extreme one. In this country it is rarely resorted to." [16]

On a number of occasions the United States has appointed consular officers who have been refused exequaturs. In 1855 the Government of Nicaragua refused an exequatur to Mr. Priest, who had been appointed United States Consul at San Juan del Sur, on the ground that he had published a private letter which was objectionable.[17] Great Britain refused to grant an exequatur to Major Haggerty, a naturalized Irishman, whom General Grant had appointed as Consul to Glasgow in 1869, on the ground that he had been engaged in the Fenian revolts.[18] The Austro-Hungarian Government refused to receive an American politician, a Czech by birth, who was appointed Consul to Prague in 1895 because he had denounced conditions in Bohemia in a speech made on a Bohemian holiday at the World's Fair Exposition in Chicago.[19] An American consul appointed to Beirut was rejected by Turkey because he was a clergyman and might be too closely connected with the missionaries.[20]

When the Chinese Government first opened its ports to American trade, inasmuch as the United States did not have available trained men, it appointed merchants as consuls. The Chinese Government did not look with favor upon this procedure and refused to grant exequaturs to these merchant consuls, believing that such appointments were not permitted under the treaties. The Chinese objections were easily overruled by the American representative, Anson Burlingame, who pointed out that the French and Russians followed a similar practice.

Although the right of refusing to accept a foreign consul would seem to be an accepted principle of international law, the treaties which put an end to World War I formulated a contrary rule for the defeated powers. By specific provisions the Treaties of Versailles, St. Germain, Neuilly, and Trianon required that the states of Germany, Austria, Bulgaria, and Hungary promise in advance to approve the designation of consuls general, consuls, vice consuls and consular agents of the Allied powers. The Allied powers, however, did not grant a reciprocal right.[21]

Revocation of Exequatur. From the instances which have occurred it would seem that there have been more cases of revocation of consular exequaturs than of refusal to grant them originally. One of the early cases in American diplomacy occurred in 1793 when the exequatur of Mr. Du-

15 Julius I. Puente, *The Foreign Consul* (Chicago, 1926), 28; Stowell, *op. cit.*, 209.
16 Moore, *op. cit.*, V, 28.
17 *Ibid.*, V, 28.
18 W. E. Hall, *A Treatise on International Law* (Oxford, 1895), 333.
19 Carlton Bailey Hurst, *Arms above the Door* (New York, 1932), 51.
20 Eugene Schuyler, *American Diplomacy* (New York, 1901), 96.
21 Paul Fauchille, *Traité de droit international public* (Paris, 1926), I, Pt. iii, 123.

plaine, French Vice Consul at Boston, was revoked because he had opposed with armed force the enforcement of the laws of the land in seizing a vessel out of the hands of an officer of justice.[22] In 1856 the exequaturs of three English consuls in the United States were revoked because it was alleged that they had attempted to recruit men for the British Army to serve in the Crimean War.[23] In 1861 the United States revoked the exequatur of Consul Bunch of Great Britain on the ground that he had violated the provisions of the Logan Act, which forbade any unauthorized person to engage in correspondence with a foreign state. Great Britain, although claiming that the charge was inapplicable to the case, did not question the right to withdraw the exequatur.[24] In this case, however, other reasons entered into the matter because the French Consul, who had acted jointly with the British Consul in the matter of corresponding with the Confederate states regarding observance of the rules of the Declaration of Paris, did not have his exequatur withdrawn.

An instance occurred in 1897 in Guatemala which brought from United States Secretary of State Sherman a clear enunciation of the accepted rule of law. The President of the Republic had ordered the withdrawal of the exequatur of Florentin Souza, United States Consular Agent at Champerico. The Legation, being uninformed, asked to be acquainted with the reason for the Government's action, at the same time stating that another person would take over the agency for the present. The Department of State said: "You were not strictly in your right in making this request. As a general rule of international intercourse a government can withdraw a consular exequatur without assigning any reason. If it voluntarily assigns cause for removal it invites discussion of the sufficiency thereof and defensive evidence can be offered with a request for a reconsideration. If it offers no reasons it can not be compelled to give them. Your inquiry, therefore, should be treated as a request for information rather than as a demand for proof of good cause, and it is hoped the Guatemalan Government will so construe it." [25]

A long controversy occurred between the United States and Great Britain when on July 18, 1922, the British Government notified the Department of State that they intended to revoke the exequaturs of the American consular officers at Newcastle because they had attempted to divert passenger trade from British to American steamship lines through the granting of visas. The United States Government made an investigation through Ambassador Harvey and found that the charges were not substantiated. The Consulate at Newcastle was thereupon closed. The British Government after considerable correspondence agreed to withdraw its charges

---

[22] Moore, *op. cit.*, V, 19.
[23] Hall, *op. cit.*, 333.
[24] Moore, *op. cit.*, V, 20.
[25] *Foreign Relations of the United States, 1897,* 338.

and permit the appointment of American Consuls Slater and Brooks to any posts in the British Empire and in return the United States agreed to reopen the Consulate at Newcastle.[26]

In June, 1941, after the Rome-Berlin Axis had been formed, the Italian Government objected to the information activities of the American consular officers and requested that they be withdrawn from Italian territory. The Department of State rejected the allegations but at the same time informed the Italian Government that "the continued functioning of Italian consular establishments in territory of the United States would serve no desirable purpose." Such action indicated that a serious situation of unfriendliness had developed between the two states.[27]

The Convention on Consular Agents adopted at Havana in 1928 follows the generally accepted rule. It stipulates that "the territorial government may at any time withdraw the consul's exequatur, but except in urgent cases, it shall not have recourse to this measure without previously attempting to obtain from the consul's government his recall." [28]

Delay in Receiving Exequatur. If for any reason there is a delay in receiving the exequatur the consul may when so directed by the Department of State proceed to his post and enter upon the discharge of his duties upon receiving permission from the proper local authorities to act in his official capacity until the exequatur arrives. Under these circumstances he should immediately notify the diplomatic mission and then if he fails to obtain permission from the local authorities or if there is an appreciable delay in receiving the exequatur, he is instructed to telegraph to the Department. If, however, it is the intention of the state not to grant the exequatur, as in the case of Turkey refusing an exequatur to the United States Consul at Erzerum until more than two years after his appointment,[29] the question is then between the foreign offices of the two states. The situation is covered by the Havana Convention as follows: "The consul can be recognized as such only after having presented his commission and obtained the exequatur of the state in whose territory he is to serve. Provisional recognition can be granted upon the request of the legation of the consul pending the delivery in due form of the exequatur." [30]

Although some authorities claim that a consular official may perform the functions of his office without an exequatur, Director of the Consular Service, Wilbur Carr, instructed the American Consul at Bucharest that a consular officer should not perform consular functions at a post until he had obtained recognition from the local authorities or his exequatur.[31]

---

[26] Green Hackworth, *Digest of International Law* (Washington, 1942), IV, 677-80.
[27] *Ibid.*, 682.
[28] *Sixth International Conference of American States, op. cit.,* Article 8.
[29] *Foreign Relations of the United States, 1898,* lxxxiii.
[30] *Sixth International Conference of American States, op. cit.,* Article 6.
[31] Hackworth, *op. cit.,* IV, 682.

18

Consular Functions in the Interest of Commerce and Navigation

THE FRENCH STATESMAN Talleyrand, who was also an accomplished diplomat, declared that the functions of a consul were infinitely varied and that even though one might have been a clever public minister one had to know a great deal more to be a good consul. In fact, when we take into consideration the numerous and varied duties of a consul it would appear that he must not only be a "Jack of all trades" but at the same time be a master of all of them. And, contrary to the status of the diplomat, in carrying out his functions the consul is not only bound by the statutes and regulations of his own country, but he is also subject to the laws of the country in which he performs his official duties.

Consular Activities in the Promotion of Trade. One of the very essential functions of the consul today is to promote his country's trade within the consular district in every legitimate way possible. According to Baron Heyking, a former Consul General of Imperial Russia, "the maintenance of their country's economic interests requires the entire attention of consuls; it forms the principal boulevard of their activity." [1]

A survey of the diverse regulations and instructions issued by the various governments bears out this statement. For example, the instructions to Brazilian consuls, which are particularly comprehensive on this point, require consuls:

To promote within their territory the commercial and industrial interests of Brazil; to observe and communicate to their government the commercial and economic development of the country in which they function with all explanations useful for the progress of Brazil; to expose the obstacles and difficulties which prevent the development of commerce with Brazil and to make suggestions; to demand within their competence from the local authorities all possible measures for the benefit of Brazilian commerce; to promote the creation of Brazilian chambers of commerce and give their support and collaboration to those existing if advisable; to organize and maintain in the consulates, sets of

[1] Alphonse de Heyking, *Les principes et la pratique des services consulaires* (Paris, 1928), 88.

samples of the principal Brazilian products furnished by the Government or by private persons; to take measures for the prompt publication of everything that refers to Brazilian industries; to maintain a register of commercial and industrial firms which operate in Brazil. . . .[2]

The instructions to Danish, Mexican, Norwegian, and Spanish consuls are almost equally explicit and comprehensive. The Netherlands instructions state that the principal duty of the Netherlands consular officer is to further the interests of the commerce, the industry, the agriculture, and the shipping of the Netherlands.[3]

The *United States Foreign Service Regulations* list five ways in which the consular officer may promote the national economic interests of the United States:

(a) By reporting on the potentialities of their districts as a market for American products.

(b) By investigating and submitting World Trade Directory Reports on the general standing of foreign firms, and upon request, trade lists of commercial firms within their districts.

(c) By looking out for and submitting immediate reports on concrete trade opportunities and by endeavoring to create a demand for American products within their districts.

(d) By facilitating and reporting on proposed visits of alien business men to the United States.

(e) By endeavoring to promote such import trade with the United States as the economic interests of the United States may require.[4]

The *Regulations* further emphasize that trade promotion should be upon the development of the export trade of the United States. However, the attention of the consul is called to the fact that mutuality of trade interests and the benefits of a well balanced commercial exchange make it desirable that American merchants and manufacturers be assisted in purchasing abroad raw materials and goods which are not in direct competition with American goods.

In order to fulfill these duties in the most efficient manner the consular officer is advised to familiarize himself with the main facts constituting the economic life of his district. This will require a study of his predecessor's reports and all published material pertinent to the subject available in his district. Coincidentally the consul is expected to make personal contact with leading local businessmen and officers. In order to facilitate the importation and sale of American goods the consular officer should be familiar with and be able to point out the products of merit usable in the district. He should also display statistical and other publications relating

---

[2] A. H. Feller and Manley O. Hudson, *Diplomatic and Consular Laws and Regulations* (Washington, 1933), I, 147-8.

[3] *Ibid.*, II, 863.

[4] *Regulations* (April, 1945), XIV, 2.

to American trade, directories of manufacturers, and encourage the use of the consulate as a center of information.

The late Frederick Van Dyne, when Consul at Kingston, Jamaica, established a commercial reading room which had on file some eighty different American trade journals, magazines and newspapers, numerous trade directories, and thousands of catalogues of American manufacturers. The Consulate thus became a sort of information bureau for American products and was visited daily by local merchants and buyers who wanted information concerning American goods. When the city constructed an opera house the city architect consulted the Consul, who was thus enabled to give information regarding American products which might be used and to make known to American manufacturers and builders a possible market.[5]

When American chambers of commerce exist they should receive the consul's support and coöperation and when such organizations have not been established and the need is evident the consul may take an active part or even the initiative in their creation. Carlton Bailey Hurst, when Consul in Barcelona, found that no American chamber of commerce had ever existed in Spain. Thinking the time ripe for such an organization he called a meeting of all American residents of Barcelona and Spanish merchants interested in import and export. An organization was formed, quarters engaged and Hurst helped furnish them by donating a hardwood table top that he had just received from the head forester of the Philippine Islands.[6]

Finding New Markets.   The consul must always be on the lookout for new outlets for his country's products. He must utilize his knowledge of the existing market situation in order to visualize the possibilities of new markets and once they are obtained he must make them known at home. He must also see to it that the national products are packed in such a way as to reach their destination in their original condition. Mr. Stowell tells of an American consul in Brazil who obtained an order for an American firm amounting to several thousands of dollars, but unfortunately the advice of the consul with regard to packing was not followed and the merchandise arrived in a very bad condition.[7]

When Consul Edward J. Norton was put in charge of the United States Consulate at Sydney, Australia, in 1919 it was his hobby to see how many profitable trade connections he might make. Since the Australian market was surprisingly misty in the minds of many manufacturers, few companies would send out direct representatives. Mr. Norton decided to work up certain markets which seemed to have prospects of success, such as the

[5] Frederick Van Dyne, *Our Foreign Service* (Rochester, New York, 1907), 166-7.
[6] Carlton Bailey Hurst, *Arms above the Door* (New York, 1932), 265.
[7] Ellery C. Stowell, *Le Consul* (Paris, 1909), Note 94.

electrical, the drug and chemical, the agricultural equipment, and office materials fields. He gave local representatives the fullest coöperation in advice regarding shipping, tariffs and credit and he joined various organizations to secure better contacts. The results were so striking that the English-controlled press made a collection of all trade letters sent by the Consulate and launched a campaign against what was called "The American Onslaught."

A few examples of specific results may be cited. Consul General Goding at Guayaquil, Ecuador, reported a trade opportunity which brought an American firm a million-dollar contract. Consul Philip Holland at Basel, Switzerland, was able to obtain an order of $14,000 worth of shoes for an American firm in competition with foreign houses. Consul Frederic Dumont helped bring about a shipment of 35,000 tons of coal to Ireland while he was Consul at Dublin. Dudley G. Dwyer, while Consul at Maracaibo, succeeded in placing several agencies for American goods in Venezuela, one resulting in an order for ten American automobiles.[8]

When George Messersmith was assigned as Consul to Antwerp in 1919, he found the seaport in a bad way as a result of the years of German occupation. It occurred to him that it would be advantageous for the automotive industry to establish assembly plants in Antwerp and he was successful in persuading both Ford and General Motors to do so. The move proved very successful and the other companies followed their example. Messersmith then persuaded other companies to establish warehouses in a free port zone to keep adequate stocks on hand for the European demand. The result was greater sales, a cut in the cost of distribution, more expeditious deliveries, and the filling of many small orders which would otherwise have been lost.

It is also expected that the consul will be alert to all contracts open to tender which might interest national firms. These include all public and private construction work, such as construction of roads, bridges, railways, telephones, buildings, and sanitation projects. Even though the principal contracts are restricted to national companies, subcontracts may often be let. Both the diplomatic and consular officers of the United States in Peru were for many years exceedingly helpful in placing and keeping the large governmental contracts in the hands of American companies. The great value of the work done by consular officials to promote American trade is shown by the following letter sent to the Paris Consulate General by a New York firm in 1932. "We appreciate your detailed report regarding the market possibilities of Pyrethrum Extract Pine Oil and Insecticide in France. Your reports are most complete and the information contained is very valuable to us. . . . We have written to all the firms whose names you were good enough to give us. Your letters contained as much or more de-

[8] Wilbur J. Carr, "What Your Consuls Do," *American Consular Bulletin* (January, 1922), 6. See also Cordell Hull, "A Statement" *Overseas Trader* (March, 1937), 11.

tailed information than would have been possible to receive from a member of our own organization had he been in France. We feel proud that our American Consular Service has built up such an efficient organization."

A statistical study made in the Department of State for the ten-year period between 1927 and 1937 estimated the results obtained by consular officers in promoting trade opportunities and by settling trade disputes to be worth over $72,000,000 to the American trader.

Trade Reports. In performing this function of trade promotion the consul must supply accurate information in the form of commercial and financial reports. Such reports should be based upon official statistics and be presented with the utmost impartiality. A consul should also analyze and interpret his figures so as to make them as valuable as possible. The United States requires its consuls to submit a comprehensive annual report on the development of commerce and industry in his district for the current year. This report places the emphasis upon the foreign trade, particularly any changes affecting the export trade of the United States. A summary of leading commodities imported should always be included as well as the official statistics of imports and exports when available.

A consul is also expected to prepare periodical and special reports during the year in order that the Department of State may be kept fully informed on all matters of interest to the American businessman. The periodical reports are made at the request of the Department. In addition to these reports the consular officer is expected to prepare from time to time voluntary reports on his own initiative concerning any matters which might be useful to the government or the business community. These voluntary reports afford an unlimited opportunity to the consular officer for original investigation and analysis along lines interesting to himself and profitable to the country. There are a number of subjects which should especially engage the attention of consuls in making voluntary trade reports, such as: general business conditions, the financial and exchange situation, crop reports, mineral and forestry development, markets for American products, tariff and customs regulations, credit and sales conditions, advertising, packing, particular lines of trade and local products marketable in the United States. Prompt information should always be given regarding expositions, particularly those devoted to commercial or technical matters.

In the seaport of Hamburg, which was formerly the leading port of entry for Germany, commercial reports were of particular importance. Consul General Erhardt at that post required weekly reports on hide and skin markets; monthly reports on dried fruit, lumber, rice, meat, and tobacco, and on commercial failures; quarterly reports on ergot, cotton, gasoline and oil prices and laid up shipping; semiannual reports on certain drugs and German crude rubber consumption, and the regularly called for annual reports. In addition to these were the voluntary weekly reports entitled "Hamburg Trade Notes"; monthly voluntary reports on such products as the walnut market, mineral oil trade, grain, rubber, fresh fruit, cocoa stocks; semiannual voluntary reports on oils and fats, canned fruits and vegetables, dried fruits, lumber; and annual voluntary reports upon fresh fruit, lumber, fish, soy beans, the Hamburg coffee market, and the market for American salmon caviar.

In certain areas trade reports are much more difficult to make than in others. In Poland, for example, where the consul is attached to the embassy in Warsaw and where the mining and steel industry is concentrated in Upper Silesia 200 miles away, the textile industry in Lodz, 90 miles away, and the shipping center, Gdynia, 250 miles away, the time and expense required for traveling necessarily limits personal contact. Furthermore, there are no trade press or specialized industrial publications nor associations of individual trade and industries to furnish information readily such as are found regularly in the older industrial states of Western Europe.

Trade Inquiries.   Replies to questions from American firms were formerly made by the commercial attachés, but this work has now been assigned to consular officers. For example, an American firm manufacturing mirrors will write to the Consulate at Copenhagen asking for names of firms and wholesalers who might be interested in their product. The consul not only sends such a list but he also includes a list of names of the jobbers with whom the real business will have to be done and the situation is carefully explained to the manufacturer. If there is no possible market, the consul will save the manufacturer further expense by frankly stating the market conditions.

Another case is that of a salesman for a firm manufacturing steam engines who comes to Paris and immediately visits the American Consulate General. He wishes to get in touch with French firms which might be interested in his product and at the same time find out what restrictions are laid upon its sale and distribution in France. A vice consul experienced in this field is sent out to look up the dealers in machinery products. He telephones personally to those most likely to be interested. He gets their credit rating through Dun or the banks or by a questionnaire. The quotas and tariffs are looked up and a memorandum prepared giving all the essential information to the agent. Oftentimes prices of similar products are included. If there is no possibility of sale, sufficient information is given to show that a careful study of the question has been made.

As perhaps might be expected, the consul often receives what to him are amusing inquiries in the requests by firms for information regarding the selling possibilities of their products. Herbert Williams when Consul at Panama received a letter from a refrigerator company which requested information not only regarding the sales possibilities of their product but also as to how much of the ice used in Panama was natural. While G. Henry Horstmann was serving as a Consul in Munich he was requested by one American to find out about the artificial breeding of fish in Bavaria and by another to send him a report including answers to sixty-one questions regarding the cultivation, production and commerce of tobacco in all the countries in which he had served.[9]

The letters from American firms often ask not only for advice as to market conditions and demand for the product but also request the names of agents or places to give or receive credit. In replying the consul may never recommend a business concern; he is only permitted to give a list of the establishments which might be interested. However, if the business relationship turns out badly, the consul is sometimes blamed for the result. So many trade inquiries are received that the *Regulations* cover the subject in considerable detail.[10]

The consul not only answers trade inquiries but upon occasions he makes special commercial investigations. In the spring of 1951, the author was invited by the American Consul in Venice, William L. Pitts, Jr., to accompany him to the little town of Schio in Vicenza to investigate an industrial plant which wanted to import, from the United States, certain chemical materials, which required a license. The plant was not easy to find since it was very small, not yet in production and the address given was merely the town. Once located, the consul found the three brothers who were establishing the business very coöperative, he obtained the necessary information to prepare a World Trade Directory Report and could promise the partners that the fulfilment of their needs would be given careful consideration.

Consular Activities in the Protection of Trade. The consul has a large number of duties which might well be classed under the general heading of protection of trade and navigation abroad. Under this heading would naturally come the various duties of a consul with regard to merchant vessels and seamen, tasks which occupy a considerable amount of his time. A consul must pay close attention to the local laws and administrative decrees concerning tariffs, customs, port administrations, warehousing, and transportation, and see to it that no discrimination shall occur in their administration to the detriment of his country's commercial interests.

An excellent example of trade protection by joint diplomatic and consular efforts is cited by Ambassador Joseph C. Grew, at that time Minister to Switzerland. Some years ago Lewis W. Haskell, the American Consul, began to receive complaints from the local importers of American automobiles that they could no longer compete with European cars owing to

[9] G. Henry Horstmann, *Consular Reminiscences* (Philadelphia, 1886), 56.
[10] *Regulations* (April, 1946), XIV, 3.

a newly applied customs ruling which levied a very high packing duty on the packing cases or containers in which the cars were imported. American cars on account of the long sea voyage had to be packed in cases whereas European automobiles could enter the country done up in burlap on flat rail cars or else could be driven in. The result was, in effect, a discrimination against American automobiles which seemed likely to drive them wholly from the market of this country leaving the field free for their European competitors. The Consul promptly brought the matter to the attention of the Minister, who spent several weeks in making representations of a forcible character and finally brought about the removal of the objectionable ruling. It would be impossible to compute in dollars and cents the gain to the American automobile industry by this intervention, but it may be said that both the Department of State and the legation received a great number of letters from automobile manufacturers, exporters and chambers of commerce, all over the United States, expressing their appreciation of the service rendered.[11]

In another instance in a Caribbean country where a decision of the local health authorities had determined that American flour contained an unduly high percentage of acidity, the consular officer made an investigation. When it was shown that the acidic content had no deleterious effects, the local authorities were induced to increase the limit of the acidic content in imported flour.

Trade Protection under Treaty Provisions.   A very important consular duty is to see that treaties of commerce and navigation are strictly observed. The consul should be familiar with any and all such treaties concluded between his own state and the state to which he is accredited. The majority of commercial treaties contain what is known as the "most favored nation" clause, and the consul must insist that his country receive as liberal treatment under this clause as any other nation obtains. A consul is usually permitted by treaties or conceded the right by usage to complain to local authorities in case of infraction of any treaty drawn to protect his country's commercial interests.

An interesting instance of trade protection under treaty provisions occurred in the international city of Tangier. The customs officials by a higher valuation arbitrarily raised the customs duties on imported flour in violation of the provisions of the Algeciras Convention to which the United States was a signatory. United States Consul General Maxwell Blake protested vigorously and proved that the French contention as regards the estimated value of flour was fallacious and could not be sustained. Although the authorities refused to refund moneys already collected, they

[11] Address by Joseph C. Grew, Under Secretary of State, at the Annual Banquet of the American Manufacturers Export Association, Hotel Astor, New York, November 12, 1925.

agreed to accept the authenticated figures of American importers as to valuation in the future.

An important case of trade protection arose in Berlin in connection with the formation in 1934 of a new fuel cartel for concerns operating in the German market. It appeared that the Consolidated Oil Corporation, an American concern which was interested in the German Sinclair Petroleum Company, would have its interests seriously jeopardized if its quota under the previous cartel arrangement were reduced, as was planned under the new arrangement. Inasmuch as the Government insisted that all firms would be bound by the terms of the new cartel whether they entered or not, the Sinclair Company appealed to the American Consulate General. Consul Geist requested the German authorities to take into consideration the representations of the American oil firm and to provide such measures as would ameliorate its position in order to protect the legitimate investments of American capital which had been made through this company in Germany.

An English company imported sample illustrated stamp albums from a Boston company and the shipment came in with no tariff. However, the second consignment of nearly two tons was held up as being forbidden by the British Revenue and Customs Act, which prohibited representations of postage stamps or similar marks. As manufacturers of stamp albums in Great Britain were allowed to make such representations, both the British and American firms protested. Mr. Gowen, the American Consul, interviewed the British officials and found that the first consignment was let in through an error. The officials pointed out that they had the right to seize the present shipment, but were willing to permit its reëxportation. But as it had already been paid for, this would not help the British firm. Seeing the unfairness to the British concern, the officials finally agreed to allow the importation of the one shipment. Both the British and American firms were profuse in their thanks to the American Consulate General.

Consuls Settle Trade Disputes.   The American consul often is able to settle trade disputes between American and foreign firms. Assistant Secretary of State Carr tells of a case where Consul Bevan at Bahia transmitted a draft of several hundred dollars through the Department of State to an American firm in settlement of a trade dispute with a Brazilian business house. In similar fashion a shipment of American goods to a Brazilian firm was unsatisfactory and when American Consul Pickerell complained, an investigation showed that a mistake had been made and a credit of $5,000 was sent to the Brazilian company by the American firm.[12]

A shipment of American rice to Marseilles that had been bought and paid for had a bad odor and taste. As a result the consignee had to dispose

[12] Wilbur J. Carr, "What Your Consuls Do," *American Consular Bulletin* 7 (January, 1922).

of it for less than half the price he had paid. Consul Thompson investigated and found that the case was *bona fide* and that the shipment had probably been spoiled by its proximity to kerosene in the boat. Although the consul was not able to raise the question of cause, there would be no further orders for American rice until an adjustment had been made. The American firm could not afford to lose its market and through the mediation of the consul a satisfactory solution was reached.

Certification of Invoices.   One of the most frequent duties of a consul is the certification of consular invoices for shipment of foreign goods exported to the United States. American customs authorities require a certified consular invoice for every shipment which with the duties imposed amounts to more than $100 in value. These invoices are prepared on special forms which may be obtained at the consulate. The invoice, which is certified in triplicate—sometimes in quadruplicate, describes the merchandise and declares its market value in the country of production or exportation. The invoice must be signed by the manufacturer or exporter who makes a declaration that the facts as declared are true. The consular official in making his certification must carefully scrutinize the shipper's declarations to be certain that the contents of each container is clearly stated, that the description of the merchandise is exact and that sufficient informaion is given to permit the customs officer to make a fair appraisal. He must also see to it that all articles and packages are clearly marked to indicate their country of origin. One of the triplicate invoices is filed at the consulate, the original is delivered to the person producing the invoice or it may be mailed by the consular officer direct to the consignee and the third is forwarded to the port of entry to which the goods are addressed. A quadruplicate copy may be delivered to the shipper.

A Turkish law required a certificate of origin to be presented to the customs officers before the goods could be cleared. However, such information was not always easy to obtain. A practice has been utilized by the American Consulate at Constantinople whereby the shipper appears before the consul, swears to an affidavit stating the origin of the goods, and although this is no more than his belief as to the facts, the affidavit is accepted by the customs authorities.

Although a number of articles no longer require a certified invoice since 1931, such as household effects used abroad, automobiles and horses brought in for temporary purposes, crude forest and agricultural products and crude minerals, newsprint paper, wood pulp and news reel films, a large consular office will certify thousands of invoices annually. For example, for the calendar year 1933 there were 3,622 consular invoices issued in Zurich, Switzerland; 7,021 in Cologne, Germany; 19,047 in Paris, France; and 25,473 in London, England. The ten leading products invoiced in London were furs, tin, tea, chemicals, provisions, wines, spirits, precious metals, books, printed matter, and antiques. Close coöperation must always be maintained with the United States Treasury attachés abroad who are equipped to investigate all cases of undervaluation or other efforts to evade requirements.

A much publicized incident of this sort occurred in France in 1925. The Tariff Act of 1922 permitted the United States to prohibit the importation of merchandise of a foreign manufacturer who refused to permit an inspection of his books by an American official to obtain an accurate figure as to the cost of production. When an American Treasury agent insisted upon examining the books of Boue Sœurs of Paris, manufacturers of chemises, he was refused. The United States forbade further importation of their product and a veritable *guerre de chemise* followed, which was only settled by a ruling of the United States Attorney General on October 21, 1927, to the effect that it would not be necessary under the Tariff Act to conduct investigation of production costs abroad, and would cease in France after February 1, 1928.

In the old days the certification of invoices was the principal function of American consuls. In a volume devoted to information concerning American consular posts prepared in response to a Senate resolution in 1901 a survey of the replies concerning the duties indicates the certification of invoices in many of the smaller ports was the sole function performed. For example, in Ecuador consular officers were stationed at Guayaquil, Bahia de Caraquez, Esmeraldas, and Manta. At Guayaquil 397 invoices were certified and 300 to 400 business inquiries answered, 28 bills of health issued and a few seamen taken care of. In Bahia the sole duty performed was the certification of 104 invoices. In Esmeraldas 92 invoices were certified and 20 trade inquiries received. In Manta the work was limited to the certification of 52 invoices.[13] George Horton tells of a consulate on the Syrian coast presided over by a former saloon keeper who regularly greeted his callers with: "Well, gentlemen, what'll it be, an invoice or a cocktail?"[14]

Consular Duties of Navigation. Merchant Vessels. It is a well established custom that merchant vessels engaging in trade carry certain papers indicating the vessel's nationality, its ownership, the nature of its cargo and its destination. They include the ship's official certificate of registry, its charter, its shipping articles, and the crew list. A number of states, including Germany, the Netherlands, and Sweden require the masters of vessels to deposit their ships' papers with the consul while in port. The custody of these papers gives the consul information which is useful to him in dealing with the port authorities and in aiding in the enforcement of the customs and quarantine regulations of the port and of his country.

[13] *Senate Document* No. 411, 57th Cong., 1st sess. (Washington, 1902), 106-9.
[14] George Horton, *Recollections Grave and Gay* (Indianapolis, 1927), 87.

The *Foreign Service Manual of the United States* provides that every master of a registered vessel of American ownership sailing from an American port should deposit his register with the United States consular officer within twenty-four hours of his arrival at a foreign port. Quite customarily the crew list and shipping articles are deposited together with the register. The requirement for the deposit of ships' papers includes all vessels engaged in commerce, also registered American pleasure craft, but excludes fishing and whaling vessels. The nationality of the vessel is determined by the certificate of registry and the flag.

A vessel which puts into a foreign port solely to obtain information does not come within the provisions of the law. Nor would a vessel driven in by a storm be required to deposit its papers.

It is the duty of the consul to see to it that the master of an American vessel is notified of this requirement in case he fails to deposit his papers. If he refuses, the consul sends a certificate of the fact to the Department of State with pertinent information and evidence and a suit will then be presented by the Government against the vessel.

The consular officer is authorized to return the ship's papers whenever the master produces the clearance of his vessel from the proper port authorities and complies with the laws of the United States regarding the seamen on board. If a master sails without his papers, the consul must transmit them to the next port of call if feasible, otherwise without delay to the Department of State with a statement of the circumstances.[15]

He must be familiar with the International Line Convention of 1930, which indicates the maximum depth to which a vessel may be loaded safely; and if the local control officer alleges a violation by an American vessel he must investigate, and if unfounded protest to the appropriate authorities, but if justified, he must report to the Department of State.[16]

Since the master of the vessel is held responsible for knowing the regulations governing entrance into ports of the United States, the consular official is required to furnish vessels clearing for foreign ports the necessary information regarding documentary requirements as to customs and immigration for the entry at a port in the United States.[17]

The consul also is instructed to receive all protests which may be presented by the master, the seamen or the passengers of any American vessel arriving in a port under his jurisdiction. Any declaration or statement so made will be duly authenticated by the consular officer under the official seal and will receive full faith in any court of the United States.

As an aid to ships' officers, the consul must keep posted in a conspicuous place the pilot charts and all notices to mariners published by the hydrographic office of the Navy Department. This includes information regard-

---

[15] *Foreign Service Manual* (November, 1951), Sect. 521.
[16] *Ibid.*, Sect. 523, 2.
[17] *Ibid.*, Sect. 523, 4.

ing new channels, new buoys, new lighthouses and lightships; also changes that have been made in the location of any of these aids to navigation. The consul is also expected to forward without delay any information to the Department of State which may be utilized for the benefit of the seafarer or to decrease the dangers of navigation.

The consular officers are required to furnish sanitary reports of ports and places designated by the Secretary of the Treasury. These are made weekly and in accordance with forms prescribed by the Treasury Department. If a disease or epidemic breaks out within the consul's district, he must telegraph or cable the State Department immediately. In Tangier for many years the consular officers were in complete charge of health and quarantine regulations for the city and even today the American consul general performs certain functions of this character. It should be noted that subsequent to February 15, 1945, vessels clearing for American ports are no longer required to obtain bills of health.

Consular Jurisdiction over Wrecked, Stranded Vessels. If by chance an American vessel may be wrecked or stranded on the coast within the jurisdiction of the consul, he is required, as far as the laws of the country permit, to take proper measures to protect the vessel and cargo, take inventories and provide for storage. He cannot, however, take possession on occasions when the master, owner or consignee is present. In the case of salvage, the local courts should permit the consul to receive the effects and the remainder of the property after salvage is paid.

In his report to the Department of State which should be made immediately by telegraph, the consular officer should give all essential information regarding the vessel, passengers and crew and the circumstances attending the disaster. The telegraphic report is to be followed by a more detailed airmail report.[18]

The Treaty of Friendship, Commerce, and Consular Rights between the United States and Germany signed December 8, 1923, provides that:

All proceedings relative to the salvage of vessels of either High Contracting Party wrecked upon the coasts of the other shall be directed by the consular officer of the country to which the vessel belongs and within whose district the wreck may have occurred. Pending the arrival of such officer, who shall be immediately informed of the occurrence, the local authorities shall take all necessary measures for the protection of persons and the preservation of wrecked property.[19]

A consul is also authorized if requested to make a survey of a wreck or a damaged vessel in order to protect the master of the ship who has been placed in a difficult and sometimes critical position. In such cases a survey carried on under the supervision of a consul is of more weight than one

[18] *Foreign Service Manual* (November, 1951), Sects. 560-62, 8.
[19] *United States Treaty Series* No. 725, Article XXVIII.

instituted and supervised solely by the master. An instance is told of the S. S. *Lake Elkwood* reaching the port of Rio de Janeiro in a damaged condition and falling into the hands of unscrupulous repairers. The United States consul was finally called upon to remove the master and assume charge of the vessel. This he did over the protest of the master and saved the Government considerable money. When the case was later brought before the courts the action of the consul was upheld.[20]

Rewards to Deserving Seamen.   In case a consul receives authentic information that seamen or citizens of the United States have been rescued from shipwreck by the master or crew of a foreign vessel, he should send a statement immediately to the Department so that the President of the United States may make suitable acknowledgments. If the consul judges that master and crew are deserving of immediate reward, he may telegraph to the Department of State for authorization to pay to the master and crew concerned cash awards to be distributed in accordance with the rank and merit of the recipients. If no cash awards are made the consular officer may recommend to the President that suitable testimonials be made; these consist of watches, binoculars, and gold medals, and are purchased from a special appropriation made by Congress for this purpose.[21]

Bret Harte, more famous for his stories than for his work as a Consul, brought about the erection of a monument in Glasgow in memory of nineteen American seamen whose lives were lost in the wreck of the *Guy Mannering* on December 31, 1865, off the coast of Ione Island.

Protection of Seamen.   American seamen are regarded as particular wards of the United States Government and many laws are found in the statute books for their protection. When a vessel flying his country's flag arrives in port the consul is regarded as possessing a sort of supervisory jurisdiction over it, and any action of the port authorities should follow consultation with him and should not be concerned with the internal administration of the vessel. Unless the peace of the port is disturbed, consuls are usually granted jurisdiction over disputes between seamen or between master and seamen which may have arisen in the course of the voyage.

The master of the vessel is required by law to give the crew full liberty to lay their complaints before the consular officer and ordinarily they should be allowed to come ashore for this purpose. The consular officer is regarded as the adviser and counsel for the seaman and he must see to it that the latter has the fullest opportunity to submit his complaint. If the consul has any reason to believe that a seaman is restrained in any way, he must go on board at once to permit his appearance. The complaints of

---

[20] Wilbur J. Carr, "What Your Consuls Do," *American Consular Bulletin* (January, 1922), 8.
[21] *Foreign Service Manual* (November, 1951), Sects. 563-5.

seamen are quite varied and are concerned with such matters as the unseaworthiness of the vessel, a lack of essential equipment, the poor quality or insufficient quantity of the provisions, harsh treatment on the part of the master and unreasonable deduction of wages.[22]

Consuls often find the problem of settling disputes between master and seamen one of their most exasperating duties. Masters resent any decision which finds against them, and the men feel that justice is always on the side of the ship and the master. The following is a typical case as related by a consul with long experience in seaport posts. A seaman would appear claiming that he had been abused criminally while on ship. According to his story he had been handcuffed, kicked and starved. A number of his fellow seamen would substantiate his claim. The testimony—always differing very considerably—would be taken, oaths would be sworn. The captain would be asked to appear. Finally, after a whole day's hearing, the matter would sift down to the real facts of the case. The master had cursed out the man and given him a kick for what appeared to be near insubordination. The dispute was a draw and the consul's routine work still remained to be done.

The Signing of Seamen.   Every master of an American merchant vessel who signs on a seaman in a foreign port is required by law to engage the seaman in the presence of the American consul stationed there. Otherwise the shipment is void and the seaman may leave the service at any time and recover the highest wage paid at the port of shipment. The consul must assist the seaman to understand the contract which he signs, because of grave abuses that have arisen through the shipping of seamen by unauthorized shipping agents. According to law, a seaman is not bound by a clause in a contract which was not read or explained to him.[23] In signing a seaman, the consul must be careful to determine the exact nationality and status of the man. This is usually done by a thorough examination of his discharge papers, identification card and credentials.

In case of desertion or casualty resulting in the loss of one or more seamen, the master is expected to ship an equal number of seamen of approximately the same rating upon arrival at port. A master may hire seamen in a foreign port for one or more round trips, or for a definite time, for any destination. The only restriction is that in order to comply with the Merchant Marine Act of 1928 (Sect. 405) the master must as far as possible see to it that throughout the period of the foreign voyage at least half of his crew shall be citizens of the United States.

All conditions of contract as to the service and pay of seamen are supposed to be contained in the shipping articles, and the consul may demand to see them whenever he thinks it necessary to the proper discharge

[22] *Foreign Service Manual* (November, 1951), Sects. 531-6.
[23] *Ibid.*, Sect. 525.

of his duties toward seamen. The shipping articles are always liberally construed in favor of the seamen.

The Discharge of Seamen. The discharge of American seamen in foreign ports is another important function of a consul. A consular officer is authorized by law to discharge a seaman in a foreign port upon his own application or upon that of the master of the vessel if the seaman has fulfilled his contract, or if he is entitled to a discharge according to the general principles of maritime law. The *Foreign Service Manual* cites many different reasons for the discharge of seamen but the most common are the following: misconduct of the seaman, unusual or cruel treatment by the master, mutual consent, completion of the shipping agreement, violation of the articles of shipment, sickness or inability of the seaman to perform his duties, and upon the sale of an American vessel abroad.[24] It is the general policy of the laws of the United States to discountenance the discharge of seamen in a foreign port, therefore the consular officer must make careful inquiries and satisfy himself that good and substantial reasons exist before granting the application for discharge; slight or venal offenses, or a single act of insubordination are not sufficient grounds.

"Gross dishonesty, habitual drunkenness, or a disposition to instigate broils and quarrels to the destruction of discipline among the crew have been held to be sufficient grounds for discharge." [25] For example, in 1938 the Department of State authorized Consul General Hurley at Marseilles to discharge a sailor who had engaged in a shooting affray which had endangered the lives of other members of the crew.

When discharging a seaman the consular officer must make an exact accounting of all wages received from the master and turned over to the seaman. This necessitates a checking of the master's books, verifying his figures and checking against the slop account. Inasmuch as the consul is held responsible for the full payment of all wages due including arrears, the most accurate accounting is required. It has been the custom of certain consulates at the seaman's request to retain his wages in trust so that he may not be tempted to spend them too recklessly. This is an extralegal practice and often occasions the consulate considerable annoyance, but is of the greatest service to the seaman.

Consul Carlton Bailey Hurst tells of a thrifty seaman who deposited over $700 at the consulate for safekeeping. But in this case temptation proved too strong, and every morning the sailor appeared at the consulate to draw a hundred dollars. Within a week his hard-earned savings had disappeared.[26]

The discharge of seamen sometimes brings about a very difficult situa-

[24] *Ibid.*, Sect. 526.
[25] *Ibid.*, Sect. 526.34.
[26] Carlton Bailey Hurst, *op. cit.*, 244-6.

tion for the consul to handle. Former Consul Lorin A. Lathrop recounts his experience as a young consul in a French port when the crew of a merchant vessel malingered the three days required to complete their shipping agreement. They then demanded a substantial increase in wages. As it was war time and no substitutes were available, the captain was at their mercy. The Consul, lacking the usual forms, wrote a contract on a large sheet of wrapping paper worded in legal phraseology but so ambiguously that it might mean almost anything. As a result, the seamen found at the next port that their contract might mean discharge instead of higher pay. They appealed to the Consul General, but he sustained the young Consul.[27]

Another case requiring even more drastic action occurred when the S. S. *Poughkeepsie*, owned by the Shipping Board, entered Bermuda in distress. The crew refused to perform their duties and demanded their discharge. The master, unable to cope with the situation, placed the matter in the hands of the consul. He held that the crew had conspired to mutiny, had them arrested, and shipped a new crew in their places. The vessel was saved considerable time and expense and the court upheld the consul.[28]

Perhaps the ruling case in regard to the refusal of a crew to perform its duties in a foreign port occurred in September, 1937, when the crew of the United States Government-owned steamship *Algic* staged a sit-down strike in sympathy with a longshoremen's strike in the harbor of Montevideo. In this case the Consul, Hector C. Adam, Jr., was authorized by the Department of State to instruct the master of the vessel to place the ringleaders in irons and to replace them with American or foreign seamen. Upon the vessel's return the guilty members of the crew were tried and convicted of inciting mutiny by the United States District Court and the conviction was affirmed in the Circuit Court of Appeals.[29]

Death of Seamen. In case a seaman dies on board ship the master takes charge of all of his money and effects. At the first port the consul should be notified; he may, if he considers it expedient, take over the money and effects and also the wages due. The effects may be sold, and all moneys from sale and wages must be remitted to the district court having jurisdiction over the port of departure or where the voyage terminates. A full report is always sent to the Department of State.

The burial expenses are chargeable to the ship and may not be deducted from the seaman's wages. The burial expenses are paid by the Government only when it had assumed responsibility for the seaman's mainte-

[27] Lorin A. Lathrop, "The Recollections of a Consul," *The Saturday Evening Post* (May 9, 1925), 49.
[28] Carr, *op. cit.*, 8.
[29] Green Hackworth, *Digest of International Law* (Washington, 1942), IV, 908.

nance and repatriation. No appropriation is available for the shipment of remains of seamen although if his family desires the return of his body at their expense the same procedure will be followed as in returning the bodies of other American citizens.

Whenever practicable the consular officer will communicate information relative to the death of the seaman to the next of kin or to other interested persons, sending all available and proper data including the location of the district court to which the wages and effects will be or have been transmitted.[30]

A typical case involving the death of an American seaman is related by Joseph Brandt, Consul at Cartagena, Colombia, in 1935. One morning he was notified that an assistant steward on an American vessel had accidentally shot and killed the second baker while on the high seas approaching the port of Cartagena. He went on board, interviewed the captain, the ship's doctor, and the assistant steward, who made an affidavit describing the incident in detail. He then proceeded to the ship's hold to view the remains before they were sealed in a casket. After obtaining a formal death certificate and an embalming certificate from the doctor, the Consul sealed his certificate on the casket. The captain took an oath and signed the necessary document for the death of a sailor at sea. The purser prepared an account of the salary due which was sworn to by the captain and the purser. An inventory was then made of the dead man's effects and the captain guaranteed their delivery in New York. The captain and Consul Brandt informed the port captain of the incident and he accepted their statement that the death had occurred on the high seas and therefore outside of his jurisdiction. After the departure of the vessel Consul Brandt sent a complete account of the affair by air mail to the Department of State, with signed copies of all the statements and certificates. After holding a hearing in New York, the District Attorney dismissed the case.

Relief of Seamen. A final duty which the consul performs for seamen is to provide for their subsistence when found destitute within his district, and their transportation home at government expense. Not only are merchant seamen who are citizens of the United States entitled to relief, but the law includes foreigners regularly shipped on an American vessel in a port of the United States. Inasmuch as only destitute seamen are eligible, and the consul must make the final decision, he often finds himself in a very delicate and disagreeable position. The law would seem to be very lenient towards the seaman but the opinions of the Comptroller General are quite the reverse.

In fact the Comptroller General, to whom the consular officer must account for the expenditure of government funds, has placed the responsibility for all ill or injured seamen regardless of the cause of their disability

[30] *Manual, op. cit.,* Sect. 555.

upon the operator of the vessel. The established rule would seem to be that the United States owners or operators are held responsible for relief and repatriation of all seamen separated from their vessels at foreign ports for any reason except desertion or shipwreck.

In providing subsistence the consular officer is expected to provide the simplest and most economical lodging and sustenance and the cheapest clothing which is serviceable and durable. Medical care should always be procured in a hospital and as economically as possible. Transportation is afforded only when it is impossible to procure employment, and impracticable to require the shipping company which owns the vessel of last service to supply the transportation. American vessels should be used whenever possible and they are compelled by law to afford transportation at the lowest passenger rate, and not in excess of two cents per mile over the established route for steam or motor vessels.

If the seaman be a deserter certain penalties are provided and the consul is authorized to make a certification of desertion at the request of the master after he has investigated the case and is satisfied that the desertion was deliberate and not connived at by the master or caused by cruel treatment. Many countries have authorized the solicitation of assistance from local authorities to return deserting seamen, but the United States has eliminated this provision from her treaties.[31]

According to Raymond Fisher, former American Consul stationed at Sydney, Australia, almost 50 per cent of office correspondence in the Australasian consulates had to do with the problems of shipping and seamen. To rid the port of American beachcombers and to provide relief wisely were the two most difficult tasks. In the latter case many seamen knew the regulations so well that they could exploit the provisions granting relief. For example, a seaman would ship from San Francisco to Newcastle, be discharged, and being destitute, demand relief. Just before he was given opportunity to ship out on an American boat, he would drift to Sydney and again obtain relief.

Even the granting of relief presented problems. If the seamen were sent to a seaman's home they prolonged their stay by remaining away when there was a chance to ship. If sent to a private family for room and board they almost always got into some sort of trouble. If they were well fed they lingered in port, if not fed sufficiently they complained loudly. In Sydney drunken and violent seamen came to the office in such numbers that the consulate lease was cancelled and it was with the greatest difficulty that a satisfactory building was obtained.

Carlton Bailey Hurst, when Consul in Barcelona, made an arrangement

---

[31] This is necessarily a very brief treatment of a highly technical subject. An excellent and detailed study has been made by Consul Charles Bridgham Hosmer entitled *Administrative Functions of Consular Officers under American Admiralty Jurisprudence*, M.LL. thesis, George Washington University, 1929.

with a small hotel on the waterfront to care for all American shipwrecked crews. The innkeeper made the mistake of furnishing wine to the first group brought in and they almost wrecked the place before the police arrived. Henceforth wine was scratched from the bill of fare. Consul Hurst was also plagued by submarined seamen who, outfitted with clothing and shoes at government expense, would sell their outfits for liquor and then claim they were robbed.[32]

According to law it is not possible to take out of a seaman's wages the amount spent on his relief. When certain seamen of the American vessel *Hilo*, wrecked near the Hawaiian Islands, reached Honolulu in a destitute condition, the American Consul General supplied their wants and shipped them back to San Francisco. When they were discharged and paid off in San Francisco the shipping commissioner at the Consul's suggestion deducted the amount expended by the Consul. The commissioner was forced to refund the amount held to the seamen.[33]

Lest it be thought that all seamen are nuisances and a drain on government funds, the following relief case deserves mention. In a despatch to John Bassett Moore, Assistant Secretary of State in 1898, a consul described the applicant for relief as intelligent, gentlemanly and well posted as a seaman; he carried extra clothing and his complaints had foundation. His request for transportation home was approved by the consul who provided the transportation costs—the sum of ten cents to carry him back to the United States from Canada.[34]

[32] Hurst, *op. cit.*, 245.
[33] John Bassett Moore, *Digest of International Law* (Washington, 1906), V, 146.
[34] *American Foreign Service Journal*, III, 85 (March, 1926).

19

Consular Services
Rendered to Nationals

AMONG THE MOST varied and interesting functions of a consular officer are those which may be grouped under the general category of services rendered to nationals. According to Pradier-Fodéré: "It is a consul's duty to see that his nationals' rights are respected in a foreign land and to take all measures which he deems necessary and useful to accomplish this end; it is through its consuls that the state extends its protecting arm over the entire surface of the globe." [1]

Consular conventions regularly place the protection of nationals as one of the first duties of a consular official. In order to carry out this function he is authorized to intervene in behalf of his nationals with the local authorities. If satisfaction is not accorded the consul is then justified in taking the matter up with the diplomatic officers of his government. In the absence of a diplomatic representative the consul may address himself directly to the national government of the country. [2]

Variety of Services Rendered. The greatest number of cases of services rendered to nationals, however, are not those which require intervention with the local authorities. They are, rather, the giving of assistance or advice by the consul to citizens who get into difficulties through ignorance or carelessness or unfortunate circumstances. Oftentimes the consul who is familiar with local laws and customs can extricate his troubled fellow countryman from a very embarrassing situation with a word in the right place. On other occasions the problem may require considerable time and attention and entail both worry and expense.

The great variety of duties which an American consul abroad performs in behalf of his countrymen may be appreciated by the report for a three-months period of a representative consulate. Consul General Coert du Bois made the following summary of aid and protection cases which were

[1] P. Pradier-Fodéré, *Traité de droit international public* (Paris, 1888), IV, 555.
[2] For a typical provision embodying the protection of nationals see Article XXI of the Treaty of Friendship, Commerce and Consular Rights of December 8, 1923, between the United States and Germany, *U. S. Treaty Series*, No. 725.

handled by the United States Consulate General in Naples for a typical three-months period:

1. Thirty-eight instances of visiting personages who, by reason of their position or their mission abroad or letters which they carried, were entitled to some form of entertainment on the part of the consular staff, the lack of which would have reflected on the United States Government; these included Congressmen, government officials, and other prominent Americans;

2. Thirty-four American citizens who happened to be abroad during a banking moratorium found themselves short of local currency with which to meet bills; the consul rendered aid in cashing paper, obtaining reasonable exchange or making arrangements for continued credit;

3. Twenty-four students desiring to enter the University of Naples, art or medical schools, or to find singing or music teachers, or private schools for their children, needed documentation or intervention.

4. Nineteen American travelers sought assistance at the consulate because of difficulties with steamship and railroad companies. These problems included the loss of tickets, the lack of accommodations and the need for special care of invalids.

5. Nineteen Americans got into trouble with the authorities through violation of police or customs regulations or through lack of proper credentials.

6. Seventeen Americans were assisted in obtaining proper medical advice and treatment, and in making arrangements for hospitalization and operations.

7. Fourteen requests for advice regarding family affairs or property were made, largely by elderly American ladies.

8. Eleven Americans were afforded protection against overcharge, persecution, annoyance, and even blackmail.

9. Thirteen destitute Americans (not seamen) were assisted.

10. Ten citizens sought advice on local marriage laws, the required documentation and the formalities for publishing the banns.

11. Ten Italian-Americans were assisted in avoiding unwarranted induction into the Italian Army.

12. Nine requests for assistance in locating relatives of Americans in Italy or the United States were handled.

13. Seven tourists were helped to obtain Italian driving licenses and permits to operate American cars in Italy.

14. Six Americans were aided in finding employment, a difficult matter.

15. In five cases intervention with other consuls was sought on behalf of American travelers.

16. Five ladies were given shopping assistance, including the services of an interpreter.

17. Four destitute Americans (not seamen) were repatriated.

18. In four cases the necessary assistance was given to deranged Americans.

19. Four Americans making protracted visits obtained houses, villas and other places of domicile through the consulate.

20. Three American journalists wanting stories, photographs and interviews were assisted.

21. In three instances lost, delayed or sequestered baggage was recovered.

22. The care taken in the disposition of two cases of suicide or attempted suicide completes the summary of aid and protection cases handled by the Naples Consulate during the quarter recorded.

Consular Protection of Citizens.   The *Foreign Service Regulations* of the United States provide that Foreign Service officers shall intervene with the appropriate foreign authorities on behalf of American citizens or nationals abroad only when it appears that the persons desiring protection are being injured, oppressed or unjustly deprived of their liberty. Consular officers are authorized to bring such cases to the attention of the local authorities unless intervention by the national authorities is required in which event the consular officer must refer the case to his diplomatic mission.[3] The consul is instructed to use every endeavor to settle all disputes in an amicable manner. If he finds it necessary to interpose with the governmental authorities, he is advised to follow the suggestion made by Thomas Jefferson to consuls in 1790: "Let all representations be couched in the most temperate and friendly terms, never indulging in any case whatever a single expression which may irritate." [4]

The question as to whether an official remonstrance in affairs of government was permissible to a consular officer was raised by the Spanish Governor General of Cuba in 1895. Consul General Williams at Havana had made representations touching the prolonged confinement of certain American citizens without trial and in contravention of existing treaties. Governor General Martinez de Campos replied that since consuls were not invested with diplomatic functions, they could not make official protests, but were limited to making inquiries and reports. Secretary of State Olney refused to accept such an interpretation of consular duties, and declared that the right of consuls to intervene with the local authority for the protection of their countrymen from unlawful acts was an accepted doctrine of international law and conventionally established by treaties. Secretary Olney thereupon pointed out that the existing treaty between the United States and Spain of February 27, 1870, made specific provision for such right of redress.[5]

Americans in Troubled Areas.   This same question was raised again in connection with the protection of American citizens in Berlin against Nazi outrages. In this case the point was made that since the United States had a diplomatic representative in Berlin, the question of protection should be one of diplomatic rather than consular representation. However, since outrages were not confined to Berlin, and Consul General George Messersmith and later Consul Raymond Geist had been constantly intervening in cases at various ports of Germany before the question was raised, the embassy preferred to act only in cases which required diplomatic action. The matter was settled by a reference to the German American Consular Convention of December 8, 1923, which provided that

[3] *Regulations* (May, 1945), XXI, 3, Note 4.
[4] *Regulations* (February, 1931), Sect. 77, Note 1.
[5] *Foreign Relations of the United States, 1895,* II, 1209.

consular officers might address national, state, provincial or municipal authorities for the purpose of protecting their countrymen.[6]

Numerous cases of protection afforded to Americans in Germany after the advent of the Hitler regime might be cited, the following instances may serve as representative examples:

An American went to Germany to visit his brother. He was arrested and accused of spreading propaganda against the German Government in the United States. The American Consul in the district learned of the case and investigated. He found that the American had in his possession a German life insurance monthly published in the United States in which appeared certain articles critical of the New Germany. A woman at the *pension* where the American was staying borrowed the paper and loaned it to a neighbor, and the unfortunate lender, who had never been guilty of the slightest word or act against Germany, was thrown into jail. Upon urgent representations from the American Consul of the district and the Consulate General at Berlin, the American was released.

Another much more serious case which received wide newspaper publicity [7] and enlisted the aid of United States congressmen and senators was that of Walter Orloff, a Brooklyn medical student at the University of Greifswald, accused of communistic activities. The matter was brought to the attention of Consul General George Messersmith by two American fellow students. Mr. Messersmith immediately got in touch with Orloff and with the authorities. It was alleged that Orloff, who frequented communistic headquarters, was attempting to reorganize the Communist Party in Germany. Apparently the police had a letter written by Orloff stating he was a Communist and eager to assist the Party. A Prussian decree made complicity in communistic and other subversive activities punishable with death.

In letters to the consulate, Orloff declared he was well treated but Consul Geist made a visit to the jail and found the youth terror stricken and quite badly treated. At first the consulate attempted to get Orloff deported, but the authorities declared it was too late since the wheels of justice had already started turning. The consulate thereupon emphasized the severity of the accusation, the youth of the prisoner, his long imprisonment before the consulate had learned of his incarceration, his ill treatment, the fact that no counsel had been allowed him, and the effect the case was having on American public opinion. The German authorities finally agreed upon deportation and Orloff was sent back to the United States.

In spite of valiant efforts made by the United States consular officials to protect Americans during this very difficult period in Germany, they were often criticized by the very people to whom they had afforded pro-

[6] *United States Treaty Series*, No. 725, Article XXI.
[7] See files of the *New York Times* (July 23-August 19, 1933).

tection. Two Brooklyn Jews who were in Berlin when the boycott commenced were arrested by police at a boarding house which they visited to see an acquaintance. The arrest was made at the request of the proprietress of the pension who became suspicious, she said, because of their appearance and their broken English.

They were put in jail and refused permission to see the Consul. The next afternoon they were released and came to the Consulate to protest. At the request of the Consul General they made an affidavit as to their treatment. The Consulate promised them no further difficulties would be encountered and that protests would be made to the proper authorities. The two men left Germany, but before leaving gave out a story which was not only false as regards the reason for their arrest, but also an accusation against the Consulate for not giving them courteous attention, and a threat to bring suit against Consul General Messersmith. Later a still more erroneous version was given to the press in New York. The version was contrary to their own affidavit and the *New York Times* correspondent in Berlin later agreed that the version in his own paper was false.

In this instance the Consul General had received the two men courteously and had promised them protection. He immediately made representations to the German police and obtained promises of no further interference with their movements. The State Department instead of criticizing Consul General Messersmith rewarded him with the position of Minister to Vienna for his excellent service in Berlin on behalf of Americans.

A somewhat different form of services to nationals occurred in connection with American armed forces in many areas during World War II. For example Carl Norden, the American Vice Consul stationed at Paramaribo in Dutch Guiana, not only paved the way for the cordial treatment accorded the American forces but served as a very satisfactory liaison officer between the American Army and the Government officials.

Violation of Local Laws and Customs. In some of the cases where Americans have been involved in difficulties with the authorities abroad the matter seems very trivial to the American but extremely serious from the standpoint of local law and custom of the foreign country. In such cases public opinion at home is inclined to blame the diplomatic or consular official for a failure to act in a sufficiently effective manner in behalf of his nationals. A much discussed case of five Americans who were arrested and held for months without bail in the Palma City jail on the Island of Majorca in 1933 illustrates the point. The alleged offense was an assault upon a member of the Civil Guard, such a serious crime from the Spanish point of view that the accused were not eligible for bail and were placed automatically under military jurisdiction. Yet the story told by the Americans made the matter a rather easy one to understand and would have been settled by a very moderate penalty in the United States.

A young American returning from a café engaged in altercation with a hotel doorman who sought the aid of the Civil Guard. When a woman onlooker remonstrated with the Guard he struck the youth, breaking his eyeglasses and knocking him over. The woman's husband rushed up and when the Guard struck his wife with a sword, hit the Guard in the eye with his fist. The whole party was arrested, including two others who were merely bystanders.[8]

The occurrence took place on June 4, and American Ambassador Bowers at Madrid received the first report on the case on June 17. He investigated and not receiving satisfactory information, sent Claude Dawson, United States Consul at Barcelona, to Majorca to investigate. Dawson reported that the military judge refused to consider any extenuating circumstances and insisted upon holding the accused in prison. The State Department now made a strong protest to the Spanish Government through Ambassador Bowers regarding the harsh conditions of confinement and the long delay in granting a trial. The five unfortunates were finally released on bail on July 20, and acquitted by a military tribunal on October 26.[9]

The strict regulations in various European countries regarding the registration of travelers' funds often causes trouble. An American woman delegate to the International Congress of University Women in Poland in August, 1936, failed to make a declaration of her letter of credit while motoring across the Polish border with her son and daughter. When the official found several one dollar bills, a few shillings and some canceled checks which she had in her pocketbook he took her to court where the judge threatening a two-years sentence committed her to the local jail in which the most elementary conveniences were lacking. The son got a telephone call through to the American Consulate General in Warsaw, which immediately despatched a member of the staff. When he finally secured her release just twenty-four hours after her incarceration the woman was hysterical. Without the consular intervention the conse-quences might have been tragic.

There are occasions, however, where the American traveler is clearly to blame and the American consul is expected to obtain mercy rather than justice. An American girl traveling from St. Moritz to Berne put her feet shod in heavy hiking boots on the seat across from her own. When the train guard objected she took them off, but protested at Swiss methods. A little later he found her again with her feet on the seat. Altercation arose and he is alleged to have seized them and placed them down none too gently. She threw a book at his head and a little later found herself

[8] *New York Times* (July 17, 1933).
[9] *New York Times* (October 27, 1933).

in jail. She was able to get in touch with the Consul, who had to pay her fine to get her out. Under the circumstances the Consul could get no satisfaction from the authorities, and received considerable criticism from the girl for his failure to obtain an abject apology.

Sometimes in spite of the consul's warning rash Americans will risk involving themselves in serious political disturbances in foreign countries. In the summer of 1935, Consul General Thomas D. Bowman in Mexico City tried in vain to prevent two American students from participating in a student movement to oust the political boss of the State of Tabasco.

Activities in Times of Revolution and War.   The consular duty of protecting his nationals during revolutionary activities is a very important one. For example when the Franco revolution broke out in Spain every effort was made both by our diplomatic and consular officers to evacuate Americans. The American Embassy at Madrid and the Consulates at Barcelona, Balboa, Valencia, Vigo and Gibraltar obtained means of transportation by bus, train, or plane to ports of embarcation. Whenever commercial vessels were unavailable American naval vessels were utilized to repatriate citizens. Of the approximately 1,500 Americans in Spain at the time all who wished to leave were safely evacuated. Oftentimes the consular officer would have to enlist the aid of the Red Cross to obtain funds for those unable to pay their passage. One woman repatriated from Seville on Red Cross funds at first demurred at traveling third class and when she was reconciled to that indignity asked for cash to get her hair waved before her departure. The consul informed her that beauticians' services were not included in necessary expenses.

Thomas J. Corcoran in Vigo, Consul General Lynn N. Franklin in Barcelona, Consul Charles A. Day in Seville, Consul Robert N. Longyear in the Balearic Islands, and above all Foreign Service Officer Eric Wendelin and Consul John D. Johnson in the Embassy at Madrid did such excellent work in evacuating all Americans who wished to leave that Secretary Hull personally commended them for their splendid services. Ambassador Claude A. Bowers embarked upon the American Coast Guard cutter *Cayuga* and turning it into a floating embassy kept himself available to all the consulates in Spain.

At the outbreak of World War II in Europe the State Department was ready for the emergency and all embassies, legations, and consulates were directed to warn all Americans to leave Europe. William Morton, American Consul in Warsaw, hastened to Brest-Litovsk and set up an evacuation center while Consul General John K. Davis remained in charge in Warsaw.

Hallet Johnson, American Consul General in Stockholm gave a preliminary warning to Americans to be prepared, suggesting Delcarlie as the best district for evacuation and urging all Americans to have their passports in order, funds available and to keep in touch with the Consulate.

Three weeks after the outbreak of the war more than 10,000 Americans had been removed from the United Kingdom and the State Department announced that during the first month of hostilities a total of 51,725 nationals had been evacuated from Europe.

Consul General Sam E. Woods and Consul Robert E. Cowan stationed at Zurich, Switzerland during World War II aided in the escape of hundreds of aviators interned in several camps in Switzerland. The aviators could get out of the camps by forged passes but the difficulty was to get out of the country. A plan was perfected whereby the aviators would call Woods at any time of day or night from a telephone box near Lucerne as alumni of Washington University. Woods would drive to Lucerne, go to a designated cathedral, take a back seat, pray, cough, drop a handkerchief, walk out and then the aviators would follow. He would then drive them to Zurich and put them up till they could escape into France. When his home was too small to accommodate them Woods rented a hospital. Woods was able to aid in the escape of over a thousand of the seventeen hundred interned in Switzerland.

The Consul's Duties Frequently Arduous and Unnoticed.   A consul is willing to undertake difficult journeys and undergo considerable hardship in order to fulfill the requirements of his office. Shortly after the close of World War I an American came into the Consulate at Cairo in great distress. His wife had disappeared after kissing him goodbye in the morning and no trace of her had been found. Consul George Wadsworth immediately made inquiries through agencies of information which were available to the Consulate. He learned that she had been seen with a dragoman with a bad record. The Consul then checked up departure statistics with the Egyptian police and learned that a caravan had left that morning. He obtained the services of a police officer and the two began a long chase over the desert. They finally caught up with the caravan before nightfall and the police officer took the dragoman in charge while the Consul with difficulty persuaded the woman to accompany him. Since she was unwilling to return to her husband the Consul placed her in a home run by an American woman. Again she disappeared and this time the Consulate located her in a cocaine dive. Once more she was brought back and by threats of arrest and deportation she was forced to take passage home on a steamer. Her husband paid her passage and the Consul put the woman on board. The husband followed and joined his wife on the boat where a reconciliation took place through the good offices of the Consul.

Oftentimes in cases which receive considerable notice in the press the work of the consular officers is an entirely overlooked factor. On September 1, 1932, the body of an American girl, Jerane Storrs Ibershoff, was found at the foot of Zermatt Mountain in Switzerland. She and her sister had been touring Europe on bicycles. As the story developed later, the younger sister had had trouble with her bicycle and had walked down to the town. The older girl, desirous of making a side trip, proceeded alone, promising to meet her sister at the station later. An itinerant Swiss saw the girl going off alone on her bicycle and followed her. When she stopped for a drink he seized her, and when she struggled he struck her several times on the head with a stone. He then attacked her, leaving her unconscious, and she died from loss of blood.[10]

While the affair received considerable attention in the press very little notice was given to the work of the American consular officials, although they took a very important part in the case. Immediately upon receipt of information of the finding of the body, the Consulate got in touch with the sister, the police and the hotel management. The Consulate made arrangements for the bringing down of the body and obtained permission from the girls' uncle for its cremation. Since the younger sister had to remain for the inquest, the Consulate took her in charge and kept her isolated from the newspapermen for three or four days. Arrangements were made for her return to the United States—a consular officer accompanied her to Cherbourg and placed her on the boat in charge of some responsible Americans who were returning home. The Consulate then followed the trial of the murderer who had been quickly caught and condemned. The only mention of the work of the Consulate in the press was that Consul General Prentiss Gilbert had reported that the body had been cremated and that the ashes would be sent back to America.

Accident Cases.   The consul is often called upon in accident cases. Consul General Dayle C. McDonough while serving in Monterey, Mexico, received a telephone call from a local hotel saying that an American registered there was locked in his room which he had not left in two days. Consul McDonough got a doctor—they broke open the room, found that the man was paralyzed and had fallen and fractured his skull. The consul had the man's brother and sister come down from Iowa and arranged for the man to be taken on a stretcher to the States for an operation. The man recovered and thanked the consul for saving his life.

Upon another occasion, when a bad automobile collision occurred in which one person was killed and several badly injured, Consul McDonough learned that one was an American girl. After visiting several hospitals, he located the girl, who was so badly injured she said she was ready to die. The consul got the best surgeon available, had the girl transferred to a better hospital, and urged her to keep up her courage. His prompt action was effective and the girl ultimately recovered.

[10] *New York Times* (September 4, 5, 7, 1932).

Consul Herbert B. Thompson in Madrid received an urgent call from an American woman in Salamanca who said that her husband had struck and killed a bicyclist and that the police had put him in jail. When the local police could give him no information, Consul Thompson drove to Salamanca. He found that the American could speak no Spanish and that according to his story the cyclist had turned suddenly into the path of the car. Consul Thompson secured the release of the man upon bail for both criminal and civil liability. The man was finally permitted to leave the country upon his sacrificing his bond. His insurance covered the civil costs, and he was only too glad to pay the criminal assessment.

An American student in Salsburg was killed in an automobile accident while driving with a friend. The American Consulate had the body embalmed and shipped home, collected the boy's effects and sent them with a letter of condolence to the parents in San Francisco. The father sent a letter of acknowledgment expressing his heartfelt gratitude for the Consul's services.

Welfare Cases. One of the constant demands upon a consul's time and energy is the assistance he renders to Americans in distress. These are generally called welfare cases and they run the whole gamut of human misfortune. A naturalized American citizen living in Indianapolis whose father died in Greece, leaving him a small inheritance, tried in vain to obtain it. He finally sold his insurance policies and got together enough money to go to Greece. He soon found the government restrictions to be of such character that he was unable to get the inheritance and he was stranded without funds. In the meantime his wife's health broke down in her efforts to carry on his shoe business in the United States. The wife appealed to her congressman, who notified the Secretary of State. As the man had not forwarded his last address there was delay in locating him. The American Consul General in Athens, Mr. Leland Morris, finally found him, but no funds were available to send him home. After considerable effort private sources were enlisted in the man's behalf and a steamship company was persuaded to give him a reduced passage back to America.

The Consulate General in Rome was appealed to one Saturday afternoon by a party of some thirty stranded Americans who were being held in the station because they had taken the wrong train. Vice Consul Achilles who was detailed to look into the matter found that the men of the party were Greeks who were being repatriated by relief agencies in Cincinnati, Ohio. It was discovered that the mistake had been made at the Franco-Italian frontier where no one had met them. As they had no funds the American Consul persuaded the Italian station agent to send them on without tickets as being cheaper than taking care of them.

The case of a young American boy who came to Italy to study after secretly marrying in the United States was a particularly sad one. His wife joined him and they soon had a baby. Their funds were very limited and when it was learned that another baby was coming they were desperate. The wife insisted upon an abortion and a doctor was found. He was a quack and the young mother died. As the doctor had made the boy help him, the case was a serious one. The American Consul notified the parents, and retained a lawyer for a very small amount, and finally after a few months in prison the boy was freed without a trial.

At times the consul finds it very difficult to decide what is the best course to pursue in giving aid to Americans in distress. A young American girl was living in Greece with her stepfather and mother. Her own father had a prison record and lived in the United States. When the stepfather killed the mother the Consulate had to decide whether it was better to have the girl stay in Greece where her estate was tied up or repatriate her to her father who was not a desirable person to act as guardian. The Consulate obtained the advice and assistance of a relief organization and the girl was apprenticed to a dressmaker in Greece.

Vice Consul Milton K. Wells at Gibraltar was notified of an American colored man and his wife who were stranded without funds. They were returning from Liberia to the United States by way of Gibraltar. An alleged steamship agent took 300 pesetas to get them by the customs in Gibraltar—one of the few ports in the world free from duties—and to get their American passport visaed by the American Consul. The swindler took their last 700 pesetas for passage in a nonexistent boat. Vice Consul Wells got in touch with the police, had the swindler arrested, and secured the return of 930 pesetas. Never were any two Americans more grateful for the services of our American consular officials abroad.

In assisting American citizens the consul is usually in a position to give the best advice possible under the circumstances. The consul's recommendations, however, are not always followed and the result is usually to the disadvantage of the national. Three American women tourists on a visit to the battlefields after World War I were badly injured when their automobile overturned. They were forced to spend their whole vacation in the hospital instead of seeing Europe. One, a teacher of physical education, was so badly injured that she would never be able to teach again. The Consulate General in Paris took up the case and obtained a settlement of 55,000 francs for the badly injured teacher and 6,500 for each of the others. A French lawyer, however, urged the woman to sue for larger amounts. Although the Consulate General urged that a settlement be made out of court, the lawyer's advice was accepted. The lawyer did secure larger amounts for them, but the insurance company appealed and the lawyer was then no longer interested. Again the Consulate was asked to intervene and was able to obtain the original offer. Unfortunately, by this time the exchange value of the franc had decreased and the women lost about $500 as a result of their refusal to settle at the first figure.

Consular Care of the Mentally Deranged. One of the most tragic types of welfare cases is that of the American who while on a visit abroad goes insane. This problem arises more often than one might expect and is sometimes a very difficult one to handle. One of the cases that was not so difficult occurred in Paris when one of a party of girl students on tour became suddenly insane. The woman conducting the tour was in a quandary because unless the tour went through on schedule all the benefits would be lost. Upon being consulted, the American Consul advised that the party continue the tour and the Consulate would take care of the girl. She was sent to a hospital, an American physician called and the father informed. Daily information concerning her condition was obtained by the consul until the arrival of her father. He was given every assistance in taking his daughter home. Both the principal of the school and the father expressed their most heartfelt thanks for the assistance rendered and ascribed no small part of the girl's subsequent cure to the prompt attention given her by the Consulate.

A more difficult case arises when the person to be aided is violently insane and commits some act infringing the laws of the foreign country. A Californian who was taken criminally insane in Chambèry Savoie picked up a tool and seriously injured two people. He was arrested and later interned in an asylum. His mother came over to France to obtain his release and to take him home. The American Consulate General in Paris finally succeeded in getting permission therefor from the authorities and then took care of all passport and other formalities.

A case was brought to the attention of the Consulate General in Rome which required very delicate handling. A mentally defective shell-shocked veteran who had come abroad with his aunt became so difficult to handle that the aunt was completely distracted. The Consul found an American doctor who was going home who agreed to allow the man to accompany him if the aunt would pay his passage. The man, himself, refused to go, however, and it was only when the Consul suggested that they all go home together that he agreed. On the night of the embarcation, however, the soldier disappeared, and just by luck was located wandering in the streets. The Consul now accompanied the soldier on the boat train and saw him aboard. The arrangement worked perfectly, the soldier was placed in a veterans' hospital and the old lady expressed her undying gratitude to the Consul.

While Consul Affeld was stationed at Kobe in 1938, he received a telephone call that an American had run amok on the NYK Line and needed a psychiatric examination. According to reports he had pestered women on the ship, had come to a costume party in a G-string and when finally he had been put in the brig he had broken out. Consul Affeld arranged for a doctor to examine the man, but the doctor refused to declare him insane. The only solution seemed to send him back on the same boat. The Consul insisted that they fix the booby hatch up more comfortably and promising the fellow he would be let out if he behaved for a probationary period, he persuaded the man to go on board. As a precautionary measure, Affeld was accompanied by a Japanese judo champion, but his services were not needed. In fact the American Consul received the thanks of the American for his assistance.

Whereabouts Cases.   Every consular post serves at some time or other as a port of missing men. In some cases the persons disappear deliberately; in other cases someone suddenly becomes interested in a member of his family or a friend of whom he has lost track for many years. One of the most complicated whereabouts cases was brought to the attention of Consul General Robert Fraser at the London Consulate General. The inquiry came from a naturalized German American living in Puerto Rico who wrote concerning the whereabouts of his son in England:

In 1913 he had married an English girl and in July, 1914, a boy was born. When the war broke, as an enemy alien he was interned for the entire period of the war. His wife and child went back to his wife's parents. Towards the close of the war he learned that his wife was living with another man whom she subsequently married. He went back to Germany and later to the United States. In 1925 he was naturalized in Chicago and changed his name. He also got a divorce from his wife and was given custody of the child. However, since the decree was not enforceable in Great Britain, the judge suggested that he wait until the boy was of age and then take up the case.

In 1934 he wrote as suggested, but his letter was returned. A second letter written by a friend brought an unsigned notation on the letter that the letter was an insult and that neither the boy nor his mother ever wanted to see the father again. As a last resort the man appealed to the American Consul.

Consul General Fraser wrote to the chief constable of the town where the boy was living, who answered that the boy also had changed his name but was still living with his mother. Letters were thereupon written to the father, giving the boy's name and address and to the son, telling the father's interest and his desire to make a will in his favor. When no reply was received, Mr. Fraser wrote the constable enclosing a copy of the letter to the son and asked him to find out if the son had received the letter. The constable interviewed the son and found that he had never heard from his father and thought that he was long since dead. He promised to write to his father immediately.

A more typical case was investigated by the American Consul in Florence. An American of means living in Tours asked that the United States Consul look up his four children who were supposedly in the custody of his divorced wife at Florence. An investigation by the Consulate indicated that the woman had left for the United States with an Italian prince, abandoning the children to the care of a governess, but without funds for food or clothing. The family was just about to be evicted from their villa for nonpayment of rent. The father sent funds to the Consulate at Florence to cover expenses and the debts left behind by the wife, and gave directions that the children and governess be sent to Paris. He later expressed his great appreciation of the work of the American Consul in the care of his family.

Sometimes the consul has to play a more direct rôle in cases of family difficulties. An American woman came to Consul Gowen in London asking that he help her trace her husband, an Englishman, who had decamped from the United States with their two older children, both born in America. With the aid of private detectives the husband was located and the woman had a visit with him. He agreed to let her have the two children for a day. She immediately brought the children to the Consulate and Consul Gowen booked passage for the same day. To avoid possible trouble he took the distraught mother to her hotel to pack, put her and the children on the boat and arranged with the captain that no one was to see her or even know that she was on board.

Often the disappearance of a person is caused by a revolution or disturbance in the country where the person is traveling or engaging in business. Assistant Secretary of State Carr tells of a New York merchant who disappeared while on a business trip to the Russian Caucasus. As a revolution had occurred in the district, his alarmed relatives appealed to the Department of State. The nearest consul was detailed on the case and reported that the man was being held by the revolutionists and was without means. Money was supplied by relatives and sent on to the consul. He employed an adventurous agent who got through the revolutionary lines, obtained the merchant's release and after much difficulty brought him back to the consul.[11]

Estates of Americans Dying Abroad. The care of the estates of deceased nationals is a very important consular function and is regularly provided for in consular conventions. In some treaties the consul takes complete control and the local authorities participate merely to protect the interests of resident creditors.[12] In others the administration is vested in local authorities and the consul merely represents the interests of the deceased national. The Consular Treaty of 1923 between the United States and Germany is of this type. It provides in Article XXIV that upon the death of a national without a will the consular officer of the district

[11] William J. Carr, "What Your Consuls Do," *American Consular Bulletin*, 2 (January, 1922).

[12] See Article XXXIII, Treaty of 1887 between United States and Peru, 25 *U. S. Statutes at Large*, 1461.

shall take charge so far as the laws of the country permit until an administrator is appointed and letters of administration granted.[13]

M. Pillaut, an outstanding authority on consular law, criticizes the first type and declares that consular conventions should be based on the following principles with reference to the care of estates: (1) the consular convention should limit itself to safeguarding the interests of the heirs; (2) the heirs should have full right of refusing consular assistance; (3) the consul's rôle should be one of supplying information and advice.[14] The Franco-Polish Treaty of 1925 in the articles pertaining to the regulation of succession follows quite closely these principles.[15]

The United States has followed a fairly consistent policy in claiming according to the custom of civilized nations the right of a consul "to receive, inventory, take care of and account for the effects of any subject of the nation by which the consul is appointed and who dies within his consulate." [16] This statement, made by Secretary of State Pickering in 1799, was repeated in approximately the same form by numerous other secretaries of state. Secretary Marcy regarded the administration of estates of American citizens dying intestate abroad as one of the most sacred and responsible trusts imposed by the consular officer.[17] It has always been recognized, however, that local law is paramount unless the matter is governed by treaty.

The instructions to American consuls today are very similar. The *Foreign Service Manual* requires a consular officer to report to the Department of State, to the legal representative and to the closest known relative the deaths of all United States citizens occurring in his consular district and in the absence of relatives or other interested persons to carry out the wishes of the deceased as to local burial, cremation, or shipment of the remains. He is further authorized to take possession and dispose of the personal estates of the deceased. These normally include convertible assets, perishable property, luggage, wearing apparel, and miscellaneous personal effects. However, he need not travel long distances to take possession—reasonable efforts are all that are required. Although he may collect and pay debts he may not act as administrator of the estate nor may he assume financial responsibility. He must inventory and appraise the personal effects on the local market value with the aid of two other persons, he must keep an account of receipts and expenditures and account directly to the parties in interest and to the courts of law. A fee of $2.00 for each $100 of total value must be collected.[18]

The number of estates abroad administered by American consuls often-

13 44 *U. S. Statutes at Large*, 2153.
14 Pillaut, *Manuel de droit consulaire* (Paris, 1910), I, 171.
15 *League of Nations Treaty Series*, LXXIII, 272.
16 John Bassett Moore, *A Digest of International Law* (Washington, 1906), V, 117.
17 Moore, *op. cit.*, V, 118.
18 *Foreign Service Manual* (December, 1951), Sects. 440-8.

times amounts to over a thousand a year. They occur in all parts of the world: the property of an American engineer in Afghanistan, the personal effects of the victim of a train wreck in Spain, the estate of an American businessman who was killed in Mexico, or the possessions of an American tourist who died in the American Hospital in Paris.

Sometimes the estate is in such an out-of-the-way place that the settlement entails considerable hardship upon the consular official charged with the duty. Consul Richard F. Boyce tells of such a case when he was Vice Consul in the West Indies. An American citizen living as a recluse on an isolated island in the West Indies passed away and the nearest American consulate was notified. Vice Consul Boyce engaged passage on a small boat which took supplies to the island twice a month. He had to live on goat meat and cocoanut water in the hottest of tropical climates while he sold at public auction the beehives, the barrel of honey, the furniture and tools of the deceased. Inasmuch as the real property by local law had to go to the eldest son and the rest could be divided, the Vice Consul spent two months tracing the children before the property could be turned over to their representative. To add to the interest of the experience, the boat barely missed going on the rocks because of engine trouble on the trip over, and almost ran into one waterspout after another on the way back.[19]

Funeral Arrangements and Shipment of the Body. The consul frequently makes all the funeral arrangements and sees to the shipment of the body home. The shipment of bodies is sometimes a rather difficult matter due to local laws and quarantine restrictions. John W. Foster relates the story of a former American minister who committed suicide in Spain. The instructions for the shipment of the body to the United States were not received until after the interment. A special suspension of the sanitary laws had to be obtained from the ministry of the interior to secure disinterment. Further difficulty arose in obtaining a small vessel in which to ship the body to Gibraltar due to the local malediction of the church against suicides. When finally an earthquake occurred during the disinterment it was too much for the superstitious sailors and they refused to touch the accursed body. It was only weeks later that the consul was able to have a British vessel touch at the port and convey the body to Gibraltar.[20]

Consul Carlton Bailey Hurst recounts the equally interesting case of an American buyer who died as a result of an appendicitis operation performed by a wholly inexperienced surgeon in Venezuela. The father was notified and cabled asking that his son's remains be sent to Paris. Consul Hurst asked permission of the Civil Governor and waited three weeks for

[19] Richard F. Boyce, "The American Consul in Action and What It Means to Be One," *Christian Science Monitor* (October 22, 1929).
[20] John W. Foster, *The Practice of Diplomacy* (New York, 1906), 228.

a reply. When it came it asked him to put his request in Spanish. When this was done he was informed that before the body could be removed, the doctor's fee of five thousand dollars for the operation and five thousand dollars more for the embalming would have to be paid. The consul protested vigorously at these extortionate demands, but as the governor and doctor were apparently leagued together, the best arrangement he could get was the reduction of the total bill to $5,000.[21]

Quite often the death of an American will take place at sea and the question comes up as to the disposition of the body. According to Vice Consul Milton K. Wells, formerly stationed at Gibraltar, bodies are quite often disembarked there, embalmed by the port doctor and shipped to the United States. The consul signs an identification certificate guaranteeing that the accompanying documents are authentic: a certificate of death signed by the doctor and captain of the boat; a certificate by the port surgeon covering the embalming; a certificate by the port doctor that the body had been placed in a lead coffin hermetically sealed; and the original bill of lading. The United States *Regulations* require that in the sealing and certifying to the contents of caskets containing the remains of deceased persons which are to be shipped to the United States the facts stated in consular certificates attached must be adequately investigated and personally known to the signing officer. The sealing at times is not a pleasant task when done seven floors down in the hot hold of a vessel by the light of a candle in an atmosphere reeking with the smell of the cargo and the sweat of the stevedores.

Disposal of the Effects of Deceased Americans.   An interesting case was presented to Vice Consul William D. Moreland, stationed at Antwerp, when a telegram from New York to the Consulate General asked that the property of an American girl who had disappeared at sea from a Red Star liner be held. Upon investigation it was found that the officials of the steamship company had already taken over the effects without notifying the American Consulate. A protest was made and the officials sent an inventory and agreed to turn over the effects if their responsibility was thereby ended. This was not acceptable and the matter was further complicated by letters to the company from the father and other heirs in France demanding the effects. The company thereupon turned over the effects to a Belgian court which held that the effects were to go to the heirs. This decision left the original American claimants outside of the settlement.

One of the numerous rules which consuls are enjoined to observe in the settling of an estate requests that all keepsakes, heirlooms, jewelry, mementos, and similar personal effects of the deceased be retained for delivery to relatives in the United States. A story is told of a consul who

21 Carlton Bailey Hurst, *The Arms above the Door* (New York, 1932), 126.

had occasion, in taking charge of the effects of a cultured, well dressed American accidentally drowned abroad, to force open a little trunk that had belonged to the dead man. It contained a first-class set of burglar's tools.[22]

Notarials. Another administrative function assigned to consuls is the performance of notarial services. Until the passage of the Act of April 5, 1906, consular officers performed notarial services at their own option and were permitted to retain the fees prescribed. As a result some of the consular posts in large cities were extremely lucrative and much sought after by political henchmen. Many tales have been told of fat fees and it has been estimated that the Consul Generalship at London, which paid $6,000 a year and fees, brought in to its fortunate officer in charge as much as $75,000 in a peak year. Former Consul Lorin A. Lathrop tells of a consul who, upon receiving an official circular which added a new service to be performed, declared it would add $3,000 to his salary. Upon being asked how he knew the service was notarial, the consul replied: "Every fee is notarial until you're told it ain't." [23] Notarial services still bring in fees, but they go to the Treasury of the United States, instead of into the pocket of the consul.

The Federal laws of the United States require every consul when an application is made to him "to administer to or take from any person any oath, affirmation, affidavit or deposition, and to perform any other notarial act which any notary public is required or authorized to perform in the United States." [24] Such acts, to be valid, must be certified by the consul under his hand and seal of office.[25] Although these services are required to be performed only for citizens of the United States, the *Regulations* permit the consular officer to perform them at his option for nationals of friendly powers.[26] A consular officer is not permitted to perform notarial services outside of his district.

Foreign Service Officer J. Rives Childs tells of an American citizen appearing at the American Consulate in Cairo with a copy of his father's will which bequeathed to him several hundred thousand dollars. The will had seemingly been probated in a Pennsylvania court. The individual who held an important position in a local commercial enterprise requested that his signature be legalized. The consul signed the document and affixed the red seal of the United States attesting that the heir had appeared before him personally and had sworn that the copy of the will

[22] Frederick Simpich, "Consul Is Uncle Sam's Trouble Man," *New York Times* (January 24, 1926).

[23] Lorin A. Lathrop, "The Recollections of a Consul," *Saturday Evening Post,* 177 (April 4, 1925).

[24] 34 *U. S. Statutes at Large,* 101.

[25] *Revised Statutes at Large,* Sect. 1750.

[26] *Regulations* (April, 1945), Sect. X, 5, Note 9.

was a true one. The fellow who was an imposter assigned his rights under the will for a hundred thousand dollars cash to some wealthy Egyptians and then disappeared. It was subsequently learned that the court was nonexistent. The validation by the Consulate had unfortunately seemed to validate the document instead of merely the signature.[27]

One of the most interesting cases of notarial services in consular annals occurred in connection with the taking of the Vice Presidential oath by William Rufus King. Mr. King, after his election, had gone to Cuba for a rest and was unable to return to Washington in time for the inauguration. An Act of Congress permitted him to take his oath of office in Cuba, and the American Consul at Havana journeyed out to the sugar plantation near Matanzos where Mr. King was staying and there administered the oath of office.[28]

The Service of Legal Processes.   Although the Consular Regulations do not authorize the consular officer to serve legal processes abroad, nevertheless the Act of July 3, 1926, provides for the service by American consuls of subpoenas issued by Federal courts in special cases of contempt. Such subpoenas may be served to compel American citizens temporarily residing abroad to testify or to serve as witness at a criminal action at home when it is deemed essential by the Attorney General or his assistants. The Walsh Act of 1926 was passed to compel the American citizens O'Neil and Blackmer to return to the United States in order to testify in the famous Teapot Dome oil case. Subpoenas had been issued in 1925, but when served with letters rogatory in French courts, the two Americans refused to return. Authorized by the new law, United States Consul at Marseilles, Bernard F. Hale, sought to subpoena Mr. Blackmer on the train between Monaco and Nice, but the much wanted oil man refused to accept the service. The American Consul thereupon confiscated Mr. Blackmer's passport. Mr. Blackmer again refused a subpoena which was subsequently served upon him in Paris.[29]

An order of a court in the United States sometimes appoints a consul as a commissioner to take testimony. Former Consul Cornelius Ferris tells of a case where most elaborate hearings were required lasting several weeks and where the fees accrued amounted to something like $1,600.[30] Vice Consul John J. Coyle recently completed an open commission to take testimony which exceeded 500,000 words at the London Consulate General; the consul fees and public stenographer charges were over $5,000. In the notorious Factor case where a number of English citizens

[27] J. Rives Childs, *American Foreign Service* (New York, 1948), 120-1.

[28] Hurst, *op. cit.*, 308.

[29] *New York Times* (April-June, 1927).

[30] Cornelius Ferris, "National Duties of American Consuls," *American Foreign Service Journal,* XI, 186 (April, 1934).

tried to prevent the Chicago bank from paying out funds from Factor's account, the official fee amounted to $21,000.

The work of taking depositions is sometimes difficult due to the hostility between lawyers and the unwillingness of witnesses to testify. Bankers and lawyers are rarely willing to testify regarding the affairs of their clients. Sometimes, however, the relations between the consulate and the parties become exceedingly cordial during a long deposition case. Consul Charles C. Broy of London tells of an admiralty case where the American lawyer, representing an English company in San Francisco, came to London and spent weeks in the long drawn out commission hearing. When the lawyer returned to the United States he not only wrote a letter of thanks to Mr. Broy, but also sent a copy to the Department of State expressing his hearty appreciation of the excellent coöperation that he had received.

Consul General Hurst tells of an interesting deposition case which concerned Johann Strauss, the Waltz King. A New York musical impresario had an arrangement with Strauss whereby his music was copyrighted in the United States under the American's name as owner. The royalties were received by the American, a commission deducted and the rest forwarded to Strauss. But upon Strauss' death the New Yorker stopped payments on the ground that Strauss had given him the rights for the payments already made. Suit was brought against the impresario and the testimony in Vienna was taken by Consul General Hurst.[31]

Services to Veterans. Another consular function whose exercise involves much detailed administration is that of rendering aid to veterans, their relatives and dependents abroad. The United States *Regulations* state that consuls are "charged with the general supervision of Veterans' Administration activities within their districts and in the absence of special instructions shall promptly submit reports of information received regarding such activities which may assist the Veterans' Administration to discharge efficiently its responsibility to its beneficiaries who reside in foreign countries." [32]

Some of the complex veterans' cases require consular investigations of alleged losses of checks, and the fraudulent reception and cashing of checks, necessitating a voluminous and detailed correspondence with the Treasury Department, the local authorities and the beneficiaries. The adjustment of veterans' fiscal relations with the Administration, arrangements for medical or mental examinations, and hospitalization of diseased veterans requires much patience and time. The work connected with veterans after World War I was particularly heavy in the Consulates at War-

[31] Hurst, *op. cit.*, 80.
[32] *Regulations* (April, 1945), Sect. IX, 9.

saw, Naples, Rome, and Athens. At Warsaw during the period immediately after World War I the Consulate General delivered between five and six hundred checks each month to beneficiaries residing in Poland.[33] This service, as well as that of authenticating claims and witnessing the signature which the veteran files in making application for compensation, is free of charge.

Consular duties in regard to the administration of veterans' affairs started during the First World War when many soldiers awarded a portion of their compensation to their parents abroad. To the ten dollars allotted by the soldier to his wife, parents, or children from his pay of thirty dollars the Government added an equal amount. These men were also persuaded by the Government to take out war risk insurance.

When the war was over the Government began awarding compensation to parents, wives, and minor children of those dead, disappeared or wounded. The first problem was one of identification of the proper person to receive the checks, questionnaires being required from both veterans and dependents for this purpose. Identification having been ascertained, the next problem was to see that the veteran or his beneficiary received his check; this was complicated by the fact that many of these people lived in small communities where no local post offices existed and there was only rural delivery.

In Greece during 1934 between 250 and 300 veterans were getting regular disability compensation and between 400 and 500 parents, wives, widows, and children were receiving death compensation through American consular officers. Approximately 1,200 checks covering $50,000 a month were distributed. Although at first these services were performed by the legations and embassies, all veterans' administration abroad since 1931 has been concentrated in the consulates because of the requirement that consuls must authenticate the claims submitted.

World War II changed the character of this work and increased it. The seventy-sixth Congress passed a law known as the Servicemen's Readjustment Act—Public Law 346—which added materially to the work done abroad for veterans by consular officers. Inasmuch as numerous foreign educational institutions in all parts of the world were approved for training of veterans much of the checking up on the enrolled veterans had to be done by consular officers. The work was so arduous that special consular attachés were assigned to a number of posts where the work was particularly heavy, such as London, Paris, Rome, Geneva, and Mexico City. For example, John N. Hayes was assigned in May, 1947 as Consular Attaché for Veterans Affairs in Geneva, Switzerland. Among specific duties he had to determine the eligibility of the veterans to educational training and subsistence allowances, he had to investigate and approve institutions

---

[33] Carr, *op. cit.*, 5.

for education and training and see to it that the veterans met the educational requirements of the institution in which they had enrolled. There were as many as 540 veterans in educational institutions in Switzerland at one time and on December 1, 1950, 363 men in training of which 189 were studying medicine. Hayes estimated that during the fiscal year 1950 some $700,000 was expended in Switzerland for veterans training.

Inasmuch as the Veterans' Administration requires that the student must show progress every four months and European universities usually have all examinations at the end of the year it is often difficult to get satisfactory coöperation. Also the student desirous of telescoping his work or wishing to work only in one specialized field needs a sympathetic consular attaché.

Marriage of Nationals. Among the many duties of a consular officer, the services rendered to nationals unquestionably furnishes the greatest diversity of interesting cases. Space alone prevents the citation of more than a few. The consul is often called upon to answer inquiries regarding local marriage regulations and in many cases to help cut official red tape which delays the culmination of a sudden courtship. The consul if requested may permit the marriage ceremony to be performed in the consulate. Although an American consul has no longer authority to celebrate marriages in a Christian country between citizens of the United States, he may act as a witness and in such cases he gives to each of the parties a certificate of the marriage and sends in a certificate to the Department of State.[34]

One of the most interesting instances of consular services in the performance of a marriage ceremony occurred some years ago in a southern European country. A woman came into the Consulate and asked the girl clerk the name of a good obstetrician. A few days later the father-to-be came in to see about the indorsement of a personal check. It finally developed that the two were having a baby but were not married. Although the Consul suggested that the baby might appreciate being born legitimately, the prospective parents seemed to manifest no interest in the matter. However, just before the happy event, the two young Americans decided to have a ceremony performed. But upon visiting the Consul to tell him of the change in plans, they were informed that the complicated requirements of the local law could not be met in the time left.

In this case the Consul felt considerable responsibility and agreed to do all in his power to reduce the formalities. He was successful but on the morning of the ceremony the man arrived late with the news that his wife was already in labor at the hospital. It was now necessary to get dispensation of the King's attorney to perform the ceremony outside of the town

[34] *Regulations* (October, 1946), Sect. XIII.

hall. This could only be done after a doctor from the public health service had examined the patient to be certain that such procedure was necessary. The Consul was equal to the occasion. He rushed the request through, and within an hour the Consul, the civil officer, the clerk and the marshal with the huge civil registry books appeared at the hospital and between the labor pains the ceremony was performed.

Locating Lost Articles.   Another form of assistance to nationals which the consul is constantly called upon to perform is to locate lost articles. Americans are notably careless about their luggage and when lost the consul is the one hope of the tourist. An American woman left her hand-bag in a Paris taxi while en route to a station. She reported the loss to the Consulate which located it in the lost articles department in the prefecture of police. It was recovered and forwarded. Another American traveler after taking the train for Pau found that he had forgotten to get his suitcase out of the check room at the Quai d'Orsay. He sent the baggage check to the Consulate General and his suitcase was sent on.

The author once left a new Borsalino hat in a hotel in Rome. He discovered the loss after he had driven some fifty kilometers en route to Venice. He stopped to telephone but as it was Sunday the Consulate General was closed. He left word at the Embassy to send the hat on to Venice. However the hat got to Venice only after its owner had gone on to Florence. It followed him to Florence but when again it arrived too late it was sent back to Rome. The Consulate then sent it to the boat but again it missed connections. Once more returned to Rome the Consulate packed it and requested a Foreign Service officer passing through on his way to the States to take it and deliver it personally. It was put in a wooden box and when the homecoming Consul arrived in New York he mailed the hat to its owner in Washington, D. C., where it arrived in excellent shape.

Nationals Involved in Customs Infractions.   Another favorite practice of American tourists which gets them into trouble is smuggling forbidden or highly dutiable articles across frontiers. In such cases where the violation of the law is deliberate the consul can do nothing, but when a mistake has been made he can often help. An American girl was stopped at the Rumanian frontier and asked whether she had any cigarettes or briquets. She thought briquets were firearms and replied in the negative. When the customs officials examined her luggage they found seven cigarette lighters in her suitcase. They took her to the station and found another. They forced her to spend the night in the station and pay a fine of 1,000 leis for each lighter. In her excitement she left her fountain pen in the customs office. The Consul General took up the case and forwarded her fountain pen and secured a promise from the officials that they would refund and send on the fine collected. At another time an American student who tried to smuggle a thousand American cigarettes into France was fined 800 francs. The American Consul on the plea of the boy's ignorance was able to have this reduced to 100 francs.

Services to Tourists. American women frequently have difficulties with shopkeepers and dressmakers and the consul is called in to obtain an adjustment. For example, an American woman touring in Europe bought a fur coat in Paris. When she received it she was not satisfied but the firm refused to do anything about it. She appealed to the Consulate General, the owner of the firm was sought and he immediately agreed to reduce the price or make a new coat. In another case where a lambskin coat was found full of defects after delivery the Consulate succeeded in getting a refund of 7,000 francs, the full amount paid.

American tourists quite often get into altercation with hotelkeepers and invoke the aid of the consul. A landlady in an Edinburgh hotel proposed to turn out unceremoniously two American girls because they kept late hours. The Consul was able to postpone the ejection until other arrangements had been made. An artist who decided to leave his hotel in Paris for a cheaper one paid his bill and informed the proprietor. The proprietor became angry, insisted upon the American staying and finally assaulted him seriously. The Consul not only obtained the artist's effects, but helped him begin suit for damages, and had the hotel blacklisted.

An amusing case of inverse protection occurred in a certain European city when the major-domo of a first class hotel came to the Consul General in great haste and trepidation and asked that he be allowed to explain an unfortunate incident before the arrival of two irate American women who were on their way to demand that he be dismissed. This woman and her daughter had asked for separate rooms and in showing them to their rooms he had thought the daughter gave him a knowing wink. When he went up to her room later he quickly realized his mistake and came to explain to the Consul. The mother and daughter appeared soon afterwards, much excited, and demanded that the Consul secure the immediate dismissal of the major-domo. The Consul calmed them down and promised to take vigorous action. They departed satisfied and the Consul, after finding that the man had an excellent record and that he gladly promised never to let such a thing happen again, dropped the case.

Miscellaneous Services. One of the most useful services performed by American consulates in all parts of the world is the receiving and forwarding of visitors' mail. In large centers where the tourists come in great numbers a miniature post office is set up. The mail room in the Paris Consulate General handles thousands of pieces of mail annually for American tourists. It has been estimated that an average of about 4,300 pieces of un-official mail are received at the Consulate General in London each year for private individuals.

Consuls are also called upon constantly by enthusiastic stamp collectors to furnish cancelled postage stamps of the country in which they are sta-tioned. Most consulates make every effort to comply with these requests. The letters come from people of all ages and many youngsters have begun this hobby through the aid of a consul. In some consulates every cancelled stamp is taken off the envelope by a clerk and then in periods of spare time small collections are prepared all ready to be sent in response to the requests which will soon come in.

Thousands of telephone calls are answered as to the names of good shops, hotels, dressmakers, florists, doctors, dentists and masseurs. Which museums should be visited and which wines should be drunk? Would the consul recommend a good night club which was rather spicy but not vulgar?

The consul is even expected to warn his nationals against confidence men. Consul General Hurst declares that so many Americans were taken in by the Spanish confidence game that a printed form was prepared to warn everyone who inquired. Even when warned, some paid no attention to the Consul's advice. One of those who spurned the Consul's warning was later found robbed of all his belongings and with a stiletto wound in his breast.[35]

Fabulous estates held by the Bank of England or the Court of Chancery only awaiting the missing heir, have been a lure to many Americans to waste thousands of dollars on a wholly mythical pot of gold. The famous Drake Estate Case is perhaps the most notorious example of this type of swindle. The allegation is made that Sir Francis Drake left a vast amount of money which was confiscated by Queen Elizabeth because no heir was discovered. Thousands of Americans have been inveigled into putting money into this scheme and over a million and a quarter dollars collected from them. In spite of the fact that one of the leading swindlers using this scheme was deported from England for defrauding Americans and later sentenced to ten years in Leavenworth, his confederates still ply their game. The Consulate General in London receives so many inquiries re-garding mythical estates that an elaborate form letter has been prepared exposing the swindle.

Shortly after V-J Day 1945, James Triolo, Vice Consul in charge of the U.S. Consulate at Medellin, Colombia, was asked by the Commanding General of the Caribbean Defense Command, Balboa, Canal Zone, to make arrangements to house, feed, and if possible, provide entertainment for 100 American young women each weekend for five weeks. The week-

[35] Hurst, *op. cit.*, 218.

end excursions were to provide short vacations for all the Canal Zone U.S.O. female volunteers who had worked uninterruptedly for months with the U.S. troops en route to the Pacific Theater of War.

Fortunately, an attractive modern tourist hotel had just been completed in Medellin, and the Vice Consul was able to arrange food and lodging at a substantial discount in the nearly empty hostelry. At his suggestion, the Mayor enthusiastically organized a reception committee which worked with the Vice Consul in formulating plans for the visits. The Automobile Club put several private cars at the disposition of the women and a full program of social events including receptions, visits to private homes, sporting events, and dinner dances was arranged.

The governor, mayor, consular corps, provincial and civil officials, many of the American colony and a police band were on hand at the airport with the Vice Consul to welcome the first contingent. All five groups were delighted with the hospitality tendered them and, in turn, made a uniformly excellent impression. The press called them "Las Sobrinas de Tio Sam" (The Nieces of Uncle Sam) and the Colombian people took them to their hearts. Here was a striking example of the Foreign Service acting as catalyst in a broad and mutually pleasant experiment in international friendship.

Ridiculous Requests for Services.   As might be expected, some requests for services are so extreme as to be ridiculous. A certain California author who was writing a book on France sent the Consulate General in Paris a questionnaire which would have taken weeks of intensive research to answer. These are a few of the questions which he wished answered: "Was M. Pol, le charmeur d'oiseaux in the Jardin de Tuileries still carrying on his pleasant occupation in 1874?" "What weather pervaded during Yuletide at Bordeaux in the years 1864, 1865, 1866, 1874, and 1875?" "What was the approximate temperature?" "Did it snow?" "Was it heavy?" "Explain the meaning of the word, 'Jacquemenot' which my dictionary does not give."

The board of health of an American municipality requested Consul Horstmann to investigate the use of a mask over the head of the ox which was used in Munich slaughter houses to prevent the ox from seeing the man with the axe. He was also to state whether the living oxen saw the others killed, whether anything was done to alleviate the pain in butchering and whether he thought that the ox was conscious of what was going on about him and was affected by the smell of fresh blood.[36]

An American student in Milan who was living with other girl students in a sort of hostel felt that they were always talking about her. She came to the Consulate and asked the Consul if he would please give her a certifi-

[36] G. Henry Horstmann, *Consular Reminiscences* (Philadelphia, 1886), 57-8.

cate of virginity. A fond mother in a Central American republic approached the Consulate General to protest the departure of a young American allegedly to go to war but in truth to avoid the obligations entailed by having violated the honor of her young daughter.

But let us conclude with the request from a western professor to a consul in Antofagasta for a cane made from wood indigenous to the district. In this case a check for ten dollars accompanied the request. As the region was mostly barren desert, however, Consul George D. Hopper regretted his inability to fulfill the request and sent back the check. Not to be denied, the professor sent a second and third request, the last time enclosing twenty dollars. The Consul finally made a trip up into the Andes, climbed a cliff ninety feet above the trail, fainted before he reached the root which he had spied, and suffered for weeks afterwards. The guide, however, got the root, which was packed and forwarded with the check to the insistent collector. Consul Hopper waited in vain for a letter of thanks.[37]

[37] G. D. H., "What a Consul Does," *American Foreign Service Journal,* VIII, 290 (July, 1931).

20

Citizenship, Passport, and Visa Services of Consular Officers

Registration of Nationals. The national laws of many states impose upon citizens temporarily or permanently living abroad the obligation of registering at the nearest national consulate. The French ordinance of 1833 provided that Frenchmen living abroad who wished to be assured consular protection must after proving their nationality inscribe their names in a register maintained for this purpose in the office of the consalute.[1] The German law of 1867 required every German consul to carry a register of all German nationals living in his district who applied to him for this purpose.[2] British *Consular Instructions* state that it is the duty of His Majesty's officers abroad to do all in their power to encourage all British residents within their districts to register.[3]

The United States *Foreign Service Regulations* provide that principal consular officers shall keep at their offices a register of persons residing in their several districts who submit satisfactory evidence of American citizenship and shall invite all persons in their districts who claim American citizenship to make the necessary applications for registration. The latter provision places a definite responsibility upon the consul to ascertain the names and addresses of persons claiming American citizenship in his district and to invite them to register. He is advised to point out that such registration provides a valuable record of citizenship and reference in case the need for protection arises.[4]

The United States Government is not officially interested in visitors or transients and although some consulates keep a register for all Americans who call, the majority do not wish tourists to register unless they are in some way connected with the Government or its work. However, if any person representing the United States Government in any capacity goes

[1] A. de Lapradelle et J. P. Niboyet, *Repertoire de droit international* (Paris, 1895), V, 85.
[2] A. H. Feller and Manley O. Hudson, *Diplomatic and Consular Laws and Regulations* (Concord, 1933), I, 552.
[3] *Ibid.*, 205.
[4] *Regulations* (May, 1945), Sect. XXI, 3.

abroad it is extremely advantageous for all concerned that he notify both the diplomatic and consular offices of his arrival.

A case came to the author's attention some years ago which caused considerable embarrassment to Consul Claude Guyant at Lima, Peru. An American rifle team consisting largely of Army men was sent down to participate in an international contest. Mail for the various members of the team came to the Consulate as well as numerous inquiries and invitations, but the officer in charge of the rifle team failed to notify the Consulate either of his arrival or address. Inasmuch as it was not the place of the consul to seek out the team, the writer, who happened to have become acquainted with the captain of the team, suggested that it was customary for visiting heads of such missions to pay their respects to the consul as well as to the ambassador. He hastened to do so and expressed his appreciation for the suggestion.

In countries where extraterritorial privileges still existed, the requirements for registration of nationals in their own consulates were more exacting. Consul Charles H. Albrecht, former American Consul at Bangkok, reported that prior to 1870 all American citizens in Bangkok had to register at the Consulate within ten days after they became residents in Siam or they would not be regarded as citizens of the United States. After 1870 a penalty of $20 fine or imprisonment of not more than five days was added.[5]

Inasmuch as the Department of State receives from various sources numerous requests for information regarding the number of Americans resident abroad, consular officers are instructed to send in such information as they can obtain upon special blanks furnished by the Department. All Americans who have been resident abroad for approximately one year are regarded as permanent residents for this classification.

Registration of Births.   Consular officers are required upon request to record the birth of American children abroad. The *Regulations* instruct them to impress upon American citizens resident in their respective districts the desirability and importance of a prompt registry of such births. In performing this duty the consul records the name and sex of the child, the date and place of birth, the names and residence of the parents, and any other facts which will help to establish fully the identity and citizenship of the child. Before recording the birth of a child consular officers must require positive proof that the father or mother is an American citizen. Either a valid passport or a certificate of registration is regarded as satisfactory proof.[6]

At the time of registration the consul is instructed to notify the parents,

[5] C. H. Albrecht, "Penalties for Non-Registration of Americans," *American Foreign Service Journal*, III (July, 1926), 234.

[6] *Regulations* (May, 1945), Sect. XIII, 6.

if both are American, that at the age of eighteen the child, if he continues to reside outside of the United States, must record his intention of becoming a citizen at an American consulate and must take an oath of allegiance upon attaining his majority. If either parent is an alien, according to the provisions of the law of May 24, 1934, the child will be divested of his American citizenship unless he resides in the United States at least five years continuously immediately prior to his eighteenth birthday.

A few states authorize their consular officers to assist in the naturalization of aliens. For example, a Russian consul is authorized to accept declarations of persons who desire to become citizens of the U.S.S.R.[7] France, Belgium, Spain, and Holland authorize consuls to receive in so far as their national laws permit declarations looking towards assuming or relinquishing the nationality of the state that they represent.[8]

Citizenship. Although the United States does not authorize its consuls to take declarations of naturalization, it is essential that the consular official be thoroughly familiar with the laws governing citizenship in the United States in order that he may perform properly his duties of protection and issuing of passports. According to the Nationality Act of 1940, it is provided that when a naturalized citizen of the United States shall have returned within five years to the foreign state from which he came, or shall have taken up permanent residence in any other state, it shall be considered prima facie evidence of a lack of intention on the part of such person to become a permanent citizen of the United States and in the absence of countervailing evidence his certification of naturalization may be canceled as having been obtained by fraud. It is the duty of the consul to report such persons within his district, and he is responsible for deciding whether a report of fraudulent naturalization should be made. In making his decision the Foreign Service officer considers such factors as whether the person still owns property in the United States, has members of his family there, pays taxes there or on the other hand owns property abroad and exercises political rights and duties abroad. If the person insists that he is an American national, he must be given every reasonable opportunity to prove his contention.[9]

Since January 13, 1941, a native born or naturalized American national loses his American citizenship if naturalized abroad, or by taking an oath of allegiance to a foreign state, serving without permission of his Government in the armed forces of a foreign state, holding a political position or voting in a political election in a foreign state, or making a renunciation of nationality before an American diplomatic or consular officer. Deserters and traitors are also included in this category.

[7] Feller and Hudson, *op. cit.*, II, 1206.
[8] de Lapradelle et Niboyet, *op. cit.*, V, 168.
[9] *Regulations* (March, 1946), Sect. XXI, Notes 12-17.

Since October 14, 1945, a naturalized citizen loses his nationality by residing two years in the state of which he was formerly a national if he acquires the nationality of that state by the operation of its laws, or by residing three years in the state of which he was formerly a national, or five years in any other state. However the provisions of the act do not apply to persons residing abroad in the employ of the United States Government or who receive compensation from the United States on account of disability in its service. Other provisions nullifying the presumption of expatriation permit persons 65 years of age and over to reside abroad without losing their citizenship if they have lived twenty-five years in the United States subsequent to naturalization, or those residing abroad because of ill health, or those representing American firms, religious, scientific, or educational organizations. A naturalized citizen may also attend a foreign university without losing his citizenship providing residence abroad does not exceed five years. A few other more technical requirements might be mentioned but the Foreign Service officer must be familiar with every provision of the nationality laws of the United States so that bona fide citizens will be protected and others be reported promptly to the Department of State.[10]

The burden of proof is upon the applicant, who must present affidavits and other evidences of the circumstances to make valid his claim under the rules laid down. Mere assertions, even under oath, will not be accepted by the consul as sufficient. For example, if the naturalized citizen declares that he resides abroad as the representative of an American firm, he should be able to show a contract with the firm, or a salary check or a letter from the firm, and he must prove that the firm does a certain amount of business abroad. Thus a naturalized German-American theatrical agent representing several American circuits in Berlin unable to show any bookings could not retain his citizenship for a period longer than two years. On the other hand Karl von Wiegand, who was engaged in Europe as the representative of American newspaper interests, was ruled as not having expatriated himself by his sojourns abroad. If the naturalized citizen is staying abroad for his health, he must submit a medical certificate proving that the treatment that he obtains abroad is better than he could receive at home. If study is the motive, a certificate of registration in a university would be sufficient. If engaged in research, affiliation with an organization for research or affidavits from outstanding authorities in the field would be proof of his bona fide purpose.

A naturalized Danish-American missionary who had lived in the United States for many years went to Denmark to collect money for founding a sanatorium. He remained thirty years. For the first ten years he retained his American citizenship as he was on a bona fide mission of American

---

[10] *Regulations,* Chap. XXI, Appendix A, Sects. 401-7.

origin. He then became a free lance and lost his citizenship, and his two daughters, born in Denmark, were not able to enter the United States as citizens.

If the applicant alleges that events beyond his control prevent his immediate return, he must prove this to the consul. Restrictive currency regulations sometimes furnish a legitimate reason. A naturalized German-American woman owned a large apartment house in Berlin. When her agent ceased to send in the rents she went over to see what was the matter. She was caught in the financial crisis, was forbidden to transfer any funds, could not sell the property, and was compelled to live on a pittance in Berlin. Under the circumstances she was granted an annual extension of her passport. Another controlling exigency regarded as a legitimate reason for continued residence abroad is the necessity to take care of a near relative who is ill or an invalid and has no one else to perform this necessary duty. Very often the citizen has come over to see his parents, one of them dies and the other cannot be left uncared for and alone. The consul is not expected to require unnatural conduct of a son or daughter for the sake of preserving his or her American citizenship.

An expatriation case somewhat out of the ordinary was presented to Consul O. G. Ellis in Budapest. An American naturalized citizen was compelled by legitimate professional reasons to reside in Denmark, so that while in Denmark the presumption of expatriation did not arise. Being divorced in Denmark and seeing his two children awarded to his wife, he fled to Hungary with his son. There in order to avoid losing the boy, he became naturalized. His wife also went to Hungary, brought an action against him and won the suit. As a result his Hungarian nationality was cancelled *ab initio*. Believing that he could resume his American nationality since the Hungarian was illegal from the beginning, he came to the American Consulate General for an extension of his passport. Instead, Consul Ellis took up his passport on the ground that he had become expatriated by his own action, in spite of the refusal of the Hungarian state to accept him.

Some cases of expatriation seem to be unduly harsh on the individual concerned—the case of René Felix, for example. Felix was born in Switzerland of a Swiss father and an American mother. He emigrated to the United States in 1940, became a citizen and remained until 1948, when he returned to Switzerland. In 1950 he returned to the United States upon a temporary passport. Unfortunately while in Switzerland he had voted in a local election and when the immigration authorities learned of this, he was declared expatriated. He appealed the case but lost, and after remaining on Ellis Island almost two months was deported.

Citizenship of Married Women. One of the problems which a consular officer often finds difficult to solve is the citizenship of married women.

Until the so-called Cable Act of September 22, 1922, the laws of the United States followed the same principles as those of most foreign nations and provided that a woman takes the nationality of her husband. Since the Act of 1922 and its amendments, and the Nationality Act of 1940, the situation is much more complicated. In substance, the law permits an American woman marrying an alien to retain her American citizenship, and it requires an alien woman marrying an American to make formal application for American citizenship. The matter is complicated by provisions which governed for a short time the special status of an American woman marrying an alien ineligible to citizenship or one who married an alien living abroad.

It should be noted that since the passage of the Act of 1940 an American-born woman living outside the jurisdiction of the United States who lost her citizenship by reason of marriage to an alien before the passage of the Cable Act may be repatriated by applying for and taking an oath of allegiance to the United States.

This is not the place for a discussion of the question of naturalization and citizenship, but a few examples will illustrate the type of case which the consul is called upon to decide.

Mrs. T——, born in the United States, was married in 1927 to a Frenchman and went to France to live. In 1930, when she wished her American passport extended, the presumption of expatriation arose, but inasmuch as the birth of a child prevented a return home within two years, the passport was extended and the trip made. She returned to France and again asked for an extension, claiming that she had to live in France with her husband because of financial reasons and the illness of her husband's parents. As soon as a legacy, then in trust, was available, she intended to go to the United States with her husband and child for permanent residence. In this case the consul approved the new application for an extension, but the Department of State refused the request.

The following interesting case came before United States Consul J. F. Huddleston in Dresden. Mrs. W——, a native American citizen, was married after the passage of the Cable Act to a German. She lived with her husband in Germany until 1924, when she visited the United States. She returned to Germany in 1925 on an American passport dated November 5, 1925, and lived with her husband until she was divorced in 1928. She married another German in 1929 and in 1934 applied for an American passport. In this case, although by the Act of July 3, 1930, an American-born woman living abroad with her husband does not lose her citizenship, Mrs. W—— was already considered to have been under the presumption of expatriation on July 3, 1930, when the new act was passed.

Passports. To Whom Issued.   The present widespread use of passports is essentially a development since World War I. Except in Russia and

Turkey, all Western Europe had eliminated the passport by 1867. France utilized it in 1870, but only for a brief period. Since the First World War, however, the majority of countries require foreigners entering their territories to possess passports properly visaed by their consular officers.

The highest number of passports ever issued by the United States prior to the Second World War was 230,000 in 1930. However, since the end of World War II the numbers have steadily increased with some 268,000 issued in 1949 and over 300,000 in 1950.

The passport today is usually a certificate of the citizenship of the bearer, although there are still a few states which will issue passports to others besides their nationals. For example, the ordinance of October 25, 1833, which is still in force, provides that French consuls are authorized in all cases where the laws and ordinances of the country in which they are established permit to issue passports for France to aliens requesting them.[11] Italy also permits the issuance of passports to foreigners in cases provided for in the regulations.[12] Great Britain, on the contrary, permits British passports to be issued only to British subjects and protected persons.[13]

In the United States, except for very short periods, the passport has always been a certificate of citizenship. Secretary of State Forsythe in 1837 declared that "passports are only granted to citizens of the United States," and Secretary of State Webster in 1843 stated that "applicants for passports are required to furnish this department with proof of citizenship."[14] A slight exception seems to have been recognized in the *Personal Instructions to the Diplomatic Agents of the United States*, issued in 1853, which stated that applications for passports from citizens of other countries "were not regularly valid and should be granted only under special circumstances as may sometimes occur in the case of foreigners coming to the United States."[15]

By an Act of Congress dated August 18, 1856, it was expressly forbidden to issue a passport to any person not a citizen of the United States. An Act of March 3, 1863, however, permitted aliens who had made a declaration of intention to become citizens, and those who were liable to military duty to obtain passports. This privilege endured only a little over three years and was repealed by the Act of May 30, 1866. The privilege was again extended to persons who had made a declaration of intention by the Act of March 2, 1907, under such rules as the Secretary of State might prescribe. The rules adopted by the State Department required a three-year residence as well as a declaration of intention and then limited the passport to a six-months period and for emergency cases only. The privilege was again withdrawn by the act of repeal of June 4, 1920.

11 de Lapradelle et Niboyet, *op. cit.*, V, 135.
12 Feller and Hudson, *op. cit.*, I, 688.
13 *Ibid.*, I, 204.
14 John Bassett Moore, *Digest of International Law* (Washington, 1906), V, 870.
15 Gaillard Hunt, *The Department of State* (New Haven, Conn., 1914), 351.

After the Spanish-American War when the United States obtained certain insular possessions, some provision was required for the issuance of passports to those inhabitants who were not citizens of the United States but owed allegiance to it. The Act of June 14, 1902, covered the situation by providing that "no passport shall be granted or issued to or verified for any other persons than those owing allegiance, whether citizens or not, to the United States." At the present time Hawaiians and the majority of the inhabitants of Puerto Rico, the Virgin Islands, Guam, and American Samoa are American citizens and as such entitled to United States passports. Passports are also issued to certain persons entitled to the protection of the United States who are inhabitants of the Canal Zone, and American possessions.[16]

Passports may be issued to minors unless there is objection on the part of parent or guardian, and children of twelve or more years of age may execute their own application. Ambassador to Italy, Henry White, noted that the State Department had authorized the issuance of a passport to a native-born child two years and eight months of age upon an application executed by the parents of the child. A passport issued to a husband may include his wife and minor unmarried children. Also a woman's passport may include her minor unmarried children.[17]

The consular officer at times has cases presented to him which are very difficult to decide. The case of Mr. E. B. C.—— is an example of the complications which sometimes arise. The applicant for a passport thought he was born in the United States in Danville, Virginia, but had no means of proving it. He was raised in an orphanage in Argentina after the separation of his parents, and in 1917 obtained a clerkship in the American Consulate. Subsequently he went to Paraguay, where he worked for Swift's and later for Wilson's. In 1927 he took a responsible position with the West Indies Oil Company. When he wished to make a business trip to the United States his passport problem arose. Inasmuch as he planned ultimately to take his Argentinian wife and three children to reside permanently in the United States the importance of his American citizenship can be appreciated.

A search was made by the State Department and his father's birth certificate found but not the son's. However since he had never registered for military service in Argentina, had always considered himself an American citizen, and was now an influential member of the American colony, his application for a passport was approved.

By Whom Issued.   Although the issuance of passports is essentially the function of a state's foreign office, the right of diplomatic and consular

---

[16] *Regulations* (May, 1945), XXI, 2, Note 46.
[17] *Ibid.,* Note 7.

officers to issue passports is accorded today in practically all national laws and consular conventions. In the United States, although the first passport seems to have been issued by the Secretary of State on July 8, 1796, no law regulated the issuance of passports until the Act of August 18, 1856. As a consequence not only were passports issued by the Secretary of State, but papers designed to serve the same purpose were issued by the governors of the states and other local authorities and even by notaries public.[18] The American ministers and consuls abroad were often embarrassed by being asked to certify such documents when they were not certain of their authenticity. Shortly before the passage of the Act of August 18, 1856, Secretary Marcy in order to help guard against fraud instructed diplomatic and consular agents of the United States abroad not to acknowledge passports or certificates of citizenship other than those issued from the Department of State.

The Act of 1856 provided that "the Secretary of State may grant and issue passports, and cause passports to be granted, issued and verified in foreign countries by such diplomatic or consular officers of the United States and under such rules as the President shall designate and prescribe. . . ." [19] It also made it a penal offense for anyone else in the United States to issue passports or any other documents serving as passports. The law was amended in 1902 to permit passports to be issued by executive officers of insular possessions of the United States.

From the very beginning the Department of State refused to issue passports to persons abroad, and when in 1810 a Virginia judge sent an application to the Department of State to issue a passport for an American in France, the Department forwarded the paper to the American Minister in Paris and asked him to issue the passport.[20] Although in this early period diplomatic officers sometimes granted passports, for the most part passports were issued abroad by consular officers until the Act of 1856 prohibited a consular officer from issuing a passport in a country where there was a diplomatic agent except in the latter's absence. This practice held until 1896 when consular officers specifically authorized by the Department were permitted to issue them. By the year 1898 about forty consular officers had the specific authority required by the regulations.[21]

It should be noted, however, that passports were issued abroad by diplomatic and consular officers only in cases of emergency. A citizen abroad in need of a passport applied through the nearest diplomatic or consular officer to the Secretary of State. If the delay would entail hardship upon the applicant, however, the diplomatic or consular officer duly authorized

[18] Moore, *Digest, op. cit.,* III, 862.
[19] 11 *U. S. Statutes at Large,* 60.
[20] Moore, *op. cit.,* III, 868.
[21] Gaillard Hunt, *The American Passport* (Washington, 1898), 88.

could issue an emergency passport good for a period not to exceed six months. It was further required that the applicant was proceeding to a country which demanded a passport to enter into its territory.[22]

When the First World War broke, the majority of Americans in Europe were without passports and as the European nations immediately insisted upon the identification of tourists, an emergency situation arose. The Department of State authorized European embassies and legations and then consulates to issue emergency passports to all American citizens who requested them. This authority to consuls was subsequently withdrawn and legations and embassies required to obtain from the applicant unquestionable proof of his identity and American citizenship.[23]

Between World Wars I and II, the issuance of service passports abroad was largely confined to consular officers. For example, the *Regulations* of August, 1930, listed 178 consular posts which might issue passports, whereas only 4 diplomatic posts had such authorization: Tirana, Peiping, The Hague, and Managua. More recent *Regulations* permit practically all diplomatic and consular posts to issue them. For example, the *Regulations* of May, 1945, list 35 embassies, 20 legations, and 144 consular posts having such authority.[24]

Over the course of the years the type of American passport has changed considerably. In the beginning it was a single sheet giving simply the name of the citizen to whom it was issued; later it became a double sheet which gave a description of the bearer; the next form was a double sheet folded into a booklet which gave at first the signature and later the photograph and a description of the citizen to whom it was issued. To prevent falsification, a red book type passport with special paper and markings was adopted. Finally the present green-book with a flexible cover contains the fingerprints of the officer issuing it as well as a signed photograph and description of the bearer.[25] The Foreign Service officer may issue, verify, renew, amend, and cancel American passports in accordance with the *Regulations* prescribed by the Secretary of State.

There are various types of American passports in general use today: diplomatic, special, regular, seamen, and service. The diplomatic passports are issued to ambassadors and ministers, Foreign Service officers, and other persons with a diplomatic status such as military and naval attachés. Special passports are issued to other government officials employed abroad. Regular passports are issued by the Department of State and service passports by Foreign Service officers abroad. Seamen's passports were first issued during World War II, and by May 1, 1945 over 300,000 of this type

---

[22] *Circular Instructions to American Diplomatic and Consular Officers,* April 19, 1907, *Foreign Relations of the United States, 1907,* I, 13-15.

[23] Charles Cheney Hyde, *International Law* (Boston, 1922), I, 694.

[24] *Regulations* (May, 1945), Sect. XXI, 2, Note 4.

[25] Graham H. Stuart, "Safeguarding the State Through Passport Control," *Department of State Bulletin* 1066-70 (June 10, 1945).

had been issued. The rules governing the issuance of service passports are exceedingly detailed so as to safeguard the proper issuance of a passport abroad.[26]

Loss of Passport. Consular officers are instructed to impress upon American citizens that the loss or destruction of a passport is a serious matter which should be reported and explained to the nearest consular officer. Before a new passport may issue, a satisfactory explanation of the loss in affidavit form must be filed and the issue of the lost passport verified by the Department of State or the office which issued it.

Upon occasions the loss of a passport, although tragic to the unfortunate tourist, has its amusing features to the officials. Consul General James B. Stewart tells of such a case happening in Budapest. An American girl in a party of tourists found that her passport had disappeared between the last and present stops on the journey. As her party was to continue its tour in the morning, she was in a predicament. The Consulate at Budapest called the consul at the previous stop and asked him to investigate. He finally discovered what was left of the precious document in the possession of the garbage man of the hotel where the party had stayed. The passport was obtained and despatched forthwith, and a member of the consular staff remained three hours at the General Post Office to get it upon arrival. A little refurbishing and the document was returned to its gratified owner. The threatened expenditure for a cable to the Department, a new passport and visas could now be utilized in a more satisfactory manner.

If a passport is lost through gross negligence, the consular officer may refuse to issue a replacement. A young American governmental official working in Berlin for one of the economic agencies came into the Consulate and asked Vice Consul Lyda Mae Francis to issue him a new passport, as he had lost his. When he explained that he had left his passport in his bag unlocked in his jeep while he went to the opera, she decided that such negligence should be punished and refused to issue a new passport. Since he could travel on travel orders, the passport was not vitally essential. He protested the refusal, but Mrs. Shipley, Chief of the Passport Division, sustained the action of Miss Francis.

A defaced passport is no longer valid and may be taken up by the consular official. A girl brought her passport to the Consulate General in Berlin to get it extended. Vice Consul Francis noticed one page was mutilated and called it to the girl's attention. The girl explained that she had put tape over the line giving her age so that her boy friend would not know that she was older than he. When she tried to pull it off, the sheet came with it. Vice Consul Francis took up the passport and issued a new one, accepting the girl's statement as to her age. When the data reached the State Department, Miss Francis was informed that the girl had made a

[26] *Regulations* (May, 1945), XXI, 2, Notes 8-39.

false declaration regarding her age. Since the girl had gone to Paris, Vice Consul Francis immediately notified the Paris Consul General.

Passport Frauds. The stringent immigration restrictions imposed by the United States since the First World War have made an American passport an exceedingly valuable document. As a result every form of fraud has been attempted to obtain them. Fraudulent birth certificates and naturalization papers have been utilized to prove American citizenship. Passports have been bought from naturalized American citizens and persons born in the United States of alien parents and altered to permit the illegal entrance of the bearers into the United States. The consular offices at Warsaw, Athens, and Naples have been particularly troubled with passport frauds and the consular officials in those offices have become experts in detecting irregularities of every sort.

A certain Franciszek Urban had a complete organization in Warsaw engaged in fraudulent practices of various sorts in connection with the effecting of illegal entry into the United States. One of the commonest practices was to charge high fees for services in assisting American-born Poles who had been brought up in Poland to obtain the necessary passports to enter the United States. In cases where the American Pole had no use for a passport he could sell it to the gang, who would alter it so cleverly that only the most minute examination with a microscope could detect the changes. The Urban gang became so brazen before it was finally broken up that it virtually blackmailed one of the officials of the Warsaw Consulate General.

J. Klahr Huddle, who had served as chief of the Division of Passport Control and for a considerable period as Consul General in Warsaw, emphasized the fact that methods had to be employed in Warsaw in dealing with persons claiming American citizenship which would be wholly uncalled for in the consulates in other large cities such as London or Paris where the emigration pressure was not nearly so great.

The following are typical examples: a supposedly American-born Pole brought both a birth certificate and a baptismal certificate and applied for a passport for return to the United States. His alleged father accompanied him and swore to the child's American birth. The Consulate has found that one of the best methods of uncovering fraud is to question the applicant regarding his relatives. In this case the candidate was unable to reply in a satisfactory manner to questions concerning the relatives of his father in Poland or the United States. The Consulate became suspicious and checked his birth in the United States and his identity and military service in Poland through the local authorities. It was discovered that the applicant had purchased the birth and baptismal certificates from a friend and had persuaded the friend's father to swear to the relationship. The town authorities had even been bribed to issue a false identity card. After the two had been convicted the original owner of the birth certificate made application.

Vice Consul Orray Taft relates the following typical incident. In 1922 an American-born Polish girl obtained a passport on the basis of her birth certificate and went to the United States. In 1928 another Polish girl of the same name obtained an American passport, this time on a baptismal certificate. In 1933 when a third member of the same family attempted to obtain a passport the earlier fraud was discovered. In this case the girl could afford reasonable proof that she had been born in the United States, but it took her exactly fifteen months to convince the Consulate that she actually had been born there.

The Consulate General at Marseilles has had considerable trouble with Armenians who claim American nationality. An Armenian will go to the United States, become naturalized, return to Armenia and get married. Political conditions prevent return, a child is born, and then all but the child massacred. A case related by Consul Charles R. Nasmith concerned the son of a naturalized American Armenian who was able to get back to the United States after his father, mother, and wife were murdered. His younger brother escaped and was brought up by a Turkish woman. The older brother learned of it and went over to bring his brother back with him. The problem of proving the American citizenship of the younger brother was a very difficult one, but was finally accomplished.

Although the passport work in a consular post is not, perhaps, as interesting as some other duties, it is one of the functions which requires unceasing vigilance and care. The Department of State has a very complete file of passport applications and all stray or fraudulent passports and irregular cases are brought to the attention of the consulates which might be concerned. The safe in the Consulate General in Naples has a great collection of fraudulent passports which have been confiscated due to the expert scrutiny of experienced consular officials. In fact upon two occasions the State Department in coöperation with the Italian Government has broken up establishments in Italy engaged in the manufacture of false passports.

Once in a while an American passport is seized by foreign authorities who question the right of one of their former nationals to possess it. The American Consulate General in Istanbul has had several instances of this kind. In such cases the United States always insists upon the return of the document, inasmuch as it reserves the right to itself of taking up or canceling a passport.

Since World War II it has become customary for the police of certain countries to take up a foreigner's passport when he checks in at a hotel and after recording the passport number and the name and address and the profession of the bearer, to return it to its owner. When this practice was followed by Peru in 1924 the United States protested, and it protested again in 1934 when Costa Rica required foreigners to deposit their passports with the captain of the port of arrival.[27] The prevalence of the custom today has forced the United States to accept it as a normal procedure.

Passport Visa Service. Closely associated with the issuance of passports, although of somewhat more recent origin, is the consular duty of granting passport visas. The visa or *visé* is an indorsement indicating that the passport has been examined and is authentic. Usually the visa is affixed in the country where the passport is issued by the diplomatic or consular officer of the country which requires it before the bearer shall be allowed to enter its territory. Occasionally it is affixed at the frontier by officials of the country to which admission is sought. More rarely it may be required from a diplomatic or consular official of the government granting the passport. In this latter case, the procedure is usually called verification.

The United States in accordance with the provisions of the law passed August 18, 1856, provided that whenever a foreign government required the visa of a passport of any citizen of the United States it should be given by the consular officer of the United States at the place where it was demanded.[28] In the instructions to diplomatic agents issued in 1885 and in the consular regulations of 1881 provision was made for verification of passports by consular officers of the place where the verification was sought. If the foreign government refused to acknowledge the validity of the consular visa the principal diplomatic official was authorized to give it. Consular agents were authorized to visé but not to issue passports. It was further provided that no visé should be attached to a passport after two years from its issue.[29]

Present Procedure in Verifying Passports. The most recent *Regulations* provide that when the laws, regulations, or practices make it desirable that an American passport be verified, diplomatic and consular officers are authorized to verify valid American passports by indorsing thereon the word "good" in the language of the country in which the officer is stationed if for use there or in English if for use at a port of entry in the United States and affixing the signature and official seal of the officer.[30]

As a security measure, the Congress passed a law on June 21, 1941, authorizing the President at his discretion to impose rules and regulations governing the entry into and the departure from the United States of all persons, aliens and citizens. A directive of the State Department dated December 16, 1941, required the verification of all American passports by the Foreign Service officer, as a prerequisite to the entry of the bearers of

---

[27] Green Hackworth, *Digest of International Law* (Washington, 1942), III, 441.
[28] *U. S. Consular Regulations* (Washington, 1868), 351.
[29] Moore, *op. cit.*, III, 995.
[30] *Regulations* (May, 1945), Sect. XXI, 2, Notes 65-8.

such passports at a port of the United States on return from a foreign country.[31] As an additional security measure, American seamen were compelled for the first time in history to carry passports.

Certain countries require their nationals when traveling in foreign countries to present their passports to the consul residing there in order to be assured of consular protection. The French law is very specific on this point.[32] Argentina, Germany, Italy, and Japan permit such verification but do not require it.

It would appear as though no requirement had ever been made by the United States that passports of foreigners be visaed until the United States entered the First World War. Assistant Secretary of State Cridler in writing to Consul McGinley in 1898 declared that the legislation of the United States did not require a consular officer to visé foreign passports but that he might do so as a matter of courtesy.[33] Shortly after the United States declared war against Germany in 1917, diplomatic and consular officers were instructed to require aliens seeking to enter the United States to have their passports visaed and the officers were further enjoined to scrutinize the applicants carefully before affixing the visas.[34] This was followed by the executive order of July 26, 1917, issued jointly by the Secretaries of State and Labor, requiring all aliens coming to the United States to bear passports visaed by American consular officers. Before a visa was granted the alien had to fill out a questionnaire giving information as to his antecedents, nationality, residence, occupation, and reason for coming to the United States.[35] The whole project of passports and entrance into the United States was taken care of by an executive order and proclamation issued by President Wilson on August 8, 1918, pursuant to an Act of May 22, 1918, to prevent in time of war departure from or entry into the United States contrary to the public safety.

Although the United States did not require visas on alien passports prior to the First World War, certain other states had for many years required this formality of Americans. In 1889 the Turkish Minister at Washington notified the Secretary of State that passports of travelers visiting Turkey must be visaed by an Ottoman consular officer.[36] The State Department issued a notice in 1901 that all persons entering Russia must have a passport visaed by a Russian diplomatic or consular official.[37] By the beginning of the twentieth century, however, except for countries of the Far East and Near East, both passports and visas had become almost obsolete.

After World War I, however, practically every state required an alien

---

[31] *Regulations* (May, 1945), XXI, 2, Note 64.
[32] Feller and Hudson, *op. cit.*, I, 526.
[33] Moore, *op. cit.*, III, 995.
[34] Hyde, *op. cit.*, I, 702.
[35] *American White Paper,* "European War," No. 2, 702.
[36] Moore, *op. cit.*, III, 997.
[37] *Foreign Relations of the United States, 1901,* 453.

entering its territory to have a passport visaed by its consul. These restrictions and the charges entailed made traveling both onerous and expensive. In fact, the handicap to travel was so great that the League of Nations held two conferences, one in 1920, and another in 1926, to try to eliminate the worst features of the passport nuisance. Although costs have been somewhat reduced, the visa system is still a very burdensome restriction upon travel. According to figures issued by the United States Passport Bureau in 1933 before the United States depreciated the dollar, an American planning to visit Europe and the Near East, stopping in Great Britain, France, Poland, Austria, Hungary, Belgium, Greece, Rumania, Spain, Portugal, Egypt, and Turkey would have to expend $10 for his passport and about $60 for visas.

More recently governments except in countries behind the Iron Curtain have welcomed visitors, particularly those willing and able to spend American dollars. As a result visa fees have been waived reciprocally or have been substantially reduced. As of March 1, 1950, out of fifty-two foreign countries all but fifteen had arranged to waive passport visa fees for Americans traveling abroad. Of these, twelve charge $2.00 or less; of the others, China charges $2.50, France $2.75 and Poland $4.75.

Although the requirement imposed upon American consuls to affix visas on the passports of foreigners desirous of entering the United States was an additional duty, it was not until the new immigration laws were put into effect that the duty became a real burden.

The Alien Visa Control System.   The Act of May 22, 1918, had been extended by the Act of March 2, 1921, and the so-called alien visa control system was inaugurated to keep out revolutionists, anarchists, fanatics, and undesirables of all sorts. A veritable flood of foreign immigrants sought entrance into the United States. In the year 1921 American consuls abroad affixed visas to over 650,000 passports of aliens bound for the United States. It was the duty of the American consul to sift out the undesirables and detect passport and visa frauds. At one port alone 31 fraudulent visas were found upon an America-bound steamer and at another a gang was ferreted out which had placed 390 passports in circulation in one month.[38]

On May 19, 1921, Congress passed the first so-called immigration quota act, a temporary emergency measure which was to stem this tide of aliens eager to escape from the miseries of war-wracked Europe. The law provided that the number of aliens of any nationality that might be admitted should be limited to 3 per cent of the number of that nationality resident in the United States, as determined by the United States census of 1910. This act was extended for two years by the Act of May 11, 1922,

[38] Wilbur J. Carr, "What Your Consuls Do," *American Consular Bulletin* (January, 1922).

and amended to approximately its present form by the Act of May 26, 1924. The latter act changed the quota basis from 3 to 2 per cent and based the quotas upon the census of 1890, instead of that of 1910. Of more importance to the consular officers, it provided a method of selection of immigrants at the source, rather than permitting them to come to the United States and then having them sent back. The United States consulates in all parts of the world where the quotas were to be filled were made responsible for the quota control by means of visas affixed to the immigrants' passports.

Former Vice Consul Raymond Fisher, stationed at London in 1924 when the new system was inaugurated, thus described the situation to the writer:

With the passage of the immigration quota law the office was in a quandary. No new visas had been granted for over six months. There was an ever increasing waiting list. No exact information could be given the applicants for visas and when finally definite word was received from Washington regarding quotas and procedure we had only the scantiest instructions on which to work. Everyone in the office, and there were some thirty of us, turned to, working night and day, taking applications, meeting the thousands of applicants who flocked around Cavendish Square urging them to bring pertinent proof of their nationality and claims. The less doubtful and more urgent applicants were given their visas first. Even then, the next ship brought back nearly half of our applicants from Ellis Island, for during the period of the voyage across new provisions had been added to the regulations.

The Nazi outrages upon the Jews before and during the Second World War made the United States seem an even greater haven for the oppressed than formerly and there was a correspondingly strong pressure upon consular officers to grant visas to permit entrance to the United States. In turn the United States tightened its restrictions somewhat and the Alien Registration Act of 1940 excluded every alien from entering the United States unless he possessed a visa, a reëntry permit or a border crossing identification card.

Passport Visas. Consular officers now make a distinction between a passport visa and an immigration visa. The latter document is issued to all aliens coming to the United States except those technically known as nonimmigrants. The passport visa is applied to the passports of nonimmigrants who comprise (1) governmental officials and those accompanying them; (2) tourists and temporary visitors; (3) aliens in transit through the United States; (4) bona fide alien seamen; (5) aliens doing business between the United States and their country under commercial treaties; and (6) alien representatives, officers or employees of recognized international organizations. When granted to a foreign diplomat or consul, the visa is called a diplomatic visa.

Under the provisions of the Information and Educational Exchange

Act of 1948 an exchange visitor under a designated program whether a student, trainee, teacher, guest instructor, professor or leader in a field of specialized knowledge could obtain a visitor's visa.

The United States is desirous of making it as easy as possible for non-immigrants to enter the United States; to that end consular officials are instructed to show them every possible courtesy and consideration. No unnecessary restrictions are to be placed in the way of granting passport visas promptly to this group. But the consul must take the responsibility for determining whether or not the applicant is entitled to enter the United States as a nonimmigrant. Therefore, he is expected to make a careful examination to obtain all pertinent facts bearing on the true status of the applicant. The burden of proof is on the applicant to show that he has a fixed domicile abroad which he has no intention of abandoning and that he is in one of the groups classed as nonimmigrants.

An interesting example showing that the American consul will do all in his power to aid a nonimmigrant who has a valid reason for visiting the United States was related to the author by Vice Consul Kathleen C. Taylor, who was at that time stationed in Rome. An Italian father was very eager to get a visa for his daughter who had been badly burned and disfigured during the German occupation of Italy during World War II. Relatives in the United States had recommended plastic surgery at a hospital in Illinois where remarkable results had been achieved. Before a visa could be issued it was necessary to get the approval of the Illinois hospital; to persuade the Italian Government to grant a passport to an unaccompanied child, which was contrary to their regulations; and to get the airlines permission for her to travel under the care of the stewardess. Arrangements then had to be made to have the girl properly bandaged and to have her met in New York and then flown to Chicago. Vice Consul Taylor with the aid of the Italian Red Cross and other welfare organizations was successful and the young girl after two years of surgical operations could face the world unashamed.

Temporary Visitors' Visas. In periods of financial depression many persons unable to obtain an immigration visa attempt to obtain a temporary visitor's visa and once in the United States, they feel that it will be possible to remain illegally. As a result consular officials have become very strict in granting nonimmigrant visas. At some ports more than 50 per cent of the applicants for passport visas as temporary visitors are refused. Figures furnished by Vice Consul E. V. Polutnik at Budapest indicated that in the fiscal year 1933 out of 1,010 applicants examined for temporary visits, 788 were refused, a ratio of over 85 per cent. In the fiscal year 1934 out of 503 applying, 344 were refused, that is, over 68 per cent.

As a rule there is no difficulty in obtaining a passport visa for the foreign businessman wishing to go to the United States. He is usually known to the consul personally or through his firm, and the matter is quickly arranged. Once in a while, however, a complaint arises. In 1926 a Bombay stockbroker who suddenly found it necessary to come to the United States on business claimed that it took him two weeks to get a visa from the Paris Consulate General. He was first required to purchase a round-trip ticket. Then he was asked to produce letters from two persons who had known him ten years. Unable to get these, he brought three letters from different banks. But the vice consul still refused a visa. The agent of the American Express Company finally pointed out that the broker's round-trip ticket was not transferable and his passport was finally visaed.[39]

Even very eminent visitors sometimes have difficulties. When Professor Albert Einstein was about to leave for the United States in December, 1932, he found that his visa was being held up. Apparently some organization in the United States objected to his coming and notified the American Consulate General in Berlin that Einstein was a Communist. The great scientist was called to the Consulate and interrogated as to his political beliefs. Becoming incensed at the questions asked, Professor Einstein refused to answer them further, and left the Consulate, declaring he would not go to the United States. However, when he found later that all visitors might be asked such questions he completed the formalities required and received his visa.[40] Some little delay occurred in the Consulate General in London in August, 1933, when certain Jewish professors, exiled from Germany, attempted to obtain visas to come to the New School for Social Research in New York. In this case the State Department gave instructions that the applications be given the utmost consideration.[41]

Bona fide tourists are always welcomed, but the consul has to be certain that the traveler really has the intention of returning. A round-trip ticket is by no means conclusive evidence, nor is a sworn statement. Chicago's Century of Progress Exposition in 1933 was thought to be the *Open Sesame* to America by many aliens but they found that the hard-hearted consul first had to be sure that they had plenty of money to go and come back and then had to be certain that they had a very definite intention of coming back. A wealthy Rumanian who wished to place his son in school in Chicago and also see the Exposition was granted a visa without hesitancy.

On occasions an alien who has applied for an immigration visa and has been refused will apply later for a passport visa. Such a situation strengthens the inference that the applicant is not entitled to nonimmigrant status and the passport visa will not be granted. Vice Consul Shiras Morris while in charge of visa work at the United States Consulate

[39] *New York Times* (May 18, 1926).
[40] *Ibid.* (December 6, 1932).
[41] *Ibid.* (August 12, 1933).

in Marseilles had such a case. A woman applying for a visitor's visa in 1934 was asked if she had ever before applied for either an immigration or passport visa at any consulate and had been refused. She answered in the negative and then swore to her statement. When she was told that the files showed that she had applied for an immigration visa in 1925 she declared that it was her cousin who had applied. When the records indicated that the cousin was born at the same place on the same day and the father had the same name the woman left in disgust.

Foreign Service Officer Robert McClintock when stationed at Panama as Vice Consul found that innumerable people went to the Canal Zone from all parts of the Western Hemisphere thinking that because the United States exercised jurisdiction over the Zone, they were automatically within the United States. It would then be quite simple, they reasoned, to take a boat bound for an American port and go right in without a visa.

A most interesting and rather exceptional passport visa case arose in connection with the visits to the United States of the Count and Countess Karolyi. Countess Karolyi came to the United States in 1924 to lecture, but was taken ill and had to abandon her lecture tour. She sent for the Count to join her, but before the United States Consulate General at London would visa his passport he had to give a pledge not to engage in public political discussions while in the United States. Count Karolyi's counsel protested to Secretary of State Hughes, but the Secretary refused to lift the ban except to permit answers to attacks by Hungarian newspapers.

When the Countess wished to return the following year to carry out her lecture tour the Consulate General in Paris refused to visa her passport. The State Department sustained this ruling and the Countess brought suit for a writ of mandamus in the Supreme Court of the District of Columbia to compel Secretary Kellogg to revise his ruling and permit her to come to the United States to visit friends and complete her lecture tour.[42] Secretary Kellogg insisted on the ban in reply to the petition and an appeal was taken to the Circuit Court. When this Court ruled against her, she dropped the suit.[43] When the Karolyis applied again in 1929, Secretary Stimson permitted them to come in and no restriction was made as regards lectures.

A somewhat similar case arose in 1938 when John Strachey, who had been granted a visitor's visa in the London Consulate General to come to the United States to conduct a lecture tour, was notified upon arriving in New York that his visa had been canceled by Consul General Douglas Jenkins. The reason given by the State Department was that Mr. Jenkins had learned after Mr. Strachey had sailed that he was a member of the

[42] *New York Times* (January 3, 1926).
[43] *Ibid.* (May 16, 1926).

Communist Party. When Strachey appeared before the Federal District Court upon a writ of habeas corpus the Court dismissed the writ thereby upholding the right of cancellation. Upon appeal, this holding was reversed by the United States Court of Appeals thereby prohibiting the London Consulate from revoking the visa.[44]

Immigration Visas. The Immigration Act of 1924 places upon American consular officers abroad the responsibility of keeping immigration into the United States within certain prescribed numerical limits. These restrictions are in addition to the various provisions of the immigration laws which generally exclude the following classes: mentally or physically defective, paupers or vagrants, diseased persons, criminals, polygamists, anarchists, prostitutes and procurers, contract laborers, persons likely to become a public charge, persons previously deported, persons financially assisted to come to the United States, stowaways, children unaccompanied, natives of some Asiatic countries and illiterates.

In the first ten-year period after the passage of the Immigration Act of 1924 American consular officers examined more than three million aliens, issued more than two million immigration visas, issued approximately half a million nonimmigrant visas and collected $24,218,022 in visa fees.[45]

The annual quota of any nationality for the fiscal year is a number which bears the same ratio to 150,000 as the number of inhabitants in the United States in 1920 having that national origin bears to the total number of inhabitants in the United States in 1920, but the minimum quota of any nationality is 100. Under this quota arrangement the countries of Western Europe are favored as against those of Eastern Europe, due to the much longer period that their nationals have been emigrating to the United States. China was first given a quota by the Act of December 17, 1943.[46]

Each quota is under the primary control of a consular quota-control officer and no consul may issue a visa chargeable against a quota unless he has previously received from that officer a definite allotment of quota numbers. For example the quota control office for Italians, no matter where they may be, is Naples. If an Italian in London wishes to go to the United States as an immigrant, he will receive a visa from the allotment of quota numbers allocated to the London Consulate General by the Consulate General in Naples. The quota control officer does not control questions of admissibility or priority of aliens applying elsewhere. He is only responsible for making available numbers for issuance to aliens on

[44] *New York Times* (October 16, 1938).
[45] "The Immigration Work of the Department of State and Its Consular Officers," *Department of State Publication* No. 703 (Washington, 1935), 1.
[46] For the quotas as of 1950 see 22 *Code of Federal Regulations*, 42.316.

the basis of reports received from other consuls and as shown by the recorded demand at his own office.[47]

Quota and Nonquota Immigrants. With respect to their admission into the United States, immigrants are divided into quota and nonquota groups. The quota group is divided into a first preference group consisting of the close relatives of citizens of the United States and skilled agriculturists up to 50 per cent of the quota. The second 50 per cent of the quota is divided into second preference aliens and nonpreference aliens. The second preference group includes children and wives of alien residents of the United States. The nonpreference aliens are those who remain after the first and second preference groups have been granted visas.[52]

Inasmuch as nonpreference applicants must be taken strictly in the order of their priority, consular officers are required to register applicants by some system which will insure correct priority status. The records of registration must be kept in registration books which are placed under lock and key. The record cards are also kept in locked filing cases and all correspondence with prospective immigrants is carefully preserved. In this way the priority status of immigrants is safeguarded against frauds or mistakes.

The nonquota immigrants are certain special classes who may be admitted to the United States at any time regardless of the quotas. Consular officers are required to verify carefully all statements made by immigrants who claim a nonquota classification. The following classes comprise the nonquota immigrants:

1. Unmarried children under 21 years of age, wives, and husbands by marriage before January 1, 1948, of American citizens;
2. Lawfully admitted aliens returning from a temporary visit abroad;
3. Aliens born in Latin American Republics or in Canada, their wives and unmarried children under 18;
4. Ministers and professors, their wives and unmarried children under 18;
5. Bona fide students at least 15 years of age who seek to matriculate in an accredited educational institution in the United States;
6. Women who have lost their American citizenship by expatriation.[48]

Results of Immigration Control. The visa system of immigration control has been extremely successful. The thorough examinations given by consuls to applicants have kept out hundreds of thousands of undesirable aliens with a minimum of inconvenience to the alien. During the ten year period July 1, 1924, to June 30, 1934, consular officers prevented almost

[47] For an excellent detailed explanation of the whole visa control system see Eliot Coulter, "Visa Work of the Department of State and the Foreign Service," *Department of State Publication* No. 3649 (Washington, 1949).

[48] *Handbook, op. cit.,* Sects. 42-208; 42-231.

7,000 criminals, prostitutes, illiterates, diseased, and other excluded aliens from entering the United States.[49]

With the coming of the period of economic depression the provision of Section III of the Immigration Act of February 5, 1917, which excludes from the United States "persons likely to become a public charge" (generally known as the L.P.C. clause) was of great assistance in reducing the number of immigrants admitted. In September, 1930, consular officers were instructed, in view of the generally unfavorable economic conditions, to take particular care that the prospective immigrant should not be admitted if he were likely to become a public charge. In consequence, in the four-year period from July 1, 1930 to June 30, 1934, consular officers withheld immigration visas from 401,564 applicants out of the 799,149 aliens examined.[50]

The rigid enforcement of the L.P.C. clause has added greatly to the mental and physical burden of the American consul's work. Every sort of pressure is put upon him to relax his vigilance. Not only does the applicant insist upon his satisfactory financial status, but his relatives and friends in the United States correspond voluminously to the same effect. Many are able to enlist congressional support, and the zealous consul has to make a water-tight case to prevent a backfire upon the Department.

A few typical instances will indicate the difficulty of the problem. Mr. X comes into the consulate at Glasgow, passes the physical and mental tests and on the whole is a very desirable type. But, although he has over $500 in cash, after paying his expenses to the United States, he has no prospect of a position nor any close friends to aid him, so the consul is forced to refuse him. A woman in Naples with 20,000 lire was kept out of the United States because in spite of these funds it was found that she had gone on relief. Mr. K of Vienna claims to be going to a brother in New York who had promised to support him, and has letters to that effect. But there is no proof that Mr. K's correspondent is his brother, nor that he is financially able to support the applicant, even if he were willing. A young lady, also Viennese, is going out to her uncle who is to support her. In this case the relationship is proved and the uncle's financial status guaranteed by Dun and Bradstreet.

Sometimes the applicant, although refused on several counts, returns again and again to the application desk. Mr. M——, a German Jew, applied with his wife and four children in 1927 at the Berlin Consulate General. He had a clear police record, but his wife was weak mentally. In 1928 a new application showed that the mental record had been cleared, but the family had no sure means of support. The next year there were almost weekly calls, letters from the applicant's father and brother

---

[49] "The Immigration Work of the Department of State and Its Consular Officers," *op. cit.*, 7.

[50] *Ibid.*, 10.

in the United States, letters from congressmen and political bosses, but it now developed that he had flat feet and was unable to earn a living. In 1933 the whole family renewed the application and one daughter was found to be mentally defective and there was still no proof as regards the income of the father and brother. In 1934 when a new police record was demanded it was found the applicant had been convicted of issuing counterfeit money. He confessed to a false statement in the first application and to bribing of a police official to obtain the first record.

The advent of the Nazi regime in Germany stimulated many German Jews, particularly professors, lawyers, and doctors, to emigrate to the United States. As Vice Consul William W. Adams pointed out,—since the German Government allowed a maximum of 2,000 marks to be taken out of the country, unless the applicant had a position in the United States, the liability to become a public charge was almost impossible to overcome. Contracts with hospitals or schools which do not violate the contract labor clause were regarded as sufficient. One case cited by him seemed to indicate there are still gaps in our legislation which was designed to protect American professional workers.

Immigration Frauds. The stringent restrictions imposed upon aliens coming to the United States have stimulated efforts to circumvent the immigration laws. Aliens who have been refused visas will spend to their limit to get into the United States, and not be overly squeamish at the methods employed. One of the instances where a steamship company was found to be implicated in immigration frauds occurred in Athens. It was learned that certain steamship agents were sending aliens illegally to the United States by providing them with fraudulent reëntry permits. The steamship company would purchase valid Department of Labor reëntry permits from persons returning from the United States and then help them obtain nonquota visas. These reëntry permits were sent to Washington for extension, then falsified to permit the illegal entry of an excluded alien. It was claimed that one company had 2,000 of these permits. The Contonis Brothers Company of Athens was the chief offender and when their establishment was finally raided at the instance of Consul General Leland B. Morris, it was discovered that they had an outfit for counterfeiting visas and other United States official documents.

The Urban gang in Warsaw, mentioned earlier, was another notorious group of swindlers which made huge sums of money at the expense of ignorant aliens. They would obtain high fees for assisting Poles to obtain necessary papers when such papers could have been obtained at no cost to the emigrant. They would also persuade the prospective immigrant that an earlier entry could be obtained for him and then send him on a circuitous journey in Europe with no result. American reëntry permits were obtained from returning aliens and the names and pictures changed to suit the immigrant applicant. Community chiefs were bribed to certify to the identity of the changed document. Passports were tampered with, visas were forged and every sort of trick utilized to make money out of the eager immigrant.

In Budapest a former cabinet officer extorted 800 pengoes from a young Jewess who wished to emigrate to the United States. In this case he collected the money on the strength of his alleged influence with the American Consul, which would enable him to obtain visas beyond the yearly contingent. When he failed to keep his promise, a threatened suit succeeded in getting a refund of the money. Consul General James Stewart made it known that the American Consulate General would investigate thoroughly all rumors pertaining to profit in visa matters and when it was learned that a minor official in the Hungarian passport bureau had declared that visas could be easily obtained by the payment of 400 pengoes to the proper person an investigation exposed the falsity of the statement.

William Russell, who worked in the immigration section of the American Embassy in Berlin when those oppressed by the Nazis were so eager to escape to America, tells how the Embassy officials were constantly being offered bribes. Food, wine, and candy were offered as well as various sums of money—one consul found seventeen boxes of expensive candy in a typist's desk—anything to speed up the precious visa required. The pressure was so great that the alien applicants besieged the offices and grabbed the consular officials on the stairways. One old refugee lady was found sitting placidly in the men's room—she couldn't read English.[51]

The ban on the entrance of Communists into the United States is sometimes circumvented. A famous case was that of Hans Eisler, one-time Communist and brother of the better known Communist leader, Gerhardt Eisler. Hans Eisler tried first to get in via Havana and later via Mexico City, but was stopped in both places. His next attempt on September 20, 1940, to cross the border-line at Mexicali was successful because Willis Meyer, the Consul, had failed to see a "stop order" which had gone out to all officials directing them to consult the State Department if Eisler applied for an immigration visa. The case gained additional notoriety since Mrs. Franklin D. Roosevelt had interceded in Eisler's behalf and Ambassador to Cuba, George Messersmith, had refused a permanent visa.

Burden of Consular Immigration Control. The very considerable burden of work imposed upon consular officials to control immigration has been increased by the constant stream of new legislation changing entrance restrictions. For example, the Alien Registration Act of 1940 required the registration and fingerprinting in duplicate of all aliens receiving visas of any kind abroad except those with "official" status. A

[51] William Russell, *Berlin Embassy* (New York, 1941), 31, 74.

departmental order of June 20, 1941, required aliens seeking permanent residence or going as visitors to the United States to submit to the State Department a biographical statement and two affidavits of sponsorship.[52]

An Act of June 29, 1946, subsequently amended, authorized the issuance of visitor's visas to the alien fiancées or fiancés of members of the armed forces of the United States under several limitations such as racial eligibility to citizenship provided they were married within three months of arrival.

The various Presidential directives regarding displaced persons and the Displaced Persons Act of June 25, 1948, amended and extended in 1950, required a vast increase of consular personnel to administer these new regulations adequately. Since this Act originally authorized the issuance of 205,000 immigration visas, later raised to 341,000 under very complicated regulations and for a limited period extending for the majority of cases from July 1, 1948, to December 31, 1951, special consular offices had to be set up in many places to deal solely with these cases.[53] Chief of the Visa Division, Hervé J. L'Heureux, estimated that by January, 1952, some 312,000 visas had been issued to refugees under the Act.

However, the law which has caused the most trouble to consular officers in recent times is the Internal Security Act of 1950 generally known as the McCarran Act. Although aimed at communism and the control of subversive activities the Act insofar as the admission of aliens is concerned excludes every alien seeking to enter the United States to engage in activities prejudicial to the public interest or likely to endanger the welfare or safety of the United States. As interpreted the Act also covers every member of any totalitarian party, past or present, regardless of its name. Hence, former Fascists, Nazis, or Falangistas are clearly excluded regardless of present beliefs. Even though the membership, as in Spain in the Falangista Party, is required by the government for all industries and business organizations automatically the ban holds. In fact, this law practically forbids any Spaniard from entering the United States even as a visitor to carry on business useful to the United States.

The consular officers had to revalidate all visas issued before the Act went into effect even though the individual possessing the visa had made all arrangements for departure to the United States. Since all clearances required a check of deportation cards, lookout cards, Safehaven file and the general consular and embassy files, and if any question remained, an opinion from the Attorney General, the time and effort consumed was so great that emigration from former totalitarian states practically ceased.

For example a German father with nine children after long efforts had obtained visas. He sold his home, bought steamship tickets and got as

[52] Graham H. Stuart, "Wartime Visa Control Procedure," *Department of State Bulletin* (Sept. 10, 1944), 273.

[53] See Coulter, *op. cit.*, 10-12 for a detailed analysis of these requirements.

far as Cherbourg. Revalidation was so slow that he could not remain there so had to return bankrupt to Munich. A German divorcée with one child had married an American who went back to the States. When he got settled she was to follow. Since she was pregnant they wanted the child born in the United States. When all was ready for her departure the Security Act required a revalidation. Since she had belonged to various youth organizations of the Nazis she was now ineligible.

Fritz Molden, son-in-law of Allan Dulles, had been forced into the German Army at the age of fifteen. He organized a resistance movement, served as a carrier between the underground and the Allies, was arrested three times and threatened with execution. After the war he had made several trips to the United States. However, when he wished to make a visit subsequent to the McCarran Act and the consul sought a waiver, the Department refused to permit the son of the owner of *Die Presse* to visit the United States. Fortunately, Minister Donnelly in Vienna, took up the matter directly with Deputy Under Secretary Mathews and a waiver was issued.

Many hundreds of American soldiers who had married German girls with the assurance that they were cleared for immigration found that the Security Act prevented their wives from departing. Since they had usually but three months to make all preparations and then were forced to return, the wives had to be left behind. It was the general opinion in our consulates abroad that the sweeping provisions and rigid interpretation of the Security Act had done inestimable harm to the spirit of friendly relationship that we had striven so hard to inspire. It would seem to be the part of wisdom for the Congress when passing laws which have to be administered abroad to consult in advance those officials made responsible for their administration.

21

Consular Privileges and Immunities

The Representative Character of Consuls. Publicists and authorities have not been able to agree as to the representative character of consular officers, hence there is a corresponding disagreement as to the privileges and immunities which should be accorded them. There seems to be almost unanimous agreement that a consul has a public character. Fauchille declares this position to be "uncontested and incontestable." [1] But when the question is raised as to whether consuls have the same character as public ministers or representatives, although some authorities take an affirmative stand, the majority reply in the negative. [2] There is no doubt, however, but that the consul possesses a status such that he is entitled to enjoy those privileges and immunities which are essential to the performance of his duties.

The position of the United States as regards consular status seems to be that while consular officials have no acknowledged diplomatic character they do possess a certain representative character. Though not having the right to claim the privileges and immunities of diplomatic officials they are under the protection of international law and may claim not only such rights and privileges as have been conceded by treaty, but also such as have been regularly sanctioned by custom and local legislation. Their authority is derived from their commissions and from their exequaturs and such authorization confers upon the consular officer all the rights and privileges necessary to the performance of the duties of the consular officer.

The United States has not always taken this stand. In fact, for many years the United States was disinclined to grant consuls any special status under international law. Secretary of State Jefferson, writing in 1791, declared that "the law of nations does not of itself extend to consuls at all." [3] When in 1835 Secretary of State Forsyth requested an opinion from

---

[1] Paul Fauchille, *Traité de droit international public* (Paris, 1926), I, Part iii, 125.
[2] See the excellent study by Irvin Stewart, *Consular Privileges and Immunities* (New York, 1926), Ch. I.
[3] John Bassett Moore, *Digest of International Law* (Washington, 1906), V, 33.

the Attorney General on the immunities of foreign consuls, Attorney General Butler declared that in his opinion "foreign consuls in the United States are entitled to no immunities beyond those enjoyed by persons coming to this country in a private capacity from foreign nations, except that of being sued and prosecuted exclusively in the United States courts. . . ." [4]

In order to discover just what are the privileges and immunities of consuls it is necessary to examine the laws of the sending and receiving states, treaties which they may have entered into, whether bilateral or multilateral, and the general customs and usages applicable to the subject. Generally speaking, considering the conventional nature of the institution, the principle of reciprocity must be recognized as governing the privileges and immunities of consular officers.[5] They inhere in the institution itself inasmuch as they are essential to the proper performance of consular duties. Since they are not personal in any respect, only the government which the consul represents can waive them.

Right of Protection of Consuls. Although a consul may not claim the absolute inviolability of a diplomatic agent, it is expected that a state will accord him the respect and protection to which his public character entitles him. Unfortunately, when public opinion is aroused against a foreign state a mob is quite likely to vent its wrath upon the unhappy consular representative of that state. During the trial of Sacco and Vanzetti in Boston it was said that practically every American consul all over the world received protests ranging from polite notes to bombs exploded in their doorways.[6]

An even more serious international situation arises when officials of the government which should guarantee protection to the consul are implicated in the assault. An incident of this sort occurred in San Salvador in 1890 when the United States Consulate was violated by the forces of the provisional government and Consul Meyers was subjected to personal indignities and hardships. Secretary of State Blaine insisted upon suitable apologies and in indemnity both for the damage to the Consulate and for the personal injury to the Consul.[7]

American Consul Goldschmidt, at La Guayra, Venezuela, was subjected to a series of insults and threats during the year 1900 by civilians and police officers. Secretary of State Hay finally took up the matter through Mr. Loomis, American Minister to Venezuela, and warned the Venezuelan

---

[4] 1 *Opinions U. S. Attorney General*, 1005.

[5] Francis Wharton, *A Digest of the International Law of the United States* (Washington, 1886), I, 768.

[6] Richard F. Boyce, "The American Consul and What It Means to Be One," *Christian Science Monitor* (October 26, 1929).

[7] Moore, *op. cit.*, V, 51.

Government that threatening the life of the consular representative of a friendly Power could not be treated with indifference or lightly put aside and the Government of the United States would hold that of Venezuela to a strict accountability for any harm or insult that might be wantonly inflicted on Goldschmidt.[8]

Several serious cases of assault upon the persons of American consular officers occurred in the Far East after the Japanese began carrying out their imperialistic policies in China and Manchuria. Vice Consul Arthur R. Ringwalt, while accompanying an American-born Chinese woman in the streets of Shanghai in an effort to find her daughter, was attacked by Japanese volunteers, although he carried a United States diplomatic passport, a *laissez-passer* from the Japanese Consulate, and a pass from the Shanghai Municipal Council. In this case Secretary of State Stimson received an apology from the Japanese Government.[9]

A much more serious incident occurred a month earlier in Mukden when three Japanese sentries beat and badly disfigured Consul Culver B. Chamberlain, who was on his way to catch a train to Harbin, where he had just been assigned. Although his motor car was flying the American flag with the American Consul General's coat of arms prominently displayed, it was stopped and entered by the Japanese sentries, who thereupon violently attacked the Consul, striking him repeatedly in the face. In this case the Acting Consul General of Japan called upon the American Consul General and expressed his deepest regrets and a representative of the Japanese Army Headquarters expressed his regret to Mr. Chamberlain. Not considering this sufficient, Secretary of State Stimson made a vigorous protest to the Japanese Government through its Ambassador in Washington,[10] demanding adequate punishment of the guilty parties. The Japanese Government agreed to punish the sentries.

With the advent of the Communist control of China, numerous indignities were perpetrated upon American consular officials. The case of Vice Consul William M. Olive is typical. While driving in July, 1949 on a street in Shanghai which, unknown to him, had been reserved for a parade, he was arrested and refused permission to telephone to the Consulate General. When he asserted his rights as a consular official he was brutally beaten, put in handcuffs and taken to a detention cell. The next morning he was forced to write out a confession of guilt including apologies to the prison guards. When officers from the Consulate General tried to see him and bring him food they were temporarily detained and threatened. Olive was released two days later, having subsisted upon bread and water and having had his requests to see a doctor to examine his injuries refused.

[8] *Foreign Relations of the United States, 1900,* 952.
[9] *New York Times* (February 14, 15, 18, 1932).
[10] *Ibid.* (January 4, 5, 1932).

When the protests of the United States Government were given no consideration the United States withdrew its consular representatives and closed the consulates in China.[11]

One of the most atrocious attacks ever made upon an American consul occurred in Teheran, Persia, on July 18, 1924. Major Robert Imbrie, American Vice Consul at Teheran, accompanied by another American and a Legation messenger, attempted to take a picture of a drinking fountain where a miracle was supposed to have happened. A large crowd had gathered around the fountain and when Major Imbrie took his photographs stones were thrown at him. The two Americans and the messenger got into a cab, but the mob followed shouting that the foreigners had poisoned the fountain. A group of soldiers and officers stopped the carriage and attacked the Americans with sabres and bayonets. The police finally rescued the badly injured occupants of the cab and took them to the hospital. The mob followed, broke into the hospital and literally beat Major Imbrie to death.

The Persian Government immediately took action and arrested some two hundred persons. The day after the murder the entire diplomatic corps sent a collective note to the Persian Government protesting its failure to accord protection. The United States demanded reparation, apology and punishment of the guilty parties. As reparation a payment of $60,000 to the widow was required. The Persian Government was also asked to pay the expenses incurred in sending an American man-of-war to receive Vice Consul Imbrie's body. A suitable Persian military guard of honor was to escort the body to the boat. The death penalty was demanded for the ringleaders of the mob. All demands were promptly met by the Persian Government. Sixty thousand dollars was paid over to Mrs. Imbrie and three thousand dollars to Mr. Seymour, who recovered from his injuries. The *Trenton* was saluted upon arrival and a guard of honor, including eight officers,—one a general, accompanied the body. Three ringleaders of the mob were executed and thirty others punished. The sum of $110,000 was paid to the United States for the expense of sending the U. S. S. *Trenton* to bring back the body.[12]

A most inexcusable attack was made upon an American Foreign Service officer in 1937, when Consul General J. Theodore Marriner was shot down in cold blood in Beirut, Syria, because he happened to be the first person to arrive at his post. The assassin, an Armenian, confessed that his motive had been revenge because a vice consul the day before had refused to grant him a visa. Mr. Marriner had served nineteen years in the Foreign Service, had been Chief of the Division of Western European Affairs in

[11] *Department of State Bulletin* (January 2, 1950), 23.
[12] For additional information see *The Near East*, XXVI, 166 (August 14, 1924) and the *American Journal of International Law*, XVIII, 768 (October, 1924).

the Department of State, and had been Counselor of Embassy in Paris just preceding his appointment to Syria. The State Department publicly stated that this post was the last before he was to be given the position of minister and later ambassador, posts to which his career had fully entitled him.[13]

Inviolability of Archives and Offices. It has become a well accepted principle of international law that the consular archives are inviolable. The term *archives* regularly includes all official documents, records and papers filed in the consulate. This immunity generally includes the inviolability of the consulate or at least that part of the building in which the archives are housed. The immunity, however, does not extend to the private papers or personal effects of the consuls, nor, in the absence of treaty provisions, is the consulate free from visit and search.

According to Dr. Irvin Stewart, "the inviolability of consular archives is covered more completely by treaty than is any other of the consular privileges." [14] In the treaty of friendship, commerce and consular rights signed by the United States and Germany December 8, 1923, it is provided that "the consular offices and archives shall at all times be inviolable. They shall under no circumstances be subject to invasion by any authorities of any character within the country where such offices are located." [15]

The multipartite convention signed by the Latin American States on February 28, 1928, at Havana is equally explicit. Article 18 declares that "The official residence of the consuls and places used for the consulate's office and archives are inviolable and in no case may the local authorities enter them without the permission of the consular agents...." [16]

In the early editions of the United States consular regulations no mention was made of the inviolability of the archives, and in the regulations of 1868, where mention is first made, the position taken is somewhat hesitant. It states that as a general rule the records and papers of the consulate are inviolable but concedes that the rule is by no means universally admitted. Subsequently the assurance becomes firmer and the present wording that the consul "may claim inviolability for the archives and official property of his office and their exemption from seizure or examination" [17] has not changed materially since it was first inserted in the regulations of 1881.

A famous exception to this now well established rule of the inviolability of consular archives occurred in 1858 when the consular property of the United States in Manchester, England, including the archives, was seized

[13] *New York Times* (October 13, 1937).

[14] Stewart, *op. cit.*, 59.

[15] *United States Treaty Series,* No. 725, Article XX.

[16] *Sixth International Conference of American States: Final Act* (Havana, 1928), Article 4, *Convention on Consular Agents.*

[17] *Regulations* (February, 1931), Sec. 73.

as security for the payment of a private debt of the Consul.[18] Although W. E. Hall relegates this case to the realm of fiction [19] an investigation by Dr. Stewart in the records of the Department of State supports the truth of the incident.[20]

Although no other exception to the rule has been discovered numerous violations of the rule have occurred. In such cases, however, the violations have been the subject of diplomatic protest and have usually brought about apologies, punishment of the guilty and reparation for the damage done.

When in 1887 in Piura, Peru, the local authorities in executing a judicial process against the furniture of the United States Consular Agent there had broken open his office desk, scattered the archives about the room and carried away several parcels of official papers, the Legation at Lima was instructed to ask for a disavowal of the acts, a reprimand for the local authorities and a guarantee that such an incident would not recur.[21]

Shortly before the outbreak of the Spanish-American War a mob attacked and demolished the American Consulate at Malaga, Spain. The Civil Governor of Malaga restored the coat of arms that had been taken away and expressed his regrets for the attack. The Spanish Government also expressed its regret and promised protection in the future for the persons and property of American consular representatives.[22]

In 1914 when the relations between the United States and Mexico were critical, the American Vice Consulate at Saltillo was entered and the records and official code book removed. The Vice Consul was imprisoned and kept in confinement for several weeks. The State Department protested vigorously and the Vice Consul was released.[23] Undoubtedly more drastic action would have been taken if the United States had not been faced at that time with more serious problems.

Pancho Villa, the Mexican bandit patriot who respected neither the American flag nor the American Consulate, was a perpetual threat to American Consul Frederick Simpich. Whenever he learned that Villa was in the vicinity he loaded the consular records and archives onto a freight car, raised the American flag and then had his office moved up or down the track for hundreds of miles if necessary to avoid being raided. Throughout this period of movable quarters Simpich kept the flag flying and his office open for business.

When the American Minister to Canada, William Phillips, in November, 1928, inquired of the State Department whether an American vice

---

[18] Lawrence's Wheaton, *Elements of International Law* (London, 1864), 427, Note 143.

[19] W. E. Hall, *A Treatise on International Law* (Oxford, 1895), 335, Note 2.

[20] Stewart, *op. cit.*, 40.

[21] Moore, *op. cit.*, V, 52.

[22] *Foreign Relations of the United States, 1898*, 1079.

[23] *Foreign Relations of the United States, 1914*, 660.

consul should comply in the event that he were served with a subpoena to produce in court the certificate of registry of an American vessel, Assistant Secretary of State Carr replied that the American Consular Agent at Lunenburg should decline to produce the certificate.[24]

Display of National Arms and Flag. It has long been considered advantageous that a consular office be designated in such a way as to indicate its official character both to the nationals of the country represented and to the inhabitants of the country in which it is located. The customary method is for the display of the national arms above the doorway or upon the façade. This symbol serves the dual purpose of assuring the customary protection and of making the office more readily known to those seeking it.

The privilege of displaying the national arms is regularly conferred by treaty, although it has become so general that it is sometimes said to be based upon international law. The United States Treaty of 1923 with Germany provides that "consular officers may place over the outer door of their respective offices the arms of their state with an appropriate inscription designating the official office." [25] The *Foreign Service Regulations* prescribe that the arms of the United States should be placed over the entrance to the consulate unless prohibited by the laws of the country. Only one coat of arms is permitted in each post and it must be placed over the office devoted to consular business.

The privilege of displaying the flag, although customary, is not so universal as is the privilege of exposing the national arms. Many consular treaties provide for it and the laws of most countries permit it. The 1923 treaty with Germany permits officers of both countries to hoist the flag of their country on their offices, including those situated in the capitals of the two countries.[26] Mexico for many years did not permit their own consuls to display the national flag, nor did they authorize foreign consulates to display theirs. In fact, in 1874, the United States Consul at Tuxpan was not permitted to raise the American flag on a holiday. When an appeal was taken to the President of Mexico the position of the local authorities was sustained. In this case, however, inasmuch as other consuls had displayed their flags without hindrance from local authorities, Secretary Fish insisted upon a like equality for the United States.[27] Subsequently Mexico appears to have accepted the general rule. However, this question was again raised in 1912 and Secretary of State Knox asserted that the flag might be displayed not merely on certain holidays but at any time to designate the consular office so that it might be easily and generally known.[28]

---

[24] Hackworth, *op. cit.*, IV, 725.
[25] *United States Treaty Series* No. 725, Article XX.
[26] *United States Treaty Series* No. 725, Article XX.
[27] *Foreign Relations of the United States, 1874*, 719, 730.
[28] *Foreign Relations of the United States, 1912*, 902.

The *Foreign Service Manual* authorizes the consul to display the national flag on all occasions when he deems it appropriate, such as national holidays of his own country and ceremonial days of the country to which he is accredited. He is always authorized to hoist it as a measure of protection. It is generally admitted that a consular officer may display his national flag on his automobile when participating in the following events: (1) local national holidays; (2) national holidays of his own country; (3) official visits of high national authorities; (4) official visits of high foreign authorities in which the consul has been invited to participate. Very strict rules are enjoined upon the consul regarding the use and display of the flag and he must not permit any disrespect to be shown it.[29]

Insults to the Flag. Occasions have arisen when insults to the flag have occurred and they are always protested vigorously. A story is told of Judge de Long, Consul at Tangier during the Civil War period, who put two Americans, sympathizers of the South, in chains for making offensive and insulting remarks concerning the American flag. When other Southern sympathizers attempted to arouse a mob to attack the Consulate, the Moorish Viceroy sent troops to disperse them. An American warship shortly afterwards appeared and the prisoners were delivered to the captain. The following day the Consulate received a scroll fastened with red cord reading as follows:

Praise to the One God!
  To the Clever and Wise Gentleman, Consul General for the American Nation.
  We continue to make inquiries for your welfare. We are deeply penetrated with the expressions of gratitude made use of at your interview with us for the assistance we rendered you in removing the insults offered to you by the Christian subjects who surrounded the consular residence thus offering indignity to the American flag . . .
  El Abbas
    Son of the Prince of the Believers. May he rest in Glory.[30]

During the World War I period the German Consul in Lausanne on January 27, 1916, raised the German flag over the Consulate in honor of Kaiser Wilhelm's birthday. A crowd collected and demanded that the German flag be taken down and the Swiss flag raised. When the Consul refused, the mob thrust aside the police and hoisted one of their number who tore down the flag. In this case the protest of the German Government was somewhat weakened by the fact that the authorities had requested the Consul not to raise the flag because of aroused public opinion and the police had made an effort to prevent the outrage.[31]

[29] *Foreign Service Manual* (August 20, 1951), 153-7, 7.
[30] Frederick W. Seward, *Reminiscences of a War-Time Statesman and Diplomat* (New York and London, 1916), 219-25.
[31] *Revue générale de droit international public* (Paris), XXIII, 340.

The Kasenkina Case. An interesting case of consular protection which involved the privileges and immunities of the Soviet Consul General and his offices in New York occurred in 1948. A Russian school teacher, Mrs. Oksana Kasenkina, brought to the United States to teach the children of the Soviet consular officials and the Russian members of the United Nations delegation, wished to avoid returning to Russia when her assignment had ended. She took refuge in a White Russian establishment run by Countess Tolstoy, but when Soviet officials in an official car went to get her she returned to the Soviet Consulate with them. A few days later she leaped from a third story window of the Consulate and was badly injured.

The consular officials at first prevented the New York police from entering the premises, but entrance was obtained into the courtyard by scaling the rear fence of the adjoining property. Admission was also refused to the ambulance driver at first. When a number of police arrived and Mrs. Kasenkina asked to be taken to an American hospital the consular officials gave a reluctant assent.

Subsequently the Soviet Embassy officials accused government agencies of the United States of tolerating the criminal activities of the "Tolstoy Fund" organization, a "White Guard gangster organization," which they alleged had kidnapped Mrs. Kasenkina and they also protested the violation of the extraterritoriality of the U.S.S.R. Consulate General by the New York police.

After a careful investigation the State Department replied that Mrs. Kasenkina had declared her unwillingness to return to Russia and had requested to be taken to the Tolstoy refugee farm. Shortly after being brought back to the Consulate General she had leaped from the window to prevent her forcible return to Russia. The United States in turn accused Consul General Lomakin of making unsubstantiated charges against the United States, and of attempting to get Mrs. Kasenkina to sign a false affidavit. He was also guilty of hindering the investigation of the competent police officials by refusing to allow them to interview Mrs. Kasenkina. On these grounds the State Department requested the President to revoke the exequatur issued to Consul General Lomakin.

The Soviet Government rejected the United States' position and demanded that its representatives have free access to Mrs. Kasenkina. The United States agreed that the Soviet representatives had the right to see Mrs. Kasenkina, but not against her wishes. As it was, she had stated to the Soviet Vice Consul in the presence of witnesses that she did not wish to see him or any other Soviet representative. The Soviet Government thereupon closed its Consulates General in New York and San Francisco and the United States closed its Consulate General at Vladivostok. Mrs. Kasenkina recovered from her fall, remained in the United

States, and broadcast over the Voice of America program a complete refutation of the Soviet version of her story as published in *Tass*.[32]

Exemption from Taxation. Although no established rule exists as yet regarding consular exemption from taxation, there is a decided trend towards the extension of the privilege. The United States has always maintained a fairly generous attitude in its treatment of foreign consular officers. Secretary Forsyth, writing in 1840, declared that all foreign consuls not engaging in trade and not citizens of the United States were exempted from all taxes, imposts and contributions except property taxes.[33] The present Federal laws exempt consuls and employees of consulates from all taxes on the income received from their consular services. In the District of Columbia they are free from personal property taxes and from the payment of licenses for their automobiles or dogs.[34]

Freedom from taxation is usually granted on a strictly reciprocal basis established by treaty arrangement. The United States has signed forty-one treaties which to a greater or less extent obtain exemption from taxation for its consular officers.[35] The Treaty of Friendship, Commerce, and Consular Rights, which was signed with Germany in 1923, provides that consular officers not engaging in trade who are nationals of the state appointing them shall be exempt from all national, state, or local taxes levied upon their persons or property. They are also exempt from all taxes on their income received for their consular services. The sole exception concerns taxes on immovable property or income from such property.[36]

Practically all states which grant any exemptions at all grant exemptions on the income of the consular officer received as compensation for his official services. Great Britain, which is notably strict in her treatment of consuls, allows an exemption in this case.[37] Secretary of State Seward wrote to Secretary of the Treasury Chase in 1863 that the Department of State was not aware that the income of any United States consul abroad derived from official sources was taxable by the governments of the countries where they resided.[38] However, some Canadian and American states impose provincial and state income taxes on foreign consuls. When in 1914 the American Consul at Moncton, New Brunswick, protested against paying an income tax on his official salary, the Canadian authorities

[32] *Department of State Bulletin* (August 29, 1948), 251; (September 26, 1948), 408.

[33] Moore, *op. cit.*, V, 86.

[34] *Foreign Service Manual* (December 3, 1951), 272, 1-272, 32.

[35] Stewart, *op. cit.*, 110.

[36] *United States Treaty Series* No. 725, Article XIX.

[37] A. H. Feller and Manley O. Hudson, *Diplomatic and Consular Laws and Regulations* (Concord, 1933), I, 216, "Finance Act, 1930," Sect. 20.

[38] Moore, *op. cit.*, V, 87.

pointed out that British consuls in the United States, particularly in New York and Boston, had to pay income taxes. The State Department instructed the Consul that no request for exemption was feasible as no guaranty of reciprocity could be given.[39] For other income the national regulations are so varied that the consular officer is expected to investigate for himself at the post to which he has been sent.

A considerable number of states exempt the sending state from payment of taxes on property used in the exercise of consular functions, although such exemption is often based upon the general principles of international law rather than upon specific treaty provisions. The American Consul General at Hamburg in 1923 refused to pay a ground tax levied by the state of Hamburg on the building housing the Consulate. Although in this case it was ruled that the levy was on the tenant in the form of additional rent the Consul General stood on his contract of a fixed rental. No action was taken.[40]

In the case of automobiles the tendency seems to be to exempt consuls from the payment of license taxes even though the automobile is used for his personal as well as consular uses. Less often the gasoline tax is also remitted. Brazil grants both diplomatic and consular officers free licenses with special plates which exempts the car from all taxes and imposts.[41]

As regards the sales taxes and other special taxes in the various states of the Union the policy varies. For example, in New York and Maryland consular officers are exempted from the sales tax in accordance with treaty provisions. Consular officers are exempt from Federal excise taxes incident to official transactions and if in accordance with treaty provisions the exemption may include personal transactions. Consular officials are not exempt from manufacturers' or retailers' excise taxes, neither do exemptions extend to the tax on cabarets, night clubs or amusements.[42]

Exemptions from Customs Duties. The majority of states have come to see the advantage of reciprocal exemption of customs duties for consular officers, particularly for their personal property and household effects upon first entrance into the country. The practice is based in some cases upon treaty provisions but more often a reciprocal exemption is granted by comity. Office supplies and stationery are commonly exempted, personal effects less often. A few examples will illustrate the varying practice: Argentina permits career consuls to bring in objects for initial installation and for public service duty free on a reciprocity basis.[43] Belgium grants practically no greater exemption to consuls than to any other foreigners establishing themselves in Belgium. This exemption, however, covers the

[39] Stewart, *op. cit.*, 127.

[40] Stewart, *op. cit.*, 106.

[41] Feller and Hudson, *op. cit.*, I, 164.

[42] *Foreign Service Manual* (December 3, 1951), 260-77, 24.

[43] Feller and Hudson, *op. cit.*, I, 43, "Decree of February 9, 1926," Article 43.

initial installation. The only exemption accorded is for official emblems and that upon a reciprocity basis. Even office furniture and paraphernalia are not exempt from the regular tariff regime.[44] Canada grants consuls general the same privileges as diplomatic officers. Consuls are given exemption for personal and household effects on their first arrival only, but office equipment and supplies sent directly by the Government are admitted free of duty.[45] Great Britain permits on a reciprocity basis free entrance of official supplies regularly and also exemption of baggage examinations of career consuls upon first arrival.[46] France admits shields, seals, flags, books, archives, and official documents addressed to consular officials duty free on a reciprocity basis. American consular officers are accorded by special favor the benefit of free entry for household goods, furniture and articles of all sorts destined for usage of their consulates.[47] Italy grants exemption for all effects and furniture on first entry upon a reciprocity basis, but the exemption does not include articles of food and drink.[48] The Netherlands grants free entry at all times to official supplies and all articles for personal and family use.[49]

The United States in the consular regulations issued in 1868 declared that no authorization had been granted to the Treasury Department to exempt consuls from customs duties.[50] The regulations issued in 1881 stated that the United States customarily admitted all articles for official use of foreign consular officers free upon a reciprocity basis.[51] The present regulations permit free entry of personal and household effects upon arrival or return to consular ports. Supplies such as office furniture and material are entered free of duty. The privilege in both cases is upon a reciprocity basis. The United States also grants foreign career consular officers assigned to the United States exemption from the payment of internal revenue taxes on imported merchandise providing the foreign country grants an equivalent exemption to United States career consular officers stationed in the foreign country.[52]

During the era of prohibition the Secretary of State refused permission for a newly appointed consul at San Francisco to enter twenty boxes of wine, but permitted the free entry of sixty-two boxes of household goods and effects.[53] It is hardly probable that since the repeal of the eighteenth amendment a consul would be asked to pay duty on such liquor as was brought in with his household effects upon arrival in the United States.

[44] *Ibid.*, I, 92.
[45] Feller and Hudson, *op. cit.*, I, 222.
[46] *Ibid.*, I, 217.
[47] *Ibid.*, I, 539.
[48] *Ibid.*, I, 716.
[49] *Ibid.*, II, 883.
[50] *Consular Regulations* (1868), Sect. 10.
[51] *Ibid.* (1884), Sect. 421.
[52] *Foreign Service Manual* (December 3, 1951), 250-55, 3.
[53] Stewart, *op. cit.*, 125.

Amenability to Civil and Criminal Process.   According to international law a consular officer is subject to both the civil and criminal jurisdiction of the local courts. It has become a well established rule in consular conventions that consuls are responsible to the laws of the place of their residence in both civil and criminal matters. There are no treaties of the United States which relieve a consul of liability to civil suit. In criminal jurisdiction no exemption can be claimed unless by specific treaty provision.

Numerous cases might be cited in support of this well established principle. In the much quoted Barbuits Case decided by the Court of Chancery in Great Britain in 1735 it was held, supporting the opinion of Barbeyrac, Wicquefort, and others, that the commercial agent of the King of Prussia in Great Britain was not entitled to the privileges of international law possessed by ambassadors. Hence the defendant was subject to suit under municipal law.[54] In another often cited case, *in re* Baiz, decided in 1889, the Supreme Court of the United States held that the Consul General of Guatemala, who alleged that he was exercising diplomatic functions, was not a public minister within the intent of the statutes of the United States, and therefore could not claim exemption from civil suit.[55]

When in 1893 the United States Consular Agent at Haida, Austria, left his post owing a number of debts, one of his creditors brought suit and obtained an order for certain of the agent's belongings. His successor refused to surrender the articles. The Austrian Government protested, maintaining that neither by law nor treaty did immunity covering archives and papers against search and seizure extend to other objects. Instructions were thereupon given by the Department of State to permit the seizure of the Agent's personal property to satisfy any claim against him.[56]

Although it is generally conceded that a consul is subject to suit, the money received from the government to pay the salary of the officers is not usually subject to garnishee before it has been paid over. A case of this sort occurred in the United States Consulate General in Berlin in 1912. When the Consul General protested against the attachment proceedings, the court dismissed the case. In a somewhat similar case which occurred in Maracaibo, Venezuela, in 1913, the Secretary of State instructed the Consul that although consuls were generally subject to the jurisdiction of the local courts, the Government of the United States did not recognize the right of the Venezuela courts to exercise control of government money in the Consul's possession due as salary to the clerk.[57]

There are very few cases of arrest in civil actions, but in criminal cases

---

[54] Edwin D. Dickinson, *The Law of Nations* (New York, 1920), Case 587.
[55] Manley O. Hudson, *Cases on International Law* (St. Paul, 1920), 848.
[56] *Foreign Relations of the United States, 1894,* 27.
[57] Cited by Stewart, *op. cit.*, 152-3.

the consul is fully subject to the local laws. However, a study of instances which have occurred would seem to indicate that consuls are rarely arrested for minor offenses and that even in serious offenses an effort is made to protect the interests of the appointing government.

A case occurred in Philadelphia in 1815 which almost caused the severance of diplomatic relations between Russia and the United States. Russian Consul General Kosloff was arrested on the charge of having raped a twelve-year-old girl who was a servant in his family. He was put in jail and later bound over to the next session of the court. The state court dismissed the case through lack of jurisdiction over a consul, and as rape was not a crime under Federal laws, no further judicial action was taken. The Russian Government, however, objected to the arrest and asked reparation through its diplomatic representative in Washington. The United States showed that Kosloff had received the full protection of the law and it was the more surprised at the Russian attitude since the Russian Government admitted that a consul deserved no protection from the law of nations in such a case.[58]

Commenting on the arrest of the United States Consul General at Montreal, Canada, in 1863, on a charge of kidnapping, Secretary of State Seward declared that the Department did not consider a consul general entitled to any diplomatic immunity.[59] When in 1895 the American Consul at Mozambique shot and wounded a native African whom he mistook for a burglar, he was tried by the Portuguese authorities. When a full acquittal was not awarded him the Consul appealed to the Department of State. The United States, however, refused to accede to his request unless there had been a plain denial of justice.[60]

The United States has upon occasion exacted severe penalties from foreign consuls. The German Consul General at San Francisco, the Vice Consul and a consular attaché were arrested in 1917 and convicted of a conspiracy to destroy munitions. All received heavy penalties, the vice consul and consular attaché receiving life sentences.[61]

An interesting case arose in Germany when United States Vice Consul Shiras Morris, who was driving from Stuttgart to Munich on his way to a vacation resort in Italy, killed a man on a bicycle who suddenly crossed the road. The damage to the automobile and the position of the body indicated a high rate of speed. The Treaty of 1923 with Germany, Article XVIII, exempted consuls from arrest except when charged with the commission of offenses locally designated as crimes. As it appeared that the Consul was guilty of fast driving resulting in the death of the cyclist, an arrangement was made whereby the Consul was transferred to Marseilles.

[58] Moore, *op. cit.*, V, 65.
[59] *Ibid.*, V, 70.
[60] *Ibid.*, V, 71.
[61] *New York Times*, January 11, 1917.

Inasmuch as the man was a ne'er-do-well and his wife, who received the insurance, did not desire to prosecute, the German Government raised no objection to the transfer.

An interesting situation occurs when a foreign consul violates the law of a state but not a Federal law in the United States. Traffic violations are offenses against state laws or municipal ordinances and in such cases the Department of Justice has ruled that state courts have no jurisdiction against consuls so that if the consul is to be prosecuted it must be in a Federal court.[62]

Serving as Witness. Although no hard and fast rules may be laid down, the following principles are generally observed in cases which raise the question of the consul's attendance as a witness. A consul is generally exempt from serving as witness in the trial of a civil case. In a criminal case a consul may be required to give testimony orally or in writing at his residence or office, or even to attend the trial personally as a witness. In such cases the requirements are enforced with due regard for the dignity and convenience of the consul. In serving as a witness the consul may not be required to disclose information received while performing his consular duties which would be incompatible with the interests of the state that he represents.[63]

A case illustrative of the procedure required occurred in Germany in 1899 when Consul General Richard Guenther was served with a subpoena to appear and give testimony in a pending suit. A threat of fine and imprisonment was attached to the summons. Consul General Guenther agreed to testify, but protested against the threats of fine and imprisonment. The Department of State, through the American Ambassador, sustained the Consul General. It was discovered that the summons had been made out in the usual form by mistake, and a polite letter was sent asking Guenther to appear, and a verbal apology was given by the official of the court.[64]

When in 1935 American Consul General Holland appeared under protest in divorce proceedings in England he was interrogated regarding the acceptance of a marriage certificate as *prima facie* evidence in courts in the United States. Assistant Secretary of State Carr asked the Embassy in London to inform the British Foreign Office that since courts in the United States did not summon British consular officers in this country to give testimony on such questions the American official should not have been obliged to leave his official duties to testify regarding questions of law and procedure. The British Foreign Office accepted the American position.[65]

A very interesting case in which the consular officer refused to give

[62] Hackworth, *op. cit.*, IV, 751.
[63] *Foreign Relations of the United States, 1899,* 567.
[64] Moore, *op. cit.*, V, 81.
[65] Hackworth, *op. cit.*, IV, 770-1.

testimony on the ground that the evidence which he could present was given to him in confidence occurred in Ontario, Canada. An American woman married to a Canadian kept a hotel in a good location. A bootlegger wished to obtain the place and when other means failed claimed that she was diseased and had contaminated a Canadian husband. The authorities insisted that she should undergo a physical examination. The woman came to the American Consul and asserting that the demand was a frame-up asked for a physical examination by a physician whom he could recommend. The examination showed that she was not diseased. Indignant at the injustice of the accusation, the woman decided to sue the Public Health Service. Again she was examined, this time by the Health Service, but no report was made. She entered suit and her attorney wished the Consul to testify. He refused and the judge thereupon sent a summons. The Consul explained that the Department had instructed him not to testify, but the judge refused to compromise and threatened jail if the Consul did not appear. Fortunately a settlement was reached on the morning of the trial whereby the woman was to receive a small sum for injury to her character.

Consuls in Times of War.   There is not the same need today as formerly to consider the situation of the consul in times of war because war conditions of the present render all consular activities impossible between belligerents. Some of the older writers, Bluntschli, for example, favored the retention of the consuls at their posts in spite of a state of war. In fact, the enemy powers did not break off consular relations during the Crimean War. However, today when war requires the mobilization of every national activity to crush the enemy, the very first step is a complete severance of both diplomatic and consular relations. The only exception conceivable is when that anomalous situation arises of a state of conflict without any declaration of war or desire on the part of either disputant to regard it as war. The Sino-Japanese conflict of 1931-1932 is such an example. In his excellent study entitled *Les Consuls en temps de Guerres et de Troubles,* Dr. Bouffanais concludes that according to actual practice consular relations between neutrals are subject to the well established rights and duties of neutrality and rest upon the basis of the principles recognized on the subject at the time of the conflict.[66]

Although the so-called "cold war" can hardly be classed as war in the legal sense, the treatment accorded American consuls by Chinese Communists in 1948-1949 flagrantly violated every principle of international law as regards consular protection. The case of Angus Ward, Consul General of the United States at Mukden, is an outstanding example. In November, 1948, the Consular office and residence were without warning cut off from

[66] Pierre Bouffanais, *Les consuls en temps de guerres et de troubles* (Paris, 1933), 239.

all communication with the rest of the world, and for over a month were not even permitted running water or electricity. Reports to the State Department were forbidden on the ground that diplomatic relations no longer existed between the United States and the Northeast Peoples Government. After seven months of remaining incommunicado a telegram from the State Department was received by Ward on June 7, 1949, ordering the closure of the Mukden Consulate General. When the Consul General requested facilities for departure his requests were ignored.

In September a Chinese employee of the Consulate named Chi quit his job suddenly. He returned later with his brother to demand his pay and when he refused a fair settlement Ward insisted that he leave the premises. His brother thereupon attacked Ward and Ward was later arrested for an alleged beating of Chi, tried, convicted, and kept in solitary confinement in an unheated, verminous cell. Finally on December 7, Consul General Ward was sent to Tientsin with his staff under armed guard in a third-class car with board shelves and no water or heat.[67]

In January, 1950, the Communists seized the American consular property in Peking in spite of the American threat to withdraw all American official personnel from Communist China. The United States thereupon closed all consulates in China except the Legation and Consulate in Taipei, the capital of Formosa, which was under the control of the Chinese Nationalists.[68]

Consuls in Extraterritorial Countries.   In concluding this survey of consular privileges and immunities a word must be said regarding the status of consuls in countries where extraterritoriality still exists. In non-Christian countries where religious law was so intertwined with civil law that the foreigner could not hope to obtain justice unless removed from local jurisdiction the practice developed of permitting foreigners to be judged in accordance with their national laws. This exceptional regime was usually established by treaties and consuls were charged with this judicial function. As a result of this special jurisdiction consuls who possessed it were necessarily public ministers with the same status as diplomats. In fact, some of them had the dual status of diplomatic agent as well as consul, as is the case of the present American representative in Tangier.

Consuls in countries where capitulations or extraterritorial privileges still exist possess in addition to the regular privileges and immunities of diplomatic agents certain judicial powers in civil and criminal matters. These powers are complete for cases arising between foreigners of the same nationality and between foreigners of different nationalities. For cases between foreigners and natives there have been several possibilities:

---

[67] *Department of State Bulletin* (Dec. 26, 1949), 955; for Ward's account of his experience see *The American Foreign Service Journal* (February, 1950), 14-44.

[68] *Department of State Bulletin* (January 23, 1950), 119.

sometimes national courts with the assistance of a consul or dragoman, as formerly in Turkey; sometimes mixed courts, as formerly in China; sometimes judgment by the officer of the nationality of the defender; and sometimes real international courts, as the international court of Tangier and the mixed courts formerly in Shanghai and Egypt. The jurisdiction of United States consular courts in Egypt expired in October, 1949, but the United States still possesses extraterritorial rights in Morocco and Muscat.

An interesting case of extraterritorial jurisdiction was brought to the writer's attention in Tangier. An American Negro who claimed to be an inventor was on his way to Ethiopia but landed in Gibraltar without funds, and the British Consul sent him over to his American colleague in Tangier. He was given a job in the Consulate General to earn funds to continue his voyage. One day when he thought the Arab servants were talking about him behind his back he seized a carving knife and went after the Arabs. He was finally subdued after stabbing several of them and put temporarily in the local jail. He quickly broke out and returned to the Consulate. He was thereupon tried by the Consular Court and found to be insane. One of the younger alien consular clerks was made responsible for him until he could be returned to the States. During the long period before his home state Oklahoma agreed to send funds for his repatriation the young consular clerk gained his confidence and the fellow would follow him everywhere and obey him implicitly. To make the long journey home it was necessary for the clerk to accompany him, which he did without the slightest incident, although the young man had never been in the United States before. The clerk liked the States so well that he subsequently returned and became an American citizen.

The question today no longer possesses the same importance as formerly because the capitulations have been suppressed in Turkey and Iran and in practically all the other countries of the Levant. Japan has long since freed herself from extraterritorial restrictions. China has suppressed all extraterritorial privileges formerly held by the foreign powers. Great Britain in draft treaties of 1929-1930 regarding the independence of Egypt recognizes that the capitulatory regime is no longer in accordance with the spirit of the times. It would seem that this piece of "medievalism stereotyped" will soon disappear and consuls in all countries of the world will have the same status in international law.

22

The American Government
Establishment in Paris

PARIS POSSESSES the dual distinction of having received the first American
legation sent to any country in the world, and of possessing the finest
building ever constructed by the United States for housing its foreign
services abroad. The American government building facing the *Place
de la Concorde* until World War II was able to house under one roof all
the employees of the Embassy, Consulate General, the military, naval, air,
commercial, agricultural, and cultural attachés. The vast expansion of the
United States overseas services required to carry out the various programs
of economic, financial, and military assistance to a stricken Europe soon
rendered this hitherto spacious building inadequate even for those services under the immediate direction of the Department of State. Inasmuch
as the Paris establishment is the largest peacetime diplomatic and consular
post in continental Europe, a survey of its organization and work will perhaps give an idea of the vast ramifications of the work carried on by the
United States as a result of its top position in the international community.

American Envoys to France. Before taking up the present establishment it is in order to say a word concerning the type of men who have
been named to conduct the diplomatic relations of the United States with
France. When Benjamin Franklin, America's first Foreign Minister, was
sent over to France by the struggling colonies in 1776 he was already well
known by the intelligentsia of the day in Paris as a scientist and a philosopher. He brought over his grandson, a youth of sixteen, to act as his secretary and set up the first American legation in Passy. Today a bronze statue
of the venerable diplomat stands overlooking the spot where he made an
unsurpassed record in the protection and furthering of American interests
abroad.

It should be noted, however, that Franklin was no tyro in the diplomatic
game. Twenty years earlier he had been sent to London by Pennsylvania
on a difficult diplomatic mission which lasted five years. After two years
at home he was again sent to London and this second mission lasted eleven

years and during most of this time he was representing four American states. These sixteen years of training in the school of diplomatic experience combined with his outstanding reputation as scientist, philosopher and wit and his ability to speak French, Italian and Spanish placed him in an enviable position to achieve a remarkable success. His colleague, John Adams, declared that "his reputation was more universal than that of Leibnitz or Newton, Frederick, or Voltaire, and his character more beloved than any of them . . . his name was familiar to government and people . . . to such an extent that there was scarcely a peasant or a citizen, a valet de chambre, coachman or footman, a lady's chambermaid or scullion in the kitchen, who was not familiar with it and who did not consider him a friend to human-kind. . . ." [1] When Voltaire returned from exile in 1778 the two great men publicly embraced and the cry went up: "Qu'il était charmant de voir s'embrasser Solon et Sophocle." [2]

The United States followed this policy of sending the best that she had to France by appointing Jefferson as Franklin's successor. No one appreciated better than Jefferson himself the difficulty of succeeding Franklin and when he was often asked the question, "C'est vous, Monsieur, qui remplace le Docteur Franklin?" he invariably replied, "No one can replace him, sir; I am only his successor." [3] Jefferson became just as great a friend of France as his predecessor and it was he who said, "To ask the travelled inhabitant of any nation 'In what country on earth would you rather live?' 'Certainly in my own, where all are my friends, my relations, and the earliest and sweetest affections and recollections of my life.' 'Which would be your second choice?' 'France.'" [4]

That Morris and Monroe, the immediate successors of Franklin and Jefferson, were not as successful in their missions as their predecessors was due more to the political situation in France than to any lack of ability in the men. This is not the place even to enumerate the eminent men who have represented the United States in France, but such names as Gallatin, formerly Secretary of the Treasury and later Minister to England, Cass, formerly Secretary of War and later Secretary of State, Richard Rush, who had served as Minister to England, as Secretary of State and Secretary of Treasury before going as Minister to Paris, Whitelaw Reid, who "added to the cleverness of the Americans the urbanity of the French," gives an idea of their calibre. In the case of Henry White, whose recall was due solely to personal reasons, the French Government went so far as to direct their representative in Washington to do what he could to secure White's retention. The outstanding achievements of Ambassador Herrick during his two missions in the difficult days of World War I and its after-

[1] Francis Wharton, *Diplomatic Correspondence of the American Revolution,* I, 488.
[2] E. E. Hale, *Franklin in France* (Boston, 1888), I, 171.
[3] Beckles Willson, *America's Ambassadors to France* (London, 1928), 22.
[4] *Ibid.,* 37.

math will never be forgotten by a grateful France. Among his successors we find such outstanding persons as William C. Bullitt and Admiral William D. Leahy. Jefferson Caffery who served for four and one-half years from 1944 to 1949 is the only career Foreign Service officer who has ever been appointed to the post. However, the present incumbent, David K. E. Bruce, served briefly as a career officer before going into the banking business. Subsequently, after a short period as Assistant Secretary of Commerce and then as Chief of the mission to France of the Economic Cooperation Administration, he was named Ambassador to France.

Lack of a Permanent Residence. We have noted that Franklin established the first American legation at Passy. It is said that more than three quarters of a century later John Bigelow, then Minister to France, visited Passy to look up the remains of the first American legation and found a part of the original building still standing and used as a school by some Sisters of Charity. A little later a plan to purchase the site and construct a suitable legation upon it was proposed but nothing came of it.[5] Jefferson found the Passy location too far removed, so he leased a house in what is now the rue Taitbout for a year and then procured a house at the Grille des Champs-Elysées suitable in every respect except for the price. Morris took a house in the Faubourg St. Germain which seems to have been equipped for abundant entertaining. He also kept up a modest place at Sainport on the Seine, about twenty miles from Paris. Minister Monroe retained the house in the Faubourg St. Germain taken by Morris. Barlow some years later established himself in the rue de Vaugirard. Gallatin found a suitable furnished residence at 21 rue de l'Université which his son described as very fine "entre cour et jardin."

So one might continue the story—*tant de ministres tant de différentes maisons.* General Porter, one of the American ministers to France, said one might as well say that "the American Legation was on wheels, year before last it was on such a street, last year on another, this year I don't know where." [6] Joseph Choate when Ambassador to England was walking one night in London when he was accosted by a policeman, "I say, old chap, what are you doing walking about in this beastly weather. Better go home." "I have no home," replied Mr. Choate. "I am the American Ambassador."

Fortunately this problem of hunting suitable quarters for an embassy residence no longer troubles the American Ambassador to France. Myron T. Herrick, knowing that the United States Congress had finally agreed to the purchase of suitable quarters for America's representatives abroad, bought in 1924 with his own money the mansion of former President Grévy at Passy. He paid 5,400,000 fr. for it, but within a week the franc had so

[5] Willson, *op. cit.*, 5.
[6] *Century Magazine,* LXXVII, 784.

risen that a very considerable profit had been made. He then offered it to the Government at the amount he paid for it, pointing out at the same time that he would be in the embarrassing situation of profiting in land speculation if the Government refused to take it. The United States thereupon took over the purchase, furnished the building suitably and possesses today in Paris one of the few adequate American embassies abroad.

Lack of a Permanent Chancery.   The chancery quarters of the United States for many years were merely certain rooms set aside in the minister's house. In fact, when James Brown terminated his service as Minister in 1829 the papers of the legation were kept in an apartment of his house where the secretary also resided. Mr. Rives found this situation unsatisfactory and rented a separate apartment for deposit of the papers and as living quarters for the secretary.[7] When John Bigelow, then Consul in Paris, took over the Legation in 1865 he said he found it in a part of Mrs. Dayton's apartments on the rue Circulaire opposite the Arc de Triomphe. It was later moved to 95 rue de Chaillot, where it remained over a grocery on one side and a laundry on the other until 1881 when more suitable quarters were found on the Place de la Bitche. As the name of this square was the same as a very unfortunate expression in English the French obligingly changed it to Place des Etats-Unis. In 1885 the chancery was moved to quarters at the corner of the avenue Marceau and the rue Galilée. Apparently these did not adequately satisfy the chancery's needs for very long as Ambassador Eustis in 1897 reported that the offices were in every way objectionable, there was not sufficient room, the drainage bad and some of the rooms small and badly lighted.[8] His successor, General Porter, found more suitable quarters at No. 8, avenue Kléber. Here they remained until 1913 when they were again moved, this time to No. 5, rue Chaillot. This was to be the last home of the American chancery until it entered its present permanent quarters in the avenue Gabriel.

The New American Government Building.   The present American government building owes its conception to a suggestion made by Senator Edge in 1925 while on a visit to Paris. He proposed to Ambassador Herrick that it might be feasible to construct a building which would house all the American governmental activities in Paris. Ambassador Herrick was enthusiastic over the idea and it was not long before he furnished Senator Edge with complete information as to the probable cost of housing as well as the approximate cost of sites and buildings. As Senator Edge was on the Senate Foreign Relations Committee he had a bill introduced authorizing the appointment of a Foreign Service Buildings Commission

[7] *Correspondence of the American Legation in Paris, October 28, 1829:* Mr. W. C. Rives to Secretary Van Buren.
[8] Willson, *op. cit.*, p. 364.

to purchase property and when necessary to construct buildings in which to carry on the manifold activities of the United States government in foreign countries. The bill was passed and $10,000,000 was appropriated to carry out its provisions.

The site chosen for the Paris building was the northern side of the Place de la Concorde where it was found possible to purchase the eighteenth-century mansion of Grimod de la Reynière occupied at the time by *le Cercle de l'Union Artistique*. The purchase was made on August 4, 1928, and the amount paid for the property was $200,000. The choice of this spot was due to the desire to build as near the business center of the city as possible and at the same time to avoid the noise and darkness of a congested area. This location met these requirements ideally and included the additional advantage of the prospect of one of the finest public squares in the world, that of the Place de la Concorde.

The following year Messrs. Delano and Aldrich of New York were appointed as architects of the building. Victor Laloux was chosen by this firm as consulting architect and John W. Chandler, an American architect practicing in France, as its Paris representative. Mr. Delano, a graduate of the Beaux-Arts, had spent many years in France, and had served as architect for some of the finest buildings in the United States.

From the very beginning it was the expressed desire of the Commission to house all the governmental activities of the United States in Paris under one roof. The architects carried out this plan in a very satisfactory fashion in the interior arrangements and at the same time made the exterior conform to the architecture of the Hotel Crillon across the street. A certain number of criticisms have been leveled at the structure by Americans who would have preferred a more original treatment, but certainly the simplicity of the building makes it fit admirably into its immediate surroundings.

The cornerstone was laid May 2, 1932, by Ambassador Edge, who had participated so actively in the formulation and execution of the plan. He expressed the wish that in thus rounding out the plans of Jacques Ange Gabriel, the architect of Louis XV, who had planned the beautiful Place de la Concorde, a contribution might also be made to a greater symmetry in Franco-American relations. The building was formally accepted as completed on September 9, 1933, and the various governmental services commenced to move in immediately.

The building is a stone-faced, three-story, steel and concrete structure. It is set back far enough to afford a view of the entire façade from the entrance gates and to permit automobiles to come in and turn inside this enclosure. Unpaved areas of the yard are planted to lawn and low shrubs and the garden is further enhanced by a fountain motif. The architecture is modeled strictly upon the French buildings of the Place de la Concorde. A seal of the United States is set into the façade facing the avenue Gabriel and two American eagles sculptured from stone mount guard atop the pillars of the main entrance gates.

The interior of the building is strictly American with simplicity of line, color, and treatment, and an abundance of light is available to practically all the rooms. An attractive staircase of stone leads from the ground floor where the Consulate offices are found to the Embassy quarters on the first floor. The building has eight beautiful crystal chandeliers presented to the American Government by the *Cercle de l'Union Artistique*. The fireplace and some of the fine old hardware also came from the old building of the Cercle.

The government building has a very large and finely proportioned hall for a library. At the present time there are some 4,000 volumes catalogued dealing with a great variety of subjects of interest to the various government services, including a complete collection of Duvergier's *French Laws and Decrees* from the first publication in 1788 to the present time. The embassy chancery also possesses the Wallace Library, a fine collection of some 2,500 volumes dealing primarily with Franco-American relations, which former Ambassador Wallace presented to the United States Government in 1930. This is housed in a beautifully furnished room which is used by the ambassador and his staff for conferences. A very large reception room tastefully furnished and approximately twenty offices complete the chancery quarters.

Inasmuch as many more people use the Consulate services than those of the Embassy, the offices of the Consulate are on the ground floor with a few on the mezzanine. The sixteen rooms and inner glass-roofed court furnish every facility for the comfortable and prompt despatch of business carried on by this agency. In addition to these rooms are the private offices of the more important consular officers.

Up to the outbreak of World War II the building was able to accommodate satisfactorily all of the official staff of the United States abroad, but at the close of the war with the vast increase of personnel required to handle postwar problems it was wholly inadequate. It will be remembered that the original building was purchased from the *Cercle de l'Union Artistique*, which still owned the neighboring building facing the avenue Gabriel. This building at the beginning of World War II was requisitioned by the French *Ministère de la Marine*. When the Germans seized Paris, they took over the building, made certain changes, and used it mostly as a depository for sailors' uniforms.

At the close of the war when the United States Government was pressed for space it was able to purchase this adjoining building from the *Cercle de l'Union Artistique* for approximately $400,000. The United States proceeded immediately to remodel and refurnish the building. Numerous offices were built and turned over to officials of the Economic Cooperation

Administration, the Foreign Buildings Office, and the Public Health Service. A large restaurant was put in for the entire Foreign Service staff to take the place of the restaurant formerly found on the third floor of the Embassy building. The swimming pool in the basement was covered over and a coöperative store was established equipped with packaged, canned, and bottled goods from the States. This building ultimately will be torn down and an addition built to the Embassy more in keeping with the original building and its beautiful surroundings.

Other Foreign Service Buildings.   With the huge development of the United States Information Service still more space was needed, and in 1947 a large residence-type building on rue du Faubourg St. Honoré was bought from Maurice Rothschild. The story is told that before the contract was signed Rothschild took out secretly some of the Louis Quinze panels and replaced them with cleverly constructed plaster reproductions. Unfortunately for the owner an anonymous informant notified the United States and a reduction in price even greater than the value of the panels was demanded and obtained.

It should be noted in passing that Public Law 547 (Utilization of foreign credits derived from surplus property and lend-lease settlements) enabled the United States to buy property and buildings abroad without the spending of American dollars, and was a means of obtaining some tangible return for war materials which otherwise might have resulted in a complete loss. This gave a great impetus to the purchase of buildings and plots of land for various Foreign Service requirements.

It was under this legislation that a large office building at number 58 rue de Boetie was purchased in May, 1950. At present it has largely been taken over by officials of the Mutual Defense Assistance Program, the Veterans Administration, and the military, naval, and air attachés.

In addition to the Ambassador's residence on the avenue d'Jena in Passy, already mentioned, some nine additional residence buildings have been acquired by the State Department to house important Foreign Service personnel. At present the Minister, the Counselor of Embassy, the Consul General, the principal Administrative Officer, and two First Secretaries are being housed in buildings owned by the United States.

Personnel of the Foreign Service Establishment.   With this brief survey of the construction and physical equipment of the American government buildings in Paris we can proceed to the more important subject—the organization of personnel. It is difficult to give the exact number of employees of the Paris establishment at the present time because of the large number of temporary agencies so closely affiliated with the Foreign Service that they are almost a part of it. For example, UNESCO, the Economic Cooperation Administration, and the Mutual Defense Assistance Program require liaison officers attached to the Embassy. Limiting ourselves to those employees qualifying as Chiefs of Mission, Foreign Service officers, Foreign Service Reserve officers, Foreign Service staff officers, and Foreign Service local employees the total number was 830 on April 1, 1951.

At the head of all American representatives is the Ambassador, who is made solely responsible for the interests of his country in France. His is the sole authority to represent his Government or to delegate such authority to an intermediary. Consequently, either he or one of his immediate assistants must deal directly with the French Government to consider various problems which arise between the two countries.

Sometimes the situation is such that it renders the position of the Ambassador a bit difficult. A case in point arose while Jesse Isidore Straus, head of the great mercantile establishment in New York—Macy's—was Ambassador to France. When the United States went off the gold standard early in the administration of Franklin D. Roosevelt the French Government resented the dollar depreciation policy since it made more difficult her sale of luxury products in the United States and also made it more of a strain to stay on the gold standard herself. The result was a policy of retaliation evidenced in further limitations placed upon American trade by both quotas and higher duties which only augmented the existing friction between the two countries.

Under these conditions Ambassador Straus' situation was not quite as happy as it might otherwise have been, and the fact that he was able to keep the economic modus vivendi, obtained by Ambassador Herrick in 1927, still functioning through this period of nationalistic sandbagging of foreign trade was proof of his ability both as businessman and diplomat. A story apropos of the situation is told which if apocryphal is nevertheless pertinent. At a diplomatic dinner tendered by a French statesman where the wines were rare and the liqueurs choice the American Ambassador was asked to say a few words. After noting the long period of very happy relations between the two countries, Straus concluded by saying that he was afraid that present-day Americans when they heard the name Lafayette thought of the Galeries instead of the General. The French host, a little nettled by the possible implications of the allusion, contented himself with saying, "Macy, beaucoup, M. l'Ambassadeur."

Relations after World War II between France and the United States were in a particularly delicate state as a result of the Soviet menace to democratic security. The United States, which had borne the brunt of assisting Europe towards economic recovery, needed Europe's assistance in maintaining European political security. France not only lagged in providing a fair quota of troops herself but opposed the rearmament of Germans even as a part of an international police force. The Ambassador, David K. E. Bruce, a successful businessman assigned to this post May 9, 1949, although able to appreciate the domestic political problem of the

French Government was able to avoid an absolute diplomatic impasse with the greatest difficulty.

THE PARIS EMBASSY

The Ambassador at Work. The work of the Ambassador in Paris is probably somewhat more arduous than in any other American diplomatic post due to the complicated relations caused by the many specialized agencies operating in the French capital. The Mutual Defense Assistance Program, the Military Assistance Advisory Group, the Economic Cooperation Administration, which under the title of Office of Special Representatives had over 1,200 officials and employees, the civilian employees of the European Command Detachment of over 100, the American Battle Monuments Commission, all of these agencies were either under the Embassy's general jurisdiction or in close liaison with it.[9] Thus, in addition to representing the United States before the French Government, negotiating important agreements, reporting upon vital political and economic questions, and protecting American interests, the American Ambassador in Paris is responsible for many other related activities.

However, the most serious problem facing the Ambassador to Paris is the stream of Americans wishing to see the Ambassador upon matters largely alien to the essential functions of the office. On a representative day in August, 1950, Ambassador Bruce had on his calendar the following items which had to be taken care of: meet with his staff; receive the French High Commissioner of Indo-China; discuss the erection of a war memorial on the landing beaches of Normandy with a representative of the Congressional Watch-dog Committee of ECA; meet a Baltimore lawyer who had served in the Maryland legislature; receive a fellow countryman with two letters from senators; lunch at the Quai d'Orsay in honor of a prominent overseas resident general; confer with an English general who had been making tests of bazookas; receive an American lawyer sent over to protect American business interests against alleged illegal discrimination; have an interview with another lawyer from Washington interested in the guarantee clauses of the E.A.A. Act to stimulate investments by American corporations abroad; receive a delegation of the Federation of Women Lawyers from the United States; discuss the question of American motion pictures abroad with two representatives of Eric Johnston's organization; meet representatives of the *Associated Press* and the *New York Times;* go to see the French Foreign Minister regarding pending matters of importance to both Governments; attend a reception given by representatives of the Suez Canal Company to meet the new Egyptian Foreign Minister; attend a dinner preceding the performance of a ballet under joint diplomatic patronage and a reception afterwards for members of the

---

9 As of October 9, 1950, there were 2,708 U. S. Government employees in Paris.

cast; go home to rest knowing that the next day and subsequent days will be approximate repetitions of the same. The Ambassador in Paris at present has a Special Assistant, an Administrative Assistant, and two Foreign Service Officers on his personal staff in addition to his secretarial assistance.

Political Section. The political section of the Embassy is under the direction of two outstanding and long experienced career Foreign Service Officers. In 1949 Charles E. Bohlen was named Minister to Paris, the first person to hold such a position. A specialist in Russian affairs, with a long detail in Moscow and as former head of the Eastern European Division of the Department of State, he was particularly well equipped to carry out Secretary Acheson's "containment of Russia" policy. Minister Bohlen was also responsible for the Embassy's liaison operation in reference to the Mutual Defense Assistance Program. The other principal adviser, Philip W. Bonsal, Counselor of Embassy and head of the Political Section, although he has been in the Foreign Service only twelve years, had had considerable business experience in Latin American countries before entering the Service.

Other Foreign Service Officers attached to the Ambassador's office or in the Political Section were also regional specialists. Philip D. Sprouse, a Foreign Service Officer, had served in China for eleven years and later in the Department as Chief of the Division of Chinese Affairs. Woodruff Wallner with fifteen years experience in the Foreign Service, largely in France and Italy, had also acted as Chief of the Division of Western European Affairs in the Department of State. Landreth M. Harrison with twenty-three years service was particularly experienced in Polish and German affairs and well equipped to deal with persons coming from behind the Iron Curtain. In similar fashion Foreign Service Officer John E. Utter was a specialist in North African affairs and the Italian colonies, William Koren Jr. in French and European affairs, and William A. Crawford in Spanish and Russian affairs.

In order to assist the Ambassador in meeting certain social requirements of the Embassy and to take care of important visitors expected and otherwise, and to handle any sudden contingency, the Paris Embassy has a Conference Attaché as a special assistant to the Ambassador. The Conference Attaché must be a master of public relations and be prepared to satisfy any important visitor's whim or desire. When the President's Secretary wanted to obtain some photographs of the Mona Lisa and was unable to explain his wishes to the attendants at the Louvre, A. John Kelly,[10] the Conference Attaché, saw to it that his plane was delayed long enough next morning so that the prized prints were obtained. Incidentally, time

[10] Mr. Kelly was transferred early in February, 1951, to be special assistant to the American Ambassador in London, and Lee B. Blanchard was assigned to Paris as Conference Attaché.

was taken out to purchase four berets which only a thorough knowledge of Parisian shops made possible. Upon another occasion when information regarding a plane with a V.I.P. came in just before the plane was due, a radio message kept the plane circling the airport till Mr. Kelly arrived to meet the visitor properly.

On one occasion when Mr. Kelly met a friend of President Truman just before Mr. Vishinsky's plane arrived, the two waited to see the reception accorded the Soviet Foreign Minister. A clever columnist saw the two Americans and knowing Mr. Kelly's status wrote an article intimating that Kelly came to meet Mr. Vishinsky surreptitiously accompanied by one of President Truman's closest friends. Kelly's secretary spent the next four hours on the telephone denying the allegation.

Economic Affairs Section. Although the American Embassy in Paris is divided into political and economic sections there has long since ceased to be a clear demarcation between the two fields. However, the economic side of the Embassy has grown much faster than the political. For example, in 1935 out of eleven officers in the Embassy only three were interested primarily in economic, financial and commercial affairs. In 1950, however, there were eighteen officers whose primary interest was political affairs while twenty-two officers were interested in some phase of French economic activity.

At the head of this section is the Counselor for Economic Affairs, whose function it is to advise the Ambassador on all economic matters. France is decidedly lukewarm to the entrance of foreign business enterprises and the rôle of the Counselor for Economic Affairs is one beset with difficulties.

In most European countries—and France is no exception—Government officials are vested with much broader powers of discretion with respect to economic and commercial affairs than in the United States. This means that the activities of American nationals who wish to trade with, or conduct business and investment activity in such countries are subject to an enormous variety of administrative rulings which are modified from time to time, and which frequently require *ad hoc* interpretation. In addition, the United States Government is party to various bilateral and multilateral agreements which, although their terms may be clearly stated, nevertheless require application from case to case. Much of the work of the Economic Sections of American embassies in European countries is concerned with the protection and promotion of the interests of American nationals within this framework. Several cases may help to illustrate the type of problems which arise and the actions which American embassy officers are called upon to take.

For example, the program of the Coca Cola Company to reëstablish itself in France after the war was met by a storm of opposition on the part of the French winegrowers, and it took months of delicate negotiation on the part of the Embassy before a conditional entrance was accomplished, and the harassments of antiquated sanitary regulations and specific measures aimed at curtailment of operations somewhat controlled.

Another problem which required many months of the most arduous negotiations resulted from French exchange control in Morocco. A few American traders who had established themselves in Casablanca after the war resented French regulations put into force in December, 1948, which restricted American imports into Morocco. The Embassy succeeded in obtaining licensing arrangements and a considerable list of commodities importable without obtaining exchange from the French financial authorities. The traders were not satisfied, established a lobby in Washington and secured an amendment to the ECA Appropriation Act which denied the use of ECA funds to any nation discriminating against American nationals in its dependent territories. Since the United States had several treaties with Morocco, one dating back to 1836, and the French Protectorate was not established until 1912, a serious problem of treaty rights was involved. It was so complicated that the question was finally turned over to the International Court of Justice for a clarifying decision. Meanwhile the crippling amendment imposing serious restrictions upon ECA funds to France was temporarily suspended.

A third type of case may be illustrated by action arising out of the bilateral air navigation agreement between France and the United States. Trans-World Airlines had been designated by the United States and authorized by the French Government to fly to Paris and points beyond and to pick up passengers in France for other foreign destinations. In September, 1950, Pan American Airways absorbed American Overseas Airlines, which had also served various points in Europe. In connection with this merger, the United States designated PAA as a second carrier on the Paris route and requested from the French Government for PAA air traffic rights similar to those enjoyed by Trans-World Airlines. This action gave rise to extensive diplomatic negotiations since the French Government's interpretation of the terms of the agreement was somewhat different from that of the United States, and the French considered it necessary to protect their national air carrier, Air France, against the increased competition which it appeared would result from the operations of a second American airline on the Paris route.

In the field of strategic materials, Embassy officials have been called upon to perform numerous functions. They have, for example, assisted in the procurement of such strategic items as manganese and industrial alcohol from France for American governmental use. The latter was of vital use in the urgent need of additional production of synthetic rubber. They also have acted to check shipments of strategic exports from the United States destined to French consignees. In such cases, the U.S. Department of Commerce, before issuing an export license, requests the Embassy to look into the proposed transaction and to determine whether the French consignee, usually a private business concern, has actually given the order, and whether the commodity is intended for its own use. In this way, transshipments to hostile nations are avoided.

In addition to representations and negotiations in connection with the difficulties of American businessmen the Economic Section must *inter alia* prepare data for ECA hearings and other conferences of an economic nature, negotiate trade agreements, take care of congressmen and other important visitors interested in economic affairs, and deal with the various exchange control problems which are forever vexing American businessmen and visitors.

The Counselor for Economic Affairs, Clarence C. Brooks, is a Class I Foreign Service Officer with some thirty years experience, first with the Bureau of Foreign and Domestic Commerce and later with the Foreign Service. He is particularly familiar with the Latin American area and its problem from long first hand contacts. His deputy, Robert P. Terrill, First Secretary in the Embassy, had served as professor of economics in several universities and had seven years experience in the Department of State in important economic agencies before being assigned to the Paris post.

Commercial Section. An important part of the economic establishment in Paris is the office of the Commercial Attaché and his staff. Divided into a Trade and Commodities Unit and a Commercial Intelligence Unit this agency is largely concerned with trade promotion and commercial reporting. Thousands of trade inquiries either by letter or personal interview are answered annually and a considerable number of required and voluntary trade reports on commodities and conditions are sent in to Washington. In 1950 the Economic Section sent in over 1,000 requested reports and about 1,800 voluntary reports and prepared over 2,200 trade promotion letters.

This agency is equipped to give the American businessman any sort of information which he needs as to credit requirements, economic conditions, possibilities for the sale of his product, competitive products—in fact, a comprehensive picture of what he may expect in merchandising his product in France. To aid further, an up-to-date file of reports on all French firms and businessmen is made available. An excellent library includes the principal publications of the Department of Commerce, numerous manufacturer's publications, directories of French businesses and industries, business magazines, the Kiplinger and Whaley-Eaton services, Dun and Bradstreet, Thomas Register of American Manufacturers, Macrais Blue Book and even telephone directories of the principal American cities.

The number of estimated official conversations carried on by the Economic Section as indicated by the Operations Report for the year October 1, 1949, to October 1, 1950, is as follows:

With American Businessmen 7,267
With Foreign Businessmen 5,596
With Foreign Officials 3,603
Others 1,929

The Commercial Section in the same year prepared 2,396 trade promotion letters and completed 43 protection cases; 702 General Economic Reports were made; 400 World Trade Directory reports and 38 Trade Lists were prepared, and 272 Commodity and Industry Reports were submitted. An excellent Monthly Economic Review is prepared by the Commercial Section under the direction of Foreign Service Officer Seymore M. Finger which gives an overall analysis of French finance, trade and industry.

The Commercial Section is headed by Commercial Attaché George L. Bell, a lawyer and businessman of wide interests with considerable governmental experience in the Foreign Economic Administration and in the Department of Commerce. He has an assistant attaché, three Foreign Service officers and one Foreign Service Staff officer as his assistants.

The other divisions of the Embassy are the Agricultural Section under Monroe McCown which covers agriculture and livestock with special attention to grains and feeds, dairy products, grapes and wines, and fisheries; the Transportation and Communications Section under Foreign Service Officer Roland G. Cleveland, which includes civil aviation, by far the most important function of the office, railways, highways, telecommunications, electric power, shipping, inland waterways and seaports and harbors; incidentally this section was most prolific in reporting, turning in, from October 1, 1949, to October 1, 1950, 316 requested reports—one on seaports and harbors of a hundred pages—and 336 voluntary reports; the Fuel and Minerals Section which has jurisdiction over all questions concerning petroleum, coal, coke, lignite and liquid fuels in France and North Africa; this Section is headed by Olaf Sundt, a geologist and geophysicist with considerable experience with oil companies; the Labor Economics Section which is concerned with labor-movement organization, social security, wages, employment, labor statistics, housing and construction, has I. J. Fasteau, a social-service worker, in charge. The last economic division is the Combined Financial Section whose duty it is to keep the Department and the Embassy informed on French and foreign exchange requirements and resources, and matters pertaining to taxes, income trends, the budget, credit policy and French policy with respect to foreign investments. Foreign Service Officer Stanley M. Cleveland is in charge of this office.

Inasmuch as the recent assistance programs approved by the American

Congress have increased both the task and the responsibilities of the Combined Financial Section, close liaison is maintained with the United States Treasury Representative in Paris who serves as Adviser to the ECA Mission to France. With regard to the Mutual Defense Assistance Program, Edward G. Trueblood, a Foreign Service Officer of some twenty-three years experience, acts as liaison officer.

THE UNITED STATES INFORMATION AND EDUCATIONAL PROGRAM IN PARIS

In Paris the United States Information and Educational Service is a huge almost autonomous organization with a staff of approximately 130 persons housed in a magnificent building at 41 rue du Faubourg St. Honoré. However, the Public Affairs Officer in charge and his assistant, and the Press Attaché or Information Officer have their offices in the chancery, 2 avenue Gabriel. This arrangement makes possible a closer coöperation with the political and economic sections of the Embassy, but is not so satisfactory for the cultural affairs section which seems to function pretty much on its own.

As officially stated, the functions of the Public Affairs Division of the Embassy are to keep the French people informed as regards the American way of life and the nature and aims of American foreign policy and at the same time to promote better understanding between the peoples of the two countries. For administrative purposes the Division is divided roughly into informational and cultural activities.

Informational Activities. At the top of the information work is the Press Attaché, who is the liaison officer between the Ambassador and all information media including the press, national and international, the radio and moving pictures. It is the duty of the Press Attaché to see to it that the Embassy has what is termed "a good press." He is responsible for the preparation of press releases, the holding of press conferences and for summaries of the French press. A ticker machine housed in the Embassy from *Agence France-Presse* gives the material of the news as it goes to the French newspapers. This was found very useful when the French press upon one ocasion confused William Foster, the new head of ECA in Europe with William Z. Foster of Communist affiliations. The Press Attaché was able to inform the French Press Agency in time to stop the story in most of the French newspapers.

A close associate of the Press Attaché is the Information Officer, whose function it is to supervise the information program of the USIE throughout France. These services include the distribution of the publications of the USIE Press Office, which will be noted later, the showing of documentary films and the exhibition of photographic displays and the direction of the Radio Section which presents broadcasts on the French system and reports on the Voice of America.

In addition to the Press Attaché there is a Press Section whose function it is to furnish the French press with texts, documents, news items, feature articles, illustrations and background information on all phases of American life. Upon request the Section will furnish exclusive feature articles to French publications.

A series of regular publications is issued by the Press Section: *USA* is a daily ten-to-twelve-page bulletin in French carrying current political, economic, and social matters in such a way as to give French journalists an excellent working source for articles on current problems in the United States. About 3,700 copies are published.

The *Bulletin Economique* is a more specialized publication covering economic and financial developments in the United States which appears weekly and has a circulation of approximately 2,500 copies.

The *Document de la Quinzaine* is a bimonthly publication devoted to a fairly exhaustive consideration of some one question of American foreign policy or important problem of current importance, as for example, the North Atlantic Pact and the Point Four Program. Ten thousand copies are printed and are sent not only throughout France but to the French speaking countries.

Arts et Lettres is a weekly bulletin devoted to features and reviews of American literature, music, and art. It has a circulation of 6,700 copies.

Finally special pamphlets are prepared when warranted on vital subjects. For example, 20,000 copies of the State Department's report on the Berlin Crisis were distributed and in coöperation with the ECA mission to France 750,000 copies of an illustrated pamphlet on the Korean situation.

The Documentary Motion Picture Section is another part of the Information Division. Some 30 to 90 films are deposited in each of the seventeen centers operated by subsidiaries of the French Ministry of Education which assures the circulation of films in a professional manner. The film office in Paris has some 190 titles in French and 320 in English, totaling over 3,000 copies, which are booked for showing all over France through the Paris office or through consulates in Public Affairs Offices. It is estimated that during 1950 USIE films were seen by over 2,500,000 people.

The Exhibits and Photo Section both designs exhibits and takes and distributes pictures. The exhibits range from designing letterheads and signs to setting up stands at international exhibitions.

The Radio Section. The principal task of this section is to maintain liaison with the officials of *Radio Diffusion Française* (RDF), which relays the French language program of the Voice of America. A monitoring service is maintained to improve the quality of the French Voice of America program and every effort is made to give it maximum publicity. In order to secure greater interest in American music some 4,000 transcriptions were loaned during 1950 to RDF. The Radio Office broadcasts a weekly program of folk music, negro spirituals and jazz. Nearly 10,000 letters from listeners were received during 1950 and it was estimated that 24 per cent of the adult French population listened to "Ici New York" to some extent.

Cultural Relations. The office of the Cultural Relations Officer is responsible for serving as the channel for France for all phases of American cultural, intellectual, and educational life. Its head, the Cultural Attaché, not only supervises the cultural relations program but he is President of the United States Educational Commission for France (Fulbright), he is the Ambassador's representative on the Board of Trustees of the American Library in Paris and *ex officio* is a member of the Administrative Council of the United States House at the *Cité Universitaire*. Finally, he serves as liaison officer with ranking officials of the Office of Cultural Relations in the Ministry of Foreign Affairs and of the Ministry of National Education.

An important requirement for a successful cultural relations program is a good library. The Paris office has a fine library of some 8,000 volumes, 20,000 pamphlets, 450 regularly received periodicals, and 7 daily newspapers. The library in the Faubourg St. Honoré building covers educational, literary, philosophical, scientific, medical, and sociological aspects of the United States. (American fiction and poetry are still covered by the previously established American library in Paris.) The reading rooms are open to the public without restrictions and without charge.

One of the principal functions of the Cultural Relations division is the exchange of persons under the Fulbright and Smith-Mundt Acts. The administration of the exchange program in France including a large number of nongovernmental exchanges is a responsibility of this section.

Closely allied with this function is the giving of information regarding educational facilities in France. French teachers of English and American teachers of French are given particular attention by the agency. Cooperation regarding every phase of music, art, and theater as media of cultural exchange, on a reciprocity or mutually advantageous collaboration basis between French and American artists is encouraged.

Finally a speaker's bureau is maintained which aims to furnish American speakers to French audiences in either language upon subjects requested.

The principal objective of the cultural relations program in France has been succinctly expressed by Public Affairs Officer William R. Tyler: "To open the eyes of the French people to the spiritual, cultural and technical resources and activities of the American people in all fields of human endeavor, and in the struggle toward a better life for the average man and woman."

Personnel of USIE. At the head of the United States Information and Educational Activities organization is Public Affairs Officer, William R. Tyler, who also serves as Counselor to the Embassy. Mr. Tyler, born in France, educated in Oxford and Harvard, experienced in radio broadcasting, was former assistant director of the Office of International Information and Cultural Affairs. Assisting him is Public Affairs Officer Davis O. Harrington. Three press attachés are assigned to the Embassy—John L. Brown in charge of regional services in other cities in France, George L. Picard, and Elias A. McQuaid, these two also serving as information officers. There are also a number of Press Officers headed by Leopold J. LeClair. Working in this capacity is Mary V. Trent, the only woman career Foreign Service Officer in the Paris office. Other assistants are Exhibit and Photo Officer Paul C. Child, Radio Officer Simon J. Copans, and Motion Picture Officer Elmer S. Dorsay.

At the head of the Cultural Relations section is Leslie S. Brady [11] with degrees from several French institutions of learning who has served in the Paris Embassy since 1946. Assisting him are Mary P. Parsons, Director of the Library, and Assistant Cultural Officers Anita Lauve in charge of educational activities, Wilfred Allard head of the library and student unit, and Dorothea Speyer in charge of art and special groups unit.

The total personnel of the USIE in Paris as of December 31, 1950, numbered 129. As might be expected, such a large organization with so little background of experience is not a smooth running organization. One weakness is the too rapid change of personnel. Another is the building, which was constructed to be a private residence and has not been reconstructed to meet the needs of the USIE services. The library is hidden away so that the ordinary Frenchman would never know of its existence unless particularly instructed. One of the French cultural centers just outside of Paris complained that it received less coöperation from the United States Information Service than from any other country's similar agency although ours was by far the largest and best equipped. There is too little coöperation between the Embassy and the St. Honoré establishment, and the ordinary American citizen seeking aid or information in this field will wonder if American efficiency is an exportable product. Compared with the similar American establishments in Germany and Austria, the Paris establishment suffers, but in its defense it must be realized that it has not had the very considerable financial support which the occupational forces have had at their disposal. The intrinsic value of informational services cannot be overestimated and the Paris Embassy should be the center of such activities in Europe.

[11] Transferred to Saigon in 1951.

THE PARIS CONSULATE GENERAL

Descending the large open staircase to the first floor we come to the offices of the Consulate General. Since Paris has the largest American colony in the world and more visitors come to Paris than to any other European capital, the American Consulate General in Paris is a very busy one. In the year 1950 it delivered 100,440 pieces of visitors' mail and forwarded 15,800 others. It must be confessed that there are occasions when it faces demands greater than its powers, as for example when a young lady from South Dakota sent a letter in care of the Consulate asking that it be forwarded to some nice young, handsome man between eighteen and twenty years of age, with the further injunction to please give it to one that can speak and write English. No information was forthcoming as to whom it was delivered. On one occasion the mail clerk was able to assist a worried mother who had written her from the States regarding her son. The boy, a student at the Sorbonne, had failed to write his mother for several months. The next time he came to the Consulate to receive his mail, Miss Nadia Cooper, the clerk for visitor's mail, upbraided him for his negligence and obtained his promise to write to his mother immediately.

In addition to the many and varied duties which the consulate is called upon to perform for the casual visitor and tourist, there is a large amount of official routine work carried on here. In the year 1950 the American Consulate General in Paris performed more than 20,000 invoice services; some 7,000 passports were issued, renewed or amended; its notarial services amounted to about 17,000; its protection and whereabouts and welfare cases amounted to about 4,200.

It handled over 2,000 cases under the G. I. bill of rights and over 600 veterans' cases. Through the budget and fiscal officer it distributed about 25,000 checks to veterans and other Federal beneficiaries for compensation, social security, pensions, and other Federal payments.

The Visa Section of the Consulate General issued over 8,000 nonimmigrant visas and almost 4,000 immigrant visas, prepared over 50,000 pieces of correspondence and held almost 28,000 interviews in connection with visa services.

Incidentally, it is the Visa Section which is considerably handicapped by sudden and ill conceived legislation in regard to immigration. When in the fall of 1950 the McCarran Bill required revalidation of all visas and forbade the issuance of visas to all communists and also to any person at any time affiliated with Nazi, Fascisti or Falangist organizations, the Visa Division was swamped with applications for revalidation. The terms of the law were so broad and the exceptions permitted so limited that the act worked a great and unnecessary hardship upon many whose admission to the United States it was not the intent of the law to prevent.

Hundreds of thousands of francs were wasted in telegrams and the airways and steamship lines were dealt a body blow.

The Visa Section headed by R. Clyde Larkin has two clerks, Miss Courant, who has been in the service thirty years, and Mrs. Illine, twenty-seven years.

The Passport Section has as its head Miss Agnes Schneider, who began working in the Berlin Embassy as a passport clerk in 1916 and has served continuously in this work for thirty-four years.

The ranking officer, however, in point of service is Miss Adele Dix, in charge of welfare and whereabouts work, who has served the Department of State for thirty-six years of which the last six have been spent in the Paris office. A few incidents will indicate the variety of problems which come under the heading—welfare and whereabouts. A young woman, the hired companion of an eighty-two-year-old woman with no sense of direction, got separated from her charge in a crowd, and in hysterics appealed to the American Consulate. The Paris police were notified, but the old lady managed to find her way back to her hotel without assistance. An American woman tearfully telephoned the Consulate to help locate her boyfriend who had decamped from their hotel with all of her money. A tourist is taken very ill, no hope of recovery—the Consulate sells his car, pays his debts—gets his rail and steamship accommodations—has a nurse accompany him—he is met with a wheel chair, taken aboard, and arrangements made with the ship's doctor to take care of him. Miss Dix and her assistant Mrs. Hamlin are prepared to meet any emergency.

The specific duties of the Consulate are divided into sections as follows: citizenship and passport; invoice; secretarial; protection and welfare; seamen, shipping and airmen; visa; services for veterans and other Federal beneficiaries and finally the public mail room. The total personnel of the Consulate General including clerks, stenographers and messengers, is ninety-seven.

Rather than adduce a specific list of the services performed in these various departments, a few examples of the many and varied cases which the Paris Consulate General has been called upon to handle will illustrate the work:

An American woman was taken ill in a Paris hotel. The manager phoned the Consulate which had her removed to the American hospital and her effects packed and stored.

An American boy went violently insane and seriously wounded two people. The Consulate aided his mother to obtain his release from the asylum to take him back to the United States.

French law is notably strict as regards the employment of foreigners, but does permit certain specialists to practice their professions. Two American specialists in acoustics who were in difficulties were able to obtain workers' permits through the American Consulate.

Two American visitors to Paris in the fall of 1949 complained to the Consulate that their passports had been stolen from their hotel rooms by chance acquaintances. One of the passports was subsequently recovered and one was not.

Flowers are placed every Decoration Day on the tomb of an American girl who died in Paris, and during the year the grave is cared for at the request of relatives who send a check regularly to the Consulate for this purpose.

An American firm shipped goods to a Paris shop which was unable to pay for them. The Consulate took over the goods and had them shipped back to the American firm.

A New York laboratory wrote the American Consulate in Paris that it appreciated its detailed report regarding the market possibilities of their product in France. "Your reports are most complete," the letter stated, "and the information contained is most valuable to us."

The Consulate General received a commission from a New York firm to take testimony from a man in Paris regarding a very important law suit.

Becoming suspicious of a woman when she was examined for a visa on her passport, the Consulate notified the immigration authorities who checked up her record and found she was a white slaver and narcotics smuggler. She was intercepted at New York and deported.

Mr. R—— refused to give a plausible statement for the purpose of his visit to the United States. A check against the office card catalogue list of undesirables indicated that he was a blackmailer who had extorted many thousands of dollars from a prominent American family. The Consulate General did not grant his visa.

Inquiries regarding entrance of various commodities such as antique furniture, seeds and plants, and pedigreed dogs are answered; also requests for information regarding marriage and divorce laws; copies of canceled postage stamps are sent; no reasonable request for service from an American citizen is refused if it can be performed.

Enough has been said to show the varied tasks which the Paris Consulate General performs and their great importance to the individuals concerned. It is perhaps these personal attentions which make the consular service better known to the ordinary American citizen than is the diplomatic branch. Perhaps, also, the performance of these services makes the consul a little more friendly and human and therefore on the whole better liked than his diplomatic colleague. But both services are equally essential and the policy of housing them together under one roof should make them more helpful to each other as well as to the government which they represent.

At the head of this businesslike establishment is a Consul General who outlines the general administrative policy of the office and has supervision over the other consular offices in France. He receives the more important visitors and keeps in contact with the American colony and with French official and commercial circles. He also maintains a close relationship with the Embassy and the commercial attaché in connection with the coördination of trade. The present Consul General and Counselor of Embassy is Cecil Wayne Gray, a career officer of over twenty-five years service before taking his present post of Counselor of Embassy and Consul General at Paris in 1948. Immediately preceding this appointment Gray was Consul General at Marseilles. As a result of his long service as executive assistant to Secretary Hull and later as Chief of the Division of Foreign Service Personnel, few men in the Foreign Service are better known, and incidentally better liked, than "Joe" Gray.

The Administrative Division. With the vast and sudden expansion of both the Department of State and of our diplomatic and consular establishments abroad as a result of the war and its aftermath,[12] the need for greater administrative coördination arose. Unfortunately what began as an essential service has grown so rapidly that in Paris as elsewhere administration has become an end in itself. The result has been an overlapping of activities which in Paris has required a general overhauling and combining. The present organization of the Paris Embassy, Consulate General, and Information Services dates from a reorganization finally worked out by the Administrative Division by the spring of 1951.

The Administrative Division of the Paris Embassy as of March 31, 1951, numbered 416 persons. It should be noted however that whereas the total staff numbered only 830 persons, this latter number did not include the American government agencies completely supported by the American Embassy such as the military, treasury, health service, ECA mission to France, and others numbering 1,479. If we include agencies partly supported by the Embassy such as ECA, European Command Detachment, SHAPE, and others, the total number is 2,549.

As organized in the spring of 1951 the Administrative Division was headed by Chief of Division Graham A. Martin, who after considerable administrative experience in various governmental agencies was given the Paris post in 1947. There are six sections under his jurisdiction: Personnel, Security, Budget and Fiscal, General Services, Conference Attaché and the USIE Administration Section. All of these titles are self-explanatory except the General Services Section which is the largest and most varied in its tasks. Under the direction of Randolph Dickens, Jr., it supervises ten units as follows: Library, Reception Desk, Procurement and Supply, Building Maintenance and Equipment, Telephone, Communications, Mail, Files, Publications, Procurement, and Garage.

[12] In the past twelve years the personnel of the Department increased 480 per cent, that of the Foreign Service 200 per cent.

Liaison Activities.   Representatives of the Department of State are today closely tied in with many activities abroad which, although neither diplomatic nor consular, are essential to the successful performance of United States policy abroad. The two most important currently are the Mutual Defense Assistance Program and the Economic Cooperation Administration,[13] both of which are an integral part of the defense program of the United States.

In each of the European countries signatory of the North Atlantic Pact there were established Military Advisory Assistance Groups (MAAGs) with a representative of the Department of State serving upon it. We have noted already that Charles E. Bohlen represented the Department of State in France. He was assisted by Foreign Service Officer Edward G. Trueblood as MDAP Coördinator. Trueblood, a career officer of more than twenty years service as a specialist on French economy, was responsible for coördinating the work of the production phases of the defense program. Assisting him was an economic analyst and three secretaries.

The Special Economic Problems Staff which was concerned with the Economic Cooperation Administration was headed by Foreign Service Officers Nat B. King and Roland M. Brandin, Economic Attaché Sidney B. Jacques and Economic Officer Frank D. Taylor with some seven secretaries and assistants.

Mention should perhaps also be made of the UNESCO Adviser Charles A. Thomson, who ranked as Counselor of the Embassy. Although regarded by some as temporary activities, the trend seems to be in the direction of increased rather than less coöperation of the United States in such multilateral activities, and the Paris Embassy will always play a major rôle in their coördination and direction.

[13] Since January 1952 absorbed into the Mutual Security Agency.

23

Observations and Suggestions

Democratic Attitude towards Diplomacy. A curious anomaly exists in the attitude towards diplomacy generally found in democracies. It might be expected that inasmuch as the foreign office and its representatives abroad are the first line of defense against international trouble, public opinion would rally wholeheartedly to the support of such an organization; yet such is not the case. In fact, diplomacy, with its taboos of secrecy, its social trappings, and caste organization, is still regarded with skepticism or suspicion by the man in the street. A very keen observer of international affairs has cogently expressed the attitude: "Not merely our own, but practically all other modern democracies have exhibited suspicion of diplomacy and diplomatists—terms which to them have seemed to smack unpleasantly of spendthrift aristocracy and of imperial intrigues. The defects of a tradition have obscured the permanent necessity of the function." [1]

The average citizen can appreciate the value of a large army and navy as necessary insurance against war. He cannot visualize the still greater worth of an agency which attempts to conduct the relations of a state with its sister states in such a way as to make the requirement of a costly army and navy as unnecessary as possible. The laboratory-like action of a solvent against war does not possess the picturesque propaganda possibilities of the giant bombing plane or the sinister deadly power of the atomic bomb. The taxpayers' representatives will sanction millions for defense in military and naval appropriations, but balk at thousands for the prevention of war through diplomatic action. Comparing the amounts expended for diplomacy versus arms by the United States today, the ratio is about 50 to 1 in favor of arms.

Is there any valid reason for such an attitude? It must be confessed that there is. Democratic governments have not hesitated to employ dubious diplomatic methods when these suited their ends. The webs of deceit and the crude machinations of early twentieth century diplomacy were not less utilized by Junker Germany and Czarist Russia than by Republican France. Democratic Great Britain found itself pledged by secret com-

[1] Paul Scott Mowrer, *Our Foreign Affairs* (New York, 1924), 193.

mitments just as deeply as Imperial Austria. When the trained diplomats failed utterly in their mission to maintain peace, and the world's salvation was once more dependent upon the largest battalions, diplomatic prestige deservedly declined in value. The diplomat was regarded as either a "hierophant or a humbug," and diplomatic practice as Machiavellian intrigue. Its successes were dubious; its failures colossal.

It is unfortunately true even today that diplomacy is rigidly ruled by the dead hand of the past. The legal equality of states is no longer questioned in international relations, yet the unnecessary distinction between ambassadors and ministers established in international law over a century ago is still rigidly maintained. Why the United States should send an ambassador to Denmark and a minister to Switzerland when both states have approximately the same size and population is as difficult to explain to the ordinary citizen as why the United States waited until 1935 to send an ambassador to China. Is it reasonable for an experienced consul general to rank lower socially than a neophyte diplomatic secretary when in the foreign service he might rank in Class I to that of his colleague's Class VI? Is it surprising that the average citizen regards diplomacy as "either a mystery beyond him or a mummery beneath him"?

Secret Diplomacy. Another less valid basis for criticism leveled at diplomacy is its secrecy. It is a natural human attribute to be suspicious of the unknown. When, therefore, the democratic citizen gets the impression that the foreign office regards itself as a sacrosanct institution whose every movement must be shrouded in the most profound obscurity, he is resentful and suspicious. Yet every intelligent citizen appreciates the fact that delicate diplomatic negotiations cannot be carried on in the pitiless glare of present day press and radio publicity. No responsible foreign office or diplomatic representative could possibly achieve a reasonable compromise on a vital question without secrecy of deliberation. President Wilson's famous leader in his Fourteen Points, "Open covenants of peace, openly arrived at, after which ... diplomacy shall proceed always frankly and in the public view," was widely misunderstood. According to Ray Stannard Baker, his biographer, this did not mean that "the birth pains of the peace" should be exposed to the world, and President Wilson, himself, later explained that he did not intend that delicate questions should not be privately discussed, but rather that no secret agreements should be entered into, and that international policies when established should be open and above-board.[2]

If foreign offices would follow such an interpretation and make public the policies determined upon and keep the press informed as far as possible on points settled after negotiations, the average citizen would be

[2] Ray Stannard Baker, *Woodrow Wilson and the World Settlement* (New York, 1922), I, 137-8.

satisfied. A British member of Parliament who has been an ardent advocate of more open diplomacy has picturesquely expressed the idea: "The spiders of intrigue which have woven undisturbed their tangled webs in secret must be chased into the open light of day. The stuffy hot-house atmosphere of diplomacy must be cleansed by the fresh air of publicity." [3]

Diplomatic Snobbishness. There is also abroad in the land the idea that ordinary diplomats are both snobs and stuffed shirts. In fact, in a recent somewhat ribald volume on Washington politics the chapter devoted to the activities of the diplomatic corps was entitled "Starched Futility". Was not Rabelais speaking of diplomats when he described a number of officials in a long room measuring how far fleas could jump, cutting the fire with knives, and emptying water with nets?

It may be that in a democracy where simplicity is supposed to be a cardinal virtue a certain resentment exists against the social side of diplomatic life. In fact, the foolish regulations regarding diplomatic costumes imposed upon American diplomats, and the century long refusal of the United States to appoint envoys with the rank of ambassador, is a clear evidence of this sentiment. Nevertheless, it is most unfortunate that the average citizen does not appreciate the arduous work done by his diplomatic representatives in protecting his national interests, political, commercial and social. And it is perhaps even more unfortunate that he fails to realize that some of the diplomats' best work is achieved through personal contacts made in the social gatherings which he so acutely resents.

Every effort should be made to counteract this caustic and for the most part undeserved criticism. Social snobbery should be regarded as a high diplomatic crime and anyone guilty of it deemed unworthy of the service. It is not enough for a profession with a past to be virtuous—it must appear to be virtuous. Inasmuch as the tendency exists to look for snobbery in the diplomatic ranks, the officers in the service should avoid the least appearance of it. The instructions as regards diplomatic uniforms, for examples, show a complete failure to appreciate democratic psychology. The American citizen has no objection to the most dazzling regalia upon the proper occasion. In fact, he indulges this flair for ceremonial costume in many of his fraternal organizations. But the same individual who would be delighted to see his representative the most elaborately attired guest at a diplomatic soirée would turn up his nose with disgust at the sight of the same diplomatic secretary decked out with morning coat, spats, and a cane, on his way to the chancery. A former American consul general has aptly said, "The conduct of foreign relations, like domestic politics, is an intensely human business." [4] The press may justly be accused of propa-

[3] Arthur Ponsonby, *Democracy and Diplomacy* (London, 1915), 114.
[4] DeWitt C. Poole, *The Conduct of Foreign Relations under Modern Democratic Conditions* (New Haven, 1924), 14.

gating to a considerable extent this exaggerated caricature of the high hat or teahound diplomat. Incidents are often related with a distorted emphasis which make fine copy for the paper, but poor publicity for the service.

Unprincipled Partisanship.   An even more serious menace to the effective conduct of our foreign relations has been the scurrilous attacks upon the Department of State and the Foreign Service by a few blatant political demagogues and their notoriety-seeking radio and columnist claque. Even though the accusations are later proved to be false the damage has been done. The prestige of the United States abroad is weakened and the morale of the governmental personnel is undermined. Few men in public life have been denounced more bitterly or continuously than Secretary of State Acheson, with less justification. A really brilliant Ambassador-at-Large, Philip W. Jessup, who outmaneuvered Vishinsky and beat him at his own game, is alleged to have an affinity for Communist causes—is guilty by association. Yet his principal associations have been with the American Legion, the American Bar Association, and the American Society of International Law, and his closest personal affiliations were with Nicholas Murray Butler and Elihu Root. Even the much maligned Institute of Pacific Relations, which he headed for a brief period, was also headed by such men as Ray Lyman Wilbur, Robert Gordon Sproul, and Gerard Swope.

The Communist threat is real, but in trying to destroy it the methods of a witch hunt are not required. It is a shameful thing when Foreign Service officers with long, honorable careers behind them can be driven out of the service by reiterated accusations of disloyalty though they have been cleared by agencies set up for the adequate handling of such cases. Foreign Service Officers John Stewart Service and Oliver Edmund Clubb were thrown to the wolves although both were declared innocent of disloyalty after most rigorous investigations. Foreign Service Officers John Carter Vincent and John Paton Davies, Jr., suffered martyrdom before they were fully exonerated.

How can it be expected that the Foreign Service officer will report sincerely, objectively and fearlessly when his most confidential findings may be blazoned in the public press, distorted and held against him? Yet, if he doesn't report fully and honestly how can the Government at home formulate a policy based upon the facts of the case? Who would care to be a specialist today on Far Eastern affairs when the experts in the Far East are pilloried, broken and if cleared sent to posts where their life-long training is of no value? How will the United States obtain top-flight applicants for a service which is looked at askance by the man in the street? The figures show that it won't. In 1949, 1,128 candidates took the Foreign Service examinations, in 1950, only 807 applied, while in

1951 when special efforts were made to encourage applications only 760 took the examinations.

Unwise Appointments. The type of political appointment which is too often made in the United States, both in the State Department and in the diplomatic service, lends itself very readily to unfavorable publicity. The appointment some years ago of an unknown lawyer whose practice and training were limited to the Great Lakes region of the United States, as Assistant Secretary of State in charge of legal matters, was not of special importance. But when this picturesque Pickwickian individual tried to startle Washington society by the extreme modishness of his attire and the appointments of his "super de luxe" automobile, as well as by the unique originality of his methods, the press could not be blamed for seizing the opportunity afforded.

When the President of the United States appoints as a foreign minister to a friendly state a campaign manager under accusation of fraud, or when another President sends an ambassador to a neighboring country to get him out of the country before an investigation might uncover an unsavory situation in his municipality, the United States suffers both at home and abroad.

A more specific criticism as to appointments which has been leveled at the Department of State by the Foreign Service officers is the abuse of the provision permitting officers to be brought back from the field to serve for a limited time in the Department. This is a very useful provision, but at times it has been utilized in a way never foreseen by the authors of the law. A Foreign Service officer is ordered to the Department for duty, permitted to resign, his salary raised, and after a term of duty he is then reappointed to the service. In this way he makes more rapid progress towards the top than his colleagues who remain in the field.

It has also been asserted by those familiar with the situation that the practice of permitting a chosen few Foreign Service officers to resign and become permanent officers at the heads of policy determining divisions is primarily for the benefit of the individual and not for the good of the service. This is particularly true as regards the geographical divisions.

Excellent arguments may be found in favor of the appointment of outstanding men with no diplomatic training to a certain number of diplomatic posts abroad. Nevertheless, one of the principal champions of noncareer diplomats was guilty of a number of inexcusable violations of ordinary good taste while ambassador at the highest post in the American diplomatic service. The employment of a professional comedian as a waiter to insult the guests at a formal dinner may have been an amusing practical joke at the time, but the incident has not enhanced the prestige of American diplomacy.

M. de Callières in his famous classic on diplomacy tells the story of the

Grand Duke of Tuscany who complained to the Venetian Ambassador to Rome that the Republic of Venice had sent as resident to his court a person of no value, with neither judgment, knowledge, or attractive personal qualities. "I am not surprised," said the Ambassador, "we have many fools in Venice." "We also have fools in Florence," retorted the Grand Duke, "but we take care not to export them." [5]

Inadequate Allowances. A long standing weakness in the organization of the diplomatic service of the United States has been the failure to provide sufficient government funds for the diplomatic representative to perform properly the necessary functions of the office. Former Secretary of State Hughes declared in 1922: "The Diplomatic Service is greatly underpaid. A man of moderate means, whatever his ability, cannot accept the more important posts of ambassador or minister. These high offices are reserved to men of wealth, when in the interest of the country they should be within the reach of men of ability, whatever their private fortune. Certainly they should be within the reach of men of talent who have ignored the opportunities to amass wealth by reason of their long employment in the service of their country." [6]

The diplomatic envoy is constantly called upon to make addresses at important gatherings which are not held in the capital. He must travel first class, put up in a suite at the best hotel, and foot the bill out of his own pocket book. Americans abroad love to be entertained, and they expect their diplomatic representative to do this in no niggardly fashion. It has been estimated that an ambassador in one of the important European posts averages at least one hundred guests a week for dinner and an even larger number at afternoon tea. If an American golf or swimming team goes abroad to represent the United States, it must be entertained properly by the American representative. A college glee club cannot be completely overlooked. Even the people's representatives in Congress who, while in Washington, insist on little or no representation allowance, when they go abroad must be most elaborately entertained by their country's foreign representatives.

The envoy must belong to several important clubs, maintaining in them an irreproachable standing. It is in this way that many of the most valuable contacts are made. He must give a fixed minimum of official dinners to governmental officials and to his diplomatic confrères, and such affairs must be up to a certain standard, or the prestige of his country is impaired. Business concerns recognize this situation and provide for it, but the wealthiest country in the world apparently regards these matters with

[5] François de Callières, *De la manière de négocier avec les souverains* (Paris, 1716), 1716.

[6] Charles Evans Hughes, "Some Aspects of the Work of the Department of State," *American Journal of International Law,* XVI (July, 1922), 362.

complete indifference. Most appropriate to the case is the French aphorism, *"c'est par les dîners qu'on gouverne les hommes."*

John W. Davis, former Ambassador to Great Britain, when asked to testify before the House Committee on Foreign Affairs in 1922, declared that "it is notorious that we never have paid to our ministers and especially to our ambassadors in the larger capitals a salary on which it was possible for them to live, let alone carry on the ceremonial activities that are indispensable in their conditions." [7]

Under Secretary of State Frank L. Polk, testifying at the same time, gave it as his opinion that an ambassador, minister, or secretary, representing the United States in whatever capacity, would probably have to expend twice as much as his salary out of his own pocket in order to get along and do the decent, reasonable thing for his country. [8] Even the rich men who spend their own funds generously object to the system. Charlemagne Tower, former Ambassador to Germany, who spent a fortune in the service, declared that it was no more in keeping with national dignity for private funds to be used in connection with the diplomatic service than it would be to pay the expenses of the post office department by popular subscription.

Not only does this parsimonious policy on the part of the United States keep able men eminently well equipped, but unable to meet the financial requirements, from being appointed, but it has forced some very successful envoys to resign from their posts. [9] Others have held the position at extreme personal sacrifice and their families have been the sufferers. The story is told that General Noyes, Minister to France from 1877 to 1881, sacrificed his entire fortune of $150,000 in order to maintain the essential expenditures of the post. As a result his widow was later compelled to sell the products of a little truck garden to gain a bare subsistence.

The Foreign Service Act of 1946 which raised ambassadors' salaries from $17,500 to a maximum of $25,000 and also permitted an expense account amounting to $25,000 has been a notable advance in meeting this weakness. However, this maximum is given only to the most important posts where the incumbent must still draw upon his personal funds to maintain a position commensurate with his colleagues of the diplomatic corps. Even if salaries might be called adequate today there is still need for a larger maximum and greater flexibility in the expense accounts. In the words of the Japanese school boy, "Poverty are no disgrace for Methodist Minister, but for Foreign Minister it are a crime."

Improvements in the Foreign Service. Unquestionably the Foreign Service today from the standpoint of organization and personnel, if not

---

[7] *Hearings before Committee on Foreign Affairs*, H. R. 68th Cong., 1st sess., 206.
[8] *Ibid.*, 212.
[9] See *supra*, p. 324.

in morale, is at an all time high; nevertheless improvements are still in order. The home leave policy of the Department is still under criticism. Not sufficient attention is paid to the debilitating conditions of tropical posts or the strain placed upon officers serving behind the Iron Curtain. A three-months period every three years instead of a two-months vacation every two years would be less expensive and more relaxing.

There seems to be a widespread objection to the selection-out system. It has already been modified as to permitting three or four reviews by selection boards before an officer of Class VI is dismissed. However, it is still felt that since conditions vary so greatly in different posts that unless the officer has had experience in large and small posts in various categories of work it is unfair to base his entire future on performance reports.

The superabundance of administrative officers seems to be an almost universal weakness in the development of the Foreign Service today; a thorough housecleaning in this field would be welcomed heartily in most posts.

One serious strain which falls upon every Foreign Service officer sooner or later would be remedied if the Government were to supply the head of every diplomatic and consular post with a sum of money to be used in exceptional cases for the repatriation of deserving Americans. Although many cases come to the attention of Foreign Service officers which can be dismissed summarily, occasionally a situation arises in which the officer is compelled to use his own funds. At present in a few large capitals American residents can be called upon to aid, but a confidential emergency fund supplied by the Government, to be used only as a last resort and in the form of a loan, would be an invaluable boon, and its abuse could be reduced to a minimum. Many countries make such provision, and the United States at one time had such a fund. Its reëstablishment is heartily recommended.

There was a time not so many years ago when the American Foreign Service was deservedly unpopular. No excuse for such an attitude exists today. A prominent former member of the British diplomatic service goes so far as to say that "Those ... who were traveling on the continent in August, 1914, and were caught in the cataclysm, were in a position to compare the way in which British and American missions or consulates dealt with the emergency. I think they will agree that so far as private individuals went, the Americans were much more hopeful and human." [10]

The American diplomatic and consular service has improved considerably since that time, and both in organization and personnel now stands second to none. Nevertheless it is well to take heed of the advice given by a career diplomat to the young officers entering the service—"You must expect neither financial rewards nor the rewards of prestige extended to

[10] George Young, *Diplomacy Old and New* (New York, 1921), 17.

officers of the Army and Navy; expect no appreciation of your services from the public nor from the Government; all that you can expect is the reward springing from the consciousness of duty faithfully performed in the service of your country."

But no service today is more important to the nation than the Foreign Service. The United States has become a world power and has taken upon itself world responsibilities vital to its very existence. Never before in history have the problems of foreign policy been more difficult and acute than they are today and never before has it been so essential that they be settled by peaceful means.

Since the primary causes of war are conflicts in Foreign Policy our first line of defense is the machinery for the conduct of foreign relations. We still need the best possible army, navy, and air force to support our foreign policy but this policy must merit defense. A well organized, adequately qualified Department of State at home and a well trained experienced Foreign Service abroad should be able to aid the President formulate such a policy. If the Government will give these agencies the necessary support and if the American people will appreciate the value of their achievements the most effective machinery existing today for the maintenance of peace and friendly relations between states will be raised to the important position that it has long merited.

Appendix A

Presidents and Secretaries of State

1789–1952

President	*Secretary of State*

Secretary of State

John Jay, of New York. Took office as Secretary for Foreign Affairs under the Continental Congress, December 21, 1784; held over without further appointment or commission and continued, though not officially, to superintend the Department under the Constitution until Jefferson took office as Secretary of State on March 22, 1790.

GEORGE WASHINGTON
   of Virginia
   April 30, 1789-March 4, 1797

Thomas Jefferson, of Virginia. Commissioned September 26, 1789, and entered upon duties March 22, 1790; retired December 31, 1793.

Edmund Randolph, of Virginia. Commissioned and entered upon duties January 2, 1794; retired August 20, 1795.

Timothy Pickering, of Pennsylvania (Secretary of War). *Ad interim* August 20-December 9, 1795; commissioned Secretary of State and entered upon duties December 10, 1795.

JOHN ADAMS
   of Massachusetts
   March 4, 1797-March 4, 1801

Timothy Pickering, continued from preceding administration; retired May 12, 1800.

Charles Lee, of Virginia (Attorney General). *Ad interim* May 13-June 5, 1800.

John Marshall, of Virginia. Commissioned May 13, 1800, and entered upon duties June 6, 1800; retired February 4, 1801; (Chief Justice of the United States) *ad interim* February 4-March 3, 1801.

THOMAS JEFFERSON
   of Virginia
   March 4, 1801-March 4, 1809

John Marshall, of Virginia (Chief Justice). *Ad interim* March 4, 1801.

Levi Lincoln, of Massachusetts (Attorney

427

President

Secretary of State

General). *Ad interim* March 5-May 1, 1801.

James Madison, of Virginia. Commissioned March 5, 1801, and entered upon duties May 2, 1801; retired March 3, 1809.

JAMES MADISON
of Virginia
March 4, 1809-March 4, 1817

(No Secretary of State or Acting Secretary of State, March 4-5, 1809.)

Robert Smith, of Maryland. Commissioned and entered upon duties March 6, 1809; retired April 1, 1811.

James Monroe, of Virginia. Commissioned (recess of the Senate) April 2, 1811, and entered upon duties April 6, 1811; recommissioned November 26, 1811; retired September 30, 1814; (Secretary of War) *ad interim* October 1, 1814-February 28, 1815; commissioned February 28, 1815, and entered upon duties March 1, 1815; retired March 3, 1817.

JAMES MONROE
of Virginia
March 4, 1817-March 4, 1825

John Graham, of Virginia (Chief Clerk). *Ad interim* March 4-9, 1817.

Richard Rush, of Pennsylvania (Attorney General). *Ad interim* March 10-September 22, 1817.

John Quincy Adams, of Massachusetts. Commissioned March 5, 1817, and entered upon duties September 22, 1817; retired March 3, 1825.

JOHN QUINCY ADAMS
of Massachusetts
March 4, 1825-March 4, 1829

Daniel Brent, of Virginia (Chief Clerk). *Ad interim* March 4-7, 1825.

Henry Clay, of Kentucky. Commissioned and entered upon duties March 7, 1825; retired March 3, 1829.

ANDREW JACKSON
of Tennessee
March 4, 1829-March 4, 1837

James A. Hamilton, of New York. *Ad interim* March 4-27, 1829.

Martin Van Buren, of New York. Commissioned March 6, 1829, and entered upon duties March 28, 1829; retired May 23, 1831.

Edward Livingston, of Louisiana. Commissioned and entered upon duties May 24, 1831; recommissioned January 12, 1832; retired May 29, 1833.

Louis McLane, of Delaware. Commissioned (recess of the Senate) and entered upon duties May 29, 1833; retired June 30, 1834.

John Forsyth, of Georgia. Commissioned June 27, 1834, and entered upon duties July 1, 1834.

MARTIN VAN BUREN
of New York
March 4, 1837-March 4, 1841

John Forsyth, continued from preceding administration; retired March 3, 1841.

WILLIAM HENRY HARRISON
of Ohio
March 4-April 4, 1841

Jacob L. Martin, of North Carolina (Chief Clerk). *Ad interim* March 4-5, 1841.

Daniel Webster, of Massachusetts. Commissioned March 5, 1841, and entered upon duties March 6, 1841.

JOHN TYLER
of Virginia
April 6, 1841-March 4, 1845

Daniel Webster, continued from preceding administration; retired May 8, 1843.

Hugh S. Legaré, of South Carolina (Attorney General). *Ad interim* May 9-June 20, 1843 (died).

William S. Derrick, of Pennsylvania (Chief Clerk). *Ad interim* June 21-23, 1843.

Abel P. Upshur, of Virginia (Secretary of the Navy). *Ad interim* June 24-July 23, 1843; commissioned (recess of the Senate) and entered upon duties July 24, 1843; recommissioned January 2, 1844; died February 28, 1844.

John Nelson, of Maryland (Attorney General). *Ad interim* February 29-March 31, 1844.

John C. Calhoun, of South Carolina. Commissioned March 6, 1844, and entered upon duties April 1, 1844.

JAMES K. POLK
of Tennessee
March 4, 1845-March 4, 1849

John C. Calhoun, continued from preceding administration; retired March 10, 1845.

James Buchanan, of Pennsylvania. Commissioned March 6, 1845, and entered upon duties March 10, 1845.

ZACHARY TAYLOR
of Louisiana
March 5, 1849-July 9, 1850

James Buchanan, continued from preceding administration; retired March 7, 1849.

John M. Clayton, of Delaware. Commissioned March 7, 1849, and entered upon duties March 8, 1849.

President	Secretary of State
MILLARD FILLMORE of New York July 10, 1850-March 4, 1853	John M. Clayton, continued from preceding administration; retired July 22, 1850. Daniel Webster, of Massachusetts. Commissioned July 22, 1850, and entered upon duties July 23, 1850; died October 24, 1852. Charles M. Conrad, of Louisiana (Secretary of War). *Ad interim* October 25-November 5, 1852. Edward Everett, of Massachusetts. Commissioned (recess of Senate) and entered upon duties November 6, 1852; recommissioned December 9, 1852; retired March 3, 1853.
FRANKLIN PIERCE of New Hampshire March 4, 1853-March 4, 1857	William Hunter, Jr., of Rhode Island (Chief Clerk). *Ad interim* March 4-7, 1853. William L. Marcy, of New York. Commissioned March 7, 1853, and entered upon duties March 8, 1853.
JAMES BUCHANAN of Pennsylvania March 4, 1857-March 4, 1861	William L. Marcy, continued from preceding administration; retired March 6, 1857. Lewis Cass, of Michigan. Commissioned and entered upon duties March 6, 1857; retired December 14, 1860. William Hunter, Jr., of Rhode Island (Chief Clerk). *Ad interim* December 15-16, 1860. Jeremiah S. Black, of Pennsylvania. Commissioned and entered upon duties December 17, 1860.
ABRAHAM LINCOLN of Illinois March 4, 1861-April 15, 1865	Jeremiah S. Black, continued from preceding administration; retired March 5, 1861. William H. Seward, of New York. Commissioned March 5, 1861; entered upon duties March 6, 1861.
ANDREW JOHNSON of Tennessee April 15, 1865-March 4, 1869	William H. Seward, continued from preceding administration; retired March 4, 1869.
ULYSSES S. GRANT of Illinois March 4, 1869-March 4, 1877	Elihu B. Washburne, of Illinois. Commissioned and entered upon duties March 5, 1869; retired March 16, 1869.

Hamilton Fish, of New York. Commissioned March 11, 1869; entered upon duties March 17, 1869; recommissioned March 17, 1873.

RUTHERFORD B. HAYES
of Ohio
March 5, 1877-March 4, 1881

Hamilton Fish, continued from preceding administration; retired March 12, 1877.
William M. Evarts, of New York. Commissioned and entered upon duties March 12, 1877.

JAMES A. GARFIELD
of Ohio
March 4-September 19, 1881

William M. Evarts, continued from preceding administration; retired March 7, 1881.
James G. Blaine, of Maine. Commissioned March 5, 1881, and entered upon duties March 7, 1881.

CHESTER A. ARTHUR
of New York
September 20, 1881-March 4, 1885

James G. Blaine, continued from preceding administration; retired December 19, 1881.
Frederick T. Frelinghuysen, of New Jersey. Commissioned December 12, 1881, and entered upon duties December 19, 1881.

GROVER CLEVELAND
of New York
March 4, 1885-March 4, 1889

Frederick T. Frelinghuysen, continued from preceding administration; retired March 6, 1885.
Thomas F. Bayard, of Delaware. Commissioned March 6, 1885, and entered upon duties March 7, 1885.

BENJAMIN HARRISON
of Indiana
March 4, 1889-March 4, 1893

Thomas F. Bayard, continued from preceding administration; retired March 6, 1889.
James G. Blaine, of Maine. Commissioned March 5, 1889, and entered upon duties March 7, 1889; retired June 4, 1892.
William F. Wharton, of Massachusetts (Assistant Secretary). *Ad interim* June 4-29, 1892.
John W. Foster, of Indiana. Commissioned and entered upon duties June 29, 1892; retired February 23, 1893.
William F. Wharton, of Massachusetts (Assistant Secretary). *Ad interim* February 24, 1893, to close of administration.

President	Secretary of State
GROVER CLEVELAND of New York March 4, 1893-March 4, 1897	William F. Wharton, continued *ad interim* from preceding administration to March 6, 1893. Walter Q. Gresham, of Illinois. Commissioned March 6, 1893, and entered upon duties March 7, 1893; died May 28, 1895. Edward F. Uhl, of Michigan (Assistant Secretary). *Ad interim* May 28-June 9, 1895. Richard Olney, of Massachusetts. Commissioned (recess of the Senate) June 8, 1895, and entered upon duties June 10, 1895; recommissioned December 3, 1895.
WILLIAM McKINLEY of Ohio March 4, 1897-September 14, 1901	Richard Olney, continued from preceding administration; retired March 5, 1897. John Sherman, of Ohio. Commissioned March 5, 1897, and entered upon duties March 6, 1897; retired April 27, 1898. William R. Day, of Ohio. Commissioned April 26, 1898, and entered upon duties April 28, 1898; retired September 16, 1898. Alvey A. Adee, of the District of Columbia (Second Assistant Secretary). *Ad interim* September 17-29, 1898. John Hay, of District of Columbia. Commissioned (recess of the Senate) September 20, 1898, and entered upon duties September 30, 1898; recommissioned December 7, 1898, and March 5, 1901.
THEODORE ROOSEVELT of New York September 14, 1901-March 4, 1909	John Hay, continued from preceding administration; recommissioned March March 6, 1905; died July 1, 1905. Francis B. Loomis, of Ohio (Assistant Secretary). *Ad interim* July 1-18, 1905. Elihu Root, of New York. Commissioned (recess of the Senate) July 7, 1905, and entered upon duties July 19, 1905; recommissioned December 6, 1905; retired January 27, 1909. Robert Bacon, of New York. Commissioned and entered upon duties January 27, 1909.

WILLIAM HOWARD TAFT
of Ohio
March 4, 1909-March 4, 1913

Robert Bacon, continued from preceding administration, and retired March 5, 1909.

Philander C. Knox, of Pennsylvania. Commissioned March 5, 1909, and entered upon duties March 6, 1909.

WOODROW WILSON
of New Jersey
March 4, 1913-March 4, 1921

Philander C. Knox, continued from preceding administration; retired March 5, 1913.

William Jennings Bryan, of Nebraska. Commissioned and entered upon duties March 5, 1913; retired June 9, 1915.

Robert Lansing, of New York (Counselor). *Ad interim* June 9-23, 1915; commissioned (recess of the Senate) June 23, 1915, and entered upon duties June 24, 1915; recommissioned December 13, 1915; retired February 13, 1920.

Frank Lyon Polk, of New York (Under Secretary). *Ad interim* February 14-March 14, 1920.

(No Secretary of State or Acting Secretary of State March 15-21, 1920).

Bainbridge Colby, of New York. Commissioned March 22, 1920, and entered upon duties March 23, 1920; retired March 4, 1921.

WARREN GAMALIEL HARDING
of Ohio
March 4, 1921-August 2, 1923

Charles Evans Hughes, of New York. Commissioned March 4, 1921, and entered upon duties March 5, 1921.

CALVIN COOLIDGE
of Massachusetts
August 3, 1923-March 4, 1929

Charles Evans Hughes, continued from preceding administration; retired March 4, 1925.

Frank Billings Kellogg, of Minnesota. Commissioned February 16, 1925, and entered upon duties March 5, 1925.

HERBERT CLARK HOOVER
of California
March 4, 1929-March 4, 1933

Frank Billings Kellogg, continued from preceding administration; retired March 28, 1929.

Henry Lewis Stimson, of New York. Commissioned March 5, 1929, and entered upon duties March 28, 1929; retired March 4, 1933.

President	Secretary of State

President

FRANKLIN DELANO ROOSEVELT
of New York
March 4, 1933-April 12, 1945

Secretary of State

Cordell Hull, of Tennessee. Commissioned and entered upon duties March 4, 1933; retired November 30, 1944.

Edward R. Stettinius, Jr., of Virginia. Commissioned November 30, 1944, and entered upon duties December 1, 1944.

HARRY S. TRUMAN
of Missouri
April 12, 1945-

Edward R. Stettinius, Jr., continued from preceding administration; retired June 27, 1945.

Joseph Clark Grew, of New Hampshire (Under Secretary). *Ad interim* June 28-July 3, 1945.

James Francis Byrnes, of South Carolina. Commissioned July 2, 1945, and entered upon duties July 3, 1945; retired January 21, 1947.

George Catlett Marshall, of Pennsylvania. Commissioned January 8, 1947, and entered upon duties January 21, 1947; retired January 20, 1949.

Dean G. Acheson, of Maryland. Commissioned January 19, 1949, and entered upon duties January 21, 1949.

Appendix B
American Diplomatic Representatives to Countries Important to the United States

Minister Plenipotentiary
> Caesar A. Rodney, of Delaware, January 27, 1823.

Chargés d'Affaires
> John M. Forbes, of Florida, March 9, 1825.
> Francis Baylies, of Massachusetts, January 3, 1832.
> William Brent, Jr., of Virginia, June 14, 1844.
> William A. Harris, of Virginia, February 19, 1846.
> John S. Pendleton, of Virginia, February 27, 1851.
> James A. Peden, of Florida, May 22, 1854.

Ministers Resident
> James A. Peden, of Florida, June 29, 1854.
> Benjamin C. Yancey, of Georgia, June 14, 1858.
> John F. Cushman, of Mississippi, July 18, 1859.
> Robert M. Palmer, of Pennsylvania, March 28, 1861.
> Robert C. Kirk, of Ohio, March 4, 1862.
> Alexander Asboth,[1] of Missouri, March 12, 1866.
> H. G. Worthington,[1] of Nevada, June 5, 1868.
> Robert C. Kirk, of Ohio, April 16, 1869.
> Julius White, of Illinois, December 12, 1872.
> Thomas O. Osborn, of Illinois, February 10, 1874.

Ministers Resident and Consuls General
> Thomas O. Osborn, of Illinois, July 7, 1884.
> Bayless W. Hanna, of Indiana, June 17, 1885.

Envoys Extraordinary and Ministers Plenipotentiary
> Bayless W. Hanna, of Indiana, July 1, 1887.
> John R. G. Pitkin, of Louisiana, July 26, 1889.
> William I. Buchanan, of Iowa, January 26, 1894.

[1] Accredited also to Uruguay.

William P. Lord, of Oregon, October 16, 1899.
John Barrett, of Oregon, July 2, 1903.
Arthur M. Beaupré, of Illinois, March 17, 1904.
Spencer F. Eddy, of Illinois, April 2, 1908.
Charles H. Sherrill, of New York, April 1, 1909.
John W. Garrett, of Maryland, December 14, 1911.

Ambassadors Extraordinary and Plenipotentiary

Frederic Jesup Stimson, of Massachusetts, October 1, 1914.
John W. Riddle, of Connecticut, November 18, 1921.
Peter Augustus Jay, of Rhode Island, March 18, 1925.
Robert Woods Bliss, of New York, February 17, 1927.
Alexander W. Weddell, of Virginia, June 3, 1933.
Norman Armour, of New Jersey, May 18, 1939.
Spruille Braden, of New York, May 8, 1945.
George S. Messersmith, of Delaware, April 12, 1946.
James Bruce, of Maryland, July 12, 1947.
Stanton Griffis, of Connecticut, September 22, 1949.
Ellsworth Bunker, of New York, March 13, 1951.

BELGIUM

Chargés d'Affaires

Hugh S. Legaré, of South Carolina, April 14, 1832.
Virgil Maxcy, of Maryland, June 16, 1837.
Henry W. Hilliard, of Alabama, May 12, 1842.
Thomas G. Clemson, of Pennsylvania, June 17, 1844.
Richard H. Bayard, of Delaware, December 10, 1850.
J. J. Seibels, of Alabama, May 24, 1853.

Ministers Resident

J. J. Seibels, of Alabama, June 29, 1854.
Elisha Y. Fair, of Alabama, June 14, 1858.
Henry S. Sanford, of Connecticut, March 20, 1861.
Joseph Russell Jones, of Illinois, March 15, 1870.
Ayres Phillips Merrill, of Mississippi, January 7, 1876.
William C. Goodloe, of Kentucky, March 4, 1878.
James O. Putnam, of New York, June 4, 1880.
Nicholas Fish, of New York, April 28, 1882.
Lambert Tree, of Illinois, July 3, 1885.

Envoys Extraordinary and Ministers Plenipotentiary

Lambert Tree, of Illinois, August 10, 1888.
John G. Parkhurst, of Michigan, October 1, 1888.
Edwin H. Terrell, of Texas, April 1, 1889.
James S. Ewing, of Illinois, April 8, 1893.
Bellamy Storer, of Ohio, May 4, 1897.
Lawrence Townsend, of Pennsylvania, April 12, 1899.
Henry Lane Wilson, of Washington, March 8, 1905.
Charles Page Bryan, of Illinois, December 21, 1909.
Larz Anderson, of District of Columbia, August 12, 1911.
Theodore Marburg, of Maryland, November 22, 1912.
Brand Whitlock, of Ohio, December 22, 1913.

Ambassadors Extraordinary and Plenipotentiary

Brand Whitlock, of Ohio, September 30, 1919.
Henry P. Fletcher,[2] of Pennsylvania, March 6, 1922.
William Phillips,[2] of Massachusetts, February 29, 1924.
Hugh S. Gibson,[2] of California, February 17, 1927.
Dave Hennen Morris,[2] of New York, May 18, 1933.
Hugh S. Gibson, of California, July 13, 1937.
Joseph E. Davies, of District of Columbia, May 14, 1938.
John Cudahy, of Wisconsin, January 12, 1940.
Anthony J. Drexel Biddle, Jr., of Pennsylvania, February 11, 1941.
Charles Sawyer, of Ohio, September 21, 1944.
Admiral Alan G. Kirk, of U. S. Navy, February 1, 1946.
Robert D. Murphy, of Wisconsin, September 22, 1949.

BRAZIL

Chargés d'Affaires

Condy Raguet, of Pennsylvania, March 9, 1825.
William Tudor, of Massachusetts, June 26, 1827.
Ethan A. Brown, of Ohio, May 26, 1830.
William Hunter, of Rhode Island, June 28, 1834.

Envoys Extraordinary and Ministers Plenipotentiary

William Hunter, of Rhode Island, September 13, 1841.
George H. Proffit, of Indiana, June 7, 1843.
Henry A. Wise, of Virginia, February 8, 1844.
David Tod, of Ohio, March 3, 1847.
Robert C. Schenck, of Ohio, March 12, 1851.
William Trousdale, of Tennessee, May 24, 1853.
Richard K. Meade, of Virginia, July 27, 1857.
James Watson Webb, of New York, May 31, 1861.
Henry T. Blow, of Missouri, May 1, 1869.
James R. Partridge, of Maryland, May 23, 1871.
Henry W. Hilliard, of Georgia, July 31, 1877.
Thomas A. Osborn, of Kansas, May 19, 1881.
Thomas J. Jarvis, of North Carolina, April 2, 1885.
Robert Adams, Jr., of Pennsylvania, March 30, 1889.
Edwin H. Conger, of Iowa, September 27, 1890.
Thomas L. Thompson, of California, April 24, 1893.
Edwin H. Conger, of Iowa, May 27, 1897.
Charles Page Bryan, of Illinois, January 19, 1898.
David E. Thompson, of Nebraska, September 26, 1902.

Ambassadors Extraordinary and Plenipotentiary

David E. Thompson, of Nebraska, January 13, 1905.
Lloyd C. Griscom, of Pennsylvania, January 29, 1906.
Irving B. Dudley, of California, December 19, 1906.
Edwin V. Morgan, of New York, January 18, 1912.
Hugh S. Gibson, of California, May 11, 1933.
Jefferson Caffery, of Louisiana, July 13, 1937.

[2] Accredited also to Luxemburg.

Adolf A. Berle, Jr., of New York, January 18, 1945.
William D. Pawley, of Florida, April 12, 1946.
Herschel V. Johnson, of North Carolina, April 14, 1948.

CANADA

Envoys Extraordinary and Ministers Plenipotentiary

William Phillips, of Massachusetts, February 17, 1927.
Hanford MacNider, of Iowa, June 20, 1930.
Warren Delano Robbins, of New York, May 11, 1933.
Norman Armour, of New Jersey, May 29, 1935.
Daniel C. Roper, of District of Columbia, May 9, 1939.
James H. R. Cromwell, of New Jersey, January 12, 1940.
Jay Pierrepont Moffat, of New Hampshire, June 4, 1940.
Ray Atherton, of Illinois, July 8, 1943.

Ambassadors Extraordinary and Plenipotentiary

Ray Atherton, of Illinois, November 18, 1943.
Laurence A. Steinhardt, of New York, August 12, 1948.
Stanley Woodward, of Pennsylvania, May 23, 1950.

CHILE

Minister Plenipotentiary

Heman Allen, of Vermont, January 27, 1823.

Chargés d'Affaires

Samuel Larned, of Rhode Island, February 29, 1828.
John Hamm, of Ohio, May 26, 1830.
Richard Pollard, of Virginia, June 28, 1834.
John S. Pendleton, of Virginia, August 16, 1841.
William Crump, of Virginia, April 10, 1844.
Seth Barton, of Louisiana, May 27, 1847.

Envoys Extraordinary and Ministers Plenipotentiary

Balie Peyton, of Tennessee, August 9, 1849.
David A. Starkweather, of Ohio, June 29, 1854.
John Bigler, of California, April 2, 1857.
Thomas H. Nelson, of Indiana, June 1, 1861.
Judson Kilpatrick, of New Jersey, November 11, 1865.
Joseph P. Root, of Kansas, September 15, 1870.
Cornelius A. Logan, of Kansas, March 17, 1873.
Thomas A. Osborn, of Kansas, May 31, 1877.
Judson Kilpatrick, of New Jersey, May 19, 1881.

Special Envoy Extraordinary and Minister Plenipotentiary

William Henry Trescot, of South Carolina, November 28, 1881.

Envoys Extraordinary and Ministers Plenipotentiary

Cornelius A. Logan, of Illinois, March 15, 1882.
William R. Roberts, of New York, April 2, 1885.
Patrick Egan, of Nebraska, March 30, 1889.

James D. Porter, of Tennessee, April 4, 1893.
Edward H. Strobel, of New York, December 13, 1894.
Henry L. Wilson, of Washington, June 9, 1897.
John Hicks, of Wisconsin, July 14, 1905.
Thomas C. Dawson, of Iowa, April 21, 1909.
Henry P. Fletcher, of Pennsylvania, December 21, 1909.

Ambassadors Extraordinary and Plenipotentiary

Henry P. Fletcher, of Pennsylvania, October 1, 1914.
Joseph H. Shea, of Indiana, March 6, 1916.
William Miller Collier, of New York, June 29, 1921.
William S. Culbertson, of Kansas, June 19, 1928.
Hal H. Sevier, of Texas, August 19, 1933.
Hoffman Philip, of New York, July 22, 1935.
Norman Armour, of New Jersey, January 17, 1938.
Claude G. Bowers, of New York, June 22, 1939.

CHINA

Envoy Extraordinary and Minister Plenipotentiary
Caleb Cushing, of Massachusetts, May 8, 1843.

Commissioners

Caleb Cushing, of Massachusetts, May 8, 1843.
Alexander H. Everett, of Massachusetts, March 13, 1845.
John W. Davis, of Indiana, January 3, 1848.
Thomas A. R. Nelson, of Tennessee, March 6, 1851.
Humphrey Marshall, of Kentucky, August 4, 1852.
Robert M. McLane, of Maryland, October 18, 1853.
Peter Parker, of Massachusetts, August 16, 1855.

Envoys Extraordinary and Ministers Plenipotentiary

William B. Reed, of Pennsylvania, April 18, 1857.
John E. Ward, of Georgia, December 15, 1858.
Anson Burlingame, of Massachusetts, June 14, 1861.
J. Ross Browne, of California, March 11, 1868.
Frederick F. Low, of California, September 28, 1869.
Benjamin P. Avery, of California, April 10, 1874.
George F. Seward, of California, January 7, 1876.
James B. Angell, of Michigan, April 9, 1880.
John Russell Young, of New York, March 15, 1882.
Charles Denby, of Indiana, May 29, 1885.
Charles Page Bryan, of Illinois, November 10, 1897.
Edwin H. Conger, of Iowa, January 19, 1898.

Commissioner

William Woodville Rockhill, of District of Columbia, July 19, 1900.

Envoys Extraordinary and Ministers Plenipotentiary

William Woodville Rockhill, of District of Columbia, March 8, 1905.
Charles R. Crane, of Illinois, July 23, 1909.
William James Calhoun, of Illinois, December 21, 1909.

Paul S. Reinsch, of Wisconsin, August 15, 1913.
Charles R. Crane, of Massachusetts, March 22, 1920.
Jacob Gould Schurman, of New York, June 2, 1921.
John Van A. MacMurray, of New Jersey, April 9, 1925.
Nelson T. Johnson, of Oklahoma, December 16, 1929.

Ambassadors Extraordinary and Plenipotentiary

Nelson T. Johnson, of Oklahoma, June 18, 1935.
Clarence E. Gauss, of Connecticut, February 11, 1941.
Maj. Gen. Patrick J. Hurley, of New Mexico, November 30, 1944.

Special Representative of the President with Rank of Ambassador

General of the Army George C. Marshall, of Pennsylvania, November 27, 1945.

Ambassador Extraordinary and Plenipotentiary [3]

J. Leighton Stuart, of New York, July 12, 1946.

CUBA

Envoys Extraordinary and Ministers Plenipotentiary

Herbert Goldsmith Squiers, of New York, May 20, 1902.
Edwin V. Morgan, of New York, November 29, 1905.
John B. Jackson, of New Jersey, December 21, 1909.
Arthur M. Beaupré, of Illinois, August 12, 1911.
William E. Gonzales, of South Carolina, June 21, 1913.
Boaz W. Long, of New Mexico, June 30, 1919.

Ambassadors Extraordinary and Plenipotentiary

Maj. Gen. Enoch H. Crowder, of the United States Army, February 10, 1923.
Noble Brandon Judah, of Illinois, November 22, 1927.
Harry F. Guggenheim, of New York, October 10, 1929.
Sumner Welles, of Maryland, April 24, 1933.
Jefferson Caffery, of Louisiana, February 23, 1934.
J. Butler Wright, of Wyoming, July 13, 1937.
George S. Messersmith, of Delaware, January 12, 1940.
Spruille Braden, of New York, December 20, 1941.
R. Henry Norweb, of Ohio, May 22, 1945.
Robert Butler, of Minnesota, May 22, 1948.
Willard L. Beaulac, of Rhode Island, June 20, 1951.

FRANCE

Chargé d'Affaires

William Short, of Virginia, April 20, 1790.

Ministers Plenipotentiary

Gouverneur Morris, of New York, January 12, 1792.
James Monroe, of Virginia, May 28, 1794.

[3] The Embassy in Nanking was closed March 5, 1950.

Charles Cotesworth Pinckney, of South Carolina, September 9, 1796.
Robert R. Livingston, of New York, October 2, 1801.
John Armstrong, of New York, June 30, 1804.

Chargé d'Affaires

Jonathan Russell, of Rhode Island, November 5, 1810.

Ministers Plenipotentiary

Joel Barlow, of Connecticut, February 27, 1811.
William H. Crawford, of Georgia, April 9, 1813.

Envoys Extraordinary and Ministers Plenipotentiary

Albert Gallatin, of Pennsylvania, February 28, 1815.
James Brown, of Louisiana, December 9, 1823.
William C. Rives, of Virginia, April 18, 1829.

Chargé d'Affaires

Leavitt Harris, of Pennsylvania, March 6, 1833.

Envoys Extraordinary and Ministers Plenipotentiary

Edward Livingston, of Louisiana, May 29, 1833.
Lewis Cass, of Ohio, October 4, 1836.
William R. King, of Alabama, April 9, 1844.
Richard Rush, of Pennsylvania, March 3, 1847.
William C. Rives, of Virginia, July 20, 1849.
John Y. Mason, of Virginia, October 10, 1853.
Charles J. Faulkner, of Virginia, January 16, 1860.
William L. Dayton, of New Jersey, March 18, 1861.

Chargé d'Affaires

John Bigelow, of New York, December 21, 1864.

Envoys Extraordinary and Ministers Plenipotentiary

John Bigelow, of New York, March 15, 1865.
John A. Dix, of New York, September 24, 1866.
Elihu B. Washburne, of Illinois, March 17, 1869.
Edward F. Noyes, of Ohio, July 1, 1877.
Levi P. Morton, of New York, March 21, 1881.
Robert M. McLane, of Maryland, March 23, 1885.
Whitelaw Reid, of New York, March 23, 1889.
T. Jefferson Coolidge, of Massachusetts, May 12, 1892.
James B. Eustis, of Louisiana, March 20, 1893.

Ambassadors Extraordinary and Plenipotentiary

James B. Eustis, of Louisiana, April 8, 1893.
Horace Porter, of New York, March 19, 1897.
Robert S. McCormick, of Illinois, March 8, 1905.
Henry White, of Rhode Island, December 19, 1906.
Robert Bacon, of New York, December 21, 1909.
Myron T. Herrick, of Ohio, February 15, 1912.
William G. Sharp, of Ohio, June 19, 1914.
Hugh Campbell Wallace, of Washington, February 27, 1919.

Myron T. Herrick, of Ohio, April 16, 1921.
Walter E. Edge, of New Jersey, November 21, 1929.
Jesse Isidor Straus, of New York, March 17, 1933.
William C. Bullitt, of Pennsylvania, August 25, 1936.
Admiral William D. Leahy, of Georgia, November 29, 1940.
Jefferson Caffery, of Louisiana, November 25, 1944.
David K. E. Bruce, of Virginia, May 9, 1949.
James Clement Dunn, of New York, March 13, 1952.

GERMANY

Envoys Extraordinary and Ministers Plenipotentiary

George Bancroft, of New York, May 31, 1871.
J. C. Bancroft Davis, of New York, June 11, 1874.
Bayard Taylor, of Pennsylvania, March 4, 1878.
Andrew D. White, of New York, April 2, 1879.
Aaron A. Sargent, of California, March 2, 1882.
John A. Kasson, of Iowa, July 4, 1884.
George H. Pendleton, of Ohio, March 23, 1885.
William Walter Phelps, of New Jersey, June 20, 1889.
Theodore Runyon, of New Jersey, March 23, 1893.

Ambassadors Extraordinary and Plenipotentiary

Theodore Runyon, of New Jersey, September 14, 1893.
Edwin F. Uhr, of Michigan, February 10, 1896.
Andrew D. White, of New York, April 5, 1897.
Charlemagne Tower, of Pennsylvania, September 26, 1902.
David Jayne Hill, of New York, April 2, 1908.
John G. A. Leishman, of Pennsylvania, August 12, 1911.
James W. Gerard, of New York, July 28, 1913.

Commissioner

Ellis Loring Dresel, of Massachusetts, November 4, 1919.

Chargé d'Affaires

Ellis Loring Dresel, of Massachusetts, November 14, 1921.

Ambassadors Extraordinary and Plenipotentiary

Alanson B. Houghton, of New York, February 10, 1922.
Jacob Gould Schurman, of New York, March 17, 1925.
Frederic M. Sackett, of Kentucky, January 9, 1930.
William E. Dodd, of Illinois, June 13, 1933.
Hugh R. Wilson, of Illinois, January 17, 1938.

Political Adviser

Robert D. Murphy, of Wisconsin, September 15, 1944.

High Commissioner

John J. McCloy, of New York, June 13, 1949.

Ambassador Extraordinary and Plenipotentiary

Walter J. Donnelly, of Connecticut, July 18, 1952.

GREAT BRITAIN

Minister Plenipotentiary
Thomas Pinckney, of South Carolina, January 12, 1792.

Envoy Extraordinary
John Jay, of New York, April 19, 1794.

Ministers Plenipotentiary
Rufus King, of New York, May 20, 1796.
James Monroe, of Virginia, April 18, 1803.
William Pinkney, of Maryland, May 12, 1806.

Chargé d'Affaires
Jonathan Russell, of Rhode Island, July 27, 1811.

Envoys Extraordinary and Ministers Plenipotentiary
John Quincy Adams, of Massachusetts, February 28, 1815.
Richard Rush, of Pennsylvania, October [day not given in record], 1817.
Rufus King, of New York, May 5, 1825.
Albert Gallatin, of Pennsylvania, May 10, 1826.
James Barbour, of Virginia, May 23, 1828.
Louis McLane, of Delaware, April 18, 1829.
Martin Van Buren, of New York, August 1, 1831.

Chargé d'Affaires
Aaron Vail, of New York, July 13, 1832.

Envoys Extraordinary and Ministers Plenipotentiary
Andrew Stevenson, of Virginia, March 16, 1836.
Edward Everett, of Massachusetts, September 13, 1841.
Louis McLane, of Maryland, June 16, 1845.
George Bancroft, of New York, September 9, 1846.
Abbott Lawrence, of Massachusetts, August 30, 1849.
Joseph R. Ingersoll, of Pennsylvania, August 21, 1852.
James Buchanan, of Pennsylvania, April 11, 1853.
George M. Dallas, of Pennsylvania, February 4, 1856.
Charles Francis Adams, of Massachusetts, March 20, 1861.
Reverdy Johnson, of Maryland, June 12, 1868.
J. Lothrop Motley, of Massachusetts, April 13, 1869.
Robert C. Schenck, of Ohio, December 22, 1870.
Edwards Pierrepont, of New York, May 22, 1876.
John Welsh, of Pennsylvania, November 9, 1877.
James Russell Lowell, of Massachusetts, January 26, 1880.
Edward J. Phelps, of Vermont, March 23, 1885.
Robert T. Lincoln, of Illinois, March 30, 1889.

Ambassadors Extraordinary and Plenipotentiary
Thomas F. Bayard, of Delaware, March 30, 1893.
John Hay, of District of Columbia, March 19, 1897.

Joseph H. Choate, of New York, January 19, 1899.
Whitelaw Reid, of New York, March 8, 1905.
Walter Hines Page, of New York, April 21, 1913.
John W. Davis, of West Virginia, November 21, 1918.
George Harvey, of New Jersey, April 16, 1921.
Frank B. Kellogg, of Minnesota, December 11, 1923.
Alanson B. Houghton, of New York, February 24, 1925.
Charles G. Dawes, of Illinois, April 16, 1929.
Andrew W. Mellon, of Pennsylvania, February 6, 1932.
Robert Worth Bingham, of Kentucky, March 23, 1933.
Joseph P. Kennedy, of New York, January 17, 1938.
John G. Winant, of New Hampshire, February 11, 1941.
W. Averell Harriman, of New York, April 2, 1946.
Lewis W. Douglas, of Arizona, March 6, 1947.
Walter S. Gifford, of Massachusetts, November 29, 1950.

ITALY

Envoys Extraordinary and Ministers Plenipotentiary

George P. Marsh, of Vermont, March 20, 1861.
William Waldorf Astor, of New York, August 4, 1882.
John B. Stallo, of Ohio, June 17, 1885.
Albert G. Porter, of Indiana, March 13, 1889.
William Potter, of Pennsylvania, November 15, 1892.

Ambassadors Extraordinary and Plenipotentiary

Wayne MacVeagh, of Pennsylvania, December 20, 1893.
William F. Draper, of Massachusetts, April 5, 1897.
George von L. Meyer, of Massachusetts, December 14, 1900.
Henry White, of Rhode Island, March 8, 1905.
Lloyd C. Griscom, of Pennsylvania, December 19, 1906.
John G. A. Leishman, of Pennsylvania, April 1, 1909.
Thomas J. O'Brien, of Michigan, August 12, 1911.
Thomas Nelson Page, of Virginia, June 21, 1913.
Robert Underwood Johnson, of New York, February 18, 1920.
Richard Washburn Child, of Massachusetts, May 26, 1921.
Henry P. Fletcher, of Pennsylvania, February 19, 1924.
John W. Garrett, of Maryland, September 11, 1929.
Breckinridge Long, of Missouri, April 24, 1933.
William Phillips, of Massachusetts, August 4, 1936.
Alexander C. Kirk, of Illinois, December 8, 1944.
James Clement Dunn, of New York, July 25, 1946.
Ellsworth Bunker, of New York, March 13, 1952.

JAPANESE EMPIRE

Ministers Resident

Townsend Harris, of New York, January 19, 1859.
Robert H. Pruyn, of New York, October 12, 1861.
Robert B. Van Valkenburgh, of New York, January 18, 1866.
Charles E. De Long, of Nevada, April 21, 1869.

Envoys Extraordinary and Ministers Plenipotentiary

Charles E. De Long, of Nevada, July 14, 1870.
John A. Bingham, of Ohio, May 31, 1873.
Richard B. Hubbard, of Texas, April 2, 1885.
John F. Swift, of California, March 12, 1889.
Frank L. Coombs, of California, April 20, 1892.
Edwin Dun, of Ohio, April 4, 1893.
Alfred E. Buck, of Georgia, April 13, 1897.
Lloyd C. Griscom, of Pennsylvania, December 16, 1902.

Ambassadors Extraordinary and Plenipotentiary

Luke E. Wright, of Tennessee, January 25, 1906.
Thomas J. O'Brien, of Michigan, June 11, 1907.
Charles Page Bryan, of Illinois, August 12, 1911.
Larz Anderson, of District of Columbia, November 14, 1912.
George W. Guthrie, of Pennsylvania, May 20, 1913.
Roland S. Morris, of Pennsylvania, August 1, 1917.
Charles Beacher Warren, of Michigan, June 29, 1921.
Cyrus E. Woods, of Pennsylvania, March 3, 1923.
Edgar A. Bancroft, of Illinois, September 23, 1924.
Charles MacVeagh, of New Hampshire, September 24, 1925.
William R. Castle, Jr., of District of Columbia, December 11, 1929.
W. Cameron Forbes, of Massachusetts, June 17, 1930.
Joseph C. Grew, of New Hampshire, February 19, 1932.

Political Advisers to Supreme Commander for Allied Powers

George Atcheson, Jr., of California, September 17, 1945.
William J. Sebald, of Maryland, acting, January 7, 1949.

Ambassador Extraordinary and Plenipotentiary

Robert D. Murphy, of Wisconsin, April 18, 1952.

MEXICO

Envoy Extraordinary and Minister Plenipotentiary

Joel R. Poinsett, of South Carolina, March 8, 1825.

Chargés d'Affaires

Anthony Butler, of Mississippi, October 12, 1829.
Powhatan Ellis, of Mississippi, January 5, 1836.

Envoys Extraordinary and Ministers Plenipotentiary

Powhatan Ellis, of Mississippi, February 15, 1839.
Waddy Thompson, of South Carolina, February 10, 1842.
Wilson Shannon, of Ohio, April 9, 1844.
John Slidell, of Louisiana, November 10, 1845.
Nathan Clifford, of Maine, July 28, 1848.
Robert P. Letcher, of Kentucky, August 9, 1849.
Alfred Conkling, of New York, August 6, 1852.
James Gadsden, of South Carolina, May 24, 1853.
John Forsyth, of Alabama, July 21, 1856.

Robert M. McLane, of Maryland, March 7, 1859.
John B. Weller, of California, November 17, 1860.
Thomas Corwin, of Ohio, March 22, 1861.
Lewis D. Campbell, of Ohio, May 4, 1866.
Marcus Otterbourg, of Wisconsin, July 1, 1867.
William S. Rosecrans, of Ohio, July 27, 1868.
Thomas H. Nelson, of Indiana, April 16, 1869.
John W. Foster, of Indiana, March 17, 1873.
Philip H. Morgan, of Louisiana, January 26, 1880.
Henry R. Jackson, of Georgia, March 23, 1885.
Thomas C. Manning, of Louisiana, August 30, 1886.
Edward S. Bragg, of Wisconsin, January 16, 1888.
Thomas Ryan, of Kansas, March 30, 1889.
Isaac P. Gray, of Indiana, March 20, 1893.
Matt W. Ransom, of North Carolina, August 24, 1895.
Powell Clayton, of Arkansas, March 22, 1897.

Ambassadors Extraordinary and Plenipotentiary

Powell Clayton, of Arkansas, December 8, 1898.
Edwin H. Conger, of Iowa, March 8, 1905.
David E. Thompson, of Nebraska, January 24, 1906.
Henry Lane Wilson, of Washington, December 21, 1909.
Henry P. Fletcher, of Pennsylvania, February 25, 1916.
Charles Beecher Warren, of Michigan, February 29, 1924.
James Rockwell Sheffield, of New York, September 9, 1924.
Dwight W. Morrow, of New Jersey, September 21, 1927.
J. Reuben Clark, Jr., of Utah, October 3, 1930.
Josephus Daniels, of North Carolina, March 17, 1933.
George S. Messersmith, of Delaware, December 4, 1941.
Walter Thurston, of Arizona, May 4, 1946.
William O'Dwyer, of New York, September 20, 1950.

PERU

Chargés d'Affaires

James Cooley, of Pennsylvania, May 2, 1826.
Samuel Larned, of Rhode Island, December 29, 1828.
Emanuel J. West, of Illinois, October 22, 1829.
Samuel Larned, of Rhode Island, May 15, 1830.
James B. Thornton, of New Hampshire, June 15, 1836.
John A. Bryan, of Ohio, August 15, 1844.
Albert G. Jewett, of Maine, March 13, 1845.
John Randolph Clay, of Pennsylvania, March 3, 1847.

Envoys Extraordinary and Ministers Plenipotentiary

John Randolph Clay, of Pennsylvania, March 16, 1853.
Christopher Robinson, of Rhode Island, June 8, 1861.
Alvin P. Hovey, of Indiana, August 12, 1865.
Thomas Settle, of North Carolina, February 18, 1871.
Francis Thomas, of Maryland, March 25, 1872.
Richard Gibbs, of New York, April 9, 1875.
Isaac P. Christiancy, of Michigan, February 11, 1879.
Stephen A. Hurlbut, of Illinois, May 19, 1881.

Special Envoy Extraordinary and Minister Plenipotentiary
> William Henry Trescot, of South Carolina, November 28, 1881.

Envoys Extraordinary and Ministers Plenipotentiary
> James R. Partridge, of Maryland, April 12, 1882.
> Seth Ledyard Phelps, of District of Columbia, June 18, 1883.
> Charles W. Buck, of Kentucky, April 2, 1885.
> John Hicks, of Wisconsin, March 30, 1889.
> James A. McKenzie, of Kentucky, April 4, 1893.
> Irving B. Dudley, of California, June 28, 1897.
> Leslie Combs, of Kentucky, December 19, 1906.
> Henry Clay Howard, of Kentucky, January 18, 1911.
> Benton McMillin, of Tennessee, July 2, 1913.

Ambassadors Extraordinary and Plenipotentiary
> William E. Gonzales, of South Carolina, September 10, 1919.
> Miles Poindexter, of Washington, February 19, 1923.
> Alexander P. Moore, of Pennsylvania, March 29, 1928.
> Fred Morris Dearing, of Missouri, January 31, 1930.
> Laurence A. Steinhardt, of New York, April 22, 1937.
> R. Henry Norweb, of Ohio, January 12, 1940.
> John Campbell White, of New York, January 29, 1944.
> William D. Pawley, of Florida, June 14, 1945.
> Prentice Cooper, of Tennessee, May 2, 1946.
> Harold H. Tittmann, Jr., of Missouri, June 18, 1948.

POLAND

Envoys Extraordinary and Ministers Plenipotentiary
> Hugh S. Gibson, of California, April 16, 1919.
> Alfred J. Pearson, of Iowa, April 2, 1924.
> John B. Stetson, Jr., of Pennsylvania, July 3, 1925.

Ambassadors Extraordinary and Plenipotentiary
> John N. Willys, of Ohio, March 8, 1930.
> F. Lammot Belin, of Pennsylvania, November 2, 1932.
> John Cudahy, of Wisconsin, June 13, 1933.
> Anthony J. Drexel Biddle, Jr., of Pennsylvania, May 4, 1937.
> Arthur Bliss Lane, of New York, September 21, 1944.
> Stanton Griffis, of Connecticut, May 15, 1947.
> Waldemar J. Gallman, of New York, July 7, 1948.
> Joseph Flack, of Pennsylvania, September 20, 1950.

RUSSIA
See also Union of Soviet Socialist Republics

Minister Plenipotentiary
> John Quincy Adams, of Massachusetts, June 27, 1809.

Envoys Extraordinary and Ministers Plenipotentiary

William Pinkney, of Maryland, March 7, 1816.
George Washington Campbell, of Tennessee, April 16, 1818.
Henry Middleton, of South Carolina, April 6, 1820.
John Randolph, of Virginia, May 26, 1830.
James Buchanan, of Pennsylvania, January 4, 1832.
William Wilkins, of Pennsylvania, June 30, 1834.

Chargé d'Affaires

John Randolph Clay, of Pennsylvania, June 29, 1836.

Envoys Extraordinary and Ministers Plenipotentiary

George M. Dallas, of Pennsylvania, March 7, 1837.
Churchill C. Cambreleng, of New York, May 20, 1840.
Charles S. Todd, of Kentucky, August 27, 1841.
Ralph I. Ingersoll, of Connecticut, August 8, 1846.
Arthur P. Bagby, of Alabama, June 15, 1848.
Neil S. Brown, of Tennessee, May 2, 1850.
Thomas H. Seymour, of Connecticut, May 24, 1853.
Francis W. Pickens, of South Carolina, January 11, 1858.
John Appleton, of Maine, June 8, 1860.
Cassius M. Clay, of Kentucky, March 28, 1861.
Simon Cameron, of Pennsylvania, January 17, 1862.
Cassius M. Clay, of Kentucky, March 11, 1863.
Andrew G. Curtin, of Pennsylvania, April 16, 1869.
James L. Orr, of South Carolina, December 12, 1872.
Marshall Jewell, of Connecticut, May 29, 1873.
George H. Boker, of Pennsylvania, January 13, 1875.
Edwin W. Stoughton, of New York, October 30, 1877.
John W. Foster, of Indiana, January 26, 1880.
William H. Hunt, of Louisiana, April 12, 1882.
Alphonso Taft, of Ohio, July 4, 1884.
George V. N. Lothrop, of Michigan, May 7, 1885.
Lambert Tree, of Illinois, September 25, 1888.
Allen Thorndike Rice, of New York, March 30, 1889.
Charles Emory Smith, of Pennsylvania, February 14, 1890.
Andrew D. White, of New York, July 22, 1892.
Clifton R. Breckinridge, of Arkansas, July 20, 1894.
Ethan A. Hitchcock, of Missouri, August 16, 1897.

Ambassadors Extraordinary and Plenipotentiary

Ethan A. Hitchcock, of Missouri, February 11, 1898.
Charlemagne Tower, of Pennsylvania, January 12, 1899.
Robert S. McCormick, of Illinois, September 26, 1902.
George von L. Meyer, of Massachusetts, March 8, 1905.
John W. Riddle, of Minnesota, December 19, 1906.
William Woodville Rockhill, of District of Columbia, May 17, 1909.
Curtis Guild, of Massachusetts, April 24, 1911.
George T. Marye, of California, July 9, 1914.
David R. Francis, of Missouri, March 6, 1916.

SPAIN

Chargé d'Affaires
> William Carmichael, of Maryland, April 20, 1790.

Minister Resident
> William Short, of Virginia, May 28, 1794.

Envoy Extraordinary
> Thomas Pinckney, of South Carolina, November 24, 1794.

Ministers Plenipotentiary
> David Humphreys, of Connecticut, May 20, 1796.
> Charles Pinckney, of South Carolina, June 6, 1801.
> James Bowdoin, of Massachusetts, November 22, 1804.
> George W. Erving, of Massachusetts, August 10, 1814.
> John Forsyth, of Georgia, February 16, 1819.
> Hugh Nelson, of Virginia, January 15, 1823.

Envoys Extraordinary and Ministers Plenipotentiary
> Alexander Hill Everett, of Massachusetts, March 9, 1825.
> Cornelius P. Van Ness, of Vermont, June 1, 1829.
> William T. Barry, of Kentucky, April 10, 1835.
> John H. Eaton, of Tennessee, March 16, 1836.

Chargé d'Affaires
> Aaron Vail, of New York, May 20, 1840.

Envoys Extraordinary and Ministers Plenipotentiary
> Washington Irving, of New York, February 10, 1842.
> Romulus M. Saunders, of North Carolina, February 25, 1846.
> Daniel M. Barringer, of North Carolina, June 18, 1849.
> Pierre Soulé, of Louisiana, April 7, 1853.
> Augustus C. Dodge, of Iowa, February 9, 1855.
> William Preston, of Kentucky, December 15, 1858.
> Carl Schurz, of Wisconsin, March 28, 1861.
> Gustavus Koerner, of Illinois, June 14, 1862.
> John P. Hale, of New Hampshire, March 10, 1865.
> Daniel E. Sickles, of New York, May 15, 1869.
> Caleb Cushing, of Virginia, January 6, 1874.
> James Russell Lowell, of Massachusetts, June 11, 1877.
> Lucius Fairchild, of Wisconsin, January 26, 1880.
> Hannibal Hamlin, of Maine, June 30, 1881.
> John W. Foster, of Indiana, February 27, 1883.
> Jabez L. M. Curry, of Virginia, October 7, 1885.
> Perry Belmont, of New York, November 17, 1888.
> Thomas W. Palmer, of Michigan, March 12, 1889.
> E. Burd Grubb, of New Jersey, September 27, 1890.

Special Envoy Extraordinary and Minister Plenipotentiary
> John W. Foster, of Indiana, March 6, 1891.

Envoys Extraordinary and Ministers Plenipotentiary

> A. Louden Snowden, of Pennsylvania, July 22, 1892.
> Hannis Taylor, of Alabama, April 8, 1893.
> Stewart L. Woodford, of New York, June 19, 1897.
> Bellamy Storer, of Ohio, April 12, 1899.
> Arthur S. Hardy, of New Hampshire, September 26, 1902.
> William Miller Collier, of New York, March 8, 1905.
> Henry Clay Ide, of Vermont, April 1, 1909.
> Joseph E. Willard, of Virginia, July 28, 1913.

Ambassadors Extraordinary and Plenipotentiary

> Joseph E. Willard, of Virginia, September 10, 1913.
> Cyrus E. Woods, of Pennsylvania, June 24, 1921.
> Alexander P. Moore, of Pennsylvania, March 3, 1923.
> Ogden H. Hammond, of New Jersey, December 21, 1925.
> Irwin B. Laughlin, of Pennsylvania, October 16, 1929.
> Claude G. Bowers, of New York, April 6, 1933.
> Alexander W. Weddell, of Virginia, May 3, 1939.
> Carlton J. H. Hayes, of New York, May 2, 1942.
> Norman Armour, of New Jersey, December 15, 1944.
> Stanton Griffis, of Massachusetts, February 1, 1951.
> Lincoln Mac Veagh, of Rhode Island, February 21, 1952.

TURKEY

Chargé d'Affaires

> David Porter, of Maryland, April 15, 1831.

Ministers Resident

> David Porter, of Maryland, March 3, 1839.
> Dabney S. Carr, of Maryland, October 6, 1843.
> George P. Marsh, of Vermont, May 29, 1849.
> Carroll Spence, of Maryland, August 23, 1853.
> James Williams, of Tennessee, January 14, 1858.
> Edward Joy Morris, of Pennsylvania, June 8, 1861.
> Wayne MacVeagh, of Pennsylvania, June 4, 1870.
> George H. Boker, of Pennsylvania, November 3, 1871.
> Horace Maynard, of Tennessee, March 9, 1875.
> James Longstreet, of Georgia, June 14, 1880.
> Lewis Wallace, of Indiana, May 19, 1881.

Envoys Extraordinary and Ministers Plenipotentiary

> Lewis Wallace, of Indiana, July 13, 1882.
> Samuel S. Cox, of New York, March 25, 1885.
> Oscar S. Straus, of New York, March 24, 1887.
> Solomon Hirsch, of Oregon, May 16, 1889.
> David P. Thompson, of Oregon, November 15, 1892.
> Alexander W. Terrell, of Texas, April 15, 1893.
> James B. Angell, of Michigan, April 15, 1897.
> Oscar S. Straus, of New York, June 3, 1898.
> John G. A. Leishman, of Pennsylvania, December 20, 1900.

Ambassadors Extraordinary and Plenipotentiary

John G. A. Leishman, of Pennsylvania, June 18, 1906.
Oscar S. Straus, of New York, May 17, 1909.
William Woodville Rockhill, of District of Columbia, April 24, 1911.
Henry Morgenthau, of New York, September 4, 1913.
Abram I. Elkus, of New York, July 21, 1916.

Commissioners

Lewis Heck, of Pennsylvania, November 30, 1918.
Gabriel B. Ravndal, of South Dakota, May 3, 1919.

High Commissioner

Rear Admiral Mark L. Bristol, of the United States Navy, August 12, 1919.

Ambassadors Extraordinary and Plenipotentiary

Joseph C. Grew, of New Hampshire, May 19, 1927.
Charles Hitchcock Sherrill, of New York, March 17, 1932.
Robert P. Skinner, of Ohio, June 13, 1933.
John Van A. MacMurray, of Maryland, January 24, 1936.
Laurence A. Steinhardt, of New York, January 12, 1942.
Edwin C. Wilson, of Florida, January 27, 1947.
George Wadsworth, of New York, August 11, 1948.
George C. McGhee, of Texas, December 8, 1951.

UNION OF SOVIET SOCIALIST REPUBLICS

Ambassadors Extraordinary and Plenipotentiary

William C. Bullitt, of Pennsylvania, November 21, 1933.
Joseph E. Davies, of District of Columbia, November 16, 1936.
Laurence Steinhardt, of New York, March 23, 1939.
Admiral William H. Standley, of California, February 14, 1942.
W. Averell Harriman, of New York, October 7, 1943.
Lieutenant General Walter Bedell Smith, of the United States Army, March 22, 1946.
Admiral Alan G. Kirk, of the United States Navy, May 21, 1949.
George F. Kennan, of Wisconsin, March 14, 1952.

Bibliography

ADAIR, E. R., *The Extraterritoriality of Ambassadors in the 16th and 17th Centuries* (London, 1929).

ADAMS, Charles Francis, *Memoirs of John Q. Adams*, 12 vols. (Philadelphia, 1874-1877).

ADAMS, Henry, *Life of John Randolph* (New York, 1910).

ADAMS, John, *John Adams Works*, 10 vols. Charles Francis Adams, ed. (Boston, 1851-1865).

ADAMS, John Quincy, *Memoirs*, 12 vols. (Philadelphia, 1874-1877).

ALDERMAN, E. A., and GORDON, A. C., *J. L. M. Curry* (New York, 1911).

D'ANETHON, Baroness Albert, *Fourteen Years of Diplomatic Life in Japan* (New York, 1912).

ANGELL, James Burrill, *Reminiscences* (New York, 1912).

ASHBURNER, Walter, *The Rhodian Sea Law* (Oxford, Eng., 1909).

DE BACOURT, Chevalier, *Souvenirs of a Diplomat* (New York, 1885).

BASDEVANT, S., *Les fonctionnaires internationaux* (Paris, 1931).

BAX, Emily, *Miss Bax of the Embassy* (Boston, 1939).

BEAULAC, Willard L., *Career Ambassador* (New York, 1951).

BEAUVAIS, Capitaine, *Attachés militaires, attachés navals et attachés de l'air* (Paris, 1937).

BEMIS, Samuel Flagg, ed., *The American Secretaries of State and their Diplomacy*, 10 vols. (New York, 1927-1929).

BENEZET, Jean Etienne, *Etude théorique sur les immunités Diplomatiques* (Toulouse, Fr., 1901).

BERNARD, M., *Four Lectures on Subjects Connected With Diplomacy* (London, 1868).

VON BERNSTORFF, Count, *My Three Years in America* (New York, 1920).

———, *Memoirs of Count Bernstorff* (New York, 1936).

BERTIE, Sir Francis, *The Diary of Lord Bertie of Thane*, 2 vols. (London, 1924).

BIGELOW, John, *Retrospections of an Active Life* (New York, 1909).

BIGELOW, Poultney, *Prussian Memories, 1864-1914* (New York, 1915).

BLAGA, Cornelius, *L'evolution de la diplomatie* (Paris, 1938).

BODIN, Albert, *Des immunités consulaires dans les pays de chrétienté* (Bordeaux, Fr., 1897).

BORCHARD, E. M., *The Diplomatic Protection of Citizens Abroad* (New York, 1915).

BOREL, F., *De l'origine et des fonctions des consuls* (Leipzig, Ger., 1831).

BOUFFANAIS, Pierre, *Les consuls en temps de guerres et de troubles* (Paris, 1933).

BOUSQUET, Georges, *Agents diplomatiques et consulaires* (Paris, 1883).

BOWEN, Herbert W., *Recollections Diplomatic and Undiplomatic* (New York, 1926).

BOWERS, Claude G., *The Spanish Adventures of Washington Irving* (Boston, 1940).

BRUNUS, Conradus, *De Legationibus* (Mainz, Ger., 1548).

BRYN-JONES, David, *Frank B. Kellogg* (New York, 1937).

BUCHANAN, Sir George, *My Mission to Russia*, 2 vols. (Boston, 1923).

DE BUNSON, Madame Charles, *In Three Legations* (New York, 1909).

BUTLER, Sir Geoffrey, and MACCOBY, Simon, *The Development of International Law* (London, 1928).

BYRNES, James F., *Speaking Frankly* (New York, 1947).

DE CALLIÈRES, F., *De la manière de négocier avec les Souverains* (Paris, 1716).

CAMBON, Jules, *Le diplomate* (Paris, 1926).

CAMPBELL, Sir Gerard, *Of True Experience* (New York, 1947).

CANDIOTI, A. M., *Historia de la institucion consular en la antiguedad y en la edad media* (Buenos Aires, 1926).

CASTRO, and CASALEIZ A., *Guia practica del diplomatico Espagnol*, 2 vols. (Madrid, 1886).

DE CHARNOY, Rousseau, *L'idée du parfait ambassadeur*, L. Delavaud, ed. (Paris, 1912).

CHILD, Maude Parker, *The Social Side of Diplomatic Life* (Indianapolis, 1925).

CHILD, Richard Washburn, *A Diplomat Looks at Europe* (New York, 1925).

CHILDS, J. Rives, *American Foreign Service* (New York, 1948).

CLERC, M., *Les metèques athéniens* (Paris, 1893).

CLIFFORD, Philip G., *Nathan Clifford, Democrat* (New York, 1922).

COLLIER, William M., *At the Court of His Catholic Majesty* (Chicago, 1912).

DE COMMYNES, Philippe, *Memoires de Philippe de Commynes*, 2 vols. (Paris, 1901-1903).

CORTISSOZ, Royal, *The Life of Whitelaw Reid*, 2 vols. (New York, 1921).

CORWIN, E. S., *The President's Control of Foreign Relations* (Princeton, N. J., 1917).

COULON, Henri, *Des agents diplomatiques* (Paris, 1889).

COX, Samuel S., *Diversions of a Diplomat in Turkey* (New York, 1887).

COX, W. V., and NORTHRUP, H. M., *Life of Samuel S. Cox* (Syracuse, N. Y., 1899).

CRESSON, W. P., *Francis Dana* (New York, 1930).

CURTIS, George W., *The Correspondence of John Lathrop Motley*, 2 vols. (New York, 1889).

DE CUSSY, Ferdinand, *Dictionnaire du diplomate et du Consul* (Leipzig, Ger., 1846).

DANGERFIELD, Royden J., *In Defense of the Senate* (Oklahoma City, 1933).

DANIELS, Josephus, *Shirt Sleeve Diplomat* (Chapel Hill, N. C., 1947).

DAVID, Paul T., and Staff, *The Administration of Foreign Affairs and Overseas Operations* (Washington, 1951).

DAVIES, Joseph E., *Mission to Moscow* (New York, 1941).

DE HAAS, J. A., *The Practice of Foreign Trade* (New York, 1935).

DENNIS, A. L. P., *Adventures in American Diplomacy* (New York, 1928).

DENNISON, Eleanor E., *The Senate Foreign Relations Committee* (Stanford, Cal., 1942).

DEPEW, Chauncy M., *My Memories of Eighty Years* (New York, 1924).

DIETRICH, Victor, *De l'inviolabilité et de l'exemption de jurisdiction des agents diplomatiques et consulaires en pays de chrétienté* (Paris, 1896).

DODD, Martha, *Through Embassy Eyes* (New York, 1939).

DODD, Wm. Jr., and Martha, *Ambassador Dodd's Diary* (New York, 1941).
DRAPER, William F., *Recollections of a Varied Career* (New York, 1908).
DUMBA, Constantin, *Memoirs of a Diplomat* (Boston, 1932).
DUMONT, Jean, *Corps universel diplomatique du droit des gens,* 8 vols. (Amsterdam, 1726-1731).
DUNHAM, Donald, *Envoy Extraordinary* (New York, 1944).
DUNN, F. S., *The Protection of Nationals* (Baltimore, 1932).

EGAN, Maurice Francis, *Ten Years Near the German Frontier* (New York, 1919).
———, *Recollections of a Happy Life* (New York, 1924).
ELLIOTT, Sir Henry G., *Some Revolutions and other Diplomatic Experiences* (New York, 1922).

FAY, Bernard, *Franklin, The Apostle of Modern Times* (Boston, 1929).
FELLER, A. H., and HUDSON, M. O., *Diplomatic and Consular Laws and Regulations,* 2 vols. (Washington, 1932).
FISHER, H. A. L., *James Bryce,* 2 vols. (Boston and New York, 1909).
FLOURNOY, R. W., and HUDSON, M. O., *Nationality Laws* (New York, 1929).
FLYNN, Robert, *British Consuls Abroad* (London, 1846).
FOSTER, John W., *A Century of American Diplomacy* (New York, 1900).
———, *Diplomatic Memoirs,* 2 vols. (Boston and New York, 1909).
———, *The Practice of Diplomacy* (New York, 1906).
FRANCIS, David R., *Russia from the American Embassy* (New York, 1921).
FRANKLIN, William A., *Protection of Foreign Interests* (Washington, 1946).
FRASER, Mrs. Hugh, *A Diplomat's Wife* (New York, 1912).
———, *Reminiscences of a Diplomat's Wife* (New York, 1912).

GADE, John A., *All My Born Days* (New York, 1942).
GARDEN, G. F., *Traité complet de diplomatie,* 3 vols. (Paris, 1833).
GARNER, J. W., *International Law and the World War* (London, 1920).
GENET, Raoul, *Traité de diplomatie de droit diplomatique,* 3 vols. (Paris, 1931).
GENTILI, Alberico, *De Legationibus, Classics of International Law,* J. B. Scott, ed. (New York, 1924).
GERARD, James W., *My Four Years in Germany* (New York, 1917).
———, *Face to Face with Kaiserism* (New York, 1918).
GIBSON, Hugh, *A Journal from Our American Legation in Belgium* (New York, 1917).
GREW, Joseph C., *My Ten Years in Japan* (New York, 1944).
GRISCOM, Lloyd C., *Diplomatically Speaking* (New York, 1940).
GROTIUS, Hugo, *De Jure Belli ac Pacis* (Oxford, Eng., 1925).
GWYNN, Stephen, *The Letters and Friendships of Sir Cecil Spring Rice* (Boston and New York, 1929).

HACKWORTH, Green H., *Digest of International Law,* 8 vols. (Washington, 1940-1944).
HALE, Edward Everett, *Franklin in France,* 2 vols. (Boston, 1888).
HARDY, Arthur Sherburne, *Things Remembered* (New York, 1923).
HARRIS, Townsend, *The Complete Journal of Townsend Harris* (New York, 1930).
HARRISON, Thomas Skelton, *The Homely Diary of a Diplomat in the East* (New York, 1917).

HAYS, Carlton J. A., *Wartime Mission to Spain* (New York, 1945).

HEARN, Walter Risley, *Some Recollections* (London, 1923).

HEATLY, D. P., *Diplomacy and the Study of International Relations* (Oxford, Eng., 1919).

DE HEGERMANN-LINDECRONE, Madame L., *In the Courts of Memory* (New York, 1912).

———, *The Sunny Side of Diplomatic Life* (New York, 1914).

HENDERSON, Sir Nevile, *Failure of a Mission* (New York, 1940).

HENDRICK, Burton J., *Life and Letters of Walter H. Page*, 3 vols. (New York, 1922-1925).

HERBETTE, L., *Nos diplomates et notre diplomatie* (Paris, 1874).

HERSHEY, Amos, *Diplomatic Agents and Immunities* (Washington, 1919).

DE HEYKING, Baron Alphonse, *La Théorie et la pratique des services consulaires* (Paris, 1928).

HILL, David Jayne, *History of Diplomacy in the Development of Europe*, 3 vols. (New York, 1906-1914).

HILL, Hamilton A., *Memoirs of Abbot Lawrence* (Boston, 1883).

HINCKLEY, Frank C., *American Consular Jurisdiction in the Orient* (Washington, 1906).

HOLMES, Oliver Wendell, *John Lathrop Motley. A Memoir* (Boston, 1889).

HOLT, W. Stull, *Treaties Defeated by the Senate* (Baltimore, 1933).

HORSTMANN, G. Henry, *Consular Reminiscences* (Philadelphia, 1886).

HORTON, George, *Recollections, Grave and Gay* (Indianapolis, 1927).

HOTMAN, Jean, *De la charge et dignité de l'ambassadeur* (Paris, 1607).

HOWARD, Esme, *Theatre of Life* (Boston, 1935).

HOWE, M. A. de Wolfe, *George von Lengerke Meyer* (New York, 1920).

HUDSON, M. O., and FELLER, A. H., *Diplomatic Laws and Regulations* (Washington, 1932).

HULEN, Bertrand D., *Inside the Department of State* (New York, 1939).

HULL, Cordell, *Memoirs of Cordell Hull*, 2 vols. (New York, 1942).

HUNT, Gaillard, *The American Passport* (Washington, 1898).

———, *The Department of State of the United States* (New Haven, Conn., 1914).

———, *The History of the Seal of the United States* (Washington, 1909).

HUNTLEY, Theodore H., *John W. Davis* (New York, 1924).

HURST, Carlton Bailey, *Arms Above the Door* (New York, 1932).

HURST, Sir Cecil, "Des immunités diplomatiques," *Recueil des Cours*, Académie de droit international (Paris, 1927).

HYDE, C. C., *International Law Chiefly as Interpreted and Applied by the United States*, 2 vols. (Boston, 1922).

JAY, John, *Correspondence and Public Papers*, H. P. Johnstone, ed., 4 vols. (New York, 1890-1893).

JAY, William, *The Life of John Jay* (New York, 1833).

JESSUP, Philip C., *Elihu Root*, 2 vols. (New York, 1938).

JOHNSON, Alan Campbell, *Viscount Halifax* (New York, 1941).

JOHNSON, Robert Underwood, *Remembered Yesterdays* (Boston, 1923).

JOHNSON, Willis Fletcher, *George Harvey* (New York, 1929).

JONES, Chester Lloyd, *The Consular Service of the United States* (Philadelphia, 1906).

JUSSERAND, Jules J., *The School for Ambassadors and Other Essays* (New York, 1925).

———, *What Me Befell* (New York, 1933).

KELLY, Hank and Dot, *Dancing Diplomats* (Albuquerque, N. M., 1950).

KNATCHBULL-HUGESSEN, Sir Hughe, *Diplomat in Peace and War* (London, 1949).

KONIG, B. W., *Hand Buch des Deutchen Konsular wesen* (Berlin, 1914).

KRAUSKE, Otto, *Die Entwickelung der Städige Diplomatie* (Leipzig, Ger., 1883).

LANE, Arthur Bliss, *I Saw Poland Betrayed* (New York, 1948).

LANE-POOLE, S., *Life of Stratford Canning* (London, 1888).

LAURENT, François, *Histoire du droit des gens et des relations internationales,* 3 vols. (Ghent, Belg., 1850).

LAWRENCE, Mary V. Tingley, *A Diplomat's Helpmate* (San Francisco, 1918).

LAY, Tracy, *The Foreign Service of the United States* (New York, 1928).

LEACH, Paul R., *That Man Dawes* (Chicago, 1930).

LEHR, Ernest, *Manuel theorique et pratique des agents diplomatiques et consulaires français et étrangers* (Paris, 1888).

LEROY, Paul, *Des consulats, des legations et des ambassades* (Paris, 1876).

LICHNOWSKY, Prince, *Heading for the Abyss* (New York, 1928).

LOCKHART, R. H. Bruce, *British Agent* (New York and London, 1933).

MACDONNELL, Lady, *Reminiscences of Diplomatic Life* (London, 1913).

MACHIAVEL, N., *Oeuvres Completes. Legations et Missions,* VII-IX (Paris, 1823-1826).

DE MARTENS, Charles, *Guide diplomatique* (Leipzig, Ger., 1866).

MARTIN, E. S., *Life of Joseph H. Choate* (New York, 1920).

MARYE, George T., *Nearing the End in Imperial Russia* (Philadelphia, 1929).

MATTHEWS, J. M., *American Foreign Relations* (New York, 1928).

MAULDE, R. H. M. de la Clavière, *La diplomatie au temps de Machiavel,* 3 vols. (Paris, 1892).

McCAMY, James L., *The Administration of American Foreign Affairs* (New York, 1950).

McCLURE, Wallace M., *International Executive Agreements* (New York, 1941).

MEISEL, August Heinrich, *Cours de style diplomatique* (Paris, 1826).

MENDE, Elsie Porter, *An American Soldier and Diplomat* (New York, 1927).

MERIWETHER, Lee, *The War Diary of a Diplomat* (New York, 1919).

MICHAEL, William H., *History of the Department of State of the United States* (Washington, 1901).

DE MILNITZ, Alex, *Manuel des consuls,* 2 vols. (London, 1837).

MONNET, R., *Manuel diplomatique et consulaire* (Paris, 1899).

MOORE, John Bassett, *A Digest of International Law,* 8 vols. (Washington, 1906).

MORGENTHAU, Henry, *All in a Lifetime* (New York, 1922).

————, *Ambassador Morgenthau's Story* (New York, 1918).

MORRIS, Gouverneur, *A Diary of the French Revolution,* 2 vols. (Boston, 1939).

MORTON, Charles, *Les privilèges et les immunités diplomatiques* (Lausanne, Switz., 1927).

MOTLEY, J. L., *Correspondence,* 2 vols. (New York, 1889).

MOTT, Colonel T. Bentley, *Myron T. Herrick, Friend of France* (New York, 1929).

————, *Twenty Years as a Military Attaché* (Oxford, Eng., 1937).

MOWAT, R. B., *The Life of Lord Pauncefote* (New York, 1929).

MOWRER, Edgar Ansel, *The Nightmare of American Foreign Policy* (New York, 1948).

MOWRER, Paul Scott, *Our Foreign Affairs* (New York, 1924).

MURRAY, Eustace C. G., *Droits et devoirs des envoyés diplomatiques* (London, 1853).

NEKLUDOFF, A., *Diplomatic Reminiscences* (New York, 1920).
NEVILL, Ralph, *Unconventional Memories* (New York, 1923).
NEVINS, Allan, *Henry White* (New York, 1930).
———, *Hamilton Fish* (New York, 1936).
NICOLSON, Harold, *Portrait of a Diplomatist* (New York, 1930).
———, *Dwight Morrow* (New York, 1935).
———, *Diplomacy* (New York, 1939).
NORADOUNGHIAN, G., *Recueil d'actes internationaux de l'Empire Ottoman* (Paris, 1897).
NYE, Russell B., *George Bancroft, Brahmin Rebel* (New York, 1944).
NYS, Ernest, *Les origines du droit international* (Brussels, 1894).

ODIER, Pierre-Gabriel, *Des privilèges et immunités des agents diplomatiques en pays de chrétienté* (Paris, 1890).
O'SHAUGHNESSY, Edith, *Diplomatic Days* (New York, 1917).
———, *A Diplomat's Wife in Mexico* (New York and London, 1916).
OUDENDYK, William J., *Ways and By-Ways in Diplomacy* (London, 1939).

DE PALENCIA, Isabel, *I Must Have Liberty* (New York, 1940).
PALÉOLOGUE, Maurice, *An Ambassador's Memoirs,* 3 vols. (New York, no date).
PARDESSUS, J. M., *Collections des lois maritimes antèrieures au XVIII siècle* (Paris, 1828-1845).
PATAU, Paul, *De la situation comparée des agents diplomatiques et consulaires* (Paris, 1910).
PAULLIN, Charles O., *Diplomatic Negotiations of American Naval Officers* (Baltimore, 1912).
PECQUET, A., *Discours sur l'art de négocier* (Paris, 1737).
PHILLIPSON, Coleman, *The International Law and Custom of Ancient Greece and Rome* (London, 1911).
PLISCHKE, Elmer, *Conduct of American Diplomacy* (New York, 1950).
PONSONBY, Arthur, *Democracy and Diplomacy* (London, 1915).
POOLE, Dewitt C., *Conduct of Foreign Relations Under Modern Democratic Conditions* (New Haven, Conn., 1924).
POTIEMKINE, Vladimir, *Histoire de la diplomatie* (Paris, no date).
PRADIER-FODÉRÉ, P., *Cours de droit diplomatique,* 2 vols. (Paris, 1890).
PUENTE, J. I., *Traité sur les fonctions internationales des consuls* (Paris, 1937).
———, *The Foreign Consul* (Chicago, 1926).

QUENNELL, Peter, *The Private Letters of Princess Lieven* (New York, 1938).

RATTIGAN, Frank, *Diversions of a Diplomat* (London, 1924).
DE RAYNEVAL, J. M. Gerard, *Institutions du droit de la nature et des gens,* 2 vols. (Paris, 1832).
REDESDALE, Lord, *Memories,* 2 vols. (New York, no date).
———, *Further Memories* (New York, 1917).
REDSLOB, R., *Histoire des grands principes du droit des gens* (Paris, 1923).
REINSCH, Paul S., *An American Diplomat in China* (Garden City, N. Y., 1922).
REYNAUD, J. E., *Des ambassadeurs chez les romans, des consulats* (Paris, 1874).
RODD, Rennell, *Social and Diplomatic Memoirs,* 1894-1901 (Oxford, Eng., 1923).

ROSEN, Baron, *Forty Years of Diplomacy* (New York, 1922).

ROSEN, Friedrich, *Oriental Memories of a German Diplomatist* (New York, 1930).

RUMBOLD, Sir Horace, *Recollections of a Diplomatist*, 2 vols. (London, 1902).

———, *Further Recollections of a Diplomatist* (London, 1903).

RUSH, Richard, *Memoranda of a Residence at the Court of London* (Philadelphia, 1833).

RUSSELL, Phillips, *Benjamin Franklin* (London, 1927).

RUSSELL, William, *Berlin Embassy* (New York, 1941).

SADOUL, Jacques, *La conditions des agents consulaires et diplomatiques au point de vue fiscal* (Paris, 1918).

SALLES, George, *Institution des consulats* (Paris, 1898).

SANDS, William Franklin, *Undiplomatic Memories* (New York, 1930).

SATOW, Sir Ernest, *A Guide to Diplomatic Practice*, 2 vols. (London, 1922).

———, *A Diplomat in Japan* (London, 1921).

SA VALLE, Raymundo, *Des agents diplomatiques* (Geneva, 1875).

DE SCHELKIN, Eugene, *Recollections of a Russian Diplomat* (New York, 1918).

VON SCHOEN, Freiherr, *The Memoirs of an Ambassador* (London, 1922).

SCHUYLER, Eugene, *American Diplomacy* (New York, 1901).

———, *Essays and Memoirs* (New York, 1901).

SCHWERDTFEGER, Rudolph, *Die völkerrechtliche Sonderstellung der diplomatischen agenten* (Wurzburg, Ger., 1914).

SCOTT, James Brown, *Robert Bacon, Life and Letters* (New York, 1923).

SECRETAN, J., *Les immunités diplomatiques des representants des états membres et des agents de la Société des Nations* (Geneva, 1929).

SEWARD, Frederick W., *Reminiscences of a War-Time Statesman and Diplomat* (New York and London, 1916).

SEYMOUR, Charles, *The Intimate Papers of Colonel House*, 4 vols. (New York, 1926).

SHARP, W. G., *War Memories* (London, 1931).

SHERRILL, Charles H., *A Year's Embassy to Mustafa Kemal* (New York, 1934).

SHERWOOD, Robert E., *Roosevelt and Hopkins—An Intimate History* (New York, 1948).

SHEPPARD, Eli T., *American Consular Service* (Berkeley, Cal., 1901).

SNELLMAN, G., *De interpretibus Romanorum* (Leipzig, Ger., 1920).

STEWART, Irwin, *Consular Privileges and Immunities* (New York, 1926).

STIMSON, Henry L., and MCGEORGE, Bundy, *On Active Service in Peace and War* (New York, 1948).

STOWELL, E. C., *Le Consul* (Paris, 1909).

———, *Consular Cases and Opinions* (Washington, 1909).

STRAUS, Oscar S., *Under Four Administrations* (Boston, 1922).

STRONG, Theron G., *Joseph H. Choate* (New York, 1917).

STUART, Graham H., *The Department of State* (New York, 1949).

———, *Latin America and the United States* (New York, 1943).

———, *The International City of Tangier* (Stanford, Cal., 1931).

DE SZILASSY, J., *Traité pratique de diplomatie moderne* (Paris, 1928).

TAFT, W. H., *Our Chief Magistrate and His Powers* (New York, 1916).

TELFER, Captain J. Buchan, *The Strange Career of the Chevalier d'Eon de Beaumont* (London, 1885).

THAYER, William Roscoe, *Life and Letters of John Hay*, 2 vols. (New York, 1915).

THAYER, William Roscoe, *The Life of Cassius Marcus Clay* (Cincinnati, Ohio, 1886).

TREAT, Payson J., *Diplomatic Relations between the United States and Japan, 1853-1895* (Stanford, Cal., 1932).

TWISS, Travers, ed., *The Black Book of the Admiralty*, 4 vols. (London, 1871).

VALFREY, Jules, *La diplomatie française au 17ième Siècle* (Paris, 1881).

VAN DOREN, Carl, *Benjamin Franklin* (New York, 1938).

VAN DYNE, Frederick, *Our Foreign Service* (Rochester, N. Y., 1909).

VARE, Daniele, *The Laughing Diplomat* (New York, 1938).

DE VATTEL, E., *The Law of Nations, Classics of International Law*, J. B. Scott, ed. (Washington, 1916).

VIDAL, Saura G., *Tratado de derecho diplomatico* (Madrid, 1925).

WADDINGTON, Mary King, *Letters of a Diplomat's Wife* (New York, 1917).

WALKER, T. A., *A History of the Law of Nations* (Cambridge, Eng., 1899).

WALSH, E. A., *History and Nature of International Relations* (New York, 1922).

WANKA, J., *Das Konsularwesen und die diplomatischen Missionem* (Prague, 1906).

WARDEN, *On the Origin, Nature, Progress and Influence of Consular Establishments* (Paris, 1813).

WASHBURNE, Elihu B., *Recollections of a Minister to France* (New York, 1899).

WHARTON, Francis, *A Digest of the International Law of the United States*, 3 vols. (Washington, 1887).

WHITE, Andrew D., *The Autobiography of Andrew D. White*, 2 vols. (New York, 1905).

WHITLOCK, Brand, *Belgium*, 2 vols. (New York, 1920).

DE WICQUEFORT, A., *L'ambassadeur et ses fonctions* (London, 1840).

WILLIS, Edward F., *Prince Lichnowsky, Ambassador of Peace* (Berkeley, Cal., 1942).

WILLSON, Beckles, *America's Ambassadors to England* (London, 1928).

——, *America's Ambassadors to France* (London, 1928).

——, *Friendly Relations* (Boston, 1934).

WILSON, Henry Lane, *Diplomatic Episodes in Mexico, Belgium, and Chile* (New York, 1927).

WILSON, Hugh, *The Education of a Diplomat* (New York, 1928).

——, *Diplomat Between Wars* (New York, 1931).

WILSON, J. M. Huntingdon, *Memoirs of an Ex-Diplomat* (Boston, 1945).

WOLFF, Sir Henry Drummond, *Rambling Recollections*, 2 vols. (London, 1909).

WOOD, Eric Fisher, *The Note-book of an Attaché* (New York, 1915).

WRIGHT, Quincy, *The Control of American Foreign Relations* (New York, 1922).

WRIGHT, R. F., *Medieval Internationalism* (London, 1930).

WRISTON, Henry M., *Executive Agents in American Diplomacy* (New York, 1929).

YARDLEY, Herbert O., *The American Black Chamber* (Indianapolis, 1931).

YOUNG, George, *Diplomacy Old and New* (New York, 1921).

ZACHARIAS, Ellis M., *Secret Missions, the Story of an Intelligence Officer* (New York, 1946).

Index

461

DATE DUE